Econometrics

Econometrics

Stephen J. Schmidt

Union College, Schenectady, New York

Boston   Burr Ridge, IL   Dubuque, IA   Madison, WI   New York   San Francisco   St. Louis
Bangkok   Bogotá   Caracas   Kuala Lumpur   Lisbon   London   Madrid   Mexico City
Milan   Montreal   New Delhi   Santiago   Seoul   Singapore   Sydney   Taipei   Toronto

McGraw-Hill
Irwin

ECONOMETRICS

Published by McGraw-Hill/Irwin, a business unit of The McGraw-Hill Companies, Inc., 1221 Avenue of the Americas, New York, NY, 10020. Copyright © 2005 by The McGraw-Hill Companies, Inc. All rights reserved. No part of this publication may be reproduced or distributed in any form or by any means, or stored in a database or retrieval system, without the prior written consent of The McGraw-Hill Companies, Inc., including, but not limited to, in any network or other electronic storage or transmission, or broadcast for distance learning.

Some ancillaries, including electronic and print components, may not be available to customers outside the United States.

This book is printed on acid-free paper.

1 2 3 4 5 6 7 8 9 0 DOC/DOC 0 9 8 7 6 5 4

ISBN 0-07-253523-7

Publisher: *Gary Burke*
Executive sponsoring editor: *Lucille Sutton*
Developmental editor: *Rebecca Hicks*
Marketing manager: *Martin D. Quinn*
Senior media producer: *Anthony Sherman*
Lead project manager: *Pat Frederickson*
Senior production supervisor: *Sesha Bolisetty*
Lead designer: *Matthew Baldwin*
Supplement producer: *Matthew Perry*
Senior digital content specialist: *Brian Nacik*
Cover design: *Jenny El-Shamy*
Typeface: *10/12 Times New Roman*
Compositor: *Interactive Composition Corporation*
Printer: *R. R. Donnelley*

Library of Congress Cataloging-in-Publication Data

Schmidt, Stephen J.
      Econometrics / Stephen J. Schmidt.
         p. cm.
      Includes index.
      ISBN 0-07-253523-7 (alk. paper)
         1. Econometrics.   I. Title.
   HB139.S334 2005
   330'.01'5195—dc22
                                                    2004042594

www.mhhe.com

For Alexandra

אשת חיל

Economists agree that her worth is far above pearls.

Brief Contents

Table of Contents

About the Author

Stephen J. Schmidt is associate professor of economics at Union College, where he has been teaching since 1994. He received his bachelor's degree in 1989 and his Ph.D. in 1995, both from Stanford University. His research interests are in industrial organization, particularly transportation, and public finance, and his articles have appeared in publications including *American Economic Review, Journal of Policy Analysis and Management, International Journal of Industrial Organization, Public Finance Review,* and *Journal of Transport Economics and Policy*. Outside economics, he spends time with his wife, Alexandra, and his children, Gideon, Josiah, and Rachel, and avidly reads 19th-century military history.

Preface

There is an ancient story about four people who, through long study and dedication, discovered a way to enter Paradise while still alive. Unfortunately, three of them were not prepared for their arrival. Of the three, one died, one went insane, and one became a heretic. The fourth one, who knew what to expect in Paradise, had a better experience. No details are given, and they would perhaps be impossible to describe anyway. All we are told of him is that he "entered in peace and departed in peace."

Studying econometrics can be a little bit like that. Econometrics is the application of statistical methods to economic theories and data. One must have some initial preparation in economics and in mathematics to approach the subject. However, not everyone's initial encounter with econometrics is positive. A few people find the experience maddening; others become convinced that "economic-tricks," as econometrics has been disparagingly labeled, is little more than a sham to allow economists to create an aura of scientific reliability around their assertions and wild guesses. (There is, at least, no record of anyone dying as a result of their initial exposure to the subject.)

Despite the opinions of others, a student who engages in the subject will not only "depart in peace" but also come away with an understanding of the way in which economic ideas and reality come together. This is because econometrics is about the use of data from the real world to evaluate economic theories. Economic theorists do not create their theories purely for the sake of having theories. Since at least 1776, economists have sought to use those theories to explain the world around them and influence its development. Adam Smith's *The Wealth of Nations* is, in part, a criticism of the mercantilist system then dominant in the world's economy and an argument in favor of a new system featuring free markets. This free-market system took form in England in the century following Smith's writing and in much of the rest of the world soon thereafter.

Econometrics is the method that permits economists to connect their ideas to the tangible world in which we live. It tells economists whether real economies behave the way that theories suggest they should. If they do, the theory is supported; if they do not, the theory is rejected and new theory must be developed to explain the results. Econometrics also allows economists to make quantitative measurements of the economy as well as recommendations for policies to improve its performance. The enormous influence that economists have acquired over public policy since the Second World War is due, in large part, to their ability to use econometrics to measure, explain, predict, and control the economy.

This book presents econometrics not as a series of statistical techniques but as a way of doing applied economics. It teaches the statistical techniques that are the basis of econometric analysis, but it teaches them in the context of important economic problems and addresses them with economic analysis. It draws on a principles-level knowledge of economic models and economic issues such as monetary policy, electric power deregulation, labor market discrimination, and welfare reform to explain the purpose and the benefits of using statistical methods to do economics. It shows not only how econometric estimates are *derived* but also how they are *used*. The large majority of chapters begin by presenting an economic problem that can be addressed with the econometric techniques presented in that chapter. As the techniques are developed, the text applies them to that problem and draws the appropriate economic conclusions that follow from the statistical results. In this way, students will learn not only how economists use econometric methods but also why they do so and why the techniques covered in this book have become the foundation of modern empirical economic work. The end-of-chapter problems continue this focus. They require students not only to apply econometric techniques, but also to apply economic logic to the results, and finally, to draw economic conclusions about the issue raised in the problem. Many of the data sets that come with the book are used in multiple problems, sometimes in more than one chapter, to demonstrate how our economic understanding of an issue changes as we learn more about it from the data.

The book also recognizes that students learn in a variety of ways. The traditional "talk-and-chalk" approach to econometrics works well for some students but not for others. This book presents results through the traditional derivations and formulas but supplements those conventional techniques with intuitive and graphical explanations of econometric methods. It assumes knowledge of basic calculus but avoids relying exclusively on calculus and algebra as a means of explaining the theorems and equations presented in the text. The result is a presentation that is mathematically rigorous but more approachable for the student than a purely algebraic exposition would be. Also, the book recognizes that some students learn better by actively exploring statistics than they do by reading about it. Each chapter of this book concludes with a computer-based Monte Carlo exercise that allows students to generate data and analyze them with the techniques in this chapter. Because the students control the process that generated the data in these exercises, they are able to make connections between the true values of the parameters of the model and the way that estimators reveal (or fail to reveal) those true values. These exercises offer students another way of developing an understanding of how econometric methods work, rather than just learning to calculate formulas. The exercises in this text help the students to see why econometrics is such a valuable part of their economics education.

ORGANIZATION

This book is divided into six parts, and it may be used in a first course in econometrics (with or without a prerequisite course in statistics), in a second course in econometrics, or in both courses. The six parts are

I. Introduction to Econometrics (Chapters 1 and 2)
II. Probability and Statistics (Chapters 3, 4, and 5)
III. Least Squares Regression (Chapters 6, 7, and 8)
IV. Specifying the Econometric Model (Chapters 9, 10, and 11)
V. Extensions of Least Squares Regression (Chapters 12, 13, and 14)
VI. Advanced Topics (Chapters 15 through 20)

A first course without a statistics prerequisite might cover Parts I, II, and III, plus some chapters from Parts IV and/or V. Part IV will probably appeal more to those teaching a course with an applied focus, and Part V to those teaching a course with a theoretical focus. A first course with a statistics prerequisite might cover Parts I, III, IV, and V. A second course would start where the first course left off, either at Part IV or Part V, and cover those parts plus as many of the chapters in Part VI as time or preference permits. A second course might also draw on the economic literature to supplement the material in Parts IV, V, and VI, selecting from applied econometric work suitable to the students' ability and the instructor's interests.

I have tried to offer the instructor flexibility in the sequence in which chapters are covered. In the first part of the book, of course, that is not really possible; the chapters in Part III depend on those in Part II, and those in Parts IV and V depend on those in Part III. Within Parts II and III, the chapters should normally be covered in sequence, although it is possible to go from Part I to Part III, returning to Part II to introduce statistical concepts as they are encountered in Part III. In Parts IV and V, the chapters, or any subset of them, can be covered in any order. It is possible to cover the chapters in Part V before (or without) covering those in Part IV, and conversely. The chapters in Part VI can be covered in any order and at any point after completing Part III, with the exception that Section 4 of Chapter 15 requires Chapter 14; Chapter 17 and Section 4 of Chapter 16 require Chapter 12; and Chapter 20 requires Chapter 19. Beyond those limits, the instructor can teach Chapters 9 through 20 in virtually any order desired once the foundation material in Chapters 1 through 8 has been covered.

SUPPLEMENTS

Supplements include an Instructor's Manual with solutions to the end-of-chapter problems in the book. Each copy of the text comes with a CD-ROM with data sets in Excel, Eviews, Stata, SAS, and plain-text formats. A website provides the data sets as well as additional material to enhance the understanding of basic econometrics. The text can also be packaged with the most recent student version of Eviews. Contact your local McGraw-Hill sales representative for the details.

ACKNOWLEDGMENTS

It is true, as it is written, that "From my teachers I have learned much, from my colleagues more, and from my students most of all." My thanks go first to those who instructed me in econometrics, among them Steven Durlauf, Tim Bresnahan, Takeshi Amemiya, Arthur Goldberger, and Tom MaCurdy. Many thanks go also to Frank Wolak, Julie Anderson-Schaffner, and John Pencavel, from whom I learned much about econometrics despite not having had the privilege of taking classes in the subject from them.

Among colleagues, I am indebted to Shelton Schmidt, who offered many helpful suggestions through the course of this project and used a draft of the manuscript in his class, and to my other colleagues at Union who have supported me through the writing of this book. I also thank the many people who reviewed the manuscript and made numerous comments, all of which have greatly improved the text. They bear no responsibility for any errors that may remain. They include: Ila Alam (Tulane University), David Bessler (Texas A&M University), Tomáš Dvořák (Union College), Leroy Gill (Ohio State University), Karen Gutermuth (Virginia Military Institute), Suleyman Ozmucur (University of Pennsylvania), Soo-Bin Park (Carleton University), Elena Pesavento (Emory University), Mark Wheeler (Western Michigan University), William C. Wood (James Madison University), and Rossitza B. Wooster (California State University, Sacramento).

Several students provided comments on the manuscript, notably Stephen Guillerm and Sarah Handler, during various stages of its evolution, and their contribution is gratefully acknowledged. My thinking about econometrics and its exposition have benefited from all of the many students to whom I have taught econometrics over the preceding decade, without whom this book could not have come into existence, and I thank them as well.

At McGraw-Hill, the book has benefited greatly from the gentle and patient editing of Lucille Sutton, Becca Hicks, Jean Lou Hess, and Pat Frederickson. Also, I appreciate the efforts of Tony Sherman, Sesha Bolisetty, Matt Baldwin, and Marty Quinn. Lucille warned me that this project would take longer than I predicted; I do not know if she realized how prophetic that statement would turn out to be. I would also like to thank my parents, John and Ellen Schmidt; Joe Shiang, who provided weekly intellectual distractions from econometrics; and especially my wife, Alexandra, who provided cookies and other forms of support too numerous to mention.

Part **One**

Introduction to Econometrics

For most of its history as an academic discipline, economics had little to do with statistics. Only in the 1940s did economists begin to use statistical methods to evaluate economic ideas; this marked the birth of econometrics. In Part I, we discuss the reasons why economists turned to statistics as a way to test economic theories, and the methods by which statistical techniques are applied to economic problems. We also discuss the way an econometric project is carried out, starting from the question that motivates the project to the writing of the report that explains the project's findings.

Chapter **One**

Econometric Concepts

Unfortunately, I must now try to explain what "econometrics" comprises. Do not confuse the word with "econo-mystics" or "economic-tricks," nor yet with "icon-ometrics." While we may indulge all of these activities, they are not central to the discipline. Nor are we concerned with measuring the heights of economists.

David Hendry

1.1 THE PURPOSE OF ECONOMETRIC ANALYSIS

In the 60 or so years that economics has been influential in the formation of public policy in the developed world, it has achieved a great deal.[1] Economic theories of fiscal and monetary policy have helped governments greatly reduce the effect of business cycles on the economy; none of the recessions following the Second World War has come close to rivaling the Great Depression. Economic analysis has supported public policies on many issues, such as the deregulation of a large number of previously public or regulated industries, usually (though not always) with great improvements in the efficiency of those industries, and the reform of the welfare system, aiming to reduce government spending on welfare and allow former welfare recipients to enter the workplace. Business and management have come to rely on workers trained in economic ways of thinking to forecast demand for their products and to improve the efficiency of their operations.

All of these uses for economics require that economic theory be applied to real-world problems, and applying economic theory to real problems requires analysis of economic data. Without being able to forecast the growth of the economy, central bankers could not know when to stimulate the economy and when to cool it off. Without measurements of production and cost functions, economists could not identify industries with competitive conditions likely to benefit from deregulation. Without knowledge of consumer incomes and preferences, businesses could not predict the profitability of the markets for their products.

---

[1] Economics has sought to influence public policy since it was born in 1776, when Adam Smith published *The Wealth of Nations,* partly as a criticism of mercantilist economic policies. However, it took a major step forward in the 1930s and 1940s when, among other key works, *The General Theory of Employment, Interest, and Money* (1936) by John Maynard Keynes proposed the first modern theoretical grounds for public policy to eliminate business cycles, and *Foundations of Economic Analysis* (1947) by Paul Samuelson established the framework of modern quantitative economic analysis.

FIGURE 1.1
Distance Fallen versus Time Fallen

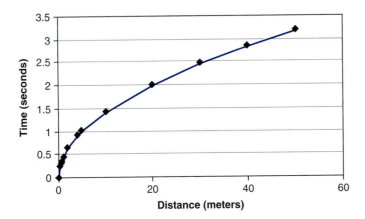

Economic theory becomes most useful when it departs from purely theoretical considerations and deals with quantitative problems whose answers are of practical importance.

However, economic data are different from data used in laboratory sciences such as chemistry and physics, because they are not generated under controlled conditions.[2] You can go into a physics laboratory, drop a heavy object from a variety of different heights, measure the time required for the object to hit the ground, and be certain of getting the same answers that someone else would get in a different laboratory elsewhere, or that you yourself would get in the same laboratory at a different time. You can therefore be sure that the differences in the times required for the object to fall are due to the differences in the height from which it is dropped, and to no other factor. The ability of physicists and other laboratory scientists to produce data in which exactly one factor influences the results of the experiment enables them to measure the influence of that factor quite precisely, without a great deal of mathematical analysis. Furthermore, the data from such an experiment will lie very close to a fixed curve, as shown in Figure 1.1. Because of this, physicists can very precisely identify the exact relationship between time fallen and distance fallen; it is, in fact, given by the equation

$$d = 4.9t^2 \qquad\qquad (1.1.1)$$

where distance is measured in meters and time in seconds. From this equation, the distance that an object will fall in any given time can be predicted quite accurately, even for distances much larger or much smaller than those used to draw the curve.

Unfortunately, economists do not have the ability to isolate a single economic effect in this way. For example, economists have long believed that, all else being held equal, a 2 to 3 percent increase in gross domestic product (GDP) will lead to a decrease of 1 percentage point in the unemployment rate. This relationship is known as Okun's law, after the

[2] This is, however, changing. The field of experimental economics studies economic decisions made by human subjects in controlled conditions where theories about those decisions can be tested. Considerable progress has been made in experimental economics in the last 20 years. However, the problems of generalizing from laboratory settings to the real economy have proved sufficiently difficult that econometric analysis remains the primary method of studying real-world economic phenomena. Also, economics experiments can rarely control for all factors affecting the decisions of their subjects; the results of experiments are often themselves subjected to econometric analysis.

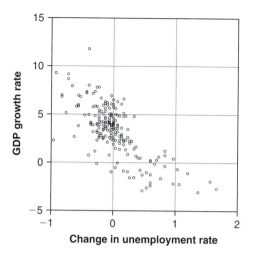

FIGURE 1.2
Historical Data on Okun's Law, 1948–2000

economist who originally proposed it.[3] Figure 1.2 shows actual changes in unemployment and GDP from 1948 to 2000. There does appear to be a negative relationship, but the data do not lie precisely on a curve, as they do in Figure 1.1. In some years, GDP growth is higher than Okun's law relationship suggests it should be; in other years, lower. This is due to a variety of other economic effects that help determine GDP in any given year. Monetary policy, fiscal policy, international trade, and a variety of other things can lead to a change in GDP and are not accounted for in Figure 1.2. Worse, the apparent negative relationship between unemployment and GDP that appears in Figure 1.2 could be due to these variables and might not have anything to do with Okun's law at all. If we could perform controlled experiments, then we would go to our laboratory, change the unemployment rate while holding monetary policy, fiscal policy, and all other relevant variables constant, and see whether GDP changed or not. We would then be able to say with certainty whether or not GDP and unemployment were related.

But we cannot do that. Instead, we have to use statistical analysis to distinguish between unemployment and the other economic variables that affect GDP in the real-world economy. Statistical analysis allows economists to separate the relationship they are interested in studying from other economic relationships that also affect the same observed data.

Definition 1.1 *Econometrics* is the study of the application of statistical methods to economic problems.

What can economists do with the results of econometric analysis? Econometrics has a wide variety of uses, but they fall into three general categories:

1. *Testing economic theories.* Any sufficiently important economic phenomenon will inevitably attract a variety of theories about why it occurs. The economic slowdown of the 1970s was not consistent with the standard macroeconomic models of that time, and a great deal of effort went into creating new theoretical explanations of macroeconomic

---

[3] Arthur Okun originally proposed that a 3 percent increase in GDP would produce a 1 percent decrease in unemployment; subsequent events have suggested that a somewhat smaller increase in GDP is required.

performance. These theories were not consistent with one another, in either their basic assumptions about how the economy worked or their suggestions about appropriate macroeconomic policy. Each theory predicted that particular relationships between economic variables would (or would not) exist. By examining whether these relationships existed, econometricians could tell whether the data supported the theories or not. During the 1980s, econometric analysis was able to show that some of these theories could not be reconciled with actual economic performance in the 1970s and 1980s, whereas others were better able to explain what had happened and what the results of economic policy decisions had been. As a result, economists gained not only a deeper knowledge about how the economy actually works but also better insights into how to make economic policy in the future.

2. *Forecasting the economy.* There is a great deal of interest, among both economists and businesspeople, in accurate forecasts of the future values of key economic variables. Indeed, economics consultants make money by producing (and selling) such forecasts to people and organizations that need them. Businesses need to know future demand for their products when making investments in new factories and equipment. The Federal Reserve Board needs to know the likely future path of the economy when deciding whether to change monetary policy and, if so, by how much. State and local governments need to know how much income and sales they can expect in their jurisdictions in order to predict the amount of money they will have for education, health care, and law enforcement. By identifying the relationships of such variables across time, econometricians can predict, with varying degrees of accuracy, the likely values of these variables. This knowledge can lead to better economic decisions by individuals, businesses, and governments.

3. *Making economic policy.* Only rarely, in modern economies, can governments directly control people's economic behavior. More often, government creates incentives for people to change their behavior, either to get a reward from the government or to avoid a penalty. For instance, the federal government gives a tax credit to people who save for their children's college educations. To make policy effectively, the government needs to understand how such incentives will affect people's behavior, to know how strong the incentive must be to achieve the goal of the policy. If we lower the sales taxes in our state, how many new businesses will move here, or be started here, as a result? If we want to reduce the use of illegal drugs by 10 percent, how much more money do we need to spend on law enforcement? Measuring these effects allows economists to advise governments on the exact policies they should pursue to achieve the economic outcomes they desire.

1.2 THE LOGIC OF ECONOMETRIC ANALYSIS

Suppose the Federal Reserve Board (the Fed) increases the money supply, hoping to stimulate the economy. Will national output rise? Most economic theories suggest that, at least in the short run, it will; as capital is injected into the economy and interest rates drop, consumers will demand more goods and firms will respond by supplying more goods to those consumers, resulting in increased national output. Other theories, however, note that this increase in demand can increase prices as well as, or even instead of, output. If the economy's aggregate supply curve is vertical, then output will not increase at all; the only

FIGURE 1.3

Historical Relationship between Money Supply and GDP, 1949–2000

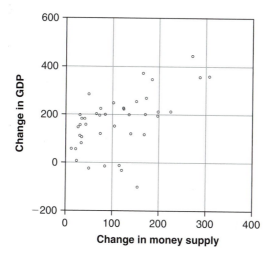

effect of the tax cuts will be higher inflation. Which of these theories is right? If output will rise, by how much will it rise? How much should the Fed increase the money supply if it wants to achieve a certain target level of output growth?

Economists answer these and other, similar questions through the analysis of data on the history of the economy. Rather than argue about the merits of the various theories, or the plausibility of the assumptions those theories are based on, econometricians look to see what has happened to output in the past when the money supply has changed. There are many reasons why economics has adapted this approach to resolving the questions it asks. For one, data analysis is (at least in part) objective; two economists using the same data to perform the same analysis should get the same answers. Objective analysis of data has been very successful in the sciences, and it appears to also be successful in economics, if not to quite the same extent.[4] For another, analysis allows us to take advantage of the inherently quantitative nature of economic data. Because the money supply and national output are easily measured in numerical terms, economists prefer an analytical method that uses those numbers to detect patterns between the two variables.

Given information about the growth of output and the money supply in the past, we look to see whether or not there is a pattern of higher growth when the money supply has been increased. Figure 1.3 shows data on increases in the money supply and increases in GDP in the United States from 1949 to 2000. From this graph it would appear that there is indeed such a pattern, although the relationship is not a strong one. Econometrics considers this relationship evidence in favor of theories that suggest that increasing the money supply

[4] The question of whether economic analysis deserves the title of *science* is a controversial one. Some argue that because economics uses objective data to test hypotheses, it is in essence scientific and should be called a science. Others argue that because the data are not derived under controlled conditions, and one economist cannot replicate another's data collection, economics should not be labeled a science, in the belief that replication of results (from different data) is a key of the scientific method. Whether economics is a science or not is not a particularly important question, at least not one of any practical importance. What is important is to realize that economics does focus on empirical testing of hypotheses with data and to that extent shares some common elements with scientific analysis, though there are other elements of scientific analysis it does not share.

increases economic growth, at least in the short run. Of course, there are other variables that affect growth, as evidenced by the fact that the data in Figure 1.3 do not lie perfectly on a line. A more sophisticated econometric analysis would use statistical techniques to deal with those other variables as well. But the basic intention of econometric analysis remains the same: to answer economic questions by looking at numerical predictions made by economic theories that bear on the questions, using data to determine what relationships exist between economic variables, and using those relationships to provide an answer to the original economic question.

1.3   THE METHODS OF ECONOMETRIC ANALYSIS

Ultimately, our goal in analyzing economic data is to understand the source of the data, which is some portion of the real-world economy whose behavior we would like to learn more about.

Definition 1.2   The *data generating process* is the collection of real-world activities that produces the data set we observe and wish to understand.

If we have collected data on U.S. interest rates, then the data generating process is the United States economy. If we are interested in studying the effects of deregulation of cable TV, and have collected data on cable TV service and prices, then the data generating process is the cable TV industry. Because of the complexity of the real economy, we will never be able to fully describe the data generating process. Instead, we must work with a simple model of the economy that we can describe fully. We must then hope that this model is sufficiently similar to the real data generating process that our analysis will describe that process well.

Definition 1.3   An *economic model* is a set of ideas about economic relationships among the values of the variables determined by the data generating process, usually expressed as lines on a graph or as mathematical equations relating the variables.

The economic model is something we choose, and we can construct models in a variety of ways. Our choice will depend on which economic relationships interest us, which ones we believe to be important in describing the data, and which ones we think are of lesser importance and can be ignored for simplicity. Different econometricians might choose different models to represent the true data generating process. Which model we pick depends on what aspects of the process we are interested in studying. Part of the art of econometric analysis is creating a model that is not too difficult to estimate but that contains all the essential features of the real economic process we are studying.

The economic model is not a complete description of the data generating process, however. The data we observe, which we get from the data generating process, will always be affected by the factors we have omitted from our economic model. Therefore, when we analyze the data we will need to allow for those factors.

Definition 1.4   An *error term* is a random variable that represents all portions of the data generating process that are not captured by the economic model.

Error terms are the reasons why our data do not fall precisely along the simple curves predicted by our economic models, as demonstrated in Figures 1.2 and 1.3. In fact, error terms can cause economic data either to fall in no visible pattern whatsoever or to fall in patterns that are purely coincidental and have nothing to do with the economic model at all.

Definition 1.5 A *spurious correlation* occurs when two economic variables that are unrelated, but random, take values that happen to be correlated.

To see a non-economic example of a spurious correlation, take a coin and flip it 25 times. Each coin toss is independent of every other coin toss; if you happen to get a heads one time, the chance that you will get a heads the next time is 50 percent. However, the odds are pretty good that, in 25 flips, you will get a run of at least five heads in a row, or at least five tails in a row. Does this mean that the coin, in some strange way, remembers what it did on the last flip and does the same thing on the next flip? Of course not; it just means that if you flip the coin enough times, sooner or later something unlikely will happen.

Economic variables are subject to unlikely coincidences in the same way. If you take 10 or 15 economic variables that, in truth, are unrelated to one another and you graph them against each other, then by coincidence a few of them will have strong relationships. Hendry (1984) reports the relationship between money supply and the price level in the United Kingdom, and also between the price level and a "mystery" variable. He shows that, because increasing the money supply is inflationary, the money supply and price levels are positively correlated but not exceptionally strongly. There is a much stronger correlation between price levels and the mystery variable, and with a little econometric magic he can make the latter correlation even stronger still. At the end, however, he reveals the secret that the mystery variable is simply cumulative rainfall in the United Kingdom. Clearly there is no real economic correlation between the amount of rain that falls and the price level, but both of those variables tend to grow over time. By coincidence, they happen to have grown very similarly. Hendry, who was making exactly this argument about the importance of economic theory in econometrics, found this relationship simply by trying lots of variables that grow over time until he found one that did what he wanted it to do. There are any number of economic or quasi-economic variables that grow; if cumulative rainfall had not been so closely related to the price level, some other variable would have been. The correlation between rainfall and price levels is completely spurious and does not demonstrate the existence of any economic relationship whatsoever. Because there is no real economic connection between the two variables, if we tried to use rainfall to predict future price levels, the predictions would be valueless. We can make use of a relationship between two variables only if we think that relationship also applies to data other than the sample we used to find the relationship. For relationships caused by economic principles, that will be true; for spurious correlations, it will not be true.

How can we tell the difference between a meaningful correlation, which indicates a true economic relationship, and a spurious one? Statistically, we cannot. Instead, our economic model tells us which relationships are economically plausible and which are not. We do not have any macroeconomic model that proposes a connection between rainfall and price levels, so we conclude that that correlation is spurious. We do have a macroeconomic model—quite a few of them in fact—that suggests correlation between the money supply and price levels. Even though the correlation between the price level and the money supply is not, statistically, as strong as the correlation between the price level and rainfall, we can believe that the former correlation is real because we have some economic reason to expect it.

Of course, we can never be sure that the correlation is *not* spurious. Some economic theories are wrong, and we don't know which; occasionally an economic model will suggest a relationship that is false, but by coincidence the data will show a correlation between the two variables anyway. There is nothing that we can do about this possibility except to set relatively high standards for concluding that correlations exist so that we will, at least, make very few positive errors. We can also compare the results of our project to those of other econometricians testing the same theory in different ways, and see if they get similar answers or different answers. If the others do not find the same correlation we do, perhaps ours was spurious. Given enough data, and enough projects, eventually the truth will come out. The economic model permits us to sort out true relations from false ones in this way.

As anyone who has taken even a single course in economics knows, many important economic models can be drawn as a set of lines, or curves, on graphs. Supply and demand curves are the bread and butter of economic analysis, cost and production functions help us understand the behavior of firms, and aggregate supply and aggregate demand curves describe macroeconomic events. Observed values of economic variables, if they obey these relations, ought to be determined by these lines. If they are, that is evidence in favor of the theories that suggest these relationships, and it may enable us to calculate the slope of the curve. If they do not, then the economic theory that predicted the relationship may be false and we should not rely on its implications.

Much of econometrics is therefore intended to let economists detect whether sets of variables lie along fixed lines and, if they do, then to measure the slopes of those lines. However, because the economic model is not a perfect description of the data generating process, errors cause the data not to lie perfectly along a straight line; in analysis, econometricians need to account for that. For example, economic theory suggests that if firms increase the amount of product they produce, their total costs should also rise. If we assume the relationship is linear,[5] we can write this as a mathematical equation:

$$TC = \beta_0 + \beta_1 Q \qquad\qquad (1.3.1)$$

which is an economic model relating total costs (TC) and quantity (Q). It states that the firm's cost is equal to a fixed cost β_0 if it produces no output, and rises by a marginal cost of β_1 when the firm increases its output by one unit. Economic theory does not tell us what the values of the fixed cost or the marginal cost should be, although it does suggest that their values should be positive, not negative. The exact values we must learn from data.

> **Definition 1.6** A *parameter* of an econometric model is an unknown constant that describes the economic relationship the econometric model predicts. We do not know the parameter's value, but we hope to use econometric methods to estimate that value.

The parameters of this economic model are β_0 and β_1. To estimate their values, we need to collect a sample of data, either from many firms in the same industry or from one firm over a period of time, and examine the relationship between output and total costs in the data we observe.

Throughout this book, we will consistently use Roman letters (A, B, C) to refer to observable data, and Greek letters (α, β, γ) to refer to things that are not observable, such as the values of parameters and error terms. When we calculate estimated values for these parameters,

---

[5] We can also assume the relationship is nonlinear if we have reason to think that, a point we will consider in Chapter 9.

FIGURE 1.4

Data on Costs and Output

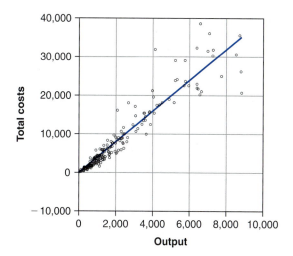

we will identify the estimates with superscripted marks; $\hat{\beta}$ and $\tilde{\beta}$ might be two different estimated (thus calculated, and hence observed) values for the unknown parameter β.

If the economic model were a perfect description of the data, then the data would lie exactly along a line if we plotted them on a graph. That will not be the case; in reality there are many reasons why one firm would have somewhat higher costs, or somewhat lower costs, than others that produced similar levels of output. Some firms may be more technically efficient than others. Some may have had labor strikes that prevented them from producing output for a period of time. Some may produce a higher-quality product than others, and higher quality products may cost more to produce. All these things are part of the data generating process that are not included in the economic model. If we wish to analyze the data we have collected, we need to include something in our analysis that represents the effect of things not included in our model on the firm's costs.

Definition 1.7 An *econometric model* combines an economic model with an error term to produce a complete representation of the true data generating process.

An econometric model of the cost function is:

$$TC_i = \beta_0 + \beta_1 Q_i + \varepsilon_i \qquad (1.3.2)$$

The econometric model differs from the economic model in two ways. First, TC and Q now have i subscripts. These subscripts indicate that we are representing the total cost and quantity of some specific firm we have observed, number i in our data, instead of the abstract idea of cost and quantity represented in the economic model. The parameters β_0 and β_1 are not subscripted because they take the same value for every observation in the sample.[6] Second, the econometric model contains an error term ε_i, which represents the effects of everything in the data generating process that is not included in the model. Therefore, this model is capable of exactly describing the data. Figure 1.4 shows data (black circles) and

---

[6] If they don't, then the observations in our sample are determined by different data generating processes, and we cannot use the sample to estimate any one of them. We can alter our model of the data generating process to allow parameter values to differ in various ways; we discuss this point in Chapter 11.

an economic model (red line) for a sample of American bus companies. The red line shows the relationship between output and total costs predicted by the economic model; the data lie above and below that line because of the error term. Data points that lie above the red line have higher total costs than the economic model predicts, and hence have positive error terms. Data points below the line have lower total costs than the model predicts, and hence have negative error terms.

The reason the data points do not all lie on the line is that there are other factors, represented by the error term, that cause the data generating process and the economic model to differ. We could try to make the economic model more sophisticated to include those concepts. To do that, we would need to identify other variables that affect a firm's total costs besides the money supply. The economic model that tells us quantity and costs are related also suggests several other variables that matter, such as the price of labor and the price of fuel. When those prices rise, firms must spend more money to purchase their inputs, and total costs will rise. Including those variables in the model produces the following equation:

$$TC_i = \beta_0 + \beta_1 Q_i + \beta_2 PF_i + \beta_3 PL_i + \varepsilon_i \qquad \textbf{(1.3.3)}$$

where β_2 and β_3 are additional parameters of the model, PF_i is the price of fuel paid by the ith firm, PL_i is the price of its labor, and we might expect β_2 and β_3 to be positive also. If a firm's total costs increase, that might have happened because of an increase in input prices, not an increase in costs. From the graph in Figure 1.4 we cannot tell whether rising costs are due to rising output, rising input prices, or something else. But if we can estimate values for all four of the parameters of this model, then we can separate the effects of increased output from the effects of increased prices in the data.

Equation 1.3.2 is a very simple econometric model of the relationship between output and costs. Equation 1.3.3 is a somewhat more complicated, but still quite simple, model of the same relationship. The additional complexity of the model makes the analysis more difficult, but it also makes the model a more accurate representation of the real economy. Whenever we choose an economic model, we must decide whether to select a model that is relatively complex or one that is relatively simple. Relatively complex models are better able to describe the data generating process but are harder to estimate. Relatively simple models are poorer representations of the data generating process but ones we can estimate more reliably, and they allow us to focus on the specific relationship that interests us. Making this trade off well is a hallmark of a good econometrician.

Given a sample from a data generating process and an economic model that we think describes that process, we then construct an econometric model and seek to estimate the parameters of the model, using the data sample. This gives us a representation of the real economy that is based on both economic theory (from the model) and observable data (from the sample), and combines those two sources of information to produce a realistic yet practical description of the data generating process that can be used to understand how the real economy works. Econometrics is the study of that combination, and it is what we will explore in the remainder of this book.

Chapter Review

- It is difficult to tell whether economic data are determined by theoretical economic relationships or not because economic data reflect the effects of many relationships all affecting the real world at once.

- Economists use statistical methods to distinguish one economic relationship in a data set from others affecting that data set. Econometrics is the study of these statistical methods and their uses in dealing with practical economic problems.

- Econometric analysis is useful for forecasting the economy, for testing theoretical ideas about the economy, and for making public policy related to the economy.

- An econometric analysis of a particular question begins with an economic theory that suggests a possible relationship between two or more observable economic variables.

- Economic models never perfectly describe data sets because real data generating processes are too complex to be described by simple mathematical models. We use error terms to represent everything that affects the real data generating process that is not included in our economic model of that process.

- This relationship is then written as an econometric model that contains both the variables of the model and the unknown parameters that describe their relationship. The theory will normally suggest particular values, or at least signs, for the parameters.

- We then obtain data on the values of the variables; determine whether the predicted relationship exists or not; and, if it does exist, estimate values for the unknown parameters of the model.

Chapter **Two**

Conducting an Econometric Project

Students are taught minor details in statistics when the hard business of econometrics is a specification search; they are taught minor details in mathematics when the hard business of mathematical economics is to make our ideas clear . . . The hard business of economic scholarship is to marshal ideas well.

D. N. McCloskey

2.1   DEVELOPING A QUESTION TO BE ANALYZED

Doing an econometric project requires many things—data, a model to organize that data, and appropriate analysis and testing of the data. But before a project requires a model or data or a hypothesis, it requires a purpose: a question that needs an answer, which the research of the project will provide. This question provides the core around which the project will be organized. What data are collected, what analysis is applied to the data, and what hypotheses are examined all depend on what we want to know about the economy. A major part—perhaps the largest part—of being a good econometrician is the ability to pick a good question to answer. An econometric project might be designed to identify the likely consequences of welfare reform on workforce participation by welfare recipients. It might be organized to see how bond yields move together and look for profit-taking opportunities. But it is important that it have some central economic idea that binds it together and gives it direction. Without that, the project can descend into mere numerical calculations that lead nowhere and provide no useful economic knowledge. In this chapter we will discuss the selection of a question to analyze econometrically, and the various steps to be followed in designing and carrying out an econometric research project to answer that question.

What makes a good question? Two things: First, the question has to be *feasible;* it has to be possible for the question to have an objective answer, which can be found using econometric methods. Second, the question has to be *practical;* it has to be possible to set up an economic model, gather data, and analyze those data within the time available for the project.

Definition 2.1 An economic question is *normative* if its answer is subjective, is not capable of being shown to be right or wrong, and depends on judgments or values about economics on which two reasonable economists might differ. An economic question is *positive* if its answer is objective, is capable of being proved right or wrong, and depends only on facts about which any two reasonable economists should agree—if the facts are known with certainty.

Questions to be answered by econometric projects must be positive questions, not normative ones. Data cannot answer questions about subjective judgments, but they can make measurements that provide the answers to questions with objective answers. The question "Should we reform welfare?" is normative. Its answer depends on subjective judgments about whether the benefits of welfare reform (increased workforce participation, reduced government spending) are more important than the costs (elimination of the social safety net, increased poverty). This is a poor question for an econometric project because data cannot tell us how that judgment should be made. In contrast, the question "How much would welfare spending be reduced if we reformed welfare?" is positive. Its answer is some number that, though it might be difficult to predict in advance, could easily be verified by comparing spending before and after welfare reform. Econometric analysis can answer that question. Identifying the effect of welfare reform on welfare spending before it happens is rather harder but still quite feasible, given a model of the determinants of welfare spending and an idea about how welfare reform will affect them.

However, to be interesting, an econometrics project should provide information that is helpful in making some kind of subjective decision. Objective knowledge about the spending consequences of welfare reform is helpful in forming a subjective opinion about whether or not reform is a good idea. Similarly, objective knowledge about the movement of bond yields can help solve the subjective question of identifying an appropriate investment strategy. Thus, although our econometrics projects will not tell us precisely which economic policies we should adopt, they will give us useful information that we can use in making that decision. An economic project needs both a topic, which is a general problem in economics that the paper will address, and a specific research question whose answer will say something interesting and useful about that topic.

2.2   DEVELOPING AN ECONOMIC MODEL TO FRAME THE QUESTION

As we noted in Chapter 1, econometrics looks for relationships between two or more variables in the sample of data. Before we can look in the data, however, we must have some ideas about what relationships might be found there. Those ideas will come to us from economic theory. Suppose, for instance, we are interested in the effect of foreign competition on prices of automobiles. How do we expect the presence of foreign competitors to affect U.S. automobile prices, and what other variables affecting automobile prices might be confused with the relation between foreign competition and prices? An economic model will help us answer those questions and give us a starting point for our econometric project.

FIGURE 2.1
Supply and Demand for Automobiles

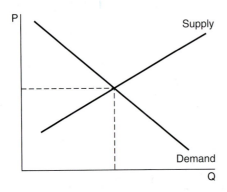

If we are willing to assume that the automobile market is reasonably competitive, then we might use a supply-and-demand model to predict the prices of automobiles and see what affects them. Such a model is shown in Figure 2.1; the price of automobiles (and the quantity of automobiles sold in the market) is determined by the intersection of the supply and demand curves. Any variable that changes demand for automobiles, or supply of automobiles, to the U.S. market will change the equilibrium price. The model gives us some ideas about what those variables might be. For example, an increase in consumer incomes will make it easier for consumers to buy automobiles and thus increase demand for them. Changes in the prices of substitute goods (such as light trucks) or complementary goods (such as gasoline) will also shift the demand curve for automobiles in predictable ways. The supply curve will be shifted by variables that affect the costs of producing automobiles: the price of steel, wages of automobile workers, and so forth. Finally, foreign competition will increase the supply of automobiles in the U.S. domestic market, shifting it out; this will decrease prices and increase quantities sold, all else equal.[1]

The model serves several purposes for us. First, it gives us a list of variables that need to be included in the econometric model. That is, it identifies all the things that affect automobile prices. We need to include those effects in our econometric model so that we can distinguish them from the effect that really interests us, which is foreign competition. If we did not have such a list, we could not know when we had included enough variables in the model to be reasonably certain that we had controlled for all important economic effects on automobile prices when trying to identify the foreign competition effect.

Second, the model gives us a list of all the variables that might be expected to affect automobile prices in some manner. Any variable not on the list is not expected to affect automobile prices. This is important because it allows us to detect correlations between two variables that are due to a spurious correlation and not to a real economic relationship. It also means that, if we have included all the variables that our economic model tells us to include, we need not worry about missing something important enough to change the results of our analysis.

Third, the model tells us which variables affect the values of other variables. Statistical analysis will tell us whether variables are related, but it cannot tell us why they are related. Statistics will tell us that people with large houses tend to have high incomes; however,

---

[1] Note that *quantity* here is the total number of all automobiles sold in the United States, foreign and domestic. One can show that, while total quantity will rise, it will rise by less than the number of automobiles imported; therefore, sales of domestic automobiles will fall.

it requires an economic model to tell us that this happens because people with higher incomes will choose to spend more on houses, and not because people who find themselves living in large houses choose to take high-paying jobs. Income influences choice of house size, not conversely. We refer to house size as a dependent variable in this model, and income as an independent variable.[2] We need to know which variables are independent and which variables are dependent in order to predict the effect of changes in the model. For example, increases in income will probably lead people to buy bigger houses, but building larger houses will not cause people to earn more income.

In other models, the direction of causality is less clear. Some economic models argue that increases in the money supply cause gross domestic product (GDP) to grow more rapidly. Other models argue that high levels of GDP growth cause the Federal Reserve Board to worry about an overheating of the economy and therefore to reduce the money supply. In a supply-and-demand model, price and quantity are both dependent variables; they are influenced by variables that shift the supply and demand curves, such as income and input prices. An increase in price does not cause a decrease (or increase) in quantity; rather, an increase in the price of a substitute good increases demand for the given product and causes both prices and quantities to rise. The economic model tells us how the variables are related and what the consequences of changes in one variable will be for the model as a whole.

2.3   FINDING DATA TO ESTIMATE THE PARAMETERS OF THE MODEL

Given an economic model that suggests relationships between certain variables, our next problem is to find a data set we can use to see if that relationship exists or not.

Definition 2.2 An *observation* of the data generating process is one set of values for all of the variables in the relationship we expect to observe.

If the data generating process is the U.S. economy, and we are interested in studying the relationship between money supply and interest rates, then we might observe the values of the money supply and the interest rate for a particular month. For instance, in November 2000, the money supply was $4,898 billion, and the interest rate (as measured by the federal funds rate) was 6.51 percent. Those two values constitute one observation. The values from another month would provide another observation; for example, in March 1999 the money supply was $4,444 billion and the federal funds rate was 4.81 percent. Each month provides an additional observation that we can use to infer the relationship between interest rates and the money supply.

Definition 2.3 A *sample,* or *data set,* is a collection of many observations of the same data generating process.

One potential problem is that all the observations must come from the same data generating process so that they will all be expected to obey the same economic relationship; in graphical terms, they will all lie around the same line. This can cause problems. If we consider a sample of observations on different automobile companies, can we be sure that

---

[2] We will provide a more formal definition of these concepts in Chapter 6.

General Motors and Ford have the same production function? Their production functions are probably quite similar, but the cars they make are not identical and each has its own proprietary technologies. We can never really know the answers to these questions, but we should select a sample in such a way that we can believe, at least as an assumption to make the analysis possible, that all the observations in the sample come from the same basic economic process and thus lie along the same line. Otherwise, we are comparing apples and oranges, and the results will not be meaningful.

There are two basic types of samples, plus a third type that is a combination of the other two.

> **Definition 2.4** A *time-series sample* contains observations on a single economic object at different periods of time.

If we form a sample by looking at interest rates and GDP in the U.S. economy for each quarter from 1960 to 1999, then we have a time-series sample; the economic object is the U.S. economy, and we have 160 different observations of that object, each from a different time period. The advantage of time-series data sets is that they observe a single object, so we need not worry about whether two countries, two firms, or two people are similar enough to compare. The disadvantage is that we must worry about whether the objects change so much over time that comparisons between early and late data are not appropriate. For example, we might worry that the oil shocks of 1973 and 1979 fundamentally changed the U.S. economy in ways that altered the data generating process and hence changed the values of the model's parameters. Also, the duration of the data collection may limit how much data we can collect. Reliable annual data on most developed economies generally goes back only to about 1946; data at more frequent intervals, such as monthly or quarterly, are not available even that far back. For developing countries, data are available for even shorter periods.

> **Definition 2.5** A *cross-section sample* contains observations from many different economic objects, all taken at a single point in time.

If we form a sample by looking at the performance of many different airline companies in 1997, then we have a cross-section sample. The advantages and disadvantages of cross-section data sets are the reverse of those of time-series data sets. With a cross-section data set we need not worry about whether the data generating process is changing over time because all observations come from the same period. We do need to worry about the comparability of the airline firms in the sample. Is American Airlines different from U.S. Airways? Is Southwest Airlines, with its alternative business strategy, different from all other U.S. airlines? How about European airlines such as Lufthansa, British Airways, or KLM? Do international alliances matter? To use cross-section data, we must assure ourselves that the different objects in our sample are sufficiently similar that we can claim our observations came from a common data generating process. We are also limited by the number of objects we can observe; there are only a certain number of airlines in the world at any one time. In some industries (say, restaurants) there may be so many firms that this is not a limit; in other industries (say, petroleum refining) there may be so few that this is a difficult limit.

One solution is to use both approaches.

> **Definition 2.6** A *panel data sample* contains observations on multiple economic objects for multiple time periods.

For example, we might consider a sample of eight different airline companies over a period of five years. If so, then American Airlines in 1997 would be one observation, United Airlines in 1997 would be a second observation, American Airlines in 1998 would be a third observation, and so forth. We might have 40 observations, if we observed all eight airlines in all five years; we might have fewer if some airlines were not observed in some years.

Definition 2.7 A panel data sample is *balanced* if it contains observations on all objects for all time periods. If it does not, then it is *unbalanced.*

It is generally better to use balanced panel data sets when possible, if only because we will have more observations that way. However, there are times when it is impossible to have a balanced panel. We might not be able to get data on some of the airlines for some of the years, or firms may go in and out of existence. If, for example, two airlines merged during the data sample (mergers were fairly common in the 1980s), then prior to the merger we would observe two airlines; afterward, only one. In such circumstances we would be forced to work with an unbalanced panel. Unbalanced panels are not a problem, although at times we might not want to use a year in which only a few firms are observed or a firm for which only a few years of data are available.

The advantage of panel data is that, by using both the time and cross-section dimensions of the data, we can create much larger samples than by using only time-series or only cross-section data. The drawback is that both the objects and the time periods must be comparable; there are two things that can shift the underlying economic relationship rather than just one. There are techniques for handling such shifts in panel data, which will be described later in the book, so this is not necessarily a problem, but it is something to be aware of when trying to decide whether or not to use panel data samples for a particular econometric project.

When gathering data for an econometric project, we must choose a sample and then find data on the variables for the observations in that sample. To a large extent, the question and model we have chosen will determine what sample we choose, but not entirely. For example, if we are interested in studying the effects of interest rates on national output, we might choose either of two approaches. We could study a time-series sample on a single country, looking to see how interest rates have varied over time and whether national output has varied together with them. Or we could study a cross-section of several countries to see if countries with higher interest rates have lower national output. In either case, there will be factors other than interest rates that affect output for which we have to control. A major difference between the two samples is what those other effects are. If we use a cross-section sample of many countries, we will have to control for other differences between the countries affecting their national output, such as population, access to technology, education and skills of workers, and international economic integration. If we use a time-series sample for a single country, some of these problems will go away, but we will have to control for other effects that change over time, such as population growth and immigration, and the development and introduction of new technology into the economy. Our choice of a sample will depend, at least in part, on which set of differences we think we can control for most effectively.

There are two other issues to think about when selecting a sample. First, the results we get from estimating our model will, strictly speaking, be applicable only to the sample on which we estimated it. We might want to apply our results to observations other than the ones in our sample. If we estimate a macroeconomic model with U.S. data, for instance, we might want to apply the results to European economies as well, or we might want to apply them to the future of the U.S. economy. This will work only if we apply the results to the same data generating process that produced the sample we analyzed. Predicting the future development of the economy using data on its past behavior is appropriate only if the economy behaves in the future as it did in the past. Normally, we would expect that to be the case; but special events—such as the Great Depression, the Second World War, or the oil shocks of the 1970s—might cause us to worry that the structure of the macroeconomy changed. Results from data taken from those periods might not be appropriate for predicting future economic performance.[3] Similarly, if we conclude that a particular economic relationship holds for the U.S. economy, then we must be careful about asserting that it also holds for the European economy, or the Chinese economy; the more different the two economies are, the less likely it is that results found by analyzing one will generalize to the other. In order to make our results as broadly applicable as possible, we want our sample to be *representative;* that is, we want it to contain observations that are similar to a broad range of cases to which we might want to apply our results. This desire leads us to want a large sample with a variety of different observations.

However, we must take care that our sample is representative of the cases to which we want to apply it, and doesn't draw on other cases that may come from different data generating processes. Suppose that we are interested in predicting the wages that welfare recipients not currently in the workforce will be able to receive if they receive training and enter the workforce. We might consider using a sample of people currently in the workforce to estimate the relationship between training and wages. But this may be a poor sample to use. Some people decide not to be in the workforce because they do not have skills that will help them earn a high wage. Therefore, people who have chosen not to be in the workforce might differ fundamentally from people who have chosen to be.[4] The wages earned by the latter group may not be very good predictors of the wages that would be earned by the former group if they came into the labor force. This problem is known as *sample selection bias.* It is important to choose a sample in such a way as to eliminate, or at least minimize, the possibility of such bias. We do that by making sure that the sample we use to estimate the model matches, as closely as possible, the population to which we intend to apply the model after we estimate it.

Second, we must believe that our economic model is a good description of every observation in the sample. If not, then our sample is being generated by two different

---

[3] Nobel laureate Robert Lucas has raised a serious concern about the use of historical data to guide future economic policy, which has become known as the Lucas critique. The results of econometric analysis are often used to guide government policies, and the people (or firms, or markets) in the sample may base their decisions on those same government policies. If governments change their policies as a result of the econometric analysis, then the behavior of the people in the sample may change; as a consequence, the old econometric results will no longer apply! This difficulty can be solved only if the economic model includes the way in which people make their decisions in response to government policy, which generally produces a complicated model that can be difficult to estimate. The Lucas critique poses, at least in theory, a deep challenge to our ability to apply econometric findings to policy problems, which we should be aware of even though dealing with the critique is difficult.

[4] Remember that people who are unemployed are part of the labor force as long as they continue to search for a job. Thus, although people do not choose to be unemployed, they do choose whether to be part of the labor force, since they decide whether to continue searching for a job, or not.

data generating processes and our analysis will not describe either one of them accurately. To be sure that our results are reliable, we want our data sample to be composed of *comparable observations*. We will never be able to get every observation to be exactly comparable to every other one, because different people and firms and countries have differences in their behavior, and people and firms and countries change their behavior over time. The relationships in economic data about those people and firms and countries may therefore change when the behavior that generated the data change. But we would like to do the best we can. This desire leads us to want a small sample of very similar observations, which directly contradicts our desire to have a large sample with a variety of observations. Choosing a sample always involves a trade-off between having the observations be representative and having them be comparable. Another part of being a good econometrician is choosing an appropriate sample to analyze that makes this tradeoff in the best possible way.

There are some things we can do to handle a sample whose observations are not strictly comparable. If we can measure the ways in which the observations are different, we can put variables into the regression to control for these differences. For example, if we know that big countries tend to have more output than small countries, then we can include population as a variable in the model we use to predict output, along with interest rates. Or we can modify the data themselves; for instance, we can compare countries on the basis of output per capita instead of on total output. The ways in which we deal with the problems of comparability in the sample are discussed in more length in later chapters. It is important to note, however, that as long as we think we can control for the differences between observations in the sample, we are usually better off having a larger and more representative sample, to make the results as broadly applicable as possible.[5]

Given a sample, the next problem is to obtain measurements on the variables of the model, in order to form a data set. Sometimes econometricians collect their own data, but far more frequently they rely on data collected by others. The problem is, then, to find out what data are available and from where. Economic data come from four broad sources:

1. *Government.* Nearly all governments in the world collect data on economic activity in their jurisdictions so that they can make policies to improve their economic performance. Much of these data are available to the public, although sometimes in limited form to protect the confidentiality of the individuals in the sample. In the United States, a great deal of economic data is available from the Census Bureau, through various arms such as the Bureau of Labor Statistics (which provides information on employment, occupation, and wages) and the Bureau of Economic Analysis (which tracks macroeconomic performance). Other government agencies collect and distribute their own data; for example, data on transportation are available through the Bureau of Transportation Statistics, and data on U.S. trade with the rest of the world are available through the International Trade Commission. Governments of most other countries collect similar data and make them available through their own government agencies. Data on a range of countries are collected by a variety of international organizations, such as the International Monetary Fund, the World Bank, and various arms of the United Nations. Subnational governments collect a variety of data relevant to their own local concerns

---

[5] There are also techniques that can be used to deal with differences between observations that we cannot observe with variables, but they are beyond the scope of this book.

and interests. Some sort of data on almost any topic related to an economic regulation, a policy, or a spending program can be obtained from the government agency responsible for that regulation or policy or program.

2. *Business.* Because of the commercial value of economic forecasts, businesses need economic data. Some companies collect their own, but others buy data from companies in the business of collecting economic data and selling them to other businesses, or to anyone else willing to pay a fee for their use. Sometimes these data are sold to colleges and universities for use by their faculty and students. Other data sets are available for individual purchase. The drawback to these data sets is that they cost money, but they are often an excellent source of data in areas that the government is not concerned with, and many colleges and universities make funds available for purchasing data.

3. *Public information sources.* Many useful economic data are available for free in the press and other public sources. Excellent financial data on stock, bond, and mutual fund prices, as well as exchange rates and commodity prices, are available every day in any major newspaper. Data on the production and salaries of professional athletes are regularly published, as is information on public expenditure on stadiums and other facilities that support professional athletic teams. Data relating to items of public interest such as welfare reform can occasionally be found in public sources as well. It can be hard, or even impossible, to find an entire sample of data this way, but public sources can often be used to supplement data obtained from government or private sources with measures of additional variables for the economic model.

4. *Other econometricians.* Many academic econometricians make data sets available to the public through their colleges and universities, and several universities have major collections of data sets that are available to the public. Furthermore, any published piece of econometric research will contain a description of the data set used in the analysis, and the source from which it was obtained. If you have a topic in mind but are not certain where to get data on it, an excellent strategy is to find papers written by other economists on the same subject and see what data they used. Unless the data they used is confidential or prohibitively expensive, you can get the same data they got and use it for your own econometric project. Doing this can turn up a number of obscure data sets that might not be easily located any other way.

Once a source is identified, obtaining data is usually simple. A large number of data sets are available on the World Wide Web; in fact, there are numerous websites dedicated to providing data sets by download. An increasing amount of government data is available this way, and many public information sources now have websites that provide the back content of their publications, including useful data. Most data available on the World Wide Web are free because of the difficulty of collecting money for data distributed that way. Other data sources, particularly those that sell data, will send you a CD-ROM or disk containing data that you can read directly into your computer. Sometimes these data come in database formats used by popular econometrics software; more frequently, they come in Excel spreadsheets or plain-text files, which you can then read into whatever software package you like. And there is still the old-fashioned method of finding data from books or newspapers in the library and typing it into the computer by hand. This is a laborious technique, but it is effective and has the advantage of not making you dependent on anyone else to provide you with anything; a few hours of effort and your data set is ready to go.

2.4 PRESENTING THE FINDINGS OF THE ANALYSIS

Once you have a question, a model that lets you convert the question into a statement about the relationship between two or more variables, and a data set that lets you look for that relationship, you can perform an econometric analysis and draw some conclusions about the answer to the question. Normally you write a paper that presents the question and conclusions—along with the model, data, and analysis that supports the conclusions—and some discussion of what the conclusions mean and why they are interesting. In this way the results of your econometric project become available to other econometricians interested in the same topic, which permits our understanding of the economy as a whole to develop step by step.

A good paper is one that uses its data and analysis to deliver an interesting message about what you learned from the analysis. The purpose of the analysis should be to correctly identify the relationships in the data and draw the correct conclusions from them. There is no fixed number of observations you must have, number of variables you must include in your economic model, or sequence of analytical steps you must go through. In each case you must use the model, data, and methods that are most appropriate for the topic that you have chosen to write about. These can vary dramatically from topic to topic. For a study of the U.S. macroeconomy using annual data, 50 observations is about as many as you could reliably hope for, and that is plenty of data for such a project (although the number of different economic effects you could hope to identify with 50 observations will not be very large). In contrast, for a study of workforce participation using census data, you could easily use thousands or even tens of thousands of observations, and in such a case 50 observations would be far too few to consider the results seriously. The number of observations you should have depends on what you are trying to do, the complexity of the model you are trying to estimate, and of course the data that are available to you. The same is true of the model and the analytical methods you use: you must use what is appropriate to your topic, and part of being a good econometrician is developing judgment about what is an appropriate model, data set, or technique and what is not.

As with papers in any discipline, the quality of your writing will affect the ability of other people to learn from your work. Therefore, good writing is essential. Grammar, vocabulary, and organization are key elements in presenting the steps of your argument. Your paper must present a question to the reader and propose an answer; a good paper is one that not only clearly and convincingly demonstrates to the reader that the proposed answer is correct but also explains the importance of that answer. Thus, there are a number of things you should do whenever you write an econometrics paper:

1. Clearly state the exact question that your analysis will answer. Stating the question prepares the reader to understand your reasons for choosing your model and your data.

2. Explain to the reader, using an economic model, what economic variables you think have relationships, and why you believe those relationships exist. For example, we believe that prices are related to incomes of consumers because increases in income tend to increase demand for the products that consumers buy, and when demand for a product increases, so does its price (and also the quantity bought and sold).

3. Also explain to the reader exactly what the variables in the data set are, including the units of measurement: Is GDP in millions or billions of dollars? Is it nominal or real? Is

"unemployment" the number of unemployed workers or the percentage of the labor force that is unemployed? Also give the reasons why you believe each variable in the data set corresponds to one of the variables in the economic model. If you use an economic model that includes the price level as a variable, you must think about whether the consumer price index or the producer price index is a more appropriate way to measure the economic concept of "price level" with real data. Which is better will probably depend on the exact nature of your project and research question. It is customary to include a table in your paper showing the means and standard deviations of every variable in the data set so that the reader can get a sense of what the data look like. Also state what the unit of observation is, how many observations are in the sample, and why you chose that particular sample to estimate the model. Give your readers enough information that they could replicate what you did if they chose to do so.

4. Present not only the statistical findings of your results but also their economic meaning. Do not, for instance, merely report, "There is a negative relationship between changes in unemployment and GDP growth." That is true, but it is not very interesting in and of itself. What matters is the economic interpretation of this relationship. Do report that this finding means that an increase in GDP growth will reduce unemployment, and that this means the government may want to consider stimulating the economy with monetary or fiscal policy if it is interested in reducing high unemployment and its attendant negative consequences.

5. If you look at several variations of your basic model (and you almost always will), identify the one you believe is best, and use that one to draw your conclusions.

6. Use good writing techniques in presenting the results. Write an outline of the paper, showing each step of the argument, before writing the first draft. Use the first person singular ("I ask whether unemployment and GDP are correlated," "I collected data on the Japanese economy from 1959 to 1994") or plural ("We ask . . . ," "We collected . . .") according to whether you are working alone or with others. Avoid the third person ("A regression was estimated," "The test was performed to answer the question").[6]

Of course, there are also some things you should not do when you write your paper:

1. Do not use excessive jargon, overly long words, or other forms of verbal obfuscation that prevent the reader from understanding what you are saying. Clear, simple, and concise language is better whenever you are in doubt—though you must not sacrifice technical accuracy to achieve simplicity.

2. Do not do analysis for the sake of doing analysis. Do analysis only when it leads to a better, more reliable economic conclusion. It is not necessary to estimate models or conduct tests simply to show that you can. Eliminate all that is unnecessary to support

---

[6] It is a matter of convention whether first-person language is permissible or not. In many disciplines, especially the laboratory sciences, it is not; but in economics it is. Pick up an issue of any economics journal at random, flip to any article, and in 95 percent of cases you will find the author(s) using first-person language. It is a matter of some historical interest why economics has evolved to allow this style in its written expression and other disciplines have not. Be that as it may, in this day and age, with a very few exceptions, economists accept first-person language because it leads to simpler and clearer writing in a field that has all too little of that. Take advantage of the power of first-person language to make your work easier for your reader to understand.

your conclusions, and focus on that which is. Not only will this keep your paper shorter, and thus save you effort, but it helps your readers understand exactly where your conclusions are coming from and prevents confusion.

3. Do not skimp on figures and graphs. Economists use graphs all the time for a simple reason; pictures convey information very effectively in ways that words cannot. If you are using a supply-and-demand model, then draw a picture with a supply curve and a demand curve, and demonstrate the economic relationship you expect to find. Similarly, when you can present your data or findings most effectively with a plot or a scatter diagram, do so. Use whatever method of written expression is most appropriate for conveying the points you are making to the reader. In economics, a good picture is worth at least 1,000 words, and often more.

4. Do not make basic spelling and grammatical errors. In particular, there are three writing errors that econometrics students regularly make that you can avoid with a little bit of care. First, use *affect* and *effect* correctly; in normal usage, *affect* is a verb and *effect* is a noun. Second, do not use the passive voice unless you have no choice. It is invariably awkward and can almost invariably be replaced with the active voice, which makes sentences shorter and clearer. "John threw the ball" is better than "The ball was thrown by John." Using the first person will help you keep your sentences in the active voice. Third, do not use vague or imprecise language; use the most precise terms that you can to convey meaning to the reader. Do not say the demand curve is "very steep"; say that it has an elasticity of 0.3. Vague language often signals that you are not certain what you are trying to say; in such a case, step away from the keyboard for a few minutes, think carefully about exactly what point you are trying to make, and start again.

Beyond these dos and don'ts, there is one final thing you should do: Do get good reference works on how to write an economics paper, and follow their advice. The article "Economical Writing" by D. N. McCloskey, cited in this chapter's opening quotation, and a number of related works that have appeared since contain a wealth of helpful suggestions (including most of the ones given above and many others besides) that can make you a better writer, and hence help you do a better job of communicating your findings to other economists. Good general writing guides are also easy to come by, and you should have one. The better your writing is, the better your work is. Even the best econometrics projects are all but useless if their findings are not written down in a way that permits other people to benefit from the author's work.

Chapter Review

- Economists conduct econometric projects to answer particular economic questions.
- A good question is a relevant question; that is, it is related to some important economic issue or problem, of which a better understanding is useful.
- A good question must be a positive question; that is, it must have a precise and objective answer that econometric analysis can determine. It should also give us information about a normative issue that helps us make better judgments or decisions about the problem to which the question is related.
- Once we choose the question, we identify an economic model that translates the question into a mathematical format that can be analyzed.

- The model lets us identify likely correlations among variables to look for in the data; it also allows us to identify spurious correlations that may exist by coincidence but that do not mean anything.
- Once we select the model, we need to find a data sample to use to estimate it. A larger data set is more powerful, but using too much data can make it more difficult to be certain that one relationship correctly describes all of the observations.
- Once we finish the analysis, we write a paper to present the findings. The findings are not valuable unless they are clearly presented in a well-written paper that allows other economists to appreciate them and make use of them.

Part Two

Probability and Statistics

Because not all the factors that affect the real economy can be captured in a simple model of the economy (or even in a complex one), the economy never does exactly what our models predict it should do. The differences between the model's predictions and the real economy are, from our perspective as econometricians, random. In order to estimate the parameters of our models, and test whether or not their values support our theory about the economy, we need to have a basic understanding of probability and statistics, so we can understand those random differences. In Part II, we provide the statistical background that is the foundation of econometric analysis. We start by discussing random variables and their properties, then turn to ways of estimating those properties from samples of data and testing hypotheses about the behavior of those variables.

Chapter **Three**

Random Variables

Do not expect to arrive at certainty in every subject which you pursue. There are a hundred things wherein we mortals . . . must be content with probability, where our best light and reasoning will reach no farther.

Isaac Watts, Improvement of the Mind

3.1 ECONOMIC VARIABLES THAT ARE UNPREDICTABLE

Few other parts of the economy receive as much popular attention as the stock market does. Major newspapers devote several pages each day to lists of the prices of the various stocks traded on each market; prices are also available almost instantaneously over cable television and the World Wide Web. Why is so much effort put into making information about stock prices so readily available? Partly it is because of their economic importance—billions of dollars' worth of stock changes hands on a daily basis—but partly it is because stock prices are random and updated information about them is therefore inherently valuable.

Even though stock prices are unpredictable, economic theory does have some ideas about how they should behave. Suppose it was known that a certain stock would rise in value next week. What would happen? Investors would rush to buy the stock while it was still cheap; next week they could resell the stock at the new, higher price and pocket the profits. However, as investors rushed to buy the stock now, they would drive its price up, as demand for it increased (and the supply of people willing to sell the stock decreased as well, for the same reason). The price would continue to rise as long as it stayed lower than the price was going to be next week; it would stop rising only when it reached the exact level that it was expected to reach next week (minus a small amount to allow for the difference in value of money today and its value next week, and to compensate for the risk of investing in a stock whose value might fall). If instead it was known that the stock was going to decline, the reverse would happen; more investors would try to sell it, fewer would be willing to buy it, and the price would fall until it reached the price that it was expected to sell at next week.

This can be summed up in a form known as the efficient markets hypothesis: *The price of a stock today is equal to its expected future value.* If a stock was expected to rise or fall in the future, then it would actually rise or fall immediately until it reached the expected price. In equilibrium, it cannot be the case that the stock is expected to rise or fall; if that was the case, the price would change until it was no longer expected to do so. Of course, in reality it will either rise or fall; our theory implies that we cannot know in advance which it will do, or by how much. Changes in stock prices are, in this sense, random.

Despite the fact that changes in stock prices are random variables, it is still important to understand them and their properties. Stocks that may rise or fall create a financial risk for their owner, which the owner may want to quantify or attempt to protect himself against. Stocks with greater risks may offer higher returns. Also, some stocks tend to fall when others rise; creating a diversified portfolio of stocks can give the owner assurance that part of the portfolio will always do well (though another part will always do poorly). And of course, there are many other random variables besides stock prices that it is important to be able to predict and understand; indeed, many economists make their living by creating (and selling) their forecasts of unpredictable variables such as interest rates, inflation rates, car prices, and new housing starts. This chapter presents the basic statistical tools econometric analysis uses to describe and analyze random variables.

What do we mean when we say that a variable is random? The word *random* is difficult to define and is used in mainstream English in a confusing variety of ways. We will adopt the following definition:

Definition 3.1 A *random variable* has four properties:

1. It takes a single, specific value.
2. We do not know in advance what value it happens to take.
3. We do, however, know all of the possible values it may take.
4. We know the probability that it will take any one of those possible values.

The result of rolling a six-sided die is a simple example of a random variable. When rolled, it will clearly take exactly one of six values; 1, 2, 3, 4, 5, or 6. Before we roll it, we do not know which it will be; but if the die is fair, we know there is a $\frac{1}{6}$ chance of each number being the result. If the die is not fair, the chance may not be equal to $\frac{1}{6}$ for each number, but if we know the properties of the die, we can still state the chance that any given number will be the result. Tommorow's price of a stock is also random by this definition; it is going to take a specific value, however, we do not know what value it is going to take until after the trading day closes, but (if we do some econometrics first) we can calculate a probability for any particular outcome.

3.2   THE PROBABILITY MASS FUNCTION AND PROBABILITY DENSITY FUNCTION

We can completely describe a random variable by listing all the values it can take, or a range of values in which it will fall, and the chance that it will take any one of them. We refer to the one that it actually does take, when and if we learn it, as the *realized value* of the random variable.

Definition 3.2 A random variable that takes a finite number of values is called a *discrete random variable*. We can represent it with a chart showing all possible outcomes and their probabilities. This chart is called the random variable's *probability mass function (PMF)*.

FIGURE 3.1
The Probability Mass Function (PMF) of a Fair Die

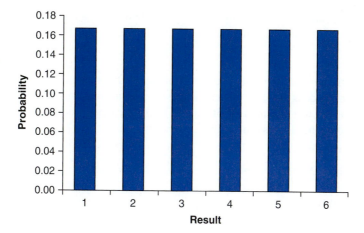

FIGURE 3.2
The Probability Mass Function (PMF) of an Unfair Die

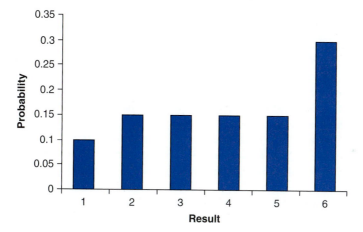

Figure 3.1 shows six possible values the die can take, and the probability that each will occur. In this case, the probability of each outcome is the same; it is $\frac{1}{6}$, or approximately 0.1667, or 16.67 percent. If the die is not fair, then the chance of each outcome will not be equal. Figure 3.2 shows the PMF of a die that rolls more 6s, and fewer 1s, than a fair die. This die has a 0.3, or 30 percent, chance of producing a 6 when thrown, only a 10 percent chance of a 1, and a 15 percent chance of any other number.

PMFs must obey some simple properties, which we can describe algebraically. Let X be a random variable, let X_i be a possible outcome of the random variable, let I be the set of all possible outcomes, and let $P(X_i)$ be the probability that outcome X_i occurs. Then it must be the case that

$$\sum_I P(X_i) = 1 \qquad\qquad \textbf{(3.2.1)}$$

That is, the sum of the probability of all possible outcomes must equal 1, since it is guaranteed that one (and only one) outcome will occur. It must also be the case that

$$P(X_i) \leq 1 \qquad\qquad (3.2.2)$$

for all values of i; that is, no single outcome can have a chance greater than 100 percent.

A stock price is different from a die roll because a stock price can take any nonnegative real value, not just a limited set of values. Thus we cannot produce a complete list of each possible outcome and its probability.[1] Instead, we can define a range of values within which the outcome must fall.

> **Definition 3.3** A random variable that can take any value within a range of values is called a *continuous random variable*. We can represent it by a graph showing the probability that it will take a value in any part of its range. This graph is called the random variable's *probability density function (PDF)*.

The difference between the PMF of a discrete random variable and the PDF of a continuous random variable comes from the fact that the continuous random variable can take an infinite number of possible values. Therefore, the probability that any particular one of them (say, 0.32358903756627815401) will occur is zero. With continuous random variables, instead of talking about the chance of any single value, we talk about the chance that the value will fall into a certain range of values. We define the PDF so that, for any range of values the random variable can take, the area under the curve is equal to the chance that the random variable will fall in that range.

For example, consider a random variable U that can take any value between 0 and 1, with each value being equally likely. Such a random variable is called a *uniform random variable*. Then the PDF looks like Figure 3.3. Values less than 0 and greater than 1 are impossible, so the PDF of U is equal to 0 both to the left of 0 and to the right of 1. For values between 0 and 1, all values are equally likely, so the function has the same height for all of them. Because the chance that U will fall between 0 and 1 is 100 percent, the area under the curve between 0 and 1 must be equal to 1. That area is a square with a width of 1, so to make its area equal to 1, its height must be 1 as well.

FIGURE 3.3
The Probability Density Function (PDF) of a Uniform Random Variable

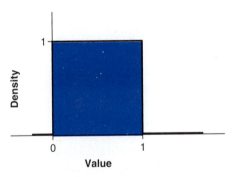

---

[1] Historically, stock prices were constrained to be a multiple of $\frac{1}{8}$ (e.g., $5\frac{1}{8}$ or $27\frac{3}{4}$) and were therefore discrete, not continuous. Today they can be any positive number with two digits after the decimal place (e.g., 25.63, 46.71). Technically they are still discrete; however, because there are thousands of possible values, for the purposes of an economic model it is often better to treat them as continuous variables and round their values off to the nearest hundredth.

We can write the PDF of U mathematically as well as graphically. The PDF for a uniform random variable is given by

$$f(U_i) = 1 \quad \text{if} \quad 0 < U_i < 1 \tag{3.2.3}$$
$$f(U_i) = 0 \quad \text{if} \quad U_i < 0 \quad \text{or} \quad U_i > 1$$

In the case of the uniform random variable, clearly the chance of getting a value between 0 and 1 must be 100 percent. Furthermore, if all values are equally likely, then the chance of getting a value between 0 and 0.5 must be 50 percent; the chance of getting one between 0 and 0.25 must be 25 percent; and similarly, the chance of getting one between 0.5 and 0.75 must also be 25 percent.

We therefore read the PDF this way: The chance that a continuous random variable will take a value between any two values X_1 and X_2 is equal to the area under the PDF between X_1 and X_2. Figure 3.4 shows two examples for the uniform PDF. The height of the pink box is 1, and its width is 0.5, so the chance of getting a value between 0 and 0.5 is 0.5, or 50 percent. The chance of getting a value between 0.5 and 0.8 is the area of the red box, which has height 1 and width 0.3, so the chance is 0.3, or 30 percent. The same method can be used to calculate the chance of the random value falling in any range we choose.

As is the case with discrete random variables, the total probability of all outcomes must be 100 percent. For a continuous random variable, this implies that the total area under the curve, between the minimum and maximum value that the variable can take, must always be equal to 1, as it is here. This is similar to the property that for a discrete random variable, the sum of all probabilities must equal 1. However, the value of the PDF of a continuous random variable can be greater than 1, as the following example shows.

Consider a random variable that is equally likely to take any value between 0 and 0.5. This variable also has a uniform distribution, but over a different range than the previous one. Its PDF is shown in Figure 3.5. The height of this PDF is 2, which it must be in order to make the total area under the curve equal to 1. This can happen because the width of the rectangle is less than 1. Although the curve has a height greater than 1, there is no way to draw an area underneath the curve with an area greater than 1—it is not wide enough. Therefore, no range of outcomes can have a probability greater than 100 percent, which matches what we would expect.

One difficulty with PMFs and PDFs is that they require us to know the exact chance of each possible outcome, or range of outcomes. For a hypothetical situation, such as the toss

FIGURE 3.4
Interpreting the Probability Density Function (PDF) of a Uniform Variable

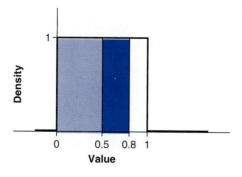

FIGURE 3.5
The
Probability
Density
Function
(PDF) of a
Second
Uniform
Random
Variable

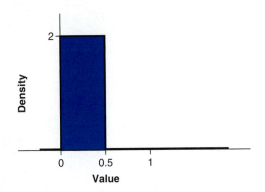

FIGURE 3.6
Empirical
Probability
Density
Function
(PDF) for
Change in
Stock Price of
Dell Computer
Corporation

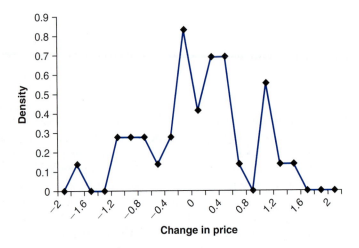

of a coin or a fair die, we know those chances. For any real economic variable, such as a stock price, we do not know the chance of each possible outcome and thus we cannot draw the PDF of the random variable. However, if we can observe many different realized values of a random variable, then we can approximate the PMF or PDF of the variable. For a discrete random variable, outcomes with higher chances will come up more often if we observe many realized values. For a continuous random variable, the realized values will more frequently fall into ranges with higher density.

Definition 3.4 The *empirical density function* of a random variable (or *empirical mass function* of a discrete variable) is a chart based on a sample of observed values of the random variable's realized values, showing the percentage of times that each value has been observed, if the random variable is discrete, or the percentage of times it has fallen into various ranges, if continuous.

Figure 3.6 shows the empirical PDF of the changes in the price of the stock of Dell Computer Corporation in May and June 2001, calculated using ranges 20 cents wide. The change in price of this stock during that period meets our definition of a random variable; it has a specific value, but at the start of each day, no one knew what that value would be.

However, the possible values were known, and we can state, at least approximately, what the chance of each possible value was.

The most likely changes were small. On 6 of the 36 trading days in the sample, Dell's price dropped by an amount between 0 and 20 cents. Thus, for the empirical PDF, the chance of a change between −20 cents and 0 cents, for example, is set equal to $\frac{6}{36}$, or 16.7 percent. This is equal to the height of the graph in that range (0.83) multiplied by the width of that range (0.2). On 9 of the 36 days, the change was between up 20 cents and down 20 cents; thus, the chance of a change between −20 cents and 20 cents is set equal to 25 percent. Changes close to 0 were relatively likely; chances of more than a dollar were relatively rare, as the function is lower in that area, generally 0.3 or below. The chance of a rise and the chance of a fall are approximately equal, as the area to the left of 0 and the area to the right of 0 are about the same (the price rose on 20 days and fell on 16 days).

It is very important to realize that this graph does not give the true PDF of the variable. Unless we know the data generating process that creates the values of the stock price (and we do not), then we cannot know the true PDF. The best we can do is create an approximation, which is what the empirical PDF is. Figure 3.6 shows what actually happened in May and June 2001, but other outcomes might have occurred. For example, the stock price never changed by more than $2 in a single day during the sample period, so this PDF shows a density of 0 for changes of that amount. However, *ex ante,* it was certainly possible that the stock might have risen or fallen by more than $2 on a single day. But it was unlikely to do so, and the true probability that it will, though not exactly equal to 0, is close to 0. In a case where we do not know the data generating process, and have to rely on observed data to calculate it, an approximately correct answer is the best we can hope for, an issue we will return to in Chapter 4.

3.3   THE CUMULATIVE DISTRIBUTION FUNCTION

Fairly frequently, we are concerned not with the chance that a random value will take exactly a certain value but with the chance that it will be less than (or perhaps less than or equal to) a certain value. For example, we might want to know the chance of rolling 4 or less on a fair die, or the chance that a stock price will fall more than $1.50. The PDF will tell us this. For the case of a discrete random variable, such as the roll of a die, the probability of getting a number less than or equal to X is equal to the sum of the probabilities of all outcomes less than X. For instance, the chance of rolling 4 or less on a fair die is $\frac{1}{6} + \frac{1}{6} + \frac{1}{6} + \frac{1}{6} = \frac{2}{3}$.

For a continuous random variable, the chance of getting an outcome less than X is the area under the PDF that is to the left of X on the curve. Figure 3.7 shows the probability that a uniform random variable with a range from 0 to 1 will be less than 0.6. The area under the curve has a height of 1 and a width of 0.6, so the chance that the realized value will be in this range is 0.6, or 60 percent. We can do the same calculation for any value of X we choose, and graph the results.

Definition 3.5 The *cumulative distribution function (CDF)* of a random variable X is a graph associating all possible values, or the range of possible values, with the chance that X will be less than or equal to X.

FIGURE 3.7
Chance That
a Uniform
Random
Variable Will
Be Less Than
0.6

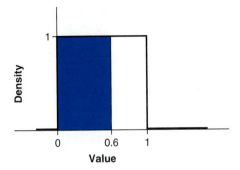

FIGURE 3.8
Cumulative
Distribution
Function
(CDF) of a Fair
Die Roll

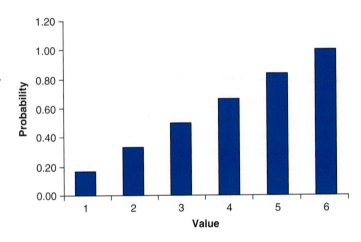

FIGURE 3.9
Cumulative
Distribution
Function
(CDF) of a
Uniform
Random
Variable

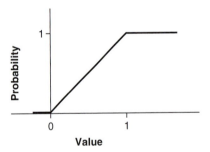

Figure 3.8 shows the CDF for a roll of a fair die; Figure 3.9 shows the CDF of a uniform random variable with a range of 0 to 1.

There are several features common to all CDFs. Because they are probabilities, they are always between 0 and 1; that is

$$0 \leq F(X_i) \leq 1 \qquad \textbf{(3.3.1)}$$

where $F(X_i)$ is the CDF. Furthermore, they are always increasing functions. This is because if we consider two possible values X and Y, and if $X < Y$, then the chance of getting a realized value less than Y must be greater than the chance of getting a realized value less than X; all values less than X are also less than Y, but some values less than Y are greater than X. Therefore, for any cumulative distribution function F, if $X < Y$, then $F(X) \leq F(Y)$, and the function must be increasing.

3.4   PROPERTIES OF RANDOM VARIABLES

A PDF is a very complete way of describing a random variable but, unfortunately, a rather cumbersome one. It will not, for instance, help us test our economic idea that stock prices should not be expected to rise or fall on any given day. In order to analyze random variables, we need to be able to simply summarize the information contained in the PDF in a way that can be compared to the predictions of economic theory.

The first and most basic description of a random value is its *expected value,* or *mean value*. The mean value is a measure of the value we expect that the random variable will take on average.

Definition 3.6 The mean value of a discrete random variable X is calculated by:

$$\mu = \sum_I X_i \cdot P(X_i) \tag{3.4.1}$$

where I is the set of all possible outcomes. The mean value of a continuous random variable is calculated by:

$$\mu = \int_I X \cdot P(X)\, dX \tag{3.4.2}$$

Using this formula to calculate the expected value of the result of tossing a fair die, we find that

$$\mu = 1(0.167) + 2(0.167) + 3(0.167) + 4(0.167) + 5(0.167) + 6(0.167)$$
$$= 0.167 + 0.333 + 0.5 + 0.667 + 0.833 + 1 = 3.5$$

For the random variable distributed uniformly between 0 and 1, the mean value turns out to be 0.5.

The expected value of a random variable has the following useful property:

Theorem 3.1 The law of large numbers: Suppose one repeatedly observes different realized values of a random variable and calculates the average of the realized values. This average will tend to be close to the expected value; the more times one observes the random variable, the closer the average will tend to be.

We can demonstrate that this is true. Let N be the total number of times the random variable is observed, and let N_i be the number of times outcome i is observed. Then N_i will be approximately equal to $N \cdot P(X_i)$, and the total of all the observations will be

$$\sum X_i \cdot N_i = \sum X_i \cdot N \cdot P(X_i)$$

Dividing the total by N to calculate the average value produces

$$\sum X_i \cdot P(X_i)$$

which is the same as the formula for the expected value.

   This suggests a use for the expected value—if you have to predict the value of the random variable before you know the realized value, predict the expected value. Over the long term you will guess correctly on average. It also suggests a way to quantify the efficient markets hypothesis, that the price of a stock today is equal to its expected future value. If you hold a stock over many days, or hold many stocks for one day, on average they should go neither up nor down; the average price change should be 0.[2] If so, then the expected value of the change on any given day should be 0 also. Having put the hypothesis into statistical terms, we can use data to test whether or not it is correct.

   However, whether a stock will go up or down is not the only thing that concerns us about it; we would also like to know how much it will go up or down. Some stocks are prone to sudden large rises and falls in value; such stocks are riskier than those whose prices are less likely to have large changes. In general, some random variables are likely to take values relatively close to their mean values; others are more likely to lie far from their mean values. Figure 3.10 shows such a case: the two variables have the same mean value, 5.5, but values of 5 and 6 are more likely for the random variable with the red PDF, and values of 1 and 10 are more likely for the random variable with the black PDF. The second measure of the random variable, its *variance,* will give us a measure of how far the value of the random variable is likely to be away from its mean; the black PDF will have a higher variance than the red one.

FIGURE 3.10

Two Random Variables with Different Variances

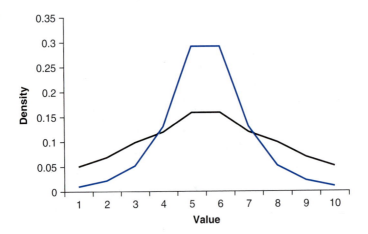

[2] Or, at least close to 0. In the simple model put forward, it would be exactly 0; in the real world, due to the time value of money and the risk involved with holding the stock, it should actually be a small positive number, though for a holding period of a single day it should be quite near 0. The difference is the result of the discrepancy between the simple model and the real world it purports to describe, a problem with all economic models; making the economic model more complicated will reduce the discrepancy but will not eliminate it.

We might consider taking the average value of the distance between the variable and its mean value; that is, the average value of $(X_i - \mu)$. Unfortunately, $(X_i - \mu)$ will be positive when the realized value is above the mean value, and negative when it will be below, and if we take the average value of $(X_i - \mu)$, positive and negative values will cancel each other out. Instead, we look at the average value of $(X_i - \mu)^2$, which is guaranteed to be positive, and the farther i is from μ, the larger $(X_i - \mu)^2$ will be.

Definition 3.7 *For a discrete random variable, the variance σ^2 is calculated by:*

$$\sigma^2 = \sum_I (X_i - \mu)^2 \cdot P(X_i) \qquad \text{(3.4.3)}$$

For a continuous random variable, the variance is calculated by:

$$\sigma^2 = \int_I (X - \mu)^2 \cdot P(X) \, dX \qquad \text{(3.4.4)}$$

where $P(X_i)$ is the probability of outcome i, as above, and the mean value μ is calculated from Equation 3.4.1 or Equation 3.4.2.

Unfortunately, because the variance is the average value of the squared distance between i and μ, it does not have an easy interpretation. It is therefore often helpful to use a second measure, called the standard deviation of the random variable.

Definition 3.8 *The standard deviation σ of a random variable is equal to the square root of the variance of the random variable.*

The standard deviation uses the square root to undo the squaring that was done in the variance formula. It is therefore, in some sense, the average difference between X_i and μ; more specifically, it is the square root of the mean squared difference.

Using these formulas, we can calculate the variance and standard deviation of the roll of a fair die. The mean value μ, as calculated before, is 3.5, and the chance of each outcome is $\frac{1}{6}$. Therefore, the variance is

$$\sum_I (X_i - 3.5)^2 \left(\frac{1}{6} \right)$$

or

$$\frac{(1 - 3.5)^2}{6} + \frac{(2 - 3.5)^2}{6} + \frac{(3 - 3.5)^2}{6} + \frac{(4 - 3.5)^2}{6} + \frac{(5 - 3.5)^2}{6} + \frac{(6 - 3.5)^2}{6}$$

which works out to approximately 2.917. The standard deviation is the square root of this, which is approximately 1.708. This means that we should expect the die roll to fall about 1.708 away from its mean value of 3.5. This is, indeed, about correct—a result of 1 or 6 is more than 2 away from the mean value; a result of 2, 3, 4, or 5 is less than 2 away from the mean value.[3]

---

[3] Note that the standard deviation is not equal to the average absolute difference between the mean and value, which is equal to 1.5 (one-third of the time the difference will be 0.5, one-third of the time it will be 1.5, one-third of the time it will be 2.5.) This happens because of the squaring in the variance formula. The standard deviation is normally slightly larger than the average absolute difference between the mean and the value.

FIGURE 3.11

Empirical
Probability
Density
Function
(PDF) for
Change in
Stock Price of
Yahoo

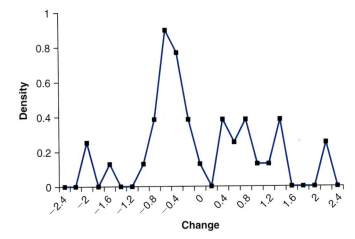

We can approximate the variance and the standard deviation of the daily change in the stock price of Dell Computer Corporation, as shown in Figure 3.6. We do not know the true mean of the change in the stock price, although the efficient markets hypothesis says it should be close to 0. However, we can take the average change in a sample of stock prices; the law of large numbers tells us that this average change should be close to the true mean, which we cannot know. Over this period, the average change in Dell's stock price was −0.099, but on most days it was rather more or less than that. How much more or less? Approximate values for the variance and standard deviation of the change in the stock price can be calculated using the same raw data that produced the empirical density function; the approximate variance is 0.524 and the approximate standard deviation is 0.724. This implies that the change in the stock price should, on average, be about 0.724 above or below the mean value, and a look at Figure 3.6 shows that this is, in fact, the case: About half the time the change is more than that; about half the time it is less.

We can use the standard deviation to compare the riskiness of Dell stock to other stocks, whose average change may be higher or lower.[4] Figure 3.11 shows the empirical PDF of Yahoo stock price changes over the same time period. Note that changes of more than $1 are substantially more likely, and changes over $2 happened several times; this PDF is wider than the PDF for Dell stock price changes. The variance of the stock price changes is 1.324 and the standard deviation is 1.15. The standard deviation is bigger for Yahoo than for Dell: 1.15 versus 0.72. This means that the daily stock price changes are more variable— likely to be farther from their mean value—for Yahoo than for Dell. On top of this, the average stock price of Yahoo was lower than the average price for Dell over the period: $19.07 and $25.11, respectively. The standard deviation of Yahoo stock price changes was 6.03 percent of the stock's average price; for Dell it was only 2.87 percent. Therefore, an investment in Yahoo was, over this period, more risky than one in Dell.

---

[4] Actually, the standard deviation is not a perfect measure of the true riskiness of holding a stock. However, in general it is true that stocks whose values have a high standard deviation are riskier than those with lower standard deviations, holding other factors constant.

3.5   THE NORMAL DENSITY FUNCTION

The two PDFs shown for Dell and Yahoo stock have a roughly similar shape: They have a high probability of being close to the mean value and lower probabilities the farther the value is from the mean, and they are roughly symmetric—the probability of getting a value a certain distance above the mean is about the same as the probability of getting the value the same distance below the mean. One of the most commonly used PDFs in econometrics takes this same shape—the *normal distribution,* also called the *bell curve.* Many real random variables have distributions that are either normal or approximately normal; for example, the PDF for the sum of the rolls of two dice is approximately normal. Figure 3.12 shows the PDF for a normally distributed random variable with a mean of 0 and a standard deviation of 1, called the *standard normal distribution.* The mathematical expression for the standard normal distribution function is given by the equation

$$P(X_i) = \frac{1}{\sqrt{2\pi}}e^{-X_i^2} \qquad\qquad \textbf{(3.5.1)}$$

A variable whose PDF takes the same shape, but has a different mean or variance, is also called a normally distributed random variable. Figure 3.13 shows two examples. The taller, narrower one has a mean of -1 and a variance of 0.25. Its peak is at a value of -1 rather than 0 for the standard normal density function, and the density at the peak is 0.798 as opposed to 0.399 for the standard normal. The flatter, wider one has a mean of 0.5 and a variance of 2, making it shorter and giving a higher chance of a result far from its mean.

In general, the PDF for a normally distributed random variable with mean μ and variance σ^2 is:

$$P(i) = \frac{1}{\sqrt{2\pi\sigma^2}}e^{-\left(\frac{X_i-\mu}{\sigma}\right)^2} \qquad\qquad \textbf{(3.5.2)}$$

and, if X is a random variable that has this distribution, we write $X \sim N(\mu, \sigma^2)$, where the $\sim$ indicates a description of the PDF of the random variable X, N indicates that the PDF is

FIGURE 3.12

The Standard Normal Density Function

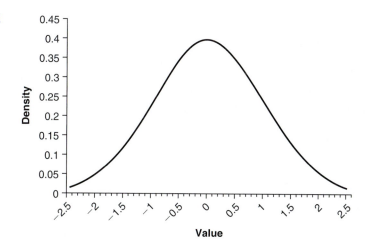

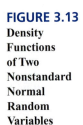

FIGURE 3.13

Density Functions of Two Nonstandard Normal Random Variables

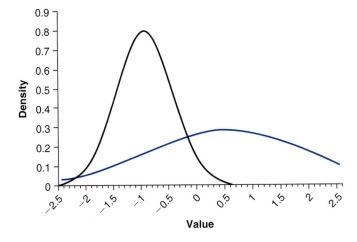

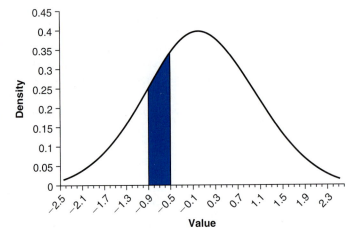

the normal PDF given by Equation 3.5.2, and μ and σ^2 are the mean and variance of X, respectively. If X happens to have the standard normal distribution function, we would write $X \sim N(0, 1)$. For the two variables in Figure 3.13, calling the first Y and the second W, we would write $Y \sim N(-1, 0.25)$ and $W \sim N(0.5, 2)$.

Calculating the probability that a normally distributed random variable will fall in a particular range is not always easy. In some cases, the probability is obvious; for example, because the normal PDF is symmetric, the probability that a normal random variable will take a value above its mean is exactly 50 percent (as is the chance that it will take a value below its mean). But for general ranges, the problem is more difficult. We can always work out an approximate answer for a specified range by working out the height of the function at two points, and using a trapezoid to approximate the area under the curve. Figure 3.14 shows this method for the chance of a standard normal random variable falling between −0.9 and −0.5. Using Equation 3.4.1, we find that the height of the left side of the trapezoid is 0.266

and the height of the right side is 0.352. The width of the trapezoid is 0.4, and using the formula for the area of a trapezoid, we get an area of 0.1236, or a 12.36 percent chance that the value of the random variable will fall between -0.9 and -0.5. We can do the same for any other finite interval we choose. However, the answer is only approximate, because the top edge of the trapezoid is a straight line, whereas the normal PDF is a curve; therefore, the area under the PDF is not quite the same as the area under the trapezoid. For small ranges, such as this one, the error is small; for larger ranges, it is greater. Furthermore, this method cannot be used to calculate the cumulative distribution function for a normal random variable, because the width of the trapezoid would be infinite, nor can we calculate the height of the left side of a trapezoid in that case. The calculation of the CDF of a normally distributed random variable requires more sophisticated methods of approximation. Rather than perform those calculations each time we need to use the normal CDF, we refer to a table of precalculated values for the standard normal distribution, which is found in Appendix A, at the end of this book. This normal distribution table shows the probability that a standard normal variable (mean 0 and variance of 1) will be greater than the values shown in the table. For instance, the probability that a standard normal variable will be greater than 0.80 is 0.2119, or 21.19 percent.

We can work out the probabilities of finite ranges using the table as well. For example, suppose we want to know the chance that a standard normal random variable will be between 0.5 and 0.8. The chance that it will be greater than 0.8, as we have seen, is 21.19 percent. The table also tells us that the chance it will be greater than 0.5 is 0.3085, or 30.85 percent. Therefore, the chance that it will be greater than 0.5 but greater than 0.8 is $30.85\% - 21.19\%$, or 9.66 percent. Or, suppose we want to know the chance that a standard normal random variable will be less than 1.1. We cannot look that up, since the table shows only the chance that the variable will be greater than a given value, but we can find it by either of two methods, demonstrated in Figure 3.15. First, we can observe that the chance that it will be greater than 1.1 is 0.1357, or 13.57 percent; therefore, the chance that it will be less than 1.1 must be 86.43 percent, since the two must add to 100 percent. Or, we can observe that the chance that it will be greater than -1.1 is 0.8643, or 86.43 percent, and since the normal density function is symmetric, the chance that it will be less than 1.1 must

FIGURE 3.15 **Two Ways of Calculating the Probability That a Standard Normal Random Variable Takes a Value Greater Than 1.1**

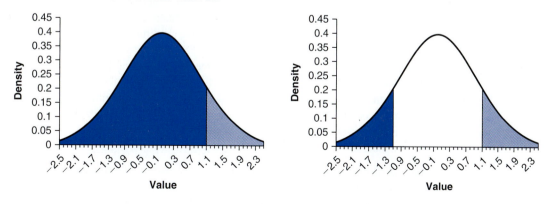

also be 13.57 percent. Using these two methods, we can calculate the probability of any range we wish to know.

Suppose the variable is normal, but not the standard normal—its mean is not 0, or its variance is not 1, or both. Then we cannot use the standard normal distribution table to find probabilities for it, at least not directly. However, we can make use of the fact that all normal PDFs have the same shape. They differ only in two ways; changing the mean shifts the PDF to the left or the right, and changing the variance makes it wider or narrower. Using this, we can state the following:

Theorem 3.2 Suppose that a variable X is distributed randomly with mean μ and variance σ^2, and we wish to know the probability that X will be less than a given value X^*. Then calculate the following:

$$Z = \frac{X^* - \mu}{\sigma}$$

The probability that X will be less than X^* is equal to the probability that the standard normal random variable will be less than Z.

Thus, to find the probability that X will be less than X^*, we calculate Z, and then look up the probability for a value less than Z on the standard normal distribution table. This process is known as transforming a nonstandard normal variable into a standard one. For example, suppose X is distributed normally with a mean of 25 and a variance of 16, and we want to know the probability that X will be less than 19. First we calculate Z:

$$Z = \frac{X^* - \mu}{\sigma} = \frac{19 - 25}{\sqrt{16}} = \frac{-6}{4} = -1.5$$

Then we look up 1.5 on the standard normal distribution table and find that the table's value is 0.0668. Therefore, the chance that a standard normal random variable will be less than -1.5 is 6.68 percent; and from Theorem 3.2, we know that the chance that X will be less than 19 is also 6.68 percent.

What does Z mean? It is the difference between X^* and μ, divided by the standard deviation of X; that is, it is the number of standard deviations between X^* and μ. In the above example, the distance between 19 and 25 is 6, which is 1.5 standard deviations, since the variance of X is 16 and thus its standard deviation is 4. Accordingly, we can think of the probability in the normal distribution table as being the chance that *any* normal random variable will be less than Z standard deviations above its mean (below its mean if Z is negative, as in the example above). From this, we can derive a useful rule of thumb. From the standard normal table, note that the value for 1 is 0.1587 and the value for -1 is 0.8413. The chance that a normal variable will be less than the value 1 standard deviation below its mean is thus 15.87 percent; the chance that it will be less than the value 1 standard deviation above its mean is 84.13 percent. Thus, the chance that it will be within 1 standard deviation of its mean is, $84.13\% - 15.87\% = 68.26\%$. Similarly, the chance that it will be within 2 standard deviations of its mean is equal to $97.72\% - 2.28\% = 95.44\%$. Rounding off a bit, we can state the following:

Theorem 3.3 A normally distributed random variable will fall within one standard deviation of its mean value about 67 percent, or two-thirds, of the time, and within two standard deviations of its mean value about 95 percent of the time.

This result will be handy to remember as we work further with normally distributed random variables in later chapters.

3.6   JOINT DISTRIBUTION OF TWO RANDOM VARIABLES

Many economic problems involve dealing with more than one variable at a time—this is why graphs, which show the relationship between two variables, are so popular in economic analysis. If both variables are random, they may be related; that is, the value that one random variable takes may depend in part on the value that the other one takes. For example, we might be interested in forecasting the price of electricity next week and the amount of electricity that will be produced. Or we might be interested in forecasting future interest rates and the number of new housing starts, the latter being an excellent leading indicator of the macroeconomy. In such cases, knowing something about what is likely to happen to one of the two variables will clearly help us predict the other one as well.

> **Definition 3.9**   The *joint probability density function* of two random variables X and Y is a function such that the area under the function for any range of X values and any range of Y values is equal to the chance that X and Y will both fall in their respective ranges.

For a simple example, consider tossing two coins. Each one can take two values, heads or tails, and there are four possible outcomes when two are tossed; heads/heads, heads/tails, tails/heads, and tails/tails. If both coins are fair, and if each toss is independent of the other, then there is a 25 percent chance of each of these outcomes occurring.[5] Figure 3.16 shows

FIGURE 3.16
Joint Probability Density Function (PDF) of Two Fair Coin Tosses

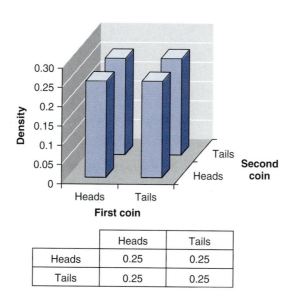

	Heads	Tails
Heads	0.25	0.25
Tails	0.25	0.25

[5] There is, however, a 50 percent chance of getting one heads and one tails. This is because that outcome can happen two ways. Either the first coin can land heads and the second one can land tails, or the reverse. There is only one way for both coins to land heads (or tails), so the chance of that is only 25 percent.

FIGURE 3.17

Supply and Demand for Oil

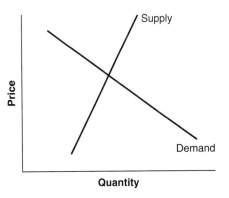

the joint PDF of two fair coin tosses. In general, we write the joint PDF as $P(X_i, Y_j)$, where X_i and Y_j are possible values of the two random variables; in this case, for instance, $P(\text{heads, heads}) = 0.25$.

We may have an economic reason to believe that two random variables are related. Suppose we are interested in forecasting the price and consumption of crude oil next month. These two variables are related by the supply and demand for oil, as shown in Figure 3.17. They will tend to move at the same time, but whether they will move together or oppositely is not clear. If the demand for oil changes, the price and quantity of oil will tend to rise and fall together; but if the supply changes, one will rise and the other will fall.

To find out, we look to see whether the variables tend to be above their means or below their means at the same time or at opposite times. If they rise and fall together, that would suggest that changes in oil prices and quantities are driven primarily by demand; if they move oppositely, then changes are driven primarily by supply. To assess this, we look at

$$(P - \mu_P)(Q - \mu_Q)$$

where P is the price of oil, Q is the quantity of oil, and μ_P and μ_Q are their mean values. If both realized values are above their means, then the product will be positive; if both realized values are below their means, it will also be positive. If one realized value is above its mean and the other is below, the product will be negative. Thus, if we know the expected value of this product, we know whether the values tend to move up and down together or oppositely. The expected value is called the *covariance* of the two variables.

Definition 3.10 For two discrete random variables X and Y, with means μ_X and μ_Y, the covariance of the two random variables is:

$$\sigma_{XY} = \sum_{I,J} (X_i - \mu_X) \cdot (Y_j - \mu_Y) \cdot P(X_i, Y_j) \qquad \textbf{(3.6.1)}$$

where X_i and Y_j are possible values of X and Y, I and J are the set of all possible values for X and Y, and $P(X_i, Y_j)$ is the joint probability density function of X and Y. For two continuous random variables, the covariance is:

$$\sigma_{XY} = \int_I \int_J (X - \mu_X) \cdot (Y - \mu_Y) \cdot P(X, Y) \, dY \, dX \qquad \textbf{(3.6.2)}$$

For the toss of two fair coins, we can calculate the covariance as follows: Let X and Y be the outcomes of each coin toss, and let a value of 1 mean *heads* and a value of 0 mean *tails*. Then the average value of each coin toss, since each outcome has a 50 percent chance, is $1(0.5) + 0(0.5) = 0.5$. There are four possible outcomes, each with a 25 percent chance of occurring. For the case of two heads, X and Y both take the value 1, so the first term of equation (3.6.1) is $(1 - 0.5)(1 - 0.5)0.25$. The entire covariance is:

$$\sigma_{XY} = (1 - 0.5)(1 - 0.5)0.25 + (1 - 0.5)(0 - 0.5)0.25$$
$$+ (0 - 0.5)(1 - 0.5)0.25 + (0 - 0.5)(0 - 0.5)0.25$$
$$= 0.125 - 0.125 - 0.125 + 0.125$$
$$= 0$$

The covariance is 0 because the coin tosses are independent; the outcome of one toss is not affected by the outcome of the other. If the covariance is not 0, then the two variables are not independent; a positive covariance means that they move up and down together, and a negative covariance means that they move oppositely.

The numerical value of the covariance of X and Y depends on the standard deviations of X and Y. If X and Y have large standard deviations, they are likely to be far from their means, $(X - \mu_X)$ and $(Y - \mu_Y)$ are likely to be large, and therefore the covariance will be large; if X and Y have small standard deviations, the covariance will be small also. We define the correlation of X and Y as the covariance of X and Y, divided by their standard deviations:

Definition 3.11 For two random variables X and Y, with means μ_X and μ_Y, the correlation of the two random variables is:

$$\rho_{XY} = \frac{\sigma_{XY}}{\sigma_X \sigma_Y} \tag{3.6.3}$$

The correlation ρ_{XY} has the useful property that it does not depend on the scale of X and Y—it is always between -1 and 1. Also, since σ_X and σ_Y must be positive numbers, it has the same sign as the covariance σ_{XY}, and has the same interpretation; positive correlations mean that variables move together, and negative correlations mean that they move oppositely. However, because the range is fixed between -1 and 1, the correlation can be interpreted quantitatively also. The closer the correlation is to 1, the more closely the variables move together, and the closer the correlation is to -1, the more closely they move in opposition. Figure 3.18 shows scatter plots of random variables with correlations of 0.95, -0.8, -0.4, and 0.1. When the correlation is positive, the variables tend to both be high or both be low, leading to a graph with a positive slope. When the correlation is negative, one tends to be high and the other low, leading to a graph with a negative slope. Correlations near 1 mean a strong relationship between the variables, and correlations near 0 indicate a weak relationship between the variables. When the correlation is 0.95, the points lie very nearly on a straight line; the variables are highly correlated. The closeness of the relation falls as the correlation falls; for a correlation of -0.8 it is still quite visible, for a correlation of -0.4 it is apparent but pronounced, and for a correlation of 0.1 it has almost vanished entirely. The correlation is thus a measure of how strong the relationship between the two random variables is. Figure 3.19 shows historical data on the correlation of oil prices and

FIGURE 3.18 **Correlations of Four Sets of Random Variables**

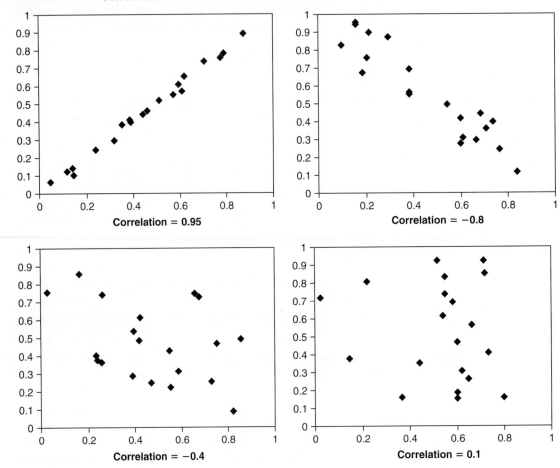

FIGURE 3.19

Correlation of Oil Prices and Quantities, 1974–2000

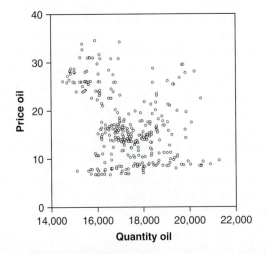

quantities between 1974 and 2000. The correlation is not very strong, but it is negative; it is −0.363. This suggests that over that time period, changes in supply were more important in determining prices and quantities of oil in the market than demand changes were, although both played a role.

Chapter Review

- Many important economic variables are *random;* we do not know what value they will take, but we know all possible values and we can assign a probability to each.
- The *realized value* of the random variable is the value it actually takes.
- The *probability density function* (PDF) is a graph showing all possible values and the chance that that value will occur.
- The *cumulative distribution function* (CDF) is a graph showing all possible values and the chance that the realized value will be less than that value.
- The *mean value* is a measure of the value that a random variable should be expected to take. If one observes the random variable many times, the average of the observed values will tend to be close to the mean value.
- The *standard deviation* is a measure of how close a random variable will be to its mean; the *variance* is the square of the standard deviation.
- *Normal random variables* are a common and important type of random variable whose probability density function is the familiar bell curve.
- To find the probability that a normally distributed random variable will be above or below a random variable, we use the normal distribution table, which shows the probability of a normal random variable being a certain number of standard deviations above or below its mean value.
- The *covariance* and *correlation* of two random variables measure the extent to which their realized values tend to rise and fall together or oppositely.

Computer Exercise

In this exercise we'll look at some computer-generated random variables and explore some of the properties of those variables discussed in the chapter.

1. In an empty Excel worksheet, type @RAND() in cell A1. You will get a decimal number between 0 and 1—the @RAND() function returns a random number with a uniform distribution between 0 and 1. Type @RAND() again in cell A2. You will get a different number between 0 and 1, and the number in cell A1 will change to a third value—each time you type a new cell entry, every random number in the worksheet is given a new value.

2. Copy the contents of cell A1 into cells A2–A20. This will give you 20 random values, all with values between 0 and 1. Select the range A1–A20, copy it to the clipboard, and then use Paste Special . . . to paste the values into cells B1–B20. Column B will now contain random values whose numbers will not change as you work in the worksheet.

3. We would expect about half the numbers in column B to be greater than 0.5. How many of them actually are? How many would you expect to be greater than 0.9? How many would you expect to be less than 0.1? How many actually are? Try again with a new set of random numbers—to do so, click on cell C1 (or any empty cell), press the Delete key, and repeat step 2 to put a new set of random numbers into column B. How different are the answers now?

4. We can also generate normally distributed random variables in Excel. In cell A1, type @NORMINV(@RAND(),0,1). This will return a normally distributed random variable with mean 0 and variance 1 (the second and third arguments are the mean and variance respectively). Copy this formula into cells A2–A20, and repeat step 2 to put a set of normally distributed random variables into column B.

5. From Theorem 3.3, how many of these 20 values would you expect to be between -1 and 1? How many actually are? How many would you expect to be bigger than 2, or less than -2? How many actually are? As in step 3, generate several different sets of random variables and see how the results change. How often do you get no values above 2 or less than -2? How often do you get more than one?

6. We can change the mean of the random variable. Retype the formula in cell A1 to be @NORMINV(@RAND(),1,1). This changes the mean of the random variable to 1. Copy this value into cells A2–A20, and copy the values into cells B1–B20. Now how many of the random numbers are greater than 1? How many would you expect? How many are between 1 and -1, and how many would you expect? (Hint: -1 is 2 standard deviations below the mean value of 1—use the standard normal distribution table.)

7. We can also change the random variable's standard deviation. Retype the formula in cell A1 to be @NORMINV(@RAND(),1,0.1). This will not change the mean, but will change the variance to 0.1 and the standard deviation to $\sqrt{0.1}$, which is about 0.31. Copy this formula into cells A2–A20, and copy the values into cells B1–B20. How many of the values should be between 1.59 and 2.31? How many actually are? What range would you expect 95 percent of the values to be in? How many are in that range? Repeat this set for several sets of random numbers and see how the answers change.

Problems

1. The following graph shows the probability mass function (PMF) for rolling two dice and adding the results together.

PMF for the Sum of Two Fair Dice

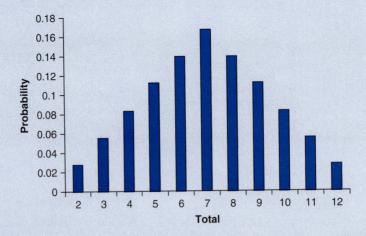

a. What is the chance of rolling either a 6, a 7, or an 8?

b. What is the chance of rolling a number greater than 9? Less than or equal to 5?

c. Find the mean value, variance, and standard deviation of this random variable.

d. Find and graph the random variable's cumulative distribution function (CDF).

2. a. Find the mean, variance, standard deviation, and cumulative distribution function for the unfair die whose probability density function is shown in Figure 3.2.

   b. Is the mean value higher or lower than the mean for the fair die? Explain why. Is the standard deviation higher or lower, and why?

3. The following graph shows the probability density function for a random variable Z:

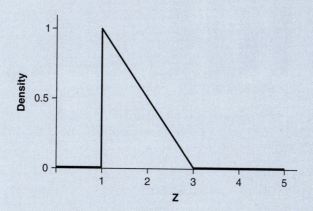

   a. What is the largest value that Z can take? What is the smallest value that Z can take?

   b. What is the probability that Z is greater than 2? (Hint: The area of a triangle is the length of the base, times the height, times $\frac{1}{2}$.) What is the probability that Z is less than 2?

   c. What is the probability that Z is greater than 4? Why?

   d. Is the expected value of Z greater than 2, less than 2, or equal to 2? Briefly explain your answer.

4. The random variable X has the following probability density function:

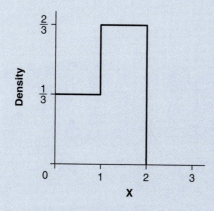

   a. What is the chance that X will be less than 1?

   b. What is the chance that X will be less than 0.5? Greater than 1.5? Less than 1.5?

   c. Find and draw the cumulative distribution function for X.

5. Explain why the following are not valid probability mass or density functions:

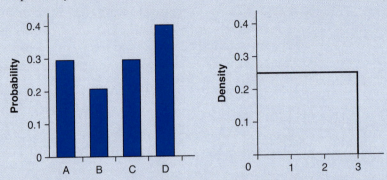

6. You are given a deck of cards that have been thoroughly shuffled—every card in the deck has a 1 in 52 probability of being the card on top of the deck. Define the random variable S as:

  $S = 1$ if the top card is a spade

  $S = 2$ if the top card is a heart

  $S = 3$ if the top card is a diamond

  $S = 4$ if the top card is a club

There are 13 cards of each suit in the deck when all the cards are present.

a. What is the probability that $S = 4$?

b. What is the expected value of S? What is the standard deviation of S?

c. Suppose instead that the ace of spades is missing from the deck; that is, there are only 51 cards in the pile. Now what is the expected value of S? Has it risen or fallen? Explain why.

d. Now suppose that all four aces are missing from the deck. What is the expected value now? How do you know?

7. Suppose the cumulative distribution function for next quarter's inflation rate is:

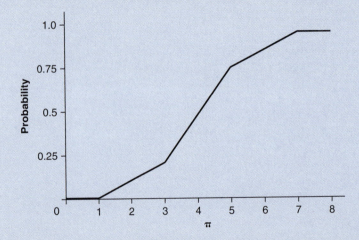

a. What is the lowest possible inflation rate? What is the highest possible rate?

b. What is the chance of a rate less than 3 percent? What is the chance of a rate more than 4 percent?

c. Is it more likely that the rate will be 2 percent or 4.5 percent?

8. Suppose the price of oil is distributed normally with a mean of $20 per barrel and a standard deviation of $5.

a. Using the normal distribution table, find the chance that the price will be less than $16 per barrel.

b. Find the chance that the price will be between $22 and $24 per barrel.

c. Is it more likely that the price will be between $22 and $24 per barrel, or between $12 and $14 per barrel? (Do not do any math to answer this question; think about the shape of the normal PDF.)

9. The current exchange rate is 125 Japanese yen per U.S. dollar. An American investor buys a Japanese bond paying 6 percent interest for 1 million yen, which therefore costs $8,000. The bond will pay 60,000 yen in interest per year; but the dollar value of this depends on future interest rates, which from today's perspective are random.

a. Suppose the exchange rate next year is distributed normally with a mean of 120 and a standard deviation of 10. Find the chance that the exchange rate will be 125 or greater next year.

b. Find the chance that the interest from the bond will be worth at least $550.

c. The investor can instead buy, for the same price, a U.S. bond paying 5.5 percent interest, which is guaranteed to pay $440. What is the chance that the U.S. bond is a better investment (i.e., will pay a higher dollar value of interest)?

10. Let C be the result of tossing a fair coin, and let $C = 1$ if the coin lands heads and let $C = 0$ if the coin lands tails.

a. Find the expected value of C.

b. If the coin is tossed 100 times, what does the law of large numbers say about the percentage of times it will land heads? What number of heads would you expect?

c. How would your answers to a and b change if the coin were unfair, with a 60 percent chance of landing heads?

11. The government is building two bridges; three contracting firms are submitting bids for the work. The government will not give both contracts to the same firm. Let $X = 1$ if the first firm gets a contract, and $X = 0$ if it does not; let $Y = 1$ if the second firm gets a contract, and $Y = 0$ if it does not.

a. There are six possible outcomes:

First Contract	Second Contract
1st firm	2nd firm
1st firm	3rd firm
2nd firm	1st firm
2nd firm	3rd firm
3rd firm	1st firm
3rd firm	2nd firm

Assuming that each outcome is equally likely, find the expected values of X and Y. What is the chance that the first firm will receive one of the contracts?

b. Find the covariance of X and Y. Are they negatively or positively correlated? Explain why. (What is implied about firm 1's chances if it is known that firm 2 will not receive a contract? What is implied if it is known that firm 2 will receive a contract?)

12. The following tables show the closing prices of four stocks plotted against the Dow Jones Industrial Average (DJIA) close for the same date:

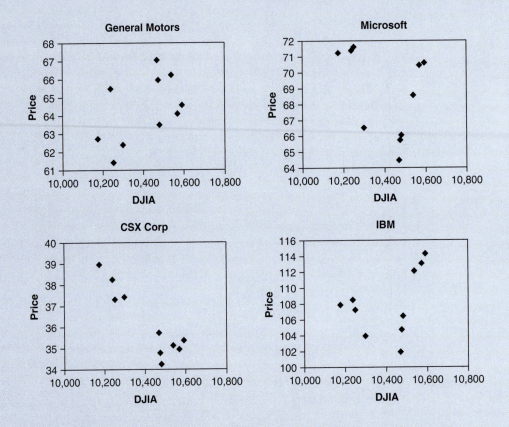

a. Which of the stocks have negative correlations with the market as a whole, and which have positive correlations? (Do not do mathematical calculations—use the graphs to answer this question.)

b. Which have the strongest correlations? Which have the weakest correlations?

c. If you were worried that the market might fall and you wished to buy one of these stocks to protect yourself against that possibility, which would you buy and why?

13. This problem uses the data file *exrates* on the data CD, which contains monthly observations on the exchange rates (against the U.S. dollar) of the German mark, the Irish pound, the Italian lira, the Japanese yen, and the British pound.

a. What is the average exchange rate of the British pound? What is the standard deviation of its exchange rate? By what percent does its value typically fluctuate in a month?

b. Answer the questions in part *a* for each of the other four currencies in the data set.

c. Which currency fluctuates the most in percentage terms? Which fluctuates the least? Which one offers the highest exchange rate risk for Americans wishing to invest overseas?

Chapter **Four**

Estimation

You can see, for example, that while the average return on common stocks for *all* of the 5-year periods was 10.9%, average returns for *individual* 5-year periods ranged from −12.4% to 28.6%. These average returns reflect *past* performance on common stocks; you should not regard them as an indicator of future returns.

Prospectus, Vanguard U.S. Stock Index Funds

4.1 PREDICTING PRICES

Suppose you wish to buy a car. If you live in a large enough city, or are willing to drive a sufficiently long distance, you will probably be able to choose the car from more than one dealer. Different dealers may offer you a different price on the same car. If you visit multiple dealers, you will get a range of prices and can select the lowest price you have been offered. However, going to car dealers takes time, and there is no guarantee that, if you visit one more dealer, you will be offered a lower price than the one you already have. At some point, the lowest price you have will be low enough that you should buy the car rather than visit more dealers. Car dealers have a similar problem; they see many potential buyers who may be willing to pay different prices. They must decide what price to offer to each customer, knowing that the next customer may be willing to pay more than this one, but it may not be worth the chance if the price this customer will pay is sufficiently high.

The price the next dealer will offer you, if you continue to search, is a random variable. It takes some specific value, but until you actually visit that dealer and ask, you don't know what it will be. To decide whether to continue searching for a lower price or to take the best one you have, you need to know the probability that the price you are offered will be lower than the lowest one you already have. You can calculate that probability if you know the probability density function (PDF) of the next offered price. Using the PDF, you can find the chance that the next offered price will be better than the best price you have now, and then you can decide whether it is worth your time and effort to continue the search, or not.

Figure 4.1 shows this problem graphically for a car shopper who has visited three dealers and received offered prices of $22,000, $23,000, and $25,000. If the PDF of offers is like the graph on the left, where the mean value of the next offer is below $22,000, then the odds of getting a better offer at the next dealer is high, in which case continued search is attractive. But if the PDF of offers is like the graph on the right, where the mean value is

FIGURE 4.1
Two Possible Probability Density Functions (PDFs) for Price Offers (Thousands of Dollars)

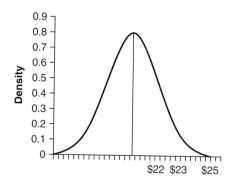
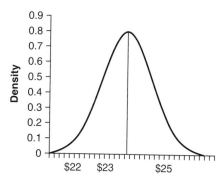

well above $22,000, then the odds of getting a better offer at the next dealer are quite low and the shopper may prefer to accept the $22,000 price.

Unfortunately, car shoppers generally do not know the exact PDF of the price any given dealer will offer them, and there is no way for them to know the exact chance that the next dealer will offer them a better price. However, after they have visited a few dealers, they will have some data on the offers they have received. If they are willing to assume that the offers of all dealers have the same PDF, then they can use this information to estimate the distribution of price offers that dealers make. They can then estimate the chance that the next dealer will offer a better price than the last one, and make an informed, if not perfectly informed, decision about whether to continue shopping or take the best offer they have.

There are many economic problems with similar structures. For example, people who are unemployed but who have received a job offer must decide whether to take the offer or decline it and continue searching. Their decision depends on their estimates of how long it will take to receive another offer and the chance that it will be better than the offers they already have. The problem of underemployment arises when skilled workers fear that the chance of finding the job for which they have been trained is low and therefore choose to take jobs that do not require their skills.

The process of using data to calculate a value to use when we need to consider the mean and variance of a random variable, or any other unobservable number whose value we need to get an idea about, is called *estimation*. The heart of econometric analysis is developing and applying good ways of calculating estimates of economic parameters whose values are unknown. If we can estimate the distribution functions of those variables, we can give advice on how those decisions should be made. This chapter presents the concepts and techniques used to estimate the parameters of the distributions of random variables in econometric analysis.

Suppose we have a random variable X, which has a mean of μ and a variance of σ^2. We would like to obtain an estimate, $\hat{\mu}$, which will be close to the true value of μ, from a data sample of observations on realized values of X. For example, if we want to know the average annual return of a stock, we might look at the return of that stock for the last 10 years. This relies on the assumption that the PDF of the stock's annual returns, or at least its mean and variance, have not changed in the 10 years that give us our data sample. That assumption might be false; companies change their market strategies and leadership, they engage in mergers and acquisitions, and the business climate changes across booms and recessions. Or we might pick 10 stocks that we assume have the same PDF, or at least the same mean and variance, as the one that interests us, and use last year's annual return for all 10 of them as our sample. That assumption might be false too because the companies are not identical; they have some differences we do not observe, and their annual returns therefore may not have exactly the same mean and variance. However, we must make some sort of assumption that allows us to generate a sample of realized values we can use in estimating μ. We should make whatever assumption we are most comfortable with and then proceed; otherwise, we cannot produce an estimate at all.[1] The better our assumption is, the better our estimate will be, and we do the best we can with the data we have.

Once we have data, however, and we believe that all of the realized values we observe are drawn from the same distribution function, the law of large numbers (Theorem 3.1) gives us an easy method for calculating an estimate from that data. The law of large numbers states that the average of a sample of realized values will be close to the mean value. We can use this to define our estimator of the mean value:

Definition 4.1 Given a random variable X with mean μ and variance σ^2, and a sample of N observations of realized values X_i, the estimator $\hat{\mu}$ of the mean of X is:

$$\hat{\mu} = \bar{X}_i = \frac{1}{N}\sum_{i=1}^{N} X_i \qquad \text{(4.1.1)}$$

For example, suppose we would like to know what the price of oil will be in two months. This is a random variable; it is going to take some specific value, but we don't know what. It has a mean value; we don't know that mean value, but if we estimated it, our estimate would be a good guess of the oil price two months from now.

We could take a sample of oil prices in past months and use their average to predict the price two months from now. This, however, is probably not a good strategy. It will work only if the price of oil has the same mean value every month—and that is probably not the case, since the price of oil is determined by supply and demand, and supply and demand factors differ from month to month. A better strategy is to take advantage of our economic knowledge of oil markets in predicting the price in two months. People can buy oil today for delivery at a fixed date in the future; to do so is called buying oil futures. Theoretically, the futures price should be about equal to the expected value of the price on the date the oil will be delivered, usually one to three months in the future (after adjusting for risk and the time value of money). If the futures price was higher, no one would buy futures, since it would be better to wait and buy at the lower price at the future date; conversely, if the futures price was lower, everyone would be willing to buy oil futures but no one would be willing to sell them, since it would be better to hold on to the oil and sell it at the higher price.

The futures price today is not a random variable; we know what value it takes. However, the difference between the futures price of oil today and the actual price it will take in two months is random. More important, whatever supply and demand factors affect the price of

[1] That is, we should proceed unless we are so uncomfortable with all of the possible assumptions that we would rather rely on our economic intuition about the mean value than on any statistical estimates we could generate. But if that happens, we should apply our econometric knowledge to some other problem.

TABLE 4.1
Future and Actual Market Oil Prices, January 1999 to March 2000

Date	Futures Price	Difference	Actual Price	Date
January 1999	12.75	−0.46	12.29	March 1999
February 1999	12.87	+2.18	15.05	April 1999
March 1999	16.76	−0.17	16.59	May 1999
April 1999	18.66	−2.36	16.30	June 1999
May 1999	16.84	+1.26	18.10	July 1999
June 1999	19.29	+0.28	19.57	August 1999
July 1999	20.53	+1.21	21.74	September 1999
August 1999	22.11	+0.28	22.39	October 1999
September 1999	24.51	−1.44	23.07	November 1999
October 1999	24.85	−0.05	24.80	December 1999
November 1999	24.59	+1.20	25.79	January 2000
December 1999	25.60	+2.20	27.80	February 2000
January 2000	27.64	+1.61	29.25	March 2000
February 2000	30.43	−4.36	26.07	April 2000
March 2000	26.90	−0.28	26.62	May 2000

oil should also affect the futures price today. It is quite possible that the difference in the two prices has the same, or at least a very similar, density function each month. Therefore, a better strategy for estimating the price of oil in three months would be to estimate the average difference in prices and add that estimate to today's futures price, which we know. This is more likely to give us an accurate estimate of the price of oil than simply looking at average oil prices.[2]

Table 4.1 shows the futures price of oil in each month from January 1999 to March 2000, the actual price of oil two months later, and the difference between the two. The two prices are generally not far apart; sometimes the actual price is higher, and sometimes the futures price is higher. Occasionally the two prices are several dollars apart, but they are usually within a dollar or two of each other (11 of the 15 data points in the sample are that close). However, they move together quite closely; the correlation between them is 0.944.

If we took the average actual price as our prediction of the price in any given month, we'd predict a value of $21.69 in each month. On average we'd be right, but we'd be off by quite a bit: $9 too high at the start of the sample and $5 too low at the end of it. The reason is simply that the price of oil was rising over this period; either demand was increasing or supply was falling or both. But the assumption that the expected price of oil was constant over this period doesn't look like a very good one to make, so the prediction of $21.69 in each month isn't very good either.

The differences between the two prices are much more stable; they are not notably larger either at the start or at the end of the sample. This is because the futures price, anticipating the supply and demand changes that will take place, rises along with the actual market difference. The average price between the two prices is $0.07. We might instead predict the actual market price of oil in two months by taking the (known) futures price today and

[2] An even better strategy, perhaps, would be to write down a supply and demand model of oil prices and estimate the equilibrium price in that model. That, however, requires us to be able to estimate the slope of supply and demand curves; we will discuss that problem (at length!) later in the book.

Date	Futures Price	Predicted Price	Actual Price	Forecast Error
April 2000	25.74	25.81	29.46	−3.65
May 2000	29.01	29.08	29.91	−0.83
June 2000	32.50	32.57	29.36	−3.21
July 2000	29.33	29.40	31.95	+2.55

TABLE 4.2
Future and Actual Market Oil Prices, April to July 2000

adding $0.07 to it. If we did that, our prediction would be off by less than $2.50 in every month except one; and in five months we'd be within 50 cents. This is clearly a much better way to predict the price of oil in the future, because it is based on an economic model of prices, which tells us that the futures price today should be expected to be the same as the actual price in two months. As a result, it makes predictions that are significantly closer to the true values.

You might ask how well it works going forward in time, predicting prices for months that are not in the sample. That depends on whether the differences in future months have the same mean and variance as the ones in the sample. The answer is that the model still predicts pretty well in the next few months after the sample, though not quite as well as before.[3] Table 4.2 shows the futures price for the next four months, the predictions obtained by adding $0.07 to the futures price, the actual price two months later, and the error of the forecast. In general it seems to predict about as well as it did within the sample, though not quite as well. (That might just be due to bad luck rather than a chance in the distribution of the differences. None of those differences is as bad as the worst one in the sample.) Because it uses our economic knowledge of the futures market, it predicts much better than the simple method of predicting $21.69 for each month.

We might be interested in knowing not only what the estimated price of oil is but also how close that estimate is likely to be to the actual value, when we learn it three months from now. To find that, we need to know the variance of the difference between the futures price and the actual price three months later. However, like the mean, the variance of that difference is unobservable. But we can estimate it. Just as we estimated the mean value of the random variable by looking at the average value of a sample of realized values, we estimate the variance of the random variable by looking at the variance of that sample:

Definition 4.2 Given a random variable X with mean μ and variance σ^2, and a sample of N observations of realized values X_i, the estimator $\hat{\sigma}^2$ of the variance of X is:

$$\hat{\sigma}^2 = \frac{1}{N-1} \sum_{i=1}^{N} (X_i - \hat{\mu})^2 \qquad (4.1.2)$$

In general, there will be a connection between the range of the realized values X_i and the estimated variance. The larger range of the observed values of X_i, the larger the values of $(X_i - \hat{\mu})$ will be, and the higher $\hat{\sigma}^2$ will be. Thus, if we observe a wider spread of observed values, we will get a high estimated variance, and if we observe a narrow spread, we will get a low estimated variance.

---

[3] Saving some data to use in checking the accuracy of your forecasts, as done here, is a very common method of evaluating the quality of the forecasts (and implicitly, the model on which they are based).

Note that we divide by $N - 1$, not by N. This is because we are calculating not the difference between X_i and its mean value μ (because we don't know it), but rather the difference between X_i and our estimate of the mean, $\hat{\mu}$. On average, the values of X_i tend to be a little closer to $\hat{\mu}$ than to the true mean μ. The estimate $\hat{\mu}$ is *exactly* the central value among the X_i values (because we calculate it that way); μ, though close to the central value, is not exactly central. This makes the squared deviations a little smaller than they ought to be, and therefore we divide by only $N - 1$, rather than N, to offset this effect.

Using these formulas, we can return to the problem of the car buyer who has received three offered prices of $22,000, $23,000, and $25,000. Assuming that the distribution of prices is normal, we can calculate the estimated mean and standard deviation; they are $23,333 and $1,528, respectively. The buyer wants to know what the chance is that the next dealer will offer a price better than $22,000. The Z statistic for this chance is given by ($22,000 - $23,333)/$1,528 = -0.87. Looking this up on the normal distribution table, we find that there is approximately a 19.2 percent chance that the next offer will be below $22,000. The chance is only approximately correct, because we have used an estimated mean and standard deviation rather than the true ones. Even so, the buyer can use this information to decide whether it is worth the time and effort to visit one more dealer.

4.2   PROPERTIES OF THE MEAN ESTIMATOR

Given the ability to calculate $\hat{\mu}$, we would like to know how close it is to the true μ. Unfortunately, we can never know this, because we don't know the value of μ. We can, however, say a surprising amount about the behavior of $\hat{\mu}$, including some things that make it a useful way to estimate the true mean of X. The first useful property it has is the most important:

> **Theorem 4.1** The expected value of $\hat{\mu}$ is μ; our estimator will, on average, give us the correct answer.

This theorem is quite easy to prove if we assert (without proving) another theorem:

> **Theorem 4.2** The expected value of a sum of terms is equal to the sum of the expected values of the terms: that is, $E(A + B + C) = E(A) + E(B) + E(C)$.

Because $\hat{\mu} = \frac{1}{N} \sum_{i=1}^{N} X_i$, the expected value of $\hat{\mu}$ is just $\frac{1}{N} \sum_{i=1}^{N} E(X_i)$ The expected value of X_i is just μ, since that is the mean value of X by definition. Therefore, the expected value of $\hat{\mu}$ is $\frac{1}{N} \cdot N \cdot \mu$, which is just μ.

But is this a useful result? After all, the expected value of each of the individual realized values is also μ. If, on average, looking at just one observation on the random variable X gives you the correct answer, why look at 20 or 30 or more? The answer is that, although both will give you μ on average, $\hat{\mu}$ will tend to be closer to μ than any particular X_i will be; it has a lower variance than a single realized value has, making it a better estimator.

> **Theorem 4.3** The variance of $\hat{\mu}$, which we write as $\sigma_{\hat{\mu}}^2$, is given by:

$$\sigma_{\hat{\mu}}^2 = \frac{\sigma^2}{N}$$

(4.2.1)

and its standard deviation is

$$\sigma_{\hat{\mu}} = \frac{\sigma}{\sqrt{N}} \qquad\qquad (4.2.2)$$

In a sample with more than one observation, N will be greater than 1, and its square root will also be greater than 1. Therefore, the variance of $\hat{\mu}$ will be smaller than the variance of a single realized value X.[4] More important, as N gets larger and larger, $\sigma_{\hat{\mu}}^2$ will get smaller and smaller. The more data we have, the closer our estimator $\hat{\mu}$ will be to the true value μ— and we can make the difference as small as we like if we can obtain enough data. That is the real advantage of using the average of a sample of observations instead of just a single observation.

Table 4.3 demonstrates the importance of averaging in reducing variance. It shows the results of taking samples of rolls of a fair six-sided die; since we know the mean and variance of this variable from Chapter 3, we can compare the results of the samples to the true values and see how good they are. We can do this because we know the data-generating process for a (hypothetical) fair die—in any real application, we wouldn't have that knowledge, and we couldn't make the comparison.[5] The figure shows calculations of $\hat{\mu}$ from eight different samples, with nine die rolls in each sample. As shown before, the mean of a single die roll is 3.5; its variance is 4.05 and its standard deviation is 2.01, which is a rather large standard deviation. The distribution of rolls reflects this; there are 16 rolls of 1 and 13 rolls of 6 in the table, so results far from the true value are pretty common. (Is this

TABLE 4.3 Eight Samples of Nine Die Rolls Each

Roll	Sample							
	1	**2**	**3**	**4**	**5**	**6**	**7**	**8**
1	5	1	2	2	3	5	1	2
2	2	1	1	6	1	6	3	5
3	3	4	3	5	6	3	3	5
4	5	3	5	1	5	2	6	5
5	1	6	2	5	6	5	6	1
6	4	6	2	6	4	6	3	5
7	4	1	1	3	1	5	4	3
8	6	5	1	1	2	1	6	4
9	2	5	6	4	1	1	3	5
Average	3.555556	3.555556	2.555556	3.666667	3.222222	3.777778	3.888889	3.888889

[4] In a sample with only 1 observation, the "average" value is exactly the same as the single realized value in the sample, and in that case Equation 4.2 reduces to $\sigma_{\hat{\mu}}^2 = \sigma^2$, which is what you'd expect; if $\hat{\mu}$ and X_i are the same number, then they should have the same variance too.

[5] That includes rolling real dice. Pick up a die off your shelf. Is it fair or not? The only way to tell is to roll it a bunch of times and see if you get what you'd expect or not, that is to say, to estimate its properties from a series of observations.

more or fewer 1s and 6s than you'd expect?) If we used a single observation to guess the mean of this random variable, our guess would tend to have a large error. On average, these die rolls do tend to give the correct answer of 3.5—the average value of the 72 die rolls in the table is 3.514. But each individual one stands a high chance of being very different from 3.5.

The average of each sample, however, tends to be much closer to the true mean value of 3.5. We can use Theorem 4.3 to calculate the variance of the average of 9 die rolls; it is 4.05/9, which works out to approximately 0.45. The standard deviation is the square root of that, which is approximately 0.67. Therefore, we can expect the average of 9 die rolls to be three times closer to the true value than a single roll will be. And in fact, nearly all the averages in Figure 4.2 are quite close to 3.5. All but one are within the range from 3 to 4, although the other one (sample 3) has a pretty poor estimate, 2.556, which is about 1.3 standard deviations away from the true value. But we are clearly better off to use the averages as a guess of the mean value of the die than we are to use a single roll.

We can, however, do even better than this; we can consider all 72 observations to be a single sample, and take the average of all 72 to be our estimate of the true mean. The variance of this estimator is 4.05/72 = 0.056, and its standard deviation is 0.237, which is almost three times better than using a single sample of nine observations. Not surprisingly, the average of all 72 rolls, 3.514, is quite close to the true mean of 3.5 (although it is actually quite a bit closer than we can really expect it to be; it turns out to be less than $\frac{1}{10}$ of a standard deviation away from the true value, which is pure luck). We could get the standard deviation to be smaller yet by using 200, or 1,000, or 10,000 rolls of the die, depending on how precise we needed our estimate to be (how small we needed its standard deviation to be) and how much time we were willing to spend rolling the die.

4.3   DISTRIBUTION OF THE MEAN ESTIMATOR

Knowing the mean, variance, and standard deviation of $\hat{\mu}$ is useful, but it's not everything. Suppose, for instance, we sample nine rolls of a fair die, and we want to know the chance that $\hat{\mu}$ will be greater than, say, 4. We don't know, because we don't know the probability density function (PDF), or cumulative distribution function (CDF), of $\hat{\mu}$. In general, finding the PDF of $\hat{\mu}$ is quite difficult, and we will not discuss it here. There are some specific cases where we can find the PDF of $\hat{\mu}$, and there are some useful things we can say about the general case that will help us deal with it as well.

First, let's consider the special case where X is not just any random variable, but happens to be a normally distributed random variable. In that case, we can say:

Theorem 4.4 Suppose that X is normally distributed; that is, $X \sim N(\mu, \sigma^2)$. Then the average value $\hat{\mu}$ of a sample of N observations of X is also normally distributed; that is, $\hat{\mu} \sim N(\mu, \sigma^2/N)$.

This lets us calculate the chance that $\hat{\mu}$ will be greater or less than any particular value using the normal distribution table. For example, assume that the daily change in value of the stock of Dell Computer Corporation is normally distributed with a mean of 0 and a variance of 0.25; that is, the daily change is distributed $N(0, 0.25)$. What is the chance that the average change over 25 days will be more than 0.1, which is 10 cents? (Or, equivalently, what is the chance that the total change over 25 days will be more than $2.50, since the total change is the average change times the number of days?)

We know, by assumption, that the variance of a single change in Dell's stock price is 0.5. Therefore, Theorem 4.3 tells us that the variance of the average of 25 daily changes is $0.5/25 = 0.02$. Its standard deviation is the square root of this, which is 0.141. Since we know that it is normally distributed, we can use the normal distribution table to find the chance that it will be greater than 0.1. The Z statistic for this problem is $(0.1 - 0)/0.141$, which is 0.71. Looking up 0.71 on the table, we find that the chance of the average daily change being greater than 10 cents is 24 percent. Therefore, the chance that it will be less than 10 cents is 76 percent. There is a 24 percent chance that Dell will rise at least $2.50 over a period of 25 trading days (if our assumption about the distribution of one day's change is correct).

Unfortunately, we can use this rule only if the underlying variable is normally distributed, and many interesting economic random variables aren't. However, we have the following rule as well:

> **Theorem 4.5** The central limit theorem: Suppose a random variable X has an unknown distribution, that is, $X \sim (\mu, \sigma^2)$, but is not necessarily normally distributed. Then the average value $\hat{\mu}$ of a sample of N observations of X is *approximately* normally distributed; that is, $\hat{\mu} \overset{\sim}{\sim} N(\mu, \sigma^2/N)$. The larger the number of observations, the better the approximation will be.

The advantage of the central limit theorem is that it doesn't matter what the distribution of the random variable X is; you don't even have to know it. As long as it has the same distribution for each observation in the sample, the distribution of the sample average $\hat{\mu}$ will be approximately normal, and the more data you have, the better your approximation will be. As long as you are working with a reasonably large amount of data (exactly how much depends on the nature of the distribution of X), you can use the normal distribution table to work out probabilities for $\hat{\mu}$ and you will be, at least approximately, correct.

Figure 4.2 demonstrates the central limit theorem in action. Graph a shows the distribution of a single fair coin toss, with $X = 0$ representing heads and $X = 1$ representing tails; it has a true mean value of 0.5. This distribution is uniform, not at all like the normal distribution. In a sample with more than one flip, the average value of X is equal to the fraction of coin tosses that come up tails in the sample, which we would expect to be about 50 percent. However, graph b shows the distribution of the average of 4 coin tosses, and graph c shows the distribution of the average of 10 coin tosses; already a distinct bell shape is starting to appear. Graph d shows the distribution of the average of 25 die rolls; it is extremely similar to the normal distribution function, and the normal distribution table gives answers for the chance of getting various results that are quite close to the true answers. This is the power of the central limit theorem—it tells us that we can use the normal distribution table to work out the probabilities of various values for our estimators, no matter what the distribution of the underlying random variables is, as long as we have enough data to make the approximation good enough for our purposes.

There is, however, a problem with this approach. Calculating the Z statistic requires us to know the variance of $\hat{\mu}$, which in turn requires us to know σ^2, the variance of X. However, we have no more knowledge of σ^2 than we do of μ; both are properties of the

FIGURE 4.2   **The Central Limit Theorem: Distribution of the Fraction of Coin Tosses That Are Tails**

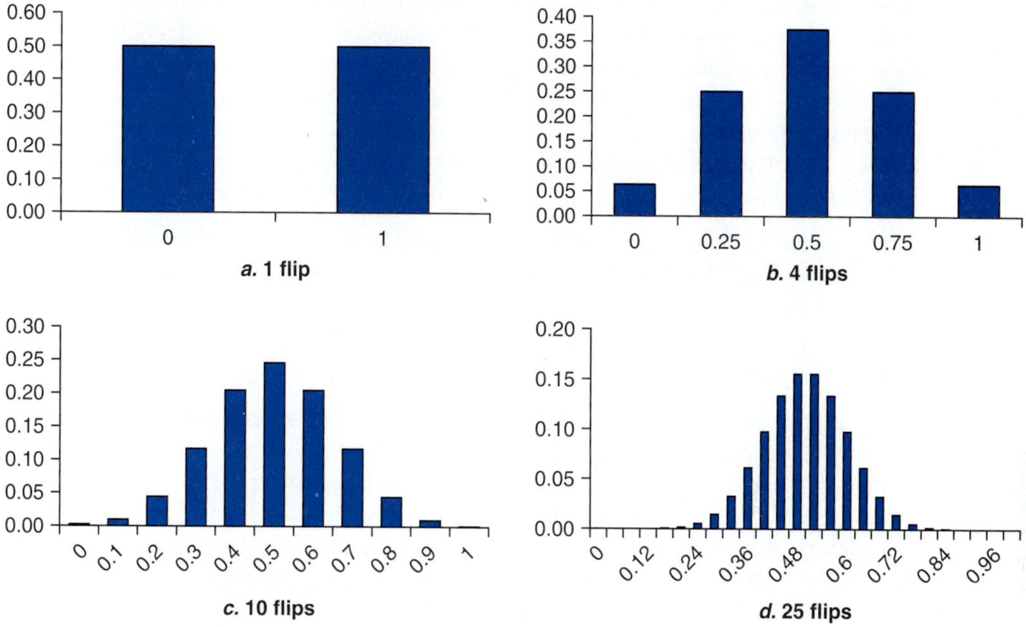

a. **1 flip**

b. **4 flips**

c. **10 flips**

d. **25 flips**

data generating process, which we do not know. In practice we are unable to calculate the Z statistic for any real economic problem. We can, however, use the sample and Definition 4.2 to calculate $\hat{\sigma}^2$, the estimated value of σ^2. Then we can use that estimated value in place of the unknown true value.

Definition 4.3 Suppose that X is a normally distributed random variable with mean μ and unknown variance σ^2. Then the *t-statistic* for the chance that $\hat{\mu}$ will be less than a given value X^* is calculated by:

$$t = \frac{X^* - \mu}{\hat{\sigma}_{\hat{\mu}}}$$

and t is a random variable which takes the *t distribution.*

The t distribution is similar but not identical to the normal distribution. The difference arises because the t statistic has the estimated standard deviation $\hat{\sigma}_{\hat{\mu}}$ in the denominator, whereas the Z statistic, which does take the standard normal distribution, has the true standard deviation $\sigma_{\hat{\mu}}$ in the denominator. If we knew the true standard deviation, we would use the Z statistic; but when we do not know the true standard deviation, which is usually the case, then we are forced to use its estimated value, which gives us the t statistic instead.[6]

---

[6] It may have occurred to you that we usually don't know the true mean, either. We will deal with this point in the next section.

The shape of the t distribution's density function is similar to the bell shape of the normal distribution function but a little bit wider and flatter. This happens because $\hat{\sigma}_{\hat{\mu}}$ is an estimated value, which will not be equal to the true value $\sigma_{\hat{\mu}}$ and may be substantially different. This increases the chance of getting a value for the t statistic that is far from 0, causing the t distribution to have more density in the tails and less in the center than the standard normal. How different the two distributions are depends on how good an estimate $\hat{\sigma}_{\hat{\mu}}$ is of the true value $\sigma_{\hat{\mu}}$. It can be shown that, just as $\hat{\mu}$ gets closer to μ as the number of observations in the sample increases, $\hat{\sigma}_{\hat{\mu}}$ gets closer to $\sigma_{\hat{\mu}}$ as the number of observations increases.

> **Definition 4.4** The *degrees of freedom (df)* of the t statistic is given by the number of observations (N) in the sample that generated the value of the t statistic, minus the number of parameters estimated to calculate the t statistic. For estimation of a mean, the degrees of freedom is $N - 1$, because calculating $\hat{\sigma}_{\hat{\mu}}$ requires an estimated value of $\hat{\mu}$.

As $\hat{\sigma}_{\hat{\mu}}$ gets closer to $\sigma_{\hat{\mu}}$, the t statistic gets closer to the Z statistic, since the difference between $\hat{\sigma}_{\hat{\mu}}$ and $\sigma_{\hat{\mu}}$ is the only difference between t and Z.

Figure 4.3 shows the PDF of the t statistic for varying numbers of degrees of freedom. If the number of observations, and thus the number of degrees of freedom (df), is small, $\hat{\sigma}_{\hat{\mu}}$ is not a very good estimator of $\sigma_{\hat{\mu}}$ and the t PDF is much wider than the normal PDF. As the number of observations and degrees of freedom rises, $\hat{\sigma}_{\hat{\mu}}$ gets closer to $\sigma_{\hat{\mu}}$ and the t and normal PDFs get more similar; as the number of degrees of freedom rises to infinity, they become identical. For 5 degrees of freedom, the t density is notably different from the normal; but for 20 degrees of freedom it is much closer to the normal. With 100 degrees of freedom it is nearly identical.

We look up critical values for the t distribution on a t distribution table, just as we do for the normal distribution; the table can be found in Appendix B at the end of this book. The t distribution table is similar to the normal distribution table. Unlike the normal table,

FIGURE 4.3

The
***t* Distribution**
for Various
Degrees of
Freedom

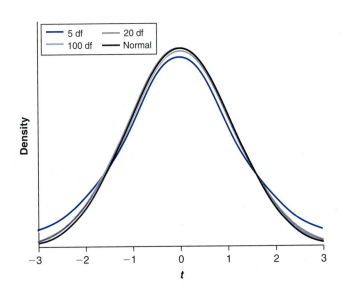

however, the t table shows this probability only for certain values of X^*; it lists the values of X^* for which the chance that t will be greater than that X^* is 0.5 percent, 1 percent, 2.5 percent, 5 percent, and 10 percent. For example, suppose the sample has 26 observations and thus the t statistic has 25 degrees of freedom. Looking at the row for 25 degrees of freedom and the column for 5 percent, we find that there is a 5 percent chance that the t statistic will be greater than 1.708, the value in the t distribution table. We refer to 1.708 as the *5 percent critical value* for the t distribution with 25 degrees of freedom. Because the t PDF is symmetric, there is also a 5 percent chance that it will be smaller than -1.708, and a 90 percent chance that it will be between -1.708 and 1.708. Looking instead at the 1 percent column, we find there is a 1 percent chance that the t statistic will be greater than 2.485 (which is the 1 percent critical value), a 1 percent chance that it will be less than -2.485, and a 98 percent chance that it will be between -2.485 and 2.485. What if we want to know the chance that the t statistic will be greater than, say, 2.2? We can't find this from the table, but we know it will be less than 5 percent and greater than 1 percent. This will be enough for econometric analysis.

Note that as the number of degrees of freedom gets large, the probabilities for t and Z become similar. From the normal distribution table, you can see that there is a 5 percent chance that Z will be above 1.64, and a 2.5 percent chance that it will be above 1.96. In the t distribution table, the 5 percent critical value is always greater than 1.64. For very small numbers of degrees of freedom, it's quite a bit bigger, but as the degrees of freedom rises, it gets closer and closer to 1.64, until at df = infinity, it is 1.64. Similarly, the 2.5 percent critical value is larger than 1.96 but gets closer to it as the number of degrees of freedom rises. For a reasonably large number of degrees of freedom (exactly how large depends on how large an error we're willing to tolerate) the t distribution and the normal distribution are similar enough that we can use the normal distribution table in place of the t distribution table if we want to know an exact critical value for a probability that isn't shown in the t distribution table.

Finally, also note that the t distribution is derived assuming that the underlying random variable X that generated the data sample is normally distributed. If that is not the case, then the statistic $(X^* - \mu)/\hat{\sigma}_{\hat{\mu}}$ does not follow the t distribution and the t distribution table cannot be used to calculate its critical values. If the assumption that X is normally distributed is implausible, then we should not use the t distribution. Instead, we should fall back on the central limit theorem, which assures us that $(X^* - \mu)/\hat{\sigma}_{\hat{\mu}}$ is approximately normally distributed, and use the normal distribution to calculate its critical values. But in this case we must remember that the critical values we get are only approximate, not exact.

4.4 CONFIDENCE INTERVALS

Both the t statistic and the Z statistic include μ, the true mean of X in the formula. But we don't know the value of μ any more than we do the value of σ. How can we use the t and Z statistics if we don't know the mean of X? The short answer is: We can't. However, if we are willing to make an assumption, or a guess, about what the true value of μ might be, then we can calculate the probability of getting our estimated value of $\hat{\mu}$. We can then use that probability to decide how much we like the original guess about the value of μ. If the probability is high, then the guessed value for μ is perhaps reasonable; if the probability is very low, then the guessed value for μ is not reasonable and we should probably discard that guess.

Consider the difference between futures prices and actual prices for oil given in Table 4.1. If we are willing to assume the difference is normally distributed, which is not unreasonable given the 15 values we have obtained, then we can see whether any particular number is plausible for the mean value. In particular, we might wish to know whether the mean difference is equal to 0 or not. The average difference in the sample is not 0—it is 0.073—but it is close to 0, and if we believed the difference should be 0, then we might think that a measured difference as small as the one we have found is evidence confirming our belief that the true mean difference is 0.

If the true value of μ is 0, is it likely that we would have gotten a sample mean of 0.073? We can use the t statistic to find out. The value whose probability we want to know, X^*, is 0.073; μ is 0, by assumption; and we can calculate that $\hat{\sigma}_{\hat{\mu}}$ is 0.456. The t statistic is therefore $(0.073 - 0)/0.456$, which is 0.16. What is the probability of getting a t statistic at least this large? We can't tell for sure, because the t distribution table in Appendix B gives only critical values for particular probabilities. But the table does tell us that, for an estimate with 14 degrees of freedom (15 observations in the sample minus 1), the chance of a t statistic of 1.76 or larger is 5 percent, the chance of a t statistic of 2.15 or larger is 2.5 percent, and the chance of a t statistic of 2.62 or larger is 0.5 percent. Because 0.16 is smaller than 1.76, the chance of getting a value this close to our assumed mean value of 0 is high, more than 5 percent. Of course, we might have gotten a negative value as well as a positive one, so we usually argue that the chance of getting a t statistic value of 0.16 or larger is bigger than 10 percent—there is a 5 percent chance of a value greater than 1.76, and a 5 percent chance of a value less than -1.76, and some chance of getting a value between 0.16 and 1.76 or -0.16 and -1.76 too. But either way, if our assumption that the mean difference between futures and actual prices equals 0 is correct, then this result is not a surprising one to get. Figure 4.4 shows the chance of getting a mean difference of 0.073 or higher; it is quite high. Therefore, the belief that the true mean difference is 0 is a reasonable one to hold, and this sample would not force us to give up that belief if we happened to hold it.

Suppose we instead assumed that the mean difference was some other number, say, 2.00. We then calculate the t statistic for getting a sample mean of 0.073 if the true μ is 2.00. The t statistic is $(0.073 - 2.00)/0.456 = -4.23$. This value is quite large. The t distribution table in Appendix B tells us that the chance of getting a value greater than 2.62 or

FIGURE 4.4

The Chance of Getting an Observed Mean Difference of 0.073 if the True Mean Difference Is 0, or If It Is 2

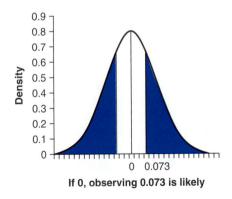

If 0, observing 0.073 is likely

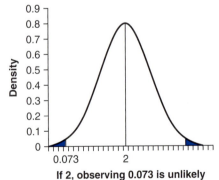

If 2, observing 0.073 is unlikely

FIGURE 4.5
An Observed $\hat{\mu}$ and Three Possible Values of μ

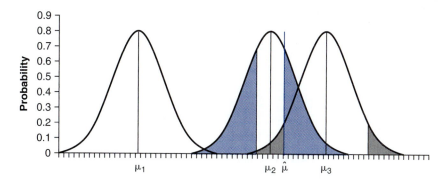

less than -2.62 is only 1 percent, so the chance of getting a value larger than -4.23 must be even less than that. Figure 4.4 also shows this probability as well, and it is very nearly 0. What does this tell us about the assumption that the mean difference in prices is $2.00? It tells us that, if that assumption is correct, there is a chance of much less than 1 percent that we would have seen a sample with an observed difference this far from the mean value. This casts a lot of doubt on the original assumption that the mean difference is $2.00. Barring some substantial evidence to the contrary, we should probably abandon that assumption, and instead assume that the true defect rate is 0 or, at least, some value much closer to 0.073.

For any particular sample, there will be some values of μ that are acceptable assumptions and others that aren't. Figure 4.5 shows a single estimated value of $\hat{\mu}$, the red vertical line on the graph, and three possible values of μ. Depending on what we believe about the value of μ, the probability of observing this particular $\hat{\mu}$ changes. Suppose we believe that the true value of μ is μ_1 in the figure. This value is far to the left of the observed $\hat{\mu}$, and we would not tend to believe this was the true value of μ; it's too unlikely to produce what we have actually observed. Suppose we instead believe that the true mean is μ_2. The distribution of $\hat{\mu}$ changes, because its mean has shifted and therefore the chance that it will take any particular value has changed also. Therefore, the bell curve shifts to the right. The observed value of $\hat{\mu}$, however, has not, and so the red line remains in the same place. If we believe the true mean is μ_2, then getting a value like $\hat{\mu}$ is quite likely; it is the area shown in pink on the graph. We would certainly maintain our belief that the true mean was μ_2 on the basis of this sample. Suppose instead we believed that the true mean was μ_3, shifting the bell curve to the right again. Then the chance of getting a value like $\hat{\mu}$ is low, but not 0; it is the area shaded in gray. We might or might not give up our belief that the true value of μ was μ_3, depending on how good we thought the sample was and how much confidence we have in our belief that the true mean really is μ_3.

In general, the closer the value of μ is to the estimated value $\hat{\mu}$, the more acceptable it is. We can find all the values of μ that are acceptable assumptions for the true value by the following procedure. Look up the critical value on the t distribution table for some particular probability, and call this value T_c^p, where p is the probability chosen. Then any value of μ that we might think to be the true value is some distance away from the value of $\hat{\mu}$ we have observed. Dividing that distance by $\hat{\sigma}_{\hat{\mu}}$ tells us how many estimated standard deviations there are between μ and $\hat{\mu}$. If that number of standard deviations is bigger than T_c^p, then the value of μ is implausible; otherwise it is plausible.

Definition 4.6 A *Q percent confidence interval* is the range of values which μ might take, for which the probability of observing a mean value at least as close to μ as $\hat{\mu}$ is no larger than Q percent. It can be calculated by:

$$[\hat{\mu} - T_c^p \cdot \hat{\sigma}_{\hat{\mu}}, \hat{\mu} + T_c^p \cdot \hat{\sigma}_{\hat{\mu}}] \qquad \text{(4.4.1)}$$

where $p = (1 - Q)/2$ is the chance that $\hat{\mu}$ will be outside the confidence interval on one particular side, and T_c^p is the critical value for probability p for the appropriate number of degrees of freedom.

The confidence interval is thus $\hat{\mu}$ plus or minus T_c^p standard deviations on either side. If we want a 90 percent confidence interval, then there is a 5 percent chance that the t statistic will be greater than the interval and a 5 percent chance that it will be below, so we use $T_c^{0.05}$ in that case. For a 95 percent confidence interval with a 2.5 percent chance of being outside on either side, we use $T_c^{0.025}$; for a 99 percent confidence interval, we use $T_c^{0.005}$; and so forth. If the t statistic is to fall in the appropriate interval, then it must be the case that

$$-T_c^p < \frac{\hat{\mu} - \mu}{\hat{\sigma}_{\hat{\mu}}} < T_c^p \qquad \text{(4.4.2)}$$

Solving the inequality for μ produces Equation 4.4.1.

Continuing the above example, we can find the 95 percent confidence interval for the true mean difference in futures and actual oil prices. In that problem, we have $\hat{\mu} = 0.073$ and $\hat{\sigma}_{\hat{\mu}} = 0.456$. Looking up the t statistic for 15 degrees of freedom and a 2.5 percent chance of being above (or below) the confidence interval, we find $T_c^{0.025} = 2.15$. Therefore the 95 percent confidence interval is given by:

$$[0.073 - 2.15(0.456), 0.073 + 2.15(0.456)] \qquad \text{(4.4.3)}$$

which simplifies to $[-0.907, 1.053]$. From this we can clearly see that a true mean difference of \$2 is outside the interval, and hence is not consistent with the observed sample; and a true mean difference of 0 is inside the confidence interval and is consistent with the sample. We can also easily see that a true value of -10 cents, 20 cents, or 70 cents would be acceptable, and that values of $-\$1.00$ and $+\$1.50$ would not.

If the underlying random variable isn't normally distributed, then the use of t critical values to calculate isn't appropriate. In that case we should use the fact that the distribution of the mean estimator is approximately normal, and use normal critical values. Suppose we run a computer chip fabrication plant and we are interested in knowing the fraction of products that are defective.[7] We can test a sample of chips produced at the plant, see how many are defective, and use that information to estimate the true defect rate. Define the random variable X such that $X = 1$ if the chip is defective and $X = 0$ if the chip works; then μ, the expected value of X, is equal to the chance that any one chip is defective, which is the defect rate. Clearly this variable is not normally distributed. We test 400 chips and we find that 36 of them are defective. Then $\hat{\mu}$ is equal to 36/400, or 0.09, or 9 percent. The variance of the sample $\hat{\sigma}^2$ turns out to be 0.0821, and $\hat{\sigma}$ is the square root of that, which is 0.287. We can use Theorem 4.3 to calculate $\hat{\sigma}_{\hat{\mu}}$, the estimated standard

---

[7] Computer chip fabrication has unusually high defect rates because of the very small scale of the product.

deviation of $\hat{\mu}$; it is $0.287/\sqrt{400} = 0.0144$. The estimated mean $\hat{\mu}$ should be within 1.96 standard deviations of its true value approximately, but not exactly, 95 percent of the time. The 95 percent confidence interval for μ is then 0.09 plus or minus 1.96(0.0144), or [0.0618, 0.1182].

We close this section with one caveat on the discussion of confidence intervals. It is often tempting to say something along the lines of "There is a 95 percent chance that the true value μ falls within the confidence interval." However, this statement is not correct, for the simple reason that μ is not random. It takes one particular value, for certain; we just don't know what that value is. The estimator $\hat{\mu}$ is random, but after we observe the sample, we know the realized value we've gotten for the estimate; it's not random anymore at that point. Therefore, there is no "chance" that μ is inside the confidence interval around $\hat{\mu}$. Either it is or it isn't, and we can't know which. What the confidence interval tells us is the range of values that, for a particular degree of certainty, we can assume to contain the true value of μ. In fact, because $\hat{\mu}$ is random, and the confidence interval is centered around $\hat{\mu}$, the location of the confidence interval itself is random. If we took many samples, and constructed a 95 percent confidence interval for each one, each confidence interval would be in a different place. However, on average, 95 percent of the confidence intervals would contain the true value, and 5 percent would not. If we used narrower 90 percent confidence intervals, then only 90 percent would contain the true value, and 10 percent would not. This is another way of thinking about what we mean by the percentage of a confidence interval.

4.5 DISTRIBUTIONS OF THE SQUARES OF NORMAL RANDOM VARIABLES

There are many problems in econometrics where we are concerned not with the value of a normally distributed random variable X, but rather with the value of X^2. The formula for the estimation of a variance involves the squares of normally distributed random variables, and when we work with variance estimates we will need to know some things about their distributions. We start with the case of a standard normal distribution:

Definition 4.7 Suppose that X has the standard normal distribution function; that is, $X \sim N(0, 1)$. Then X^2 is also random, and takes the *chi-square (χ^2) distribution* with one degree of freedom; we write $X^2 \sim \chi_1^2$.

Why do we say it has one degree of freedom? Because this is a special case of a more general chi-square (χ^2) distribution, which is the distribution of a sum of squared standard normal random variables.

Definition 4.8 Suppose that N independent random variables $X_1, X_2, \ldots, X_N$ are all distributed $N(0, 1)$. Then the sum of their squares $X_1^2 + X_2^2 + \cdots + X_N^2$ is also random and has the chi-square distribution with N degrees of freedom, which we write as χ_N^2.

Note that the term *degrees of freedom* has a somewhat different definition for the χ^2 distribution than it does for the t distribution we discussed earlier. There it is the number of

FIGURE 4.6
**Density
Function of the
Chi-Square
Distribution,
Various
Degrees of
Freedom**

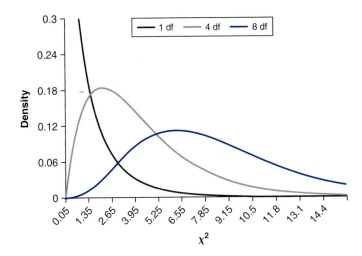

observations in the sample, minus 1 for the estimated mean; but here it is the number of random variables in the sum. Figure 4.6 shows the χ^2 distribution for 1, 4, and 8 degrees of freedom.

Like the normal distribution function, the χ^2 distribution does not have a mathematical expression—it has to be calculated by approximation. A table of values for the χ^2 distribution is found in Appendix C at the end of this book. Using this table, we can find the chance that a random variable with the χ^2 distribution will take a certain value. Suppose $Y \sim \chi_1^2$. What values for Y are likely to occur, and what values are unlikely? Like the t distribution table, the χ^2 table gives a critical value such that the chance Y will be above that value is 1 percent, 5 percent, or some other value. For instance, from the 10 percent column and the first row of the chart, we see that the chance that Y will be greater than 2.71 is 10 percent. The chance that it will be greater than 6.63 is 1 percent, and so forth. For random variables with more degrees of freedom, use a different row. If $Z \sim \chi_4^2$, for instance, then there is a 5 percent chance that it will be greater than 9.49, and a 10 percent chance that it will be greater than 7.56.

What if X is normally distributed but does not have the standard normal distribution? Then we can transform it in the same way we did previously.

Theorem 4.6 Suppose that $X \sim N(\mu, \sigma^2)$. Then $\left(\frac{X-\mu}{\sigma}\right)^2 \sim \chi_1^2$. Suppose that $X_1, X_2, \ldots, X_N$ are all $\sim N(\mu, \sigma^2)$. Then $\sum_{i=1}^{N} \left(\frac{X_i-\mu}{\sigma}\right)^2 \sim \chi_N^2$.

That is, the same transformation that allowed us to find the distribution of a nonstandard normal random variable can be used to find the distribution of its square, or of the sum of a series of squared, nonstandard normal random variables.

Unfortunately, these transformations require us to know σ, and often we won't know it. But we may have an estimate $\hat{\sigma}$ that we can use instead. When we do that, however, we change the distribution of the resulting sum of squares, because $\hat{\sigma}$ is not exactly equal to σ, and $\hat{\sigma}$ is itself random. In the case of our mean estimator, using $\hat{\sigma}$ in place of σ changed the

FIGURE 4.7
Density Function of the *F* Distribution, Various Degrees of Freedom

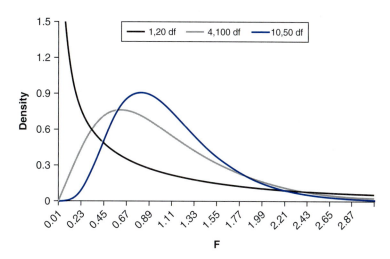

distribution from the normal distribution to the *t* distribution. A similar change takes place in this case.

Definition 4.9 Suppose that $X_1, X_2 \ldots X_N$ are all $\sim N(\mu, \sigma^2)$, and $\hat{\sigma}$ is an estimator of σ that is estimated with M degrees of freedom. Then $\frac{1}{N} \sum_{i=1}^{N} \left(\frac{X_i - \mu}{\hat{\sigma}}\right)^2$ is random and takes the *F distribution* with N degrees of freedom in the numerator, and M degrees of freedom in the denominator. We write this distribution as $F_{N,M}$.

The *F* distribution requires two different measures of the degrees of freedom; the first is the number of terms in the summation, and the second is the number of degrees of freedom used to estimate $\hat{\sigma}$. Like the χ^2 table, the *F* distribution table shows the critical value for which there is a certain chance of the random variable being above that value. The columns of each table are the degrees of freedom in the numerator, and the rows are the degrees of freedom in the denominator; Appendix D at the end of this book shows 5 percent critical values and 1 percent critical values. For example, if $Z \sim F(2, 10)$, then there is a 5 percent chance that Z will be greater than 4.1 and a 1 percent chance that it will be greater than 7.56. Figure 4.7 shows a plot of the density function of the *F* distribution for various degrees of freedom.

The better our estimate of $\hat{\sigma}$ is, the more likely it will be close to the true value of σ. Just as the *t* distribution grew similar to the normal distribution in that case, so does the *F* distribution grow similar to the χ^2 distribution.

Theorem 4.7 As the number of degrees in the denominator M gets large, the $F_{1,M}$ distribution becomes equal to the χ_1^2 distribution.

You can see this from the first line of the χ^2 table and lower left-hand corner of the *F* table in the appendixes. If $X \sim \chi_1^2$, then there is a 5 percent chance of a value greater than 3.84 and a 1 percent chance of a value greater than 6.63. If Y has the *F* distribution with 1 degree of freedom in the numerator and many degrees of freedom in the denominator, then the *F* tables show exactly the same values. For reasonably large degrees of freedom in the denominator (say, above 20) the *F* table value is only slightly larger than the corresponding χ_1^2 table value.

It doesn't quite work if there is more than 1 degree of freedom in the numerator, because of the $1/N$ term in the formula for the F statistic. If $Y \sim \chi_3^2$, then there is a 5 percent chance that it will be 7.81. If Z has the F distribution with 3 degrees of freedom in the numerator and many degrees of freedom in the denominator, then there is a 5 percent chance that it will be greater than 2.60, which is exactly $\frac{1}{3}$ of 7.81. With this correction, the values in the F table for many degrees of freedom in the denominator are exactly the same as the values in the χ^2 table. We will work extensively with the χ^2 and F distributions in the remainder of the book.

Chapter Review

- *Estimation* is the process of using a data sample to obtain estimated values for the unknown parameters of a statistical model.
- Our estimator of the mean of a random variable is the average value of a sample of realized values of that random variable.
- The mean estimator gives the correct answer on average, and we can calculate its variance and standard deviation. The larger the sample, the smaller the variance and standard deviation will be.
- If a random variable is normally distributed, so is our estimator of its mean.
- Even if a random variable is not normally distributed, our estimator of its mean is approximately normally distributed. The larger the sample, the better the approximation (the central limit theorem).
- The central limit theorem allows us to calculate the probability of getting particular values for the estimator from the normal distribution table.
- For any given data sample, some assumptions about the true value of the mean make the observed estimator likely; others make it quite unlikely.
- A *confidence interval* is the set of all possible values of the true mean that have at least a specified percentage chance of producing the observed estimator.
- The sum of squared standard normal random variables takes the *chi-square* (χ^2) distribution. If the normal random variables are not standard, but we know their variance, we can transform them and the transformed variables take the χ^2 distribution. If we do not know the variance, we can transform by the estimated variance, and then the transformed variables take the F distribution. The χ^2 and F distributions are related in the same way that the normal and t distributions are related.

Computer Exercise

In this exercise we'll use Excel's random-number generator to create samples and take their averages, and see how well they predict the true mean of the random numbers in the sample, testing the predictions of the central limit theorem and the rule for calculating confidence intervals.

1. In an empty Excel worksheet, type +RAND() in cell A1 to get a uniform random number between 0 and 1. Its mean is 0.5, and its variance is 0.0833; this gives it a standard

deviation of 0.288. Copy this formula into the range A2—A16 to get a sample of 16 such random numbers.

2. Copy the values in column A and, using Paste Special, copy the values into column B so that the values will not change when you work on the spreadsheet.

3. In cell B17, type +average(b1..b16) to take the average value in the sample. How close is it to 0.5? (You may want to type "Mean" in cell A17 for a label.)

4. In cell B18, type +var(b1..b16) to calculate the estimated variance, and in B19, type +stdev(b1..b16) (or +sqrt(b18)—you'll get the same thing either way—to calculate the estimated standard deviation. How close are they to 0.0833 and 0.288?

5. Using the estimated value for the mean and standard deviation in cells B17 and B19, find the 90 percent confidence interval for the true mean. Does 0.5 fall in this confidence interval or not?

6. Select the values in column A again (they'll be different now) and, using Paste Special, copy them into column C. Then repeat steps 3 through 5 for column C. How did the estimator do this time?

7. Repeat step 6 for columns D through J so that you have 10 different estimates of the mean, variance, and standard deviation. Does the mean seem to be consistently coming out near 0.5? How near? How many times did 90 percent confidence interval *not* contain 0.5?

8. Let's look at the properties of these 10 estimators. In square K17, type +average(b17..j17). This will work out the average of the 10 estimates of the mean. How close is it to 0.5?

9. Type +var(b17..j17) in cell K18 and +stdev(b17..j17) in cell K19 to find the variance and standard deviation of the 10 estimates.

10. Now, let's figure out what we ought to get in question 9 and compare it to our results. As stated above, X's mean is 0.5 and its standard deviation is approximately 0.288. Find the mean and standard deviation of the average value of 16 observations of X. How close is this to what you actually got in question 9?

11. Using the Z statistic (because we know the true variance) find a range in which it is 90 percent likely that the sample average will fall. How many of your sample averages did *not* fall in this range?

12. *Optional* Plot the histogram of the 10 sample estimates of the mean. Does it look approximately bell-shaped?

Problems

1. Assume that the daily price change of Dell Computer Corporation stock is normally distributed with a mean of 0 and a standard deviation of 50 cents.

   a. What is the expected change in the price over a 10-day period? What is the expected average daily change over the 10 days?

   b. What is the standard deviation of the average daily change in the price for a sample of 10 days? (You can calculate the true standard deviation because we have assumed a value for the true standard deviation of a single day's change.)

   c. What are the odds that the stock would fall more than 50 cents over 10 days? (Hint: What average daily change is implied by such a fall?)

2. The following table shows unemployment rates and inflation rates for France and the United States from 1991 to 1998.

Year	France		United States	
	Unemployment	Inflation	Unemployment	Inflation
1991	9.5	3.15	6.8	4.20
1992	10.4	2.47	7.5	3.01
1993	11.8	2.06	6.9	2.99
1994	12.3	1.67	6.1	2.56
1995	11.8	1.71	5.6	2.83
1996	12.5	1.95	5.4	2.95
1997	12.4	1.25	4.9	2.29
1998	11.8	0.71	4.5	1.55

Assume that these four variables are randomly distributed and that each variable's PDF is the same in all years.

a. Estimate the mean and variance for each of the four variables.

b. Calculate 95 percent confidence intervals for the mean for each of the four variables.

c. Do the confidence intervals for average unemployment for the two countries overlap or not? What do you conclude from that?

d. Do the confidence intervals for average inflation rates for the two countries overlap or not? What do you conclude from that?

3. E-Widgets Inc. has had the following monthly sales:

January	February	March	April	May	June	July	August	September
$733,000	$588,000	$457,000	$538,000	$680,000	$631,000	$635,000	$508,000	$572,000

Assume that the amount of sales for each month is a random variable, and that the PDF is the same for each month.

a. Find an estimate of the expected value of sales.

b. What would you predict sales will be in October? Why do you make that prediction?

c. Find an estimate of the variance of sales and standard deviation of sales. How far would you expect sales to be from your prediction in October?

d. E-Widgets Inc. believes that its sales in December have a different PDF; it has the same variance as the PDF for the other months, but its mean is $100,000 higher. What would you predict for the company's December sales?

4. E-Widgets Inc. wishes to build a new factory. It will have to borrow money to do so, and will have to repay the loan in four months. To do that, the company will have to generate $1.8 million in sales over those four months.

a. To generate $1.8 million in four months, what must E-Widgets' average monthly sales be?

b. Find an estimate of E-Widgets' average monthly sales for those four months. Also find an estimate of the standard deviation of average monthly sales for those four months.

c. Is your estimate of average monthly sales greater or less than the required amount? Is the difference larger or smaller than the variance of the estimate?

d. Based on your predictions, would you recommend that E-Widgets Inc. build the factory or not? Explain your recommendation.

5. The CEO of E-Widgets Inc. is very interested in sales forecasts but wants to know how reliable they are before he makes any decisions.

a. The estimate of the mean value of sales is itself a random variable. Find the standard deviation of that estimate. (Hint: The sample used to calculate that estimate has nine observations.)

b. Find a 90 percent confidence interval for the true mean value of sales. Also find a 95 percent confidence interval for the true value. Which is narrower?

c. Is it reasonable to believe that the average value of monthly sales is $550,000? Is it reasonable to believe it is $700,000? Is it reasonable to believe it is $650,000?

6. Recall from introductory economics that an increase of $1 in government spending may increase GDP by more than $1. The exact amount by which GDP goes up is the multiplier. Using a sample of 41 observations, we estimate the multiplier; its estimated value is 4.0 and its standard error is 0.4.

a. Find a 90 percent confidence interval, a 95 percent confidence interval, and a 99 percent confidence interval for the true value of the multiplier.

b. Would you believe that the value of the multiplier was 4.2? Would you believe that it was 2.8?

c. If government spending increases by $20 billion, how much do you predict that GDP will rise? Find an interval in which it is 90 percent likely that the resulting true rise in GDP will be found.

7. Consider the roll of a single six-sided die, which may or may not be a fair die. As shown in Chapter 3, if the die is fair, then the mean value of a single roll is 3.5 and the variance of a single roll is 4.05.

a. Assume that the die is fair. If we make this assumption, then what is the expected value of the sample average value of 100 rolls? What is the variance of the sample average value? What (approximately) is the distribution function of the sample average value?

b. Find the chance that, in a sample of 100 rolls, we would get a mean value greater than 3.6. Then find the chance that we would get a mean value less than 3.2.

c. Find a value X such that the chance of the sample average being above X is only 2.5 percent.

d. What can we say about the distribution of the sample average if we assume the die is not fair?

8. You are handed a coin and told that it may be a fair coin or it may be weighted. If it is fair, then the chance of a flip of the coin resulting in a heads is 50 percent. If it is weighted, then it is weighted in such a way that the chance of a flip of the coin resulting in a heads is 75 percent.

a. Let X be a variable that is 1 if the coin comes up heads on one toss and 0 if the coin comes up tails. Assume the coin is fair. What is the expected value of X? Now assume the coin is weighted. What is the expected value of X now?

b. If you flipped the coin 50 times, how many heads would you expect if it was fair? How many if it was weighted?

c. You flip the coin 50 times and get 27 heads. Calculate an estimate of the expected value of X, and its standard deviation.

d. Calculate an estimate of the standard deviation of your estimated mean.

e. Calculate a 95 percent confidence interval for the expected value of X. Of the two possible expected values you calculated in part a, how many fall inside the confidence interval? What can you conclude about the coin?

9. A company wishes to know what fraction of customers prefers its product to that of its competitors' products. Let π be the fraction of customers that prefer the given company's product. A sample of 100 customers shows that 28 prefer the company's product and 72 prefer a competitor's product.

a. Estimate the value of π. Also estimate the variance of your estimate of π.

b. The company takes a larger sample of 500 customers, of whom 140 prefer the company's product and 360 prefer a competitor's product. Does this sample produce the same estimate of π, or a different estimate? Does this sample produce the same variance for the estimate of π, or a different variance? If different, is the variance of this estimator larger or smaller?

c. Calculate 95 percent confidence intervals for both estimators. Which is narrower?

d. How many customers would the company have to sample in order to estimate π to within plus or minus 1 percent? (Assume that the sample continues to show that 28 percent of consumers prefer the company's product.)

10. You roll a single six-sided die 100 times and you observe the following results:

	Roll					
	1	**2**	**3**	**4**	**5**	**6**
Number	13	16	11	21	15	24

a. Calculate an estimate of the expected value of one roll from this sample. Also calculate an estimate of the variance of one roll from this sample. Is the variance estimate higher or lower than you would expect if the die is fair?

b. If the die is fair, what are the chances of observing a sample average value this high or higher? What are the chances of observing a sample average value this far from 3.5 or farther?

c. Calculate a 95 percent confidence interval for the true expected value of a single roll (which does not require the assumption that the die is fair). Does 3.5 lie inside this range? What does this suggest about the assumption that the die is fair?

Chapter **Five**

Hypothesis Testing

It shall be an unlawful employment practice for an employer—(1) to fail or refuse to hire or to discharge any individual, or otherwise to discriminate against any individual with respect to his compensation, terms, conditions, or privileges of employment, because of such individual's race, color, religion, sex, or national origin.

The Civil Rights Act of 1964 (Pub. L. 88-352), Title VII, section 703

5.1 DETECTING LABOR MARKET DISCRIMINATION

Since 1964 it has been illegal to discriminate in hiring workers (and in many other aspects of economic life as well) on the basis of race and other personal characteristics. However, demonstrating that an individual has been the subject of discrimination is not easy; without access to documentation about a firm's hiring practices, or the testimony of witnesses who observed discrimination taking place, it is quite difficult to prove beyond a reasonable doubt that a given individual was discriminated against.

But if a firm engages in systematic discrimination against many possible workers, not just one, then econometric analysis can reveal the presence of discrimination against them as a group. For example, if a firm discriminates against women in the hiring process, it will probably end up with a lower fraction of women among its employees than would be the case if it did not discriminate. If we can observe a sample of the firm's employees, we can calculate the fraction that are women and see if it is consistent with the fraction of the relevant workforce that are women and the variance of the random factors in the hiring decision.

In doing so, we have turned an *economic hypothesis*—that the firm does (or does not) discriminate against women in its hiring practices—into an *econometric hypothesis*—that the fraction of the firm's employees that are women should be lower than (or equal to) the fraction of relevant workforce that are women.[1] The economic hypothesis is very interesting to an economist but difficult to test in and of itself. The econometric hypothesis is easy to test but not very interesting in and of itself, except so far as it is linked to an economic hypothesis by

---

[1] The difficulty, in practice, is identifying the relevant workforce. From how large an area should a firm be expected to draw its workers? What qualifications are necessary for the firm's work, and what fraction of the people in the labor force in that area has those qualifications? Without answers to these questions, one cannot determine the fraction of the "relevant labor force" that is female, and without that, one has nothing to which to compare the fraction of the firm's workers that are female. In econometric analysis, the devil is often in the details.

some sort of economic model of what the data sample should be like if the hypothesis is true, or false. Much of the art of being a good econometrician lies in finding a way to transform a given, even obvious, economic hypothesis into an econometric hypothesis that is testable with the data available. Then, knowing whether the econometric hypothesis is true or false, one can in turn conclude whether the original economic hypothesis is true or false and can return to the economic argument that motivated the hypothesis in the beginning.

In general, we create an econometric hypothesis from an economic hypothesis by finding a numerical prediction of the economic hypothesis. For example, a supply curve should have a positive slope; the marginal propensity to consume should be between 0 and 1; unemployment and inflation should have a negative correlation. In the above example, the economic hypothesis is that the firm selects workers at random from the population of qualified applicants.[2] If so, then the chance that any one worker will be female will be equal to the fraction of women in the applicant pool (μ). Then we know from the law of large numbers that the fraction of women the firm hires ($\hat{\mu}$) should tend to be close to μ but will not be identical to it; and we know from the central limit theorem that $\hat{\mu}$ is, at least approximately, normally distributed, with a variance we can estimate. We can check to see whether $\hat{\mu}$ is as close to μ as its variance implies it should be. If so, we conclude that the firm is not discriminating; if not, then we consider the possibility that it might be (or the possibility that some assumption of the model is wrong; perhaps the qualified applicant population is not what we think it is). This allows the data to speak to us about the economic issue with which we are ultimately concerned, discrimination in hiring. This chapter presents the statistical methods used to formally state hypotheses about economic questions in an econometric form and to test those hypotheses with data.

5.2 THE NULL HYPOTHESIS

To understand how to turn an economic hypothesis into an econometric hypothesis, we need to know what an econometric hypothesis looks like. An econometric hypothesis has two parts: a parameter of the economic model, and a value that it would take if the economic hypothesis is true (or sometimes, if it is false).

Definition 5.1 The *null hypothesis,* which we write as H_0, is an econometric hypothesis of the form

$$H_0 : \mu = k$$

That is, some parameter μ of an economic model takes exactly a particular value k.

In the previous example, the parameter μ of the model is the chance that a worker hired by the firm is female, and the value k that it would take is the fraction of the workforce that is

---

[2] Random from the perspective of the econometrician, at least. In reality the firm is undoubtedly picking applicants with high abilities, good communication skills, and specific job-related qualifications—or perhaps something less savory such as connections with the firm or the identity of the college the applicant attended. Though the firm knows these things about the applicants, the econometrician generally does not, because they are difficult to observe in real data. Therefore, though the firm is picking whichever of the applicants is most qualified, the econometrician does not know which one that will be, and to the econometrician the identity of the most-qualified applicant is random, in the sense that we defined the word *random* in Chapter 3.

female. We can observe the value that we expect the parameter to take—if the firm is likely to hire only workers within the same city as the firm, and the city's workforce with the appropriate qualifications is 55 percent female, then we would expect that, if the firm does not discriminate, the chance that any one of its workers would be female is also 55 percent. The null hypothesis would then be $\mu = 0.55$, where μ is the chance that a given worker is female. But we cannot observe the actual chance that one of the firm's workers is female. To test whether the null hypothesis is true or not, we will have to estimate the value of μ and see whether or not the estimated value is close to the hypothesized value 0.55.

What if the null hypothesis is not true? Then the parameter takes some other value.

Definition 5.2 The *alternative hypothesis,* which we write as H_A, is an econometric hypothesis that we expect to be true if the null hypothesis is not true. It can take any of several forms:

$$H_A : \mu \neq k$$

or

$$H_A : \mu > k$$

or

$$H_A : \mu < k$$

or possibly other forms, depending on the values of μ that are allowed by the underlying economic model.

Note that the null hypothesis involves an equality: The parameter μ is expected to take exactly a certain value k, not any other. The alternative hypothesis, in contrast, need not be an equality; it can be an inequality. Why is that? Because we can predict a value for our estimator $\hat{\mu}$ only if we have a specific value in mind for μ. If our idea about the value of μ is wrong, then we have no idea what values we might expect $\hat{\mu}$ to take. The null hypothesis will give us a specific value for μ. Our testing strategy will then be as follows:

1. Assume the null hypothesis is true, that is, that $\mu = k$.
2. Calculate the distribution of $\hat{\mu}$ based on that assumption.
3. Test to see whether the sample gives us a value for $\hat{\mu}$ that is likely given the distribution we calculate.
4. If the value we get for $\hat{\mu}$ is very unlikely, then we will *reject* the null hypothesis; if it is likely, then we will *fail to reject* the null hypothesis.

We do not have to have a specific value for the alternative hypothesis, because we never assume the alternative hypothesis is true. We will turn to the alternative hypothesis only if the null hypothesis is rejected.

This, in turn, influences the way we set up the null hypothesis; we always set up the null hypothesis in such a way that it predicts a single value for the unknown parameter of the model. Otherwise our testing strategy cannot be used. To see this, suppose we wanted to adopt the null hypothesis that the firm discriminated—that is, that $\mu < 0.55$. We cannot test this null hypothesis because if the firm does in fact discriminate, we do not know what fraction of its employees will be female. It will be less than 55 percent, but how much less? We do not know. Instead, we must adopt the null hypothesis that the firm does not discriminate. If that is true, then we know (from the economic model) that $\mu = 0.55$. We then know that the fraction of female workers it has should be close to 55 percent. How close it should be depends on the variance of $\hat{\mu}$, which we can also estimate from the sample.

Note that failing to reject the null hypothesis does *not* mean that the null hypothesis must be true. It only means that the data are consistent with the null hypothesis, so we have no basis for discarding it. However, there may be many other possible hypotheses that are also consistent with the data, and there is no reason to prefer the null hypothesis to them. The same is not true if we reject the null hypothesis. If we observe that only 26 percent of workers hired by the firm are female, then we would reject the null hypothesis that the firm is not discriminating. A test can never establish that the null hypothesis is true, but it can establish that it is false. Many explanations of economic data are possible, and though a test cannot show that one of those explanations is the only one that can be correct, it can show that one of them definitely is incorrect. Thus, hypothesis tests are much better at proving that our economic ideas are wrong than they are at proving that our ideas are correct. This is unfortunate, but we can hope that if we can use econometrics to eliminate enough wrong answers, then economic theory can guide us to the right answers. Or, in the words of Sherlock Holmes, "When you have eliminated the impossible, whatever remains, however improbable, must be the truth." That is the basic idea behind using hypothesis tests to determine which economic ideas are true and which are not.

5.3   TESTING THE NULL HYPOTHESIS

To test the null hypothesis, we have to be able to calculate a $\hat{\mu}$ to estimate the value of μ, and we have to know its variance so that we can tell whether it is close to the value k that the null hypothesis tells us it should be close to. For the discrimination example, the way to calculate an estimate of the chance that any one worker is female is to examine a sample of the firm's workers and calculate the fraction that is female. If the null hypothesis that the chance that the firm hires a woman is 55 percent is correct, then the mean of that fraction is 0.55. Since the worker will be female with chance k and male with chance $1 - k$, the variance of a single observation, from Definition 3.7, is $(1 - k)^2 k + (0 - k)^2(1 - k)$, which reduces to $k(1 - k)$, and therefore the variance of the fraction of N workers that are female is, from Theorem 4.3,

$$\sigma_{\hat{\mu}}^2 = \frac{k(1 - k)}{N} \tag{5.3.1}$$

which tells us how close we can expect our sample fraction of female workers to be to k, the hypothesized true value.[3]

Suppose we look at a sample of 36 workers and find that 17 of them are female. This means that $\hat{\mu} = 0.472$, a bit below the 0.55 we expect if the firm is not discriminating; we would have expected $0.55 \cdot 36 = 19.8$, or about 20 female workers. Is this just the result of random chance, or is it so low that the firm must be discriminating? To answer that, we need to find out how unlikely it would be to get a value that is $(0.55 - 0.472) = 0.078$ away from the value we expected. To answer that, we calculate the Z statistic for the chance of getting this

---

[3] In this case we can use the true variance of the fraction of women in the sample, because the null hypothesis tells us its variance as well as its mean. In most applications, we won't be able to calculate the true variance of the estimator and will have to estimate it.

FIGURE 5.1

The Chance of Observing 17 Female Workers or Fewer in a Sample of 36

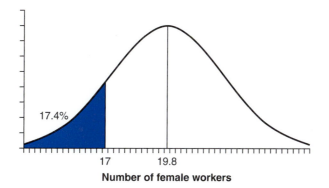

value. To know that, we need the variance of $\hat{\mu}$, which we find from Equation 5.3.1:

$$\sigma_{\hat{\mu}}^2 = \frac{0.55(1 - 0.55)}{36} = 0.0069 \qquad \textbf{(5.3.2)}$$

Then we can find Z:

$$Z = \frac{0.472 - 0.55}{\sqrt{0.0069}} = -0.941 \qquad \textbf{(5.3.3)}$$

Looking up -0.941 on the normal distribution table, we find that the chance of getting a value less than -0.941 is 17.4 percent. This means that, if the firm is not discriminating, the chance of getting 17 female workers or fewer in a sample of 36 workers is also 17.4 percent, as Figure 5.1 shows. This is not highly unlikely (especially because there is an equal chance that we might have observed too many workers), and therefore this seems like evidence that the firm is not discriminating.

Suppose instead we had found only 12 female workers in the sample of 36. Then the sample estimate of $\hat{\mu}$ would be $12/36 = 0.33$, much less likely if the true value of μ is 0.55. The Z statistic in that case would be:

$$Z = \frac{0.33 - 0.55}{\sqrt{0.0069}} = -2.65 \qquad \textbf{(5.3.4)}$$

That is, the value of $\hat{\mu}$ we are getting from the sample, 0.25, is more than two and a half standard deviations below the hypothesized true value of 0.55. The normal distribution table shows that the chance of a value this low, or lower, is only 0.4 percent, as Figure 5.2 shows. This is strong evidence that the true mean is *not* 0.55 and that the firm perhaps is discriminating (at least, if we are confident that 0.55 is the correct fraction of women in the qualified workforce).

Note, however, that in neither case does the test tell us anything about whether the alternative hypothesis is true, because the alternative hypothesis does not suggest a particular value of μ, and thus we cannot calculate a Z statistic for the alternative hypothesis. As Figure 5.3 shows, we cannot claim to have stated anything about the probability that we would have gotten 12, or 17, or any other number of female workers in a sample of 36, since the alternative hypothesis doesn't tell us what the distribution of $\hat{\mu}$ should be. All we can conclude is that μ is not equal to 0.55. This leaves over many possible values for μ, some of which are quite consistent with a sample fraction of 12 female workers in a sample of 36.

FIGURE 5.2

The Chance of
Observing
12 Female
Workers or
Fewer in a
Sample of 36

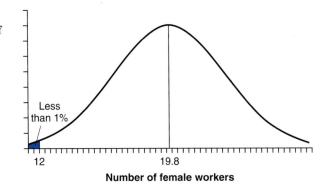

FIGURE 5.3

The Chance of
Observing a
Sample of 33%
Females under
Three Possible
Values of μ
Consistent with
the Alternative
Hypothesis

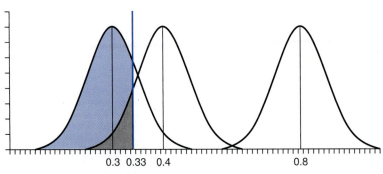

If μ were equal to 0.4, for example, the chance of getting a value of 0.33 or lower would be the red area in the graph, which is reasonably large. If μ were equal to 0.3, the chance of getting a value of 0.33 or lower is even higher; it is the sum of the red and gray areas, which is more than 50 percent. Other values of μ that are consistent with the alternative hypothesis $\mu \neq 0.55$ are even less consistent with a sample of 12 female workers out of 36 than $\mu = 0.55$ is. For example, if $\mu = 0.8$, there is virtually no chance of generating a sample with only 12 female workers out of 36. If we want to know whether, say, 0.3 is a plausible value for μ, then we need to conduct another test with the null hypothesis $\mu = 0.3$, and work out the Z statistic for that hypothesis. But we probably should not do this unless we have some economic reason to believe that the firm really does hire exactly 30 percent female workers, not more and not less. For any estimate we get for the sample, there will be many possible values of μ that are consistent with that estimate—the confidence interval tells us all of them. There is no reason on statistical grounds to prefer one to another; only an economic model can give us a reason to specify one particular value as the one we believe might be the true value, which the data can then either support or not.

5.4 CHOOSING WHETHER TO REJECT THE NULL HYPOTHESIS

Under what circumstances should we reject the null hypothesis? And under what circumstances should we accept the null hypothesis? The latter question is easy to answer: No statistical sample can ever prove that the null hypothesis is true. There are two reasons for this.

FIGURE 5.4

The
Distribution of
$\hat{\mu}$ **When the**
Null
Hypothesis Is
Slightly Wrong

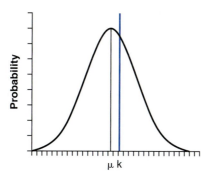

First, as Figure 5.4 shows, if the null hypothesis is wrong, and μ is not equal to k, but it is equal to some value that is very close to k, then it is difficult to prove that the null hypothesis is wrong. The value of $\hat{\mu}$ will most likely be close to μ, by the law of large numbers; therefore, it will most likely be close to k also. It is unlikely that one will get a value of $\hat{\mu}$ that is so far from k as to allow rejecting the (false) null hypothesis that $\mu = k$; for that to happen, $\hat{\mu}$ has to be far from the true μ, which is unlikely. The farther k is from the true μ, the more likely we are to get a value of $\hat{\mu}$ that is far from k also, and hence will convince us to reject the null hypothesis. Conversely, if we get a value of $\hat{\mu}$ that is close to k, it does not mean that μ is exactly equal to k; just near it.

For example, suppose that we observe that the firm has 52 percent female workers. Can we conclude that the firm is not discriminating? We cannot; the firm's chance of hiring a woman should be close to 55 percent but may be somewhat less. For example, if the chance of the firm hiring a woman is 51 percent rather than 55 percent, then the firm is discriminating—and the null hypothesis is false—but a sample of 52 percent female workers is quite likely. In this case, we have not proved that the firm is not discriminating, although we have found that the extent of the discrimination should not be very great. For this reason, we can never claim to have statistically proved the null hypothesis; there are always values other than k that the true parameter might take that are equally consistent with the data.

Second, the idea that the firm should be hiring 55 percent female workers depends on the accuracy of the economic model that generated the null hypothesis. Suppose that we have mismeasured the number of women in the firm's potential workforce; in particular, suppose there are 70 percent women in the workforce, but the firm discriminates, so that the chance of this (discriminating) firm hiring a woman is 55 percent. Then, observing a sample with close to 55 percent women in it, we would conclude the firm was not discriminating; but because the model is in error, the test is wrong also. We can never, statistically, rule out the possibility that the null hypothesis is wrong because the model may be wrong too, in such a way that the wrongness of the model and the null hypothesis cancel out, giving us an estimated value close to the true value we expected.

But the reverse is not true; we can reject the null hypothesis. If we find that the firm has 15 percent female workers, then we can be quite sure that something is wrong in our assumptions; either the model is wrong, the null hypothesis is wrong, or both. To whatever extent we have confidence in our model, we can claim to have shown that the null hypothesis is incorrect; the sample is not consistent with it. For this reason, we will speak of rejecting a null hypothesis, but we will not speak of accepting a null hypothesis. Instead, we will say either that we have rejected the null hypothesis or that we have failed to reject it.

Failing to reject the null hypothesis lends credibility to it, but does not rule out different economic models and different economic hypotheses that might have generated the same statistical prediction. To do that, we have to find a different parameter for which the two models do have different predictions and see if we can obtain data that will allow us to estimate that parameter and let us tell them apart.[4]

More interesting is the question of when we can reject the null hypothesis. We should reject a null hypothesis when the data sample is so unlikely if the null hypothesis is true that it causes us to lose our confidence in the hypothesis. How unlikely does that have to be? That depends on how much we like the null hypothesis; it may vary from problem to problem, and from person to person for a given problem. Our solution is to give people a choice of how quick to be in rejecting the null hypothesis.

> **Definition 5.3** The *level of significance* of a test is the probability of observing a sample that will cause us to reject the null hypothesis if the null hypothesis is true.

A test with a 5 percent level of significance will reject the null hypothesis if there is a 5 percent chance or less of observing a result as unlikely as the sample if it is true. A test with a 10 percent level of significance is quicker to reject; it will reject if there is a 10 percent chance or less of observing a result as unlikely as the sample. If we get a sample with an 8 percent chance of occurring, then the test with the 10 percent level of significance will reject the null hypothesis, but the test with the 5 percent level of significance will not. We can be stricter if we like; we can choose a 1 percent level of significance, in which case we will not reject the null hypothesis unless the sample is so unlikely that there is only a 1 percent chance of observing a result so unusual as the sample. By a somewhat ad hoc convention, econometricians usually choose a 5 percent level of significance when performing tests, although it is possible to speak of a result as being significant at the 10 percent level, which means it can be rejected with a test with a 10 percent level of significance, but not one with 5 percent. Or one can speak of it as being significant at the 1 percent level, which means it cannot even be rejected with a test with a level of 1 percent significance, and surely not with a test of 5 percent or 10 percent significance. Or we can report the level of significance that is just big enough to cause rejection.

> **Definition 5.4** The *p value* of a test result is the level of significance at which we begin to reject the null hypothesis. At any larger level of significance, we will reject; at any smaller level, we will fail to reject.

Continuing from the above example, the chance of getting a sample of 17 or fewer female workers in a random sample of 36, if the true probability is 0.55, is 17.4 percent. We could not reject the null hypothesis on the basis of this sample even at a 10 percent level of significance, and certainly not at a 5 percent or 1 percent level. On the other hand, at a 20 percent level of significance, we would reject the null hypothesis. The *p* value of this test statistic is 17.4 percent; we will reject the null hypothesis at any level of significance larger than 17.4 percent and fail to reject with any smaller level. In contrast, the chance of getting

---

[4] What if the models have the same predictions for all parameters we can estimate? Then there is no meaningful difference between them, at least not from an econometric point of view. Two such models are called *observationally equivalent,* and we can prefer one to the other only on aesthetic or intuitive grounds; statistically they are indistinguishable.

12 or fewer female workers is 0.4 percent, and this would permit us to reject the null hypothesis at any of these three levels of significance. The p value of this null hypothesis is only 0.4 percent. The lower the p value of a test result is, the more confident we are that we can safely reject the null hypothesis.

What should we do if, instead of getting 12 female workers in the sample, we get 28? This is just as unlikely as getting 12 (in fact, slightly less likely) but in the other direction; it implies that the firm is hiring too many female workers, not too few. Should we, in such a case, conclude that the firm is discriminating, or not?

That depends on our view of whether discrimination in favor of women, and against men, is possible or not. Suppose we believed, on economic grounds, that it was utterly impossible that firms might discriminate in favor of women. Then in this case we would be inclined to accept the idea that the firm does not discriminate at all. If the firm does not discriminate, then it is unlikely that we would see a sample with 28 female workers, but it is even more unlikely that we would get a sample with 28 female workers if the firm was discriminating. So we would choose the lesser of two evils, and not reject the null hypothesis. If instead we believed that discrimination in favor of women was possible, then that is clearly a better way to explain the finding of 28 female workers, and in that case we would want to reject the null hypothesis of no discrimination, in favor of believing that there is discrimination in favor of women.

Formally, the two tests have different alternative hypotheses. If we don't believe that discrimination in favor of women is possible, then we don't believe that it is possible for μ to be greater than 0.55. In that case we would test the null hypothesis,

$$H_0 : \mu = 0.55$$

against the alternative hypothesis,

$$H_A : \mu < 0.55$$

Setting up the test this way denies the possibility that μ could be greater than 0.55. In this case, if we chose a test with a 5 percent level of significance, we would want to reject if we got a sample with so few female workers that there was less than a 5 percent chance of observing that few or fewer. From Theorem 3.2 we can calculate the critical number of female workers that would be so unlikely. The normal distribution table shows that for a 5 percent chance, $Z = -1.64$. We will reject the null hypothesis if we see a fraction of female workers that is 1.64 standard deviations below the expected 0.55, and we will fail to reject otherwise. Since the variance of $\hat{\mu}$ is 0.0069, as calculated above, the standard deviation of $\hat{\mu}$ is 0.083, and 1.64 standard deviations is 0.136. We will reject if we get a fraction of female workers less than 0.414, which is 14.90. Rounding off to the nearest integer, this means that we reject with a sample of 14 women or fewer, and fail to reject with a sample of 15 women or more, as Figure 5.5 indicates.

Definition 5.5 The *rejection region* of a hypothesis test is the set of all values of the test statistic that will cause us to reject the null hypothesis.

The rejection region of the discrimination test is the set of numbers 14 or lower, because if $\hat{\mu}$ falls below 14.9, we will reject the hypothesis. This type of test is called a *one-tailed test,* because the rejection region is entirely in one tail of the distribution. We will reject for a sufficiently low number of women in the observed sample, but never for a high number.

FIGURE 5.5
The Rejection Region of a One-Tailed Test

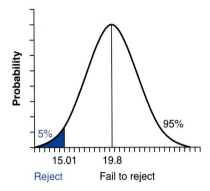

FIGURE 5.6
The Rejection Region of a Two-Tailed Test

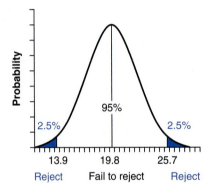

If we believe instead that there might be discrimination in favor of women, then we believe that values of μ greater than 0.55 are possible. In that case we would test

$$H_0 : \mu = 0.55$$

against a different alternative hypothesis,

$$H_A : \mu \neq 0.55$$

which allows for the possibility that μ might be greater than 0.55. Now, when we decide whether a sample is so unlikely that there is less than a 5 percent chance of observing it, we have to include some chance of a very high value of $\hat{\mu}$ as well as a very low one; specifically, we have to allow for a 2.5 percent chance of each, since the distribution of $\hat{\mu}$ is symmetric. We would then only reject if the Z statistic of the fraction of female workers in the sample was 1.96 or higher, or -1.96 or lower. 1.96 standard deviation of $\hat{\mu}$ is equal to $1.96 \cdot 0.083 = 0.163$; now we would reject only if the fraction of female workers in the sample is below $0.55 - 0.163 = 0.387$, or if it was greater than $0.55 + 0.163 = 0.713$. These fractions imply a total of 13.9 female workers in the lower case and 25.7 in the higher case, as Figure 5.6 demonstrates. The rejection region is now the two-part region of 13 or fewer women or 26 or more, and we call this a two-tailed test, since it can reject for either a very high or very low number of female workers in the sample.

Does it make a difference whether we use a two-tailed or one-tailed test? Usually not, but there are two cases when it does. The first is the obvious one: if we get a very high value for $\hat{\mu}$. If we got a sample of 28 female workers, we would reject the null hypothesis of no discrimination with the two-tailed test, but fail to reject it with the one-tailed test. The other case where it matters is a case with a low, but not extraordinarily low value for $\hat{\mu}$; this case arises because the one-tailed test has twice as much rejection region on the left side of the graph as the two-tailed test has. Suppose we got a sample with 14 female workers in it. The chance of a value this low or lower is more than 2.5 percent but less than 5 percent; specifically, it is 2.7 percent. The one-tailed test would reject the null hypothesis of no discrimination, since this is fewer than 15 female workers; the two-tailed test would fail to reject, because it is more than 13.

Since it can make a difference, how do we know which test to use? It depends on our belief about discrimination in favor of women. If we think it is impossible, then we should use the one-tailed test, since doing so makes it more likely that we'll reject the null hypothesis of no discrimination when the firm is discriminating against women. If we think discrimination in favor of women is possible, then we had better use the two-tailed test so that we can reject the null hypothesis of no discrimination if we get a very large fraction of female workers in the data.

5.5   THE SIZE AND THE POWER OF TESTS

Does our test give us the right answer or not? Unfortunately, we can't know, because (as always) we can never know the true value of μ. There are four possibilities: The null hypothesis is either true or false, and we either reject or fail to reject it. Figure 5.7 shows the possible outcomes of the test. In two of the four cases, we get the right answer: when we reject a false null hypothesis, and when we fail to reject a true null hypothesis. In the other two cases, we get the wrong answer: when we reject a true null hypothesis, and when we fail to reject a false one.

Definition 5.6 Rejecting the null hypothesis when it is true is called a *Type 1 error*. The *size* of a test is the probability that we will reject the null hypothesis when it is true.

Because we know the distribution of $\hat{\mu}$ when the null hypothesis is true, we can calculate the size of a test; it is the same as the level of significance. Since we do not want to make errors, we prefer the size of the test to be low.

Definition 5.7 Failing to reject the null hypothesis when it is false is called a *Type 2 error*. The *power* of a test is the probability that we will reject the null hypothesis when it is false; that is, the chance that we will not make a type 2 error.

Unlike the size of the test, we cannot calculate the power of the test, because the alternative hypothesis doesn't give us a precise value of μ and so we cannot calculate the distribution

FIGURE 5.7
Possible Outcomes of a Hypothesis Test

	Null hypothesis true: $\mu = k$	Null hypothesis false: $\mu \neq k$
Fail to reject null hypothesis	Correct decision	Incorrect decision: Type II error
Reject null hypothesis	Incorrect decision: Type I error	Correct decision

of $\hat{\mu}$ when the null is false. However, we can say a few things about it. If we truly believe that discrimination in favor of women is impossible, then we would prefer the one-tailed test to the two-tailed test in the discrimination example, because it is more powerful. It has a larger rejection region on the left-hand side of the graph and so is more likely to reject when the true value of μ is below 0.55. If we do not think so, then we cannot say which test is more powerful in general—the two-tailed test will be more powerful if the true value of μ is greater than 0.55; otherwise the one-tailed test will be.

As a general principle, we want to use the most powerful hypothesis tests we can so as to have the greatest confidence that we will reject a false null hypothesis. However, the only way we can make a given test more powerful is to increase the test's rejection region. But if we do this, then we increase the size of the test, because a larger rejection region makes it more likely that we will reject when the null hypothesis is true, which is not desirable. The reverse is true if we try to reduce the size of the test (that is, reduce the chance of falsely rejecting the null hypothesis). We do that by making the rejection region smaller; but by doing that, we decrease the power of the test.

5.6 TESTS INVOLVING VARIANCE ESTIMATES

On occasion we may want to conduct tests about estimates of variances instead of estimates of means. For example, suppose we want to know whether two stocks have the same variance in their prices. Of course, you would calculate $\hat{\sigma}^2$, the estimate of the variance, for samples of each stock, and see how close your estimates were. But they won't be exactly equal to one another. How close would you expect them to be? To answer that you need to know their distribution.

> **Theorem 5.1** If X and Y are two random variables with the same variance σ^2, and we estimate their variances from samples of N and M observations, respectively, then the ratio of the estimates of their variance, $\hat{\sigma}_X^2/\hat{\sigma}_Y^2$, takes the F distribution with $N - 1$ degrees of freedom in the numerator and $M - 1$ degrees of freedom in the denominator.

We can use this to test whether the variance of the daily price change of Yahoo stock was greater than the variance of the daily change of General Electric (GE) stock. Our null hypothesis is that the ratio of the true variances should be 1; the alternative hypothesis is that it is not. The estimated variance of GE's daily change is 2.00; the estimated variance of Yahoo's daily change is 1.32. The ratio of the estimated variances is therefore 1.51. The samples have 41 and 40 degrees of freedom, respectively, and the 5 percent critical value for the F distribution with (40, 40) degrees of freedom is 1.69. Since the estimate is lower than this, if the null hypothesis is true, there is more than a 5 percent chance of getting a value of 1.51 or larger. We therefore fail to reject the null hypothesis; we cannot say that there was any difference between the variances of the daily price changes of the two stocks.[5]

---

[5] Note that there is a 5 percent chance that F is above 1.69, but we are not considering the possibility that F might be smaller than 1. We are thus implicitly performing a one-tailed test. It is possible to conduct two-sided tests with the F distribution, but in virtually all econometric applications of the F distribution, only a one-sided test makes sense, so we discuss only that case.

However, that may not be the interesting question. GE stock has a much higher average value in the sample ($49.78 for GE versus $19.07 for Yahoo) and therefore a $1 drop in the price of Yahoo causes a larger loss, in percentage terms, for the investor than does a $1 drop in the price of GE. For comparability, we should put each daily change into percentage terms and compare the variances that way. The variance of the percent daily price change of Yahoo stock is 38.4 (implying a standard deviation of about 6.2 percent change per day), while the variance of the percent daily change of GE stock is only 0.76 (implying a standard deviation of about 0.87 percent change per day). Viewed this way, it is apparent that the Yahoo stock was considerably riskier over the sample period. The ratio of these variances is $38.4/0.76 = 50.5$, which is much larger than the 5 percent critical value of 1.69 and even the 1 percent critical value of 2.11. We overwhelmingly reject the null hypothesis that the variance of the percentage changes is equal.

Chapter Review

- In order to test an economic hypothesis, we must transform it into an *econometric hypothesis,* based on an economic model, in which the economic hypothesis suggests a particular value for one (or more) of the parameters of the model. We can then estimate the parameter and see if our estimated value is consistent with the econometric hypothesis or not.

- The *null hypothesis* states that the parameter takes the value suggested by the economic hypothesis. The *alternative hypothesis* states that it does not, but takes some other value or range of values. We assume that the null hypothesis is correct, then test to see if the data supports that assumption. If it does not, we *reject* the null hypothesis, leaving us with only the alternative hypothesis. If the data is consistent with the null hypothesis, then we *fail to reject* the null hypothesis.

- The *level of significance,* or *size,* of a test is the chance that we will reject the null hypothesis if it is true. The *power* of a test is the chance that we will reject the null hypothesis if it is wrong.

- The *rejection region* of a test is the range of estimated values for the parameter being tested which will cause us to reject the null hypothesis.

- A *one-tailed test* places the rejection region entirely in one tail of the distribution of the estimator. A *two-tailed test* places some part of the rejection region in both tails of the distribution. We use a one-tailed test if we can be certain that the null hypothesis, if wrong, will be incorrect in one direction only. Otherwise we use a two-tailed test.

Computer Exercise

In this exercise we'll test a null hypothesis using computer-generated data samples and see how well the tests do at correctly rejecting wrong hypotheses and failing to reject true ones.

1. In an empty Excel worksheet, type +RAND() in cell A1 to get a uniform random number between 0 and 1. Its mean is 0.5 and its variance is 0.0833. Copy this formula into the range A2..A16 to get a sample of 16 random numbers.

2. Copy the values in column A, and use Paste Special to copy the values into column B, so the values will not change while you work on the spreadsheet.

3. In cell B17, type +average(b1..b16) to take the average value of the sample.

4. Now we'll use that estimate to test some null hypotheses. First, consider a true null hypothesis, $\mu = 0.5$. If this null hypothesis is true, then the variance of $\hat{\mu}$ is $(0.5 \cdot 0.5)/16 = 0.0156$ and the standard deviation of $\hat{\mu}$ is 0.125. Test the hypothesis that $\mu = 0.5$. Do you reject, or fail to reject, this hypothesis? Do you get a correct or incorrect inference?

5. Now we'll instead test the false null hypothesis that $\mu = 0.1$. If so, then the variance of $\hat{\mu}$ is $(0.1 \cdot 0.9)/16 = 0.0056$ and its standard deviation is 0.075. Test the hypothesis that $\mu = 0.1$. Do you reject, or fail to reject, this hypothesis? Do you get a correct or incorrect inference?

6. Now we'll instead test the false null hypothesis that $\mu = 0.6$. If so, then the variance of $\hat{\mu}$ is $(0.6 \cdot 0.4)/16 = 0.015$ and its standard deviation is 0.122. Test the hypothesis that $\mu = 0.6$. Do you reject, or fail to reject, this hypothesis? Do you get a correct or incorrect inference?

7. Repeat steps 2–6 to get new numbers in column B, and hence a new estimate. How often do you reject the null hypothesis $\mu = 0.5$? How often do you reject the null hypothesis $\mu = 0.1$? How often do you reject the null hypothesis $\mu = 0.6$? Why is one of the two false null hypotheses harder to reject than the other?

Problems

1. A sample of 18 randomly selected economics majors shows that, when they took their first job, they received the following starting salaries:

$30,200	$37,500	$36,700	$40,300	$30,300	$43,200
$40,500	$37,100	$30,400	$29,900	$40,900	$23,100
$38,800	$37,800	$31,200	$36,200	$34,100	$36,700

a. Estimate the expected starting salary of an economics major using this sample. Find a 95 percent confidence interval for the true starting salary.

b. Assume the true expected starting salary is $39,000. Find a range, with $39,000 at the center, in which there is a 95 percent chance that the estimated starting salary would fall.

c. Test the null hypothesis, at the 5 percent level, that the true starting salary is $39,000 against the alternative hypothesis that it is not. Do you reject or fail to reject?

2. Suppose we have estimated the slope of a supply curve and wish to test whether the supply curve is flat, that is, whether its slope is 0. What is the null hypothesis? Should we use a one-tailed test or a two-tailed test? What is the alternative hypothesis?

3. On December 4, 2002, after the stock market closed, United Airlines was denied loan guarantees by the federal government, making it likely the company would go bankrupt. The following table shows the change in stock prices (in percentage terms) of 10 other airlines on December 5:

Alaska	American	America West	British	Continental
+7.74%	+7.67%	−0.89%	−2.52%	+4.12%

Delta	JetBlue	Northwest	Southwest	US Airways
+4.45%	+3.14%	+4.84%	+3.53%	No change

Assume that the change in the stock price of each airline is an independent random variable and that all 10 airlines have the same density function.

a. Estimate the expected percent change in the stock price. Calculate an estimate of the variance of your estimator.

b. Test whether the expected change is equal to 0 at the 10 percent level.

c. The same day, the Standard & Poor's index as a whole fell 1.2 percent. Test whether the expected change of airline stocks that day was equal to 1.2 percent at the 10 percent level.

d. Was the denial of United's loan guarantees good news or bad news for other airlines?

4. The following table shows the percent change in the price of the stocks of the airlines listed in problem 3 for the following day, December 6:

Alaska	American	America West	British	Continental
+5.71%	+5.54%	+0.90%	+1.08%	+1.98%
Delta	JetBlue	Northwest	Southwest	US Airways
+3.80%	+1.25%	+2.50%	+0.74%	+3.70

Assume that the change in the stock price of each airline is a random variable and that all 10 airlines have the same density function, but the density function may be different than it was on the previous day.

a. Test whether the expected change on December 6 is equal to 0 or not at the 10 percent level.

b. On that day, the Standard & Poor's 500 rose 0.66 percent. Test whether the expected change in airline stocks on that day was equal to 0.66 percent or not at the 10 percent level.

c. Do these data suggest that the announcement of the denial of loan guarantees had an effect on the price of airline stocks on December 6, or not?

d. How would your answers to parts a, b, and c change if you did the tests at the 5 percent level instead of the 10 percent level?

5. a. Estimate the variance of the percent change in airline stock price on December 5, using the data in problem 3.

b. Estimate the variance of the percent change in airline stock price on December 6, using the data in problem 4.

c. Test the null hypothesis that the variance of the change on December 5 is equal to the variance of the change on December 6 against the alternative hypothesis that the December 5 variance is greater, using an F test. What economic conclusions might you draw from the test result?

6. Amangalated Systems Inc. has bid on 25 government contracts and received 14 of them. It wishes to estimate the probability that it will win the next contract, assuming that the chance of it winning is the same for all bids it makes.

a. Estimate the probability that Amangalated will win a contract that it bids on. Also calculate the estimated standard deviation of your estimate.

b. Test the null hypothesis that Amangalated has a 50 percent chance to win a contract. Is it more appropriate to use a one-sided or a two-sided test?

c. Amangalated is planning to make 10 more bids and believes it will win 8 of them. Is its belief consistent with the data?

7. A manufacturer claims that there is only a 1 percent chance that its product will be returned for defects within the warranty period. You observe a sample of 1,500 of its products, of which 19 are returned.

   a. Calculate an estimate of the true chance of its product being returned. Also calculate an estimate of the variance of that estimate.

   b. Test, at the 5 percent significance level, the null hypothesis that the return rate is 1 percent against the alternative hypothesis that the defect rate is not 1 percent. Do you use a one-sided or two-sided test? Do you reject or fail to reject the manufacturer's claim of a 1 percent return rate?

   c. Test, also at the 5 percent significance level, the null hypothesis that the return rate is 1 percent against the alternative hypothesis that the return rate is greater than 1 percent. Do you use a one-sided or a two-sided test now? Which test seems more appropriate?

8. Let Q be a random variable that is equal to 1 with probability μ and equal to 0 with probability $1 - \mu$.

   a. Calculate the expected value of Q and the variance of Q.

   b. In a sample of 50 observations, Q is equal to 1 in 18 cases and equal to 0 in 32 cases. Calculate an estimate of μ and an estimate of the variance of Q.

   c. One way to test the null hypothesis that $\mu = 0.3$ is to make the assumption that $\mu = 0.3$ but to use our estimated variance of Q in calculating the Z statistic. Do the test this way at the 10 percent significance level. What is the rejection region of the test?

   d. Another way to do the test is to use the fact that, if $\mu = 0.3$, then the variance of Q must be 0.21. Do the test at the 10 percent significance level, making the assumption that the variance of Q is in fact 0.21. What is the rejection region of this test?

   e. Which of the two tests is more powerful? (Hint: Think carefully about the chance of falling inside the rejection regions.)

9. A firm that is a monopolist will always choose a quantity of output at which its elasticity of demand is elastic, that is, is less than -1. A firm in a competitive industry can choose a quantity of output with any demand elasticity. Using a data sample with 54 observations, you estimate the elasticity of demand for Acme Motors. The estimated elasticity is -0.86 and the estimated standard deviation of this estimate is 0.11.

   a. Does this estimate have a normal distribution or a T distribution? Briefly explain why.

   b. Test, at the 5 percent significance level, whether the elasticity of demand is equal to -1 or not.

   c. Find a 95 percent confidence interval for the true elasticity of demand. Based on this information, would you conclude that Acme Motors is a monopolist, that it is not a monopolist, or that the data are not sufficient to determine whether Acme is a monopolist or not?

d. Suppose instead you get an estimated elasticity of -0.71 and a estimated standard deviation of 0.11. What would you conclude in that case?

10. Using a sample of 100 observations on a random variable X, we estimate an expected value of 10.25. The estimated variance of the sample mean is 0.36.

    a. Test the null hypothesis that the true expected value is equal to 10, using a two-sided test and 5 percent significance. What is the rejection region of this test?

    b. Assume that the null hypothesis is wrong, and that the true expected value of X is actually 11. Also assume that the true variance is, in fact, 0.36. What is the chance that we will (falsely) fail to reject the null hypothesis? What is the power of this test?

11. In this problem we'll consider a die that may or may not be fair. If it is not fair, then there is a 30 percent chance that it rolls a 1 or a 6, and a 10 percent chance of any other number.

    a. Draw the probability mass function (PMF) of the die if it is not fair. Calculate the expected value of a single roll in that case.

    b. If we rolled the die 100 times and took the sample average, would we be able to test whether this die is fair or not? Explain why or why not.

    c. Instead let's define the variable X, which is equal to 1 if a single die roll comes up 6 and is equal to 0 otherwise. What is the expected value of X if the die is fair? What is it if the die is not fair? Can we use this variable to tell the two dice apart? Explain why or why not.

    d. We roll the die 100 times and in 27 cases get a roll of 6. Test the null hypothesis that the die is fair. Then test the null hypothesis that the die is weighted. What do you conclude about the die?

    e. Propose two other methods of determining whether or not the die is fair.

Part Three

Least Squares Regression

Many economic models can be written as lines on a graph or as a system of linear equations. If we can measure the slopes and intercepts of those lines, we can use them to predict the behavior of the economy; we can also test whether the data lie along the lines that our theories predict they should. In Part III, we present least squares regression, the basic statistical method used to estimate slopes and intercepts of lines through data. We start with the simple case of an equation with only two variables, calculating estimators of the slope and intercept of the line relating them and deriving some properties of those estimators. Few economic models, however, involve only two variables. We therefore turn to the more complex, but more realistic, case of models with more than two variables, showing how the simple estimates can be extended to the multivariate case.

Chapter **Six**

Ordinary Least Squares

The fundamental psychological law, upon which we are entitled to depend with great confidence both *a priori* from our knowledge of human nature and from the detailed facts of experience, is that men are disposed, as a rule and on the average, to increase their consumption as their income increases, but not by as much as the increase in their income.

John Maynard Keynes

6.1 THE PROBLEM OF MEASURING SLOPES

Many economic models are solved by the intersection of two curves on a graph; finding the solution requires knowing the slopes and intercepts of the curves. For example, consider the multiplier model of national income, as graphed in Figure 6.1.[1] In this model, when consumers see their incomes increase, they have a choice of what to do with the extra money; they can spend it, or they can save it. Either decision has consequences for the macroeconomy. If consumers spend the money, then their spending is income for someone else in the economy, who in turn faces the same choice of whether to spend or save it. This cycle leads to the multiplier effect, which causes national income to rise by more than the initial income increase as money circulates around the economy. How much more depends on the slope of the aggregate expenditure (AE) function; the steeper the AE line is, the more national income increases. In order to keep national income growing at a steady rate, we would like to know how government fiscal policy affects it, and that requires us to know, or at least to estimate, the slope of the AE line.

The key underlying relationship of this model is the consumption function, which relates the amount that consumers want to spend to their incomes. We write:

$$C = a + bY \qquad\qquad \text{(6.1.1)}$$

where a is autonomous consumption, the amount of money that consumers would spend if they had no income, and b is the slope of the consumption function. If Y rises by $1, that

---

[1] This model is very basic and does not capture many important real-world issues with the macroeconomy and with the problem of measuring it. However, it can be handled with the simple econometric tools discussed in this chapter. As we cover more advanced econometric techniques, we will be able to refine the model accordingly.

FIGURE 6.1

The Keynesian Cross Model of National Consumption and Income

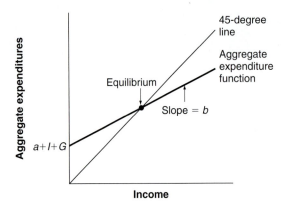

is, if consumers received an additional dollar of income, then C will rise by $\$b$. We call b the marginal propensity to consume (MPC). Because consumers will spend some of the additional income, but not all of it, we expect that $0 < b < 1$.

The MPC is directly related to the effect of government spending on national income. National income is determined by the identity that any dollar of spending by one person is a dollar of income for some other person in the economy. Therefore, aggregate expenditures must equal aggregate income. In a simple economy with no international trade, aggregate expenditures are given by the sum of consumption (C), investment (I), and government spending (G):

$$AE = C + I + G \tag{6.1.2}$$

or, using Equation (6.1.1) for C,

$$AE = a + I + G + bY \tag{6.1.3}$$

which is shown on the graph in Figure 6.1. The equilibrium is the point where $AE = Y$, that is, where the aggregate expenditure curve crosses the 45-degree line.

What happens if the government decides to spend more money? Then the curve shifts up as G rises, and hence the intercept rises. However, equilibrium income rises by more than the rise in G, because the equilibrium point shifts up along the 45-degree line, as shown in Figure 6.2. We can use $AE = Y$ and solve Equation 6.1.3 to get

$$Y = \frac{1}{1 - b}(a + I + G) \tag{6.1.4}$$

which shows that if G rises by $\$1$ (or $\$1$ billion) then Y will rise by $1/(1 - b)$ (or billion). We refer to $1/(1 - b)$ as the multiplier. Normally we expect that, because b is less than 1, the multiplier is greater than 1; an increase in government spending increases national income by more than the amount that government spending rose.

There are two reasons to want to know the value of b. First, it allows us to test the economic hypothesis that $0 < b < 1$, and thus helps us verify whether the economic model is a good description of the real economy, or not. Second, it lets us calculate the multiplier and thus helps us understand how the economy should respond to changes in government spending; this helps us make good economic policy. To get a value for b, we need to be able

FIGURE 6.2

**Effect of an
Increase in
Government
Spending on
National
Income**

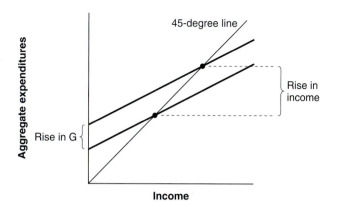

to measure the slope of the consumption function using economic data. This chapter presents the basic methods of measuring slopes of curves through data, which is the foundation for most modern econometric analysis.

6.2   MODELS, DATA, AND ERROR TERMS

In general, measuring the slope of a curve is difficult because the economic model of which the curve is part is not a perfectly accurate model of the real economy. In subjects such as physics and chemistry, we can perform laboratory experiments in which many factors are eliminated or controlled for. Doing so gives us data regarding a simple problem that a physical or chemical model can describe very accurately. In economics we cannot do that. We cannot, for instance, ask the Federal Reserve Board to cut the money supply by 20 percent while holding everything else in the economy constant so that we can see what happens and measure it.[2] As a result, there are always factors that affect the data that are not incorporated in the economic model we are using to describe the data.

Suppose we have a simple economic model that takes the general form

$$Y = \beta_0 + \beta_1 X \qquad\qquad \textbf{(6.2.1)}$$

that is, a line whose slope is β_1 and whose intercept is β_0, and we have a data sample of N observations on the variables X and Y that was generated by the real economy.

Definition 6.1 In Equation 6.2.1, we refer to Y as the *dependent variable* in the model, and to X as the *independent variable* in the model, because Y is calculated from the value of X. We refer to β_0 and β_1 as the *parameters* of the model, which we wish to estimate. We say that we are regressing Y on X; more generally, we say that we are regressing the dependent variable on the independent variable.

[2] But wouldn't it be interesting if we could? Actually, there is a growing field of experimental economics, in which subjects make a variety of simple economic decisions in laboratory conditions where at least some external factors are controlled for; and on rare occasions, policymakers have been induced to change public policies in controlled ways for economists to analyze (the negative income tax experiments of the early 1970s being the most famous case). However, these experiments cannot eliminate or control for all factors that affect subject decisions, even the simple ones made in the experiments, so statistical analysis is still necessary to study the results of those experiments.

FIGURE 6.3
Hypothetical
Economic
Model and
Data

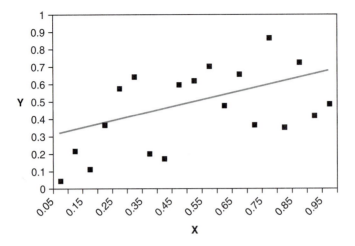

The data generating process will not perfectly follow the model. As Figure 6.3 shows, some points will have values of Y that are higher than the model predicts, others lower; a few will lie almost exactly on the line, but only by coincidence. The data do not lie exactly on the line implied by the model because of the factors that are important in the data generating process in the real world but that are omitted from the economic model, which is an imperfect model of the real data generating process. Accordingly, we write the econometric model as

$$Y_i = \beta_0 + \beta_1 X_i + \varepsilon_i \qquad \text{(6.2.2)}$$

where X_i and Y_i represent the values of X and Y for the ith observation, and ε_i, which we call the error term, represents all factors that are important in reality but omitted from the economic model. There are several different sources of error terms in economic models.

1. There may be some factors that affect Y that are difficult or impossible to measure. For example, in the case of the consumption function, household wealth is an important factor in determining the amount of money people consume, but it is difficult to measure household wealth accurately in the actual economy. Expectations of future income are equally important but are nearly impossible to measure with data.

2. The real relationship between X and Y may not be a straight line. If the relationship is a curve whose slope is changing, then the data will not lie exactly on any line.

3. Y may not be measured with perfect accuracy. National income is measured by a census sample that includes only a fraction of the national population, not every consumer in the country; it should be very accurate, but it will not be exactly correct.

4. There may be purely random factors that determine outcomes. For example, weather is important in determining food consumption and tourist activity.

Any or all of these can cause the value of Y in the data, determined by Equation 6.2.2, to differ from the one predicted by the economic model of Equation 6.2.1, and hence to lie above or below the line. If there were no error terms in the model, and the data lay perfectly on the straight line predicted by the economic model, then measuring the slope of the line would require nothing more than a protractor. Because of the error terms, however, we cannot directly read the slope of the line from the data and therefore need to use more sophisticated methods to infer it.

6.3   THE ORDINARY LEAST SQUARES ESTIMATORS

We do not know the true values of β_0 and β_1 because we do not know the exact data generating process; but we would like to use observed data to create estimates, $\hat{\beta}_0$ and $\hat{\beta}_1$, that are close to the true value. Our problem is to find a way of creating those estimates that will assure us that they are close to the true value. We would like them to be equal to the true value, of course, but since we do not know the true value, we cannot guarantee that they will be. Instead, $\hat{\beta}_0$ and $\hat{\beta}_1$ are our best guesses about what the true values might be equal to. They will not take the same values as the true β_0 and β_1, but we know the values we picked for them. Whenever, in the course of our economic analysis, we need to use values for the (unknowable) β_0 and β_1, we will use our (known) values for $\hat{\beta}_0$ and $\hat{\beta}_1$ instead.

We can pick any values we choose, but some will be better than others. Figure 6.4 shows two possible sets of values for $\hat{\beta}_0$ and $\hat{\beta}_1$; one set corresponds to the red line and the other corresponds to the pink line. The red line is a fairly good estimate; its slope and its intercept are close to the true slope β_1 and the true intercept β_0. The pink line is a rather bad estimate, since its slope and intercept are very different from the true values. If we used the red line to make guesses about the locations of the data points, we would guess reasonably well, because the red line runs fairly close to the true data; but if we used the pink line, we would predict poorly. We need a method of picking estimates for the slope and intercept of the line that are likely to produce estimates like the red line, and unlikely to produces estimates like the pink line.

To state that method, we use the following definition:

Definition 6.2 The *residual* for each data point is the distance between the estimated line and that data point.

FIGURE 6.4
Two Estimates of the True Model

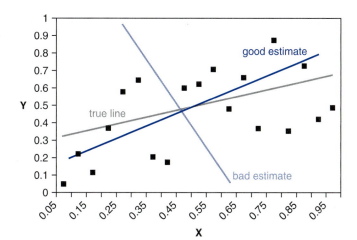

FIGURE 6.5
The Difference between the Error Term and the Residual

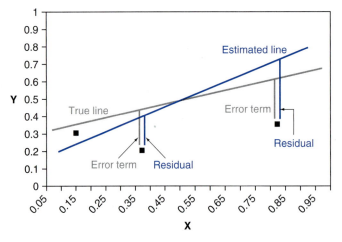

And we can write:

$$Y_i = \hat{\beta}_0 + \hat{\beta}_1 X_i + \hat{\varepsilon}_i \qquad (6.3.1)$$

where we use $\hat{\varepsilon}$ to represent the residual. Note that the residual $\hat{\varepsilon}$ is not the same as the error term ε; as shown in Figure 6.5, the residual is the distance between the data point and the *estimated* line, whereas the error term is the distance between the data point and the *true* line. We can never know the value of the error term, because we do not know β_0 and β_1, the slope and intercept of the true line. But we can know the value of the residual, since we choose $\hat{\beta}_0$ and $\hat{\beta}_1$, the slope and intercept of the estimated line. Note also that, if our estimated line is close to the true line, then the residuals will be close to the error terms; and if our estimated line is far from the true line, then the residuals and the error terms will be quite different. In some cases the error term will be smaller than the residual and in other cases the error term will be larger, depending on whether the data point lies closer to the true line or the estimated line. If the data point lies in between the true and estimated lines, then the error term may be negative and the residual positive, or vice versa.

In general, an estimated line will be better if it produces smaller residuals; it will mean that it is closer to the data, and that will tend to mean that it is closer to the true line as well. We might therefore want to pick the estimated line that produces the smallest possible residuals. In fact, that is what we do:

Definition 6.3 The *least squares principle* is to choose the estimated line, by choosing a slope and intercept $\hat{\beta}_0$ and $\hat{\beta}_1$, that has the smallest possible sum of the squared residuals.

How do we do that? We write an equation for the sum of the squared residuals, and we find the values of $\hat{\beta}_0$ and $\hat{\beta}_1$ that minimize it. Solving Equation 6.3.1 for the residual:

$$\hat{\varepsilon}_i = Y_i - \hat{\beta}_0 - \hat{\beta}_1 X_i \qquad (6.3.2)$$

Definition 6.4 The *sum of squared residuals (SSR)* is given by:

$$\text{SSR} = \sum_{i=1}^{N} \hat{\varepsilon}_i^2 = \sum_{i=1}^{N} (Y_i - \hat{\beta}_0 - \hat{\beta}_1 X_i)^2 \qquad (6.3.3)$$

Using calculus, we can find the values of $\hat{\beta}_0$ and $\hat{\beta}_1$ that minimize the SSR. The answers are:

$$\hat{\beta}_1 = \frac{\sum_{i=1}^{N}(Y_i - \bar{Y})(X_i - \bar{X})}{\sum_{i=1}^{N}(X_i - \bar{X})^2} \tag{6.3.4}$$

$$\hat{\beta}_0 = \bar{Y} - \hat{\beta}_1 \bar{X} \tag{6.3.5}$$

where $\bar{Y}$ and $\bar{X}$ are the average values of Y and X, respectively. These formulas depend only on the observable data, that is, only on the values of X_i and Y_i. Given the data sample, we can calculate these estimated values directly, and hence we refer to them as the *ordinary least squares (OLS) estimators* of the true, unknown values β_0 and β_1. They are called ordinary least squares estimators to distinguish them from other estimators based on the least squares principle, which we will study in later chapters. They are, however, the most commonly used least squares estimators and are often referred to simply as least squares estimates.

Given values of $\hat{\beta}_0$ and $\hat{\beta}_1$, we can use Equation 6.3.2 to calculate the residuals as well. The residuals have two useful properties, which we will use later:

> **Theorem 6.1** The sum of the residuals, $\sum_{i=1}^{N} \hat{\varepsilon}_i$, will always equal 0. The estimated line will always run through the center of the observed data; that is, the point $(\bar{X}, \bar{Y})$ will always lie on the estimated line. Because the sum of the residuals is equal to 0, the average residual is also equal to 0.

The formal proof of this is derived from the derivative of the SSR with respect to $\hat{\beta}_0$. Intuitively, it is true for the following reason. Suppose that the estimated line did not run through the center of the data; suppose, for sake of illustration, that it ran below it. (The argument would be the same if it ran above.) Then the estimated line would look like Figure 6.6. Most of the residuals would be positive and large; only a few would be negative,

FIGURE 6.6

An Estimated Line Passing below the Center of the Data

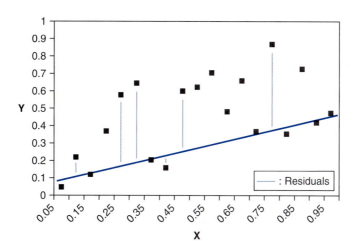

and these would be small. Raising the estimated line would decrease the positive residuals, and most of the residuals are positive. It would increase the negative residuals, but there are few of those. Furthermore, the large residuals tend to be positive, and because we are minimizing the sum of squared residuals, we gain more by reducing a large residual than we lose by increasing a small one. Therefore, raising the line would reduce the SSR and produce an estimated line that better fit the data. The line that will minimize the SSR is one for which the average residual is 0—one that runs through the center of the data.

We can also show:

Theorem 6.2 The sum of each residual multiplied by its associated value of X, $\sum_{i=1}^{N} \hat{\varepsilon}_i X_i$, will equal 0 also.

This result, which follows from the derivative of the SSR with respect to $\hat{\beta}_1$, implies that the correlation between X and the residuals $\hat{\varepsilon}$ will always be exactly equal to 0, a fact whose implications will be developed in later chapters.

We can use the least squares estimators to calculate a value for the marginal propensity to consume in the U.S. economy. Suppose we have the data shown in Table 6.1. The average value of consumption is \$4,903.9 billion, and the average value of income is \$5,841.6 billion. We can then write the economic model

$$C = a + bY \qquad (6.3.6)$$

where C is the independent variable, Y is the dependent variable, the slope is b, and the intercept is a. To estimate this, we need to write an econometric model that includes an error term, since we know there will be real-world factors other than gross domestic product (GDP) that influence consumption:

$$C_t = \beta_0 + \beta_1 Y_t + \varepsilon_t \qquad (6.3.7)$$

where the econometric parameter β_1 corresponds to the economic parameter b, the marginal propensity to consume, and the econometric parameter β_0 corresponds to the economic parameter a, the level of autonomous consumption. We can then produce estimates for β_0 and β_1 using Equations 6.3.4 and 6.3.5. You can verify, either with a calculator or by typing the above data into an econometric analysis program, that the answers are $\hat{\beta}_0 = 24.58$ and $\hat{\beta}_1 = 0.835$. This does not tell us the true value of the marginal propensity

TABLE 6.1
U.S. Consumption and National Income, 1990–1999 ($ billion)

Source: Economic Report of the President, January 2001.

Year	Consumption	Income
1990	$3,831.5	$4,642.1
1991	3,971.2	4,756.6
1992	4,209.7	4,994.9
1993	4,454.7	5,251.9
1994	4,716.4	5,556.8
1995	4,969.0	5,876.7
1996	5,237.5	6,210.4
1997	5,529.3	6,618.4
1998	5,850.9	7,038.1
1999	6,268.7	7,469.7

to consume in the U.S. economy, which we will never know, but it does tell us that 0.835 is a good estimate of it.

Observe that this estimate does conform to our expectation from economic theory that $0 < b < 1$, and that we can calculate an estimate of the multiplier from it: $1/(1 - 0.835) = 6.06$. This suggests that an increase of \$1 billion in government spending will increase U.S. national income by about \$6.06 billion.[3]

6.4   THE DIFFERENCE BETWEEN CORRELATION AND CAUSE

Can we conclude from this regression that an increase in national income will cause consumption to rise? We cannot. Regression analysis tells us that two variables have a mathematical relationship; it does not say anything about *why* they have it. To understand why two variables are related, we need to have an economic theory that explains the relation. Otherwise we could not know which of the two variables was the one causing the other to increase. For example, instead of putting consumption on the left-hand side of the regression equation, we might have put income there, and put consumption on the right-hand side, estimating the regression equation:

$$Y_t = \beta_0 + \beta_1 C_t + \varepsilon_t \qquad \textbf{(6.4.1)}$$

If we estimated that regression instead of the one in Equation 6.3.7, we would get different estimates for the parameters. This regression would show that a line with a slope of 1.194 fits the data for C and Y very well when C is placed on the horizontal axis and Y on the vertical axis, the reverse of the way these variables are normally graphed. Should we conclude that an increase in national consumption of \$1 billion induces people to go out and earn \$1.194 billion more income in order to support their consumption after the fact?

Clearly this interpretation of the data is not correct, but not because the regression is invalid. This interpretation is wrong because it is inconsistent with the economic model given in Section 6.1, which tells us that people determine a level of consumption based on their income, not vice versa. Only an economic model can tell us which variables are taken as given and which variables are determined within the context of the model.[4] In this case, the multiplier model tells us that the correct way to specify the regression equation is to write $C = a + bY$, not $Y = a + bC$, and that the multiplier can be calculated only from the first equation and not the second.

In general, only an economic model can tell us that the value of one variable is determined by another variable. The variable whose value is to be determined should be the dependent variable in the econometric model, and the variable that determines that value should be the independent variable. That is, if the value of the variable Y is determined by

---

[3] Note that this isn't a very good estimate of the multiplier, which is generally believed to be much smaller, probably around 2. This estimate is poor because it is based on a poor model of the macroeconomy; in particular, this model does not take account of the role of international trade in removing income from the U.S. multiplier cycle. We can get better estimates with better macroeconomic models, but they require more powerful estimation methods, which will be covered in later chapters.

[4] Variables taken as given by an economic model are referred to as *exogenous;* those determined within the model are referred to as *endogenous.* We will see this distinction again in the following chapters.

the variable X, then we should write our econometric model as $Y = \beta_0 + \beta_1 X + \varepsilon$, rather than as $X = \beta_0 + \beta_1 Y + \varepsilon$. There are two reasons why this is so. First, there will be factors outside the model that affect the value of Y, which are represented by the error term. The error term affects the value of the dependent variable, but not the value of the independent variable. Second, economically we will wish to talk about how an increase in X affects the value of Y. This makes sense if we write the econometric model as $Y = \beta_0 + \beta_1 X + \varepsilon$; a one-unit increase in X, holding all else constant, changes Y by β_1 units. But if we have written X as the independent variable, then the econometric model will be much more difficult to interpret. Therefore, it is best to use Y as the dependent variable.

6.5 USING THE ESTIMATED REGRESSION LINE TO FORECAST Y

How good is our estimated line? The first question we might ask is: How close is the estimated line to the true line? That question is difficult to answer because we do not know the location of the true line; we will deal with it in Chapter 7. Another question we might ask, and one that is easier to answer because it depends only on things we can observe, is: How close is the estimated line to the data points we observe? That is useful to know if we intend to use the regression to forecast values of Y. The closer the data lie to the estimated line, the closer that predictions of Y based on the estimated line are likely to be to the actual values.

If we could, we would want to base our forecasts of Y on the true econometric model that generates the data:

$$Y_i = \beta_0 + \beta_1 X_i + \varepsilon_i \tag{6.5.1}$$

But we cannot do that because it requires values for β_0 and β_1, which we do not know. Instead, we base our forecasts on the estimated model:

$$Y_i = \hat{\beta}_0 + \hat{\beta}_1 X_i + \hat{\varepsilon}_i \tag{6.5.2}$$

because the least squares estimators gives us values for $\hat{\beta}_0$ and $\hat{\beta}_1$. We also know X_i, since it is observed in the data. The only variable on the right-hand side of Equation 6.5.2 for which we do not have a value is $\hat{\varepsilon}_i$, the residual. If we knew Y_i we could calculate the residual directly, but we are trying to forecast Y_i and so we have to guess a value for the residual. Since the data point is equally likely to fall above or below the line, and since we know the average value of all the residuals is 0, the law of large numbers suggests that we should guess 0 for the value of any particular residual. We can then calculate a predicted value of Y, which we call $\hat{Y}_i$, from the following equation:

$$\hat{Y}_i = \hat{\beta}_0 + \hat{\beta}_1 X_i \tag{6.5.3}$$

The difference between Y_i and $\hat{Y}_i$ is that Y_i includes the residual but $\hat{Y}_i$ does not, as Figure 6.7 shows. The predicted value falls directly on the estimated line, because the (unknown) residual is not included in the predicted value.

We can use the estimated values from our macroeconomic equation to predict values of consumption for 2000. National income in 2000 was \$8,002.0 billion. Putting in our estimated values for $\hat{\beta}_0$ and $\hat{\beta}_1$, we get:

$$\hat{C}_{2000} = 24.58 + (0.835 \cdot 8002.0) = 6706.3 \tag{6.5.4}$$

FIGURE 6.7
True and
Predicted
Values of Y

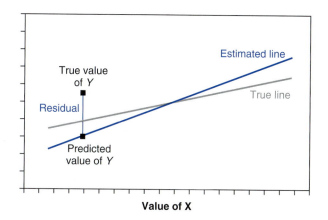

and we would predict consumption of $6,706.3 billion for the United States for 2000. The prediction would be quite accurate in this case: The actual value was $6,757.3 billion, a difference of $51 billion, or less than 1 percent.

6.6   MEASURING THE FIT OF THE ESTIMATED REGRESSION LINE

How good are our forecasted values of the dependent variable Y? That depends on how far the actual data point is from our estimated line, and that depends on the variance of the residuals. The smaller the residuals are, the better our forecasts will be.

To assess the ability of the regression to predict the dependent variable, one thing we might do is look at the size of the average residual; the larger the average residual is, the farther the data points lie from the line. However, as stated in Theorem 6.1, the average residual is always exactly 0. Instead, to eliminate the problem of negative residuals, we square the residuals, calculate an average squared residual, and then take its square root.

Definition 6.5 The *standard error of the regression (SER)* is given as follows:

$$\text{SER} = \hat{\sigma}_\varepsilon = \sqrt{\frac{1}{N-2} \cdot \text{SSR}} = \sqrt{\frac{1}{N-2} \sum_{i=1}^{N} \hat{\varepsilon}_i^2} \qquad \textbf{(6.6.1)}$$

If we want an estimate $\hat{\sigma}_\varepsilon^2$ of the variance of the errors σ_ε^2, we can get one by squaring the SER:

$$\hat{\sigma}_\varepsilon^2 = \frac{1}{N-2} \cdot \text{SSR} = \frac{1}{N-2} \sum_{i=1}^{N} \hat{\varepsilon}_i^2 \qquad \textbf{(6.6.2)}$$

Note that instead of dividing the SSR by N, as we would usually do to take an average value, we divide by $N - 2$. We do that because the residuals are not variables given to us by the data generating process, but rather are calculated from our values of $\hat{\beta}_0$ and $\hat{\beta}_1$. Because we picked $\hat{\beta}_0$ and $\hat{\beta}_1$ to minimize the sum of the squared residuals, SSR is as small as it can possibly be, and therefore the residuals tend to be slightly smaller than the underlying error terms. We divide by $N - 2$ to correct for the fact that we calculated the SSR based on two other estimated values; of course, as the number of observations gets large, the difference between $1/N$ and $1/(N-2)$ becomes very small, and the distinction becomes unimportant. For the macroeconomic regression above, the SER is 44.03, indicating that the average residual should be around $44 billion. This suggests that our forecasts are pretty good—$44 billion is a small error compared to consumption, whose value is in the trillions of dollars.

Knowing the SER tells us how big the average error term is likely to be, and in that sense it also tells us how close the data are to the line. However, the SER depends on the scale of the data. When the dependent variable is national consumption, whose value will be in the trillions of dollars, then the typical error term (or average residual) will be in the tens of billions of dollars (positive or negative). If the dependent variable is the price of a gallon of gasoline, whose value is around $1.50 or $2.00, then the error term will typically be much smaller, perhaps 10 or 20 cents depending on the data sample. An error of $100 would be fantastically good in the first case; terrible in the second case. In that sense, the SER does not really help us understand how close the data are to the line, unless we also know how big Y is.

A better way to ask the question is to ask how much the regression helps us predict the value of Y. If we did not know anything about the relation between X and Y, and had to predict the values of Y_i for a particular observation, we would use the law of large numbers and guess the mean value of Y, that is, $\bar{Y}$. Not knowing X, we would have to pick the same guess no matter for which observation we were forecasting the value of Y. But with the regression, we can instead guess $\hat{Y}_i$, which will be different for each observation since it depends on X_i; and this will be a better forecast, since we use the information the regression gives us about the relationship between X and Y to make the forecast. How much better will it be?

To answer that question, we calculate predicted values for each observation in the data set, with and without using the information from the regression, and see how much better we do with the regression information. Suppose we did not use the regression, and predicted $\bar{Y}$ for every observation. Then our error for each data point would be the difference between Y_i and $\bar{Y}$.

Definition 6.6 The *total sum of squares (TSS)* is given by

$$\text{TSS} = \sum_{i=1}^{N} (Y_i - \bar{Y})^2 \tag{6.6.3}$$

The TSS measures the extent to which Y moves above or below its mean value, and tells us how well we can forecast Y if we do not use any information about X to forecast it.

Now suppose we do use the regression, and we use $\hat{Y}_i$ as our predicted value. Then the error for each data point will be the difference between Y_i and $\hat{Y}_i$, which is just the residual $\hat{\varepsilon}_i$, as we saw in Figure 6.7. Therefore, the total squared error in this case would be the SSR. We claim the following:

Theorem 6.3 The sum of squared residuals (SSR) from the regression will always be smaller, or at worst equal to, the total sum of squares (TSS).

Why is that true? Because we pick $\hat{\beta}_0$ and $\hat{\beta}_1$ in order to make the SSR as small as possible. If we want to, we can choose $\hat{\beta}_1 = 0$; that is, we can make the line flat. If we do that, then since $\hat{\beta}_0 = \bar{Y} - \hat{\beta}_1 \bar{X}$, we will pick $\hat{\beta}_0 = \bar{Y} - 0\bar{X}$, which means $\hat{\beta}_0 = \bar{Y}$. Then our predicted value will be $\hat{Y}_i = \bar{Y} + 0X_i = \bar{Y}$, and the sum of squared residuals will be exactly equal to the total sum of squares. It's possible that this would be the lowest possible value for the sum of squared residuals, but it's extremely unlikely; unless X and Y are totally uncorrelated, some other choice of $\hat{\beta}_0$ and $\hat{\beta}_1$ will produce a lower SSR than the choice of $\bar{Y}$ and 0 will, and then the SSR will be lower than the TSS.

The amount by which the SSR is lower than the TSS is a measure of how much the regression has done to explain the variation in Y.

Definition 6.7 The *explained sum of squares (ESS)* is the amount of variation in Y that can be explained using information on X, and is given by:

$$\text{ESS} = \text{TSS} - \text{SSR} = \sum(Y_i - \bar{Y})^2 - \sum(Y_i - \hat{Y}_i)^2 \quad \textbf{(6.6.4)}$$
$$= \sum(\hat{Y}_i - \bar{Y})^2$$

Thus we have divided the TSS into the portion the regression has explained, ESS, and the portion it has not, SSR. What fraction of the TSS has the regression explained?

Definition 6.8 The fraction of variance in Y explained by X is called R^2 and is given by:

$$R^2 = \frac{\text{ESS}}{\text{TSS}} = 1 - \frac{\text{SSR}}{\text{TSS}} \quad \textbf{(6.6.5)}$$

We interpret R^2 as a measure of how well the model fits the data. Since SSR will always lie between 0 and TSS, R^2 will always lie between 0 and 1, no matter what the units of Y may happen to be. If the model fits the data perfectly—all residuals are 0—then SSR $= 0$ and $R^2 = 1$. The larger the residuals get, the larger SSR gets and the smaller R^2 is. In the worst case, SSR $=$ TSS, ESS $= 0$, and $R^2 = 0$. In general, the higher R^2 is, the closer the data lie to the regression line, as Figure 6.8 indicates. Note that R^2 is fundamentally a property of the linearity of the data. If, as in the graph on the right, the data happen to lie close to a line, then least squares will put the estimated line directly through the data, and the R^2 will be high. If the data are scattered in a cloud, as in the graph on the left, then they will not lie near any line, and the R^2 will be low.

Therefore, R^2 is a measure of how well the estimated line predicts the data. In that context it can be useful. However, it does not say anything about how close the estimated

FIGURE 6.8
Regressions with R^2 of 0 and 1

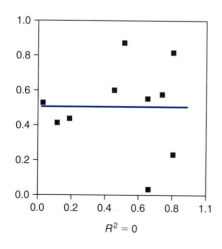

$R^2 = 0$

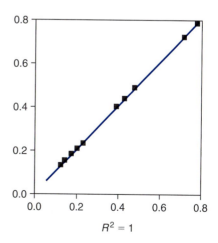

$R^2 = 1$

values of $\hat{\beta}_0$ and $\hat{\beta}_1$ are to their true values, and it cannot be used to say whether $\hat{\beta}_0$ and $\hat{\beta}_1$ are good estimates or not. There are regressions with very high R^2 but very poor estimates of $\hat{\beta}_0$ and $\hat{\beta}_1$, and conversely, there are regressions with very low R^2 but with excellent estimates of $\hat{\beta}_0$ and $\hat{\beta}_1$. Some data sets are inherently easy to predict. For example, the U.S. economy normally grows between about 1 percent and about 4 percent per year. A forecast that GDP will be, say, 2.5 percent higher than this year's GDP is unlikely to be off by more than one or two percentage points, simply because next year's total GDP is not inherently very variable—the economy does not grow or shrink by 20 percent in a given year. Conversely, other data sets are inherently very hard to predict. For example, data on the wages of U.S. workers have very large error terms, and very large residuals, because a worker's wage depends on many factors that are difficult to measure with economic data—the quality of their education, the skills they have acquired on the job, their personal motivation, their work history, and so forth. Nonetheless, if we have enough data, we can estimate the parameters of models of wage determination very precisely, despite the fact that the residuals will be large and the R^2 will therefore be small. It is important *not* to rely on R^2 as a measure of the quality of the regression as a whole. It is useful as a measure of the model's ability to predict the data. Depending on whether or not you intend to use the regression for forecasting, the value of R^2 may be important or may be irrelevant.

Chapter Review

- Many economic problems require knowing the slopes of curves that are part of economic models.

- Real economic data do not lie precisely on those curves; our econometric models must include an error term to allow for observations that deviate from the curves.

- The *residual* is the distance between the data and the estimated line. We choose estimated values for the slope and intercept of the line by minimizing the sum of the squared residuals.

- We can use the estimated line to forecast values for data points we do not observe.

- The *standard error of the regression (SER)* is an estimate for the average distance between the true line and the data.

- The R^2 of the regression is a measure of the amount of variation in the dependent variable that can be explained using the econometric model and the value of the independent variable.

Computer Exercise

In this exercise we'll generate some random data and run regressions on it; we'll change the size of the error term, and we'll see how the residuals, SER, and R^2 values change as we do so.

1. Start Eviews, and create a new worksheet, undated, with 100 observations. Then, on the command line, type genr x = rnd()*20 to create an independent variable, which we'll keep fixed throughout the exercise.

2. Type genr err = rnd()*5 to create some initial error terms. Then type genr y = 10 + 0.5*x + err to create a dependent variable.

3. Type ls y c x to estimate a regression with Y as the dependent variable and X as the independent variable (C represents the intercept term). Is the estimated slope close to 0.5? Is the estimated intercept close to 10?

4. What is the R^2 for this regression? Does the regression explain most of the variance in the independent variable, or not very much of it? How large is the SER? Is it consistent with the value for R^2, given that the average value Y should be around 15?

5. Double-click on the RESID variable, which contains the residuals for the regression. How big are the residuals? Click the View button and select Descriptive Statistics, then Histogram and Stats. What is the average value of the residual? What is its standard deviation?

6. On the command line, type fit yhat. This command will calculate the predicted values for each observation for this regression. Open a group containing y and yhat. How close are the predicted values to the true values? (They should differ by exactly the amount of the residual for that observation.)

7. Open a group containing x and y, then click View, then Graphs, then Scatter, then Scatter with Regression. You will see the data and the regression line.

8. Type genr err = rnd()*2 to create a new error sequence with much smaller errors, and type genr y = 10 + 0.5*x + err to recreate the dependent variable. Then repeat steps 3 through 7 with the new dependent variable. How much smaller are the SER and the R^2, and how much better are the predicted values? How has the graph changed?

9. Type genr err = rnd()*30 to create a new error sequence with much larger errors, and type genr y = 10 + 0.5*x + err to re-create the dependent variable. Then repeat steps 3 through 7 with the new dependent variable, and see how the R^2, SER, and predicted values are now.

Problems

1. Consider an economic model $Y_i = \beta_0 + \beta_1 X_i$, which is estimated with the following data points:

Y	X
150	4
180	6
200	7

Suppose that the true values of the parameters are $\beta_0 = 80$ and $\beta_1 = 17$.

a. Using Equations 6.3.4 and 6.3.5, or using a computer, calculate the least squares estimates of $\hat{\beta}_0$ and $\hat{\beta}_1$.

b. Using these values of $\hat{\beta}_0$ and $\hat{\beta}_1$, calculate the predicted value for each observation and the residual for each observation.

c. Using the true values of β_0 and β_1, calculate the error term for each observation. For which observations are the residuals larger than the error terms? For which are the error terms larger?

d. Verify that the sum of the residuals is 0 (Theorem 6.1) and that the sum of X_i times the residual is also 0 (Theorem 6.2). Verify that the sum of the error terms is *not* 0.

2. Suppose you have the following five data points:

Y	X
64	10
68	12
47	8
73	11
34	5

and you wish to estimate a relationship of the form $Y_i = \beta_0 + \beta_1 X_i$.

a. One possible estimate is $\beta_0 = 0$, $\beta_1 = 7$. Find the residuals and the SSR associated with this estimate.

b. Another possible estimate is $\beta_0 = 10$, $\beta_1 = 5$. Find the residuals and the SSR associated with this estimate.

c. According to the least squares principle, which of these estimates is better?

d. Could either of these estimators be the least squares estimator? Why or why not? (Hint: Calculate the sum of the residuals for each.)

3. a. Using the estimated consumption function CONSUMPTION $= 24.58 + (0.835 \cdot$ INCOME), calculate the predicted value of consumption if national income is equal to $4,392 billion, as it was in 1989.

b. The actual value of consumption in 1989 was $3,597 billion. What is the difference between the predicted and actual values? Is it smaller or larger than the SER?

4. Suppose that when estimating the consumption function, instead of getting the estimated value $\hat{b} = 0.835$, we had instead gotten the estimated value $\hat{b} = 0.65$. What would the value of the multiplier then be? Would we expect government spending to have a greater or lesser effect on the economy if we had gotten this different estimate?

5. Load the data file buscost, which contains two variables describing the operation of 246 bus companies in U.S. cities. Totalcost is the total operating expense of the company, in thousands of dollars; RVM is the total output of the firm, in thousands of revenue vehicle miles (miles driven by buses in service). Estimate the following cost function:

$$\text{Totalcost}_i = \beta_0 + \beta_1 \text{RVM}_i + \varepsilon_i$$

a. If RVM rises by 1, how much will total cost rise? What is the estimated marginal cost of an additional RVM of output?

b. Predict the total cost of providing 0 RVM. What are the estimated fixed costs of the firms in this industry? (Remember that total costs are measured in thousands of dollars.)

c. Predict the total cost of providing 5 million RVM. (Remember that the variable RVM is measured in thousands.)

d. What is the standard error of the regression? By how many thousands of dollars do the average bus company's actual costs differ from the predicted value?

e. What is the R^2 of the regression? Graph the data. How close are the data points to a line? Does it appear from the graph that the marginal cost (the slope of the line) is constant or not?

6. Load the data file wages1, which contains two variables from the U.S. Census Bureau's *Current Population Survey* on American workers. The variable Wages is the individual's annual earnings from wages and salary income; the variable education is the individual's level of education. All individuals with more than 18 years of education (beyond master's degree) receive a value of 18 in the data. Estimate the following equation:

$$\text{Wages}_i = \beta_0 + \beta_1 \text{Education}_i + \varepsilon_i$$

a. If you get one more year of education, by how much does your annual income from wages and salaries rise? Does this seem like a reasonable value or not?

b. Predict the average wage for a high school graduate (12 years of education) and a college graduage (16 years of education). What is the value of a college degree, in terms of increasing your wage income?

c. What is the R^2 of this regression? What is the standard error of the regression? Is this regression reliable for predicting wages of individuals or not?

7. Load the data file taxrecpt, which contains data from 1960 to 1995 on two variables. receipts is the federal government's total tax receipts; gdp is the U.S. gross domestic product. Both are measured in billions of dollars. Estimate the following equation:

$$\text{receipts}_i = \beta_0 + \beta_1 \text{GDP}_i + \varepsilon_i$$

a. If GDP rises by $1 billion, how much do tax receipts rise? What is the effective marginal tax rate in the United States, according to this regression?

b. The values of GDP from 1996 to 1999 were (in billions of dollars):

1996	$7,813
1997	8,318
1998	8,790
1999	9,299

Predict federal tax collections in each of those years.

c. Calculate the difference between the predicted values and the actual values, which are (in billions of dollars):

1996	$1,499
1997	1,625
1998	1,754
1999	1,874

How many are positive and how many are negative? Is the average forecast error equal to 0 or not? If not, explain why not.

Chapter **Seven**

Properties of the Least Squares Estimators

Three econometricians go on safari together, and decide to go out hunting big game. The first one takes aim at an elephant and misses ten feet to the left. The second one takes aim at the same elephant and misses ten feet to the right. The third one jumps up and shouts, "We got him!"

7.1 DESIRABLE PROPERTIES OF ESTIMATORS

The ability to calculate estimates of the slopes and intercepts of economic relations is tremendously useful, but it is still more useful if we know something about the reliability of the estimates and their relationship to the true, unknown values. The estimates are random variables and not guaranteed to take any particular values. But if we understand the distribution function of the estimates, then we can talk about what values they are likely to take, or unlikely to take—and from their statistical properties we can get some measure of how dependable they are in economic applications. In this chapter we first present the distributions of the least squares estimators and some of their properties and then explain why those properties make them good estimators to use in economic analysis.

We start by defining three properties that we like estimates to have. We will say that estimators are good ones if they have those properties. The first one is that, like the third econometrician, we would like to get the right answer on average.

Definition 7.1 An estimator $\hat{\beta}$ is *unbiased* if its expected value is equal to β, the true value of the parameter it estimates. Otherwise it is *biased*. It is unbiased if $E(\hat{\beta}) = \beta$; it is biased if $E(\hat{\beta}) \neq \beta$.

Another way to put it is that if an estimator is unbiased, then the expected difference between $\hat{\beta}$ and the true β is 0; the estimate does not tend to be too high or too low. If it is biased, then it tends to give an answer that is either too high (if the expected difference is positive) or too low (if the expected difference is negative). If we know that our estimator is unbiased, then we know that, although the estimator probably does not take the true value, it does not tend to be off in one particular direction or the other.

Unbiasedness, however, is not all that useful a property, because you do not get the average value; you get whatever value you get. It is not necessarily comforting to know that a huge positive error and a huge negative error are equally likely. We would perhaps prefer to know that the errors are small, whichever side they happen to be on.

> **Definition 7.2** An estimator $\hat{\beta}$ is *consistent* if, as the data sample gets arbitrarily large, the difference between the estimated value and the true value β gets arbitrarily small. With more and more data, the chance of being close to the true value approaches 1. Otherwise it is *inconsistent*.

More formally: An estimator is consistent if, for any small range around the true value β, the chance that $\hat{\beta}$ will fall in that range approaches 1 as the number of data points in the sample goes to infinity. What this means is that if our estimator is consistent, then we can all but guarantee that it will be as close to the true value as we need it to be, if we can collect enough data to use in estimating it. This property is useful because it assures us that we can, with enough data, reduce the probability of a damagingly large error as close to 0 as we need to. It gives us some assurance that $\hat{\beta}$ is, in some sense, close to the true β.

However, this property has its limits as well, because we never have an infinite amount of data, or even as large an amount as we'd like to have. For finite samples of data, the probability of being in any given range around the true value is less than 1, and we don't know exactly how much less. We would like to use an estimator that is as likely as possible to be close to the true value; even if it's not very likely, it's the best option we have if our estimator has a better chance than any other estimator.

> **Definition 7.3** An estimator $\hat{\beta}$ is *efficient* if there is no other unbiased estimator whose variance is lower than the variance of $\hat{\beta}$. An estimator is efficient within a class of unbiased estimators if no other estimator in the class has a lower variance than the variance of $\hat{\beta}$.

We would like to use an estimator with all three of these properties—unbiasedness, consistency, and efficiency—if we can find one. Of course, to have a choice, we have to know two different estimators, one of which is least squares. To see a simple example of a case where there are several different estimators to choose from, with different variances, consider the following problem.[1]

Suppose, for the sake of simplicity, that we know that the true value of β_0 is 0, so that we only need worry about estimating β_1. Suppose further that we have only one data point and thus our information is described by Figure 7.1. In this case it is clear that the best way to estimate the slope of the line is to pick the line connecting the known intercept to the one data point we have. The data point is just as likely to be above the true line as below it, since the average value of the error term is 0. Therefore, an estimated line through the data point is just as likely to be below the line as above it, and hence unbiased.

Now suppose that we have two data points. They might, by coincidence, lie exactly on a line through the origin, in which case that line is obviously the right estimate; but more likely, they will not. If they do not, then we have the situation shown in Figure 7.2. Clearly the estimated line should be in between the two data points somewhere. What is the best way to estimate the slope of the line in this case?

---

[1] This example is taken from Murray (1999).

FIGURE 7.1
**Estimating a
Slope with a
Single Data
Point**

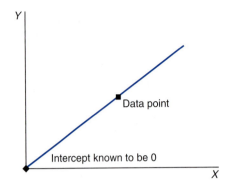

FIGURE 7.2
**Estimating a
Slope with Two
Data Points**

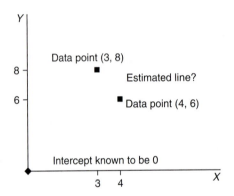

You may be able to think of several different ways to proceed. One option is to take the slopes of the lines through each point and average them to produce an estimate of β_1. Another is to find the point exactly halfway between the two data points and take the slope of the line through that point as the estimate of β_1. Those will generally not produce the same answer. For example, suppose the two points are (4, 6) and (3, 8). Then the slope of the line through the first point is 1.5, and the slope of the line through the second point is 2.667. The average slope is therefore 2.083. However, the point halfway between those two points is (3.5, 7), and the slope of the line through that halfway point is 2. Thus, these two methods of estimating the slope, both of which seem reasonable, give different estimates.

And, as it turns out, neither of them is the same as the least squares estimate. To produce the least squares estimate, we would choose the line with the smallest sum or squared residuals, or the smallest vertical distances between the line and the two data points. For any given $\hat{\beta}_1$, the formula for the estimated line will be just $\hat{Y} = \hat{\beta}_1 X$ (because we know the intercept is 0) and for any value X_i, the line will pass through the points $(X_i, \hat{\beta}_1 X_i)$. For the two data points in this example, the line will pass through $(3, 3\hat{\beta}_1)$ and through $(4, 4\hat{\beta}_1)$. The residuals, which are the difference between the true value of Y and the predicted value $\hat{Y}$, will therefore be $(8 - 3\hat{\beta}_1)$ for the first point and $(6 - 4\hat{\beta}_1)$ for the second point. The least squares estimator is the value of $\hat{\beta}_1$ that minimizes the sum of the squared residuals $(8 - 3\hat{\beta}_1)^2 + (6 - 4\hat{\beta}_1)^2$. The derivative of this with respect to $\hat{\beta}_1$ is $6(8 - 3\hat{\beta}_1) + 8(6 - 4\hat{\beta}_1)$; setting this equal to 0 and solving for $\hat{\beta}_1$ shows that the value that minimizes the sum of squared residuals (SSR) is 1.92. So we now have three different estimates for the slope of the true line: 2.083, 2, and 1.92. There are other ways to produce plausible estimated values for β_1 as well. Which is the best estimate to use?

To answer that question, we need to know the properties of the various estimators. Are they biased or unbiased? Consistent or inconsistent? Which is most efficient? To answer these questions, we need to know some things about the mean and variance of each estimator. The mean and variance of the estimators depends on the properties of the error terms that are causing the data not to lie exactly on the line; we cannot know which estimator is better without knowing some things about those error terms. In the next section, we introduce some assumptions that, if true, guarantee that the least squares estimator is the best one to use.

7.2 THE CLASSICAL REGRESSION MODEL

To find out whether the least squares estimators $\hat{\beta}_0$ and $\hat{\beta}_1$ are unbiased, consistent, or efficient, we have to make some assumptions about the properties of the error terms. The most basic set of assumptions we make about the error terms, and about the regression more generally, are called the classical regression model.

> **Definition 7.4** The *classical regression model* is composed of the following five assumptions, known as the *Gauss-Markov assumptions:*
>
> A1. We have the correct model; that is, the true data generating process is of the form
>
> $$Y_i = \beta_0 + \beta_1 X_i + \varepsilon_i$$
>
> A2. X does not take the same value for all observations.
> A3. Given the values of X_i, the variance of ε_i is σ^2 for all observations; that is, the variance of the error term for each observation is the same.
> A4. The error terms are not correlated with one another.
> A5. The error terms are not correlated with the value of X_i; the mean value of ε is 0 no matter what the value of X is.

Assumption A1 guarantees that our econometric model of the data matches the actual economic process we're studying. There's nothing much we can do to verify this assumption or to correct for it if it's wrong, so we generally produce the best model we can and hope that it works. Assumption A2 requires that some observations have different values for X than others so that the data can tell us how changes in X affect Y. Mathematically, this assumption guarantees that $\sum_{i=1}^{N}(X_i - \bar{X})^2$ is not equal to 0 (if X takes the same value for all observations, it will equal 0), which will be important below. The other three assumptions, however, are testable, and we can change the way we estimate the model if we find that they are false. Those tests and changes to the model are the subject of later chapters in the book.

Assumption A3 asserts that each error term has the same variance, that is, that each data point is likely to lie just as far from the true model as any other.

> **Definition 7.5** If the variance of ε_i is σ^2 for all observations, then the error terms are *homoskedastic* (homo- is the Latin root meaning "the same"). If the variance of

ε_i is σ_i^2, and differs from observation to observation, then the error terms are *heteroskedastic* (*hetero-* is the Latin prefix meaning "different").

Assumption A3 assumes that the error terms are homoskedastic, or that the regression has homoskedasticity.[2]

Assumption A4 asserts that the error terms are uncorrelated and do not influence each other:

> **Definition 7.6** If the error terms are correlated with one another, that is, if the correlation of ε_i and ε_j is not equal to 0 for some values of i and j, then we say the error terms are *serially correlated*. If the error terms are uncorrelated, then we say that the errors terms are not serially correlated.

Assumption A4 assumes that the error terms have no serial correlation.

Assumption A5 asserts that the values of ε do not differ for different values of X; that is, knowing X does not tell you anything about what the value of ε is likely to be.

> **Definition 7.7** If the error terms are uncorrelated with a variable, we say that the variable is *exogenous*. If the error terms are not correlated with the variable, then we say that the variable is *endogenous*.

Y is an endogenous variable by construction; clearly, if $Y_i = \beta_0 + \beta_1 X_i + \varepsilon_i$, then if ε_i rises, Y_i will also, and the two will be positively correlated. The variable on the left-hand side of any regression will always be endogenous. The variable on the right-hand side might or might not be. Assumption A5 requires that it be exogenous.

With these five assumptions, we can say some useful things about the properties of $\hat{\beta}_0$ and $\hat{\beta}_1$.

> **Theorem 7.1** In the classical regression model, $\hat{\beta}_0$ and $\hat{\beta}_1$ are unbiased. The expected value of $\hat{\beta}_0$ is β_0, and the expected value of $\hat{\beta}_1$ is β_1; on average, the estimators produce the correct answer.

Intuitively, this happens because each error term is equally likely to be above or below the true line, and therefore it is just as likely that the estimated regression line will be above or below the true line. On average it will be exactly on the true line. Therefore, a line drawn through the center of the data will also be equally likely to be above or below the true line, and will be the true line on average. Figure 7.3 shows the distribution of a biased and an unbiased estimator. The distribution of the unbiased estimator has an expected value equal to the true value of β; the biased one does not.

We can also assert the following:

> **Theorem 7.2** In the classical regression model, $\hat{\beta}_0$ and $\hat{\beta}_1$ are consistent. As the number of observations in the data set gets larger and larger, the chance that $\hat{\beta}_0$ and $\hat{\beta}_1$ will be within any desired distance of the true β_0 and β_1 goes to 1.

Intuitively, this is because each error term is uncorrelated with the others, so it will tend to take its mean value of 0 and therefore will tend to improve the estimates. Adding more and

---

[2] This is an American spelling; English econometricians tend to use *homoscedasticity* (and *heteroscedasticity* for the opposite case). It means the same thing no matter how you spell it.

FIGURE 7.3
Distributions of Unbiased and Biased Estimators

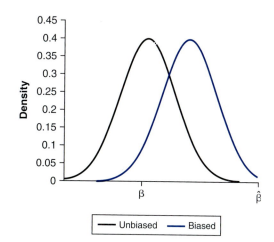

FIGURE 7.4
Change in the Distribution of a Consistent Estimator as N Increases

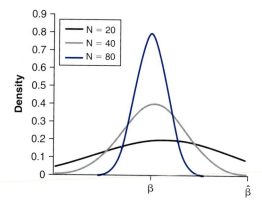

more observations will improve the estimates as much as we desire. Figure 7.4 shows how the density function of a consistent estimator changes as the number of observations increases. With more observations, the density function becomes narrower and taller, so the probability of getting an estimated value that is close to the true value of β gets closer to 1.

The next property of least squares requires some definitions beforehand:

Definition 7.8 An equation is *linear* with respect to a set of variables Z if it can be written in the form

$$a_0 + a_1 Z_1 + a_2 Z_2 + \cdots + a_K Z_K = 0 \qquad (7.2.1)$$

where the a terms do not depend on Z. Otherwise it is *nonlinear*.[3]

[3] To be precise, we might speak of this model as being linear to the β parameters. A model can be linear in the parameters, linear in the X variables, both, or neither. Generally, when we speak of a model as linear or nonlinear, we will mean linear in the parameters.

The equation $Y = 5 + Z_1 + 3Z_2$ is linear with respect to the Zs, since it can be written as $(5 - Y) + 1Z_1 + 3Z_2 = 0$. The equation $Z^2 + 5ZY - 2Y = 0$ is linear with respect to Y, because it can be written as $(Z^2) + (5Z - 2)Y = 0$, and the Z^2 term does not depend on Y. However, it is not linear with respect to the Zs, because the Z^2 term cannot be written as (a_0) or as $(a_1 Z)$. Therefore, this equation is linear with respect to one variable but not with respect to the other. The equation $\log Y = \beta_0 + \beta_1 \log X_1 + \beta_2 \log X_2$ is linear with respect to the β parameters, but not with respect to the X variables, because of the log terms.

The concept of linearity is used in several ways in econometrics, and we will see it again later. At the moment, we are concerned with estimators, so we define what it means for an estimator to be linear.

Definition 7.9 An estimator is *linear* if the equation that defines it is linear with respect to the dependent variable Y. Otherwise it is *nonlinear*.

The least squares estimator is linear because we can rewrite the formula for the least squares estimator in the following way:

$$\hat{\beta} = \sum_{i=1}^{N} \left(\frac{(X_i - \bar{X})}{\sum_{j=1}^{N}(X_j - \bar{X})^2} \right) Y_i \tag{7.2.2}$$

which shows that, if we choose

$$a_i = \frac{(X_i - \bar{X})}{\sum_{j=1}^{N}(X_j - \bar{X})^2}$$

which does not depend on Y, then Equation 7.2.2 is of the form given by Equation 7.2.1, and therefore least squares is a linear estimator. With that said, we can show:

Theorem 7.3 The Gauss-Markov Theorem: In the classical regression model, $\hat{\beta}_0$ and $\hat{\beta}_1$ have a lower variance than any other possible linear estimator. In the class of linear estimators, $\hat{\beta}_0$ and $\hat{\beta}_1$ are efficient.

Figure 7.5 shows the density functions of an efficient and an inefficient estimator. Both are unbiased, but the efficient estimator has a lower variance, making it narrower and taller than

FIGURE 7.5

Distribution of Inefficient and Efficient Estimators

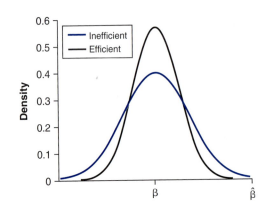

the inefficient estimator. The efficient estimator is more likely to produce an estimated value close to the true value of b than the inefficient estimator is.

The Gauss-Markov theorem is our justification for using the least squares estimators instead of any other linear estimators. If we are trying to choose from several different estimators, and all of them are linear and unbiased, then we should choose the least square estimators. They have smaller variances than any other estimators, and hence are more likely to be close to the true value. However, the Gauss-Markov theorem so far only asserts that least squares is efficient within the class of linear estimators. It's possible that there might be some nonlinear estimator out there that is more efficient. If we are willing to add one more assumption to the classical regression model, we can eliminate that possibility.

Theorem 7.4 Add the following assumption to the classical regression model:

A6. ε_i is distributed normally; that is, $\varepsilon_i \sim N(0, \sigma^2)$.

Then $\hat{\beta}_0$ and $\hat{\beta}_1$ have a lower variance than any other possible unbiased estimator. Thus $\hat{\beta}_0$ and $\hat{\beta}_1$ are efficient.

We have two mnemonics to help us remember these properties:

Definition 7.10 In the classical regression model, the least squares estimators are the *best linear unbiased estimator (BLUE)*. If we add assumption A6, then the least squares estimators are the *best unbiased estimator (BUE)*.

And, if the assumptions of the classical regression model are true, and certainly if assumption A6 is true as well, then least squares is the best way to estimate β_0 and β_1 from the data.

7.3 DISTRIBUTION OF THE LEAST SQUARES ESTIMATORS

The assumptions of the classical model not only let us prove that the ordinary least squares (OLS) estimator is the most efficient unbiased estimator; they also allow us to say something about the difference between the true values of β_0 and β_1, and the estimates $\hat{\beta}_0$ and $\hat{\beta}_1$. Because we don't know β_0 and β_1, we can't know how far off our estimated values are from the true values. But with assumptions A1 through A5, we can estimate the variance and standard deviation of $\hat{\beta}_0$ and $\hat{\beta}_1$, which are random variables. Knowing them, we will know how much our estimates might have been higher or lower if the random error terms had taken different values, and that will give us an idea of their reliability.

$\hat{\beta}_0$ and $\hat{\beta}_1$ are random because they depend (indirectly) on the random error term ε_i; the smaller the errors are, the closer the data will lie to the true line, and therefore the more reliable $\hat{\beta}_0$ and $\hat{\beta}_1$ will be. In general, the larger σ_ε^2 is, the larger each individual error will be. We don't know σ_ε^2, but we can use the standard error of the regression, defined in Equation 6.6.2 as an estimate of it. Then we can estimate the variances of $\hat{\beta}_0$ and $\hat{\beta}_1$. They turn out to be:

$$\hat{\sigma}_{\hat{\beta}_1}^2 = \hat{\sigma}_\varepsilon^2 \left(\frac{1}{\sum (X_i - \bar{X})^2} \right) \tag{7.3.1}$$

$$\hat{\sigma}_{\hat{\beta}_0}^2 = \hat{\sigma}_\varepsilon^2 \left(\frac{\sum (X_i^2)}{N \sum (X_i - \bar{X})^2} \right) \tag{7.3.2}$$

where $\hat{\sigma}^2_{\hat{\beta}_1}$ is the estimated variance of $\hat{\beta}_1$, which is an estimate of its (unknown) true variance $\sigma^2_{\hat{\beta}_1}$, and similarly $\hat{\sigma}^2_{\hat{\beta}_0}$ is the estimated variance of $\hat{\beta}_0$. The standard errors of $\hat{\beta}_0$ and $\hat{\beta}_1$, which we call $\hat{\sigma}_{\hat{\beta}_0}$ and $\hat{\sigma}_{\hat{\beta}_1}$, are the square roots of $\hat{\sigma}^2_{\hat{\beta}_0}$ and $\hat{\sigma}^2_{\hat{\beta}_1}$, respectively. Econometrics software will report these standard errors when you use it to estimate a regression. For example, in the regression of consumption on national income from Chapter 6, where the estimated equation is $C = \beta_0 + \beta_1 Y$, these formulas give a standard error of 88.9 for $\hat{\beta}_0$ and 0.0150 for $\hat{\beta}_1$. Note that these estimated variances will tend to get smaller and smaller as we add more observations to the sample. In the formula for $\sigma^2_{\hat{\beta}_1}$, the more observations there are, the more terms there will be in the summation in the denominator; and because the term in the denominator is a sum of squares, each term is positive. The more terms there are, the larger the denominator will be, and the smaller $\sigma^2_{\hat{\beta}_1}$ will be. In the formula for $\hat{\sigma}^2_{\hat{\beta}_0}$, there are sums of squares in both the numerator and the denominator, which tend to offset one another; but the N term in the denominator assures us that $\hat{\sigma}^2_{\hat{\beta}_0}$ will tend to decrease as N increases.

Do these formulas tell us how far the estimated values of $\hat{\beta}_0$ and $\hat{\beta}_1$ are likely to be from the true values of β_0 and β_1? Not quite. To know that, we need to know the distribution functions of $\hat{\beta}_0$ and $\hat{\beta}_1$ so that we can construct confidence intervals for them and test hypotheses about their true values, such as $\beta_1 < 1$. Knowing the means and standard deviations of the estimates isn't enough to allow us to draw their density functions. Fortunately, we can show the following:

Theorem 7.5 If the classical regression assumptions A1–A5 are true, and if assumption A6 (normally distributed error terms) is also true, then the estimators $\hat{\beta}_0$ and $\hat{\beta}_1$ are normally distributed. Even if assumption A6 is not true, $\hat{\beta}_0$ and $\hat{\beta}_1$ are still approximately normally distributed, and the more observations used to estimate the regression, the better the approximation.

Using this theorem, and the estimated values $\hat{\beta}_0 = 24.58$ and $\hat{\beta}_1 = 0.835$, we can make some assertions about the true values of β_0 and β_1. If assumption A6 is true, then we know that $\hat{\beta}_1$ is distributed normally with a mean of the true β_1, whatever value that has. We don't know its standard deviation, since we don't know the true value of $\sigma_{\hat{\beta}_1}$; but we do know that it is approximately 0.015. Because we are using an estimated standard deviation, we use the t distribution instead of the normal distribution to do hypothesis tests about the true value. For example, we can test the economic hypothesis that the marginal propensity to consume is less than 1, as theory predicts it should be. The null hypothesis (which we expect to reject) is $\beta_1 = 1$, and the alternative hypothesis is $\beta_1 < 1$. Then we know:

$$t = \frac{\hat{\beta}_1 - \beta}{\hat{\sigma}_{\hat{\beta}_1}} \sim t_8 \qquad (7.3.3)$$

That is, the t statistic has 8 degrees of freedom, since we have 10 observations and have estimated two parameters. The value of the t statistic for this particular data sample works out to $(0.835 - 1)/0.015$, which is approximately -11. For a one-tailed test with 5 percent significance level, the critical value of t_8 is 1.86: The calculated value of t is larger than that (in absolute value), so we would reject the null hypothesis $\beta_1 = 1$ in favor of the alternative $\beta_1 < 1$: The marginal propensity to consume is indeed less than 1, as we expected it would be.

We can also work out a confidence interval for the true value of β_1 on the basis of the estimates, using Equations 4.4.1 and 4.4.2. In general, we expect that

$$-T_c^p < \frac{\hat{\beta}_1 - \beta_1}{\hat{\sigma}_{\hat{\beta}_1}} < T_c^p \qquad (7.3.4)$$

so that the confidence interval for the true value of β_1 is given by

$$\left[\hat{\beta}_1 - T_c^p \hat{\sigma}_{\hat{\beta}_1}, \hat{\beta}_1 + T_c^p \hat{\sigma}_{\hat{\beta}_1}\right] \qquad (7.3.5)$$

In the example above, for 8 degrees of freedom $T_c^{0.05} = 2.306$, so we expect that the t statistic with 8 degrees of freedom, if we use the true value of β_1 to calculate it, should be less than 2.306 in absolute value 95 percent of the time. The confidence interval works out to [0.80, 0.87], and our estimates are consistent with a belief that the true marginal propensity to consume is between 80 percent and 87 percent of an additional dollar of income.[4] They are not consistent with beliefs outside that range. Specifically, they are not consistent with the belief $\beta_1 = 1$, which is another way of showing that that null hypothesis is rejected by the data.

Figure 7.6 shows this graphically. We do not know the density function for $\hat{\beta}_1$, because we don't know its mean value β_1, and the density function is centered around the mean value (because least squares is unbiased). We do know its shape; it is the same shape as a t distribution with 8 degrees of freedom.[5] We don't know its standard deviation either, but we have 0.015 as an estimate of its standard deviation, and we can use that to draw the figure for various assumptions about what the true mean might be. The vertical red bar in the figure shows the estimated value of 0.835, and the leftmost density function assumes that the true value of b is 0.825. This is close to the estimated value—less than 1 estimated standard deviation away—and an estimated value of 0.835 is quite likely if the true value of β_1 is 0.825. Therefore, this value is inside the confidence interval and we cannot reject

FIGURE 7.6
The Probability of Observing $\hat{\beta}_1 = 0.835$ for Three Possible Values for the True Marginal Propensity to Consume

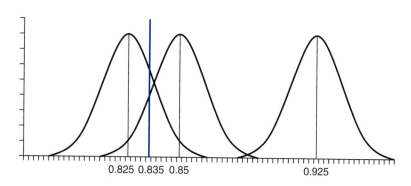

0.825 0.835 0.85   0.925

[4] Any value in this range is (with 95 percent confidence) equally believable as a true value for β_1. In particular, the point estimate 0.835 is not inherently more believable than other values in the confidence interval.

[5] It is not exactly the same as a t distribution because its mean is not 0 and its standard deviation is not 1. The transformed variable defined by Equation 7.3.3 has a t distribution, though, and undoing the transformation doesn't change the shape of the density function; it just makes it narrower (from dividing by 0.015) and shifts it rightward (by adding 0.835).

the null hypothesis $\beta_1 = 0.825$. The middle density function assumes the true value of β_1 is 0.85. Under this assumption, an estimated value of 0.835 is somewhat less likely than under the assumption that the true value is 0.825, because the difference would be 0.15 instead of only 0.1, but this is still reasonably likely. We would not reject the null hypothesis $\beta_1 = 0.85$ either. The rightmost density function assumes that the true value of β_1 is 0.925. This assumed true value is quite far from the estimated value of 0.835—the distance is 0.9, which is 6 estimated standard deviations. This is highly unlikely to have occurred. Therefore, 0.925 is not inside the confidence interval for the true value of b, and we reject the null hypothesis $\beta_1 = 0.925$. The figure does not draw the density function for the assumption $\beta_1 = 1$, as it would be off the graph to the right, but you can easily see that the estimated value of 0.835 would be even more unlikely under that assumption than under the assumption that $\beta_1 = 0.925$, and the null hypothesis $\beta_1 = 1$ is also rejected by this estimate, as shown above.

Chapter Review

- An estimator is *unbiased* if its expected value is the true value; that is, if it produces the correct answer on average.
- An estimator is *consistent* if the chance of the estimated value being within any given distance of the true value rises to 1 as the sample size rises.
- An estimator is *efficient* within a class of unbiased estimators if it has a lower variance than other estimators in that class.
- Under the five assumptions of the classical regression model, the least squares estimator is unbiased, consistent, and more efficient than any other linear, unbiased estimator; it is the *best linear unbiased estimator (BLUE)*.
- Under the additional assumption that the error term is normally distributed, least squares is more efficient than any unbiased estimator, linear or nonlinear; it is the *best unbiased estimator (BUE)*.
- The standard error of the regression (SER) is an unbiased and consistent estimator of the variance of the error terms.
- The larger the SER, the larger the variances of the least squares parameters $\hat{\beta}_0$ and $\hat{\beta}_1$; the more observations, the smaller their variances.
- $\hat{\beta}_0$ and $\hat{\beta}_1$ are normally distributed if the error terms are normally distributed, and are approximately normally distributed even if the error terms are not normally distributed.
- We can use estimated values for $\hat{\beta}_0$, $\hat{\beta}_1$, and their standard deviations to calculate confidence intervals for the true values of β_0 and β_1, and to test hypotheses about those true values.

Computer Exercise

In this exercise we'll generate some regressions and look at the distributions of the estimated parameters to see how closely they match the distributions as calculated in this chapter.

1. Start Eviews, and create a new worksheet, undated, with 100 observations. On the command line, type genr x=rnd()*20 to get a randomly generated independent variable.

2. Type genr err=rnd()*5-2.5 to produce some error terms. Then type genr y=10+0.5*x+err to create a dependent variable.

3. Type ls y c x to regress Y on X. What estimated values do you get for $\hat{\beta}_0$ and $\hat{\beta}_1$? What are the estimated standard errors of these estimates? The true values, we know, are 10 for β_0 and 0.5 for β_1. Are the estimated values within 1 estimated standard error of the true values? Are they within 2 estimated standard errors?

4. Test the null hypotheses that $\beta_0 = 10$ and that $\beta_0 = 0.5$, which we know to be true. Do you reject these hypotheses, or fail to reject them?

5. Open an Excel spreadsheet, and enter the values you've gotten for $\hat{\beta}_0$, $\hat{\sigma}_{\hat{\beta}_0}$, $\hat{\beta}_1$, and $\hat{\sigma}_{\hat{\beta}_1}$.

6. Repeat steps 2 through 5 twenty times. How many times do you reject the null hypotheses $\beta_0 = 10$ and $\beta_0 = 0.5$? (You've done 40 tests, so if you test at a 5 percent level of significance, you should expect to reject twice.)

7. Look at the 20 values you've gotten for $\hat{\sigma}_{\hat{\beta}_0}$ and $\hat{\sigma}_{\hat{\beta}_1}$. How close are they to one another? In the 20 trials, how many times was $\hat{\beta}_0$ within 1 estimated standard deviation of 10, and how many times was $\hat{\beta}_1$ within 1 estimated standard deviation of 0.5? It should have been about two-thirds of the time, that is, about 13 or 14 times. Would you say they are good estimators of the true variances of $\hat{\beta}_0$ and $\hat{\beta}_1$?

8. *Optional.* Plot the histograms of your estimates of $\hat{\beta}_0$ and $\hat{\beta}_1$. They are not normally distributed, because the error terms are uniformly distributed rather than normal, but the estimates are approximately normally distributed. How good is the approximation? That is, are your histograms close to being bell-shaped, or far from it? If you like, produce 20 more estimates using normally distributed random variables—generate these with the command genr err = nrnd()*1.4. (Multiplying by 1.4 gives them approximately the same variance as the original, uniformly distributed errors.) Are the histograms more bell-shaped in this case than before?

Problems

1. Load the data set carspend, which contains three variables. The first, carspend, is total expenditure on new automobiles in the United States. The second, disposinc, is national disposable income in the United States. The third, cpi, is the consumer price index. The data is observed quarterly from the first quarter of 1959 through the third quarter of 2003.

   a. Draw supply and demand curves for automobiles. If income rises, which way will the demand curve shift? What will happen to price and quantity of automobiles?

   b. Consider the economic model

   $$\text{Carspend} = \beta_0 + \beta_1 \text{Disposinc}$$

   What sign does economic theory predict for β_1? Why does it predict that?

   c. Estimate the econometric model

   $$\text{Carspend}_t = \beta_0 + \beta_1 \text{Disposinc}_t + \varepsilon_t$$

   What is your estimate of β_1? If income rises by $1 billion, how much does car spending rise? Does this seem like an economically reasonable value?

   d. Test the null hypothesis that $\beta_1 = 0$ against the alternative hypothesis $\beta_1 > 0$. Do you reject, or fail to reject, the null hypothesis? Does the result support the theory of automobile supply and demand, or not?

   e. How would the test be different if you tested the null hypothesis against the alternative hypothesis that $\beta_1 \neq 0$? Would it alter the conclusion or not?

2. Load the data file carspend, which is described in problem 1.

   a. Plot a graph with car spending on the vertical axis and time on the horizontal axis. Is car spending generally rising or falling over time?

   b. Plot a graph with the consumer price index (CPI) on the vertical axis and time on the horizontal axis. Is the CPI generally rising or falling over time?

   c. To correct for inflation, calculate real car spending and real disposable income, using CPI as the price deflator. Then estimate the regression

   $$\text{Realcarspend}_t = \beta_0 + \beta_1 \text{Realdisposinc}_t + \varepsilon_t$$

   What is your estimate of β_1? Based on this regression, if real income rises by \$1 billion, how much does car spending rise?

   d. Test the null hypothesis that $\beta_1 = 0$ against the alternative hypothesis $\beta_1 > 0$. Do you reject, or fail to reject, the null hypothesis?

   e. What does this result suggest about the supply and demand of automobiles? How might you explain this result?

3. Load the data file homers, which has two variables. The variable salary is the salary of major league baseball players, measured in thousands of dollars. The variable homers is the number of home runs they hit. Both variables are for the 2000 season. There are data on 254 position players (no pitchers).

   a. Estimate the regression equation:

   $$\text{Salary}_i = \beta_0 + \beta_1 \text{Homers}_i + \varepsilon_i$$

   What is your estimate for β_1? Does it take the sign you would expect?

   b. If a player hits one more home run, how much does his salary rise? If he hits five more home runs, how much does his salary rise?

   c. What would you predict for the salary of a player who hits no home runs?

   d. Estimate the regression:

   $$\text{Homers}_i = \gamma_0 + \gamma_1 \text{Salary}_i + \varepsilon_i$$

   If a player's salary rises by \$1 million, how many additional home runs does he hit?

   e. Which of the two variables is more likely to be endogenous, and which of the two variables is more likely to be exogenous? Which of the two regressions do you think is a better model of the salary market? Can you suggest a different way of estimating this equation?

4. Load the data file buscost, which contains two variables describing the operation of 246 bus companies in U.S. cities. The variable totalcost is the total operating expense of the company, in thousands of dollars; the variable rvm is the total output of the firm, in thousands of revenue vehicle miles.

   a. Estimate the equation:

   $$\text{Totalcost}_i = \beta_0 + \beta_1 \text{RVM}_i + \varepsilon_i$$

   Find a 90 percent confidence interval and a 95 percent confidence interval for the true marginal cost of an additional RVM. Would you believe that the true marginal cost is equal to \$4.90, or not?

b. What is the chance that the true marginal cost is equal to $4.90?

c. Using a one-sided test, test the null hypothesis that fixed costs are equal to 0 in this industry against the null hypothesis that they are positive. Do you reject or fail to reject this null hypothesis? What is disturbing about the result?

d. Using your estimates of the parameters, calculate an estimated average cost function for this industry. Draw graphs showing the predicted marginal cost, average cost, and total cost functions.

5. Load the data file taxrcpt, which contains two variables. The first, gdp, is U.S. gross domestic product (GDP), and the second, receipts, is total tax receipts of the federal government. The variables are measured annually from 1960 to 1995.

a. Most federal tax receipts come from sources that are linked to income, such as the income tax, the payroll tax, and the corporate income tax. If GDP rises, what should happen to tax receipts?

b. Consider the economic model:

$$\text{Receipts} = \beta_0 + \beta_1 \text{GDP}$$

What sign would you expect for β_1? If you wanted to test the theory that GDP does not affect tax receipts against the theory that it does, what null and alternative hypotheses would you use?

c. Estimate the equation

$$\text{Receipts}_t = \beta_0 + \beta_1 \text{GDP}_t + \varepsilon_t$$

Test the null hypothesis you proposed in the previous part of the question. What do you find?

d. Find a 95 percent confidence interval for β_1. If GDP rises by $10 billion, how much do you predict tax receipts will rise? Would you believe, or not believe, a proposal that they would rise by $2 billion?

6. A critical issue in macroeconomics is the slope of the aggregate supply curve (AS). If the aggregate supply curve is vertical, then changes in monetary policy, which shift the aggregate demand curve (AD), cannot affect GDP and can only change the price level (see figure). If the AS curve is positively sloped, then changes in monetary policy can change both GDP and the price level.

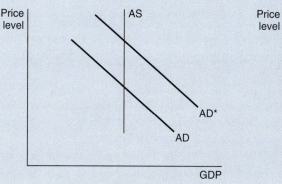

If AS is vertical

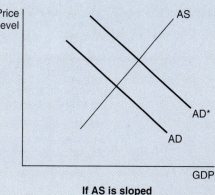

If AS is sloped

Load the data file macro1. It contains data on four variables: realgdp is the real GDP of the United States, cpi is the consumer price index, money is the level of the real money supply, and govtdebt is the real federal debt. All variables except cpi are measured in billions of dollars, and data is observed from 1959 to 2001.

a. Graph realgdp against time. Does it generally rise or decline? In what years is it declining? What was happening in the economy in those years? Also graph money against time. Is it declining at the same time that GDP declines, or at different times?

b. Estimate the equation:

$$\text{CPI}_t = \beta_0 + \beta_1 \text{Money}_t + \varepsilon_t$$

Test whether an increase in the money supply increases the CPI or not. Does the result match your expectation from the graphs above? What does this result tell you about the slope of the AS curve?

c. Estimate the equation:

$$\text{GDP}_t = \beta_0 + \beta_1 \text{Money}_t + \varepsilon_t$$

Test whether an increase in the money supply increases GDP or not. What does this result tell you about the slope of the AS curve?

d. By how much does a $1 increase in the money supply increase real GDP?

7. The theory of aggregate supply and aggregate demand described in problem 6 also predicts that fiscal policy, which shifts the AD curve, increases CPI, and may increase GDP as well.

a. Estimate the equation:

$$\text{CPI}_t = \beta_0 + \beta_1 \text{Govtdebt}_t + \varepsilon_t$$

Test whether an increase in government debt (i.e., a deficit) increases the CPI or not. Does the result match your expectation from the graphs above?

b. Estimate the equation:

$$\text{GDP}_t = \beta_0 + \beta_1 \text{Govtdebt}_t + \varepsilon_t$$

Test whether an increase in government debt increases GDP or not. What does this result tell you about the slope of the AS curve? Is your answer consistent with your answer to problem 6c?

c. By how much does a $1 increase in the federal deficit increase real GDP? The answer should be the same as the answer to problem 6d. How close are the estimates? Is the difference relatively large or relatively small compared to the standard errors of the estimates?

8. Load the data file wages1. The data file contains observations on two variables, wages and salaries for 826 workers, taken from the *Current Population Survey.* The variable wages is wage and salary income, measured in dollars per year; the variable education is measured as the highest grade level completed.

a. According to the economic theory known as human capital theory, education increases a worker's productivity and thus leads to higher wages. Consider the economic model

$$\text{Wages} = \beta_0 + \beta_1 \text{Education}$$

What sign would you expect β_1 to take? Briefly explain why. Graph the data with wages on the vertical axis and education on the horizontal axis. Does it look like the data support human capital theory, or not?

b. Estimate the equation

$$\text{Wages}_i = \beta_0 + \beta_1 \text{Education}_i + \varepsilon_i$$

Test whether β_1 is equal to 0 or not. Do you get the expected result?

c. What is the estimated standard deviation of the error term? How does it compare to the average wage? If a data point was two standard deviations above the regression line, how far would the worker's wage be from its predicted value? Do wages seem to be easy to forecast, or hard to forecast?

d. Graph the residuals from the model. Are there more large positive errors or large negative errors? Do the errors appear to have a normal distribution? Does this suggest that ordinary least squares (OLS) is the best estimator, or is a better estimator possible?

Chapter **Eight**

Multivariate Regression

Vehicles Produced Per Worker: U.S. and Japanese Firms		
	1960	**1983**
GM	8	11
Ford	14	15
Chrysler	11	11
Nissan	12	30
Toyota	15	38

Source: Michael A. Cusumano, *The Japanese Automobile Industry*, pp. 187–88.

8.1 ESTIMATING A PRODUCTION FUNCTION

In the early 1980s, the American automobile industry was in trouble, facing a wave of Japanese and other foreign imports. The share of foreign automobile manufacturers in the U.S. market rose from less than 5 percent in the early 1950s to well over 20 percent by 1980. By that time, imports were widely believed to be both cheaper and better than the American cars. As the above figures show, Japanese automobile production per worker rose dramatically between 1960 and 1983, while American production per worker changed only slightly. In the 1980s, the advance of imports into the American market was at least partly halted. Market shares of foreign producers, which had reached 23 percent by 1983, stayed almost the same for the next 10 years, although many foreign companies began producing their models in the United States to avoid trade barriers erected by the U.S. government.[1]

Why did the American automobile industry lose so much of its market to foreign companies, and how did it halt the erosion of its market share? There are many possible explanations, but one common one suggests that American automobile manufacturers learned to produce more efficiently in response to Japanese competition. This explanation is easy to examine by estimating a production function for the American automobile industry and testing to see whether productivity increased in the late 1980s and 1990s, and if so, by how much.

A production function relates the amount of output of a firm, industry, or nation to the amount of inputs used to produce that output:

$$Y = f(X_1, X_2 \ldots X_K) \tag{8.1.1}$$

---

[1] The evolution of the American automobile industry is described in Walter Adams and James Brock, *The Structure of American Industry,* 9th ed., pp. 65–92.

where Y is the amount of output produced and the Xs are the K different inputs used to make that output. To estimate a production function for a particular industry, we need to list the inputs used and pick a specific mathematical form for the function, rather than the general form given in Equation 8.1.1.

Definition 8.1 The *functional form* of a regression equation is the precise mathematical equation used in estimating it. The equations:

$$Y = \beta_0 + \beta_1 X_1 + \beta_2 X_2 + \cdots + \beta_K X_K$$

$$Y = \beta_0 + \beta_1 X_1 + \beta_2 X_1^2 + \beta_3 X_2 + \beta_4 X_2^2 + \cdots + \beta_{2K-1} X_K + \beta_{2K} X_K^2$$

$$\sqrt{Y} = \beta_0 + \beta_1 X_1 + \beta_2 X_2 + \cdots + \beta_K X_K$$

are three different possible functional forms for the general form
$Y = f(X_1, X_2 \ldots X_K)$.

One cannot estimate an equation like $Y = f(X_1, X_2 \ldots X_K)$; one must pick some functional form in order to calculate residuals. A common choice for production functions is the Cobb-Douglass functional form:

$$Y = A \cdot X_1^{\beta_1} \cdot X_2^{\beta_2} \cdot \cdots \cdot X_K^{\beta_K} \qquad (8.1.2)$$

This form has the difficulty that it is not linear, because the β parameters appear in the exponents of the equation.[2] This problem can be solved by taking logarithms on both sides of the equation:

$$\log Y_t = \beta_0 + \beta_1 \log X_{1t} + \beta_2 \log X_{2t} + \cdots + \beta_K \log X_{Kt} \qquad (8.1.3)$$

where the t subscripts refer to different years in the data sample, and which is now a linear form with regard to the βs.[3] We replace the term $\log A$ with the term β_0, to make clear that the $\log A$ term, which does not vary across observations, is really the intercept term in the equation. Doing this does not change the mathematics at all but rather makes clearer what is going on in the equation; this is called *reparameterizing* the model, and it is done whenever mathematical manipulation of an equation, such as taking logs above, has made it desirable to simplify the notation a little bit.

The choice of inputs is somewhat subjective. Producing automobiles requires thousands of different inputs, and in principle one should include each of them as a separate variable in the production function. In practice this is impossible, because data with that level of detail are not generally available. Instead, we aggregate the inputs into groups that we believe are economically similar and on which we can observe data. For example, we might be willing to assert that a welder and a machine operator, though they represent two

---

[2] It is not impossible to estimate a nonlinear form of an equation, but it is more difficult, and in general econometricians prefer to use linear forms. Estimation of nonlinear equations is discussed in Chapter 18.

[3] Even though the X variables now appear in logs, it is still linear with respect to the βs, and for the purposes of ordinary least squares (OLS), linearity with respect to the βs is what matters, because the βs are what we are trying to estimate. It doesn't matter if the equation is linear with respect to the Xs because we know their values already. If you like, think of the dependent variable as being ($\log Y$) rather than Y, and the independent variables as ($\log X$) rather than X; the relationship between $\log Y$ and $\log X$ is linear. To the equation, ($\log Y$) and ($\log X$) are strings of numbers just like any other string of numbers; it doesn't know or care that ($\log X$) happens to be the logarithm of some other set of numbers.

different types of labor with different skills, are similar enough that they can be grouped together. We might be less willing to group a welder and a painter together, but we might be forced to do so if our data do not break down employment in enough detail to tell us how many welders and how many painters the industry is employing. In actually specifying the equation, we aggregate as little as possible, because aggregation may result in not having the correct equation and violating assumption A1 of the classical model, but we aggregate as much as necessary, because we have to use the data that we have available. For the automobile industry, we might specify the equation as follows:

$$\log Y_t = \beta_0 + \beta_1 \log \text{PW}_t + \beta_2 \log \text{NPW}_t + \beta_3 \log \text{CAPEXP}_t$$
$$+ \beta_4 \log \text{MAT}_t + \beta_5 \log \text{YEAR}_t + \varepsilon_t \qquad \textbf{(8.1.4)}$$

where we have chosen the four inputs PW (production workers), NPW (nonproduction workers), CAPEXP (capital expenditure), and MAT (material inputs) to match the data available from the U.S. Census Bureau's Annual Survey of Manufactures (ASM) that we will use to estimate the regression. This represents a fairly high level of data aggregation, as we have grouped all types of capital together and all material inputs together. We have, however, been fortunate enough to be able to separate production labor (roughly defined by the ASM as workers who produce automobiles directly) and nonproduction labor (managers and others whose jobs are one step removed from producing automobiles) so that labor is disaggregated into two separate categories.

Measuring output is relatively difficult for the automobile industry, since it manufactures many models of cars, some of which are substantially larger and more expensive than others. Instead of counting the number of cars produced, we define output by its value; that way, a car costing $30,000 will count as twice as much output as one costing $15,000. This is probably reasonable given that the more expensive car is larger, contains more sophisticated equipment, and probably required more labor to make. Measuring by value does, however, raise problems of inflation; a car that cost $10,000 in 1983 costs considerably more than that now. To correct for this problem, we divide output value by the consumer price index (CPI) for the automobile industry so that we use the log of the real value of automobile output as the dependent variable in the regression. We do the same for materials and capital expenditure, since those variables are also measured in dollars, in order to aggregate many different types of material and capital into two variables. But in this case we use the producer price index (PPI) since these are intermediate goods, not final goods.

We have also included YEAR as a right-hand-side variable. This variable is included to allow for the possibility that American firms have become more efficient and therefore the production function has shifted over time. Such a variable is called a *time trend variable,* or simply a trend variable. If American firms, operating more efficiently, have managed to produce more output from the same inputs over time, then we would expect β_5 to be positive. If so, then the passage of time, as represented by an increase in YEAR (say, from 1981 to 1982) will cause Y to rise. If the productivity of American firms is falling over time, then a one-unit increase in YEAR should be correlated with a decrease in Y, and then β_5 would be negative. If the efficiency of American firms has not changed, than β_5 should be 0. This allows us to turn our economic hypothesis—that American car companies increased productivity—into an econometric hypothesis—that $\beta_5 > 0$. Formally, of course, we will choose $\beta_5 = 0$ as the null hypothesis and $\beta_5 > 0$ (or perhaps $\beta_5 \neq 0$, if we prefer a two-sided test) as the alternative hypothesis, since the null hypothesis must be in the form of an equality. But we expect to reject the null hypothesis in favor of the alternative, if our economic ideas are correct.

Note, however, that proving that the productivity of American firms rose will not prove that Japanese competition was the cause of it. Econometrics cannot prove that one thing causes another; economic theory is required to establish that. But if we can document from the data that productivity did rise in this period, then it adds credibility to the theory that the rise was caused by Japanese competition, which is what we would hope to achieve with this regression. Conversely, if we show that productivity was not rising during this period, then the theory that Japanese competition increased American productivity is certainly false, and that would be a useful conclusion also.

Note also that we have added an error term to the right-hand side of the equation. This error term represents all factors affecting automobile production that we have not listed in the variables. In terms of the production function, it captures any inputs we have not included as right-hand-side variables (though hopefully there are none of those). It may also allow for changes in the production function over time that are more complicated than a constant outward shift. These and other factors that cause the data points not to lie exactly along the estimated production function are accounted for in the regression equation through the error term.

8.2   EQUATIONS WITH MORE THAN ONE RIGHT-HAND-SIDE VARIABLE

Estimating this production function, or any equation with the general form $Y = \beta_0 + \beta_1 X_1 + \beta_2 X_2 + \cdots + \beta_K X_K$, is a little more complicated than estimating the simpler equation $Y = \beta_0 + \beta_1 X_1$, because this equation has more than one variable on the right-hand side of the equation.

Definition 8.2 A *multivariate model* has more than one right-hand-side variable. A *univariate model* has only one right-hand-side variable.

Multivariate models allow us to estimate relations where two or more independent variables affect a dependent variable. For example, in the production function, the amount of output produced depends on all four inputs, as well as the passage of time. In general, we will use K to indicate the number of independent variables, which we will refer to as $X_1, X_2, \ldots X_K$. The number of parameters we estimate is equal to $K + 1$: one for each variable, plus β_0, the intercept. Because there is more than one right-hand-side variable, we have to alter our interpretation of the regression coefficients $\beta_0, \beta_1, \ldots \beta_K$.

Theorem 8.1 If we have the regression equation
$Y = \beta_0 + \beta_1 X_1 + \beta_2 X_2 + \cdots + \beta_K X_K$, then:

1. β_i is the amount that Y will rise if X_i rises by 1 unit, holding all other X variables constant.

2. β_0 is the value of Y if all X variables are equal to 0.

Often these coefficients can be given economic meanings as well. In the production function $Y = \beta_0 + \beta_1 K + \beta_2 L$, β_1 is the amount by which output Y will rise if one more unit of capital K is added to the production process, and labor use is held constant. This corresponds to the economic concept of the marginal product of capital. Similarly, β_2, which is the amount by which output rises if one unit of labor L is added to production, is the marginal product of labor. β_0 is the amount of output that would be produced if 0 units of capital and 0 units of labor were used; we might expect this to be 0. The interpretation of these parameters, and the interpretation of the parameters of any multivariate regression, are based on the *ceteris paribus* assumption—that one of the independent variables is changed, with all others held constant, to produce the measured effect on the dependent variable.

In the Cobb-Douglass production function given in Equation 8.1.3, the coefficients are interpreted slightly differently, because the variables are in logs. From Theorem 8.1, it must be the case that if log PW rises by 1, then log Y rises by β_1. What does this mean in economic terms? You may know that if X rises by 1 percent, then the log of X rises by approximately 0.01. Therefore, the Cobb-Douglass equation implies that if PW rises by 1 percent, then Y rises by β_1 percent. This corresponds to the economic concept of elasticity. In the Cobb-Douglass production function, the parameters $\beta_1, \ldots \beta_N$ are the elasticities of output with respect to each of the inputs $X_1, \ldots X_N$. Economic theory has several predictions about these elasticities. They should be positive, since adding more of an input should produce more output, not less, and they should be less than 1, since inputs should have diminishing marginal products. We can also associate them with properties of the production function. For instance, if the elasticities of the inputs add up to 1, then the production function has constant returns to scale. We can use this property, and our estimates of the $\beta_1, \ldots \beta_K$ parameters, to test whether the production function has constant returns to scale, increasing returns, or decreasing returns.

When estimating a multivariate model, we can still use the least squares principle, but we have to modify it slightly. We now define the residual as:

$$\hat{\varepsilon}_i = Y_i - \hat{\beta}_0 - \hat{\beta}_1 X_{1i} - \hat{\beta}_2 X_{2i} - \cdots - \hat{\beta}_K X_{Ki} \qquad (8.2.1)$$

and the sum of squared residuals is now given by

$$\text{SSR} = \sum_{i=1}^{N} (Y_i - \hat{\beta}_0 - \hat{\beta}_1 X_{1i} - \hat{\beta}_2 X_{2i} - \cdots - \hat{\beta}_K X_{Ki})^2 \qquad (8.2.2)$$

Figure 8.1 shows residuals for a case with two right-hand-side variables X_1 and X_2. The graph is three-dimensional because there are three variables (the independent variables X_1

FIGURE 8.1
Fitting a
Regression
Line with Two
Right-Hand-
Side Variables

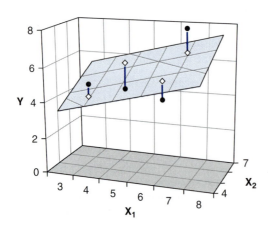

and X_2 and the dependent variable Y), and the regression "line" is now a plane because for each possible value for X_1 and X_2 there is a corresponding value of $\hat{Y}$. The residuals (red lines in the figure) are the distances between the data points (black circles) and the fitted regression equation (pink plane). We choose the slope of the plane to minimize the sum of squared residuals. If there are more than two right-hand-side variables, we can no longer draw the data graphically, but the principle is the same: Choose estimated values for the β parameters that minimize the sum of the squared residuals. The resulting formulas are quite complicated but easily calculated by computer. It turns out that the least squares method is just as good a way to estimate multivariate equations as it is to estimate univariate ones, as long as one condition is met.

> **Definition 8.3** A group of variables $X_1, X_2, \ldots X_{\hat{K}}$ is *perfectly multicollinear* if there exist constant numbers $a_0, a_1, \ldots, a_K$, not all equal to 0, so that the equation
>
> $$a_0 + a_1 X_1 + a_2 X_2 + \cdots + a_K X_K = 0 \qquad \textbf{(8.2.3)}$$
>
> is true for every observation. Such variables are also called *linearly dependent,* because Equation 8.2.3 is linear. If no such constants exist, the variables are called *linearly independent.*

It is probably not immediately obvious why this property is important; an example may make it clearer. Suppose we are interested in currency exchange rates. In particular, we want to know whether inflation or interest rates are more important in determining exchange rates. If we had only the data shown in Table 8.1, we would be unable to tell, because the two variables move together. Whenever the interest rate rises by 1 point, the inflation rate rises by 2 points, and similarly when they fall. Figure 8.2 plots these two variables. Because of their perfect relationship, they lie on a straight line, which is a graphical method of demonstrating that they are perfectly multicollinear.

In this case it is not possible to tell whether it is changes in interest rates or inflation that is causing changes in the exchange rate, because rises in the two variables occur at exactly the same time and in exact proportion. The only way we could tell which of the two was responsible for exchange rate changes is to observe a year of data in which one rose and another didn't, and see whether exchange rates changed or not that year.[4] But if that doesn't

TABLE 8.1 Hypothetical Data on Exchange Rates			
Year	Exchange Rate	Inflation Rate	Interest Rate
1990	2.5	8%	5%
1991	3.2	6	4
1992	2.7	8	5
1993	3.3	4	3
1994	2.1	10	6
1995	2.9	6	4
1996	3.6	2	2

[4] Actually, we could tell the effects apart even if the other one rose, as long as it didn't rise in exactly the 2:1 ratio observed in the past. It would also be fine if the other one fell. It is the fact that the rises are exactly proportional that causes the problem. Any change that breaks up the proportionality is enough to let us distinguish the effects of the two variables in theory, although if the proportionality remains very high, it will still be quite difficult to tell which variable is causing the dependent variable to change in practice.

FIGURE 8.2
Perfectly Multicollinear Variables

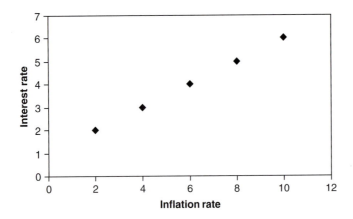

TABLE 8.2
Hypothetical Data on Drink Prices

P_{coffee}	P_{tea}	P_{soda}	P_{beer}
$2.77	$1.30	$1.12	$2.70
2.77	1.36	0.84	2.39
2.57	1.14	1.18	3.04
2.66	1.22	1.06	2.79
2.31	1.30	1.18	3.22
2.46	1.26	1.11	3.02
2.69	1.10	1.15	2.91

happen, then we are powerless to distinguish between the effects of the inflation and interest rates. You can quickly see that if we choose the constants $a_0 = 2$, $a_1 = 1$, $a_2 = -2$, then the equation

$$2 + \text{Inflation} - 2 \cdot \text{Interest rate} = 0 \qquad \textbf{(8.2.4)}$$

is true for all seven years of the data, and in fact Figure 8.2 is a graph of this equation. Therefore, these variables are perfectly multicollinear.

Not all cases of perfect multicollinearity are as easy to see as this one, however. For example, the four price variables in Table 8.2 are also perfectly multicollinear; it is not at all obvious from the table, but the equation

$$5 - P_{coffee} - 0.5P_{tea} + P_{soda} - P_{beer} = 0 \qquad \textbf{(8.2.5)}$$

holds for all observations, so these variables meet the definition of perfect collinearity, and it is not generally possible to tell their economic effects on a fifth variable (say, coffee sales) apart from one another.

There are two important things to know about perfectly multicollinear variables. First, if the number of variables is equal to, or greater than, the number of observations available, the variables will always be perfectly multicollinear. To avoid perfect multicollinearity you must have more observations in the data set than you have variables you wish to observe. Second, if two variables in a group of variables are perfectly multicollinear, then the whole group is also. This happens because you can always pick $a = 0$ for all the variables other than the two multicollinear ones. That is to say, if you have five variables $X_1 \ldots X_5$, and it happens that (say) $6 + 2X_1 + X_2 = 0$, then it is also the case that $6 + 2X_1 + X_2 + 0X_3 + 0X_4 + 0X_5 = 0$. If a set of variables is perfectly multicollinear, adding more variables won't eliminate the multicollinearity. Instead, you have to either drop one of the variables causing the multicollinearity or add observations to the data set for which the equation doesn't hold (if that is possible).

With perfect multicollinearity defined, we can now say some things about the effectiveness of least squares estimation of multivariate equations.

Theorem 8.2 To the assumptions A1–A5 of the classical regression model, add a new assumption:

A7. The variables X_1, X_2, $\ldots X_K$ are not perfectly multicollinear.

Then the least squares estimator is unbiased, consistent, and the best linear unbiased estimator (BLUE). If we add assumption A6, it is the best unbiased estimator (BUE).

This theorem assures us that least squares is just as good for multivariate models as it is for univariate ones.

8.3 INTERPRETING A MULTIVARIATE EQUATION

We use least squares to estimate Equation 8.1.3 using data from the ASM from 1979 to 1996. Table 8.3 shows the results. The first column of the table lists the different right-hand-side variables, including the intercept as a "variable" on the right-hand side of the equation. The second column lists the parameters associated with each variable. It is important to distinguish between the variable and the parameter associated with it. Variables, such as log of production workers (log PW), take known values, which are different for each observation in the data set. Parameters, such as β_1, have constant values, which are unknown and must be estimated.[5] The third column of the table gives the estimated values calculated by the

TABLE 8.3
Estimation Results of Automobile Production Function

Variable	Parameter	Estimate	Standard Error	t Statistic
Intercept	β_0	0.731	0.875	0.835
Log PW	β_1	0.668	0.244	2.727
Log NPW	β_2	0.128	0.117	1.089
Log CAPEXP	β_3	−0.070	0.021	−3.217
Log MAT	β_4	0.386	0.161	2.398
Year	β_5	0.034	0.0108	3.131

$R^2 = 0.988$ SER = 0.0270
$N = 18$ SSR = 0.008767

[5] Unfortunately, economists are often sloppy in spoken and, sometimes, written language and use these terms interchangeably, though it would be better if they didn't. The output from your regression software will not show a column of parameters, because the computer doesn't know the names you've chosen to give to the parameters of the model; it only knows about the variables.

least squares regression. Thus we have $\hat{\beta}_0 = 0.731$, $\hat{\beta}_1 = 0.668$, and so forth. The fourth column gives the estimated standard error of each estimate. Thus $\hat{\sigma}_{\hat{\beta}_1}$, the estimated standard error of $\hat{\beta}_1$, is 0.244. The fifth column gives the t statistic for the null hypothesis that each parameter is equal to 0. We can calculate formulas for the standard error of the regression (SER) and R^2 in the same way we calculated them for the single-variable regression model, using the formula for the sum of squared residuals (SSR) given by Equation 8.2.2, and those values are shown at the bottom of the table. We can also calculate predicted values for the dependent variables using the values of the $\hat{\beta}$ estimates:

$$\hat{Y}_i = \hat{\beta}_0 + \hat{\beta}_1 X_{1i} + \hat{\beta}_2 X_{2i} + \cdots + \hat{\beta}_K X_{Ki} \qquad \textbf{(8.3.1)}$$

Why do we calculate the t statistic for the hypothesis that each parameter is equal to 0? Sometimes that hypothesis makes sense as an economic hypothesis. For instance, the null hypothesis that $\beta_5 = 0$ is equivalent to the economic hypothesis that the production function has not shifted over time and that the American automobile industry has not become more efficient, a clearly interesting hypothesis. Sometimes that hypothesis does not make sense. For example, the hypothesis $\beta_1 = 0$ is equivalent to the economic hypothesis that adding production workers to a factory does not produce any more output, that is, that the elasticity of output with respect to production workers, and also the marginal product of production workers, is 0. That hypothesis is not very interesting, since it is almost certainly false; if we failed to reject it, we would be more likely to conclude that the model, the data, or both were flawed than to conclude that the marginal product of auto workers is really 0. Why then do we test this hypothesis for every parameter? The answer is purely mathematical. If the regression equation is

$$Y = \beta_0 + \beta_1 X_1 + \beta_2 X_2 + \beta_3 X_3 + \beta_4 X_4 \qquad \textbf{(8.3.2)}$$

and, say, $\beta_3 = 0$, then we can rewrite the regression equation as

$$Y = \beta_0 + \beta_1 X_1 + \beta_2 X_2 + 0 X_3 + \beta_4 X_4 \qquad \textbf{(8.3.3)}$$

But $0X_3$ is going to be 0 no matter what value X_3 happens to take, so we can drop that term from the equation altogether, and just write

$$Y = \beta_0 + \beta_1 X_1 + \beta_2 X_2 + \beta_4 X_4 \qquad \textbf{(8.3.4)}$$

That is, we can regress Y on X_1, X_2, and X_4 only. Dropping a variable from the model increases the degrees of freedom of the regression by 1. It therefore improves the precision of the estimates, and allows us to have smaller confidence intervals for the parameters. Note, however, that dropping the variable for this reason has no basis in economic theory. If economic theory suggests that a variable should be included in an econometric model, then it may well be wise to retain it even if its parameter its not statistically significantly different from 0.

In this case, the most interesting hypothesis—the economic hypothesis that led us to estimate the regression in the first place—is $\beta_5 = 0$. The t statistic for this hypothesis, the regression tells us, is 3.13. We could have calculated this ourselves $(0.0340 - 0)/0.0108$ and gotten the same answer, of course. The reported t statistic will always be equal to the reported parameter estimated divided by the estimated standard error, because that is what the t statistic formula reduces to when the hypothesized value of the parameter is 0. To find the critical t value for the test, we need to know how many degrees of freedom the regression has.

Theorem 8.3 The number of degrees of freedom for t tests in a multivariate regression is the number of observations in the regression (N) minus the number of parameters estimated in the model ($K + 1$ if the model has an intercept and K if it does not).

This is a generalization of the rule for the univariate case, where the number of degrees of freedom was $N - 2$, and two parameters were being estimated (β_0 and β_1). In this case, the model has 18 observations and 6 parameters estimated (the intercept plus one for each of five variables), so it has $18 - 6 = 12$ degrees of freedom. If we perform a two-tailed test with the alternative hypothesis, the critical t value for 12 degrees of freedom and 5 percent significance is 2.18; if we perform a one-tailed test in the belief that efficiency could not have dropped over time, then the critical t value is 1.78. Either way, the t statistic is larger than the critical value, and we would reject the null hypothesis $\beta_5 = 0$ in favor of whichever alternative we chose. Economically, we would conclude that the automobile industry's production function is, in fact, shifting out over time, meaning that efficiency has increased. The regression does not prove that Japanese competition is responsible for the increase, but the time period and the economic model certainly suggest that that is the case.

We can also look at the tests that the other parameters are equal to 0. The intercept is not statistically significantly different from 0; its t statistic is 0.835, well below the critical values for either alternative hypothesis. However, this finding is very difficult to interpret economically. It is the value that $\log Y$ would take if the log of each input was 0—that is, if exactly 1 input was being used, since $\log(1) = 0$; 1 production worker, 1 manager, \$1 of materials, and \$1 of capital expenditure—and if this was done in the year 0. But this is clearly meaningless. Therefore, we need not worry about the significance of the intercept, or even its reported value; they have no economic meaning for us to worry about.

The tests of the parameters on the input variables do have an economic meaning, since they are the elasticities of output with respect to each input, as described above. We would expect that all four of the inputs would have positive elasticities, and probably less than 1, since we would expect that inputs have diminishing returns; increasing an input by a certain percentage should increase output by a smaller percentage. We can test whether each parameter is significantly different from 0, we can test whether it is significantly different from 1, and we can find a confidence interval for it and see whether the confidence interval lies entirely between 0 and 1. (The results are related; if we reject the null hypothesis that one of the elasticities equals 0, or 1, then that value will not be inside the confidence interval.)

For example, the estimated elasticity of output with respect to changes in the number of production workers is 0.668 with an estimated standard error of 0.244. The critical t statistic for a two-sided test is, as noted above, 2.18. The t statistic for the hypothesis that $\beta_1 = 0$ is $(0688 - 0)/0.244 = 2.72$, which is the same answer the table gives, of course. That hypothesis we can reject; the elasticity of output with regard to production workers is positive. The t statistic for the hypothesis that $\beta_1 = 1$ is $(0.668 - 1)/0.244$, which is -1.36. This is closer to 0 than the critical t value, and therefore we fail to reject the null hypothesis that $\beta_1 = 1$. This doesn't mean that the true value is exactly equal to 1, although it means we can't conclude it isn't. The data are also consistent with the null hypothesis $\beta_1 = 0.7$, or $\beta_1 = 0.9$, or some other number less than 1, but not much less, so that our estimated parameter will not be very far from 1, relative to its estimated standard error. The confidence interval for the true value of β_1 is equal to the estimated value 0.688 plus or minus the estimated standard error (0.244) times the critical t value (2.18), which works out to (0.156,

1.219), and we would not reject any hypothesized value for the true elasticity that fell in that interval. Since most of that confidence interval is indeed between 0 and 1, we can safely say that this estimated elasticity is consistent with our expectations about what it would be.

By the same procedure, we can work out test results and confidence intervals for each of the four elasticities. The results don't always come out as well as they did for production workers. The elasticity of output with regard to materials, β_4, works well. Its confidence interval is $(0.035, 0.736)$, which falls entirely between 0 and 1, and we can reject the null hypotheses that $\beta_4 = 0$ and $\beta_4 = 1$. The other two give us surprising results. The elasticity for nonproduction workers, β_2, has a confidence interval of $(-0.127, 0.383)$. We can reject the null hypothesis $\beta_2 = 1$, but not the hypothesis $\beta_2 = 0$; we cannot be certain that the marginal product of nonproduction workers is positive. However, most of the confidence interval is positive; the reason part of it is negative is that the estimated value of β_2, 0.128, is relatively low. This should not surprise us. After all, nonproduction workers are those who work on things other than automobiles. They cannot directly increase production; they increase production only if they enable production workers to work more effectively, or materials to be used more efficiently, or some similar thing. For this reason, their marginal productivity might be lower than those of production workers and materials that affect the level of output more directly.

We could drop the variable from the model if we wanted to—its parameter is not statistically significantly different from 0—but we do not need to. The advantage to dropping it is that we will gain one degree of freedom, but the disadvantage is that it might cause us to have an incorrect functional form for the regression, violating assumption A1 of the classical model and causing OLS to no longer be BLUE. On the balance, it's probably better to keep the variable, since economic theory makes it pretty clear that nonproduction workers are an input and the variable really does belong on the right-hand side of the production function. Although we would have preferred to be able to reject the null hypothesis $\beta_2 = 0$, we need not be terribly disturbed that we can't. There are plenty of reasonable values for the true β_2 in the confidence interval we've calculated for it, and they do not suggest that there is a problem with the regression.

Unfortunately, we can't say the same for β_3, the elasticity of output with respect to capital expenditure. Its estimated value is negative, when it should have been positive; and worse, we can reject the null hypothesis that $\beta_3 = 0$. We can only conclude that the true value of β_3 is negative; the confidence interval works out to be $(-0.115, -0.024)$. This is not consistent with economic theory and suggests that, in fact, there is a problem with the regression. Perhaps the economic theory that says elasticities of inputs are positive is wrong, but probably not. More likely, we have misspecified the production function in some way. In this particular case, it is probably because capital expenditure is not the same thing as capital used up in producing automobiles. The latter, which is the right way to measure input use, is better captured by depreciation than it is by capital expenditure. If the automobile industry was keeping its capital stock at a constant value, then depreciation would be equal to capital expenditure every year; but it is probably not doing that. The regression would probably work better if depreciation was used as an input instead of capital expenditure. Unfortunately, the ASM doesn't include depreciation as a variable, so there is no easy way to do so. Perhaps we should drop this variable from the regression? Unfortunately, we cannot drop it, because the parameter is statistically significantly different from 0. For the moment, we have no choice but to keep it, even though it is giving us a surprising result.

8.4 TESTS INVOLVING MORE THAN ONE PARAMETER: THE *F* TEST

Some of the tests we might like to conduct involve more than one parameter of the model. For example, we might like to know whether the industry's production function has constant returns to scale or not. If it does, as noted above, then we would expect $\beta_1 + \beta_2 + \beta_3 + \beta_4 = 1$. However, we cannot use a *t* test to conduct this test, since a *t* test is only able to test the value of one parameter at a time. We need a more general way to test hypotheses that can handle hypotheses with more than one parameter in them. In fact, we have three ways of doing so, and we'll discuss each of them in turn.

Consider, for instance, the effect of fiscal policy on the national economy. The government can stimulate the economy in one of two ways—by increasing spending or by cutting taxes. We might consider a very simple econometric model of the U.S. economy:

$$GDP_t = \beta_0 + \beta_1 GDP_{t-1} + \beta_2 Tax_t + \beta_3 Spend_t + \varepsilon_t \qquad \textbf{(8.4.1)}$$

where GDP_{t-1} is the previous year's value of GDP, and Tax and Spend are the amount of federal taxation and spending in the current year. Some economic theories suggest that what really affects the economy is whether the government runs a deficit, that is, spends more than it takes in. That is to say, we can stimulate the economy equally effectively by increasing spending by \$1 or by reducing taxes by the same amount. In this model, a \$1 increase in taxes changes GDP by β_2 and a \$1 increase in spending changes it by β_3. If the two effects are in fact equal, that implies that $\beta_3 = -\beta_2$. If that is the case, then we can rewrite the model as

$$GDP_t = \beta_0 + \beta_1 GDP_{t-1} + \beta_2 Tax_t - \beta_2 Spend_t + \varepsilon_t \qquad \textbf{(8.4.2)}$$

or

$$GDP_t = \beta_0 + \beta_1 GDP_{t-1} + \beta_2 (Tax_t - Spend_t) + \varepsilon_t \qquad \textbf{(8.4.3)}$$

where Tax − Spend is, of course, just equal to the deficit.

Now, suppose that it is true that $\beta_3 = -\beta_2$. If so, then Equation 8.4.3 should be just as good a way to describe real data as Equation 8.4.1. However, if it is not true that $\beta_3 = -\beta_2$, then the steps used to derive Equation 8.4.3 are invalid and Equation 8.4.3 should not be able to describe the data as well as Equation 8.4.1 does. One way we can test to see whether the hypothesis is true is to estimate both equations and see how well each one does. If they do about equally well, then the hypothesis $\beta_3 = -\beta_2$ is acceptable. If Equation 8.4.1 does much better, than we should reject the hypothesis. The idea of the test is to impose the hypothesis on the equation and see how much worse the estimation is when we do that; the worse it gets, the more likely we are to reject the hypothesis.

Definition 8.4 The model that has the hypothesis mathematically imposed on it is called the *restricted model;* the model that does not have the hypothesis imposed is called the *unrestricted model*. The hypothesis itself is referred to as the *restriction* being tested.

In this case, the restriction is $\beta_3 = -\beta_2$, the unrestricted model is Equation 8.4.1 and the restricted model is Equation 8.4.3. Note that we can impose more than one restriction this way if we wanted to. Suppose we wanted to test whether fiscal policy had any impact on

GDP at all. In that case we would impose not only that $\beta_3 = -\beta_2$ but also that they both equal 0. Then we would write the model as

$$\text{GDP}_t = \beta_0 + \beta_1\text{GDP}_{t-1} + 0\text{Tax}_t + 0\text{Spend}_t + \varepsilon \qquad \textbf{(8.4.4)}$$

Or just

$$\text{GDP}_t = \beta_0 + \beta_1\text{GDP}_{t-1} + \varepsilon \qquad \textbf{(8.4.5)}$$

which imposes two restrictions on the model; $\beta_2 = 0$ and $\beta_3 = 0$. We can impose as many restrictions on the model as we like in this fashion.

How do we measure how well each equation does? We measure it by the SSR of each model.

Theorem 8.4 The unrestricted model will always have a lower SSR than the restricted model (or at worst, the same SSR).

An intuitive proof of this theorem is easy. When picking values of β_2 and β_3 to minimize the SSR in the restricted model, we pick only a single number for β_2 and then use the restriction $\beta_3 = -\beta_2$ to determine a value for β_3, since it has to obey the imposed restriction. But when picking values for β_2 and β_3 to minimize the SSR in the unrestricted model, we can choose any values for β_2 and β_3 that we like. If it makes the SSR smaller to do so, then we can pick values that happen to obey the restriction $\beta_3 = -\beta_2$. But we're not forced to do so; if we can produce a lower SSR by choosing values that don't obey that restriction, we will, since our objective is to get the lowest SSR possible. Therefore, the unrestricted model can always get at least as low a SSR as the restricted model, and can almost always get a lower one, since it's extremely unlikely that picking a β_3 that was exactly equal to $-\beta_2$ would be optimal. The question is, How much lower should the unrestricted SSR be before we reject the hypothesis?

Theorem 8.5 If the null hypothesis is true, then the F statistic calculated by

$$F = \frac{(\text{SSR}_R - \text{SSR}_{UR})/r}{\text{SSR}_{UR}/df} \qquad \textbf{(8.4.6)}$$

takes the F distribution with r degrees of freedom in the numerator and df degrees of freedom in the denominator, where SSR_R is the sum of squared residuals in the restricted model, SSR_{UR} is the sum of squared residuals in the unrestricted model, r is the number of restrictions imposed, and df is the number of degrees of freedom in the unrestricted regression equation (number of observations minus number of parameters estimated).

If the null hypothesis is true, we would expect the F statistic to be 0, or at least close to it. This is because, if the null hypothesis is true, then we'd expected SSR_R to be close to SSR_{UR}, leading the numerator to be small. If the null hypothesis is false, however, then SSR_R will be much larger than SSR_{UR}, the numerator will be large, and the F statistic will take a large value, one that it would be unlikely to take if the null hypothesis was true. Small F values suggest the hypothesis is true; large F values suggest it is not.

Estimating Equations 8.4.1 and 8.4.3 with data from 1949 to 2000 produces SSRs of 74,721 for the former and 184,498 for the latter. These are quite different; the SSR is more than twice as large in the restricted model as in the unrestricted model. To find out if we should reject the hypothesis, we calculate the F statistic, which is

$$F = \frac{(184{,}498 - 74{,}721)/1}{74{,}721/48} \qquad (8.4.7)$$

where we have imposed one restriction ($\beta_3 = -\beta_2$) and the unrestricted model has 48 degrees of freedom—52 observations minus four parameters to be estimated. The F statistic works out to 70.5. The critical value for 5 percent significance for the F distribution with 1 and 48 degrees of freedom, 4.04, is much lower than this.

What does this tell us about the null hypothesis? If the hypothesis were true, we'd expect SSR_R to be pretty close to SSR_{UR}; specifically, there is a 95 percent chance that it would be less than 4.04. In this case, the odds that we would get an F statistic as large as 70.5, if the hypothesis is true, is extremely small. We conclude that SSR_R is substantially larger than SSR_{UR}, the unrestricted model fits the data better than the restricted model, and we therefore reject the null hypothesis.

One common F test is the test of whether all the parameters $\beta_1, \ldots \beta_K$ (excluding the intercept β_0)[6] are equal to 0 or not. The restricted model for this hypothesis is just $Y = \beta_0 + \varepsilon$, because if all other βs are 0, then all the right-hand-side variables drop out of the model. Econometric software that reports an F statistic as part of its standard regression output is probably reporting the F statistic for this particular hypothesis. Why this hypothesis? It usually has no economic meaning; in most problems it would be unreasonable for all right-hand-side variables to drop out of the equation. There are exceptions, such as the efficient markets hypothesis discussed in Chapter 4, which states that no variables should be able to influence stock returns, and in that case the test is meaningful. More often, however, this statistic is reported simply as a test to see if the independent variables are having any effect on the dependent variable at all. If they are not, then there is probably a serious problem with some part of the analysis—either the model, the data, or both. If we reject the hypothesis that the independent variables have no effect on the dependent variable, then we move on to the real economic question at hand.

Turning back to the automobile production function, we can test whether the industry production function has constant returns to scale or not. As discussed above, if it does, then increasing all four inputs in the same proportion should increase output by the same proportion, and if that's so, then the four elasticities should add up to 1. We write that mathematically as $\beta_1 + \beta_2 + \beta_3 + \beta_4 = 1$. How do we impose this restriction on the model? First, we solve that equation for one of the elasticities: $\beta_4 = 1 - \beta_1 - \beta_2 - \beta_3$. Then we substitute that equation into the unrestricted model, Equation 8.1.3, which produces:

$$\log Y_t = \beta_0 + \beta_1 \log \text{PW}_t + \beta_2 \log \text{NPW}_t + \beta_3 \log \text{CAPEXP}_t$$
$$+ (1 - \beta_1 - \beta_2 - \beta_3) \log \text{MAT}_t + \beta_5 \log \text{YEAR}_t + \varepsilon \qquad (8.4.8)$$

Rearranging the terms produces

$$\log Y_t - \log \text{MAT}_t = \beta_0 + \beta_1(\log \text{PW}_t - \log \text{MAT}_t) + \beta_2(\log \text{NPW}_t$$
$$- \log \text{MAT}_t) + \beta_3(\log \text{CAPEXP}_t - \log \text{MAT}_t)$$
$$+ \beta_5 \log \text{YEAR}_t + \varepsilon \qquad (8.4.9)$$

[6] We exclude β_0 because we are asking whether any of the independent variables affect the dependent variable, and β_0 has no independent variable associated with it. If we included β_0, we would also be requiring that the mean value of Y has to be 0 (because then $Y = \varepsilon$), which will almost always be false.

TABLE 8.4
Estimation Results of Restricted Auto Production Function

Variable	Parameter	Estimate	Standard Error	t Statistic
Intercept	β_0	1.377	0.255	5.398
log PW − log MAT	β_1	0.546	0.184	2.966
log NPW − log MAT	β_2	0.059	0.075	0.786
log CAPEXP − log MAT	β_3	−0.062	0.019	−3.306
Year	β_5	0.027	0.006	4.344

$R^2 = 0.712$
$N = 18$

SER = 0.0266
SSR = 0.009202

which we can estimate with least squares, once we calculate the new variables (log $Y-$ log MAT), (log PW − log MAT), (log NPW − log MAT), and (log CAPEXP − log MAT). The results of estimating this equation are shown in Table 8.4. Note that β_4 doesn't appear in the list anymore, since we've eliminated it from the equation. We can calculate its implied value from the restriction: $\beta_4 = 1 - \beta_1 - \beta_2 - \beta_3 = 1 - 0.546 - 0.059 - (-0.062) = 0.457$. There are several things to note about the results of this estimation:

1. Most of the standard errors are lower than before. This is because imposing restrictions reduces the number of parameters in the model, increasing the number of degrees of freedom and making it easier to accurately estimate each parameter that remains.
2. The SSR is larger than before. This is because imposing the restriction cannot make the SSR smaller and usually makes it larger, as it has here.
3. As a result of the SSR being larger, the SER is larger and the R^2 is smaller than before.
4. None of the parameter values have changed very much, and none have changed their significance; those that were significantly different from 0 still are, and the one that wasn't (β_2) still isn't.

Is the restriction acceptable? The F statistic is:

$$F = \frac{(0.009202 - 0.008767)/1}{0.008767/12} \tag{8.4.10}$$

because we are imposing one restriction (we have eliminated one parameter from the model), and the unrestricted model has 18 observations and 6 estimated parameters. The F statistic works out to 0.59541. The critical value for 1 and 12 degrees of freedom is larger than this; it is 4.75. Therefore there is a 5 percent chance of getting an F value smaller than 4.75, and much more than a 5 percent chance of getting a value as small as 0.595. This result is consistent with the null hypothesis of constant returns to scale in the industry, and therefore we do not reject that null hypothesis with this data. We would continue our analysis using the restricted regression, because the restriction is economically reasonable and econometrically acceptable and, most important, because we get better estimates of the parameters (ones with smaller standard errors) when we impose it. For instance, the confidence interval for β_1 is now substantially smaller than it was previously. There are now 13 degrees of freedom in the unrestricted model, so the critical t statistic is 2.16, and the confidence interval is 0.546 plus or minus 2.16 · 0.184, which works out to (0.148, 0.943). This confidence interval is entirely inside the earlier one, so we clearly have improved our knowledge about the true value of β_1. Also, we can now reject the null hypothesis $\beta_1 = 1$, as we expected, since 1 is no longer inside the confidence interval (alternatively, the t statistic for that test is $(0.546 - 1)/0.184 = 2.467$, which is larger than the critical value of 2.16.

8.5 TESTS INVOLVING MORE THAN ONE PARAMETER: THE WALD AND LM TESTS

Using the F test is not, however, the only way to test the hypothesis of constant returns to scale. Intuitively, there is a much simpler test available. If we expect $\beta_1 + \beta_2 + \beta_3 + \beta_4 = 1$, then why don't we just add up $\hat{\beta}_1 + \hat{\beta}_2 + \hat{\beta}_3 + \hat{\beta}_4$ and see if we get something close to 1? In this case, Table 8.3 shows that we'd get $0.668 + 0.128 - 0.070 + 0.386 = 1.112$. The problem is determining whether 1.112 is "close enough" to 1, or if it is far away enough to reject the hypothesis. That is, we need to know the standard error of the sum $\beta_1 + \beta_2 + \beta_3 + \beta_4$ so that we can know how far away from 1 we would expect it to be if the null hypothesis were true.

Observe that the standard errors of the $\hat{\beta}$s are mostly larger than 0.112; they are 0.244, 0.117, 0.021, and 0.161, respectively. Surely if most of the individual $\hat{\beta}$s are plus or minus at least 0.1, then the sum is also? Unfortunately, that need not be the case. The standard error of the sum of the $\hat{\beta}$s depends on the standard error of each individual $\hat{\beta}$ and also on their covariance. In particular, if two coefficients are negatively correlated (that is, one is high when the other is low, and conversely)—that is, if $\hat{\sigma}_{\hat{\beta}_i \hat{\beta}_j}$ is negative—then the sum of those coefficients can have a smaller standard error than either one of the coefficients individually, because their errors tend to cancel one another out when the two estimates are added together. The test that calculates the standard error of $\beta_1 + \beta_2 + \beta_3 + \beta_4$ and compares it to 1, the *Wald test,* is an alternative way of testing multivariate hypotheses.

Theorem 8.6. Given the econometric model $Y_i = \beta_0 + \beta_1 X_{1i} + \beta_2 X_{2i} + \cdots + \beta_K X_{Ki} + \varepsilon_i$, and the null hypothesis $\sum_{k=0}^{K} a_k \beta_k = r$, the Wald test statistic is calculated by

$$W = \left(\sum_{k=0}^{K} a_k \hat{\beta}_k - r \right)^2 \left(\sum_{i=0}^{K} \sum_{j=0}^{K} a_i a_j \hat{\sigma}_{\hat{\beta}_i \hat{\beta}_j} \right) \qquad \textbf{(8.5.1)}$$

and takes the chi-square distribution with one degree of freedom.

The Wald test can also be used to test multiple hypotheses, just as the F test can, although the formula for the test statistic is more complicated in that case, and the degrees of freedom of the chi-square distribution is equal to the number of hypotheses tested. Most econometric software packages will calculate the test statistic for you. In this case, we are testing the single hypothesis $\beta_1 + \beta_2 + \beta_3 + \beta_4 = 1$, and the formula for the test statistic is

$$W = (\hat{\beta}_1 + \hat{\beta}_2 + \hat{\beta}_3 + \hat{\beta}_4 - 1)^2 \left(\sum_{i=1}^{4} \sum_{j=1}^{4} \hat{\sigma}_{\hat{\beta}_i \hat{\beta}_j} \right) \qquad \textbf{(8.5.2)}$$

The test statistic works out to 0.596, which is less than the 5 percent critical value of 3.84 for a chi-square statistic with 1 degree of freedom. So we would fail to reject the null hypothesis that $\beta_1 + \beta_2 + \beta_3 + \beta_4 = 1$, and economically, we would conclude that the data are consistent with constant returns to scale in the automobile industry.

Note that we got the same answer with the Wald test that we did with the F test; we failed to reject the null hypothesis in both cases. Are the two tests guaranteed to give you the same answer each time? Unfortunately, they are not, although they should be similar, and the more degrees of freedom in the estimation, the more similar they will be, becoming identical as the number of degrees of freedom grows large. This means that normally either both will reject or both will fail to reject. If not, however, if one rejects and the other fails to reject, then because they are similar, both will be close to their critical values. The one that rejects will not reject by much, and the one that fails to reject will not fail to reject by much. In that case, you should be very hesitant about any conclusion you draw, since whether you decide to reject or not to reject, either way you were close to doing the opposite.

If that is the case, what reason is there to prefer one to the other? In most applications, there is not much difference between them and you can perform either one. There is one advantage to the Wald test: It only requires you to estimate one model, the unrestricted model, whereas the F test requires you to estimate both the restricted and the unrestricted model. Before the advent of cheap and powerful computers with good econometrics software, this was an excellent reason to prefer the Wald test; even a small regression, with few observations and variables, could take the better part of a day to calculate by hand.[7] However, now that computers can estimate regressions in tiny fractions of a second, this is no longer a compelling reason to favor the Wald test. This can still be an advantage in the rare cases where it is difficult or impossible to estimate the restricted model. Such cases are rare, but they do exist.[8] At present, the econometrics profession does not seem to have any strong preference for one test or the other.

You might be wondering whether it would also be possible to conduct a hypothesis test by estimating only the restricted model. The answer is yes; one estimates the restricted model, then calculates the extent to which the SSR could be reduced by getting rid of the restriction. Such a test is called an *LM test*. LM is an abbreviation for Lagrange multiplier, which is the name of the mathematical technique used to calculate the effect of the restriction on the SSR. However, this test is almost never used when the F test is possible, and we will not discuss it further here. It is used only when estimation of the unrestricted model is impossible. That does not happen often, but we will see one example of it in Chapter 13.

Chapter Review

- The precise mathematical specification of the regression equation is called its *functional form.*

- An econometric model is called *multivariate* if it has more than one variable on the right-hand side of the equation.

- A set of right-hand-side variables is *perfectly multicollinear* if a linear equation involving those variables holds for each observation in the data sample.

- If the right-hand-side variables of an equation are perfectly multicollinear, then it is impossible to estimate the parameters of the model because the effects of the variables cannot be distinguished from one another.

---

[7] Be grateful you live in the modern era and not in the bad old days of econometric analysis.

[8] For example, suppose you are estimating a (nonlinear) model with a term such as $(\beta_1/\beta_0)X$, and you wish to impose the restriction $\beta_0 = 0$. Dividing by 0 is mathematically impossible.

- If the right-hand-side variables of an equation are not perfectly multicollinear, then the least squares estimator is BLUE; and if the error terms are normally distributed it is BUE, just as it was in the univariate case.
- Multivariate hypotheses about a model's parameters can be tested by creating a *restricted model* imposing the hypothesis and seeing how much the SSR increases when the restriction is imposed; this test is called an *F* test.
- Multivariate hypotheses can also be tested by calculating the standard error of a combination of parameters; this test is called a *Wald test*.
- *F* tests and Wald tests give answers that are guaranteed to be similar but not guaranteed to be identical. Normally, both will reject a hypothesis or both will fail to reject it. If one rejects and the other fails to reject, then one should not place great confidence in either finding.

Computer Exercise

In this exercise we'll generate some multivariate regressions with some parameters equal and others not, and see how well our various tests work at detecting the differences.

1. Start Eviews, and create a new worksheet, undated, with 100 observations.

2. On the command line, type genr x1=rnd()*20 to get a randomly generated independent variable. Then type genr x2=rnd()*20 and type genr x3=rnd()*20 to get two more independent variables. Finally, type genr z1=x1+x2 and genr z2=x1+x3 for later use in *F* tests.

3. Type genr err=rnd()*5-2.5 to produce some error terms. Then type genr y=10+5*x1+5*x2+2*x3+err to create a dependent variable. In this model, $\beta_0 = 10$, $\beta_1 = 5$, $\beta_2 = 5$ also, and $\beta_3 = 2$.

4. Type ls y c x1 x2 x3 to regress Y on the X variables. How close are your estimated values of $\hat{\beta}_1$ and $\hat{\beta}_2$? Their estimated standard errors should be roughly the same size. Are they within one standard error of each other? Two standard errors? How close are your estimated values of $\hat{\beta}_1$ and $\hat{\beta}_3$?

5. In the window with the regression results, select View, then Coefficient Tests, then Wald tests to do a Wald test of the hypothesis $\beta_1 = \beta_2$. Enter c(2)=c(3) for the hypothesis to be tested. Do you reject or fail to reject?

6. Also do the Wald test of the hypothesis $\beta_1 = \beta_3$, entering c(2)=c(4) for the hypothesis to be tested. Do you reject or fail to reject?

7. Type ls y c z1 x3 to estimate a restricted model where the (true) restriction $\beta_1 = \beta_2$ is imposed. Which equation has the higher SSR? Do the *F* test of this restriction. Do you reject or fail to reject?

8. Type ls y c z2 x2 to estimate a restricted model where the (false) restriction $\beta_1 = \beta_3$ is imposed. Which equation has the higher SSR? Do the *F* test of this restriction. Do you reject or fail to reject?

9. Repeat steps 3 through 8 ten times. How many times do you fail the *F* tests? How many times do you fail the Wald test? Does it happen at the same time or different times? When you fail, how many standard errors apart (roughly) are the estimates of $\hat{\beta}_1$ and $\hat{\beta}_2$ (or $\hat{\beta}_1$ and $\hat{\beta}_3$ for the second hypothesis)?

Problems

1. Load the data file **stateed**, which contains data on a sample of the 50 U.S. states for five variables: stateaid is the amount of money the state spends on aid to local school districts (millions of dollars), income is the total income in the state (billions of dollars), population is the population of the state (in thousands of people), elderly is the fraction of the state's population that is over age 65, population is the state's population, and attend is the fraction of the state's school-age population (children ages 6 to 18).

    a. Would you expect a state with high income to give more aid or less aid to local schools? Would you expect a state with a population with a higher fraction of the elderly to give more aid to schools, or less? Briefly explain why.

    b. Estimate the regression $Stateaid_i = \beta_0 + \beta_1 Income_i + \beta_2 Population_i + \beta_3 Elderly_i + \beta_4 Attend_i + \varepsilon_i$. Which of the variables have statistically significant effects and which do not?

    c. Test the null hypothesis that $\beta_3 = \beta_4 = 0$ (note that this is one test of a joint hypothesis, not two separate tests). Does the composition of the state's population appear to affect spending, or not? Given these results, why do some states spend more on school aid than others?

2. Load the data file **stateed**, which is described in problem 1. In this problem we'll control for the fact that large states spend more money than small states do by looking at the relationship in per capita terms rather than in terms of total dollars spent.

    a. Create two new variables, aidpc and incomepc, by dividing aid and income by the state's population, multiplying by 1,000 in the former case and by 1 million in the latter case to correct for the different units of measurement. (Elderly and Attend need not be transformed because they are already measured as percentages of the population.)

    b. Estimate the regression $Aidpc_i = \beta_0 + \beta_1 Incomepc_i + \beta_2 Population_i + \beta_3 Elderly_i + \beta_4 Attend_i + \varepsilon_i$. Test the null hypothesis $\beta_1 = \beta_2 = \beta_3 = \beta_4 = 0$. Do these variables seem to affect per capita school aid, or not?

    c. If state per capita income rises by $1,000, how much does per capita school aid spending rise? Is the result statistically significantly different from 0, or not?

    d. If the fraction of the state's school-age population rises by 1 percent, how much does state spending on education increase? Is the effect statistically significantly different from 0, or not?

    e. According to this regression, what is the most important determinant of state spending on school aid? Provide an economic (or perhaps political) reason why this might be so.

3. Open the data file **dollar**, which contains data on the following three variables: inflation is the U.S. inflation rate, tbillrate is the interest rate on six-month U.S. treasury notes, and dollarvalue is the value of the U.S. dollar against a basket of foreign currencies, indexed so that $1995 = 100$. The sample is composed of monthly observations from 1967 to 2001. One theory of the value of the dollar is the theory of purchasing power parity (PPP), which says that currency values adjust to keep the real world prices of commodities equal. This theory implies that inflation in the United States should lower the value of the dollar. An alternative theory is the theory of interest rate parity (IRP), which says that currency values adjust to keep real interest rates equal. This theory implies that

higher U.S. interest rates should raise the value of the dollar.

a. Display a graph of the dollar's value over time. When was it particularly strong, and when was it particularly weak?

b. If we wanted to look only at the PPP theory, we might look at the economic model Dollarvalue $= \beta_0 + \beta_1$ Inflation. What sign do you expect for β_1? Estimate the regression equation Dollarvalue$_t = \beta_0 + \beta_1$ Inflation$_t + \varepsilon_t$. Test whether β_1 is significantly different from 0. Do you get what you expect or not? What would you conclude about the PPP theory from this?

c. If we wanted instead to look at the IRP theory, then we'd look at the model Dollarvalue $= \beta_0 + \beta_1$ Tbillrate. What sign do you expect for β_1 in this model? Estimate the regression equation Dollarvalue$_t = \beta_0 + \beta_1$ Tbillrate$_t + \varepsilon_t$. Test whether β_1 is significantly different from 0. Do you get what you expect or not? What would you conclude about the IRP theory from this?

d. In reality, it may be the case that both theories have some ability to explain the value of the dollar. Estimate the equation Dollarvalue$_t = \beta_0 + \beta_1$ Tbillrate$_t + \beta_2$ Inflation$_t + \varepsilon_t$. Do you get the expected signs for both β_1 and β_2? Are the results statistically significant? Do you find evidence in support of both theories, only one, or neither?

e. If the U.S. inflation rate rises by 1 percent, and interest rates stay the same, how much will the dollar's value change? How much will it change if interest rates rise by 2 percent and the inflation rate stays the same? How much will it rise if interest rates and the inflation rate both rise by 2 percent?

4. Open the data file football, which contains data on four variables measured on a sample of 30 NFL teams for the 1997 season: attendance is the number of tickets sold for the team's home games, and wins, losses, and ties are the team's number of wins, losses, and ties for the 1997 season, respectively.

a. The number of tickets sold is determined by the market for tickets. Assume that buyers have a higher demand to see a team that wins most of its games than they do to see a team that loses most of its games. When a team's number of wins increases, which way does its demand curve shift? What should happen to its ticket sales (that is, attendance) and ticket prices?

b. We'll use the data on attendance to test the model's prediction about ticket sales. Consider the economic model Attendance $= \beta_0 + \beta_1$ Wins $+ \beta_2$ Losses $+ \beta_3$ Ties. What sign do you expect for β_1? What signs do you expect for β_2 and β_3?

c. Now estimate the regression equation Attendance$_i = \beta_0 + \beta_1$ Wins$_i + \beta_2$ Losses$_i + \beta_3$ Ties$_i + \varepsilon_i$. What happens, and why? (Remember that each team plays a total of 16 games in a season.)

d. Instead estimate the equation Attendance$_i = \beta_0 + \beta_1$ Wins$_i + \beta_2$ Ties$_i + \varepsilon_i$. What attendance do you predict a team would get if it had a record of 0 wins, 0 ties, and 16 losses? How much would attendance rise if it won an additional game (and therefore had one fewer loss?) How much would it rise if it tied one game instead of losing it? How much would attendance rise if it tied one game instead of winning it?

e. Suppose we instead estimated the equation Attendance$_i = \beta_0 + \beta_1$ Losses$_i + \beta_2$ Ties$_i + \varepsilon_i$. Use these estimates to answer the same questions as in part d. Do you get different answers, or the same answers? Does it matter whether you drop Wins or Losses from the original regression equation?

5. Load the data file football, described in problem 4, and estimate the equation Attendance$_i = \beta_0 + \beta_1 \text{Wins}_i + \beta_2 \text{Ties}_i + \varepsilon_i$.

a. We might expect that a win would increase attendance more than a tie would. What does this imply about the relationship between β_1 and β_2? Test this null hypothesis. Do you reject or fail to reject?

b. How do you explain your finding that $\hat{\beta}_1 < \hat{\beta}_2$? (Hint: Count the total number of ties observed in the data set.)

6. Open the data file tests, which contains data on 10 variables: math and english are the percentages of students that achieved passing grades (65 percent or better) on standardized math and English tests within a given school district; highmath and higheng are the percentages of students that achieved high passing grades (90 percent or better) on the same exams; expperpup is the total amount of money spent by the school district on education divided by the total number of pupils in the district; stateexp and localexp are the per-pupil expenditures by state and local governments, respectively; stateshare is the percentage of expenditure provided by the state; poverty is the poverty rate in the district; and dropout is the dropout rate in the district.

a. Economists often think of education as a good that is produced with inputs; spending more money on inputs should produce more "output," that is, better-educated students. Consider an economic model of educational production, Math $= \beta_0 + \beta_1 \text{Localexp} + \beta_2 \text{Stateexp}$ and English $= \gamma_0 + \gamma_1 \text{Localexp} + \gamma_2 \text{Stateexp}$. What signs would you predict for $\beta_1, \beta_2, \gamma_1,$ and γ_2 if this model is correct?

b. Estimate the equation Math$_i = \beta_0 + \beta_1 \text{Localexp}_i + \beta_2 \text{Stateexp}_i + \varepsilon_i$. Which parameters are statistically significantly different from 0, and which are not? Estimate the equation English$_i = \gamma_0 + \gamma_1 \text{Localexp}_i + \gamma_2 \text{Stateexp}_i + \upsilon_i$. Which of this equation's parameters are statistically significant?

c. Consider the economic hypothesis that it does not matter whether educational inputs are bought with state or local money; that is, suppose that state and local spending have the same effect on test scores. What null hypothesis about the parameters corresponds to this economic hypothesis? Test it, being sure to specify an alternative hypothesis as well in the test. What do you find?

d. Test the null hypothesis that $\beta_1 = \beta_2 = 0$ against the null hypothesis that at least one of them is not equal to 0, and the null hypothesis that $\gamma_1 = \gamma_2 = 0$ against the null hypothesis that at least one of them is not equal to 0. What do you find? What do you conclude about the model of education as a production process?

7. Open the data file tests, which is described in problem 6. In this problem we'll include the data on state and local spending in a somewhat different way. Instead of putting each type of spending in separately, we'll put in one variable for total spending, plus a second one indicating what fraction of the money was spent by the state.

a. Estimate the equation Math$_i = \beta_0 + \beta_1 \text{Expperpup}_i + \beta_2 \text{Stateshare}_i + \varepsilon_i$. Test the economic hypothesis that it does not matter whether expenditures are provided by the state or by local governments. Do you use an F test or t test? What do you find?

b. Test the null hypothesis that spending (of either type) does affect test scores against the alternative hypothesis that it improves them. What do you find?

c. Repeat parts *a* and *b* for the equation $English_i = \beta_0 + \beta_1 Expperpup_i + \beta_2 Stateshare_i + \upsilon_i$.

d. Do we get the same economic conclusions, or different economic conclusions, from this equation compared to the one from problem 6?

8. Open the data file tests, which is described in problem 6. One problem with the production model of education is that one of the inputs into education is the students themselves, and not all school districts have equally talented students. In this problem we'll include variables that we hope will control for such effects.

a. Estimate the equation $Math_i = \beta_0 + \beta_1 Expperpup_i + \beta_2 Stateshare_i + \beta_3 Poverty_i + \beta_4 Dropout_i + \varepsilon_i$. Test the null hypothesis $\beta_3 = 0$ against the alternative $\beta_3 \neq 0$. Does the poverty rate of a school district appear to affect its test scores? If so, does it raise them or lower them?

b. Test the null hypothesis that districts with high dropout rates have a lower fraction of passing scores. What economic conclusions do you draw from the result?

c. Test the null hypothesis $\beta_1 = \beta_2 = \beta_3 = \beta_4 = 0$. Do these variables seem to affect student test scores, or not?

d. Repeat the tests in parts *a* through *c* on the equation $English_i = \gamma_0 + \gamma_1 Expperpup_i + \gamma_2 Stateshare_i + \gamma_3 Poverty_i + \gamma_4 Dropout_i + \upsilon_i$. Do you get similar results, or different ones? If you get different ones, what differences might there be in English education and math education to explain them?

9. Open the data file tests, which is described in problem 6. In this problem we'll look at the fraction of students who get high passing grades, instead of all students who pass.

a. Estimate the equation $Highmath_i = \beta_0 + \beta_1 Expperpup_i + \beta_2 Stateshare_i + \beta_3 Poverty_i + \beta_4 Dropout_i + \varepsilon_i$. What parameters are statistically significant now?

b. Estimate the equation $Highengh_i = \gamma_0 + \gamma_1 Expperpup_i + \gamma_2 Stateshare_i + \gamma_3 Poverty_i + \gamma_4 Dropout_i + \varepsilon_i$. What parameters are statistically significant in this equation? Are they the same as in the equation in part *a*, or not?

c. What do you conclude about the effect of state spending on test scores from these regressions? Suggest two economic reasons why this might occur.

Part Four

Specifying the Econometric Model

If economic data were always explained by simple models with straight lines, we could do all our econometric analysis with the basic least squares model. But that is not the case. There are often many ways to write a mathematical equation to describe the economic theory explaining the data, and we need to know which of them describes the data best. We do not know exactly which independent variables affect the dependent variable. Different theories may predict different independent variables; even when it is clear that a particular economic variable matters, there are often many different data series we could use to represent that economic variable in the analysis. Different parts of the economy may have somewhat different behavior, or the economy may evolve over time, causing the values of the parameters of our models to change. In Part IV, we present techniques to deal with these problems and (along with economic theory) to help us determine the right model to use in econometric analysis.

Chapter **Nine**

Selecting a Functional Form

. . . d) The commission has found, after an extensive public review process, that the interests of ratepayers and the state as a whole will be best served by moving from the regulatory framework existing on January 1, 1997 . . . to a framework under which competition would be allowed in the supply of electric power and customers would be allowed to have the right to choose their supplier of electric power.

(e) Competition in the electric generation market will encourage innovation, efficiency, and better service from all market participants, and will permit the reduction of costly regulatory oversight.

California Public Utilities Code, Section 330

9.1 NATURAL MONOPOLY AND THE SHAPE OF THE COST FUNCTION

In most industrial societies, the electric power industry was either regulated or nationalized shortly after coming into existence. This was done because the industry tended toward monopoly; most customers had only a single firm to provide them with electricity and, in the absence of any competition, were forced to pay whatever price that firm requested, or do without electricity. Why did these monopolies exist? Economists have long understood that the electric power industry is a case of natural monopoly, that is, it has an average cost curve that is decreasing over practical ranges of output (see Figure 9.1). In such a case, large firms can produce electricity more cheaply than small ones, and if two firms merge, they will have a cost advantage over their smaller rivals. This process continues until only one firm remains in the industry. Introducing new competitors will not help; the incentive to merge, or to expand to drive rivals out of business, will quickly result in the restoration of monopoly. The solution is to accept the fact of monopoly, but to control prices to prevent electricity consumers from being exploited.

FIGURE 9.1
Cost Curve of
a Natural
Monopoly

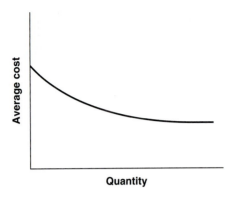

Since the 1990s, however, restructuring of the electric power industry has become increasingly common. The British electricity industry was broken into three electricity-generating companies and a single transmitting company in 1990. Subsequently, first California and then many other American states created markets with many generating companies, though still with a single transmitting company, which remained regulated. This was done because of a belief that natural monopoly conditions no longer applied in the generation of electricity. Power demand had grown so large, and power transmission costs fallen so low, that a community could be served by many different power plants, not a single one. Advocates of restructuring felt that the industry would operate more efficiently if plants were required to compete with one another for the business of customers. How can we tell if the electric power industry is indeed no longer a natural monopoly? We can estimate its cost curve and see whether or not its costs are truly declining. If they are, then the industry remains a natural monopoly and restructuring is probably a bad idea. If they are not, then competition may be effective at reducing prices and increasing efficiency.

However, estimating the cost curve of the electricity industry requires some careful consideration of the functional form to be used in specifying the cost function. Choosing an inappropriate cost function can cause serious problems with the analysis, either because the function doesn't fit the true shape of the data very well, because it implies economic properties that aren't true in the industry, or both. This chapter presents a variety of common functional forms and their economic and statistical properties. For each form we'll discuss economic situations in which it is commonly used and why it is a good way to represent that particular economic model.

9.2 RISING AND FALLING COSTS: QUADRATIC TERMS

Economic theory tells us that the costs of producing any product depend on the prices of each input used and the amount of output produced. That is, a general cost function can be written as:

$$C_i = f(Q_i, P_{1i}, P_{2i}, \ldots P_{Ki}) \qquad (9.2.1)$$

where C_i is the total cost of producing the product, $P_1, P_2, \ldots P_K$ are the prices of K different inputs used to produce the product, Q_i is the amount of output the firm produces, and the i subscript indexes different firms in the sample. Of course, this general form is not useful for estimating the cost function; we have to choose a particular functional form. The simplest one is a linear function:

$$C_i = \beta_0 + \beta_1 Q_i + \beta_2 P_{1i} + \beta_3 P_{2i} + \cdots + \beta_{K+1} P_{Ki} + \varepsilon_i \quad \textbf{(9.2.2)}$$

where the expression for costs is linear with respect to the prices.[1] This functional form has several advantages. The first is its simplicity; this is the most direct and intuitive way of assembling these variables into an equation. The linear functional form is usually what one uses if one doesn't have any other ideas about what sorts of functional forms might be appropriate.

The second is that its economic interpretation is fairly straightforward, because of the simplicity of the graphs that result from it. For example, consider what happens to costs if the firm increases output by 1 unit: Q rises by 1; none of the input price variables change. Therefore, costs will rise by a total of β_1. Economically, we interpret β_1 as the marginal cost (MC) of producing more output. The linear functional form gives us a single number, $\hat{\beta}_1$, which we can take as an estimate of that marginal cost; we do not need to do any complicated calculations to find it. We can also see this from the graph of cost against output, which is shown in Figure 9.2. This graph is a straight line, as is the graph of any linear function, and its slope is just β_1. Theory tells us that cost functions slope up, as drawn in the graph; we would expect $\beta_1 > 0$, and we could test this econometrically. The graph also shows the fixed cost, that is, the cost of producing 0 output; it is the intercept of the line. This value is $\beta_0 + \beta_2 P_{1i} + \beta_3 P_{2i} + \cdots + \beta_{K+1} P_{Ki}$, which is the result of plugging $Q = 0$ into Equation 9.2.2. We would normally expect this to be positive, or at worst 0, and we could test for that from estimates of the cost function also.

We can also determine the relationship between total costs and prices from this function. An increase of \$1 in P_1 will result in an increase of β_2 in total costs C. We don't have an economic name for this term, but we do have some ideas about it: An increase in the price

FIGURE 9.2
Fixed and Marginal Costs When the Cost Function Is Linear

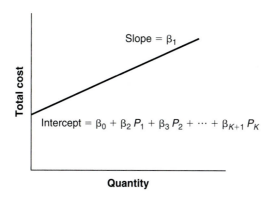

y-axis: Total cost
x-axis: **Quantity**
Slope = β_1
Intercept = $\beta_0 + \beta_2 P_1 + \beta_3 P_2 + \cdots + \beta_{K+1} P_K$

---

[1] Be sure to distinguish between an equation that is linear in the P variables, and an equation that is linear in the β parameters. To use ordinary least squares (OLS), the equation must be linear in the parameters, but it need not be linear in the variables. The linear functional form is distinguished by being linear in the variables and the parameters; other functional forms in this chapter will be linear in the parameters but not the variables.

of an input should cause total costs to rise.[2] Therefore, we would expect $\beta_2 > 0$, and we could test that as well.

However, there are several reasons why the linear functional form is not a good one to use for estimating cost functions. The first is that marginal costs are not usually constant; normally, we expect marginal costs to rise as output increases, holding other factors fixed. The linear functional form, which implies that $MC = \beta_1$, does not permit marginal costs to change when Q changes. If we believe that marginal costs do rise, then the linear functional form cannot be the correct one; this violates assumption A1 of the classical linear model, and leads to ordinary least squares (OLS) being biased and inconsistent. A better functional form is:

$$C_i = \beta_0 + \beta_1 Q_i + \beta_2 Q_i^2 + \beta_3 P_{1i} + \beta_4 P_{2i} + \cdots + \beta_{K+2} P_{Ki} + \varepsilon_i \qquad \text{(9.2.3)}$$

In this functional form, marginal costs can either rise or fall. We can see this by taking the derivative of C with respect to Q, which is the slope of the cost function and, hence, is the marginal cost of additional output:

$$MC = \beta_1 + 2\beta_2 Q_i \qquad \text{(9.2.4)}$$

When $Q = 0$, the marginal cost will be β_1; we would normally expect this to be positive, so we should find $\beta_1 > 0$. But as Q_i rises, the marginal cost will change, because the Q_i^2 term in the original cost function causes Q_i to remain in the marginal cost equation.

Definition 9.1 A functional form is called a *quadratic* with respect to a variable X if it contains an X^2 term in the equation. The functional form

$$Y = \beta_0 + \beta_1 X_1 + \beta_2 X_1^2 + \beta_3 X_2 + \beta_4 X_3$$

is quadratic with respect to X_1, but linear with respect to X_2 and X_3. The functional form

$$Y = \beta_0 + \beta_1 X_1 + \beta_2 X_1^2 + \beta_3 X_2 + \beta_4 X_2^2 + \beta_5 X_3 + \beta_6 X_3^2$$

is quadratic with respect to all three of the right-hand-side variables.

There are three possibilities for the shape of a quadratic cost curve, all of which are shown in Figure 9.3. First, if $\beta_2 > 0$, then marginal costs will rise as Q_i gets larger, and the cost curve will get steeper. Second, if $\beta_2 < 0$, then marginal costs will fall as Q_i gets larger, and the cost curve will get flatter. In both of these cases, marginal costs will be different for firms making different amounts of output. Third, if $\beta_2 = 0$, then marginal costs are constant and the slope of the curve does not change; that is, it is a straight line.

The quadratic cost function has two advantages over the linear one. The first is that it is economically more realistic; it permits marginal costs to rise as quantity rises, which we expect to be true. The second is that, mathematically, it is capable of representing either a straight or a curved cost curve, whichever may happen to be true. If the true cost function is linear, then the quadratic cost function can always pick $\hat{\beta}_2 = 0$, in which case the quadratic term cancels out of the equation and it becomes exactly the same as the linear

---

[2] Of course, if the price of the input rises, the firm will try to use less of it, which will reduce costs. However, it can be proved that the effect of the higher price of the input is larger than the effect of the reduced quantity of the input; total costs will always rise when the price of an input rises.

FIGURE 9.3
Marginal Costs When the Cost Function Is Quadratic

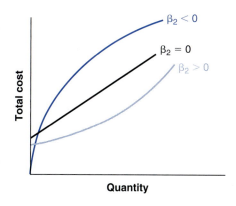

FIGURE 9.4
Fitting Linear and Quadratic Functional Forms to Data

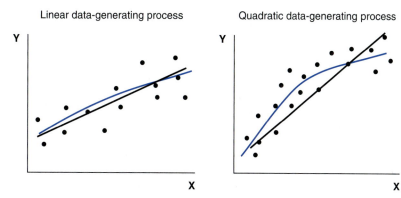

equation. If the true cost function is not linear, then the quadratic cost function can pick some other value for β_2 and it can take shapes that the linear cost function cannot.

> **Definition 9.2** If we have two functional forms, the first of which can be made equivalent to the second by imposing restrictions on the parameters, then we say that the first functional form is more *flexible* than the second. The first one can take any shape that the second one can take, by imposing the restriction; it can also take additional shapes by not imposing the restriction.

The quadratic functional form is more flexible than the linear functional form because the quadratic functional form can be made linear by imposing the restriction $\beta_2 = 0$ if that helps to fit the data. Figure 9.4 demonstrates this point. If the true, unknown cost curve that generated the data is in fact linear, as in the graph on the left, then it would be correct to use the linear functional form, but it would also be correct to use the quadratic functional form, since it will fit the data just as well as the linear one will. But if the true, unknown cost curve is actually quadratic, as in the graph on the right, then it is correct to use the quadratic functional form, but not the linear functional form.[3] It will fit the data much better than the

---

[3] If the true functional form is neither linear nor quadratic, then strictly speaking, it is not correct to use either functional form; however, the quadratic functional form will be closer to the true, unknown functional form than the linear form will be, because it can curve to match the true form while the linear one cannot. It will generally therefore suffer less bias from violating assumption A1 and will be preferable even in this case.

FIGURE 9.5
Changing
Slopes in
Quadratic
Functional
Forms

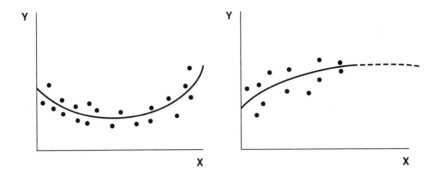

linear one will because the quadratic one will curve through the data, whereas the linear one cannot do so. As a general principle, it is better to use functional forms that are more flexible rather than less flexible, because the flexible ones give you the best chance of matching up to the data generating process that produced the sample of observations.

There are, however, three possible concerns about using the quadratic functional form. The first is that the quadratic functional form, if extended far enough, will eventually change the sign of its slope, because it ultimately must take the shape of a parabola. This may cause problems of economic interpretation. For instance, a cost curve should always slope upward; but a quadratic cost function will always take a negative slope somewhere, either to the left or the right depending on whether the function is concave (U-shaped) or convex (hill-shaped), as Figure 9.5 shows. Where the cost function is negatively sloped, the marginal cost will be negative, which is economically impossible. This, however, is not necessarily as bad as it sounds. The quadratic functional form must slope down somewhere, but it need not do so in the range of the data. If, as on the right-hand graph of Figure 9.5, the pattern of the data is upward-sloping, then the best-fitting curve will be positively sloping throughout the region where the data lie. The quantity where the slope becomes negative will be greater (or lesser) than anything observed in the data—and so the slope, and marginal cost, will be positive for all the quantities of interest.[4] Conversely, if the pattern of the data is U-shaped, then the quadratic functional form will capture that shape correctly, as shown in the left-hand graph of Figure 9.5. Therefore, one can generally estimate a quadratic functional form without worrying about the fact that the fitted curve will change slopes at some point. It will only change slope at a meaningful quantity if the data really show a change in slope; if the data have a positive (or negative) slope, then so will the estimated quadratic function be over the observed range of data.

The second concern is that the quadratic form requires estimating an additional parameter, thus reducing the degrees of freedom of the estimation, and reducing the power of the estimates. The third concern is that the changing slope makes it more difficult to talk about what the marginal cost really is. If we estimate a linear functional form and get $\hat{\beta}_1 = 12$, then we can say "The estimated marginal cost of generating one more unit of output is $12." But if we estimate the quadratic functional form and get $\hat{\beta}_1 = 10$ and $\hat{\beta}_2 = 0.1$, then

---

[4] This is, however, one of many reasons why econometricians should be careful not to extrapolate results too far outside the sample range of the data set. If one tried to predict the marginal cost for a firm much larger than those shown in the data, a result like the right-hand side of Figure 9.4 would produce a negative prediction for a sufficiently large quantity of output.

no such simple statement is possible. About the best we can say is something like "The marginal cost is $10 when the firm produces no output, and it rises by $1 for each 10 additional units of output. When the firm produces 10 units of output, the marginal cost is $11; when it produces 20 units of output, the marginal cost is $12; when it produces 50 units of output, the marginal cost is $15, and so forth." Of course, if the marginal cost of output really does vary as the amount of output varies, and if our economic question requires us to deal with that variation, then we have no choice but to estimate the quadratic cost function. But it makes the task of explaining the results more difficult and, for that reason, should be avoided unless we believe that the quadratic regression will fit the data significantly better. Of course, if we try the quadratic term in the equation and find that $\hat{\beta}_2$ is statistically significantly different from 0, then we have no choice; we must keep the quadratic term in the equation and cannot drop it out to get back to the linear functional form. If we did, we would be imposing an inaccurate restriction on the equation and violating assumption A1 of the classical regression model.

9.3 MORE COMPLICATED CHANGES IN COSTS: INTERACTION TERMS

Lack of flexibility is not, unfortunately, the only problem with the linear cost function. As noted above, the linear cost function suggests that dC/dP_1, the increase in total costs that occurs when a price rises, is just β_3. This is also a constant that doesn't vary with the price, or with the amount of output made. That seems unlikely. If a firm is producing a large amount of output, then it is using a large amount of each input, and a price rise should increase its costs by a lot, whereas if it is making a small amount of output and using a small amount of each input, then a price increase should have a smaller effect on total costs. Also, in the linear function form, the marginal cost β_1 doesn't depend on the prices of the inputs. Even in the quadratic form, the marginal cost ($\beta_1 + 2\beta_2 Q_i$) still doesn't depend on the prices of the inputs. That seems unlikely too; if you have to buy more coal to produce one more kilowatt of electricity, then the higher the price of coal is, the higher the marginal cost should be. If we are willing to accept a more complicated functional form, then we might try something like this:

$$C_i = \beta_0 + \beta_1 Q_i + \beta_2 Q_i^2 + \beta_3 P_{1i} Q_i + \beta_4 P_{2i} Q_i$$
$$+ \cdots + \beta_{K+2} P_{Ki} Q_i + \varepsilon_i \tag{9.3.1}$$

Now, when we take the derivative of total costs with respect to Q, while holding all the prices constant,[5] we get the marginal cost

$$MC = \beta_1 + 2\beta_2 Q_i + \beta_3 P_{1i} + \beta_4 P_{2i} + \cdots + \beta_{K+2} P_{Ki} \tag{9.3.2}$$

which has the advantage that a change in any input price, as well as a change in quantity, will cause the marginal cost to change. This happens because, when we take the derivative of total costs with respect to Q; the term $\beta_3 P_1 Q_i$ in the original cost function produces a term $\beta_3 P_{1i}$ in the marginal cost function.

---

[5] If you have studied partial derivatives, then you may recognize that what we are taking here is really the partial derivative of C with respect to Q, which we would write as $\partial C/\partial Q$.

Definition 9.3 A term in a functional form that is the product of two variables is called an *interaction term* between the two variables. The functional form

$$Y = \beta_0 + \beta_1 X_1 + \beta_2 X_2 + \beta_3 X_1 X_2 \qquad (9.3.3)$$

contains an interaction term between X_1 and X_2. An interaction term guarantees that the derivative of Y with respect to one variable will depend on the other.

The interaction terms in Equation 9.3.1 permit the marginal cost to depend on each price. Since higher prices should lead to higher marginal costs, we would expect $\beta_3 > 0, \beta_4 > 0, \ldots \beta_{K+2} > 0$. They also take care of the problem of costs changing with price. In this functional form, if P_1 rises by \$1, then total costs rise by $\beta_3 Q$. If $Q = 0$, then an increase in P_1 has no effect on costs. This is exactly what we would expect; if we are not making any output, then a rise in the price of an input should not affect costs because we're not buying any inputs. Further, since we expect $\beta_3 > 0$, the more output we're making, the larger the effect of a price increase on costs will be; and that is exactly as we expect. This functional form, containing interaction terms, does a better job of matching our expectations about what the cost function should look like than the linear or quadratic functional forms do, and therefore is more likely to satisfy assumption A1—that we are estimating the correct functional form—and more likely to produce unbiased and consistent estimates of the true cost function.

9.4 A BRIEF HISTORY OF ELECTRICITY COST ESTIMATION

As with production functions, economists like to talk about elasticities when they discuss cost functions. One difficulty with all of the above functional forms is that they produce relatively messy expressions for the elasticity of costs with respect to output. In general, the elasticity of cost with respect to output can be found from

$$\varepsilon_Q = \frac{dC}{dQ} \cdot \frac{Q}{C} \qquad (9.4.1)$$

In the case of the linear functional form, Equation 9.2.1, this works out to

$$\varepsilon_Q = \beta_1 \frac{Q_i}{C_i} \qquad (9.4.2)$$

For the quadratic and interaction functional forms, the formulas are more complicated still. One solution is to do as we did in Chapter 8 and use the Cobb-Douglass functional form for the cost function:

$$Y_i = A \cdot Q_i^{\beta_1} \cdot P_{1i}^{\beta_2} \cdot P_{2i}^{\beta_3} \cdot \cdots \cdot P_{Ki}^{\beta_{K+1}} \qquad (9.4.3)$$

and again take logarithms on both sides to get a functional form that is linear in the βs:

$$\log Y_i = \beta_0 + \beta_1 \log Q_i + \beta_2 \log P_{1i} + \beta_3 \log P_{2i}$$
$$+ \cdots + \beta_K \log P_{Ki} \qquad (9.4.4)$$

which has the simple elasticity $\varepsilon_Q = \beta_1$. One of the first econometric studies of the electric power industry, Nerlove (1963), used this functional form. This functional form is called the *log linear functional form,* or *linear in logs.*

However, a drawback to this functional form is that it requires the elasticity of scale to be constant at all points on the cost curve. If the cost function has this functional form, then

FIGURE 9.6
Average Cost
Curve Shapes

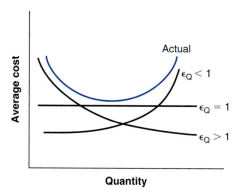

average costs must be everywhere falling (if $\varepsilon_Q < 1$), everywhere rising (if $\varepsilon_Q > 1$), or flat (if $\varepsilon_Q = 1$), as shown in Figure 9.4. However, this is not the shape of average cost curves that economic theory suggests, because of fixed costs and decreasing marginal product of the inputs. Real production processes tend to have falling average costs at low levels of output (because the fixed costs are distributed over more and more units of output) and rising average costs at high levels of output (because decreasing marginal product becomes more important). This causes the average cost curve to take a U-shape, as shown in red in Figure 9.6. The log-linear functional form cannot take this shape; it can rise or fall, but not both. This means that the log-linear functional form is not likely to be the true relationship of the data generating process and therefore violates assumption A1 of the classical regression model. Recognizing this, Nerlove estimated his cost function on five subsets of his data: the smallest 20 percent, the next smallest 20 percent, and so on up to the largest 20 percent. In this way, he could allow the curve to bend in one direction for small firms and in another direction for large firms, as theory predicts—and indeed he did find that the curve got flatter as firms got larger. However, he had to estimate five regressions instead of one; each regression had only one-fifth the number of observations of the whole data set and hence was much less powerful for estimating the parameters of the equation.

Christiansen and Greene (1976) proposed to add quadratic terms and interaction terms to the log-linear functional form to allow the elasticities of scale to vary with Q:

$$\log Y_i = \beta_0 + \beta_1 \cdot \log Q_i + \beta_2 \cdot \log Q_i^2 + \sum_{i=1}^{K} \beta_{3k} \cdot \log P_{ki}$$

$$+ \sum_{k=1}^{K} \beta_{4k} \cdot \log Q_i \cdot \log P_{ki} + \sum_{j=1}^{K}\sum_{k=1}^{K} \beta_{5jk} \cdot \log P_{ji} \cdot \log P_{ki} + \varepsilon_i \qquad \textbf{(9.4.5)}$$

This functional form, which has a large number of parameters to estimate but which is very flexible, is called the *translog functional form* and is widely used in econometrics. In the translog functional form, the elasticity of scale is

$$\varepsilon_Q = \beta_1 + 2 \cdot \beta_2 \cdot \log Q_i + \sum_{k=1}^{K} \beta_{4k} \cdot \log P_k \qquad \textbf{(9.4.6)}$$

The important parameter, economically speaking, is β_2. We expect $\varepsilon_Q < 1$ for low levels of output, but $\varepsilon_Q > 1$ for high levels of output. This is possible if β_2 is positive; then ε_Q will rise as Q gets larger. If so, the average curve will start with a region of falling costs, pass through a flat point where $\varepsilon_Q = 1$, and then rise again, matching the expected shape shown in red in Figure 9.4. The translog is plausibly the true relationship between costs and output, and therefore it is more likely to satisfy least squares assumption A1 than the other functional forms are. The translog also has the advantage that the elasticity of scale can vary with the input prices, although it is less clear economically that this should be the case.[6]

Christiansen and Greene estimated a translog cost function for the electric power industry, using Nerlove's original data from 1955, and updated data from 1970. Their estimate for β_2 was 0.079 with a standard error of 0.01. The t test for the hypothesis that $\beta_2 = 0$ has a t statistic of 7.96; they rejected the hypothesis that returns to scale were constant in the industry. They concluded, on the basis of this and other results, that the average cost curve did indeed take the expected U shape; returns to scale were initially increasing, but reached a point, around 20 or 30 billion kilowatt-hours, where returns to scale began to decrease. They found that in 1955, most of the firms were producing a quantity of output where the average costs were still falling, although some of the largest firms had reached the bottom of the curve. However, by 1970 almost half of the firms were on the flat part of the average cost curve, and the largest firm was well up onto the rising part of the average cost curve. From this they concluded that the industry could support a relatively large number of firms and that economies of scale were not a reason to resist policies to promote competition in the industry.

9.5 SOME ADDITIONAL USEFUL FUNCTIONAL FORMS

There are a few other functional forms that are commonly used in econometric analysis, either because they have useful economic interpretations or because they take shapes that quadratic and translog functions cannot. Consider the *semilog functional form,* so called because it has logs on one side of the equation but not the other:

$$\log Y = \beta_0 + \beta_1 X_1 + \beta_2 X_2 + \varepsilon \qquad (9.5.1)$$

This functional form takes the shape shown in Figure 9.7. It is similar to a quadratic functional form, but it slopes upward everywhere; its slope is given by

$$\frac{dY_i}{dX_{1i}} = \beta_1 Y_i \qquad (9.5.2)$$

which is always positive, though it gets closer and closer to 0 (the curve gets flatter and flatter) as X_i gets larger. However, this is not the primary reason to use it. The major advantage of the semilog functional form is the interpretation of the β_1 and β_2 parameters, which is: A one-unit increase in X_1 (or X_2) will result in a percentage increase of $\beta_1 \cdot 100$ percent (or $\beta_2 \cdot 100$ percent) in Y. That is, if we have

$$\log Y = 2.2 + 0.1 X_1 + 0.25 X_2 + \varepsilon \qquad (9.5.3)$$

---

[6] Of course, if it is not, the regression can always choose $\beta_{4k} = 0$ and eliminate the possibility. We can even test whether this is the case or not if we are interested in the economic question of whether the efficient scale of the firm changes as input prices change.

FIGURE 9.7

Shape of the Semilog Functional Form

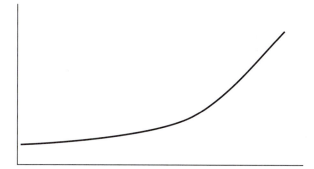

then a one-unit increase in X_1 causes Y to rise by 10 percent, and a one-unit increase in X_2 causes Y to rise by 25 percent. This is useful in cases where the dependent variable Y has a very large range, and one would not expect a change in X to have the same (absolute) effect for observations with small values of Y as it does for ones with large values of Y. For example, the semilog functional form is often used in regressions with wages, salaries, or incomes on the left-hand side, because of the wide variation of those variables in the actual population. Consider the economic model

$$\text{Salary} = f(\text{Education, Experience, Gender}) \qquad \textbf{(9.5.4)}$$

where we might be interested in testing whether or not gender affects a person's salary (perhaps because of gender discrimination in the labor market) but where we know that we must control for differences in education and experience among different workers—those with more education and experience will earn more, all else being equal.

We would not expect an additional year of experience to have the same effect on the salaries of all workers. Consider a professional athlete who, with one year of experience in his or her sport, earns $2 million a year; consider also a worker who sells popcorn during the game, also with one year of experience, who might earn $10,000 a year. An additional year of experience will raise the athlete's salary by considerably more than it will raise the popcorn seller's salary. If we estimated a linear functional form:

$$\text{Salary} = \beta_0 + \beta_1 \text{Educ} + \beta_2 \text{Exp} + \beta_1 \text{Gender} + \varepsilon \qquad \textbf{(9.5.5)}$$

and got an estimated value of, say, $\hat{\beta}_2 = \$20,000$, then we would have to conclude that an additional year of experience increased salary by $20,000. For the athlete, this would seem too small, as it would imply a rise from $2 million to only $2.02 million. For the popcorn seller, it would seem much too large, as it would imply a rise from $10,000 to $30,000, which is absurd. But any estimate we might get for $\hat{\beta}_2$ would be just as bad; no matter what it was, it would be much too small for the athlete, much too large for the popcorn seller, or both.

We would do much better to use the semilog functional form to construct the econometric model:

$$\log \text{Salary} = \beta_0 + \beta_1 \text{Educ} + \beta_2 \text{Exp} + \beta_3 \text{Gender} + \varepsilon \qquad \textbf{(9.5.6)}$$

In this case, we might get an estimate around $\hat{\beta}_2 = 0.05$. This would imply that an additional year's experience adds $(0.05 \cdot 100) = 5\%$ to one's salary, and 5 percent of the

FIGURE 9.8
Shape of the Reciprocal Functional Form

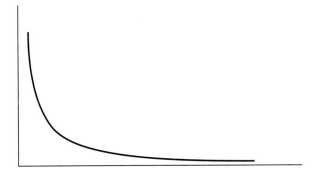

athlete's salary is much larger than 5 percent of the popcorn seller's salary. The athlete's salary would rise by $100,000, to $2.1 million, but the popcorn seller's salary would rise by only $500, to $10,500. Both of these numbers seem reasonable. The semilog functional form produces much more plausible predictions and is therefore much easier to interpret in sensible ways.

Another useful functional form is the *reciprocal functional form:*

$$Y = \beta_0 + \beta_1 \frac{1}{X_1} + \varepsilon \qquad (9.5.7)$$

The primary reason to use the reciprocal functional form is its shape, which is shown in Figure 9.8. It is downward-sloping (assuming $\beta_1 > 0$) but, since $1/X_1$ cannot be negative, it cannot go below β_0; as long as β_0 is positive, it cannot cross the horizontal axis. This is useful for estimating curves that must stay above the horizontal axis, such as demand curves.[7] If one estimated a linear demand curve:

$$P = \beta_0 + \beta_1 Q + \varepsilon \qquad (9.5.8)$$

then at any quantity greater than (β_0/β_1), the predicted market price would be negative.

A reciprocal functional form

$$P = \beta_0 + \beta_1 \frac{1}{Q} + \varepsilon \qquad (9.5.9)$$

is guaranteed to predict a market price greater than β_0 no matter how large the quantity gets and, if $\beta_0 > 0$, is guaranteed to predict a positive quantity. However, the reciprocal functional form can be awkward to interpret because it does not have a constant slope, constant elasticity, or other useful properties. For this reason it is not as widely used as those functional forms that do have economic interpretations of their shapes.

There are many other functional forms that one can use. The functional forms available to the econometrician are limited only by the mathematical creativity of the econometrician in constructing equations and by the patterns of the data. If one has stringent economic beliefs about the shape of the economic function, or if one has data that take an odd shape,

---

[7] If $\beta_1 < 0$, then the reverse is true; the curve is always positively sloped but cannot rise above β_0. This shape is less useful in economic applications, however.

then one may need a functional form much more complicated than the ones presented in this chapter to meet one's needs. However, no matter what functional form one chooses, two things remain true: One must be able to give an economic interpretation of the parameters when estimated, and the more parameters one uses, the fewer degrees of freedom one has to estimate them. For this reason, simpler functional forms are generally preferable to more complicated ones, as long as they are complicated enough to conform to economic theory about the shape of the curve and to fit the data well. Within those guidelines, the choice of functional form is up to the researcher and is one of the factors that make econometric analysis something of an art rather than a purely automatic technique.

However, one has to be careful about trying too many different functional forms. Because of the error terms, the location of the data points are random; they are likely, by coincidence, to fall into some sort of pattern. If an econometrician tries many different functional forms for an econometric model, looking for one that produces an estimated parameter significantly different from 0, sooner or later one will turn up, just by coincidence. The econometrician would then conclude that the relationship in the data was caused by the underlying economic model, when it was not; it was just caused by the random pattern the data happen to fall into.

This sort of thing can happen even if the econometrician uses only one or two functional forms. But it's not very likely that the data would, coincidentally, fall into exactly that one or two functional forms. However, if we try 5 or 10 or 20 different functional forms, then the odds that we will run into a coincidental pattern rise, and such a pattern can lead us to false conclusions about the underlying economics. It is therefore best to choose a small number of functional forms to try, according to an economic theory of what patterns the data ought to contain. If they do not, then the theory is probably wrong, and one should draw that conclusion rather than keep trying more and more functional forms until one happens to match your prior expectations.

Chapter Review	
Chapter Review	• A regression equation can be estimated with many different functional forms. Economic theory will often suggest shapes and properties that a functional form for an estimation should have.

Chapter Review

- A regression equation can be estimated with many different functional forms. Economic theory will often suggest shapes and properties that a functional form for an estimation should have.

- The data may also require that the functional form take particular shapes to fit the observations well.

- When comparing two functional forms, the first form is more *flexible* than the second form if the first form can take all the shapes the second form can take, plus additional shapes the second form cannot. More flexible functional forms will always fit the data better (have a lower SSR) than less flexible functional forms.

- *Quadratic* terms of the form βX_1^2 permit the marginal effect of an independent variable X_1 on the dependent variable Y to rise or fall as X_1 changes.

- *Interaction* terms of the form $\beta X_1 X_2$ permit the marginal effect of one independent variable on the dependent variable Y to rise or fall as the other independent variable changes.

- A *translog* functional form permits elasticities to vary as the independent variables vary; it is a highly flexible functional form that is widely used in studies of production and cost functions.

- The *semilog* functional form, with log Y as the dependent variable, permits a one-unit rise in a dependent variable X_1 to cause a percentage change in Y, and is useful where percentage changes in Y are economically more plausible than unit changes in Y are.
- The *reciprocal* functional form, with $1/X_1$ as the independent variable, guarantees that the function stays above a lower bound (or below an upper bound), and is useful for estimating economic functions that are constrained to be positive (or, less often, constrained to be negative).

Computer Exercise

In this exercise we'll generate data using a true model that is quadratic in one variable and linear in another, and see how well different functional forms estimate the true model.

1. Start Eviews, and create a new worksheet, undated, with 100 observations.

2. On the command line, type genr x1=rnd()*10 to get a randomly generated independent variable. Then type genr x2=rnd()*10 to create a second one. Last, type genr x1sq=x1*x1 and genr x2sq=x2*x2 to get quadratic terms for X_1 and X_2.

3. Type genr err=rnd()*20–10 to produce some error terms. Then type genr y=10+5*x1– 10*x2+ 2*x2sq +err to create a dependent variable. In this model, $\beta_0 = 10$, $\beta_1 = 5$, $\beta_2 = -10$, and $\beta_3 = 2$. Note that this true model is quadratic with respect to X_2 but is linear with respect to X_1, because we didn't include x1sq in the equation that generates Y.

4. Type scat x1 y to create a graph with Y on the vertical axis and X_1 on the horizontal axis. Does it look linear, or does it appear to curve?

5. Type scat x2 y to create a graph with Y on the vertical axis and X_2 on the horizontal axis. Does it look linear, or does it appear to curve? Click on the Options button, and turn on the Regression Line option. Where are the data above the regression line through this plot? Where are they below the line?

6. First, let's estimate this model using (incorrectly) a purely linear functional form. Type ls y c x1 x2 to regress y on only the linear terms. What is the sum of squared residuals for this model? How large is the standard error of the regression? Is the estimated value for β_1 significantly different from the true value of 5? Is the estimated value for β_2 significantly different from the true value of -10?

7. Next, let's try adding an (inappropriate) quadratic term for X_1, to see what happens. Type ls y c x1 x1sq x2 to run this regression. Is the parameter on x1sq significantly different from 0 or not? How much has the SSR dropped? How has the SER changed?

8. Instead, let's add the quadratic term on the correct variable, X_2. Type ls y c x1 x2 x2sq to run this regression. Is the parameter on x2sq significantly different from 0 or not? How much has the SSR dropped? How has the SER changed? Is it significantly different from its true value of 2? Look at the estimated value of β_2. Is it significantly different from -10 now?

9. Type ls y c x1 x1sq x2 x2sq to run a regression with both quadratic terms. Now is the parameter on x1sq significantly different from 0 or not? How much has the SSR dropped? How has the SER changed? Are the parameters on x2 and x2sq still taking the correct values?

Problems

1. Open the data file buscost, which is described in problem 5 in Chapter 6. Estimate the following linear cost function: $\text{Totalcost}_i = \beta_0 + \beta_1 \text{RVM}_i + \varepsilon_i$.

   a. What is the estimated marginal cost of providing one more RVM of output?

   b. What is the estimated elasticity of cost with respect to output when the firm produces 2,000 units of output? (Elasticity is equal to marginal cost, multiplied by output and divided by total cost. You will need to calculate the predicted value of total costs when output is equal to 2,000.) What is it when the firm provides 5,000 units of output? Is the elasticity constant or not?

   c. Generate the variables logtcost and logrvm, which are the logs of Totalcost and RVM, respectively, and estimate the log-linear cost function: $\log \text{Tcost}_i = \gamma_0 + \gamma_1 \log \text{RVM}_i + \varepsilon_i$. What is the estimated elasticity of cost with respect to output when the firm provides 5,000 units of output? Is it constant or not?

   d. How different are the results using the two different functional forms? Does one seem better and, if so, which?

2. Open the data file buscost, which is described in problem 5 in Chapter 6. Generate a quadratic term rvm2, which is equal to the square of RVM. Estimate the quadratic cost function $\text{Totalcost}_i = \beta_0 + \beta_1 \text{RVM}_i + \beta_2 \text{RVM}_i^2 + \varepsilon_i$.

   a. Find an expression for the marginal cost as a function of output, and graph it on a graph with Output on the horizontal axis and marginal cost on the vertical axis. Is your graph rising or falling as output rises?

   b. What is the estimated marginal cost of producing one additional unit of output when RVM = 5,000?

   c. Test whether marginal costs are constant against the alternative hypothesis that they are rising. What do you find?

   d. Is there a quantity of output at which we would predict marginal costs to be equal to 0? If there is, find it. If there is not, explain why not.

3. Open the data file buscost, which is described in problem 5 in Chapter 6. Generate the variables logtcost and logrvm, which are the logs of Totalcost and RVM, respectively, and then generate a quadratic term log2rvm, which is equal to $\log \text{RVM}^2$. Estimate the log-quadratic cost function $\log \text{Tcost}_i = \beta_0 + \beta_1 \log \text{RVM}_i + \beta_1 (\log \text{RVM}_i)^2 + \varepsilon_i$.

   a. Find an expression for the elasticity of total cost with respect to output. Does elasticity appear to rise or fall as output rises?

   b. What is the estimated elasticity when RVM = 5,000?

   c. Test whether the elasticity is constant as output rises against the null hypothesis that it is changing (in either direction). What do you conclude?

   d. Find the point at which the estimated elasticity is equal to 1. Find a value of output for which the cost function has increasing returns to scale, and one for which it has decreasing returns to scale.

   e. Find the average firm size in the data. Would you characterize an average-sized firm as a natural monopoly, or not? (That is, would two firms half the size have higher costs or lower costs?)

4. Open the file buscost2, which contains six variables describing the operation of 246 bus companies in U.S. cities: Totalcost is the total operating expense of the company, in

thousands of dollars; RVM is the total output of the firm, in thousands of revenue vehicle miles; Plabor and Padmin are the prices of driver labor and administrative labor, respectively, in dollars per hour; Pmaint is the price of maintenance service in dollars per hour; and Pfuel is the price of diesel fuel in dollars per gallon. Generate new variables for the logarithms of total cost, RVM, and all four of the price variables. On the basis of the economic model of a Cobb-Douglass cost function $TC = K \cdot P_L^{\beta_1} \cdot P_A^{\beta_2} \cdot P_M^{\beta_3} \cdot P_F^{\beta_4} \cdot RVM^{\beta_5}$, estimate the equation $\log Tcost_i = \beta_0 + \beta_1 \log P_{Li} + \beta_2 \log P_{Ai} + \beta_3 \log P_{Mi} + \beta_4 \log P_{Fi} + \beta_5 \log RVM_i + \varepsilon_i$.

a. What are your estimates for the elasticity of costs with respect to each price? Are they significantly different from 0 or not? If they are, do they take the sign you would expect them to take, or not?

b. What is your estimate for the elasticity of output? Does it suggest decreasing or increasing returns to scale? Test whether the elasticity is equal to 1 (i.e., constant returns to scale) or not.

c. Generate a quadratic term for the square of the log of output, and estimate the equation $\log Tcost_i = \beta_0 + \beta_1 \log P_{Li} + \beta_2 \log P_{Ai} + \beta_3 \log P_{Mi} + \beta_4 \log P_{Fi} + \beta_5 \log RVM_i + \beta_6 (\log RVM_i)^2 + \varepsilon_i$. Find an expression for the elasticity of costs with respect to output. Test whether that elasticity is constant or not.

d. According to the regression in part c, is the elasticity of cost with respect to price constant or not? Briefly explain why.

5. Open the file buscost2, which is described in problem 4. Estimate the equation $\log Tcost_i = \beta_0 + \beta_1 \log P_{Li} + \beta_2 \log P_{Ai} + \beta_3 \log P_{Mi} + \beta_4 \log P_{Fi} + \beta_5 \log RVM_i + \varepsilon_i$, generating the necessary variables to do so.

a. Economic theory suggests that if bus firms are cost-minimizers, then if all prices rise by the same percentage, then total costs should rise by the same percentage. This implies that $\beta_1 + \beta_2 + \beta_3 + \beta_4 = 1$. Test this null hypothesis. Do you reject, or fail to reject?

b. This equation might not be correctly specified if the elasticity of total costs with respect to output is not constant. Generate the quadratic term for log RVM, and estimate the equation $\log Tcost_i = \beta_0 + \beta_1 \log P_{Li} + \beta_2 \log P_{Ai} + \beta_3 \log P_{Mi} + \beta_4 \log P_{Fi} + \beta_5 \log RVM_i + \beta_6 (\log RVM_i)^2 + \varepsilon_i$. Again test the null hypothesis $\beta_1 + \beta_2 + \beta_3 + \beta_4 = 1$. Does the addition of the quadratic term to the cost function change the result?

6. Open the file wages1, which is described in problem 6 in Chapter 6. Estimate the equation $Wages_i = \beta_0 + \beta_1 Education_i + \varepsilon_i$.

a. If a person has an annual wage of $25,000 and his education increases by one year, what do you expect his new wage to be? If another person has an annual wage of $2 million and her education increases by one year, what do you expect her new wage to be?

b. Instead, estimate the equation using the semilog functional form: $\log Wages_i = \beta_0 + \beta_1 Education_i + \varepsilon_i$. If a person has an annual wage of $25,000 and gets one more year of education, by what percentage do you expect his wage to rise? What dollar amount is this? If a person has an annual wage of $2 million and gets one more year of education, by what dollar amount do you expect her wage to rise?

c. Which of the two functional forms gives more economically reasonable results? Briefly explain why.

7. Open the file wages1, which is described in problem 6 in Chapter 6. In this problem we'll add a quadratic term to the wage equation. Generate a quadratic term for education squared, and estimate the equation $\log \text{Wages}_i = \beta_0 + \beta_1 \text{Education}_i + \beta_2 \text{Education}_i^2 + \varepsilon_i$.

   a. Find an expression for the percentage increase in annual wage from a one-year increase in education. Graph this relationship on a graph with *Education* on the horizontal axis and *log Wages* on the vertical axis. By what percentage does wage increase if one's education increases from 4 years to 5? By what percentage does wage increase if one's education increases from 13 years to 14? Which is more valuable, the 5th year of a person's education or the 14th year?

   b. Test whether that expression is constant with respect to the amount of education or not. If it is not, does the return to education increase or decrease as the amount of education rises?

   c. Test whether $\beta_1 = 0$. Provide an economic interpretation of your finding.

   d. Test the joint hypothesis that $\beta_1 = 0$ and $\beta_2 = 0$. Does education affect wages or not?

8. Open the file cars, which contains quarterly observations from 1960 to 2002 on four variables: carexpend is annual expenditure on new automobiles, disposinc is disposable personal income, wages is wage and salary income, and dollarvalue is the value of the U.S. dollar against a basket of foreign currencies. The first three variables are measured in billions of dollars; the last is an index with 1997 value = 100. Economic theory suggests that consumption depends on income and prices. In this case, we expect that higher income will lead to greater spending on cars, and that a higher dollar value (which makes foreign automobiles less expensive domestically) will also lead to greater spending on cars.

   a. Estimate the regression $\text{Carexpend}_i = \beta_0 + \beta_1 \text{Disposinc}_i + \beta_2 \text{Dollarvalue}_i + \varepsilon_i$. Test whether $\beta_1 = 0$ and whether $\beta_2 = 0$. Are our expectations correct or not? How much does car expenditure rise when disposable income rises by \$1 billion?

   b. Perhaps it matters whether we include a quadratic term in the regression or not. Estimate the equation $\text{Carexpend}_i = \beta_0 + \beta_1 \text{Disposinc}_i + \beta_2 \text{Disposinc}_i^2 + \beta_3 \text{Dollarvalue}_i + \varepsilon_i$. Is the quadratic term significant, or not? When disposable income is equal to \$5,000, as it was in 1993, how much does car expenditure rise when disposable income rises by \$1 billion?

   c. Perhaps we would do better to use a log-log functional form so that we could talk about the income elasticity of automobile purchases. Estimate the equation $\log \text{Carexpend}_i = \beta_0 + \beta_1 \log \text{Disposinc}_i + \beta_2 \log \text{Dollarvalue}_i + \varepsilon_i$. In this functional form, are our expectations that higher income and higher dollar value will increase car expenditure correct? What is the income elasticity of car purchases?

   d. Perhaps this regression needs a quadratic term. Estimate the equation $\log \text{Carexpend}_i = \beta_0 + \beta_1 \log \text{Disposinc}_i + \beta_2 \log \text{Disposinc}_i^2 + \beta_3 \log \text{Dollarvalue}_i + \varepsilon_i$. Is the quadratic term significant, or not? When disposable income is equal to \$5,000, what is the income elasticity of car purchases?

   e. How different are the economic conclusions we would draw from these four regressions? Which of them do you prefer, and why?

   f. Perhaps disposable personal income is not the right way to measure income. Rerun the four regressions with wage income as the income measure. Does it make a difference? If so, how is it different?

Chapter **Ten**

Determining the Econometric Specification

Making profits on Wall Street is a bit like eating the stuffing from a turkey. Some higher authority must first put the stuffing into the turkey . . . One of the benevolent hands doing the stuffing belonged to the Federal Reserve. That is ironic, since no one disapproved of the excesses of Wall Street in the 1980s so much as the chairman of the Fed, Paul Volcker. At a rare Saturday press conference, on October 6, 1979, Volcker announced that the money supply would cease to fluctuate with the business cycle; money supply would be fixed, and interest rates would float. The event, I think, marks the beginning of the golden age of the bond man.

Michael Lewis

10.1 FINDING THE BEST REGRESSION EQUATION

In most cases, an economic model will suggest some general concepts that need to be included in a regression equation but will not suggest precise variables. For example, consider an economic model that determines the yield on corporate bonds in U.S. capital markets, which became a very interesting topic in October 1979. If the market is competitive (which is a pretty reasonable assumption), then a supply and demand model should be a good one for predicting prices and thus yields. Anything that affects the supply of bonds that corporations wish to sell on the market, or the demand of investors to buy them, should change the bond yield; increases in demand should lower yields, and increases in supply should raise them. As economists, we have some general idea about what sorts of things will change supply and demand. On the supply side, anything that increases the future prospects of the U.S. economy, and thus makes investment more attractive, will encourage companies to offer more bonds for sale. On the demand side, wealthier investors will want to buy more bonds, and the returns on alternative investments will also matter. When stocks or foreign assets offer higher returns, demand for U.S. corporate bonds will drop. All of these things will affect corporate bond yields and should be included in any regression that is interested in any one of those effects. A good understanding of the way bond yields move can be worth a lot in the bond-trading markets of the world.

Unfortunately, there are many different ways to measure those concepts with real economic data, and it's not clear which of the choices is the best. In measuring future economic prospects, should we look at gross domestic product (GDP)? At GDP growth? How about inflation rates, or price levels? Of course, those variables might affect demand for bonds also. On the demand side, how do we measure the attractiveness of alternative investments in stocks? Should we look at a narrow market measure like the Dow Jones Industrial Average or a broader measure like the Standard & Poor's (S&P) 500 index? Should we look at national income, personal income, after-tax income? We probably also need to see what is going on in other parts of the capital market. How much government debt is being floated? Does it matter how much new debt is being floated, or is the total debt outstanding the key variable? Economic theory doesn't do much to help us answer these questions; they are practical questions that require practical answers. Given that there are usually many different variables in the data that might capture any particular economic effect that interests us, we have to choose which of those variables we want to use in our regression analysis, and we'd like to allow the data to identify which variables work well, and which ones work poorly. This chapter presents the econometric techniques used to decide which variables belong on the right-hand side of an equation, the consequences of using the wrong variables, and ways to detect and rectify the problem.

For an initial regression explaining why bond yields are higher at some times than at others, we might try something like the following (rather large) regression:

$$
\begin{aligned}
\text{Bondyield} = \beta_0 &+ \beta_1 \text{GDP} + \beta_2 \text{RealGDP} + \beta_3 \text{Grossinv} + \beta_4 \text{Grosspdinv} \\
&+ \beta_5 \text{GDPdef} + \beta_6 \text{Inflation} + \beta_7 \text{Money} + \beta_8 \text{DowJones} + \beta_9 \text{SP500} \\
&+ \beta_{10} \text{NYSEvol} + \beta_{11} \text{SPdivyield} + \beta_{12} \text{Personalinc} + \beta_{13} \text{Nationalinc} \\
&+ \beta_{14} \text{Feddebt} + \beta_{15} \text{Pubheldfd} + \varepsilon
\end{aligned}
\qquad \textbf{(10.1.1)}
$$

The dependent variable, Bondyield, is the return on corporate bonds rated AAA investment grade. The first four variables on the right-hand side are intended to measure U.S. productivity: GDP is gross domestic product in nominal dollars, RealGDP is GDP in real dollars, Grossinv is gross investment in the U.S. economy, and Grosspdinv is gross private domestic investment. None of these variables really perfectly captures the notion of investment productivity that we're interested in, but all of them should be at least somewhat related to it; when expansion of the U.S. economy is profitable, GDP should go up, both in nominal and real terms, and investment should be high.

Definition 10.1 A *proxy variable* is one that we use as an independent variable in a regression, not because we believe it really directly affects the dependent variable, but because we can measure it and because we think it is related to another variable that does directly affect the dependent variable but that we can't measure.

In this case the four variables listed are intended as proxies for the desire of U.S. corporations to supply bonds to the U.S. market. They may or may not be very good ones, but they are at least easily obtained from public data sources and should capture the broad intention of including things that affect the supply side of the market for corporate bonds.

The next three variables on the right-hand side are intended to measure the effects of future inflation on the return to investment: GDPD is the GDP deflator, Inflation is the current (not future) inflation rate, and Money is the money supply.[1] Increases in any of these variables should suggest that inflation will be higher in the future, and proxy for the variable we'd really like to use, expectations of future inflation, which isn't measurable. The next four variables measure the effect of stock markets as alternative investments: Dowjones is the Dow Jones Industrial Average, and SP500 is the S&P 500 index. Higher values of these change the desirability of stock investments relative to bond investments, although not in predictable ways; higher values of stock prices may suggest increasing corporate value, or it may suggest that stocks are overpriced and will fall in the future. NYSEvol is the volume of shares traded on the New York Stock Exchange, and SPdivyield is the average dividend yield on S&P 500 firms. These suggest higher interest in the stock market and might be expected to drive down bond yields.

The last four variables have to do with the demand for investments as a whole: Personalinc and Nationalinc are personal and national income in the United States as a whole, Feddebt is the total amount of outstanding federal debt (a prime competitor for corporate debt in bond markets), and Pubheldfd is the amount of federal debt held by the U.S. public. Higher incomes should increase demand for investment in corporate bonds; higher federal debt may crowd out demand for corporate debt in the market.

Table 10.1 shows the results of estimating this equation, using a sample of quarterly observations from the first quarter of 1968 to the first quarter of 1998, 121 total observations. The results are not very good; although we have a high R^2 of 0.949, very few of the parameter estimates are significantly different from 0. Most have rather high standard errors, suggesting that we have estimated the effect of these variables rather poorly. Furthermore, many of the ones that are not statistically significantly different from 0 take unexpected signs, although because they are not significant, they have at least a 5 percent chance to take

TABLE 10.1
Results of Estimation of Equation 10.1.1

Variable	Parameter	Estimate	Standard Error	t Statistic for $\beta = 0$
Intercept	β_0	19.019	2.498	7.61
GDP	β_1	−0.0031	0.0031	−0.98
RealGDP	β_2	−0.5079	0.0764	−6.65
Grossinv	β_3	0.0025	0.0030	0.84
Grosspdinv	β_4	0.0045	0.0027	1.67
GDPdef	β_5	0.1954	0.0622	3.13
Inflation	β_6	−0.0170	0.0591	−0.28
Money	β_7	−0.0032	0.0013	−2.38
DowJones	β_8	−0.0008	0.0006	−1.36
SP500	β_9	−0.0071	0.0066	−1.08
NYSEvol	β_{10}	−0.00000414	0.0002	−0.02
SPdivyield	β_{11}	−0.4264	0.1470	−2.89
Personalinc	β_{12}	0.0055	0.0028	1.95
Nationalinc	β_{13}	0.0047	0.0028	1.65
Feddebt	β_{14}	0.0058	0.0028	2.09
Pubheldfd	β_{15}	−0.0145	0.0036	−4.07
$N = 121$	$R^2 = 0.949$		$SSR = 26.22$	$SER = 0.499$

[1] Several different measures of the money supply are possible; the definition used here is M2, which includes liquid noncash assets such as savings accounts and money market funds in addition to cash.

either sign and we should not attach any importance to the one they happen to take. For example, we would expect the parameter of the inflation variable, β_6, to take a positive sign rather than a negative one. Clearly we have picked a fairly poor way to represent this equation; we are including too many variables. On the one hand, we have some reason to believe that all of them might matter, at least indirectly. On the other hand, for each economic concept in our supply and demand model, we have two or three measured variables. These variables tend to be highly multicollinear, and they are probably insignificant because of the multicollinearity, not because they don't belong in the economic model. With only 121 observations, we are not going to be able to estimate 15 parameters very precisely. And worse, these are not the only variables we might have wanted to include in the model—it might be desirable to include a measure of exchange rates, for instance, to allow for the possibility that foreign demand for U.S. bonds might depend on the value of U.S. dollars overseas. How can we choose a better representation of this equation, from which we can draw economic conclusions that are more reliable than the ones from this regression will be?

Remember that we do not know, and can never know, the exact process that generated the data we are studying. Instead, we estimate a model of that process that describes it well, and we decide which model we prefer on the basis of its properties. The problem of selecting a good model is the problem of finding one with desirable properties; economically plausible, and with precise estimates of its parameters. Although there are some guidelines for doing that, and there are some mistakes to be avoided, the selection of the "best" regression equation to describe a particular data set remains somewhat subjective. Two reasonable economists might come to different conclusions about which regression is the best description of the data, depending on their prior expectations about what is economically important and the precise questions they want the regression to answer.

10.2 TO INCLUDE OR NOT TO INCLUDE A VARIABLE

Searching for the right specification involves deciding which variables to include in the regression and which ones to drop from it. There are two ways we can make a wrong decision—we can either drop a variable that we should have kept, or we can keep a variable that we should have dropped. In either case, ordinary least squares (OLS) is no longer the best linear unbiased estimator (BLUE) because we violate the first assumption of the Gauss-Markov theorem, which is that we have used the correct functional form the best linear unbiased estimator (BLUE). What does happen to OLS if we make this mistake, and is there an approach that minimizes the problems caused by OLS not being BLUE anymore?

Suppose we make the mistake of including a variable that does not belong in the regression. That is, suppose the true model is given by

$$Y = \beta_0 + \beta_1 X_1 + \beta_2 X_2 + \varepsilon \qquad \textbf{(10.2.1)}$$

but we mistakenly include an irrelevant variable; we estimate the regression

$$Y = \beta_0 + \beta_1 X_1 + \beta_2 X_2 + \beta_3 X_3 + \varepsilon \qquad \textbf{(10.2.2)}$$

The consequences of this are not so bad, because we can always rewrite the true model as if it were

$$Y = \beta_0 + \beta_1 X_1 + \beta_2 X_2 + 0 X_3 + \varepsilon \qquad \textbf{(10.2.3)}$$

where Equations 10.2.1 and 10.2.3 are in fact identical because the term $0X_3$ will cancel out of Equation 10.2.3, leaving us with Equation 10.2.1 exactly. In such a case we can say the following things:

Theorem 10.1 Suppose one mistakenly includes one or more irrelevant variables in a regression equation. Then, the following things are true:

1. $E(\hat{\beta}_i) = 0$ for every $\hat{\beta}_i$ that is a parameter on an irrelevant variable.
2. $E(\hat{\beta}_i) = \beta_i$ for every $\hat{\beta}_i$ that is a parameter on a relevant variable; that is, OLS remains unbiased.
3. OLS remains consistent also.
4. Unless the irrelevant variable is uncorrelated with all the other right-hand-side variables, OLS is no longer efficient; estimating the model without the irrelevant variable would produce smaller standard errors of the parameters on the variables that belong in the equation.

Intuitively, this occurs because if the truth is that, say, X_3 doesn't belong in the regression specification, then that is mathematically equivalent to allowing X_3 to enter the regression specification but with the true value of $\beta_3 = 0$. In such a case, OLS should pick $\hat{\beta}_3 = 0$ on average anyway, because OLS (on the correct specification) is unbiased. Furthermore, given an infinite amount of data, OLS will pick $\beta_3 = 0$ exactly, because OLS is consistent. However, in a finite sample of data, OLS will not pick $\hat{\beta}_3 = 0$ exactly, except by sheer coincidence: Even though the true β_3 is 0, OLS will pick an estimated $\hat{\beta}_3$ that is slightly higher or lower than 0, because OLS estimates are not equal to the true parameters. Although the estimated value of $\hat{\beta}_3$ should not be significantly different from 0, occasionally it will be, because the test is imperfect and may commit a Type 1 error. Even if $\hat{\beta}_3$ is not statistically significantly different from 0, its presence creates uncertainty about the effects of the other variables, which increases their standard errors. This causes OLS to become inefficient, with larger standard errors than we would get if we correctly realized that X_3 does not belong in the specification and therefore didn't include it, thus forcing OLS to implicitly pick $\hat{\beta}_3 = 0$ exactly (to cancel X_3 out of the equation).

Thus we see that including an irrelevant variable, although not desirable, is not all that bad. We still get correct estimates for the parameters of the model—they are just less well estimated than they could be. Furthermore, we can use the estimated value of $\hat{\beta}_3$ to test the hypothesis that $\beta_3 = 0$, and that test is a valid one. If we include an irrelevant variable in the model, we have the ability to detect our mistake by this test and correct it in the next version of the regression we run.

The same is not true if we fail to include a variable that we should include. That is to say, suppose the truth is

$$Y = \beta_0 + \beta_1 X_1 + \beta_2 X_2 + \varepsilon \qquad \textbf{(10.2.4)}$$

but we mistakenly omit the relevant variable X_2; we estimate the regression

$$Y = \beta_0 + \beta_1 X_1 + \varepsilon \qquad \textbf{(10.2.5)}$$

Now we have a problem, because X_2 really affects the value of Y, but our estimated regression has no way of accounting for that effect, because we didn't include X_2 in the specification.

Theorem 10.2 Suppose that one mistakenly omits one or more relevant variables in a regression equation and that the omitted variable is correlated with at least one of the included variables. Then the following things are true:

1. In general, $E(\hat{\beta}_i) \neq \beta_i$ for the parameters of every variable in the regression. The OLS estimators become biased. We say that the regression suffers from *omitted variable bias.*

2. OLS becomes inconsistent also; the estimated value for $\hat{\beta}$ does not become close to the true β as the sample size grows.

Omitting a relevant variable is much worse than including an irrelevant one, because the omission creates bias and inconsistency, whereas the irrelevancy creates inefficiency but preserves unbiasedness and consistency. With an included irrelevant variable, you still have good odds to get close to the right answer; with an omitted variable, you get the wrong answer on average, and adding data will not solve the problem. Worse, if you omit X_2 from the regression, you cannot estimate a value for $\hat{\beta}_2$, so you cannot do a test of whether $\beta_2 = 0$ or not. If you could, you could at least find that $\beta_2 \neq 0$ and you could detect the error; but with no value of $\hat{\beta}_2$ to use in the test, you have no way of proving that the variable you didn't include should have been included! Furthermore, you cannot even correctly test whether or not X_1 should be included in the model. Although you have an estimate for $\hat{\beta}_1$, it is biased and inconsistent, and so it can't tell you whether the true β_1 is equal to 0 or not. When there is omitted variable bias in a regression, it is very difficult to salvage anything from it.

Given these two facts, it is clearly better to put in too many variables than to put in too few, and we should use that knowledge when we search for the best specification for a regression. Thus, when we do not know exactly which variables belong on the right-hand side of the regression equation, it is best to start by using all of the possible right-hand-side variables (knowing that we are probably including irrelevant variables) and then test to see which variables can be dropped and which cannot, until we have eliminated as many variables as seems desirable. This way, at each step of the process (except for the specification of the initial model) every decision is justified by a statistical test, which produces a correct specification as long as the initial specification was acceptable. This is because an equation with too many variables is still an unbiased, consistent equation in which we can ask whether a particular variable should be dropped or not, and get the right answer.

The same is not true if we start with a small specification and work our way up. Suppose we start with a model such as Equation 10.2.4 and test to see whether a new variable, X_3, becomes significant when we add it to the equation. Suppose it does not; then we continue on and see if another new variable, X_4, becomes significant when we add it. Suppose it does; then we know that our regression needs to include X_4. We also learn, however, that our test of whether X_3 belongs in the model or not was invalid! This is because we have just shown that the regression containing only X_1, X_2, and X_3 suffers from omitted variable bias: It does not include the variable X_4, now known to be relevant, and therefore its estimate of the parameter on X_3 was biased and inconsistent. The test of whether that parameter is equal to 0 is therefore not a correct test of whether or not X_3 belongs in the equation. If we started with a small specification and added variables, then each time we added a variable to the regression we'd have to start over and retest every variable we previously had chosen not to add. Clearly, this is a very inefficient way of searching for a specification.

Starting with a large specification and dropping variables is not subject to this problem, because all the variables are used in the initial equation. There is no possibility of discovering omitted variable bias halfway through the process and needing to start over.[2] For this reason, starting with the largest possible specification is the accepted way to search for the correct specification of a regression model when there is uncertainty (as there almost invariably is) about which variables belong in the model and which do not.

There are, however, occasions when there is a variable that we strongly believe to be in the model but cannot measure in data. In such a case we cannot fix the omitted variable bias that is caused by omitting this variable. We can, however, say something about the likely size and direction of the bias so that we at least know in which direction the estimates we do get are likely to be off. Suppose that the true data generating process is

$$Y = \beta_0 + \beta_1 X_1 + \beta_2 X_2 + \varepsilon \qquad \text{(10.2.6)}$$

but because we are unable to measure X_2, we instead estimate the regression

$$Y = \beta_0 + \beta_1 X_1 + \upsilon \qquad \text{(10.2.7)}$$

where $\upsilon = \beta_2 X_2 + \varepsilon$, reflecting the fact that the variable we could not measure is now part of the error term in the regression we do estimate; it is one of the reasons why the data will not lie exactly along the line we estimate with the variables we have. Then we can say the following:

> **Theorem 10.3** Suppose that the data generating process is $Y = \beta_0 + \beta_1 X_1 + \beta_2 X_2 + \varepsilon$, but the econometric model omits X_2. If X_1 and X_2 are uncorrelated, OLS will provide unbiased and consistent estimates of β_1. But if X_1 and X_2 are correlated, OLS estimates of β_1 become biased and inconsistent.

This theorem tells us that omitted variables are not a problem as long as they are uncorrelated with the variables we do include in the regression. The regression that omits them is not as efficient as a regression that includes them, but since we cannot include them if we cannot measure them, the regression that omits them is the next best thing. Omitted variable bias is a problem only when the omitted variable is correlated with one or more of the right-hand-side variables in the regression.

We can even say something about the direction of the bias when it is not 0. Suppose that the true model is Equation 10.2.6, that X_1 and X_2 are positively correlated, and that $\beta_2 > 0$. Then, when X_1 is high, X_2 will tend to be high also because of the positive correlation between those two variables, and Y will tend to be high also because, when $\beta_2 > 0$, higher values of X_2 lead to higher values of Y. Then the data will look like Figure 10.1. In this case the estimated OLS line will tend to be steeper than the true line because it is pulled up by the unusually high errors when X_2 (and therefore Y) are high, and down when X_2 (and therefore Y) are low. OLS will produce a positive bias; it will, on average, estimate a $\hat{\beta}_1$ that is higher than the true β_1.

---

[2] It is, however, possible that there might be a relevant variable that was not included in the data set at all, in which case the first regression will suffer from omitted variable bias, and all subsequent ones will too. But no amount of testing can find an omitted variable that isn't in the data to begin with, nor can we include the variable even if we want to if we do not have data on it. We start with the largest regression we can estimate and then work our way down; if a relevant variable is unmeasurable, there is nothing we can do about it except to be careful in interpreting the estimates we get.

FIGURE 10.1
Effect of Omitted-Variable Bias

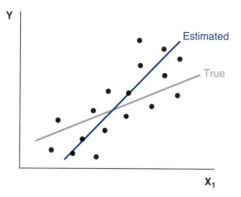

TABLE 10.2
Direction of Omitted Variable Bias in OLS

	X_1, X_2 Positively Correlated	X_1, X_2 Negatively Correlated
$\beta_2 > 0$	Bias is positive	Bias is negative
$\beta_2 < 0$	Bias is negative	Bias is positive

The reverse is true if $\beta_2 < 0$. In that case, when X_1 and X_2 are high, Y will be low, and conversely. The data will tend to lie below the line for high values of X_1 and above the line for low values of X_1, causing a negative bias; $\hat{\beta}_1$ will tend to be lower than the true β_1. And the bias reverses again if X_1 and X_2 are negatively correlated. In that case, high values of X_1 tend to have low values of X_2. If $\beta_2 > 0$, then high values of X_1 get low values of Y and we get a negative bias, or if $\beta_2 < 0$, then high values of X_1 get high values of Y and we get a positive bias. Table 10.2 shows the relationship between the correlation of X_1 and X_2, the sign of β_2, and the direction of the bias of OLS. And finally, if either $\beta_2 = 0$ (meaning X_2 doesn't belong in the regression after all) or if the correlation between X_1 and X_2 is 0 (meaning the υ error terms are uncorrelated with X_1), then the bias is 0 and OLS is an acceptable method of estimating β_1.

In practice, we can almost always imagine some variables that are not included in our data set, and thus not included in our regression, that might affect our dependent variable. Therefore, nearly all equations suffer, potentially, from omitted variable bias. In order to use OLS, we must hope that either the variables we omit do not have a very large effect on the dependent variable (so that we do not reject the hypothesis that their parameters are equal to 0) or that they are at least uncorrelated with the variables we use so that our estimated parameters remain unbiased.

10.3 IMPERFECT MULTICOLLINEARITY

As we search for the "best" specification, one thing that is clearly not desirable is to have a lot of parameter estimates with high standard errors. High standard errors mean low confidence about the true values of the parameters, and low confidence makes it hard to determine which variables belong in the regression and which do not. What causes high standard errors in a regression like the one shown in Table 10.1, and what can we do to reduce them?

TABLE 10.3
More Hypothetical Data on Exchange Rates

Year	Exchange Rate	Inflation Rate	Interest Rate
1990	2.5	8.0%	5%
1991	3.2	6.0	4
1992	2.7	8.0	5
1993	3.3	4.0	3
1994	2.1	10.0	6
1995	2.9	7.0	4
1996	3.6	2.5	2

High standard errors occur when it is difficult to tell from data whether an independent variable is having an effect on the dependent variable and, if so, how much of an effect. We have already seen, in Chapter 8, one case in which it is not just difficult but actually impossible to tell whether an independent variable is having an effect on the dependent variable: the case of perfect multicollinearity. If two variables move perfectly together, then it is impossible to know which of the two is affecting the dependent variable. For least squares estimation to work, we cannot have two perfectly multicollinear variables in the regression.

Suppose instead that the variables are not perfectly multicollinear but are quite close to it. That is, suppose we look at inflation rates and interest rates—but the data, shown in Table 10.3, are a little different than they were in Chapter 8. The relationship $2 \cdot$ interest rate $-$ inflation rate $= 2$ holds for the first five observations, but not for the last two; in 1995 the inflation rate was 7 percent rather than 6 percent, and in 1996 it was 2.5 percent rather than 2 percent. Technically, this is sufficient for us to be able to determine whether inflation rates or interest rates affect exchange rates. The variables are not in perfect proportion in the last two years, and we can see whether the changes in the exchange rate for those years are more closely aligned with the changes in the inflation rate or the changes in the interest rate.

However, while it will be possible to tell them apart, it won't be easy. Five of the seven observations in the data are not helpful in distinguishing the effects; only the last two are, and an unusual error term in one of those two years could cause us to make a wrong inference about which variable is driving the changes in interest rates.

Definition 10.2 When two variables move together closely, but not perfectly, they are *imperfectly multicollinear,* or just *multicollinear*. The more multicollinear two variables are, the harder it is to distinguish their effects on the dependent variable, and the larger the standard errors of the estimates of their parameters will be.

In the case of two variables, multicollinearity can be easily detected by looking at a scatterplot, or at the correlation coefficient, of the variables in question. If the variables are highly correlated, their correlation coefficient will be close to 1 (or close to -1 if their correlation is negative and they move oppositely) and they will be tightly grouped along a line in the plot. In the case of estimating Equation 10.1.1, that is the case for many of the variables on the right-hand side of the regression. Figure 10.2 shows a scatterplot of two of these variables, the Dow Jones Industrial Average and the S&P 500, which move very closely together over time, and whose effects are therefore almost impossible to distinguish. Similarly, Table 10.4 shows the correlation matrix of the four variables proxying for economic production; all of them are very highly correlated, and the multicollinearity among them is severe. All the correlations are at least 0.95, and some are as high as 0.99.

FIGURE 10.2
Scatterplot of Imperfectly Multicollinear Variables

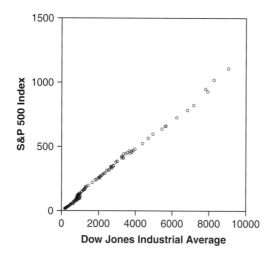

TABLE 10.4
Correlations between Four Productivity Measures

	GDP	RealGDP	Grossinv	Grosspdinv
GDP	1.000	0.957	0.993	0.990
RealGDP	0.957	1.000	0.973	0.963
Grossinv	0.993	0.973	1.000	0.996
Grosspdinv	0.990	0.963	0.996	1.000

When any one of these four variables rises, all four of them rise together, and usually in very similar (though not identical) proportion. For this reason it is extremely difficult to tell which of the four is "causing" changes in bond rates. The reality, of course, is that none of them is causing changes in bond rates by itself; all of them are different, imperfect ways of measuring the real economic effect at work, which is that highly productive economies offer better investment opportunities than less productive ones do. The solution is to not use all four of them, but rather to drop one or more of the ones whose parameters are not statistically significantly different from 0, thus eliminating the multicollinearity problem.

Which of the four variables should we drop and which should we retain? Unfortunately, that question does not have a single correct answer. Clearly, we must not drop RealGDP, which is statistically significantly different from 0 and belongs in the regression. Grosspdinv is not quite significant at the 5 percent level, but it is at the 10 percent level; we can drop it if we want to, but it might make some sense to keep it, at least initially, and see if it becomes significant when some other variables are dropped first. As for the other two, both are insignificant at all conventional significance levels, and there is no strong reason to prefer to drop one or the other on statistical grounds. At this point, economic judgment comes in. Do you have a reason, based on economic knowledge or intuition, to think that one variable is more likely to belong in the regression than another? Is one of them more important to the underlying economic theory than the other? If so, we had better retain that one and drop the other. We go through a similar process with each of the other groups of variables that we believe are related to each other. Each time we identify a variable, or group of variables, we want to drop, we perform the appropriate t test or F test to verify that dropping those variables is acceptable.

TABLE 10.5
Results of Reestimation of Equation 10.1.1 Dropping Insignificant Variables

Variable	Parameter	Estimate	Standard Error	t Statistic for $\beta = 0$
Intercept	β_0	21.085	1.540	13.69
RealGDP	β_2	−0.4969	0.0530	−9.37
Grossinv	β_3	0.0067	0.0021	3.15
Money	β_7	−0.0033	0.0007	−4.75
SP500	β_9	−0.0143	0.0012	−11.83
SPdivyield	β_{11}	−0.2632	0.1204	−2.18
Personalinc	β_{12}	0.0105	0.0008	11.87
Pubheldfd	β_{15}	−0.0086	0.0006	−15.05
$N = 121$	$R^2 = 0.943$		SSR = 29.81	SER = 0.514

Doing so might produce a final regression like the one in Table 10.5. We have dropped at least one variable from each of the four groups of variables, and we have retained at least one in each group, sometimes two. All the parameters now have lower standard errors than before, in some cases much lower. (For example, the standard error of $\hat{\beta}_{15}$ is now 0.0006, as opposed to 0.0036 in Table 10.1.) Almost all the t statistics are higher, though not all are; the t statistic on SPdivyield is now −2.18, whereas before it was −2.89. This happened because its parameter estimate dropped, from −0.4264 to −0.2632. Even though its standard error is now smaller, because it is closer to 0, it is fewer standard errors away from 0, giving it a lower t statistic. It does not really matter, however; it is greater (in absolute value) than the critical value of 1.98, so it remains statistically significant.

To verify that this regression is an acceptable simplification of the original one, we should do an F test to verify that collectively dropping the eight dropped variables is acceptable. The F statistic is

$$\frac{(29.807 - 26.223)/8}{26.223/105} = 1.79$$

and the 5 percent critical value for the F distribution with 8 restrictions and 105 degrees of freedom is 2.03. Because the F statistic of 1.79 is lower than 2.03, these restrictions are acceptable and we can proceed using the restricted model.

Clearly, the parameters of this model are much better estimated than the parameters in the original, larger regression. For the parameters that remain, we have much more precise estimates of their values; for the parameters that were dropped when their associated variables were dropped, we can be fairly certain that the true parameters are not statistically significantly different from 0, given our ability to estimate them in the face of the multicollinearity of the variables, and that it is acceptable to treat them as if they were 0. Note, however, that the R^2 of the regression has fallen; R^2 always falls when variables are dropped, because dropping variables cannot improve the fit of the model. It is, in fact, perhaps surprising that it has not fallen very much; it was 0.949 and is now 0.943, a very small change given that the regression is using less than half as many variables to predict bond yields as before. Similarly, the SSR and the standard error of the regression have risen, but not a great deal. We are much better off having more precise estimates of the parameters, whose values are typically what interests us, and accepting a slightly poorer fit of the model, than having a model that fits slightly better but having very little idea about the economic relationships that underlie that model.

FIGURE 10.3

Age, Income, and Price of First Home Purchase

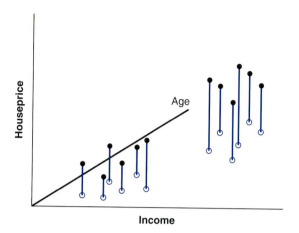

Unfortunately, not all multicollinearity is due to multiple measurements of the same underlying variable. Sometimes multicollinearity occurs because two conceptually separate economic variables happen, coincidentally, to be highly correlated. For a simple example, consider the following regression estimated on a sample of first-time home buyers:

$$\text{Houseprice} = \beta_0 + \beta_1 \text{Income} + \beta_2 \text{Age} + \varepsilon \qquad \textbf{(10.3.1)}$$

and suppose the data look like those in Figure 10.3. We would normally expect $\beta_1 > 0$, because buyers with greater incomes will be able to afford larger and more expensive homes. We would also expect $\beta_2 > 0$, because older first-time buyers are more likely to already have children or possessions, and need a larger and more expensive home. Because people's incomes rise with time, however, people who are older are likely to also have higher incomes, and therefore the Age and Income variables are likely to be multicollinear. The figure shows two groups of data points, one of younger and poorer buyers and one of older and richer buyers. It is clear that the older, richer group spends more on its first home purchase than the younger, poorer group. But it is impossible to tell whether age or income is responsible for the increase, because any buyer that has a high value of one has a high value of the other as well. Therefore, the standard errors of the estimated values for β_1 and β_2 will be high, and neither variable will be significantly different from 0. Clearly, there is some effect, but it is impossible to reject the null hypothesis that age is irrelevant (because maybe the effect is caused by income) or the null hypothesis that income is irrelevant (because maybe the effect is caused by age).

In this case, the problem can be solved in either of two ways. The best way is to collect some more data, observing some people who are young and rich, some who are old and poor, or both; observing these types of people will quickly clarify whether age or income is responsible for buying more expensive homes. The second way is to collect more data of the same type as before. Because age and income are not perfectly correlated, we can look at people who are just a little richer than their age suggests, or just a little younger than their income suggests, and distinguish the two effects. If we can observe enough people, we will eventually get one of the two variables (or even both) to be statistically significant, because larger samples produce more precise estimates of the parameters of the model and hence lower standard errors and higher t statistics. But if the correlation between age and income is high, it may take a lot of observations to achieve this, perhaps more than we can get. And it may also be impossible to find a sample of people for whom income and age are not correlated this way. Multicollinearity is, ultimately, a property of the sample, not of the estimation; the only way to eliminate it is to change the data sample. When that is possible, it is the right solution. When that is not possible, which is often the case, then we must accept that the data limits what we can learn about the underlying economic relationship. In a case like this we will be able to tell that age and income together have some effect on house purchases, but we will not be able to distinguish which of the two is the cause. We will have to draw the best economic conclusions we can in the face of this difficulty.

10.4   ECONOMIC INTUITION AND SPECIFICATIONS

Not all questions about specifications deal with whether or not to include certain variables. Many questions deal with the exact mathematical relationship to use when including variables in a regression. This section considers a variety of questions of that form and discusses ways to choose an appropriate specification based not on formal testing but rather on economic intuition about how variables ought to be related.

For example, we know that there is a relationship between unemployment and the money supply; an increase in the money supply tends to stimulate the economy, increase output, and reduce unemployment. We might be tempted to write a simple regression equation to represent this relationship:

$$\text{Unemployment}_t = \beta_0 + \beta_1 \text{Moneysupply}_t + \varepsilon_t \qquad \textbf{(10.4.1)}$$

expecting that β_1 will be negative; increasing the money supply will reduce unemployment. This is, however, unlikely to be the true long-term relationship between the two variables. The money supply tends to rise over time; in 1960 it was \$304 billion, but by 2000 it had risen to \$4.8 trillion, and as time passes it will undoubtedly rise higher yet. Equation 10.4.1 suggests that these two variables are linearly related—that as the money supply increases over time, the unemployment rate will increase with it. But we know that this is not so; the unemployment rate is a percentage, and it does not tend to increase over time. It is usually somewhere between 3 and 10 percent, and could not possibly rise over 100 percent or even get very close to it. Therefore, this specification for the regression equation, while mathematically possible, is economically implausible. Because the unemployment rate cannot consistently rise as the money supply does, this regression will tend to produce estimates of β_1 close to 0, and the larger the sample is, the closer to 0 the estimates will be, as the money supply rises more and more while unemployment doesn't.

Better is to calculate a new variable that is the change in the money supply (Changems) from the past year to the present:

$$\text{Changems}_t = \text{Moneysupply}_t - \text{Moneysupply}_{t-1} \qquad \textbf{(10.4.2)}$$

and write the regression as:

$$\text{Unemployment}_t = \beta_0 + \beta_1 \text{Changems}_t + \varepsilon_t \qquad \textbf{(10.4.3)}$$

because, while the money supply is steadily growing, the amount of its yearly change grows somewhat slower. This is known as taking the *difference* of the money supply (or to be more precise, the *first difference*) and using the differenced variable in the regression, producing a variable that is somewhat more comparable to unemployment than the original variable is. Of course, because the money supply, like most macro variables, tends to grow exponentially (by a certain percentage each year), even the annual changes in the money supply tend to get larger over time; in 1960 the money supply grew by $20 billion, but in 2000 it grew by $420 billion. Still better, perhaps, is to calculate the percentage change in the money supply (Pctchgms) in a given year:

$$\text{Pctchgms}_t = \frac{\text{Moneysupply}_t - \text{Moneysupply}_{t-1}}{\text{Moneysupply}_{t-1}} 100 \qquad \textbf{(10.4.4)}$$

and use that as the independent variable in the regression:

$$\text{Unemployment}_t = \beta_0 + \beta_1 \text{Pctchgms}_t + \varepsilon_t \qquad \textbf{(10.4.5)}$$

where the percentage change in the money supply is, like the unemployment rate, fairly stable over time; Figure 10.4 shows their values between 1960 and 2000. This relationship, because it regresses one percentage on another and conforms best to our prior economic knowledge about the behavior of the two variables, is probably the best one to use. (This is why the Okun's law example in Chapter 1 uses GDP growth rates, rather than GDP, as the variable in the Okun's law relationship.) Another alternative would be to use two variables that grow over time; for example, one could use the total number of unemployed people in the economy:

$$\text{Unemployed} = \beta_0 + \beta_1 \text{Moneysupply}_t + \varepsilon_t \qquad \textbf{(10.4.6)}$$

and this would also conform to our economic knowledge, since both variables may plausibly grow together over time. However, equations in which both variables grow together over time suffer from a different set of econometric problems, which we will discuss in Chapter 17.

Similar issues can arise when comparing cross-section observations of vastly different sizes. Suppose that we are interested in welfare spending by states and that we believe states with greater poverty should spend more on welfare. Then we might regress:

$$\text{Welfspend} = \beta_0 + \beta_1 \text{Poverty} + \varepsilon \qquad \textbf{(10.4.7)}$$

FIGURE 10.4
Money Supply Growth Rate and Unemployment Rate, 1960–2000

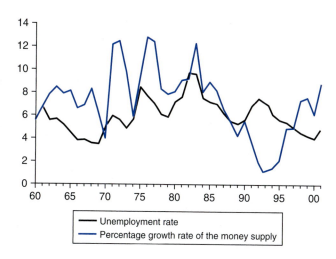

Unemployment rate
Percentage growth rate of the money supply

where Welfspend is a state's welfare spending and Poverty is the poverty rate in that state, expecting that $\beta_1 > 0$. However, poverty rates are expressed as percentages; California and Delaware might have similar poverty rates, but we would expect California to spend much more on welfare because its population is much larger and it has, all else equal, more households that qualify for welfare. We might allow for this by including population in the regression:

$$\text{Welfspend} = \beta_0 + \beta_1 \text{Poverty} + \beta_2 \text{Population} + \varepsilon \qquad \textbf{(10.4.8)}$$

but that may not capture the true relationship very well either. This suggests that a 1 percent increase in the poverty rate would increase welfare spending by β_1 in both California and Delaware, whereas we would expect a larger change in California. One option is to use, instead of the poverty rate, the number of households below the poverty line:

$$\text{Welfspend} = \beta_0 + \beta_1 \text{Poorhholds} + \varepsilon \qquad \textbf{(10.4.9)}$$

where California, the larger state, would tend to have more poor households. Another option is to use welfare spending per capita as the dependent variable:

$$\text{Welfspendpc} = \beta_0 + \beta_1 \text{Poverty} + \varepsilon \qquad \textbf{(10.4.10)}$$

where we might think that, if the poverty rates were the same, California might spend exactly the same amount per family as Delaware, and would spend more in total in exact proportion to the number of families in each state. Either Equation 10.4.9 or Equation 10.4.10 will probably work better than Equation 10.4.8, and any of these three will surely work better than Equation 10.4.7, which takes no account of this difficulty.

Even simpler than the question of whether or not to state variables in per capita terms is the question of what units to state them in. Should we state per capita welfare spending in dollars, hundreds of dollars, or thousands of dollars? If the poverty rate in our state is 15 percent, should we enter that as 15 in the data, or as 0.15? Since the choice of units for measuring our data is essentially arbitrary, it would be disturbing if the choice of units affected the regression results in some way. Fortunately, it does not, at least not in any meaningful way. Table 10.6 shows the effect of estimating Equation 10.4.10 on two different data sets. Data set A measures welfare spending in dollars and the poverty rate in percentage terms: for Illinois, welfare spending per capita is 602 (dollars) and the poverty rate is 11.6 (percent). Data set B measures welfare spending in thousands of dollars and the poverty rate in fractional terms: for Illinois, welfare spending per capita is 0.602 (thousand dollars) and the poverty rate is 0.116 (fraction of the population).

TABLE 10.6
Two Estimates of Equation 10.4.10

	Data Set A			Data Set B		
Variable	Parameter	Standard Error	t Statistic	Parameter	Standard Error	t Statistic
Intercept	484.4	106.6	4.544	0.4844	0.1066	4.544
POVERTY	8.671	8.042	1.078	0.8671	0.8042	1.078
	$R^2 = 0.02465$	SER $= 193.82$		$R^2 = 0.02465$	SER $= 0.19382$	

The parameter estimates are numerically different, but their economic meanings are identical. With data set A, we get an intercept of 484, measured in dollars, meaning that a state with 0 poverty would have welfare spending of $484 per capita. With data set B, we get an intercept of 0.484, measured in thousands of dollars, meaning that a state with 0 poverty would have welfare spending of $484 per capita, the exact same value. The slope estimates also have identical economic meanings. With data set A, the slope of 8.671 indicates that a 1 (percent) rise in poverty causes welfare spending to rise by $8.67 per capita. With data set B, a rise of 1 (fraction of the population) in poverty causes welfare spending to rise by 0.867 thousand dollars. A rise of 1 in the fraction of the population in poverty corresponds to going from no poverty to complete poverty; this is an absurdly large change. A more interesting rise of 0.01 in the fraction of the population in poverty (or 1 percent) corresponds to a rise of $0.01 \cdot 0.867 = 0.00867$ thousand dollars in welfare spending, which is of course just $8.67 per capita, the exact same answer as in data set A. The t statistics and R^2 are identical for the two regressions, and the standard errors of the regressions are identical also, since one represents $193 and the other represents 0.193 thousand dollars, which is again $193.

It doesn't matter in which units we choose to measure our variables; the economic answers will be the same either way, although the numerical estimates of the parameters will change. We choose units for our variables based on convenience, of two types. First, we should choose units that make the interpretation of the parameters easier. It is much more natural to talk about a poverty rate of 11.9 percent than to talk about a poverty rate of 0.119; percentage points are the appropriate unit for this variable. Second, we choose units that keep the β parameters in reasonable ranges. If we regress the prime interest rate on GDP, for example, and we measure GDP in dollars, we will find that a $1 increase in GDP causes the prime rate to rise by 0.00000000000093 percent. This is an accurate estimate (it's statistically significantly different from 0, with a t statistic of 4.91), but it's not a very useful number because a $1 change in GDP is so small as to be virtually meaningless. Better is to express GDP in hundreds of billions of dollars. Then we would estimate $\beta_1 = 0.093$, meaning that a hundred-billion-dollar rise in GDP would cause the prime rate to increase by about one-tenth of 1 percent. The choice of appropriate units for variables leads to reasonable ranges for the parameter estimates and makes the economic interpretation of the results considerably clearer.

Chapter Review

- Given an economic relationship, it is usually not apparent exactly how the regression equation that describes that relationship should be written. We must search for the best specification for the regression.

- We may have to choose one or more variables to serve as *proxies* for other variables we cannot include in the regression because we do not have data for them or because they are unmeasurable.

- Including an irrelevant right-hand-side variable in a regression causes OLS to become inefficient, but OLS remains unbiased and consistent.

- Omitting a relevant right-hand-side variable, in contrast, causes OLS to become biased and inconsistent.

- Because omitting a relevant variable is much worse than including an irrelevant one, we search for the correct specification by starting with the largest possible model and work our way down to the smallest acceptable specification.
- Two (or more) variables that are highly correlated, but not perfectly related, are called *multicollinear*. When variables are multicollinear, it is difficult to separate their effects on the dependent variable.
- When there are multicollinear variables in a regression, normally we must drop some of them in order to get precise estimates of the others.
- We can avoid dropping variables if we can either get sufficient data or collect observations that eliminate the multicollinearity of the variables, but this is not always possible.
- We must also be careful not to estimate regressions that imply implausible economic relationships. Using first differences of variables or measuring variables in percentage or per capita terms can change implausible equations into plausible ones.
- It does not matter what units we measure our variables in; normally, we choose units that keep the values of the β parameters in reasonable ranges.

Computer Exercise

In this exercise we'll look at the bias caused by an omitted right-hand-side variable and see how it distorts the results for the variables that are included in the regression.

1. Start Eviews, and create a new worksheet, undated, with 100 observations.
2. On the command line, type genr x1=rnd()*10 to get a randomly generated independent variable. Then type genr x2=rnd()*5 + 0.6*x1 to create a second one; X_1 and X_2 will be positively correlated.
3. Type genr err=rnd()*20–10 to produce some error terms. Then type genr y=10+ 5*x1+3*x2+ +err to create a dependent variable. In this model, $\beta_0 = 10$, $\beta_1 = 5$, and $\beta_2 = 3$.
4. Type scat x1 x2 to create a graph with X_2 on the vertical axis and X_1 on the horizontal axis. Do they move together? How strongly?
5. First, let's estimate this model using the correct specification that includes both X_1 and X_2. Type ls y c x1 x2. Is the estimated value for β_1 significantly different from the true value of 5? Is the estimated value for β_2 significantly different from the true value of 3?
6. Next, let's try omitting X_2 and see how the results change. Type ls y c x1 to run this regression. Now what estimate do you get for β_1? Is it significantly different from the true value of 5? Is it higher or lower? Is this what you expected or not?
7. Type genr errors = resid to store the residuals from this regression in a variable. Then type scat x2 errors to plot the errors against X_2. Are they related and, if so, how?
8. Repeat steps 3–7 five times. How often do you find that β_1 is significantly different from its true value due to the omitted variable bias?
9. Generate a new set of X_2 values by typing genr x2=rnd()*5 – 0.6*x. Now X_1 and X_2 will be negatively correlated instead of positively correlated. Repeat steps 3–7 another five times with the new values of X_2. Now which way does the bias go?

Problems

1. Open the data file schoolspend, which contains data on 50 U.S. states for seven variables: totalspend is the amount of money that school districts in the state spend on education from kindergarten through 12th grade, measured in millions of dollars; totalstateaid is the amount of money provided by the state to school districts, measured in millions of dollars; income is the total state income in millions of dollars; population is the total population of the state in thousands; and elderly, minority, and schoolage are the fraction of the state's population that are 65 or over, members of ethnic minorities, and ages 6 to 17, respectively.

    a. School spending decisions are made by school district officials, based on revenue raised locally and state aid. If more state aid is available, local officials could either spend more money on schools, cut back on local revenue, or do some of both. In an economic model of the form Totalspend $= \beta_0 + \beta_1$ Totalstateaid, what values would you expect β_1 to take, and what values would you expect it not to take?

    b. However, we also know that bigger and richer states will be able to afford to spend more money on school aid as well. Estimate the equation Totalspend$_i = \beta_0 + \beta_1$ Totalstateaid$_i + \beta_2$ Income$_i + \beta_3$ Population$_i + \varepsilon_i$. How many of the variables are statistically significant?

    c. Test the null hypothesis that $\beta_3 = 0$. Do you reject or fail to reject? Estimate the regression equation Totalspend $= \beta_0 + \beta_1$ Totalstateaid$_i + \beta_2$ Income$_i + \varepsilon_i$. How much have your estimates of β_1 and β_2 changed? How much have their standard errors changed?

    d. Suppose we (incorrectly) dropped income from the model instead of population. Estimate the equation Totalspend $= \beta_0 + \beta_1$ Totalstateaid$_i + \beta_3$ Population$_i + \varepsilon_i$. Use the results of this equation to test the null hypothesis that $\beta_3 = 0$. What do you find this time?

    e. Calculate the correlation coefficient between population and income, and graph a scatterplot of the two variables. Why do you get different results in the two regressions? Do states with larger populations spend more on schooling, or not? Briefly explain why.

    f. Suppose we had failed to control for the size of the state in our analysis at all, and estimated the regression Totalspend $= \beta_0 + \beta_1$ Totalstateaid$_i + \varepsilon_i$. Estimate this equation and test whether $\beta_1 = 0$. Calculate the correlation coefficients between totalstateaid and population and income. How does omitted variable bias affect our estimate of β_1 in this case?

    g. Perform an F test to test whether it is acceptable to drop both income and population from the original regression. Does an increase in state aid, holding population and state income constant, increase spending on schooling or not?

2. Open the data file schoolspend2, which contains data on 50 U.S. states for seven variables. In this data file, the spending variables are measured in per-student terms rather than as total amounts of money for the entire state. Specifically, spending is the amount of money per pupil that school districts in the state spend on education from kindergarten through 12th grade, measured in dollars per pupil. stateaid is the amount of money provided by the state to school districts, measured in dollars per pupil. incomepp is the state income per pupil (i.e., total state income divided by number of pupils in

the state). population, elderly, minority, and schoolage are the same as they are in problem 1.

a. Looking at the data in per pupil terms may make it easier to compare big states to small states. Draw a scatterplot of Stateaid against Incomepp, and Stateaid against Population. Do they appear to be highly multicollinear or not? Calculate the correlation coefficients of Stateaid, Incomepp, and Population.

b. We would expect that increases in state aid per pupil might increase state spending per pupil, but we would still think that higher income per pupil would also increase spending on education. Estimate the equation $Spending = \beta_0 + \beta_1 Stateaid_i + \beta_2 Incomepp_i + \beta_3 Population_i + \varepsilon_i$. How many of the variables are statistically significant?

c. Does population affect state spending per pupil on education or not? How do you know? Does population affect total state spending on education? If it does, how does it do so?

d. Drop any insignificant variables from the regression and re-estimate it. Perform an F test (or if you dropped only one variable, a t test) to verify that the restricted model is acceptable. Are the parameters of the restricted model similar to those of the unrestricted model, or different?

e. Calculate the correlation coefficient between Stateaid and Incomepp. How multicollinear are these variables?

f. Does an increase in state aid, holding population and state income constant, increase spending on schooling or not? Does the regression in this problem provide a better answer to the question than the regression in problem 1, a worse answer, or an equally reliable answer? Briefly explain.

3. In this problem, we'll consider the fact that school spending is driven by factors other than financial ones. In particular, we'll look to see if age profiles and ethnic composition of populations affect the way school spending decisions are made. Open the data file schoolspend, which was described in problem 1.

a. Estimate the regression $Totalspend_i = \beta_0 + \beta_1 Totalstateaid_i + \beta_2 Income_i + \beta_3 Elderly_i + \beta_4 Minority_i + \beta_5 Schoolage_i + \varepsilon_i$. Calculate the change in total spending that should occur if a state's fraction of school-age children rises by 1 percent. Does this seem like a reasonable amount, or not? Why do you think you get this result?

b. Would you expect a state with a high proportion of school-age children in its population to spend more or less on schools than other states do? Would you expect a state with a high proportion of the elderly in its population to spend more or less on schools? Briefly justify your answers. Do the signs you get match the signs you expected, or not?

c. How many of the three demographic variables are statistically significant in the regression in part a? Do an F test to test whether the three demographic variables can be jointly dropped from the equation. What do you find?

4. In this problem we'll ask the same question using data for per pupil spending. Open the data file schoolspend, which was described in problem 2.

a. Estimate the equation $Spending = \beta_0 + \beta_1 Stateaid_i + \beta_2 Incomepp_i + \beta_3 Elderly_i + \beta_4 Minority_i + \beta_5 Schoolage_i + \varepsilon_i$. How many of the three demographic variables are statistically significant now?

b. Do an F test to test whether the three demographic variables can be jointly dropped from the equation. Then do a second F test to see whether only Elderly and Schoolage can be dropped. What is your preferred version of the regression? Do demographics affect spending, or not?

c. Using the preferred version, if the fraction of the school-age population rises by 1 percent, how much does spending per pupil change?

d. Using the preferred version, if the fraction of the population that is a member of an ethnic minority rises by 1 percent, how much does spending per pupil change? Does this seem like a small or large amount? Write a short essay explaining the implications of this finding.

5. Professional athletes are among the highest-paid people in society, and both economists and non-economists have asked why that is so. There is also considerable variation in salary among major league athletes, the lowest-paid receiving minimum salaries set by the league, and the highest paid receiving tens of millions of dollars per year. If major league baseball teams, like other firms, maximize their profits, then they should be willing to pay a player any salary up to his marginal revenue product—that is, the amount of additional revenue they will earn by hiring that player. Since teams that are successful have higher revenues (through higher ticket and merchandise sales), economists have asked whether players who perform better, and hence help their team be successful, have higher marginal revenue products, and hence higher salaries. In this problem we'll look at data on salaries of major league baseball players and see whether variations in their salaries can be explained by their performance on the field.

   Open the file baseball, which contains data on 254 major league baseball players. The data set contains 21 variables: salary is the player's salary, measured in thousands of dollars, and amerleague is a variable that is 1 if the player plays in the American League and 0 if he plays in the National League. The remaining variables all measure different aspects of the player's performance: atbats, hits, battingavg, singles, doubles, triples, homeruns, walks, strikeouts, runs (runs scored), rbi (runs batted in), onbasepct (on-base percentage), stolenbases, and caught (times caught stealing).

   a. Regress Salary on all the other variables in the data set. What happens, and why? (Hint: There are four types of hits: singles, doubles, triples, and home runs. Therefore, Singles + Doubles + Triples + Homeruns = Hits.)

   b. Remove Hits from the equation, and estimate it again. How many of the parameters are statistically significant?

   c. Perform an F test of the null hypothesis that the variables Stolenbases and Caught can be dropped from the regression. Is this acceptable?

   d. Continue dropping other variables until you find a final specification in which all remaining variables are statistically significant. Perform an F test to verify that this specification is acceptable. (If you fail the F test, then you need to put back at least one of the variables you dropped.)

   e. On the basis of your preferred final specification, if a player increases his batting average from .250 to .300, how much would his salary rise?

   f. On the basis of your preferred specification, if a player hit 20 fewer singles and 20 more home runs (leaving his batting average unchanged), how much would his salary rise?

6. When governments plan budgets, they do not know for certain how much tax revenue they will have in the coming year. They must predict how much revenue they will receive on the basis of information they have at the time of planning. In this problem, we'll use data on federal tax collections and a variety of economic indicators to identify variables that affect government revenues that might be used to plan fiscal policy.

   Open the data file receipts. This data set contains 42 annual observations from 1959 to 2001 on the following variables: nextrevenues is the tax revenues for the year following the observation year, which the government wishes to predict; currentrevenues is the tax revenues for the observation year; consumption is national consumption; investment is national investment; persincome is personal income; inflation is the inflation rate; unemployment is the unemployment rate; priceoil is the price of a barrel of oil; corpbondrate is the interest rate on grade AAA corporate bonds; tbillrate is the interest rate on 3-month Treasury bonds; cpi is the consumer price index; democrat is a dummy variable that is 1 if the president is a Democrat in the observation year; and republican is a dummy variable that is 1 if the president is a Republican in that year. All financial variables are measured in billions of real dollars, 1982–1984 = 100.

   a. The federal government collects the majority of its tax revenues from three sources—taxes on personal income (both from salaries and from investments), taxes on corporate income, and taxes on payrolls. Which of the variables in this data set do you think would be good measures of the tax base? Which ones do you think are not likely to be good measures?

   b. Run a regression with Nextrevenues as the dependent variable and all other variables in the data set, except Currentrevenues, as independent variables. What happens? (Hint: What is true about the variables Republican and Democrat?)

   c. Rerun the regression, dropping either the Republican or the Democrat variable. (It does not matter which one you drop.) How many of the parameters are statistically significantly different from 0?

   d. Calculate the correlation coefficients for the variables Consumption, Investment, and Persincome. Why are they so highly correlated? Pick one other pair of variables that you think might be highly correlated with one another, and calculate their correlation coefficient. Were you right or wrong?

   e. Using your knowledge of the correlation coefficients you have calculated, begin removing variables from the regression equation to reduce multicollinearity. At each state, verify by t test or F test that the removal is acceptable. Continue to remove variables until you reach a final regression for which all independent variables are statistically significant.

   f. Are tax revenues affected by whether the president is a Republican or a Democrat? If so, how much higher (or lower) are they when the president is a Republican, versus when he is a Democrat? Do you find your answer reasonable?

   g. Are the variables that have been kept in your final regressions the same as the ones you thought would be good measures in part a? Write a short essay explaining what you have learned from seeing which variables have turned out to be important and which ones have not.

Chapter **Eleven**

Models with Structural Shifts

Whip Inflation Now!

Anti-inflation political slogan of the Ford Administration, 1975

11.1 SHIFTING CURVES AND STAGFLATION

In the 1960s, macroeconomists grew very interested in the relationship between unemployment and inflation. In 1958, A. W. Phillips had pointed out that British macroeconomic data showed a negative correlation between the two variables; unemployment tended to be low when inflation was high and vice versa. Econometricians quickly confirmed that U.S. data showed the same pattern, which was given the name *Phillips curve*, illustrated in Figure 11.1. There was not a very solid theoretical basis for the correlation, but economists became very interested in deriving one. They produced a variety of models that suggested that economic policies that stimulated the economy, and thus reduced unemployment, would be inflationary, and those policies that cooled the economy off and increased unemployment would reduce inflation also.[1]

In the early 1970s, however, inflation and unemployment rose simultaneously to levels not seen since the 1930s. As a result, data on unemployment and inflation rates fail to show the predicted pattern. From 1960 to 2000, there appears, in fact, to be a positive relationship between unemployment and inflation, as shown in Figure 11.2. Table 11.1 shows the results of regressing inflation on unemployment; it confirms that the slope of the relationship between the two variables is positive, though it is significantly different from 0 only at the 10 percent level, not at the 5 percent level. This presented a serious challenge to the theory of the Phillips curve, which suggested the two variables should not rise simultaneously. The poor performance of the U.S. economy during this period led to a variety of policies to deal with it, from the wage and price controls of the Nixon administration, to the Whip Inflation Now campaign of the Ford administration, to the accommodative policies of the Carter administration.

---

[1] Sargent (1987) discusses the history of the Phillips curve at some length, including earlier observations of the same point by other economists.

FIGURE 11.1
A Theoretical
Phillips Curve

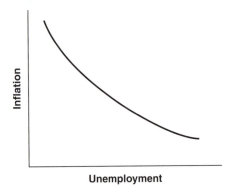

FIGURE 11.2
Historical
Data on
Unemployment
and Inflation
Rates,
1960–2000

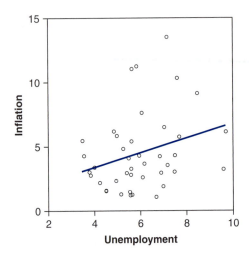

TABLE 11.1
Results of
Regressing
Inflation on
Unemployment

Variable	Parameter	Estimate	Standard Error	t Statistic for $\beta = 0$
Intercept	β_0	1.069	1.897	0.56
Unemployment	β_1	0.570	0.308	1.84
$N = 41$	$R^2 = 0.080$		SSR $= 333.3$	SER $= 2.924$

Economists were reluctant to abandon the Phillips curve. They realized that a shift of the curve, as shown in Figure 11.3, could explain the macroeconomic events of the 1970s. During the 1960s, the low Phillips curve would permit the economy to enjoy relatively low levels of unemployment and inflation, or to have very low levels of one in return for a modest rise in the other. When the curve shifted out, sometime around 1970, this become impossible; the economy would then have fairly high levels of both inflation and unemployment, and could have a low level of one only by tolerating very high levels of the other. If the Phillips curve moves over time, however, it will be difficult to estimate it econometrically. We locate an economic relationship in data by observing many points derived from that relationship,

FIGURE 11.3
A Shift in the
Phillips Curve

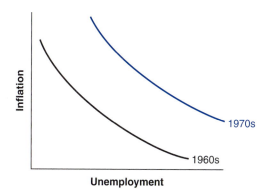

FIGURE 11.4 Two Versions of Wage Discrimination

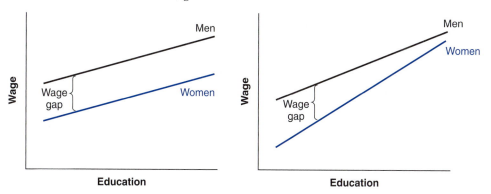

expecting that the error terms will tend to average out if we observe enough points. But this works only if the underlying relationship doesn't move. If the relationship changes over time, then each point is created by a different version of the regression equation and we never get more than one observation on each version. Only if we are willing to make some assumptions about how the relationship changes over time can we use those assumptions to estimate both the slope and intercept of the line, and the amount by which it has shifted.

There are many other economic problems in which we expect an economic relationship to lie in two different places, and not all of them involve a line shifting over time. For instance, consider the relationship between wages and education. We believe that people with higher educations earn higher wages, because in their education they acquire skills that make them more productive on the job. However, we also know that there are factors besides education that affect wages, such as discrimination. We might believe, for example, that given the same amount of education, women will tend to receive lower wages than men. If so, then there are two relationships between education and wages: one for men and one for women, with the line for women's wages lying below the line for men's wages. If women's wages are lower than men's by the same amount for any level of education, then these lines might look like the left side of Figure 11.4; both would have the same slope, but the intercept would be higher for men. Or, if higher education helped women overcome the effects of discrimination, then the lines might look like the right side of Figure 11.4; in this case, the women's line would have a steeper slope, and the wage gap between men and women would decrease as education increased, perhaps vanishing altogether at a sufficiently high level of education. This chapter presents the econometric techniques that permit us to determine whether there are one or two different economic relationships in a data set and, if there are two, how they differ. These techniques will allow us to address a variety of economic questions that turn on whether two groups are similar or different.

11.2 DUMMY VARIABLES

To deal with the question of whether a data set contains two distinct groups of data, drawn from true equations in two different locations, we need a way of defining which group each observation is in.

Definition 11.1 A *dummy variable* is a variable that takes only two values, 1 or 0.

Dummy variables have myriad uses in econometrics. For the Phillips curve example, we can define the dummy variable Shift to be equal to 1 in years between 1974 and 1983, the years in which the curve appears to have shifted out, and equal to 0 in all other years. This divides the data set into two groups, in which we believe the Phillips curve may have been in different places, allowing us to test whether the regression is in the same place for the two groups. In the wages example, if we have a sample of workers, we can define the dummy variable Male to be equal to 1 if the worker is male, and 0 if the worker is female, and see whether wages are lower for women than for men.

Alternatively, we could define the dummy variable Female to be equal to 1 if the worker is female and 0 if the worker is male. If we did this, however, the Male and Female dummy variables would be redundant. Either one of them is sufficient to tell us what gender every worker in the sample is; if we know the value of one we can instantly infer the value of the other, so it adds no new information. Furthermore, since every worker is either male or female but not both, we know that

$$\text{Male}_i + \text{Female}_i = 1 \qquad\qquad \textbf{(11.2.1)}$$

for all observations in the sample. This makes Male and Female perfectly multicollinear, and makes it impossible to use both of them in the same regression. Either one tells us all the information we need to know to measure the effects of gender on wages.

The same is true if we have dummy variables that describe more than two possible cases. For example, we may be interested in studying house prices, and we may think that house prices are different in urban, suburban, and rural areas. We can create three dummy variables: Urban is equal to 1 if the house is in an urban area and 0 if it is not, Suburban is equal to 1 if the house is a suburban area and 0 if it is not, and Rural is equal to 1 if the house is in a rural area and 0 if it is not. These three dummy variables divide the data sample into the three groups for which we think the underlying economic relationship varies. In this case, no one variable tells us everything about the house; if Urban = 1 it must be urban, but if Urban = 0 it could be either suburban or rural. Two variables, however, are sufficient to give us complete information. If Urban = 1 and Suburban = 0, then the house is urban; if Urban = 0 and Suburban = 1, then the house is suburban; if Urban = 0 and Suburban = 0, then the house must be rural by process of elimination.[2] Therefore, we need only use two of the three variables, and again the equation

$$\text{Urban}_i + \text{Suburban}_i + \text{Rural}_i = 1 \qquad \textbf{(11.2.2)}$$

will be true for each observation. The three variables together are perfectly multicollinear, and only two can be used in any particular regression.

What does a regression equation look like when it contains a dummy variable? Consider the following regression equation for the Phillips curve:

$$\text{Inflation}_t = \beta_0 + \beta_1 \text{Unemployment}_t + \beta_2 \text{Shift}_t + \varepsilon_t \qquad \textbf{(11.2.3)}$$

What does this regression equation imply about the Phillips curve? For any given observation, there are two possibilities: Either the observation is from the shifted period, in which case Shift = 1, or it isn't, in which case Shift = 0. Suppose that it is not. Then, for this observation, we can rewrite Equation 11.2.3 as

$$\text{Inflation}_t = \beta_0 + \beta_1 \text{Unemployment}_t + \beta_2 0 + \varepsilon_t \qquad \textbf{(11.2.4)}$$

which simplifies to

$$\text{Inflation}_t = \beta_0 + \beta_1 \text{Unemployment}_t + \varepsilon_t \qquad \textbf{(11.2.5)}$$

This is a linear relationship with a slope of β_1, which we expect to be negative, and an intercept of β_0, which we expect to be positive.

Suppose instead that the observation is drawn from the period of the shift. In this case we can rewrite Equation 11.2.3 as

$$\text{Inflation}_t = \beta_0 + \beta_1 \text{Unemployment}_t + \beta_2 1 + \varepsilon_t \qquad \textbf{(11.2.6)}$$

which simplifies to

$$\text{Inflation}_t = (\beta_0 + \beta_2) + \beta_1 \text{Unemployment}_t + \varepsilon_t \qquad \textbf{(11.2.7)}$$

This is also linear; its slope is also β_1, but its intercept is $(\beta_0 + \beta_2)$, which is β_2 points higher (lower, if β_2 is negative) than the relationship for non-Shift observations. Both relations are graphed in Figure 11.5, which matches, at least roughly, what economists have

FIGURE 11.5

Phillips Curve with 1970s Dummy

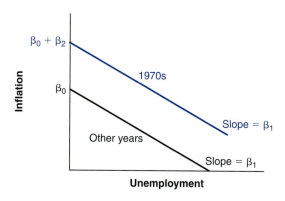

[2] It's not possible that Urban = 1 and Suburban = 1; the house can be in only one place.

TABLE 11.2
Results of Estimating Equation 11.2.3

Variable	Parameter	Estimate	Standard Error	t Statistic for $\beta = 0$
Intercept	β_0	5.934	1.400	4.24
Unemployment	β_1	−0.503	0.248	−2.03
Shift	β_2	6.291	0.854	7.36
$N = 41$	$R^2 = 0.621$		SSR = 137.4	SER = 1.901

come to believe: The Phillips curve shifted out in the 1970s, for a variety of reasons, leading to stagflation. The dummy variable allows us to write a single regression equation, Equation 11.2.3, which captures the shift in the curve and allows us to measure the extent of the change. When we calculate $\hat{\beta}_2$, we have an estimate of the difference in the intercepts of the two curves, which tells us how far the curve shifted.

Table 11.2 shows the result of estimating Equation 11.2.3. They are much better than previously. The slope of the curve is now negative, as expected, and statistically significantly different from 0. The estimated value is reasonable; $\hat{\beta}_1 = -0.503$ implies that a 1 percent rise in unemployment will decrease inflation by about 0.5 percent. This matches economic intuition about how the macroeconomy works, which Table 11.1 definitely did not. Also, the fit of the regression is much improved; the R^2 has risen from 0.08 to 0.62, and the SSR and SER have correspondingly improved.

We can also measure the amount by which the curve shifted. $\hat{\beta}_2 = 6.29$ implies that the Phillips curve moved up on the graph a bit more than 6 percentage points of inflation. Holding the unemployment rate constant, inflation was about 6 percent higher during the stagflation period than it was in other years, and the intercept, normally 5.93 percent, rose to $5.93 + 6.29 = 12.22\%$. Of course, unemployment was not held constant; it rose, and the slope of the curve tells us how much this reduced inflation. Allowing unemployment to rise 2 percent lowered inflation to 5 percent above its initial value prior to the shift, allowing unemployment to rise 4 percent lowered inflation to 4 percent above its initial value, and so forth.

Furthermore, because $\hat{\beta}_2$ is an estimate of how much the curve shifted, we can test whether the curve shifted or not. If the curve did not shift, then the intercepts would have to be the same in the two periods; this would imply $\beta_0 = \beta_0 + \beta_2$, or $\beta_2 = 0$. We can test this with a simple t test. The t statistic for this null hypothesis is $(6.29 - 0)/0.854 = 7.36$, far above the 5 percent critical value of 2.024 for 38 degrees of freedom. We (strongly) reject this null hypothesis, and we can conclude that the curve did in fact shift during the 1970s and early 1980s. This is evidence in favor of the stagflation theory explaining the economic slowdown of that decade.

11.3 ALLOWING SLOPES TO VARY

Powerful though it is, the analysis in the previous section is based on an assumption: When the curve shifts, only its intercept changes; its slope remains the same. This implies two things that may be unlikely. First, in the 1970s, the inflation rate was higher than in other years by the same amount no matter what the unemployment rate was. Second, the change in the unemployment rate required to reduce the inflation rate by one point was the same in both decades. We may not want to make that assumption; we might want to allow the slope of the curve to shift. We might want to do that simply because we are not comfortable with the assumption that the slope is constant and would like to test that assumption. Or we might have an economic reason to think the slope is different for two groups in the data set, as in the wage discrimination example in Section 11.1, where the economic belief that the wage gap is smaller for higher education levels implies that the wage-education curve is steeper for women than it is for men. In either case we would like to have a method of writing the regression equation that permits the slope of the curve to change instead of (or in addition to) the intercept.

We can do this by making use of an interaction term between the variable on the horizontal axis and the dummy variable that distinguishes the two groups. In the Phillips curve example, we can write the regression equation as

$$\text{Inflation}_t = \beta_0 + \beta_1 \text{Unemployment}_t + \beta_2 \text{Unemployment}_t \cdot \text{Shift}_t + \varepsilon_t \quad \textbf{(11.3.1)}$$

As with Equation 11.2.3, there are two possible cases for any one observation: Either it is a year in the 1970s, in which case $\text{Shift}_t = 1$, or it is not, in which case $\text{Shift}_t = 0$. In the latter case, we can write the regression as

$$\text{Inflation}_t = \beta_0 + \beta_1 \text{Unemployment}_t + \beta_2 \text{Unemployment}_t \cdot 0 + \varepsilon_t \quad \textbf{(11.3.2)}$$

which simplifies to

$$\text{Inflation}_t = \beta_0 + \beta_1 \text{Unemployment}_t + \varepsilon_t \quad \textbf{(11.3.3)}$$

This is a linear relationship with a slope of β_1 and an intercept of β_0; it is exactly the same as the curve we got in the previous section when Shift $= 0$. However, when we consider the case when Shift $= 1$, we get a different result. When Shift $= 1$, Equation 11.3.1 reduces to

$$\text{Inflation}_t = \beta_0 + \beta_1 \text{Unemployment}_t + \beta_2 \text{Unemployment}_t \cdot 1 + \varepsilon_t \quad \textbf{(11.3.4)}$$

which can be rewritten as

$$\text{Inflation}_t = \beta_0 + (\beta_1 + \beta_2) \text{Unemployment}_t + \varepsilon_t \quad \textbf{(11.3.5)}$$

which is a line with intercept β_0 and slope $(\beta_1 + \beta_2)$. In this case, the intercept remains the same in the 1970s but the slope changes; the slope has increased by β_2 in the 1970s compared to its level in earlier years (or decreased, if $\beta_2 < 0$). These equations are graphed in Figure 11.6. This specification of the equation assumes that, in the 1970s, the Phillips curve rotated around a fixed vertical intercept. This also has the effect of allowing the curve to be higher in the 1970s, but in a way that allows the gap to be different in different years. Specifically, the gap is larger when unemployment is higher, and falls to 0 when unemployment falls to 0.

Results of estimating Equation 11.3.1 are shown in Table 11.3. Again, allowing for the curve to shift produces an estimated slope in the nonshift period that is negative and statistically significantly different from 0 (the t statistic is -2.08), and the estimated value is reasonable; the estimated slope is -0.633, which is quite similar to the estimated slope of -0.503 from the previous regression, given the standard errors of the two estimates. We

FIGURE 11.6
Phillips Curve with 70s Interaction

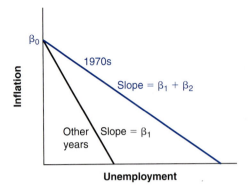

TABLE 11.3
Results of Estimating Equation 11.3.1

Variable	Parameter	Estimate	Standard Error	t Statistic for $\beta = 0$
Intercept	β_0	6.767	1.688	4.01
Unemployment	β_1	−0.633	0.303	−2.08
Shift · Unemployment	β_2	0.808	0.136	5.92
$N = 41$	$R^2 = 0.522$		SSR = 173.4	SER = 2.136

find that the change in slope in the 1970s was significantly different from 0; the slope rose (became less negative and flatter) by 0.808. However, this is a little too much of a change. These results show an intercept of 6.767 percent for both periods, a slope of −0.633 for the nonshift period, and a slope of −0.633 + 0.808 = +0.175 for the shift period. In order to reach the data from the late 1970s, holding the intercept fixed, the Phillips curve line has to rotate around so far that its slope becomes positive! This is economically untenable. Further, the fit of Equation 11.3.1 is not as good as that of Equation 11.2.3—the SRR is 173.4 rather than 137.4, and the R^2 is lower, 0.52 instead of 0.62. Both on statistical and economic grounds, Equation 11.2.3 is a better model of the true shift in the Phillips curve than Equation 11.3.1 is.

However, this does not prove that the slope of the Phillips curve did *not* change during the stagflation period. It only shows that assuming the slope changed *and* the intercept did not is untenable. But perhaps both of them changed; in reality, it seems plausible that that might happen. We can go one step further and write the regression equation in a way that allows for both the slope and the intercept to change at the same time:

$$\text{Inflation}_t = \beta_0 + \beta_1 \text{Unemployment}_t + \beta_2 \text{Shift}_t$$
$$+ \beta_3 \text{Unemployment}_t \cdot \text{Shift}_t + \varepsilon_t \qquad \textbf{(11.3.6)}$$

This equation contains both the dummy variable, which shifts the intercept of the curve, and the interaction term, which shifts the slope of the curve. It allows for much more general shifts of the curve over time, as shown in Figure 11.7. Now when the curve shifts, it can both rise and rotate, because the Shift variable appears in two terms. If Shift = 0, the equation reduces to

$$\text{Inflation}_t = \beta_0 + \beta_2 \text{Unemployment}_t + \varepsilon_t \qquad \textbf{(11.3.7)}$$

FIGURE 11.7
Phillips Curve with Slope and Intercept Shifts

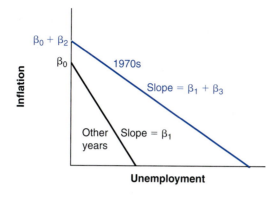

TABLE 11.4
Results of Estimating Equation 11.3.6

Variable	Parameter	Estimate	Standard Error	t Statistic for $\beta = 0$
Intercept	β_0	3.825	1.586	2.41
Unemployment	β_1	−0.118	0.284	−0.41
Shift	β_2	14.51	3.523	4.12
Shift · Unemployment	β_3	−1.202	0.591	−2.39
$N = 41$	$R^2 = 0.671$	SSR $= 118.9$		SER $= 1.793$

and when Shift $= 1$, it reduces to

$$\text{Inflation}_t = (\beta_0 + \beta_2) + (\beta_1 + \beta_3)\text{Unemployment}_t + \varepsilon_t \quad \textbf{(11.3.8)}$$

so that we can interpret β_2 as the difference in the intercept in the two cases and β_3 as the difference in the slopes.

> **Definition 11.2** A regression equation is *fully interacted* with a set of dummy variables if it contains every dummy variable (minus one to prevent perfect multicollinearity) and interaction terms between every slope coefficient and every dummy variable (again, minus one to prevent perfect multicollinearity).

Equation 11.3.6 is fully interacted by this definition. More generally, if we have the equation

$$Y = \beta_0 + \beta_1 X_1 + \beta_2 X_2 + \beta_3 X_3 + \varepsilon_t \quad \textbf{(11.3.9)}$$

and we have three dummy variables D_1, D_2, and D_3 that describe three possible subsamples, then the regression equation

$$Y = \beta_0 + \beta_1 D_1 + \beta_2 D_2 + \beta_3 X_1 + \beta_4 D_1 X_1 + \beta_5 D_2 X_1$$
$$+ \beta_6 X_2 + \beta_7 D_1 X_2 + \beta_8 D_2 X_2 + \varepsilon_t \quad \textbf{(11.3.10)}$$

is a fully interacted regression.

Table 11.4 shows the results of estimating the fully interacted Equation 11.3.6. It shows that both the intercept and the slope changed significantly during the stagflation era; Shift

FIGURE 11.8
Phillips Curve
Estimation
Results

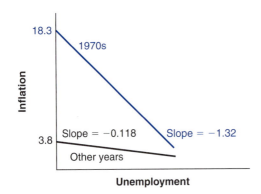

is positive and significant, and Shift · Unemployment is negative and significant. The results suggest that the intercept changed from 3.825 to 18.335 during the stagflation, and the slope actually became steeper, changing from −0.118 to −1.320 during the stagflation. The implied curves are graphed in Figure 11.8, and they clearly show the dramatic change in the Phillips curve in the shift period that these results demonstrate.

11.4 TESTING FOR SHIFTING CURVES: THE CHOW TEST

You might ask why, if we believe there are two different curves in the data, and both their slopes and intercepts are different, we are estimating a single regression equation. Couldn't we just estimate one regression for each time period and get the estimates of the slopes and intercepts that way? In fact, we could do that—and if we did, we'd get exactly the same answers. Table 11.5 shows the results of regressing inflation on unemployment for each of the two time periods separately. Note that the parameter estimates of the slopes and intercepts exactly match those in Figure 11.8. And not only that, but the sum of the SSRs of the two separate regressions—56.5 and 62.4—add up exactly to the SSR of the single, fully interacted regression, 118.9.

This happens because the two problems are, mathematically, identical. In the first case, we are picking two slopes and two intercepts; in the second, we are picking one slope, one intercept, one slope change, and one intercept change. Either way, we can put each of the two curves wherever we like to minimize the sum of squared residuals, and ordinary least squares (OLS) will put the curves in exactly the same place both times.[3] So we get the same slopes and intercepts either way.

---

[3] Note, however, that the standard errors don't match. The reason is that we have used the Gauss-Markov assumptions, including homoskedasticity—all errors have the same variance. When we run one unified regression, we are assuming the variance of the errors is the same for all 41 observations. When we run two separate regressions, the variance of the errors takes one value in 1974–1983 and a different value for the other years, because the variance is estimated separately for each regression. This doesn't change the estimates of the β parameters but does change the estimate of σ, the standard error of the error terms, and thus changes the estimated standard errors of the β parameters also, which depend on the estimate of σ. If we ran the one unified regression, properly allowing for heteroskedasticity in the two periods, then we could make the standard errors match as well.

TABLE 11.5 **Phillips Curve Estimates for Separate Time Periods**

Variable	1974–1983			All Other Years		
	Parameter	Standard Error	t Statistic	Parameter	Standard Error	t Statistic
Intercept	18.33	4.663	3.93	3.825	1.298	2.95
Unemployment	−1.319	0.612	−2.15	−0.118	0.232	−0.51
	N = 10	SSR = 56.5		N = 31	SSR = 62.4	

Does it then make any difference which way we do it? You might think it does, because in the case of the fully interacted regression, we can test whether the curve has shifted. If the curve has not shifted, then the intercepts must be the same and the slopes must be the same. That implies that $\beta_0 = \beta_0 + \beta_2$ and $\beta_1 = \beta_1 + \beta_3$, or $\beta_2 = \beta_3 = 0$. This can be easily tested by an F test. But if we run two separate regressions, there is no easy way to impose the restriction that the intercepts, or the slopes, or both be the same in each of the two regressions. How then can we test whether the curves are in statistically significantly different places if we run two separate regressions?

It turns out that we can perform this test in the following way. Suppose we believe that the values of the parameters are exactly the same in both time periods; that is, $\text{Inflation}_t = \beta_0 + \beta_1 \text{Unemployment}_t + \varepsilon_t$ in the 1970s, and also $\text{Inflation}_t = \beta_0 + \beta_1 \text{Unemployment}_t + \varepsilon_t$ in other years. Then we can legitimately run a single regression on the whole sample, and let it serve as the restricted model that imposes equality of slopes and intercepts in both time periods, while the unrestricted model is the regression estimated separately on each of the two time periods. More generally:

> **Theorem 11.1** Suppose you have a sample of N observations, and you believe that the sample can be divided into M subsamples, with the regression equation (with k variables) in a different place in each subsample. Let SSR be the sum of squared residuals from estimating the regression on the entire sample, and let SSR_i be the sum of squared residuals from estimating the regression on the ith subsample. Then the F statistic calculated by
>
> $$F = \frac{[\text{SSR} - (\text{SSR}_1 + \text{SSR}_2 + \cdots + \text{SSR}_M)]/[(M-1)(k+1)]}{(\text{SSR}_1 + \text{SSR}_2 + \cdots + \text{SSR}_M)/[N - M(k+1)]} \quad \textbf{(11.4.1)}$$
>
> can be used to test the null hypothesis that the curve is in the same place in each of the M subsamples, versus the alternative hypothesis that the curve is in a different place in at least one of the subsamples.

This is true because we can think of SSR as the restricted sum of squared residuals, and $(\text{SSR}_1 + \text{SSR}_2 + \cdots + \text{SSR}_M)$ as the unrestricted sum of squared residuals. If the regression is in the same place for each time period, then there is only 1 intercept instead of M different intercepts, and there is only 1 slope for each right-hand-side variable instead of M different slopes, so the number of restrictions being imposed is $(M-1)(k+1)$. In the unrestricted model, we pick $(k+1)$ parameters for each of M equations, so the degrees of freedom in the unrestricted model is $N - M(k+1)$. The formula then follows from the usual definition of the F statistic given in Equation 8.4.6. This test is called the *Chow test,* after the economist who first proposed it.

We can do a sample Chow test with the regressions given above. The Phillips curve sample is divided into two subsamples; letting 1974–1983 be the first subsample and the rest of the years be the second subsample, we have SSR $= 333.3$ from Table 11.1, and $SSR_1 = 56.5$ and $SSR_2 = 62.4$ from Table 11.5. We have two subsamples, so $M = 2$, and there is one variable in the regression equation, so $k = 1$. The F statistic becomes:

$$F = \frac{[333.3 - (56.5 + 62.4)]/1 \cdot 2}{(56.5 + 62.4)/[41 - (2 \cdot 2)]} \qquad \textbf{(11.4.2)}$$

because we are imposing two restrictions (equal slopes and equal intercepts) and we are choosing four parameters in the unrestricted model (the two separate equations). This statistic works out to $F = 33.35$, which is greater than the 5 percent critical value of 3.26.

Note that this works out to exactly the same F statistic we would get if we tested the null hypothesis $\beta_2 = \beta_3 = 0$ in Equation 11.3.6. This is true because, as shown above, the SSR for Equation 11.3.6, which is 118.9, is exactly the same as $56.5 + 62.4$ from the two separate estimations. Also, $\beta_2 = \beta_3 = 0$ implies two restrictions, and the degrees of freedom of Equation 11.3.6 is 37. Therefore, the F statistic is exactly the same as the Chow test F statistic and will produce exactly the same answer; the curve is in a different place from 1974 to 1983.

Again you may ask, Does it then matter which way we do the test? The answer is again yes. We can do the Chow test if we want to impose equal value for all parameters on the model, but we cannot do it if we want to impose only equal slopes or only equal intercepts. If we estimate the fully interacted regression, we can test $\beta_2 = 0$ (while allowing β_3 to take any value), $\beta_3 = 0$ (while allowing β_2 to take any value), or $\beta_2 = \beta_3 = 0$. With the Chow test we can do only the latter. In that sense, the fully interacted regression is more powerful; it permits us to test more possible restrictions than the two separate estimates do. In this particular case, the fully interacted model shows, by appropriate t tests, that both the slope and the intercept are different in the period of the shifted curve; the Chow test can demonstrate only that at least one of them changed.

However, the fully interacted model is somewhat more cumbersome to estimate, particularly if there are many right-hand-side variables, many subsamples, or both. Since the results will be the same either way, it may be easier just to do separate regressions for each sample than to estimate the fully interacted model, especially in the larger cases. If we are not interested in testing whether particular slopes or intercepts do or do not vary, but are interested instead only in whether the curve (with all its parameters) has shifted or not, then the Chow test may be the better one to use. But econometrician's convenience is the sole standard to judge by; you get the same answer either way.

It is worth noting that the quality of the estimates you get depends on the number of observations in each subsample. If one subsample has very few observations, then the parameter estimates for that subsample will tend to have high standard errors and be statistically insignificant. The Chow test is not very powerful in that case either; when one set of parameters is poorly estimated, it is hard to tell whether or not their values are different from those of the other set. If you have choice about how to divide the data into subsamples, it is desirable to divide the sample as evenly as possible so that the smallest subsample has as many observations as possible. If your economic model suggests a specific break point in the data, however, you may not have discretion and you will have to work with whatever sized subsamples you have in your data.

11.5   USING DUMMY VARIABLES WITH PANEL DATA: TIME AND FIXED EFFECTS

One problem with the model in section 11.2 is that, although it allows the curve to shift once, or even a few times, it still requires the curve to remain in place long enough to generate an adequate number of observations for each position to which it shifts. Even with the assumption that the Phillips curve remained in place from 1974 to 1983, a fairly long time as business cycles go, we still have only 10 observations to estimate the regression on the sub-sample where the curve shifted out. If we thought that the curve moved more often—every three to five years, perhaps—we would not be able to detect the shifts because we would not have enough observations on any one position of the curve to accurately identify it.

If, however, we use panel data, we can get around this requirement. Panel data sets contain both a cross-section and a time-series component; they allow us to make many observations on an economic relationship within a single time period. If we have a panel data set, we can allow for the curve to be in a different position every year and still be able to estimate its position in each year. Similarly, they allow for the curve to be in a different position for every observation in the cross-section component of the data set, since we can estimate that curve with data observed over time. More powerfully, and somewhat less obviously, we can do both of these things at once and obtain a great deal of flexibility in the location of the curve across observations and over time.

Consider, for example, the following economic relationship:

$$\text{Educspend}_{it} = \beta_0 + \beta_1 \text{Income}_{it} + \varepsilon_{it} \qquad \textbf{(11.5.1)}$$

where Educspend_{it} is the amount of money per capita a state government spends on K–12 education, Income_{it} is the per capita income of its citizens, the i subscript indicates different states, and the t subscript indicates different time periods. We expect that richer states will be able to spend more money on education for their citizens, implying that $\beta_1 > 0$. Because there are 50 states, we can create a panel data set with states as the unit of observation, observed over a period of years. Table 11.6 shows results of estimating Equation 11.5.1 on a sample of 528 observations—the 48 continental states (Alaska and Hawaii are excluded from the data set) for the years 1984 to 1994. Somewhat surprisingly, the results show no relation at all between income and education spending; the estimated parameter is positive, but is not statistically significantly different from 0, and the R^2 is extremely close to 0. Furthermore, the estimated parameter is extremely small; it predicts that an extra dollar of income in the hands of state citizens will produce a mere 0.036 cent of spending on education.

TABLE 11.6
Results of Estimating Equation 11.5.1

Variable	Parameter	Estimate	Standard Error	t Statistic for $\beta = 0$
Intercept	β_0	434.37	31.670	13.7
Income	β_1	0.0003	0.0017	0.20
$N = 528$	$R^2 = 0.00008$	SSR $= 8.03\text{e}6$		SER $= 123.5$

Why did this occur? One possibility is that different states have different attitudes toward education spending and therefore the relationship between education spending and income is different for each state, making the observations noncomparable. Certainly there are historical patterns to education spending across states that might produce a lack of pattern. In 1994, average per capita income was $19,795 and average per capita education spending was $499; but states varied around these averages. Maryland, for example, is a wealthy state that has chosen not to spend much on education; its per capita income was $23,859 and its education spending was $354. West Virginia, conversely, is a relatively poor state that chooses to spend heavily on education. Its per capita income was $16,116 and its education spending was $685. A variety of factors might explain why some states spend more or less on education, such as the percentage of children in the state's population or the fraction of children who attend private schools. Indeed, Figure 11.9, which shows a scatter plot of per capita spending and per capita income, suggests that there is no particular pattern between income and education spending.

However, the question of whether states with higher incomes spend more on education than states with lower incomes may not be the interesting question. We may instead want to ask whether if a given state received an increase in its income, it would choose to spend more on education. The difference is that the latter question compares two levels of income while holding other factors about the state constant; the former compares two different states with incomes different but with other factors about the two states differing also. We may get very different answers to the two questions, depending on the influence of factors other than education that are particular to each state.

We can address the latter question by including a dummy variable for each state in the regression equation:

$$\text{Educspend}_{it} = \beta_0 + \beta_1 \text{Income}_{it} + \sum_{j=2}^{48} \beta_j \text{Sdum}_i^j + \varepsilon_{it} \qquad \textbf{(11.5.2)}$$

where Sdum^j is a dummy variable which is 1 if this observation is on the jth state, and 0 if not. This formulation allows the intercept of the model to be different for each state; if a state has a particularly high intercept, then in all years it spends more on education than

FIGURE 11.9

State Income and Spending on K–12 Education, 1984–1994

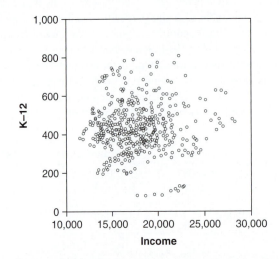

other states with similar incomes (e.g., West Virginia), and if it has a particularly low intercept, then it spends less on education than other states with similar incomes (e.g., Maryland).

> **Definition 11.3** A group of dummy variables that correspond to each cross-section unit in a panel data set are called *fixed effects;* they measure the effects of all factors that vary across cross-section units but do not change over time.

When using fixed effects in regression using panel data, one dummy must be dropped to avoid perfect multicollinearity; in this case we have chosen to drop Sdum[1], for the state of Alabama, though any dummy would do (and choosing a different one would not change the results). Fixed effects control for all effects that, like the dummy variable, are specific to that particular state and do not vary over time.

Results of estimating Equation 11.5.2 are shown in Table 11.7; estimates for the parameters on dummy variables are shown, but to conserve space, their standard errors are not shown.[4] With the inclusion of the fixed effects, we now find that income has a statistically significant effect on education spending, and a reasonably large one; an extra dollar of income in the hands of state residents will increase education spending by 2.9 cents, holding other time-invariant factors about the state constant (because of the inclusion of the fixed effect for the state). Figure 11.10 shows why we get different results in the two cases. Because of the fixed effects, each state has its own relationship between income and spending on kindergarden through 12th grade (K–12) education; those with positive fixed

TABLE 11.7
Results of Estimating Equation 11.5.2

Variable	Parameter	Estimate	Standard Error	*t* Statistic for $\beta = 0$
Intercept	β_0	−31.02	20.54	−1.51
Income	β_1	0.0295	0.0011	25.3
$N = 528$	$R^2 = 0.921$		SSR = 6.35e5	SER = 36.41

Fixed Effects

Alabama	0.0	Maine	−29.2	Ohio	−78.2
Arizona	−44.1	Maryland	−285.6	Oklahoma	46.8
Arkansas	34.2	Massachusetts	−293.5	Oregon	−144.1
California	−6.4	Michigan	−165.2	Pennsylvania	−160.1
Colorado	−149.4	Minnesota	32.7	Rhode Island	−156.7
Connecticut	−318.5	Mississippi	91.1	South Carolina	55.4
Delaware	−79.7	Missouri	−68.5	South Dakota	−162.3
Florida	−122.1	Montana	48.9	Tennessee	−153.3
Georgia	12.9	Nebraska	−213.4	Texas	−49.3
Idaho	53.8	Nevada	−50.0	Utah	139.8
Illinois	−224.1	New Hampshire	−476.6	Vermont	−113.9
Indiana	−74.6	New Jersey	−189.1	Virginia	−153.1
Iowa	8.1	New Mexico	320.0	Washington	161.2
Kansas	−63.7	New York	−86.1	West Virginia	182.0
Kentucky	62.5	North Carolina	74.4	Wisconsin	−76.4
Louisiana	58.0	North Dakota	28.7	Wyoming	266.7

[4] It is fairly standard practice not to even report values for the parameters of the dummy variables unless their values are of particular interest.

FIGURE 11.10
State-Level
Relationships
between
Income and
K–12
Spending

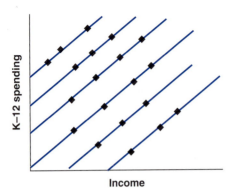

effects have relationships higher up the curve (e.g., West Virginia) and those with negative fixed effects have relationships lower down the curve (e.g., Maryland). For each state, a fairly strong positive relationship exists. However, states with higher curves tend to have lower incomes, and so when comparing different states, rather than different observations on the same state, the relationship breaks down. Including the fixed effects, so as to examine the question of how K–12 spending varies with income within a given state, reveals the expected economic pattern. It allows us to control for effects specific to given states that do not vary over time, even though we cannot explicitly measure them in the data, and lets us observe the financial effect that we expected to see.

Just as we can use dummy variables to allow a curve to have a different intercept for each state, we can also use them to allow the curve to have a different intercept for each time period.

> **Definition 11.4** *Time effects* are a group of dummy variables that correspond to each time period in a panel data set. They measure the effects of all factors that vary over time but do not change across cross-section units.[5]

Time effects allow for the possibility that the curve is shifting over time, just as the dummy variable in Equation 11.2.3 did, but they allow for it to shift every year, not just once or twice. The regression with time effects is:

$$\text{Educspend}_{it} = \beta_0 + \beta_1 \text{Income}_{it} + \sum_{s=2}^{11} \beta_s \text{Tdum}_s^t + \varepsilon_{it} \qquad \textbf{(11.5.3)}$$

or, if we wish to include both fixed effects and time effects,

$$\text{Educspend}_{it} = \beta_0 + \beta_1 \text{Income}_{it} + \sum_{j=2}^{48} \beta_j \text{Sdum}_i^j \qquad \textbf{(11.5.4)}$$

$$+ \sum_{s=2}^{11} \beta_{s+47} \text{Tdum}_t^s + \varepsilon_{it}$$

where Tdum^s is a dummy that is 1 in year s, and 0 otherwise.

Results for estimating Equation 11.5.4 are not terribly different from those of Equation 11.5.2 (they are not shown here). The estimate of β_1 falls slightly, to 2.4 cents

---

[5] There is no standard name for such dummy variables; they are referred to by a fairly wide variety of names in the literature. The name *time effects* makes the parallel between them and fixed effects clear.

FIGURE 11.11
Time Effects in Equation 11.5.4

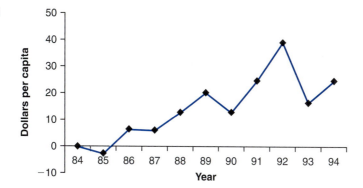

increased K–12 spending, per dollar of increased income, and remains statistically signifi-cant (*t* statistic of 7.47). The state fixed effects change slightly but not greatly. The estimated parameters for the time effects are shown graphically in Figure 11.11. Over time, spending has grown fairly steadily, although the curve seems to have shifted up slightly during the recession of 1991–1992; this probably occurred because state governments, even in the face of stagnant or falling incomes, could not cut (or even slow the growth of) school spending for a recession they expected to be temporary. The use of time effects allows us to track the movement of a curve over each year in our panel data sample, and gives us the ability to understand the evolution of an economic relationship over time in considerably more detail than we can do with time-series data.

11.6   THE REASONS WHY CURVES SHIFT

The techniques discussed in the preceding sections are very good for demonstrating that curves have moved, and if they have, by how much. However, they are extremely unsatis-factory for one deep reason: They do not explain *why* the curve shifted. To an economist, the fact that the Phillips curve shifted in the 1970s raises as many questions as it answers, if not more. What happened around 1973 that caused the curve to shift out? Did it have something to do with the oil shock that occurred that year? The growth rate of productivity fell sharply about the same time—was that related to the movement of the Phillips curve? If so, did the slowdown in productivity cause the curve to shift out, did productivity fall because the Phillips curve had shifted out, or did some third reason cause both?

Dummy variables are incapable of answering questions like the ones above, because they do not contain any economic information. They merely assert the existence of a partition in the data set, with each half of the partition being described by a different relationship. In some cases, this is sufficient, particularly if the difference between the two groups is not essential to the economic question. If, for example, one is interested in measuring the slope of the Phillips curve, and is not concerned with whether or why the curve's intercept may change, then adding a dummy variable to the regression solves the problem very nicely. But one interested in understanding the determinants of inflation and unemployment rates cannot stop there.

Indeed, once it became fairly clear that the Phillips curve had shifted, economic theorists very quickly started trying to explain why it had done so. They advanced many theories, of which we will only consider one simple one here. Consider a firm that observes a rise in the price at which its products can be sold. Is this due to a rise in demand or just to inflation? At least immediately, the firm cannot know whether or not demand has risen. If demand has risen, the firm should produce more output and hire more workers. If not, and the price rise is due solely to inflation, it should do nothing. The firm must form some guess about how much inflation has occurred and how much its product's price has risen as a result. Then, it hires more workers (reducing unemployment) only if it sees a price rise greater than the one it expects. If it sees a price rise, but smaller than it expects, it might even conclude that demand for its products had fallen and therefore would lay workers off, increasing unemployment. This theory suggests the following economic relationship:

$$\text{Inflation}_t - \text{Inflation}_t^{\text{pred}} = \beta_0 + \beta_1 \text{Unemployment}_t + \varepsilon_t \quad \textbf{(11.6.1)}$$

where $\text{Inflation}_t^{\text{pred}}$ is the amount of inflation firms predict, which can be solved to produce

$$\text{Inflation}_t = \beta_0 + \beta_1 \text{Unemployment}_t + \text{Inflation}_t^{\text{pred}} + \varepsilon_t \quad \textbf{(11.6.2)}$$

which is generally known as the *expectations-augmented Phillips curve*. How do firms choose a prediction about the amount of inflation to expect? Suppose they behave very simply, and just assume inflation will be what it was last year. Then

$$\text{Inflation}_t^{\text{pred}} = \text{Inflation}_{t-1} \quad \textbf{(11.6.3)}$$

which can be substituted into Equation 11.6.2 to produce

$$\text{Inflation}_t = \beta_0 + \beta_1 \text{Unemployment}_t + \beta_2 \text{Inflation}_{t-1} + \varepsilon_t$$
$$\textbf{(11.6.4)}$$

where we expect $\beta_2 = 1$ as well as $\beta_1 < 0$. If so, then this theory offers an explanation of why the Phillips curve shifted out. The oil shocks of the early 1970s caused unexpectedly high inflation. In following years, consumers expected this high inflation to continue, and so it did, increased by another round of oil shocks in 1979 when the Iran-Iraq war broke out. The deep recession of the early 1980s, with its high levels of unemployment, lowered inflation, again unexpectedly, and consumers began (slowly) to shift their expectations of inflation downward, bringing the Phillips curve back to its original location.

Table 11.8 shows the results of estimating Equation 11.6.4. This equation is highly successful at explaining the data; all estimated parameters are statistically significant, and it produces a lower SSR than any of the preceding models despite having only three parameters rather than four. β_1 is negative as expected and takes a quite reasonable value; perhaps more impressively, β_2 is quite close to 1 and is not statistically significantly different from it. The t test for the null hypothesis $\beta_2 = 1$ is $(1.025 - 1)/0.102 = 0.245$, much less than the critical

TABLE 11.8
Results of Estimating Equation 11.6.4

Variable	Parameter	Estimate	Standard Error	t Statistic for $\beta = 0$
Intercept	β_0	4.138	1.042	3.97
Unemployment	β_1	−0.705	0.205	−3.43
Inflation$_{t-1}$	β_2	1.025	0.102	10.03
$N = 40$	$R^2 = 0.752$		SSR $= 87.53$	SER $= 1.538$

value of 2.02. This result is strikingly close to what our theory predicted and lends a great deal of credibility to the idea that expectations of inflation are important in determining the location of the Phillips curve in any given year. Certainly this regression is much more satisfying than one that shows that the Phillips curve moved but gives no idea why it did so.

Dummy variables, then, are a two-edged sword. They are excellent for explaining whether curves move but terrible for explaining why. They are useful for dealing with the possibility that a curve has moved while trying to measure some other aspect of the curve, but they cannot give deeper insights about why the curve behaves the way it does. At their best, however, they at least enable us to ask more penetrating questions about the economic relationships we are trying to measure that can help us gain a better understanding of the real economic process that generated the data.

Chapter Review

- Economic relationships may shift over time as the economy grows, or they may be in different places for different groups of observations. This can make estimation of those relationships complicated, because not all observations are described by the same curve.
- We can use *dummy variables* to divide the sample into the different groups and allow the intercept of the curve to vary for each group.
- We can use *interaction terms* with dummy variables to allow the slope of the curve to differ for each group as well.
- An econometric equation is *fully interacted* if all variables have interaction terms with all dummy variables (minus 1 to prevent perfect multicollinearity). Estimating a fully interacted model produces the same parameter estimates as estimating the equation separately for each different group.
- The *Chow test* can be used to test whether or not the curve has shifted. The F test can be used on the fully interacted model to test whether or not the curve has shifted and, if it has, which parameters have changed and which have not.
- If we have panel data, we can allow the curve to have a different intercept for each cross-section unit in the panel by including *fixed effects,* and for each time period by including *time effects.*
- Dummy variables do not explain why the curve shifted; we may be able to learn more about the changes in the underlying economic relationship if we can use nondummy variables that test economic theories about why the curve shifted.

Computer Exercise

In this exercise we'll generate data from two different groups, see how estimation works if we fail to allow for the difference, and try to detect the difference using the Chow test.

1. Start Eviews, and create a new worksheet, undated, with 100 observations.
2. Press the Sample button and enter 1 60. Then, on the command line, type genr group1=1 to generate a dummy variable which is 1 for the first 60 observations. Then press the Sample button again and enter 61 100. On the command line, type genr group1=0 to set

the dummy variable equal to 0 for the last 40 observations. Last, press the Sample button one more time and enter 1 100 to restore the full sample. (Do *not* omit this!)

3. Type genr educ = 12 +nrnd()*4 to generate random education levels for each observation in the sample. Then type genr wage = 10 + educ*2 + group1*5 + nrnd()*3 to generate random wages for each observation based on wage and membership in group 1. Which group gets higher wages on average, and how much higher? Does the slope vary between groups, or just the intercept?

4. Show a scatter plot of wage versus educ. Can you see two distinct groups in the plot?

5. Type ls wage c educ group1. Is group1 significant? Is its parameter about equal to 5?

6. Set the sample to 1 60, then type ls wage c educ. Then set the sample to 61 100 and type ls wage c educ again. Use the results to perform the Chow test. Does the test show two different curves, or not? (We know that in reality the data set does, in fact, have two separate curves in it.)

7. Reset the sample to 1 100, then type genr wage = 10 + educ*2 + group1*0.2 + nrnd()*3 to generate new wages with much less discrimination in them. Repeat steps 4–6. Is the difference in the two groups visible now? Does the dummy variable show up as significant, and does the Chow test find the distinction?

8. Reset the sample to 1 100, then type genr wage = 10 + educ*2 + group1*2 + educ*group1*0.4 + nrnd()*3. This time the slope will vary as well as the intercept. Type genr educg1 = educ*group1 to generate the interaction variable, and run steps 4–6 again, except this time in step 5 type ls wage c educ group1 educg1. Is educg1 significant? How about group1? Do the F test and see if the curve has moved. Does it produce the same answer as the Chow test?

Problems

1. In the United States, men earn substantially more money in labor markets than women do. This may be evidence of discrimination, or it may have other causes, such as differences in educational levels between men and women. In this problem we'll look at data on labor market earnings of men and women, taken from the U.S. Census Bureau's Current Population Survey, and identify the causes of the difference between male and female wages.

   Load the data set wages2. This data set contains observations on 827 single men and women (to avoid issues regarding the income of spouses) for the following variables: Wagesalary is wage and salary income, measured in dollars per year; Earnings is total earned income, also measured in dollars per year; Female, Africamer, and hispanic are dummy variables that are 1 if the observed person is female, African American, or Hispanic, respectively, and 0 if not; Age is the person's age (older people have more work experience and may be more productive); Education is the number of years of schooling the person has (more educated workers are more productive—anyone with more than 18 years of education is given a value of 18); and Hours is the number of hours the person worked during the year.

   a. First, we'll measure the total gender gap in wage and salary income. Calculate the average wage income for men and the average wage income for women. Which is higher, and how much higher is it? Does this seem like a small difference or a large one? Because averages can be distorted by a few high-income individuals, also calculate the median values. Which median is higher? Is the gap about the same, larger, or smaller?

b. Some of the gender gap may be caused by men having more education, or being older. Calculate average education and age for men and women. Are there differences or not?

c. Now we'll look to see how much of the difference in wage income can be explained by age and education, and how much remains to be explained by gender. Estimate the equation $\text{Wagesalary}_i = \beta_0 + \beta_1 \text{Education}_i + \beta_2 \text{Age}_i + \beta_3 \text{Female}_i + \varepsilon_i$. How many parameters are statistically significantly different from 0?

d. How much does your annual wage and salary income go up if you acquire one more year of education? Multiply this by the average difference in education between men and women. How much of the gap is explained this way?

e. How much does wage and salary income go up if your age rises by one year? Multiply this by the average difference in age between men and women. How much of the gap is "explained" by age difference?

f. After controlling for education and age, how much difference remains between wage incomes of men and women? Whose incomes are higher? Is this what you expected? Does the remaining gap seem large or small? (Hint: What fraction of the average value is it?)

2. One possible reason for remaining differences in wage income between men and women is that men receive different types of education that prepare them for higher-paying jobs. For example, economics majors at most U.S. colleges are disproportionately male. If so, then education should raise the wage income of men by more than it raises the wage income of women. In this problem we'll examine that possibility. Load the data set wages2, which was described in problem 1.

a. Generate an interaction variable equal to Female · Education. What value does this variable take for women? What value does it take for men?

b. Consider the economic model $\text{Wagesalary} = \beta_0 + \beta_1 \text{Education} + \beta_2 \text{Female} + \beta_3 (\text{Female} \cdot \text{Education})$. In this model, if a woman receives one more year of education, how much does her wage rise? If a man receives one more year of education, how much does his wage rise? If education is more valuable for men than it is for women, then what should be true about the value of β_3?

c. If a man and a woman have the same level of education, what is the difference in their wages? If $\beta_3 > 0$, then is the gender gap larger for more educated people, or larger for less educated people?

d. Estimate the regression $\text{Wagesalary} = \beta_0 + \beta_1 \text{Education}_i + \beta_2 \text{Female}_i + \beta_3 (\text{Female}_i \cdot \text{Education}_i) + \beta_4 \text{Age}_i + \varepsilon_i$. Is the interaction parameter statistically significantly different from 0? If so, is it positive or negative? What other parameters are insignificant?

e. To test whether gender affects wage income, what null hypothesis do we test? Using an F test, conduct this test. Does gender affect wages or not?

f. Estimate the regression $\text{Wagesalary} = \beta_0 + \beta_1 \text{Education}_i + \beta_2 (\text{Female}_i \cdot \text{Education}_i) + \beta_3 \text{Age}_i + \varepsilon_i$. Is this model an acceptable restricted model or not? According to these results, is education more valuable for men or for women? What does that imply about the effect of education on the gender gap?

g. Is the gender gap affected by education, not affected by education, or are we unable to tell from these regressions? Write a short essay using the results of these regressions (and the regression from problem 1 if you did that problem) explaining your answer.

3. In this problem we'll consider the possibility that there is discrimination on the basis of race as well as gender. Load the data set wages2, which was described in problem 1.

   a. Calculate the average values of the Africamer and Hispanic variables. What fraction of the sample is African American? What fraction is Hispanic American? Does the sample seem representative of the U.S. population as a whole?

   b. What is the average wage income of African Americans in this data set? What is the average wage income of Hispanic Americans? What is the average education of the other observations in the sample? Does the difference in wage income by race seem to be large or small?

   c. Estimate the model $\text{Wagesalary} = \beta_0 + \beta_1 \text{Education}_i + \beta_2 \text{Age}_i + \beta_3 \text{Female}_i + \beta_4 \text{Africamer}_i + \beta_5 \text{Hispanic}_i + \varepsilon_i$. Does there appear to be discrimination against African Americans in this data? Does there appear to be discrimination against Hispanic Americans?

   d. Test the null hypothesis that race has no effect on wages. What do you find? How do you explain this finding in light of your answer to part *b*? (Hint: What other variables in the regression are capable of explaining differences in wages?)

   e. What policies would you suggest in order to reduce differences in wage incomes by race in the United States, on the basis of this regression?

4. Open the file buscost2, which was described in problem 4 in Chapter 9. In this problem we'll use the variable Private to test whether privately operated bus companies are more cost-efficient than publicly operated ones. Privately operated companies may be more sensitive to financial issues and opportunities to reduce costs than publicly operated companies are, and that may be the reason for such efficiencies.

   a. Calculate the mean value of the variable Private. What fraction of the bus companies in the United States is privately operated? What fraction is publicly operated?

   b. Estimate the equation $\text{Totalcost}_i = \beta_0 + \beta_1 P_{Li} + \beta_2 P_{Ai} + \beta_3 P_{Mi} + \beta_4 P_{Fi} + \beta_5 \text{RVM}_i + \beta_6 \text{Private}_i + \varepsilon_i$. How much lower are the costs of private firms estimated to be? Test whether the difference is statistically significant, or not.

   c. How many of the other parameters in the model are statistically significant? Do any of parameter estimates have implausible signs? Are those ones significant or not?

   d. If some of the other parameters in the regression from part *b* were not statistically significant, then reestimate the equation, dropping variables (and verifying by appropriate *t* and *F* tests that it is permissible to drop them) until all remaining parameters are significant. Again test whether private companies have lower costs, holding input prices and output constant. Has your answer changed? If so, why has it changed?

   e. This equation assumes marginal costs (the derivative of output with respect to RVM) is constant. Add a quadratic term for RVM to the equation, and reestimate the model. Is it significant? Does its addition change the test result or not?

5. In this problem we'll consider whether the result from problem 4 is dependent upon the functional form chosen. Open the file buscost2, which was described in problem 4 in Chapter 9.

   a. We'll try estimating the production function using the double-log (Cobb-Douglass) functional form instead of the linear functional form. Generate the logs of the relevant variables, then estimate the equation $\log \text{Totalcost}_i = \beta_0 + \beta_1 \log P_{Li} + \beta_2 \log P_{Ai} + \beta_3 \log P_{Mi} + \beta_4 \log P_{Fi} + \beta_5 \log \text{RVM}_i + \beta_6 \text{Private}_i + \varepsilon_i$. In this functional form, is there a difference between public and private costs, or not? Drop any other insignificant variables in the regression. Does β_6 become significant when you do this, or not?

b. Perhaps the difference is more complicated than just an intercept shift. Estimate the regression $\beta_0 + \beta_1 \log P_{Li} + \beta_2 \log P_{Ai} + \beta_3 \log P_{Mi} + \beta_4 \log P_{Fi} + \beta_5 \log \text{RVM}_i + \varepsilon_i$ separately on the public subsample and the private subsample. Perform a Chow test for the equality of the parameters in the two samples. What do you find?

c. Which of the parameters appears to have changed their values most between the two samples? Estimate the fully interacted model in which all independent variables are multiplied by the private variable. Then drop as many interaction terms as you can until the remaining ones are significant.

d. How does the cost function of a private firm differ from that of its public counterpart? Write a short essay explaining what the regressions of this problem tell us about the answer to that question. Are the results consistent with our expectations that private firms are more cost-conscious than public ones, or not?

6. One problem with the Chow test is that it depends on an assumption about where the break in the sample occurred. The timing of the beginning of the oil shock is pretty easily identified as late 1973. However, the timing of the end is more difficult to pin down, because the price of oil came back down over a period of time longer than one year. In this problem we'll redo the Chow test, assuming the shift ended in 1982 instead of 1984, and see how the results change.

Load the data file phillips, which contains annual observations from 1960 to 2000 on the following variables: inflation is the inflation rate, unemployment is the unemployment rate, year is the year of the observation, shift is the dummy variable described in the text, and altshift is a dummy variable which is 1 from 1974 to 1981 and 0 otherwise.

a. Suppose we instead dated the last year of the shift as 1981 instead of 1983. Estimate the regression $\text{Inflation} = \beta_0 + \beta_1 \text{Unemployment}_i + \varepsilon_i$ for the entire sample. What is the sum of squared residuals?

b. Now estimate the regression separately on the sample for which Altshift is equal to 1 (1974 to 1981) and on the subsample for which it is equal to 0 (1960 to 1973 and 1982 to 2000). Add the sum of squared residuals from these two equations. What is the total? Is it higher or lower than the total of the SSRs from the two subsample regressions given in the chapter? Is it much different?

c. Do the Chow test of the null hypothesis that the parameters of the model are the same in the two subsamples. What exactly is the alternative hypothesis of this test? What do you find?

d. Based on this Chow test and the one in the chapter, what can we really conclude about the movement of the Phillips curve during the 1970s and 1980s, and what are we forced to make assumptions about?

7. A great deal of economic analysis, going all the way back to the 1800s, has been done on the conflict between the owners of a firm and its workers over how much of the revenues of the firm should be paid to the workers as wages and how much should be retained by the

owners as profits. One way of dealing with this problem is to have employee-owned firms, for which the employees are the owners and the conflict between the groups disappears. Employee ownership is not common, but there are some prominent employee-owned firms, among them (as of 2002) United Airlines and United Parcel Service. Economists have suggested that employee-owned firms might be more profitable than traditional firms, either because management conflicts should be reduced or because employees who own the firm will be more conscious of opportunities to improve efficiency and hence profitability. In this problem and the next one, we'll look at a panel data set of 20 firms, 10 employee owned and 10 not, over an eight-year period, and see if the employee-owned firms did better on some simple accounting measures of financial success.

Load the data set empown, which contains 128 observations on the following variables: revenues is the firm's revenues, netincome is its net income, employees is its number of workers, empowned is a dummy which is 1 if the firm is employee owned and 0 if not, firm is the number of the firm (1–20), and year is the year of the observation (1995–2002). Firms 1–10 are employee-owned, and firms 11–20 are not. The data set also contains a fixed-effect dummy variable for each firm (df1 to df20) and a time-effect dummy variable for each year (dy95 to dy02).

a. The panel is not balanced—that is, not all 20 firms appear in all eight years of the data. Calculate the mean value of the Empowned variable. What fraction of the observations are employee-owned firms?

b. Estimate the equation $\log \text{Netincome}_i = \beta_0 + \beta_1 \log \text{revenues}_i + \beta_2 \log \text{employees}_i + \beta_3 \text{Empowned}_i + \varepsilon_i$, generating the logs of the variables as necessary. We use logs to reduce problems of comparing large firms to small ones. Test whether employee-owned firms have higher or lower profitability than other firms. Is the different significant at the 5 percent level? Is it large or small?

c. It may be important to include time effects in the regression. In particular, there was a recession in 2001, and the curve may have shifted down. Reestimate the regression, including the variables dy96 to dy02. (You must omit one time effect to avoid perfect multicollinearity; omit dy95.) Do the results of the test of employee ownership effects change? If so, how do they change?

d. Do an F test to see if the time effects are statistically significantly or not. Does the curve appear to be shifting over time, or stable?

e. It may also be important to include fixed effects in the regression, since there may be many things other than employee ownership that vary between firms. Reestimate the regression from part *b*, this time including the variables df1 to df19 (omit df20). Include the time effects if they were significant in the F test in part *d*; otherwise exclude them. What happens, and why? (Hint: There are no firms in the sample that changed ownership status during the sample period.)

f. Estimate the regression again, dropping the Empowned variable. Test whether the fixed effects are significant or not. What do you find? Look at the individual coefficient estimates. Do the fixed effects for the employee-owned firms (1–10) seem different from those for the other firms (11–19)?

g. What do you conclude from these regressions about the effect of employee ownership on firm's net income? Write a short essay explaining your findings.

Part **Five**

Extensions of Least Squares Regression

Ordinary least squares regression is the best choice of statistical technique for econometric analysis only if the Gauss-Markov assumptions are satisfied. But in real economic data, those assumptions are often not satisfied. In Part V, we introduce variations of least squares analysis that produce more efficient estimators than ordinary least squares when the data suffer from autocorrelation, heteroskedasticity, or endogenous right-hand-side variables, all of which violate the assumptions of the classical regression model. We also present tests for detecting these problems in data and discuss the consequences of these problems if they remain undetected.

Chapter **Twelve**

Autocorrelation

The term "business cycles" refers to the joint time-series behavior of a wide range of economic variables such as prices, outputs, employment, consumption, and investment. In actual economies, this behavior seems to be characterized by at least two broad regularities: (1) Measured as deviations from trend, the ups and downs in individual economies exhibit a considerable amount of persistence. (2) Most important, measures of various economic activities move together . . . These and other more specific regularities appear to be quite general features of market economies.

John Long and Charles Plosser (1983)

12.1 CORRELATED ECONOMIC SHOCKS

Real-world economies are characterized by business cycles: alternating periods of booms and recessions. Although they can be smoothed out, at least partially, through appropriate monetary and/or fiscal policy, they seem to be a reflection of some underlying tendency of the economy to periodically speed up and slow down. Consider the growth rate of the U.S. economy, shown in Figure 12.1. If we regress this variable on a time trend, then the growth rate tends to run above trend for several years at a time, then goes below the trend for a few years during recession, then returns above trend for several years, and so on.

The error terms of this model do not appear to be independent of one another, or even uncorrelated with one another. Instead, they appear to be correlated with the errors in adjacent years. If a given year (say, 1986) is a boom year, with a positive error term, then the next and previous years (1987 and 1985) probably are boom years also, with positive error terms themselves. Conversely, if a given year is a recession year (say, 1981), then adjacent years tend to also be recessions. We can easily explain this behavior if we assume that the error terms are positively correlated with one another over time; then one good year will tend to be followed by another, and one bad year will tend to be followed by another. Eventually, of course, something unusual will happen and a bad year will be followed by a good year; this represents the end of the recession and the start of the next boom. Conversely, we will eventually get a good year followed by a bad year, through random chance, and that will make the start of the next recession. We say the economy is subject to *shocks;* these shocks move the economy up or down in the period that they occur, then persist for a period of time

FIGURE 12.1
Growth Rate
(Percent) of the
U.S. Economy,
1959–1999

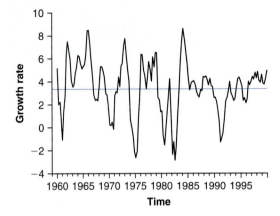

FIGURE 12.2
Randomly
Generated
Correlated
Data

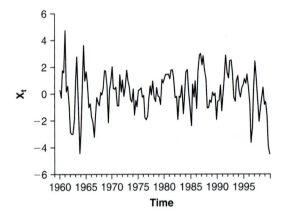

before their influence decays. These shocks are represented in econometric models by the values of the error term (and the error term is sometimes itself referred to as the shock).

Economically, we can explain this sort of pattern in the data by assuming that the underlying shocks to the economy, which make it grow faster or slower in any given year, persist for more than one year. For example, suppose one sector of the economy has unusually high technological progress in a given year. It will probably take more than one year to develop and deploy the new technology. Also, other sectors of the economy will learn to take advantage of the better technology of the new sector, and resources will shift to that sector to take advantage of the higher productivity there—and these changes will take more than one year as well. As a result, the year in which growth is high due to the initial technological progress will tend to be followed by more years in which growth is high, as the development spreads to the rest of the economy. Conversely, a negative shock such as increases in barriers to international trade could take several years to be resolved, and this could cause a low growth rate to similarly persist for several years. Figure 12.2 shows some randomly generated data created by a time trend with correlated error shocks; it looks surprisingly like the growth rate in Figure 12.1, enough so to make econometricians suspect that models with correlated error terms might be a good way to represent macroeconomic time series data.

There is, however, one problem: Correlated error shocks violate the assumptions of the Gauss-Markov theorem. Specifically, they violate assumption A4, which explicitly assumes that error terms are uncorrelated with one another. In the presence of correlated error terms, ordinary least squares (OLS) is no longer the best linear unbiased estimator (BLUE). We need to adjust our method of estimating the parameters of our model to account for the presence of the correlation in the error terms. Doing so, we can find estimators that are better (more efficient) than the OLS estimator is when the data contains serial correlation. This chapter presents the econometric techniques that handle the case of serially correlated shocks and then shows how they are applied to some simple macroeconomic problems.

12.2   CONSEQUENCES OF AUTOCORRELATION

Suppose that we have a data set that has serial correlation, but we do not realize that we have it and we use OLS to estimate the parameters. What are the consequences for the resulting estimates?

Theorem 12.1 If all the assumptions of the Gauss-Markov theorem are true except A4, and the errors are serially correlated, then:

1. The OLS estimates ($\hat{\beta}$) of the true values of the β parameters remain unbiased;
2. OLS estimates of β parameters remain consistent;
3. OLS estimates of the β parameters become inefficient; there exist other estimators that are unbiased and have smaller variances;
4. The usual standard errors of the OLS estimates become biased and inconsistent.

Intuitively, this happens because, although the error terms are serially correlated, their average value is still 0. They are still equally likely to lie above or below the true regression line; therefore, an estimated line through the center of the data will still tend to lie close to the true line. With enough data, it can be made to lie as close to the true line as desired. However, because the errors tend to come in patterns, and OLS assumes they do not, it is possible to estimate the model more efficiently by accounting for this tendency of the errors to come in patterns, and not distorting the estimated slope and intercept of the line to try to eliminate those patterns.

If all we need to do is estimate the slope and intercept of the relationship, serial correlation does not present a very serious problem. The estimates we get still give us the right answer on average, and they get more reliable as we get more data. They are not the best possible estimates we could get with the data, and it would be nice to do better if we can, but the OLS estimates still work fairly well. The problem comes if we need to know how reliable our estimates are; for example, if we wish to test hypotheses about their true values. Because our standard errors are biased, we do not have reliable information about how far off our estimates of the true βs are likely to be. Worse, the standard errors are biased downward, meaning that the standard errors we calculate are lower than the actual standard errors. In the presence of serial correlation, OLS claims to be more accurate than it really is. This can lead to incorrect hypothesis test results, which will tend to find that parameters are more precisely estimated than they in fact are, and will tend to find that parameters are significantly different from 0 when they are not. Although it is possible to find alternate formulas for the standard errors of the OLS estimates when there is serial correlation, it is typically better to try to fix the problem than to proceed with inefficient estimates.

12.3 DETECTING SERIAL CORRELATION

Suppose instead that we do recognize the possibility of serial correlation. We would like to have a method of testing to see whether it exists so that we know whether we should estimate with OLS or seek a better estimator. To test for serial correlation, we have to have some idea of what form the serial correlation is taking so that we know what patterns to look for in the residuals of the regression. Serial correlation can take a wide variety of forms, since in principle any error term can be correlated with any other. One simple possibility, which occurs often in time-series data, is that each error term is related to the one in the previous time period.

> **Definition 12.1** An error term is said to have *first-order autoregression,* or to follow a *first-order autoregressive process,* if it obeys the relationship
>
> $$\varepsilon_t = \rho\varepsilon_{t-1} + u_t \qquad\qquad \textbf{(12.3.1)}$$

where ρ is called the *autocorrelation coefficient* and u_t is a random variable that is not serially correlated: The covariance between u_t and u_{t+s} is 0 for all t and s. We say the errors are *autocorrelated.*

This type of serial correlation is called autoregression because the value of the error term at time t depends on its past values; it is called first-order autoregression, or AR(1) for short, because only the value from one previous period, time $t-1$, affects the value of the present term. We refer to this as a process because it is a rule that governs the evolution of the error term, and hence of the economy, over time.

This form is useful because, if, $\rho > 0$, it corresponds to the economic notion of persistent shocks. Suppose at time $t-1$, that the dependent variable takes an unusually high value, due to a variety of unmeasurable effects in the error term. Then at time t, some fraction of those effects will continue to influence the dependent variable and the rest will have dissipated. The autocorrelation coefficient is the fraction of the effect that continues to affect the economy and hence remain present in ε_t, and u_t represents new effects on the dependent variable that did not exist at time t.[1] If this is the case, and if $-1 < \rho < 1$, then ε_t and ε_{t-1} will be correlated, and their correlation coefficient will be ρ.[2]

First-order autocorrelation is most likely to occur in time-series data, because in time-series data the observations are naturally ordered chronologically—it makes sense to talk

---

[1] It is much less clear what economic interpretation should be given if $\rho < 0$. In that case, positive error terms at time $t-1$ tend to be followed by negative error terms at time t, and conversely. This would happen not only if the unmeasurable effects on the economy represented by the error term vanished in the following time period but also if there was some sort of overshooting effect by which the dependent variable went past its expected value. For example, if a market has unusually high prices in one period, perhaps additional suppliers will enter the market and cause an oversupply, hence unusually low prices, in the next period. Although such effects can happen in economic data, they are rare; in most data sets with first order autoregression in the error terms, the autocorrelation coefficient is positive.

[2] If $\rho > 1$ or $\rho < -1$, then the shocks do not partly dissipate over time; instead they multiply over time, the variance of the error terms becomes infinite, and the correlation coefficient of ε_t and ε_{t-1} becomes ill-behaved. For present purposes we assume $-1 < \rho < 1$. We will deal with the case of $\rho = 1$ in a later section of this chapter.

about "the previous observation" and "the next observation" because the data set develops over time. For this reason, AR(1) error terms are usually used with time-series data sets. Cross-section data sets are much less likely to have a natural order in which the concepts of "previous" and "next" observation make sense. If one has data on the 50 U.S. states, there are many ways to order them—largest to smallest in area, largest to smallest in population, east to west, north to south, or even alphabetically. It is not necessarily plausible that the error terms would happen to be correlated in this way. If we order the data by population, and it turns out that the error terms for, say, California and Texas are correlated with one another, then it is more likely that this is caused by an omitted variable that varies with the size of the state than that there is some economic shock that is common to California and Texas but does not affect Arizona and New Mexico. This applies even more if we order the data alphabetically—it is hard to believe that some economic shock would be common to Alabama and Alaska but not to Mississippi or South Carolina, simply because of the names of the states! For this reason, we do not worry greatly about the possibility of autocorrelation in data that is purely cross-sectional, unless there is something other than time that provides a natural order to the data in which it is plausible that common shocks affect adjacent observations. But we do worry about it in time-series data, where economic shocks lasting more than one period affect the data we use in the estimation.

If we do believe that our data set has autocorrelation, and we are willing to assume that the autocorrelation is AR(1), then we can test for its presence by looking for patterns in the residuals for the regression. If adjacent residuals are correlated, either positively or negatively, and the correlation is significant, then we have a problem; if they are not significantly correlated, then there is no first-order autocorrelation and we can proceed to estimate the model by OLS.

Definition 12.2 The *Durbin-Watson test statistic* for first-order autocorrelation is given by:

$$\text{DW} = \frac{\sum_{t=2}^{T} (\varepsilon_t - \varepsilon_{t-1})^2}{\sum_{t=1}^{T} (\varepsilon_t)^2} \tag{12.3.2}$$

To understand why this test statistic detects autocorrelation of the first-order autoregressive type, multiply out the numerator and divide the fraction to get

$$\text{DW} = \frac{\sum_{t=2}^{T} (\varepsilon_t)^2}{\sum_{t=1}^{T} (\varepsilon_t)^2} - \frac{\sum_{t=2}^{T} 2\varepsilon_t \varepsilon_{t-1}}{\sum_{t=1}^{T} (\varepsilon_t)^2} + \frac{\sum_{t=2}^{T} (\varepsilon_{t-1})^2}{\sum_{t=1}^{T} (\varepsilon_t)^2} \tag{12.3.3}$$

The first term in the sequence is almost exactly equal to 1; it differs from 1 only because the summation is from 2 to T in the numerator, and 1 to T in the denominator. As T gets larger and larger, the difference goes to 0. The third term in the sequence is similarly close to 1; rewrite the numerator of that term as $\sum_{t=1}^{T-1} (\varepsilon_t)^2$, and now it differs from 1 only because the summation is 1 to $T - 1$ in the numerator and 1 to T in the denominator. Because $E(\varepsilon_t) = 0$ by assumption, the second term can be rewritten as

$$2 \cdot \frac{\sum_{t=2}^{T} (\varepsilon_t - 0)(\varepsilon_{t-1} - 0)}{\sqrt{\sum_{t=1}^{T} (\varepsilon_t - 0)^2} \sqrt{\sum_{t=1}^{T} (\varepsilon_t - 0)^2}} \tag{12.3.4}$$

which is almost identical to the definition of the sample correlation between ε_t and ε_{t-1}:

$$\hat{\rho} = \frac{\sum_{t=2}^{T}(\varepsilon_t - 0)(\varepsilon_{t-1} - 0)}{\sqrt{\sum_{t=2}^{T}(\varepsilon_t - 0)^2}\sqrt{\sum_{t=2}^{T}(\varepsilon_{t-1} - 0)^2}} \qquad \textbf{(12.3.5)}$$

where again the difference is only that some of the summations are from 1 to T instead of from 2 to T, and that difference goes to 0 as T gets large. Thus we can say

$$\text{DW} \cong 2 - 2\rho \qquad \textbf{(12.3.6)}$$

Because the correlation coefficient must be between -1 and 1, the Durbin-Watson statistic will be between 0 and 4. The Durbin-Watson statistic permits us to test the null hypothesis that $\rho = 0$ against the alternative hypothesis that $\rho > 0$. If $\rho = 0$, then the correlation between ε_t and ε_{t-1} is 0 and there is no autocorrelation. In this case the Durbin-Watson statistic will be equal to 2, and it will be appropriate to estimate the model by OLS—the Gauss-Markov assumptions hold in that case. If $\rho > 0$, then the correlation between ε_t and ε_{t-1} is positive, there is autocorrelation, and we should seek a more efficient estimator that accounts for the correlation.

Of course, the Durbin-Watson statistic is only approximately equal to $2 - 2\rho$, and thus even if $\rho = 0$, the Durbin-Watson statistic will not be equal to 2; it will only be close. We would like to know the probability density function (PDF) of the Durbin-Watson statistic, to know how close it should be to 2, and to be able to perform hypothesis tests about its value. Unfortunately, this is difficult to do, because the distribution of the Durbin-Watson statistic depends not only on the number of observations but also on the values of the X variables used in the regression. For some regressions, the Durbin-Watson statistic tends to be closer to 2 when $\rho = 0$ than it does for other regressions, and therefore it is not possible to establish a precise critical value for the Durbin-Watson statistic that is a cut-off between "close to 2" and "far from 2" that would distinguish autocorrelation from its absence.

However, it is possible to establish a range into which the critical value will fall, regardless of the values of X. That is to say, we can find a lower critical value that is based on worst-case assumptions about the values of X, and an upper critical value that is based on best-case assumptions. We can then evaluate the Durbin-Watson statistic as shown in Figure 12.3. The figure shows the range in which the Durbin-Watson statistic will fall, and the upper and lower critical values (UC and LC, respectively). If the Durbin-Watson statistic is so close to 2 that it is closer than even the upper critical value, or if it is greater than 2, then it falls in the gray region of Figure 12.3. This implies that the data are consistent with the null hypothesis that $\rho = 0$. In that case we do not reject the null hypothesis of no autocorrelation, and we can use the OLS estimates of the parameters. If the Durbin-Watson statistic is below

FIGURE 12.3 **Possible Outcomes of the Durbin-Watson Autocorrelation Test**

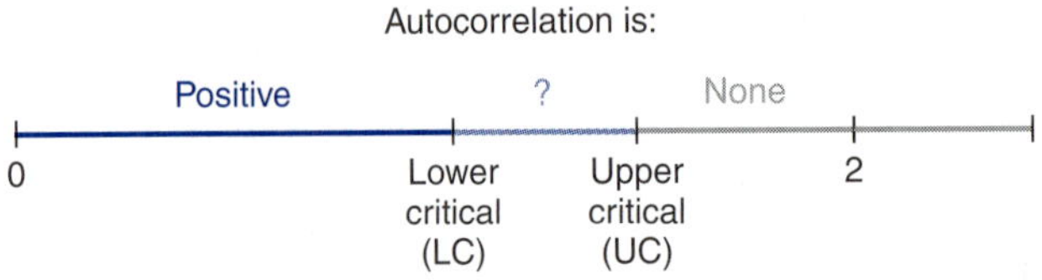

TABLE 12.1
Results of
Estimation of
Equation 12.3.7

Variable	Parameter	Estimate	Standard Error	t Statistic for $\beta = 0$
Intercept	β_0	5.502	0.207	26.6
Interestrate	β_1	0.149	0.028	5.22

even the lower critical value, and falls in the red region of Figure 12.3, then we can reject the null hypothesis that $\rho = 0$, and we can conclude that we have positive autocorrelation.[3]

The final possibility is that the Durbin-Watson statistic falls closer to 2 than the lower critical value but farther from 2 than the upper critical value, falling in the pink region of Figure 12.3. In this case we do not know what the result of the test should be; depending on the exact values of the X variables, the Durbin-Watson statistic might be farther from or closer to 2 than the exact critical value. We cannot conclude whether or not there is autocorrelation. In such a case it is usually best to assume that there is autocorrelation. If we assume that the errors are autocorrelated and allow for a general first-order autoregressive structure, we can test whether $\rho = 0$; if the data are truly not autocorrelated, we should fail to reject that hypothesis. We can then drop the autocorrelation correction. But if we assume that there is no autocorrelation, then we cannot test whether that assumption is correct. It is better to allow for the correction, even though it requires us to estimate one more parameter (ρ is a parameter of the model) and therefore gives us one less degree of freedom in the model.

Table 12.1 gives an example of a regression that suffers from autocorrelation of the errors. The dependent variable is the U.S. savings rate, defined as personal savings as a percentage of gross domestic product (GDP). We would expect this to be affected by interest rates; higher interest rates should encourage consumers to save, whereas lower interest rates should discourage them from doing so. Using quarterly data from 1964 to 1992, we estimate the regression

$$\text{Savingsrate}_t = \beta_0 + \beta_1 \text{Interestrate}_t + \varepsilon_t \qquad \textbf{(12.3.7)}$$

where GDP is the measure of national income used, and consumption and GDP are measured in real terms. As expected, $\hat{\beta}_1 > 0$, indicating that higher interest rates lead to higher personal savings, and it is statistically significantly different from 0. In fact, the standard error is quite small, leading to a t statistic of 5.22 for the significance test.

Unfortunately, the results suffer from autocorrelation. Figure 12.4 plots the predicted and actual values of the savings rate for this equation. The residuals (differences between the predicted and actual values) show very strong patterns over time. For some periods the true value tends to be consistently above the predicted value (for example, 1973 to 1976), and in other periods it is consistently below the predicted value (1987 to 1991). These residuals have the characteristic appearance of positive first-order autocorrelation. The Durbin-Watson statistic calculated from these residuals is 0.567, suggesting a value for ρ of about 0.71. The lower critical value for the Durbin-Watson statistic, with one right-hand-side

---

[3] We assumed that the autocorrelation was positive, not negative, when we chose $\rho > 0$ as the alternative hypothesis. The Durbin-Watson critical values are calculated for a one-tailed test. We can also test for negative autocorrelation. In that case, the upper and lower critical values are greater than 2; to find them, subtract the values given in the Durbin-Watson table from 4. For example, if the critical values are 1.654 and 1.694 for positive autocorrelation, then the critical values are 2.306 and 2.346 for negative autocorrelation. We can also perform a two-tailed test with the alternative hypothesis $\rho \neq 0$ using both sets of critical values; however, in this case we must remember there is a 5 percent chance of being below one set of critical values and a 5 percent chance of being above the other, so the test is of size 10 percent rather than 5 percent.

FIGURE 12.4
Predicted and
Actual Values
of Savings
Rate from
Equation 12.3.7

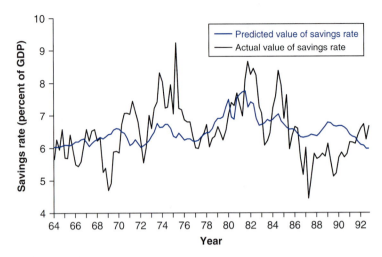

variable and 116 observations, is 1.654, and the upper critical value is 1.694. A Durbin-Watson statistic above 1.694 would indicate no autocorrelation; a value below 1.654, as is the case here, indicates positive autocorrelation. Our equation suffers from inefficiency and from biased standard errors. This is why the t statistics for this regression are as large as they are. Because the reported standard errors are lower than the true standard errors of the parameters, the variables appear to be more standard deviations from 0 than they actually are, and the t statistics are correspondingly high. Because of the autocorrelated errors, the parameters are not in fact as well estimated as they appear to be, and although they appear to be significantly different from 0 from these results, they may not actually be.

12.4   CORRECTING FOR AUTOCORRELATION

If we find that a regression has autocorrelation, we need to find a new method of estimating the parameters of the model, one that is more efficient than OLS and for which we can calculate valid standard errors. There are a variety of ways to do so; most of them involve rewriting the model in such a way that the errors become uncorrelated over time and therefore the transformed model can be efficiently estimated by OLS. Suppose we have the following regression:[4]

$$Y_t = \beta_0 + \beta_1 X_t + \varepsilon_t \tag{12.4.1}$$

and we believe that ε_t follows a first-order autoregressive process:

$$\varepsilon_t = \rho\varepsilon_{t-1} + u_t \tag{12.4.2}$$

Then we can substitute Equation 12.4.2 into Equation 12.4.1 to get

$$Y_t = \beta_0 + \beta_1 X_t + \rho\varepsilon_{t-1} + u_t \tag{12.4.3}$$

[4] We have specified only one right-hand-side variable, for simplicity, but the method works with any number of right-hand-side variables as long as we don't run out of degrees of freedom in the model.

If Equation 12.4.1 holds at time t, then it must hold at time $t - 1$ also:

$$Y_{t-1} = \beta_0 + \beta_1 X_{t-1} + \varepsilon_{t-1} \qquad \textbf{(12.4.4)}$$

Multiply Equation 12.4.4 by ρ:

$$\rho Y_{t-1} = \rho \beta_0 + \rho \beta_1 X_{t-1} + \rho \varepsilon_{t-1} \qquad \textbf{(12.4.5)}$$

Subtracting Equation 12.4.5 from Equation 12.4.3 and rearranging terms produces:

$$Y_t = (1 - \rho)\beta_0 + \rho Y_{t-1} + \beta_1 X_t - \rho \beta_1 X_{t-1} + u_t \qquad \textbf{(12.4.6)}$$

where two things are true; first, the ε terms have canceled out, because both equations contain a $\rho \varepsilon_{t-1}$ term, and second, the remaining error term u_t is, by assumption, not serially correlated! Therefore, it is efficient to use OLS to estimate Equation 12.4.6, which we reparameterize as

$$Y_t = \gamma_0 + \gamma_1 Y_{t-1} + \gamma_2 X_t + \gamma_3 X_{t-1} + u_t \qquad \textbf{(12.4.7)}$$

where $\gamma_1 = \rho$, $\gamma_2 = \beta_1$, and we can calculate an estimate of β_0 by dividing γ_0 by $(1 - \gamma_1)$ to get estimates of all three of the original parameters of Equation 12.4.1, and of the autocorrelation coefficient. This transformation is known as the *Cochrane-Orcutt transformation*.

The Cochrane-Orcutt transformation has two significant drawbacks. First, because it requires us to include both X_t and X_{t-1} as independent variables on the right-hand side of the equation, we lose one observation from the sample when we use it—we cannot observe X_{t-1} for the first period of our data set. Second, it produces a fourth estimated parameter, γ_3, which should be equal to $\rho \beta_1$ according to the model, but typically will not be exactly equal to $\gamma_1 \gamma_2$ and may be very different.[5] There are several different variations on this transformation that eliminate these problems and produce parameter estimates that are efficient in the presence of autocorrelation of type AR(1). Different software packages use different variations, and their derivations are beyond the scope of this book; consult your software's reference manual if you wish to know exactly how it performs autocorrelation corrections.

Table 12.2 shows the results of estimating Equation 12.3.7 using a correction for first-order autocorrelation. Note that the estimated values for the β parameters are not very different between Table 12.1 and Table 12.2. This happens because both sets of parameters are unbiased; even though the OLS estimates in Table 12.1 suffer from autocorrelation, they still produce the right answer on average. However, the reported standard errors are about twice as large in Table 12.2. Because of this, the t statistics in Table 12.2 are lower as well.

TABLE 12.2 **Results of Estimation of Equation 12.3.7 with Autocorrelation Correction**

Variable	Parameter	Estimate	Standard Error	t Statistic for $\beta = 0$
Intercept	β_0	5.971	0.382	15.6
Interestrate	β_1	0.083	0.049	1.71
Autocorrelation	ρ	0.735	0.064	11.5

[5] If the model has more than one right-hand-side variable, then we get one "extra" parameter for every right-hand-side variable in the model, none of which is guaranteed to take the predicted value.

This occurs because the standard error estimates in Table 12.1 are incorrect, due to bias induced by the autocorrelation, and make the parameters appear more precisely estimated than they really are. The standard errors in Table 12.2 do not suffer from this bias, and correctly indicate the likely deviations between the estimated β parameters and their true values. Indeed, because the estimates in Table 12.2 are efficient while those in Table 12.1 are not, the true standard errors of the estimates in Table 12.1 (as distinct from the biased estimates of the standard errors shown in the table) are higher than the standard errors in Table 12.2. The estimates in Table 12.2, which correct for the autocorrelation in the data, are the more reliable of the two, even though the bias in the first set of standard errors makes the estimates in Table 12.1 falsely appear to be more reliable.

Table 12.2 also reports an estimated value and standard error for ρ, the autocorrelation coefficient. The value of 0.735 is quite close to what the Durbin-Watson statistic suggested. It indicates that, given a quarter when there is a positive error and the savings rate is 1 percent higher than we would expect on the basis of interest rates, the next quarter's interest rates will also be higher than we would expect—about 0.735 percent higher. In the quarter after that we should expect interest rates to be $(0.735)^2 = 0.54$ percent above the level suggested by interest rates, and so forth.

The standard error of 0.064 gives us a measure of the accuracy of our estimate of ρ; the 95 percent confidence interval for its true value ranges about 0.13 to either side of 0.735, or from about 0.605 to about 0.865. This suggests a very high level of persistence for shocks to savings rates. An event that causes savings to be unusually high in a given quarter can persist in the economy for some years before its effect dissipates. A series of several consecutive shocks to consumption can change consumer behavior substantially and produce unusually high, or unusually low, savings rates for several years. This appears to be what happened in 1973 and again in 1986.

This regression has corrected the autocorrelation problem. Figure 12.5 plots the predicted and actual values of the savings rate, including the prediction of the residual based on the previous quarter's residual. There is no tendency for the predicted value to stay above or below the true value for long periods of time. This graph is consistent with the idea that the error terms in this regression are uncorrelated over time, as desired.

FIGURE 12.5
Predicted and Actual Values of Savings Rate from Equation 12.3.7 Including Autocorrelation Correction

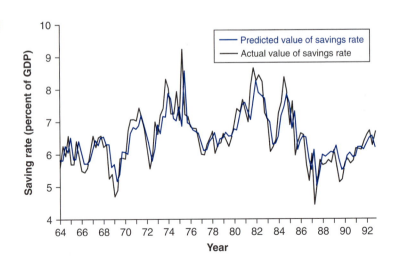

Note also that the predicted values now lie much closer to the actual values than in Figure 12.4, without the autocorrelation. This occurs because once we know there is a pattern of autocorrelation in the residuals, we can use that pattern to predict the next quarter's error term, and hence improve our prediction of the next quarter's savings rate. We don't understand why the correlation exists, but as long as we can see that it does, it tells us that upward or downward shocks to the savings rate will tend to persist—and knowing that helps us predict them into the future.

12.5 THE CASE OF $\rho = 1$

The method for correcting autocorrelation discussed in the preceding sections assumes that ρ is less than 1. If ρ is equal to 1, the problem of autocorrelation is substantially more difficult. Intuitively, the reason is that when $\rho < 1$, then the effect of a shock in one period is diminished in the next period when it is multiplied by ρ. Over time it eventually dies out altogether. But if $\rho = 1$, then that does not happen. Because in this case $\varepsilon_t = \varepsilon_{t-1} + u_t$, whatever unpredictable shocks affected the economy at time $t - 1$ are still present in full force in time period t. They do not diminish over time; when the dependent variable is increased due to a positive shock, it stays increased forever, instead of returning to normal after a period of time, and when it is decreased due to a negative shock, it stays decreased forever. Because a new shock hits the dependent variable in each time period, the cumulative effect of the shocks builds over time without limit, and the error term can become arbitrarily large as time goes on.

> **Definition 12.3** If $\varepsilon_t = \varepsilon_{t-1} + u_t$, then ε_t is a *random walk*. We also say that ε_t contains a *unit root*.

The term *random walk* comes from the failure of the error terms to tend back to 0 following a shock. If they "walk" away from 0 due to a shock in one period, they have no tendency to "walk" back and are just as likely to get farther from 0 as to get closer.[6] The term *unit root* derives from the fact that $\rho = 1$ in such a case. Figure 12.6 shows some data generated by a random walk process; observe that after the value drops to about -10 early in the evolution of the process, it shows no tendency to return, and stays negative for the remainder of the graph; indeed, it drops even further, down to about -15, then wanders back and forth between -10 and -15. If the error term of a regression has this behavior, then the assumption that the data will lie evenly around the true model will be false, and OLS will not produce consistent estimates of the model's parameters. Mathematically, we can show:

> **Theorem 12.2** If $\varepsilon_t = \rho\varepsilon_{t-1} + u_t$, then
>
> $$\sigma_\varepsilon^2 = \frac{\sigma_u^2}{(1 - \rho^2)}.$$

As ρ approaches 1, the variance of the error terms approaches infinity, and is undefined when $\rho = 1$.

---

[6] The original term comes from a story involving an inebriated individual standing in the center of a dock, taking steps in random directions. If he has some tendency to step back toward the center of the dock (corresponding to $\rho < 1$) then on average he will stay safely in the center. But if he has no tendency to return to the center of the dock (corresponding to $\rho = 1$) then his random motion will eventually carry him off the edge of the dock and into the water, no matter how large the dock is.

FIGURE 12.6

A Random Variable with a Unit Root

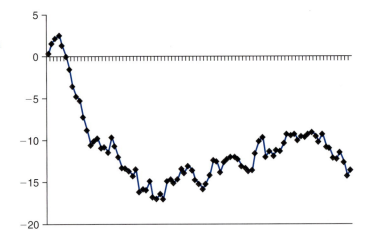

In Chapter 7 we showed that the variances of the estimated $\hat{\beta}_i$ parameters are proportional to the variance of the error terms; when $\rho = 1$ and the variance of the error terms goes to infinity, then the variances of the $\hat{\beta}_i$ do also. OLS estimates of the parameters become completely unreliable; they are still unbiased, because the error terms still average 0, but they are inconsistent and inefficient. Unlike the case where $-1 < \rho < 1$, where using OLS is inefficient but still a reasonable estimation strategy, in the case where $\rho = 1$ OLS is inappropriate and we must find a better estimation strategy.

Fortunately, the same logic that provided the Cochrane-Orcutt transformation provides a solution in this case also. Suppose that we have a regression whose error contains a unit root, that is, $\varepsilon_t = \varepsilon_{t-1} + u_t$. We write the regression as

$$Y_t = \beta_0 + \beta_1 X_t + \varepsilon_{t-1} + u_t \qquad \textbf{(12.5.1)}$$

At time $t - 1$ we have:

$$Y_{t-1} = \beta_0 + \beta_1 X_{t-1} + \varepsilon_{t-1} \qquad \textbf{(12.5.2)}$$

Subtracting Equation 12.5.2 from Equation 12.5.1 (we do not need to multiply by ρ, as we did before, because $\rho = 1$) and rearranging terms produces:

$$Y_t - Y_{t-1} = \beta_1(X_t - X_{t-1}) + u_t \qquad \textbf{(12.5.3)}$$

where the β_0 and ε_{t-1} terms have canceled out, and the β_1 terms can be grouped together. Using the notation ΔY_t and ΔX_t to stand for $Y_t - Y_{t-1}$ and $X_t - X_{t-1}$, that is, for the changes in Y and X from one period to the next, we can rewrite Equation 12.5.3 as

$$\Delta Y_t = \beta_1 \Delta X_t + u_t \qquad \textbf{(12.5.4)}$$

This technique is known as *estimating in first differences* because we refer to ΔY_t as the first difference of Y_t (and to ΔX_t as the first difference of X_t). The advantage of estimating in first differences is that it solves the problem of ε_t following a random walk, and produces consistent estimates of the β parameters of the model (except for β_0). However, it has some drawbacks as well. Suppose Y and X are growing together, with the same rate of

FIGURE 12.7

Two Variables with a Common Growth Trend

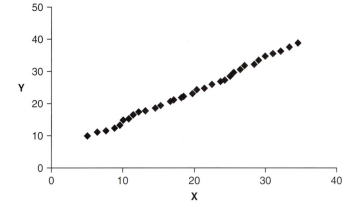

FIGURE 12.8

Uncorrelated Changes in Two Variables with a Common Growth Trend

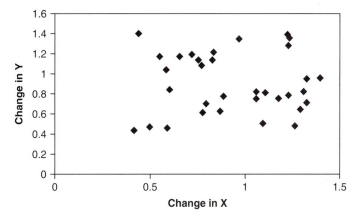

growth, but their deviations from their common growth path are independent of one another. Figure 12.7 shows hypothetical data on variables that have that behavior. Because they are growing together, they clearly have a useful relationship; knowing whether X is high or low will help predict whether Y is high or low. But taking first differences destroys this relationship, because the changes in X and Y over time are independent of one another, as Figure 12.8 shows. Taking first differences removes the information about their relationship conveyed by their common trend, and that is often undesirable. This is especially true because many important macroeconomic variables tend to grow together in much this fashion as the economy grows over time. There are techniques that can be used to analyze such data without removing the information conveyed by the long-run trend of the variables, and they are covered at greater length in Chapter 17.

12.6   MORE COMPLICATED AUTOCORRELATION STRUCTURES

First-order autoregressive models of autocorrelation are quite powerful, especially for annual data series, and are capable of solving autocorrelation problems in many data sets. However, there are some data sets in which the autocorrelation takes more complicated forms, particularly if the data are not annual but rather quarterly, monthly, or even of a shorter time period. One way in which autocorrelation might be more complicated is that it might depend on more than one past value of ε.

Definition 12.4 If the error term follows the process $\varepsilon_t = \rho_1 \varepsilon_{t-1} + \rho_2 \varepsilon_{t-2} + u_t$, then ε follows a *second-order autoregressive (AR) process.* More generally, if the error term follows the process

$$\varepsilon_t = \sum_{s=1}^{P} \rho_s \varepsilon_{t-s} + u_t \tag{12.6.1}$$

Then ε follows an order P autoregressive process, which we call an *AR(P) process.*

Or perhaps it is not the past values of ε, but the past values of u that affect the current value of ε.

Definition 12.5 If the error term follows the process $\varepsilon_t = \lambda u_{t-1} + u_t$, then ε follows a *first-order moving average (MA) process.* More generally, if the error term follows the process

$$\varepsilon_t = \sum_{s=1}^{Q} \lambda_s u_{t-s} + u_t \tag{12.6.2}$$

Then ε follows an order Q moving average process, which we call an *MA(Q) process.*

Or perhaps past values of both ε and u matter.

Definition 12.6 If the error term follows the process

$$\varepsilon_t = \sum_{s=1}^{P} \rho_s \varepsilon_{t-s} + \sum_{s=1}^{Q} \lambda_s u_{t-s} + u_t \tag{12.6.3}$$

Then ε follows a process with both autoregressive and moving average components, which we call an *ARMA(P, Q) process,* where P is the number of lags of ε and Q is the number of lags of u in the process.

How do we know whether to use an autoregressive process or a moving average process, or a combination of both, to test for autocorrelation? It turns out it doesn't matter. Suppose that we have an AR(1) process:

$$\varepsilon_t = \rho \varepsilon_{t-1} + u_t \tag{12.6.4}$$

Then it must also be the case that $\varepsilon_{t-1} = \rho \varepsilon_{t-2} + u_{t-1}$. Substituting that equation for ε_{t-1} into Equation 12.6.4 produces

$$\varepsilon_t = \rho^2 \varepsilon_{t-2} + \rho u_{t-1} + u_t \tag{12.6.5}$$

It must also be the case that $\varepsilon_{t-1} = \rho \varepsilon_{t-2} + u_{t-1}$, and substituting this into Equation 12.6.5 produces

$$\varepsilon_t = \rho^3 \varepsilon_{t-3} + \rho^2 u_{t-2} + \rho u_{t-1} + u_t \tag{12.6.6}$$

This step can be repeated indefinitely: the result will be

$$\varepsilon_t = \sum_{s=0}^{\infty} \rho^s u_{t-s} \qquad\qquad \textbf{(12.6.7)}$$

which is a MA(∞) process (the $s = 0$ term equals u_t no matter what the value of ρ is). The implication is that an AR(1) process can alternatively be written as a purely MA process, as long as the lag length is long enough to produce the desired degree of accuracy.

This holds true not just for an AR(1) process, but generally.

Theorem 12.3 Any ARMA(P, Q) process can be written as a purely AR or purely MA process with a sufficiently large (possibly infinite) number of lags.

So it doesn't matter if we choose to use an autoregressive model of the error term, or a moving average model, or a combination of both; any approach is capable of representing any autocorrelation structure we might have as long as we add enough terms to the model. Of course, as a practical matter we wish to use as few terms as we can, because each term we use requires us to estimate one more parameter. Normally, we will try a few terms of each type until we get a satisfactory model of the autocorrelation.

How do we choose which terms to try? To detect first-order autocorrelation, we estimated the uncorrected model, then looked at the correlations between $\hat{\varepsilon}_t$ and $\hat{\varepsilon}_{t-1}$. To detect more general ARMA processes, we look at the correlations between $\hat{\varepsilon}_t$ and past values of $\hat{\varepsilon}_t$ to detect higher order autocorrelation. To do that, we define two properties of time series variables:

Definition 12.7 The *autocorrelation coefficient* of a time series ε_t for time lag s is given by:

$$\frac{\sum_{t=s+1}^{T} \varepsilon_t \varepsilon_{t-s}}{\sum_{t=1}^{T} \varepsilon_t^2} \qquad\qquad \textbf{(12.6.8)}$$

and the *autocorrelation function* of the time series, which we write as $\rho(s)$, gives the autocorrelation coefficients as a function of s.

Definition 12.8 The *partial autocorrelation coefficient* of a time series ε_t for time lag s is the coefficient β_s from the regression

$$\varepsilon_t = \beta_1 \varepsilon_{t-1} + \beta_2 \varepsilon_{t-2} + \cdots + \beta_s \varepsilon_{t-s} \qquad\qquad \textbf{(12.6.9)}$$

and the *partial autocorrelation function* gives the partial autocorrelation coefficients as a function of s.

The correlation is called partial because it shows the relationship between ε_t and ε_{t-s} controlling for the fact that ε_t is also related to $\varepsilon_{t-1}, \varepsilon_{t-2} \ldots \varepsilon_{t-s-1}$, which the simple correlation between ε_t and ε_{t-s} does not control for.

To determine how best to represent the error term of an actual regression, we first estimate the model and calculate the residuals. We then calculate the correlation coefficients and the partial autocorrelation coefficients of the observed residuals.

Theorem 12.4 If the error term ε_t of a regression follows an ARMA(P, Q) process, then the autocorrelation coefficients of the residuals $\hat{\varepsilon}_t$ are consistent estimates of the MA parameters λ_s, when the error term is written as an MA( ) process, and the partial autocorrelation coefficients are consistent estimates of the AR parameters ρ_s when the error term is written as an AR( ) process.

We then look to see which of the two (or perhaps combination of the two) can describe the sequence with the fewest parameters to model with sufficient accuracy. We can also show that the standard error of the calculated estimates of λ_s and ρ_s is approximately equal to $1/\sqrt{N}$, where N is the number of time periods in the data set.[7] We can use this to do tests of significance; if an estimated autocorrelation coefficient or partial autocorrelation coefficient is less than approximately $2/\sqrt{N}$, then it is not statistically significantly different from 0.

Figure 12.9 shows the autocorrelation and partial autocorrelation coefficients for a random variable which follows the process $\varepsilon_t = 0.9\varepsilon_{t-1} + u_t$. A graph showing these coefficients is also known as the correlogram of the variable. The partial autocorrelation coefficients show that ρ_1 is very close to 0.9 and all later values of ρ, if we choose to use them, are close to 0. As shown above, we can rewrite this process as an MA process

$$\varepsilon_t = \sum_{s=0}^{\infty} 0.9^s u_{t-s}$$

and the autocorrelation coefficients show this pattern; they are approximately 0.9, 0.81, 0.729, and so forth for successive powers of 0.9. This occurs because if 90 percent of each

FIGURE 12.9 **Autocorrelation and Partial Autocorrelation Coefficients of a Simulated AR(1) Process**

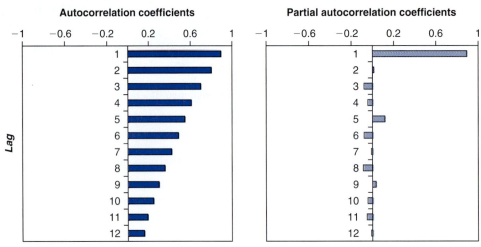

[7] This result relies on the assumptions that the values of u_t are uncorrelated over time and identically distributed. Standard errors can also be found if those assumptions are incorrect.

TABLE 12.3   **Results of Estimation of Equation 12.6.10**

Variable	Parameter	Estimate	Standard Error	t Statistic for $\beta = 0$
Intercept	β_0	4.145	0.206	20.2
Primerate	β_1	0.210	0.026	8.09

year's shock survives to the next year and 10 percent decays, then a shock of 1 at time t will have an effect of 0.9 in year $t + 1$, 0.81 in year $t + 2$, 0.729 in year $t + 3$, and so on, getting weaker with each passing year but never decaying completely to 0. We have the choice to view this as either an AR process or an MA process, but clearly it is better to view it as an AR process (requiring only 1 correction term) than as an MA process (requiring many corrective terms). Most autocorrelation in economic data is better represented by AR terms, because it models shocks that persist over time in this way, but in some models MA terms are useful to help clear up some autocorrelation that the pattern of decay in an AR process doesn't quite catch.

Table 12.3 shows the results of estimating the equation

$$\text{Unemployment} = \beta_0 + \beta_1 \text{Primerate} + \varepsilon \qquad \textbf{(12.6.10)}$$

using quarterly data from the first quarter of 1948 to the fourth quarter of 2002. We might expect a relationship between these variables because firms can substitute between capital and labor inputs in production. When interest rates rise and capital is more expensive, firms can demand more labor, reducing unemployment. We find results that are contrary to what is expected: The regression predicts that increases in the prime rate will increase unemployment, not reduce it. Moreover, the effect appears to be statistically significant, although we might suspect that there is autocorrelation that biases the standard error estimates and makes the estimated value look more precise than it is.

In fact, the Durbin-Watson statistic is equal to 0.125, suggesting that there is, at least, first-order autocorrelation. But there may be more autocorrelation than just first-order. Figure 12.10 shows the correlogram of the residuals from this regression. We used 220 observations to estimate Equation 12.6.10, so any coefficient greater than about 0.135 is statistically significantly different from 0. Most of the autocorrelations are greater than 0.135, but most of the partial autocorrelations are not, suggesting that the error term of this regression is best modeled as an AR process, with at least two lags. Estimating the model with an AR(2) correction reveals that a little more correction is necessary, but the addition of MA(4) and MA(8) terms, corresponding to lags of one and two years, respectively, produces a correlogram with all estimated coefficients not significantly different from 0.

Table 12.4 shows the results of estimating Equation 12.6.10 with the necessary corrections. The AR and MA correction terms are all statistically significant. Better, the estimated parameter for the prime rate is statistically significant and now takes the expected negative sign; firms do in fact substitute away from capital into labor when the price of capital rises, as theory predicts. The effect, however, is quite small; a 1 percent rise in the prime rate only reduces unemployment by 0.054 percent. Thus the substitution opportunities, though real, appear to be limited.

TABLE 12.4
Results of
Estimation of
Equation
12.6.10 with
Autocorre-
lation
Corrections

Variable	Parameter	Estimate	Standard Error	t Statistic for $\beta = 0$
Intercept	β_0	6.330	0.661	9.57
Prime Rate	β_1	−0.054	0.019	−2.80
AR(1)	ρ_1	1.641	0.053	31.1
AR(2)	ρ_2	−0.652	0.052	−12.4
MA(4)	λ_4	−0.414	0.070	−5.89
MA(8)	λ_8	−0.228	0.069	−3.28

FIGURE 12.10 **Autocorrelation and Partial Autocorrelation Coefficients of Residuals from Equation 12.6.10**

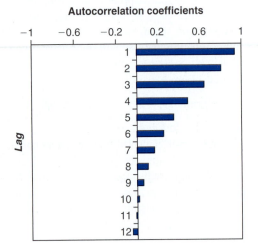
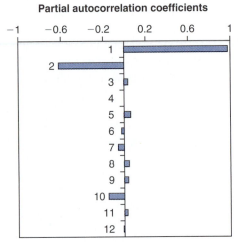

Chapter Review

- When unobserved, persistent shocks affect the value of a dependent variable, and regressions involving that variable will tend to suffer from serial correlation. Many time-series data sets, especially macroeconomic data, have this feature.

- If a regression has serial correlation, then OLS estimates of the parameters remain unbiased and consistent, but are inefficient.

- The usual standard errors of OLS estimates, however, are biased—and biased downward, causing variables to appear more precisely measured and more likely to appear to be statistically significantly different from 0 than they really are.

- A simple but very useful way to model serial correlation is *first-order autoregression,* in which $\varepsilon_t = \rho \varepsilon_{t-1} + u_t$. The autocorrelation can be positive or negative, although positive autocorrelation is much more common in economic data.

- The *Durbin-Watson test statistic* can be used to test for first-order autoregression in the error terms.

- The *Cochrane-Orcutt transformation* or other, similar methods can be used to produce an estimator of the parameter of the models that is more efficient than OLS in the presence of autocorrelation and that produces correct estimates of the standard errors of the estimated parameters.

- An error term is a *random walk,* or has a *unit root,* if $\rho = 1$. Regression in first differences is a solution to this problem, but an imperfect one because it eliminates information about the common trend of the variables.
- More complicated *autoregressive (AR)* and *moving average (MA)* structures for autocorrelation can be detected and corrected for using autocorrelation and partial autocorrelation coefficients.

Computer Exercise

In this exercise we'll generate two sets of error terms, one with autocorrelation and one without, and run otherwise identical regressions with each set of errors. We'll see how the properties of the two regressions differ due to the autocorrelation of the errors.

1. Start Eviews, and create a new worksheet, undated, with 120 observations.

2. At the command line, type genr err1 = nrnd() to create one set of errors that is not autocorrelated.

3. Type genr u = nrnd()/2.294 to create a set of *u* variables that will be used in creating errors that follow an autoregressive process.

4. Type smpl 1 1, then type genr err2 = nrnd() to create an initial value for the autocorrelated error sequence.

5. Type smpl 2 120, then type genr err2 = 0.9*err2(–1) + u to generate a second set of errors that follows the process $\varepsilon_t = 0.9\varepsilon_{t-1} + u_t$. Then type smpl 1 120 to restore the full sample for analysis.

6. Find the means and standard deviations of err1 and err2. How close are they? (Both should have means close to 0 and standard deviations close to 1.)

7. Open err1, press the View button, and view Correlogram, which will produce a plot of the autocorrelations and partial autocorrelations of the variable. Are any of them very large? Now open err2. What does its correlogram look like?

8. Plot both err1 and err2 as line graphs. Which looks more like typical macroeconomic data?

9. Now we'll use these errors in regressions. Type genr x = 30+rnd()*20 to create an independent variable; then type genr y1 = 2+0.1*x + err1 and y2 = 2+0.1*x + err2 to create two dependent variables, one with each error term.

10. Type ls y1 c x and do the Durbin-Watson test. Do you reject, or fail to reject, autocorrelation? Under the View button, select Residual Tests, then Correlogram and Q statistics to check for more complicated types of autocorrelation. How does it look?

11. Type ls y2 c x and do the Durbin-Watson test. Now do you reject or fail to reject? Check the correlogram for this regression also.

12. Look at the standard error for β_1 in this regression. Is it higher or lower than the standard error for β_1 in the first regression, which had no autocorrelation?

13. Type ls y2 c x ar(1) to estimate the regression with an autocorrelation correction. Do you get an estimated value close to 0.9? View the correlogram one more time. Does it look like the correlogram from the regression with no autocorrelation in part 10?

Problems

1. a. Suppose you have the model $C_t = \beta_0 + \beta_1 Y_t + \varepsilon_t$, where C is consumption and Y is income, and that the error term follows an AR(1) process with $\rho = 0.881$. Suppose you were told that the value of $\varepsilon_{97:2}$, the error term for the second quarter of 1997, was $10 billion. What value would you predict for the error term for the third quarter of 1997? What value would you predict for the first quarter of 1998? Do you predict that unusually high consumption will disappear quickly or persist for some time?

   b. Suppose the estimated value of β_1 is 0.62 and the estimated value of β_0 is $220 billion. In the third quarter of 1997, U.S. GDP was $8,931 billion. If you knew nothing about the value of the error term from the second quarter, what value would you predict for consumption in the third quarter? If you knew the second quarter error term was $10 billion, what would you predict for the third quarter? What would you predict if the second quarter error term was −$5 billion (that is, was $5 billion below its expected value)?

2. Open the data file taxrcpt, which was described in problem 7 in Chapter 6.

   a. Estimate the regression $\text{Receipts}_t = \beta_0 + \beta_1 \text{GDP}_t + \varepsilon_t$. What are the values and standard errors of the parameter estimates?

   b. What is the Durbin-Watson statistic? What are the upper and lower critical values? Do you find positive autocorrelation, negative autocorrelation, no autocorrelation, or are you in the uncertain region?

   c. Reestimate the equation using a correction for an AR(1) process in the error term. Have the estimated parameter values risen or fallen? Have they changed much, or are they about the same as before? Have the standard errors of the estimated parameters risen or fallen? Have they changed much, or are they about the same as before?

3. Load the data file macro2, which contains quarterly observations on consumption, GDP, and the prime rate from the first quarter of 1947 to the fourth quarter of 2001.

   a. Estimate the regression $\text{Consumption}_t = \beta_0 + \beta_1 \text{GDP}_t + \beta_2 \text{Primerate}_t + \varepsilon_t$. What is the Durbin-Watson statistic for this regression? Find the lower and upper critical values for the Durbin-Watson test. Does this regression have autocorrelation and, if so, is it positive or negative?

   b. Reestimate the regression, including a correction for first-order autocorrelation. What is the estimated value of ρ?

   c. Estimate the regression in first differences; that is, $\text{Consumption}_t - \text{Consumption}_{t-1} = \beta_0 + \beta_1 (\text{GDP}_t - \text{GDP}_{t-1}) + \beta_2 (\text{Primerate}_t - \text{Primerate}_{t-1}) + \varepsilon_t$. What is the Durbin-Watson statistic for this regression? Has the first differencing dealt with the autocorrelation problem or not?

4. In a famous article on expectations, Robert Barro (1977) argued that changes in the money supply would affect the economy only if they were unexpected, because anticipated changes in the money supply would not cause anyone to change his or her behavior. In this problem we'll predict changes in the money supply and see if the errors are serially correlated in ways that would help with prediction. Load the data file money, which contains quarterly observations from the first quarter of 1960 to the fourth quarter of 2002 on changefedexp (the change in federal expenditures in the given quarter); unemployment (the unemployment rate in the given quarter); and changem1 and futurechangem1 (the change in the money supply in the given and following quarter, respectively), the last being the variable Barro wished to predict.

a. Estimate the regression $\text{Futurechangem1}_t = \beta_0 + \beta_1 \text{Changefedexp}_t + \beta_2 \text{Unemployment}_t + \varepsilon_t$. What are the standard errors of the three parameters? Which of the parameters are significantly different from 0?

b. This regression may suffer from autocorrelation, in which case the standard error estimates are biased. Perform a Durbin-Watson test on this regression. Is there autocorrelation or not? On the basis of this finding, if you knew there had been an unusually large increase in the money supply this quarter, what would you predict about the change in the money supply for the next quarter, all else held equal?

c. Reestimate the equation adding a correction for first-order autocorrelation. Is the value of ρ significantly different from 0? What are the standard errors of the three parameter estimates now? How many are larger and how many are smaller? Did any of them change their significance?

d. If the error term for the fourth quarter of 2002 was known to be $2 billion, what value would you predict it would take in the first quarter of 2003?

e. Instead of using an autocorrelation correction, Barro addressed the problem by including the present quarter's change in money supply as a right-hand-side variable. Estimate the regression $\text{Futurechangem1}_t = \beta_0 + \beta_1 \text{Changefedexp}_t + \beta_2 \text{Unemployment}_t + \beta_3 \text{Changem1}_t + \varepsilon_t$. What value do you get for β_3? How similar is it to your estimated value of ρ from part c? If Changem1 rose by $2 billion in the fourth quarter of 2002, how much would you predict it would rise in first quarter 2003?

5. Load the data file carspend, which was described in problem 1 in Chapter 7. In this problem we'll consider whether this regression suffers from autocorrelation, and how the results change if an autocorrelation correction is used.

a. Estimate the equation $\text{Carspend}_t = \beta_0 + \beta_1 \text{Disposinc}_t + \varepsilon_t$. What is your estimated value for β_1? Find a 95 percent confidence interval for its value. If disposable income rises by $1 billion, how much do you expect car spending to rise?

b. Perform the Durbin-Watson test on the regression. Do you have positive autocorrelation, negative autocorrelation, no autocorrelation, or are you in the uncertain region?

c. Plot the residuals from this regression. What sort of pattern do they appear to have?

d. Estimate the equation again, this time using a correction for an AR(1) process in the error term. What is the estimated value of ρ? Is it significantly different from 0?

e. What is the value of $\hat{\beta}_1$ now? Has it changed a lot, or not very much? Is the standard error of $\hat{\beta}_1$ larger or smaller than it was without the autocorrelation correction? Find the 95 percent confidence interval for β_1 on the basis of this regression. If disposable income rises by $1 billion, how much do you expect car spending to rise?

f. Which confidence interval is a better estimate of the range of possible values for β_1, the first one or the second one? Briefly explain why. Is a rise of $10 million in car spending an acceptable prediction for the effect of a $1 billion rise in disposable income, or not?

6. In this problem we'll consider whether the error term in the car spending equation might suffer from an autocorrelation problem more complex than first-order autocorrelation. Load the data file carspend, which was described in problem 1 in Chapter 7.

a. Estimate the equation $\text{Carspend}_t = \beta_0 + \beta_1 \text{Disposinc}_t + \varepsilon_t$, and estimate the correlogram of the residuals, using 10 lags. How many significant autocorrelation terms are there? How many significant partial correlation terms are there? Will it be easier to describe this error term as an AR process, or an MA process?

b. Estimate the equation $\text{Carspend}_t = \beta_0 + \beta_1 \text{Disposinc}_t + \varepsilon_t$, including corrections for an AR(2) process in the error term. What are the estimated values of ρ_1 and ρ_2? Are they statistically significantly different from zero?

c. Find a 95 percent confidence interval for β_1 on the basis of this regression.

d. Suppose we thought there might be an AR(3) process in the error term. Add the correction for AR(3). Is the estimated value of ρ_3 statistically significantly different from 0?

7. In this problem we'll look at the behavior of stock prices over time, and see if they support some simple economic theories about their correlations. Load the data file stockprices, which has 37 daily observations on the prices of three stocks: Dell, General Electric, and Yahoo. If stock markets are unpredictable, then the value of a stock on any given day should be equal to its value the day before, plus or minus a random (unpredictable) change. That is, we should have $\text{GE}_t = \text{GE}_{t-1} + \varepsilon_t$. Note that this regression has no intercept term.

a. In the regression $\text{GE}_t = \beta_1 \text{GE}_{t-1} + \varepsilon_t$, suppose the error terms have positive auto-correlation. If the error term on one day is negative (that is, GE was priced below its expected value), what would you predict would be true the next day? What might you want to do the next day in that case? What would you predict if the autocorrelation was negative?

b. If markets are unpredictable, then there should not be any autocorrelation, of either sign. Reestimate the regression with a correction for an AR(1) process in the error term, and test the null hypothesis that $\rho = 0$. What do you find?

c. Repeat parts *a* to *c* for Dell and Yahoo stock prices. What do your results suggest about the unpredictability of markets?

Chapter **Thirteen**

Heteroskedasticity

And the people saw . . . the noise of the trumpet, and the mountain smoking; and when the people saw it, they removed, and stood far off.

Exodus 20:15

13.1 DATA POINTS OF DIFFERING RELIABILITY

Suppose that you are in charge of awarding a prize for scholarship, and suppose further that you have chosen to use grade point average (GPA) as one criterion for choosing the recipient. You narrow your choice down to two students, with identical GPAs of 3.7. One of them is a junior with 20 courses on her record; the other is a freshman with only 4 courses on his. To which of the two would you award the prize?

In each case the student's GPA is an estimate of his or her true scholarly abilities; it is based on a measurement of the student's abilities made through exams, papers, and other graded assignments. However, no assignment covers all the material that was included in an entire college course. Sometimes a student gets lucky and finds all the questions on the exam to be easy ones. Other times a student gets unlucky and discovers that the single item in the course that he or she did not understand well is the one that the big essay question on the final exam asks about. Therefore, a GPA is an estimate of scholarly ability based on a sample of data about the student's ability; like any other estimate based on sample data, it is subject to error in either direction.

Assuming that the exams and papers the student has taken are reasonably comprehensive, GPA should be an unbiased estimator of scholarly ability; on average, a student's GPA is just as likely to be above the level implied by his or her ability as it is to be below that level. However, a junior with 20 courses to her credit has taken more courses, and hence has taken more exams and written more papers, than a freshman with only 4; the GPA of the junior is an estimate based on a larger sample. As we know from studying the central limit theorem in Chapter 4, the variance of an estimator decreases as the sample size rises.[1] Thus, the GPA of the junior is more likely to be close to her true scholarly ability than the GPA of the freshman. A freshman with a single semester under his belt may have gotten lucky

[1] Strictly speaking, the central limit theorem can be applied only if each observation in the sample has the same distribution, and that is usually not true in the case of college courses, whose grade curves can differ considerably across departments and across sections. However, the intuition conveyed by the central limit theorem—that the GPA of the student with more courses to her credit is a more reliable indicator of underlying ability—is correct in this case as well.

(or unlucky) on a final exam and gotten an unusually high (or low) grade. Or he may have had a class in an unusually difficult discipline, or his learning style may have matched the professor's teaching style particularly well. Any such factor can contribute to an unusual grade in either direction; for a freshman with only 4 courses, one unusual grade can raise or lower the GPA quite a bit. The same factors can contribute to an unusual grade for a junior as well, but they do not affect the student's overall GPA nearly as much. For this reason, we can have more confidence that 3.7 GPA measures the true scholarly ability of the junior than it does for the freshman. (However, it does not necessarily follow that we should award the prize to the junior. The freshman is just as likely to be better than his 3.7 GPA as he is to be the opposite, if the estimator is unbiased.)

Data in regression analysis are, at least potentially, subject to the same concerns; some data points may be more accurate measures of the true relationship between the variables than other data points are. This can happen for any of a variety of reasons:

1. *Larger random numbers have larger variances.* The gross domestic product (GDP) of the United States is about $10 trillion. Its variance is correspondingly large. If we were predicting U.S. GDP and got a prediction that was within, say, $20 billion of the correct value, this would be a very good estimate. The GDP of Albania, in contrast, is only about $3 billion, Albania being a much smaller and poorer country than the United States. If we were predicting the GDP of Albania and were off by $20 billion, we would be embarrassed; this would be a terrible estimate. Given a regression equation like $GDP = \beta_0 + \beta_1 X + \varepsilon$, we might find that the variance of the error for the U.S. observation was larger than the variance for Albania, and this would imply heteroskedasticity.

2. *Averages have smaller variances as the number of observations that produced the average rises.* This is the case of the junior and the freshman. It tends to apply any time data are measured in per-person or per-household terms, or when data points are inferred from a representative sample (poll results, for instance) and the number of observations used in the inference differs from data point to data point.

3. *Quality of data measurement varies.* Some economic data are more reliable than other data, particularly when different parts of the sample are drawn from different sources. For example, when comparing data from different countries, data from countries experiencing civil disruptions may not be as accurately calculated as that from more stable countries. This may cause the errors in regressions using such data to be heteroskedastic, as the poorly measured data may be farther from the line.

4. *Inherent variance in the unobserved factors can cause error terms in our models.* If we are forecasting stock prices, the variance of our errors in blue-chip stocks will probably be smaller than the variance of our errors in small initial public offering (IPO) stocks, just because the stocks of established firms are inherently less volatile and less likely to move far away from whatever economic relationship we expect them to obey.

When, for any of these four reasons, the variances of the errors differ from observation to observation in this way, some data points are more reliable than others. This violates assumption A3 of the Gauss-Markov theorem, which requires that the error terms all have the same variance. As a consequence, ordinary least squares (OLS) will no longer be an efficient way to estimate the data. As with autocorrelation, we need to know how to detect heteroskedasticity if we have it, and how to improve our estimators if we find that we do. This chapter presents the econometric techniques for detecting and correcting for heteroskedaticity, as well as some procedures for cases when correcting the heteroskedasticity is not possible.

13.2   THE GOOD, THE BAD, AND THE UGLY

When some data points are more reliable than others, putting the line through the center of the data is still a useful way to estimate the true model, because the data are just as likely to lie above the line as below it. Figure 13.1 shows 10 data points, 5 with low values of X and 5 with high values. The five observations on the left have a standard deviation of 1; those on the right have a standard deviation of 4. Because the ones on the left have a lower standard deviation, they are more likely to fall close to the line than the ones on the right. The ones on the right may fall close to the line, by coincidence, and one or two do, but they are more likely to fall a long distance away from the line. When we fit a line to the data, the "good" observations on the left give us a better estimate of where the line belongs than do the "bad" observations on the right.

However, in practice it is unlikely that the unreliable options will nicely divide themselves equally above and below the line. Instead, there are likely to be a small number of data points with relatively large errors. If they happen to be mostly above or mostly below the line, then the estimated line can differ substantially from the true line. Figure 13.2 shows an example. The gray line is the true model that generated the data, but by

FIGURE 13.1
Regression with Observations of Differing Reliability

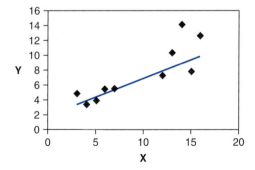

FIGURE 13.2
Regression with One Highly Inaccurate Observation

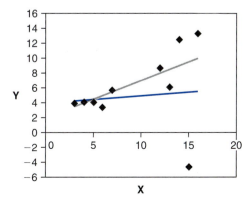

coincidence, one data point has an extremely large negative error term. Fitting a line to these data by least squares will cause the red estimated line to be pulled down toward this data point, resulting in estimates of the slope and intercept of the line that are quite far from their true values. This does not create bias—the line could equally well have been pulled up—but it does produce estimates with high variances, because the chance that the estimated slope and intercept will be far from the true value is higher than it would be if all the error terms had the same standard deviation, and no one observation was likely to distort the estimated line in this way.

What does this imply about the estimates of the parameters of the model? When the data used in estimating a regression suffer from heteroskedasticity, assumption A3 of the Gauss-Markov theorem, which is that every error term has the same variance σ^2 and hence the same standard deviation σ, is violated. As a result, the OLS estimates are no longer the best linear unbiased estimator (BLUE); but as was the case with autocorrelation in Chapter 12, the consequences are not as bad as they might be.

> **Theorem 13.1** If all the assumptions of the Gauss-Markov theorem are true except A3, and the errors are heteroskedastic, then:
>
> 1. The OLS estimates of the $\hat{\beta}$s remain unbiased;
> 2. The OLS estimates of the $\hat{\beta}$s remain consistent;
> 3. The OLS estimates of the $\hat{\beta}$s become inefficient; that is, there exist other estimators that are unbiased and have smaller variances;
> 4. The usual OLS estimates of the standard errors of the $\hat{\beta}$s become biased and inconsistent.

The intuition behind this result is much the same as it was for the similar result of Chapter 12; although the errors are heteroskedastic, they still average 0. Thus the data still tend to lie evenly around the true line, and since OLS puts the estimated line through the center of the data, the estimates will remain unbiased and consistent. The inefficiency arises because OLS places greater emphasis on the observations with high variances than is warranted, and not enough emphasis on the ones with low variances, allowing one "ugly" observation to distort the estimates of the parameters more than it should be allowed to.

The real problem is, again, the bias of the standard errors of the parameter estimates; which tends to be downward, making the parameters appear more precisely estimated than they really are. This causes them to have narrower confidence intervals than they really have and falsely increases the chance that they will appear to be statistically significant. If we are interested in performing any tests on those estimates, or assessing their reliability, then heteroskedasticity will cause problems that we will have to deal with.

13.3 DETECTING HETEROSKEDASTICITY OF A KNOWN FORM

In general, our approach to detecting heteroskedasticity is similar to our approach for detecting autocorrelation—run the regression with OLS, and examine the residuals for a pattern that suggests heteroskedasticity. The primary difference is that when we are looking for autocorrelation, a first-order autoregressive process is an obvious form to look for first, but with heteroskedasticity it is less obvious what patterns we should expect. Even if the data are truly homoskedastic, and all the observations have the same variance, there will still be some large residuals and some small ones, because of their underlying randomness. We can detect heteroskedasticty easily only if we suspect some sort of pattern about *which* observations tend to have high variances and which tend to have low variances. In some cases we will have such a suspicion. If heteroskedasticity is based on scale, then larger countries (measured by GDP or population or some similar scaling variance) may have larger variances; in the case of GPAs, students with fewer courses may have larger variances. In other cases we will not have any very strong ideas about which observations are reliable and which are not. For this reason, heteroskedasticity methods can be divided into two groups—those that assume we know the form of the heteroskedasticity, and those that assume we do not know it. In this section we will discuss the former, and in section 13.5, we will turn to the latter.

Suppose we have a variable that we think influences the variance of the error terms. It may be one of the right-hand-side variables in the regression, or it may be a completely separate variable.[2] In what follows we will call this variable Z, to emphasize its relationship to the variance of the error terms rather than its possible relationship to the dependent variable Y, but remember that it is possible that Z is also one of the X variables in the regression equation.

Definition 13.1 Suppose that the variance of the error terms is given by:

$$\sigma_i^2 = \sigma^2 Z_i^2 \qquad \text{(13.3.1)}$$

Then the standard deviation of each error is proportional to the value of Z for that observation; the larger Z is, the farther the data point is likely to be from the line. Then we say that the data have *proportional heteroskedasticity.*

If we are estimating a regression on a sample of countries, and we think larger countries have larger errors, we might choose the population of the country to serve as a Z variable, or the GDP, or another variable that is proportional to the scale of the country and thus to the size of the error terms.[3]

What if we believe that the relationship is an inverse one—that is, that observations with larger values of the variable causing the heteroskedasticity have smaller errors? Then we let Z be equal to the reciprocal of the variable we measure so that observations with large values of the variable in question, which have small errors, have small values of Z as well. We can also do mathematical transformations if we wish. If we are using GPA data, and from the central limit theorem we believe that

$$\sigma_i^2 = \frac{\sigma^2}{N_i} \qquad \text{(13.3.2)}$$

where N_i is the number of courses the ith student has taken, then we write the equation as

$$\sigma_i^2 = \sigma^2 \left(\frac{1}{\sqrt{N_i}} \right)^2 \qquad \text{(13.3.3)}$$

---

[2] It cannot be the dependent variable, however—the dependent variable is correlated with the error terms by construction.

[3] Unfortunately, when we have several candidates, there is rarely a reliable guide to use in picking one.

and we choose $Z = 1/\sqrt{N_i}$. By similar rearrangement, we can write most reasonable forms of heteroskedasticity as being proportional to some variable Z that is a transformation of the observed variable we believe is related to the variance of the errors.

Supposing that we have proportional heteroskedasticity and can identify the variable Z or at least make a guess about it, what do we expect to see when we look at the residuals of the regression? We should expect to see larger errors associated with larger values of Z. One simple way to check our hypothesis is to plot the residuals from the regression against Z. If the data are heteroskedastic, and if the heteroskedasticity is proportional to Z, then they should produce a plot that looks something like the left side of Figure 13.3. As Z increases, the residuals get larger, both above and below the line, causing the graph to take a trumpet shape, with the bell opening out to the high Z side. If the data are homoskedastic, then this will not happen and the figure will look like the right side of Figure 13.3—the size of the residuals will tend to be about the same no matter what the value of Z is. Unfortunately, this will also happen if the true errors are heteroskedastic but not proportional to Z. Thus the absence of a pattern does not show that the errors are homoskedastic. It shows only that the errors are not heteroskedastic in the form we thought. This could be because the errors are truly homoskedastic, or it could happen because we chose a bad variable to serve as Z. The only way to verify that the data were really homoskedastic would be to graph the residuals against all possible choices for the Z variable, which is plainly impossible.

For a practical example, consider the following regression of electricity use:

$$\text{Elec} = \beta_0 + \beta_1\text{Agric} + \beta_2\text{Aid} + \beta_3\text{Computers} + \beta_4\text{GDP}$$
$$+ \beta_5\text{GDPgrowth} + \beta_6\text{Illitf} + \beta_7\text{Illitm} + \beta_8\text{Industry}$$
$$+ \beta_9\text{Life} + \beta_{10}\text{Roads} + \beta_{11}\text{Popgrowth} + \beta_{12}\text{Urban} + \varepsilon \quad \textbf{(13.3.4)}$$

where Elec is electricity consumption of a particular nation, Aid is the amount of foreign aid the country receives, Agric is the fraction of the country's GDP from agriculture, Industry is the fraction of the country's GDP from industry, Computers is the number of personal computers per 1,000 people, Life is life expectancy in years, Roads is miles of paved roads, Popgrowth is the annual population growth rate, and Urban is the fraction of the country's population that lives in cities. Computers, Life, Illitf, Illitm, Agric, Industry, and

FIGURE 13.3
Patterns of
Heteroskedas-
tic and
Homoskedastic
Residuals

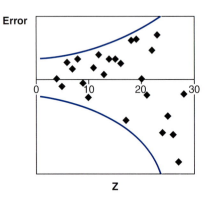

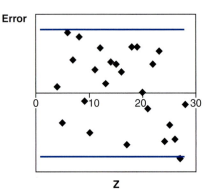

Roads are all measures of a country's technological development, which we expect to increase its demand for electricity. Aid is the variable of interest we might want to know whether increasing foreign aid to a country will cause it to require more electricity and hence increase its energy needs and perhaps exacerbate environmental problems within the country.

Results of estimating Equation 13.3.4 by OLS, on a sample of 57 countries using data from 2000 (except for Computers, which is from 1998), are shown in Table 13.1. Only 3 of the 13 estimated parameters are statistically significant; and of those, two have t statistics only barely greater than the critical value. This regression has more right-hand-side variables than the 57 observations can precisely estimate. Also, because so many of the right-hand-side variables are proxies for technological development, there are some moderately serious multicollinearity problems, which explains why several indicators that should have positive effects (notably Computers) turn out to have negative, but not significant, effects. The solution is to drop some variables according to tests of their statistical significance.

It turns out, by testing to drop irrelevant variables, that *every* variable in the equation can be dropped except GDP, leaving the final regression shown in Table 13.2. This is not an economically very satisfying result. Although the parameter on GDP takes the expected positive sign, and is very precisely estimated, it seems unlikely that none of the other variables in the equation affect electricity demand. Furthermore, it seems at least reasonably likely that this equation suffers from heteroskedasticity. Different countries are of different sizes and have vastly different demands for electricity—and therefore the variance of their

TABLE 13.1
Results of Estimation of Equation 13.3.4 by Least Squares

Variable	Parameter	Estimate	Standard Error	t Statistic for $\beta = 0$
Intercept	β_0	174,739	108,134	1.62
Agric	β_1	−887.1	1,135.5	−0.78
Aid	β_2	371.5	455.7	0.81
Computers	β_3	−98.42	196.6	−0.50
GDP	β_4	456.5	80.38	5.68
GDPgrowth	β_5	−5,078.9	2,526.6	−2.01
Illitf	β_6	470.4	1,522.3	0.31
Illitm	β_7	−652.0	2,189.2	−0.30
Industry	β_8	687.1	1,495.1	0.46
Life	β_9	−2,684.3	1,366.2	−1.96
Roads	β_{10}	351.1	481.7	0.73
Popgrowth	β_{11}	−11,231.1	12,757.0	−0.88
Urban	β_{12}	341.4	684.8	0.49

TABLE 13.2 **Results of Eliminating Insignificant Variables from Equation 13.3.4**

Variable	Parameter	Estimate	Standard Error	t Statistic for $\beta = 0$
Intercept	β_0	12,588	9.316	1.35
GDP	β_4	345.3	9.890	34.9

FIGURE 13.4
Graph of Residuals from Equation 13.3.4 versus Population

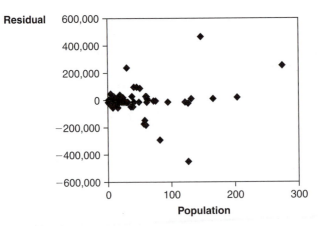

demands probably varies by the size of the country as well. To test whether this is the case, we need to pick a variable to measure the "size" of the country and thus to serve as the Z variable that we think will be proportional to the heteroskedasticity. The remaining variable in the regression, GDP, is one option; other measures of country size such as population and surface area are also possibilities. Let us choose, somewhat arbitrarily, population as the Z variable; that is,

$$\sigma_i^2 = \sigma^2 \text{Population}_i^2 \qquad \textbf{(13.3.5)}$$

Figure 13.4 shows a graph of the residuals from this regression against the population of each country in the sample.[4] Most of the observations on the smallest countries, with populations of less than about 20 million, have residuals fairly near 0. As population increases, the residuals get larger; although some of them remain close to 0, some get larger and a handful get very far away from the graph. This pattern suggests that population might in fact be correlated with the size of the residuals in the model, and it might be reasonable to try to correct for heteroskedasticity that is proportional to population.

However, we can't be sure from this evidence alone that heteroskedasticity (of this form or some other) exists, because the graphical method of detecting heteroskedasticity is not a formal test for heteroskedasticity. There is no way to quantify how much the graph looks like it has a pattern and how much it does not, so there is no way to create any kind of critical value for how "trumpet-shaped" the graph should look before one concludes that there is heteroskedasticity. There are, however, several ways to create a formal test for heteroskedasticity that draw on the same basic intuition as the graphs do: the size of the residuals should be larger as Z gets larger.

One simple possibility is to divide up the sample, placing large countries in one subsample and small countries in another, and look at the residuals for each sample, expecting them to be significantly larger in the sample with larger values of Z. This test is known as the *Goldfeld-Quandt* test for heteroskedasticity. For this test, the null hypothesis is that the variances in the two subsamples are equal and the alternative hypothesis is that they are not

---

[4] The graph omits the observations from the largest two countries, which if included would distort the scale of the graph so much as to obscure the pattern. Their populations are 949 million and 1,242 million, and their errors are +200,000 and +557,000, respectively.

equal. If we fail to reject the null hypothesis, we conclude the data are homoskedastic; if we reject it, we conclude they are heteroskedastic. It turns out that doing this requires us to estimate the regression separately on each of the two subsamples so that the residuals in each of the subsamples will be independent of one another. (If they are taken from the same regression, then they're not quite independent since they have to add up to 0 across both subsamples.) Rather than splitting the sample exactly in half, it is customary to leave some of the observations with middle values of Z out of the subsample regressions altogether, since one cannot be sure which of the two subsamples they should be in. Then calculate the test statistic:

$$GQ = \frac{SSR_1/df_1}{SSR_2/df_2} \qquad \textbf{(13.3.6)}$$

where SSR_1 and SSR_2 are the sums of squared residuals from the large-Z and small-Z subsample regressions, respectively, and df_1 and df_2 are the degrees of freedom from each of the two regressions (normally the same if one has put the same number of observations in each of the subsamples). This statistic takes the F distribution. If there is no homoskedasticity, then SSR_1/df_1 should be equal to SSR_2/df_2, and therefore GQ should be approximately equal to 1. If there is heteroskedasticity, then we expect that the residuals are larger in sample 1, and therefore SSR_1/df_1 should be greater than SSR_2/df_2, and GQ should be greater than 1. If it is larger than the critical F statistic for the appropriate number of degrees of freedom, then we reject homoskedasticity in favor of heteroskedasticity.

The Goldfeld-Quandt test, though it closely follows the intuition that the residuals should be larger on one side of the graph than the other, has two drawbacks. First, the outcome depends on exactly which observations one chooses to include in the large-Z sample and which one chooses to include in the small-Z sample, and there is no obvious rule for choosing how to create the subsamples. If different choices produce different answers— and that can happen—then it is unclear which answer to believe. Second, and conceptually more important, the Goldfeld-Quandt test does not take advantage of the proportional form of the heteroskedasticity.[5] It divides the observations into a "large" group and a "small" group, whereas in reality each error term has a different variance of its own, based on its own particular value of Z.

An alternative test is to see whether the residuals are correlated with the values of Z; if so, that is strong evidence in favor of the proportional heteroskedasticity hypothesis. This test is known as the *Breusch-Pagan-Godfrey* test for heteroskedasticity. One problem is that the residuals are both positive and negative; thus, if we look purely at the correlation between the residual and Z, it will tend to be 0 whether the data are homoskedastic or heteroskedastic, since the positive and negative residuals will tend to cancel each other out. To solve this problem, we square the residuals and look to see whether observations with high values of Z have higher squared residuals. In particular, since our assumption of proportional heteroskedasticity is that $\sigma_i^2 = \sigma^2 Z_i^2$ (Equation 13.3.1), we run the following regression:

$$\hat{\varepsilon}_i^2 = \gamma_0 + \gamma_1 Z_i^2 + u \qquad \textbf{(13.3.7)}$$

---

[5] However, this can be an advantage, since it means that the test still works pretty well even if the heteroskedasticity is not strictly proportional.

If there is heteroskedasticity, then we expect $\gamma_1 > 0$, that is, as Z^2 gets larger, the squared residual gets larger also. (One can include more than one Z variable in the test equation if one suspects that heteroskedasticity is related to more than one variable.) To perform the test, we look at the R^2 for this regression. If the error terms are homoskedastic, then there should be no correlation between the squared residuals and Z^2, and we should get an R^2 close to 0. If, however, there is heteroskedasticity as we suspect, and larger values of Z have larger residuals, then Z^2 should be correlated with the squared residuals and this regression will have an R^2 significantly greater than 0. It turns out that the appropriate test statistic is $\text{BPG} = N \cdot R^2$, where R^2 is taken from estimating Equation 13.3.7 and N is the number of observations used in estimating it. BPG takes the chi-square distribution with 1 degree of freedom. (If we have included more than one variable in the test equation, then the BP statistic takes the chi-square distribution with the number of degrees of freedom equal to the number of variables included.) The null hypothesis is that $\text{BPG} = 0$, indicating homoskedasticity; the alternative hypothesis is that $\text{BPG} > 0$, indicating heteroskedasticity. As shown in Figure 13.5, if the data are homoskedastic, we expect to get a test statistic below the critical value, and if the data are heteroskedastic, then we expect to get a test statistic above the critical value.[6]

We perform this test for the residuals graphed in Figure 13.4, from the restricted version of Equation 13.3.4, estimating the regression

$$\hat{\varepsilon}_i^2 = \gamma_0 + \gamma_1 \text{Population}_i^2 + u \qquad \textbf{(13.3.8)}$$

Results are shown in Table 13.3. The test statistic is $119 \cdot 0.404 = 48.1$; the critical value from the χ_1^2 chart in Appendix C is 3.84. The BPG statistic is much greater than the

TABLE 13.3
Results of Estimating Equation 13.3.8

Variable	Parameter	Estimate	Standard Error	t Statistic for $\beta = 0$
Intercept	γ_0	5.79e9	2.91e9	1.99
Population^2	γ_1	1.56e3	1.75e4	8.91
$N = 119$				$R^2 = 0.404$

FIGURE 13.5
The Distribution of the BPG Heteroskedasticity Test Statistic

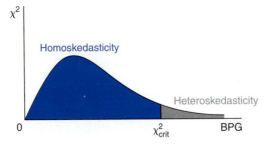

[6] This test is an example of the Lagrange multiplier test discussed back in Chapter 8, which is estimated using only the restricted model (where the restriction is homoskedasticity) and where an unrestricted model that allows for general heteroskedasticity is not estimated. The test statistic $N \cdot R^2$ is, in a very general sense, a measure of how much better we could fit the data if we allowed for the possibility that some errors were larger than others.

critical value. We reject the null hypothesis of homoskedasticity in favor of the alternative hypothesis of homoskedasticity that is proportional to population.

13.4 CORRECTING FOR HETEROSKEDASTICITY OF A KNOWN FORM

Now that we know we have heteroskedasticity, what do we do about it? The approach is basically the same as we used in Chapter 12 to correct for autocorrelation; we transform the model mathematically into a form in which it is homoskedastic and can be estimated by least squares. We have, in general, the equation

$$Y_i = \beta_0 + \beta_1 X_{1i} + \beta_2 X_{2i} + \cdots + \beta_K X_{Ki} + \varepsilon_i \qquad \textbf{(13.4.1)}$$

where we have found, using the methods of the previous section, that ε has proportional heteroskedasticity, that is:

$$\sigma_i^2 = \sigma^2 Z_i^2 \qquad \textbf{(13.4.2)}$$

where Z may be one of the X variables, or may not be. To transform the model, we divide both sides by Z_i:

$$\frac{Y_i}{Z_i} = \beta_0 \frac{1}{Z_i} + \beta_1 \frac{X_{1i}}{Z_i} + \beta_2 \frac{X_{2i}}{Z_i} + \cdots + \beta_K \frac{X_{Ki}}{Z_i} + \frac{\varepsilon_i}{Z_i} \qquad \textbf{(13.4.3)}$$

which we rewrite as

$$\frac{Y_i}{Z_i} = \beta_0 \frac{1}{Z_i} + \beta_1 \frac{X_{1i}}{Z_i} + \beta_2 \frac{X_{2i}}{Z_i} + \cdots + \beta_K \frac{X_{Ki}}{Z_i} + \tilde{\varepsilon}_i \qquad \textbf{(13.4.4)}$$

where $\tilde{\varepsilon}_i = \varepsilon_i / Z_i$ is a new error term, equal to the old one divided by Z_i. What are the properties of this new error term? First, $\tilde{\varepsilon}_i$ has an average value of 0 and is not serially correlated, because ε_i has those properties and dividing by Z_i doesn't change them. However, $\tilde{\varepsilon}_i$ does have a different standard deviation and variance, because dividing by Z_i does decrease the size of ε_i (or increase it, if $Z_i < 1$). The standard deviation of ε_i is σZ_i, because of Equation 13.4.2; and when we divide by Z_i, we scale down ε_i in exact proportion to its standard deviation. The resulting $\tilde{\varepsilon}_i$ therefore all have a standard deviation of σ and thus a variance of σ^2. This, however, means that they all have the same variance—that is, they are homoskedastic! This, in turn, means that Equation 13.4.4 can be efficiently estimated by least squares.

Intuitively, what is happening is this: When we apply OLS to the original Equation 13.4.1, we are minimizing the sum of the squared residuals $\sum \hat{\varepsilon}_i^2$, and the problem with this method of choosing values for $\hat{\beta}_0$ and $\hat{\beta}_1$ is that it places "too much" emphasis on the observations with large errors, caused by their large value of Z. When we apply OLS to the transformed Equation 13.4.4, however, we are minimizing the sum of the squared residuals $\sum \tilde{\varepsilon}_i^2$, which is equal to $\sum (\hat{\varepsilon}_i / Z_i)^2$. The larger the value of Z_i is, the more we are scaling down that particular value of $\hat{\varepsilon}_i$; we are thus reducing the influence of precisely those observations that have large variances and are thus relatively unreliable. Conversely, the smaller the value of Z_i is, the more we increase the importance of $\hat{\varepsilon}_i$ in the sum of squared residuals and the more we increase the influence of those observations which are relatively reliable. Each observation is given a weight in the summation that is proportional to its value of Z, and hence proportional to its reliability. We refer to $1/Z_i$ as the *weight* placed on each observation in minimizing the sum of squared residuals, and we refer to the technique of transforming the equation in this way as *weighted least squares*. We can think of Equation 13.4.4 as being produced by multiplying each observation by the amount of weight, $1/Z_i$, that we wish to put on it in drawing the line through the center of the data we have observed. Observations with high values of Z_i get low weight, and those with low values of Z_i get high weight.

Note that the transformed Equation 13.4.4 has no constant term; the old constant term β_0 has been divided by Z_i. The only way the transformed equation can have a constant is if the heteroskedasticity is proportional to one of the X variables in the equation. Suppose, for the sake of illustration, that the heteroskedasticity is proportional to X_2. Then we choose $Z = X_2$, and the transformed equation is

$$\frac{Y_i}{X_2} = \beta_0 \frac{1}{X_{2i}} + \beta_1 \frac{X_{1i}}{X_{2i}} + \beta_2 \frac{X_{2i}}{X_{2i}} + \cdots + \beta_K \frac{X_{Ki}}{X_{2i}} + \tilde{\varepsilon}_i \quad \textbf{(13.4.5)}$$

The fraction X_{2i}/X_{2i} can be reduced to 1, producing the equation

$$\frac{Y_i}{X_2} = \beta_0 \frac{1}{X_{2i}} + \beta_1 \frac{X_{1i}}{X_{2i}} + \beta_2 + \cdots + \beta_K \frac{X_{Ki}}{X_{2i}} + \tilde{\varepsilon}_i \quad \textbf{(13.4.6)}$$

where β_2, which used to be the parameter on X_2, now functions as an intercept, since it has been transformed into one by the division. The interpretation of the coefficients, however, remains unchanged from the original regression; β_2 is the amount by which Y rises when X_2 rises by 1 unit (and similarly for $\beta_1 \ldots \beta_K$) and β_0 is the value that Y takes when all of the X variables are equal to 0. The economic meaning of the coefficients is not changed by the transformation of the equation in which they are written.

Table 13.4 shows the results of estimating Equation 13.3.5 by weighted least squares, using population as a weight (that is, by dividing Equation 13.3.5 by Population$_i$ and estimating the resulting equation by least squares). Observe that nearly all the standard errors are substantially smaller than in Table 13.1, which estimates the same equation by least squares; recognizing and allowing for the heteroskedasticity greatly increases the precision

	Variable	Parameter	Estimate	Standard Error	t Statistic for β = 0
TABLE 13.4 **Results of** **Estimation of** **Equation** **13.3.4 by** **Weighted Least** **Squares**	Intercept	β_0	−3,021.2	10,429.1	−0.29
	Agric	β_1	−79.40	119.7	−0.66
	Aid	β_2	33.68	48.35	0.70
	Computers	β_3	−37.57	16.87	−2.22
	GDP	β_4	495.6	51.46	5.68
	GDPgrowth	β_5	−129.1	214.6	−0.60
	Illitf	β_6	−10.93	155.7	−0.07
	Illitm	β_7	42.89	191.0	0.22
	Industry	β_8	184.1	103.9	1.77
	Life	β_9	96.68	124.3	0.78
	Roads	β_{10}	20.35	45.90	0.44
	Popgrowth	β_{11}	−1146.1	997.7	−1.14
	Urban	β_{12}	−104.9	63.0	−1.66

TABLE 13.5
Final Results of Estimation of Equation 13.3.4 by Weighted Least Squares

Variable	Parameter	Estimate	Standard Error	t Statistic for $\beta = 0$
Intercept	β_0	−972.7	6014.3	−0.16
Agric	β_1	−237.4	74.10	−3.20
Aid	β_2	90.98	23.81	3.82
Computers	β_3	−41.07	12.38	−3.32
GDP	β_4	482.5	46.05	10.5
Life	β_9	137.5	61.99	2.22
Roads	β_{10}	52.32	21.44	2.44
Urban	β_{12}	−119.2	49.42	−2.41

of the estimates. This equation suffers from the same problems with multicollinearity as the previous one did; however, the process of eliminating variables works much better than it did when we used least squares to estimate the data. The final estimation of this model, after eliminating five variables and verifying their elimination by a suitable F test, is shown in Table 13.5. The remaining seven independent variables are all statistically significant, and their standard errors are all far smaller than those of the original least squares estimates. With weighted least squares, we can accurately measure the effect of various measures of technological development on electricity demand. Not all the variables take the expected sign—it is quite surprising to see that an increased number of computers reduces electricity consumption—but their influence is now appropriately reflected in the final regression, as is the effect of aid on electricity consumption, which provides the answer to our original economic question. Increased aid will indeed increase electricity consumption in the country that receives it.

13.5 WHEN HETEROSKEDASTICITY IS OF UNKNOWN FORM

All of the foregoing, however, depends on being able to identify some particular variable (or variables, in the case of the Breusch-Pagan-Godfrey test) as proportional to the heteroskedasticity. This is not always possible; there are certainly cases where we may be concerned about the possibility of heteroskedasticity without being able to identify a variable that is proportional to it. Or, we may have an idea about a variable that causes the heteroskedasticity but be unable to measure it—for example, we may have data based on averages without knowing how many samples each average is based on. In those cases, OLS still has the flaws listed in Theorem 13.1, but it is not possible to use weighted least squares to eliminate them; another method is needed. Fortunately, it is possible to detect and correct, at least in part, for heteroskedasticity even without knowing the particular form it takes. Unfortunately, the tests and corrections for heteroskedasticity of unknown form are not nearly as powerful as those for heteroskedasticity of known form, simply because there is less information to go on when looking for heteroskedasticity or when dealing with its consequences.

The basic idea behind testing for heteroskedasticity of unknown form is a simple one: If heteroskedasticity exists, it must be correlated with some variable. We may as well try all the ones we have got and see what happens. The test based on this approach to detecting heteroskedasticity is known as the *White test* for heteroskedasticity of unknown form.

Specifically, suppose we have the following regression:

$$Y_i = \beta_0 + \beta_1 X_{1i} + \beta_2 X_{2i} + \cdots + \beta_K X_{Ki} + \varepsilon_i \qquad \textbf{(13.5.1)}$$

and we wish to search for heteroskedasticity. Then, following the same intuition as that which supports the Breusch-Pagan-Godfrey test, we estimate Equation 13.5.1 by least squares, calculate the squared residual for each observation, and estimate:

$$\hat{\varepsilon}_i^2 = \gamma_0 + \sum_{k=1}^{K} \gamma_k X_{ki} + \sum_{k=1}^{K} \gamma_{K+k} X_{ki}^2 + \sum_{k=1}^{K-1} \sum_{l=k+1}^{K} \gamma_{kl} X_{ki} X_{li} + u_i \qquad \textbf{(13.5.2)}$$

That is to say, we regress the squared residuals on every right-hand-side variable, the square of every right-hand-side variable, and all possible interaction terms of all right-hand-side variables.[7] If there is heteroskedasticity, hopefully it is related to one or more of those variables. If it is, one or more of the γ coefficients will pick up the relationship. If not, then we have done the best we can—and we can conclude, for lack of an alternative, that there is no heteroskedasticity. In this case we have only shown that there is no heteroskedasticity proportional to the variables we have used in the test. We have not excluded the possibility that there is heteroskedasticity of other forms.

One drawback of the White test is that the number of possible interaction terms can be very large if K is big, and if the sample is not large, Equation 13.5.2 can have more variables than parameters and we will run out of degrees of freedom. An alternative is to drop the interaction terms and only use the quadratic terms, estimating:

$$\hat{\varepsilon}_i^2 = \gamma_0 + \sum_{k=1}^{K} \gamma_k X_{ki} + \sum_{k=1}^{K} \gamma_{K+k} X_{ki}^2 + u_i \qquad \textbf{(13.5.3)}$$

The former test is known as the *White test with cross-terms* and the latter is known as the *White test without cross-terms*. In general it is better to use the cross-terms as long as sufficient degrees of freedom are available, since they may pick up heteroskedasticity if used, and to drop them only when necessary due to many variables and a small sample.

In either case the test statistic is, as with the Breusch-Pagan-Godfrey test, equal to $N \cdot R^2$ from Equation 13.5.2 or 13.5.3, as the case may be, and it is distributed chi-square with the number of degrees of freedom equal to the number of variables used in the estimation of the test (not the original) equation. If this is greater than the critical value, then the residuals are related to one or more of the X variables, or their quadratic terms and cross-terms, and there is heteroskedasticity. If it is below the critical value, then the squared residuals are unrelated to the X variables and their quadratic and cross-terms, and we have failed to detect any heteroskedasticity.

A harder question is what to do about heteroskedasticity if we find it this way. If we are lucky, only one of the variables in Equation 13.5.2 (or 13.5.3 if we use that) will be stastistically significant. If we are even luckier, it will be a quadratic term or linear term rather than an interaction term. If it is a quadratic term, and every other variable is not statistically significant in the equation (and an appropriate F test confirms that), then we have found that

$$\hat{\varepsilon}_i^2 = \gamma_0 + \gamma_{K+k} X_{ki}^2 + u_i \qquad \textbf{(13.5.4)}$$

---

[7] We do make some obvious exceptions where necessary. For example, if X_k is a dummy variable that takes only the values 0 and 1, then we do not include X_k^2 in Equation 13.5.2, since it would also take only the values 0 and 1 and be perfectly multicollinear with (in fact, identical to) the original X_k.

in which case we can use $1/X_{ki}$ as a weight and perform weighted least squares. Failing that, perhaps we find that a linear term is the only significant term, in which case we have

$$\hat{\varepsilon}_i^2 = \gamma_0 + \gamma_k X_{ki} + u_i \qquad \textbf{(13.5.5)}$$

in which case we can use $1/\sqrt{X_{ki}}$ as a weight.

If we are somewhat less lucky, we may get a single interaction term to be significant, in which case we have

$$\hat{\varepsilon}_i^2 = \gamma_0 + \gamma_{k1} X_{ki} X_{1i} + u_i \qquad \textbf{(13.5.6)}$$

In this case, we could use $1/\sqrt{X_{ki} X_{1i}}$ as a weight, and statistically it will work fine, but as economists we should start to wonder a bit—what could the underlying economic model be that would cause the variance of the residuals to not be correlated with X_k or X_1, but only with both of them multiplied together? More frequently, however, the White test equation will contain several significant variables on the right side, and there will be no obvious way to choose one of them to serve as a weight. Thus the White test regression is not usually a helpful way to identify possible weights.

In such a case, we fall back on the conclusion of Theorem 13.1—OLS remains unbiased and consistent even when there is heteroskedasticity, and we ignore it. The only problems are the bias and inconsistency of the standard error estimates for the parameters, and we work on fixing these instead. The solution is to use a different formula to estimate the standard errors of the parameters, one that is not as efficient as the standard formula but that is consistent in the presence of heteroskedasticity. This formula was also developed by White, and it is sufficiently complex that we will not present its details here. These standard errors are known as *heteroskedasticity-consistent standard errors*. Their main advantage is that they permit us to perform correct tests of hypotheses about the values of our parameters even in the presence of heteroskedasticity that we can't fix by weighting the regression appropriately—they report consistent estimators of the standard deviations of our parameters in that case.

The drawback is that these standard deviations are even larger than the ones reported by OLS originally, because the bias tends to be downward and OLS reports the standard errors as smaller—the estimates as more precise—than they really are. Table 13.6 shows the results of estimating Equation 13.3.4 using the corrected standard error formula. Note that the

TABLE 13.6
Results of Estimation of Equation 13.3.4 with Heteroskedas-ticity-Consistent Standard Errors

Variable	Parameter	Estimate	Standard Error	t Statistic for $\beta = 0$
Intercept	β_0	174,739	115,628	1.51
Agric	β_1	−887.1	871.0	−1.02
Aid	β_2	371.5	320.3	1.16
Computers	β_3	−98.42	126.5	−0.77
GDP	β_4	456.5	108.8	4.19
GDPgrowth	β_5	−5,078.9	3,161.8	−1.61
Illitf	β_6	470.4	770.6	0.61
Illitm	β_7	−652.0	1,117.0	−0.58
Industry	β_8	687.1	822.5	0.83
Life	β_9	−2,684.3	1,649.7	−1.62
Roads	β_{10}	351.1	313.9	1.12
Popgrowth	β_{11}	−11,231.1	8,299.4	−1.35
Urban	β_{12}	341.4	517.9	0.66

parameter estimates are exactly the same as they are in Table 13.1—using the corrected standard error formula doesn't change the choice of estimated values for the parameters, which are just as inefficient as they were before. However, now the standard error column correctly reflects this inefficiency; some (though not all) of the standard error estimates are larger than previously, and in particular, the two variables that appeared to be borderline significant in Table 13.1 now are clearly insignificant (which explains why we were able to drop them, after all, in generating the restricted model in Table 13.2). These standard errors remain vastly greater than the ones produced by weighted least squares when we correct the heteroskedasticity problem, and thus we can calculate more efficient estimates of the parameters.

Thus, it is preferable to correct for heteroskedasticity when it is possible to do so. This, however, depends on identifying a correct weight; and unless we have some economic intuition about where the heteroskedasticity is coming from, we usually do not have a way to find an appropriate weight. Although the White test may suggest a weight, it may suggest the wrong weight—and using the wrong weight can make the estimates even less efficient than if no weight at all is used. As a result, heteroskedasticity of unknown form remains a difficult problem. It is clearly better to use the corrected standard error formula than not to use it, but that does not deal with the root problem of inefficient estimates that heteroskedasticity causes. It leaves us less able to correctly assess the economic relationships that drive the data than we are when our data are homoskedastic.

Chapter Review	• *Heteroskedasticity* occurs whenever some data points are more reliable than others, meaning that they have a smaller variance (and standard deviation), lie close to the true relationship between the variables in the regression, and are better indicators of what the true data generating process actually is.

- Scale, averaging, and data quality are three possible causes of heteroskedasticity in econometric data.

- In the presence of heteroskedasticity, OLS remains unbiased and consistent, because the data still tend to be centered around the true model.

- However, because one high-variance observation can significantly shift the location of the estimated line, OLS becomes inefficient. It is possible to create a better estimator that identifies high-variance observations and does not overreact to them.

- Furthermore, the estimated standard errors of the parameters become biased, and we cannot correctly assess the precision of the estimates or test hypotheses about them.

- When heteroskedasticity is of known form, we can use *weighted least squares* to correctly de-emphasize high-variance observations and produce efficient estimates of the parameters of the model.

- The *Goldfeld-Quandt test* and the *Breusch-Pagan-Godfrey test* are both capable of detecting heteroskedasticity when we have reason to suspect some variable of being proportional to the variance of the error terms.

- When we do not have reason to suspect any particular variable as proportional to the variance of the errors, we must fall back on methods for dealing with heteroskedasticity of unknown form, which are not as powerful or effective.

- The *White test,* with or without cross-terms, can detect heteroskedasticity of unknown form.

- The White test may be able to suggest a weight to use in weighted least squares, though usually it will not.
- We can calculate alternative standard errors that are consistent in the presence of heteroskedasticity and permit correct testing of hypotheses.
- The use of the *heteroskedasticity-consistent standard errors* does not address the root problem of inefficiency of the estimates themselves. Thus it is a less than fully satisfactory solution, though it is better than no solution at all.

Computer Exercise

In this exercise we'll create data with heteroskedastic errors and see how much the heteroskedasticity techniques discussed in the chapter improve the estimation.

1. Open Eviews, and create a new workfile, undated, with 50 observations.

2. Type genr x1 = rnd()*20 and genr x2 = rnd()*20 to create two independent variables.

3. Next, type genr z = x2*0.7 +rnd()*6 to create a third variable that will control the heteroskedasticity. The variable Z will be correlated with X_2 but not identical to it.

4. To increase the chance that we get one far outlying observation, we'll give the variable Z one very large value. Type smpl 1 1, then type genr z=200, then type smpl 1 100 to restore the full sample. (Note that doing this reduces the correlation between X_2 and Z.) Then type genr zsq = z*z for use in testing later.

5. Next we'll create a set of heteroskedastic errors. Type genr err=nrnd()*z to create a set of randomly distributed errors whose variance is proportional to Z. Create a group with the variables err and Z, then graph it as a scatterplot. What happens to err as Z gets larger? What shape does the graph take?

6. Finally, type y = 500 − 2*x1 + x2 + err to create a dependent variable. Then type ls y c x1 x2 to estimate the regression. (Observe that Z is not in the regression.) How close are the estimated parameters to the true values? How big are the standard errors? Do the parameters appear to be unbiased and consistent?

7. In the regression window, click the View button, then select Actual, Fitted, Residual . . ., then select Residual Graph. Is the residual for the first observation (the one for which we set $Z = 200$) unusually large?

8. If we didn't know the variable that controlled the heteroskedasticity, we'd have to fall back on the White test for heteroskedasticity of unknown form. In the regression window, click the View button, then select Residual Tests, then select White Heteroskedasticity (cross-terms). Do you find heteroskedasticity or not?

9. Click the Estimate button to reestimate the equation. This time, select Options and turn on the White heteroskedasticity-consistent errors option. How much do the estimates change?

10. Instead, let's use the fact that we know the variable that controls the heteroskedasticity. Type genr errsq = resid*resid to generate the squared residuals from this regression. In the regression window, press the Name button to give the original equation a name (any name you like) so that we won't lose it when we run the next regression. Then type ls errsq c zsq to test whether the squared residuals are proportional to Z^2 or not. Are they?

11. Close the errsq regression window. Type genr weight=1/z to create an appropriate weighting variable. Then go back to the original regression window, click the Estimate button to estimate again, and click the Options button. Turn off the White standard errors, and turn on the weighted least squares option, using weight as the weighting variable. Now how are the estimated parameters? Are the standard errors smaller or larger than before? How much has weighted least squares improved the quality of the estimates?

12. *Optional:* Weighted least squares works well only if we use the right weight. Estimate the model again, this time using x_2 as the weight. What does this do to the standard errors of the estimates?

Problems

1. Load the data file manufactures, which contains data from the U.S. Census Bureau's American Survey of Manufactures on 455 industries from 1994 on the following variables: shipments (value of output shipped), materials (value of materials inputs used in production), newcap (expenditure on new capital by this industry), inventory (value of inventories held), managers (number of supervisory workers employed), and workers (number of production workers employed). The first four variables are measured in thousands of dollars.

a. Estimate the regression $\text{Shipments}_i = \beta_0 + \beta_1 \text{Managers}_i + \beta_2 \text{Workers}_i + \beta_3 \text{Materials}_i + \beta_4 \text{Newcap}_i + \beta_5 \text{Inventory}_i + \varepsilon_i$. If a firm employs one more manager, how much do shipments rise? If a firm employs one more production worker, how much do shipments rise? Does this match your intuition about the salaries earned by managers and manufacturing workers?

b. Perform the White test, no cross-terms, for heteroskedasticity of unknown form. How many right-hand-side variables does the test regression have? What is the test statistic, and what is the critical value? Does this test find heteroskedasticity or not?

c. Now perform the White test with cross-terms. How many right-hand-side variables does the test regression have? What is the test statistic, and what is the critical value? Does this test find heteroskedasticity or not? Does it match your answer to part *b*?

d. Which of the four reasons for the existence of heteroskedasticity listed in the chapter do you think might apply here? What types of industries would have larger errors, and what types would have smaller? (You might want to look at the distribution of the workers or materials variables.)

e. Reestimate the equation, using the correction for heteroskedasticity-consistent standard errors. How much do the standard errors change? How many variables change their reported statistical significance as a result?

2. In this problem we'll use weighted least squares to correct for heteroskedasticity. Load the file manufactures, which was described in problem 1.

a. Estimate the regression $\text{Shipments}_i = \beta_0 + \beta_1 \text{Managers}_i + \beta_2 \text{Workers}_i + \beta_3 \text{Materials}_i + \beta_4 \text{Newcap}_i + \beta_5 \text{Inventory}_i + \varepsilon_i$, and save the residuals. Then estimate the regression $\hat{\varepsilon}_i^2 = \beta_0 + \beta_1 \text{Materials}_i + \upsilon_i$. What is the R^2 from the latter regression? Calculate the Breusch-Pagan-Godfrey test statistic for proportional heteroskedasticity. Do you reject the null hypothesis, or fail to reject it? Does this imply homoskedasticity or heteroskedasticity?

b. Reestimate the first regression using weighted least squares, using $1/\sqrt{\text{Materials}_i}$ as the weight. You can do this by multiplying every variable in the regression by the weight (including the constant) or by using the weighted least squares command if your software package has one. How much do the estimated parameter values change? How much do their standard errors change? Has the weighting improved the estimates or not?

3. In this problem we'll consider some alternative weights. Load the file manufactures, which was described in problem 1.

    a. First we'll consider the possibility that the heteroskedasticity is proportional to Materials_i instead of its square root. Estimate the regression $\text{Shipments}_i = \beta_0 + \beta_1 \text{Managers}_i + \beta_2 \text{Workers}_i + \beta_3 \text{Materials}_i + \beta_4 \text{Newcap}_i + \beta_5 \text{Inventory}_i + \varepsilon_i$, and save the residuals. Then estimate the regression $\hat{\varepsilon}_i^2 = \beta_0 + \beta_1 \text{Materials}_i^2 + \upsilon_i$. Calculate the BPG statistic for this regression. Can we conclude that there is heteroskedasticity proportional to Materials_i, or not?

    b. Estimate the original regression using weighted least squares with $1/\sqrt{\text{Materials}_i}$ as the weight. Compare the estimated parameters and their standard errors to those of the unweighted regression. Does it appear that weighting improved the estimates, or not?

    c. If you did problem 2, also compare the results of weighted least squares with $1/\sqrt{\text{Materials}_i}$ as the weight to the results using $1/\sqrt{\text{Materials}_i}$ as the weight. Are the results identical, or different? If they are different, are they slightly different or very different? Can we tell which weight is the better one to use?

    d. Next, we'll consider the possibility that the heteroskedasticity is proportional to Inventory_i instead of Materials_i. Regress the residuals from the original (unweighted) equation on inventory; $\hat{\varepsilon}_i^2 = \beta_0 + \beta_1 \text{Inventory}_i^2 + \upsilon_i$. Calculate the BPG test statistic. Do you find heteroskedasticity of this form or not?

4. One approach to getting rid of heteroskedasticity is to change the functional form of the equation. In particular, when the linear functional form shows heteroskedasticity that appears to be caused by scale, using the logarithmic functional form can reduce heteroskedasticity substantially. Load the file manufactures, which was described in problem 1.

    a. Estimate the equation $\log \text{Shipments}_i = \beta_0 + \beta_1 \log \text{managers}_i + \beta_2 \log \text{Workers}_i + \beta_3 \log \text{materials}_i + \beta_4 \log \text{newcap}_i + \beta_5 \log \text{inventory}_i + \varepsilon_i$. If the firm hires 10 percent more managers, how much do shipments rise? If they hire 10 percent more workers, how much do shipments rise?

    b. Perform the White test with cross-terms on this regression. What is the test statistic? Do you reject homoskedasticity, or fail to reject it?

    c. Another thing that can help is to drop irrelevant variables. Which parameters in the regression for part *a* are not statistically significant? Drop the associated variables (verify by the appropriate F test that it is acceptable to do so). Then repeat the White test. Do you pass now?

5. In this problem we'll perform the Goldfeld-Quandt test for heteroskedasticity and see what it finds. Load the file manufactures, which was described in problem 1.

    a. We'll assume that the heteroskedasticity depends on materials. What is the median value of the materials variable? Estimate the regression $\text{Shipments}_i = \beta_0 + \beta_1 \text{Managers}_i +$

β_2Workers$_i$ + β_3Materials$_i$ + β_4Newcap$_i$ + β_5Inventory$_i$ + ε_i, using only those observations for which materials has a value less than 90 percent of the median value. How many observations are used in this regression? What is the sum of squared residuals? Then estimate it using only those observations for which materials has a value greater than 110 percent of the median value. How many observations are used, and what is the sum of squared residuals for this regression?

b. Calculate the Goldfeld-Quandt test statistic. What value do you get? What is the critical value? Does this test detect the heteroskedasticity or not?

6. Heteroskedasticity can also depend on a variable that is not one of the right-hand-side variables in the regression. Load the data file schoolspend, which was described in problem 1 in Chapter 10.

a. Consider the regression Totalspend$_i$ = β_0 + β_1Totalstateaid$_i$ + β_2Income$_i$ + β_3Minority$_i$ + ε_i. Would you expect this regression to suffer from heteroskedasticity or not? Why or why not?

b. Estimate the regression and conduct the White test (because of the small number of observations, don't use cross-terms). What do you find?

c. Perhaps we can do better if we change to per capita spending. Generate variables spendpc, stateaidpc, and incomepc by dividing the totals by population and multiplying by 1,000 (because spending is in millions of dollars but population is in thousands). Estimate the regression Spendpc$_i$ = β_0 + β_1Stateaidpc$_i$ + β_2Incomepc$_i$ + β_3Minority$_i$ + ε_i, and perform the White test. Does this regression appear to suffer from heteroskedasticity or not?

d. Use the squared residuals from the regression in part c to estimate the equation $\hat{\varepsilon}_i^2 = \beta_0 + \beta_1$Population$_i^2 + \upsilon_i$. Calculate the BPG statistic. Do you reject or fail to reject the hypothesis of homoskedasticity? How do you reconcile this result with your results from the White test in part c?

e. Estimate the regression from part c again using 1/Population$_i$ as a weight. Do the estimates change much? Do they get more precise when the weighting correction is applied? Which set of estimates do you prefer?

7. Load the data file schoolspend, which was described in problem 1 in Chapter 10. We'll see if changing to the log functional form helps remove heteroskedasticity from this regression.

a. Estimate the regression log Totalspend$_i$ = β_0 + β_1 log Totalstateaid$_i$ + β_2 log income$_i$ + β_3Minority$_i$ + ε_i. If state income rises by 10 percent, how much does school spending rise? If state aid rises by 10 percent, how much does spending rise? Test whether $\beta_1 = 1$. If state aid rises by 1%, does school spending rise by 1%, or by less?

b. Perform the White test (no cross-terms) on the regression from part a. What do you find?

c. Perhaps there is heteroskedasticity proportional to population in this regression. Use the squared residuals from the regression in part a to estimate the equation $\hat{\varepsilon}_i^2 = \beta_0 + \beta_1$Population$_i^2 + \upsilon_i$. Calculate the BPG statistic. What do you find now? Has the log transformation solved the heteroskedasticity problem?

Chapter **Fourteen**

Endogenous Right-Hand-Side Variables

We have shown that violence aimed at children can be reduced by increasing the tax on beer. Specifically, a 10 percent increase in the excise tax on beer . . . would have lowered the number of abused children by about 151,800.

Sarah Markowitz and Michael Grossman (1998)

14.1 CALCULATING THE EFFECTS OF EXCISE TAXES

There are a number of goods that, when consumed, affect the well-being of people other than the one who consumes them. Smoking tobacco creates secondhand smoke, which many people find displeasing; burning coal to produce electricity, or gasoline to power a car's engine, creates pollution that lowers the air quality of an entire region; excessive consumption of alcohol can lead to violence and a host of related social problems. Such goods are said to create negative externalities, and government sometimes proposes to control or limit their consumption.[1] To provide economic advice to political leaders, we would like to be able to use our knowledge of economics and econometrics to predict the effects of those proposals.

The most common method by which governments seek to limit consumption of certain goods is a tax known as an excise tax. Figure 14.1 shows the effect of a tax on sellers. This tax increases the price at which sellers will provide the good, causing the equilibrium price to rise and the equilibrium quantity to fall.[2] The vertical distance between the two supply curves is equal to the amount of the tax per unit sold. Suppose we want to calculate the amount by

---

[1] Some goods increase the well-being of people other than the consumer; such goods create positive externalities. The government often seeks to encourage, rather than limit, the consumption of such goods, usually through subsidies.

[2] One could alternatively place a tax on the buyers of the good, which would shift demand to the left, also causing equilibrium quantity to fall; equilibrium price would fall too, but buyers would have to pay the tax in addition to the market price of the good (and the price falls by less than the amount of the tax, so the buyers end up paying more in total). Both policies have exactly the same economic effects.

FIGURE 14.1

Effects of a Tax on Sellers

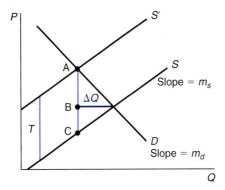

which the equilibrium quantity of the good falls. We can do this if we know the slope of the demand curve, which we call m_d, and the slope of the supply curve, m_s. The distance between points A and B on the graph is equal to the change in quantity times the slope of the demand curve; the distance between points B and C is equal to the change in quantity times the slope of the supply curve. Adding the two together equals the total tax, which implies

$$T = \Delta Q m_d - \Delta Q m_s \qquad (14.1.1)$$

where the minus sign is necessary because the tax represents a reduction in the amount of money collected by the supplier. We can solve this for ΔQ to find the change in quantity as a function of the tax amount:

$$\Delta Q = \frac{T}{m_d - m_s} \qquad (14.1.2)$$

which will be negative, because m_d is negative and m_s is positive. Or, if we know how much we want the quantity to fall, then we can use Equation 14.1.1 directly to calculate the amount of tax required. For example, if the slope of the demand curve is -0.5 and the slope of the supply curve is 1, then a tax rate of 3 units will change quantity by 2 units.

Note that this economic model contains more than one equation—it contains two, one describing the behavior of consumers (the demand equation) and the other the behavior of suppliers (the supply equation). Many interesting economic models contain multiple equations. Finding the equilibrium price and quantity in the supply and demand model requires us to know the slopes of the supply and the demand curve. At first glance this seems simple enough; obtain data on prices and quantities, and estimate the supply and demand curve. But if we estimate the equation

$$Q = \beta_0 + \beta_1 P + \varepsilon \qquad (14.1.3)$$

are we estimating the demand curve or the supply curve? Or something else altogether?

Economic models with more than one equation present a serious problem for least squares analysis, because they represent more than one relationship between the variables in the model. Least squares assumes that there is only a single relationship between the two variables of interest. But in this case there are two relationships, the supply curve and the demand curve, which have different slopes and intercepts. Thus, we need to extend the least squares method so that it can estimate the intercepts and slopes of two or more different economic relationships relating a set of variables. This chapter presents two different methods for estimating models in which two different curves determine the equilibrium of the economic model, which will allow us to estimate the slopes not only of supply curves and demand curves but also generally of relationships in economic models with two (or more) equations.

14.2 CAUSES OF ENDOGENOUS RIGHT-HAND-SIDE VARIABLES

The reason that there are two equations in a supply and demand model is that there are two variables—equilibrium price and equilibrium quantity—whose values the model explains.

> **Definition 14.1** A variable is *endogenous* to an economic model if its value is determined within the model. A variable is *exogenous* to the model if its value is taken as given by the model.

In the case of the supply and demand model, price and quantity are both endogenous variables; their values are determined by the crossing point of the supply and demand curves. In general, economic models will have the same number of endogenous variables and equations.[3] Any other variable that affects the model will be exogenous; its value must be taken as given because there are not enough equations in the model to determine its value inside the model. For example, in the supply and demand model, income is a relevant variable; higher income should shift the demand curve out, increasing both price and quantity. However, the model assumes that buyers know their incomes and that they determine the quantity of the product they wish to buy on the basis of those incomes. The amount of income that buyers have determines the location of the demand curve; if it rises or falls, the demand curve rises or falls with it, and so do the equilibrium price and quantity. Conversely, drawing the demand curve in any one place on the graph implies a particular level of income that produces that demand schedule. There are other variables—the price of material inputs and labor, for instance—that suppliers take as fixed, which are thus exogenous to the model, and which shift the supply curve if their values change.

This definition of endogenous and exogenous variables appears to differ from the one given in Definition 7.7, where we defined an exogenous variable as one uncorrelated with the error term in the econometric model, and that an endogenous variable as one correlated with the error term. It turns out, however, that these two definitions are equivalent, as Figure 14.2 shows. Suppose we write the demand curve as

$$Q = \beta_0 + \beta_1 P + \varepsilon_D \qquad \textbf{(14.2.1)}$$

and the supply curve as

$$Q = \gamma_0 + \gamma_1 P + \varepsilon_S \qquad \textbf{(14.2.2)}$$

---

[3] If the equations are linear, then they will always have the same number of endogenous variables as equations. Only if the equations are nonlinear (so that the curves could possibly cross at more than one point, or none) can the number of endogenous variables and equations differ. Even in such cases, economists normally make assumptions to prevent multiple solutions to the model (such as strictly increasing marginal costs) to ensure that this will not happen and, if that is done, the number of equations and endogenous variables will again be equal.

FIGURE 14.2
Correlation of
***P* and *Q* with**
Errors in
Demand

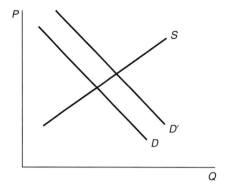

where the use of the γ parameters in the supply curve reflects the fact that these are two different relationships with different slopes.[4] We expect $\gamma_1 > 0$, since the supply curve has a positive slope, but $\beta_1 < 0$, since the demand curve has a negative slope. Now suppose that, for one particular observation, ε_D takes an unusually high value; for any given price, there is a higher-than-usual quantity demanded. Then the demand curve shifts up, as shown in the graph. As a result of the shift, both P and Q take higher values as well. Conversely, if ε_D takes an unusually low value, the demand curve will shift inward, and P and Q will both fall. This implies that both P and Q are positively correlated with ε_D; their values all rise and fall together. This presents no difficulty for Q, the left-hand-side variable in the equation; it will obviously be correlated with ε_D, which affects it directly. But the correlation of P and ε_D, which appears on the right-hand side of the equation, is a more serious problem. It violates assumption A5 of the Gauss-Markov theorem, that the error terms are uncorrelated with the right-hand-side variables, and causes ordinary least squares (OLS) estimates to no longer be the best linear unbiased estimator (BLUE). The same is true, by a similar argument, of the supply error. If ε_S changes, the supply curve will shift, and both P and Q will change with it. Therefore, P will be correlated (negatively, in this case) with ε_S, so we cannot correctly estimate the supply curve by least squares either.

This problem will occur whenever two or more equations in an economic model determine the values of a like number of endogenous variables. A change in any one of the error terms in those equations will change the solution of the entire model, and thus will change the values of all of the endogenous variables. They will therefore all be correlated with the error terms of any given equation in the model, and will be endogenous to the econometric model as stated in Definition 7.7. Thus the two definitions are effectively identical. Anytime a variable in a regression is endogenous according to the economic model that generated the regression, it must be treated as econometrically endogenous as well, and least squares cannot be used to estimate an equation in which it appears on the right-hand-side.

---

[4] We put Q on the left-hand side of these equations, and P on the right-hand side, because from the standpoint of an individual buyer or seller, in a competitive market P is fixed and given, and the buyer or seller is choosing his or her individual quantity. It has therefore become conventional to write these equations with Q as the left-hand-side variable. But from the standpoint of the entire market, P is not fixed, but endogenous. It is unfortunate that economists have also conventionally chosen to put P on the vertical axis of supply and demand graphs—in many regards it would be better to put Q on the vertical axis—but it is too late to change it now.

14.3   THE CONSEQUENCES OF ENDOGENOUS RIGHT-HAND-SIDE VARIABLES

What happens if we ignore an endogenous right-hand-side variable and estimate the equation by least squares anyway? There will be serious problems, because when we draw a line through the center of the data, it will not represent either the supply curve or the demand curve; it will represent the pattern of the various equilibrium points as both the supply and demand curves shift over the sample. Because the OLS line will not match any of the economic relationships in the data, its parameters will not be meaningful estimates of the slopes of those relationships.

> **Theorem 14.1** If all the assumptions of the Gauss-Markov theorem are true except A5, and one of the right-hand-side variables of the regression equation is endogenous, then:
>
> 1. The OLS estimates of the $\hat{\beta}s$ become biased;
> 2. The OLS estimates also become inconsistent;
> 3. The OLS estimates also become inefficient;
> 4. The usual standard error estimates also become biased and inconsistent.

If a right-hand-side variable is endogenous, then it is correlated with the error term. In that case, the error terms do not have an average value of 0; the average will be higher or lower depending on the value of the endogenous variable. Figure 14.3 shows a case of two endogenous variables Y_1 and Y_2, where the error terms in the equation with Y_1 as the left-hand-side variable are positively correlated with the Y_2, which is a right-hand-side variable. When Y_1 has an unusually high value, the errors tend to be positive, causing most of the data to lie above the line. When Y_2 has an unusually low value, the errors tend to be negative, causing most of the data to lie below the line. This causes the least squares best-fit line to slope more steeply than the true model does. The estimated $\hat{\beta}_1$ tends to be greater than the true β_1, meaning that there is positive bias and inconsistency—we do not get the right answer on average, nor do we tend toward the right answer as we get more and more data.

Figure 14.4 shows the results of this bias in a supply and demand system. In the supply and demand model given in Equations 14.2.1 and 14.2.2, the supply and demand curves will be

FIGURE 14.3

Endogenous Variable Bias

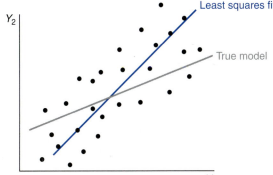

FIGURE 14.4
OLS with an
Endogenous
Right-Hand-
Side Variable

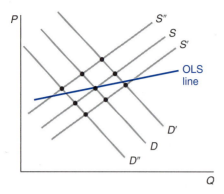

in different locations for each observation in the sample, because each observation will have different values of ε_S and ε_D. The observed values of P and Q in the data will be determined by the location of the intersection of the supply and demand curves. A line through those values, marked by the intersections of the different supply and demand curves in Figure 14.4 will produce neither the demand curve nor the supply curve, but rather a mix of both of them. If the equilibrium changes because the demand curve shifts up (or down), then the equilibrium point will shift along the supply curve, which creates a tendency toward positive slope in the data. But if the equilibrium changes because the supply curve shifts up (or down), then the equilibrium point will shift along the demand curve, which creates a tendency toward negative slope. The actual OLS line can take either a positive or negative slope depending on which effect is stronger in the data. In Figure 14.4, the demand curves are drawn as shifting more than the supply curves do, so the OLS line has a mildly positive slope; but if the supply curves are drawn as shifting more, the OLS line will have a mildly negative slope. In either case, it will not take the slope of either the supply curve or the demand curve, but some average of the two. Thus it will not produce consistent estimates of either one.

14.4 SOLVING THE PROBLEM: SOLVING THE MODEL

One solution to the problem of an endogenous right-hand-side variable is to use the fact that, if a right-hand-side variable is endogenous, then there must be some second relationship between it and the left-hand-side variable. This implies that there must be a second equation relating the two endogenous variables that can be used to eliminate the one on the right-hand side from the model. In general, if we have N endogenous variables and N equations relating them, we can solve the equations so that each endogenous variable appears on the left-hand side of one equation, and on the right-hand side of none of the equations.

> **Definition 14.2** The system of equations that is produced by solving the model for its endogenous variables is called the *reduced form* of the model. The original equations are called the *structural equations,* and the solved equations, which have only exogenous variables on the right-hand side, are called the *reduced-form equations*.

We can find the reduced form of a supply and demand model as follows. Let the demand equation be given by:

$$Q = \beta_0 + \beta_1 P + \beta_2 I + \varepsilon_D \qquad \textbf{(14.4.1)}$$

and the supply curve as

$$Q = \gamma_0 + \gamma_1 P + \gamma_2 W + \varepsilon_S \qquad \textbf{(14.4.2)}$$

where I is the income of buyers in the market, which should affect demand but not supply, and W is the wage rate of the seller's employees, which should affect the cost of producing the product and hence the supply curve, but not the demand curve. We wish to eliminate P from Equation 14.4.1, because of its endogeneity. Solving Equation 14.4.2 for P produces

$$P = \frac{Q - \gamma_0 - \gamma_2 W - \varepsilon_S}{\gamma_1} \qquad \textbf{(14.4.3)}$$

Plugging this into Equation 14.4.1 eliminates P, producing

$$Q = \beta_0 + \beta_1 \left(\frac{Q - \gamma_0 - \gamma_2 W - \varepsilon_S}{\gamma_1} \right) + \beta_2 I + \varepsilon_D \qquad \textbf{(14.4.4)}$$

Solving this equation for Q produces

$$Q = \frac{\beta_0 - (\beta_1/\gamma_1)(\gamma_0 + \gamma_2 W + \varepsilon_S) + \beta_2 I + \varepsilon_D}{1 - (\beta_1/\gamma_1)} \qquad \textbf{(14.4.5)}$$

which can be reparameterized as

$$Q = \delta_0 + \delta_1 W + \delta_2 I + \varepsilon_Q \qquad \textbf{(14.4.6)}$$

where

$$\delta_0 = \frac{\beta_0 - (\beta_1/\gamma_1)\gamma_0}{1 - (\beta_1/\gamma_1)}, \quad \delta_1 = \frac{-(\beta_1/\gamma_1)\gamma_2}{1 - (\beta_1/\gamma_1)}, \quad \delta_2 = \frac{\beta_2}{1 - (\beta_1/\gamma_1)},$$

$$\varepsilon_Q = \frac{-(\beta_1/\gamma_1)\varepsilon_S + \varepsilon_D}{1 - (\beta_1/\gamma_1)} \qquad \textbf{(14.4.7)}$$

Equation 14.4.6 has two right-hand-side variables, but both are exogenous; it can therefore be estimated by OLS. Its parameters are complicated combinations of the parameters of both structural equations 14.4.1 and 14.4.2, but reparameterizing removes that complexity from consideration.

We can similarly find an equation for P if, instead of plugging Equation 14.4.3 into Equation 14.4.1, we do the reverse, plugging Equation 14.4.1 into Equation 14.4.3 to eliminate Q:

$$P = \frac{\beta_0 + \beta_1 P + \beta_2 I + \varepsilon_D - \gamma_0 - \gamma_2 W - \varepsilon_S}{\gamma_1} \qquad \textbf{(14.4.8)}$$

Solving for P produces:

$$P = \frac{\beta_0 + \beta_2 I + \varepsilon_D - \gamma_0 - \gamma_2 W - \varepsilon_S}{\gamma_1[1 - (\beta_1/\gamma_1)]} \qquad \textbf{(14.4.9)}$$

which we reparameterize as

$$P = \pi_0 + \pi_1 W + \pi_2 I + \varepsilon_P \qquad \textbf{(14.4.10)}$$

where

$$\pi_0 = \frac{\beta_0 - \gamma_0}{\gamma_1[1 - (\beta_1/\gamma_1)]}, \quad \pi_1 = \frac{-\gamma_2}{\gamma_1[1 - (\beta_1/\gamma_1)]}, \quad \pi_2 = \frac{\beta_2}{\gamma_1[1 - (\beta_1/\gamma_1)]},$$

$$\varepsilon_P = \frac{\varepsilon_D - \varepsilon_S}{\gamma_1[1 - (\beta_1/\gamma_1)]} \tag{14.4.11}$$

Equations 14.4.6 and 14.4.10 are the reduced-form equations of the model. They describe the equilibrium of the model; one equation describes equilibrium price and equilibrium quantity. If we know the values of the exogenous variables W and I, we can use them to quickly calculate the equilibrium price and quantity that result.

This also gives us an economic interpretation of the new δ and π parameters; they describe the way in which the system reacts to a change in one of the exogenous variables. If income rises by 1 unit, then quantity will rise by δ_2 units and price will rise by π_2 units. Because an increase in income should shift the demand curve out, resulting in higher quantities and prices, we would expect both $\delta_2 > 0$ and $\pi_2 > 0$.[5] Similarly, if W rises, shifting the supply curve to the left, then we would expect quantity to fall and price to rise, which implies that $\delta_1 < 0$ and $\pi_1 > 0$. Some algebra will show that these signs are also what one would expect using Equations 14.4.7 and 14.4.11 assuming that $\beta_1 < 0$, $\gamma_1 > 0$, $\beta_2 > 0$ and $\gamma_2 < 0$.

The strength of the reduced-form approach is exactly this: It provides a simple description of the equilibrium of the model and of how it changes when the exogenous variables change. For many problems, this is sufficient to answer the economic question at hand. For example, the reduced form is perfect for calculating how much equilibrium prices and quantities of a good will change if a new union contract results in increased wages; β_1 and γ_1 provide that answer directly. Or suppose we have an aggregate supply–aggregate demand model of the macroeconomy in which GDP and inflation are endogenous, and want to know how much government spending will increase gross domestic product (GDP). All we need do is solve the model for GDP (we do not even need to calculate the equation for the price level), estimate the resulting equation, and the parameter on government spending is the answer we need. If we want to estimate the response of the model to changes in exogenous variables, then the reduced form gives us precisely what we need to know.

The weakness of the reduced-form approach, however, is that it does not provide values of the parameters of the structural equations of the model. Although the δ and π parameters have useful and interesting economic interpretations, they are not the slopes of the supply and demand curves. If we have an economic problem that requires us to know those slopes, such as the calculation of the effects of an excise tax, then we cannot yet solve it.

One possibility is to work backward from the values we have. If we know the values of δ_1, δ_2, π_1, and π_2, then we can, in principle, use Equations 14.4.7 and 14.4.11 to calculate the values of β_1, β_2, γ_1, and γ_2. This, however, will take a considerable amount of algebra. Also, it will not provide estimates of the standard errors of the β and γ parameters, which we will need if we want to calculate confidence intervals for the slopes of the supply and demand curves, or test hypotheses about them. It would be preferable to have a method of

---

[5] This assumes that the good is a normal good; its consumption increases as income rises. It would not be true if the good is an inferior good, whose consumption falls as income increases. Throughout this chapter we will assume that goods are normal; the changes are minimal for the case of an inferior good.

estimating the values of the β and γ parameters directly. That can be done; but before we turn to that problem, we will state one theorem that is useful for working with reduced forms.

> **Theorem 14.2** Suppose that we have N endogenous variables $Y_1 \ldots Y_N$, M exogenous variables $X_1 \ldots X_M$, and N independent structural equations,[6] all of which are linear. Then the reduced form can be written as N equations of the form
>
> $$Y_{ni} = \delta_{n0} + \delta_{n1}X_{1i} + \delta_{n2}X_{2i} + \cdots + \delta_{nM}X_{Mi} + \varepsilon_{ni} \quad \textbf{(14.4.12)}$$
>
> That is, the reduced-form equations will be linear, and will contain all of the exogenous variables in the entire model (though it is possible that some of the δ parameters may be equal to 0).

This theorem guarantees us that the reduced form exists and contains linear equations. That permits us to skip the algebra involved in calculating the reduced form, as long as we don't need to know the exact reparameterization required. If we write the structural equations as linear in the variables, then the solution we get will also be linear and we can simply write it that way from the start rather than calculate a complicated reparameterization that we do not intend to use.

14.5   SOLVING THE PROBLEM: ESTIMATING THE STRUCTURAL EQUATIONS

If we want to estimate the slopes of the supply and demand curves themselves, then we cannot use least squares. The least squares estimated line goes through the center of the observed data, and the data points do not lie around either the supply curve or the demand curve. This happens because we never observe the entire supply curve or the entire demand curve; we observe only the one point where they happen to cross. Estimating the curves requires us to use the economic model to infer the existence of something that is not directly visible in the data.

To do that, we need to observe a variable that causes one curve to shift, thus causing the equilibrium point to move along the curve that remains stationary. Figure 14.5 shows the approach graphically. Suppose we observe an increase in income, holding all other exogenous variables equal. This will cause the demand curve to rise but will not shift the supply curve. Quantities and prices will rise as the equilibrium shifts along the supply curve, and the ratio of the price change to the quantity change is equal to the slope of the supply curve. If we can see how prices and quantities change when income changes, all else held constant, then we can infer the slope of the supply curve from that information.

> **Definition 14.3** The parameter of an endogenous right-hand-side variable is *identified* if it is possible to infer its value from the effects of one or more exogenous variables in the economic model.

---

[6] The structural equations must be independent because, if two of the equations were dependent, then we would not have enough equations to solve for all of the independent variables. In such a case the economic model would have no solution for its equilibrium and would thus be unsuitable for estimation anyway.

FIGURE 14.5
**Identifying the
Slope of One
Curve through
a Shift in the
Other Curve**

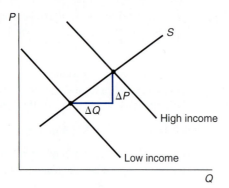

In the above example, γ_1 is identified by the exogenous variable income. The slope of the supply curve can similarly be identified by an exogenous variable, such as wages, that affects the supply of the good but not the demand for it.

Note that this technique works only because of the economic assumption that income does not affect the supply curve and wages do not affect the demand curve. It is because we are willing to assume that changes in a particular variable leave one curve stationary that we can figure out its slope.

> **Definition 14.4** A variable that is exogenous in an econometric model, and is excluded from at least one equation of a system of equations, is called an *instrumental variable*. The method of estimating parameters using them is called the *instrumental variables method*. The restriction that an instrumental variable does not appear in one equation of the system, and thus can be used to identify the parameters of that equation, is called an *exclusion restriction*.

The instrumental variables method relies critically on the correctness of the exclusion restriction. If the exclusion restriction is wrong, and the instrumental variable appears in both equations, then when the instrumental variable changes, both equations will shift. If that happens, then the ratio of the price change to the quantity change will not reflect the slope of either of the two curves. It is necessary to use an assumption from economic theory—the exclusion restriction—to estimate a relationship from economic theory, even though the data do not lie around a line defined by that relationship. Thus the estimates it produces are only as good as the assumptions that support it. However, the ability to use theory to infer the slope of a curve that is one part of a complex economic system is an extremely powerful technique. It enables us to measure the fundamental economic relationships in our models and test whether or not they conform to our expectations from economic theory, even though those relationships, because they generate the data jointly and not individually, cannot be directly observed.

How do we use an instrumental variable to actually calculate an estimated slope? Suppose we have a model of the general form

$$Y_1 = \beta_0 + \beta_1 Y_2 + \beta_2 X_1 + \beta_3 X_2 + \varepsilon_1 \qquad \textbf{(14.5.1)}$$

$$Y_2 = \gamma_0 + \gamma_1 Y_1 + \gamma_2 X_1 + \gamma_3 X_3 + \varepsilon_2 \qquad \textbf{(14.5.2)}$$

where Y_1 and Y_2 are endogenous, and X_1, X_2, and X_3 are exogenous. X_3 is omitted from Equation 14.5.1 and can be used as an instrumental variable to estimate that equation; X_2 is excluded from Equation 14.5.2 and can be used as an instrument to estimate it. We use the following procedure, known as *two-stage least squares* because it requires us to use OLS regression twice:

1. Using OLS, regress the endogenous variables on all of the exogenous variables of the entire model:

$$Y_1 = \delta_0 + \delta_1 X_1 + \delta_2 X_2 + \delta_3 X_3 + \upsilon_1 \qquad (14.5.3)$$

$$Y_2 = \pi_0 + \pi_1 X_1 + \pi_2 X_2 + \pi_3 X_3 + \upsilon_2 \qquad (14.5.4)$$

(Observe that these equations are the reduced form equations of the model.) Calculate the predicted values $\hat{Y}_1$ and $\hat{Y}_2$ from these two equations.

2. Now estimate the structural equations by OLS, replacing the endogenous variables with their predicted values from stage 1:

$$Y_1 = \beta_0 + \beta_1 \hat{Y}_2 + \beta_2 X_1 + \beta_3 X_2 + \varepsilon_1 \qquad (14.5.5)$$

$$Y_2 = \gamma_0 + \gamma_1 \hat{Y}_1 + \gamma_2 X_1 + \gamma_3 X_3 + \varepsilon_2 \qquad (14.5.6)$$

Then we can show the following:

Theorem 14.3. The estimated $\hat{\beta}$ and $\hat{\gamma}$ parameters from the second-stage regressions of Equations 14.5.5 and 14.5.6 are consistent estimators of the true β and γ parameters. They are biased, but the bias diminishes as the sample grows larger.

A formal proof of this theorem is difficult, but we can suggest the following intuition. The problem with estimating Equation 14.5.1 directly is that Y_2, as an endogenous variable, is correlated with ε_1. However, its replacement $\hat{Y}_2$ is not correlated with ε_1; it depends only on X_1, X_2, and X_3, all of which are exogenous by assumption. Anytime $\hat{Y}_2$ shifts, it must have done so because one of the exogenous variables shifted, and those shifts in exogenous variables are exactly what enable us to identify the slopes of the structural equations.

Mathematically, because $\hat{Y}_2$ does depend on the instrumental variable X_3, the indirect effect of X_3 on Y_1 is included in the model via $\hat{Y}_2$. Of course $\hat{Y}_2$ also depends directly on X_1 and X_2, but they are separately included in the model; it is the exclusion of X_3 from Equations 14.5.5 and 14.5.1 that allows its effect to be included in the equation *only* through $\hat{Y}_2$ and thus to estimate the shift along the curve that takes place when X_3 changes, changing both Y_1 and Y_2 in the ratio of β_1. Observing this ratio gives us a consistent (but not unbiased) estimate of β_1.

The second regression of the two-stage least squares process also gives us a way to test whether a variable is exogenous or endogenous, in the sense of being correlated with the error terms. We know from Equation 14.5.4 and the formula for calculating predicted values that

$$Y_2 = \hat{Y}_2 + \hat{\upsilon}_2 \qquad (14.5.7)$$

Y_2 may be endogenous, but $\hat{Y}_2$ must be exogenous, since it depends only on the exogenous X variables. If Y_2 is correlated with ε_1, and hence endogenous, it must be because $\hat{\upsilon}_2$ is correlated with ε_1; $\hat{Y}_2$ cannot be correlated with ε_1. If $\hat{v}_2$ is not correlated with ε_1 either, then Y_2 must not be—and must therefore be exogenous. This method of testing for endogeneity of a right-hand-side variable is known as a *Durbin-Wu-Hausman test* or sometimes just as a *Hausman test.*

There are many ways to test the null hypothesis that $\hat{v}_2$ and ε_1 are uncorrelated (implying that Y_2 is exogenous) against the alternative hypothesis that they are correlated (implying that Y_2 is endogenous). One is to calculate not only the predicted values of $\hat{Y}_2$ from Equation 14.5.2 but also the values of the residuals $\hat{v}_2$. Then estimate the regression:

$$Y_1 = \beta_0 + \beta_1 \hat{Y}_2 + \beta_2 X_1 + \beta_3 X_2 + \beta_4 \hat{v}_2 + \varepsilon_1 \qquad \textbf{(14.5.8)}$$

and test the null hypothesis $\beta_4 = 0$, using the critical values from the normal distribution (β_4 does not follow the exact t distribution in this regression, due to the estimated values of $\hat{v}_2$, but it is approximately normally distributed). If $\hat{v}_2$ and ε_1 are uncorrelated, then $\hat{\beta}_4$ should not be significantly different from 0. If it is, then we can reject the null hypothesis, conclude that $\hat{v}_2$ and ε_1 are correlated, and conclude that therefore Y_2 is endogenous.[7]

One problem with the two-stage least squares process is that it requires two estimations instead of only one. It is also possible to calculate two-stage least squares in a single estimation step, and most econometrics software packages do so. Note that, if we perform two-stage least squares in the two-step method, then the OLS standard errors reported by the second stage regression will be incorrect because the OLS formula for standard errors does not take account of the fact that the independent variables are predicted values from the first-stage regression. It is possible to find a corrected formula for the standard errors that accounts for the increased variability caused by predicting the independent variables. Econometrics software will report those standard errors, which will usually be slightly larger than the ones calculated by OLS in the second-stage regression.

14.6 CONDITIONS FOR APPLYING TWO-STAGE LEAST SQUARES

An equation can be estimated by two-stage least squares only when there are available instrumental variables to identify the parameters of the model. In the example given in the preceding section, there was one instrumental variable available to identify each of the parameters on endogenous right-hand-side variables. But that need not be the case. Consider, for example, the following model of the money market:

$$R = \beta_0 + \beta_1 M + \beta_2 Y + \beta_3 \Pi + \varepsilon_D \qquad \textbf{(14.6.1)}$$

$$R = \gamma_0 + \gamma_1 M + \varepsilon_S \qquad \textbf{(14.6.2)}$$

where Equation 14.6.1 is the demand function, Equation 14.6.2 is the supply function, R is the interest rate, M is money, Y is income, and Π is the inflation rate. These equations are

---

[7] Note that Y_2, $\hat{Y}_2$, and $\hat{v}_2$ are perfectly multicollinear, because of Equation 14.5.7. The Hausman test can therefore be constructed by including any two of them in the test equation. Some software packages use a different combination than the one used in this derivation. The test results are identical any way you do it.

FIGURE 14.6
Money Supply and Money Demand

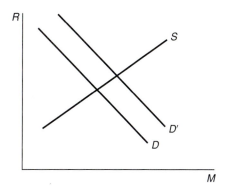

graphed in Figure 14.6. If we want to find the slope of the money supply curve, we can use Y (which shifts the demand curve but not the supply curve) to identify it. Or, we can use Π; it also shifts the demand curve and should produce the same response in interest rates and quantities of money. Of course, in observed data, it will not produce exactly the same response because of the randomness of the data. Better, then, is to use both Y and Π as instruments, and use information on how R and M change in response to both of them to infer the slope of γ_1. On the other hand, if we want to find the slope of the money demand curve, we have a problem; there is no variable in the model that shifts the supply curve. The error term does, but we cannot observe the error term and therefore cannot use it to infer movements along the supply curve.

We may need more than one instrumental variable to estimate an equation if it has more than one endogenous right-hand-side variable. Consider the following three-equation model:

$$Y_1 = \alpha_0 + \alpha_1 Y_2 + \alpha_2 Y_3 + \alpha_3 X_1 + \alpha_4 X_2 + \varepsilon_1 \qquad \textbf{(14.6.3)}$$

$$Y_2 = \beta_0 + \beta_1 Y_1 + \beta_2 Y_3 + \beta_3 X_2 + \beta_4 X_3 + \beta_5 X_4 + \varepsilon_2 \qquad \textbf{(14.6.4)}$$

$$Y_3 = \gamma_0 + \gamma_1 Y_1 + \gamma_2 Y_2 + \gamma_3 X_3 + \varepsilon_3 \qquad \textbf{(14.6.5)}$$

The system has three endogenous variables and four exogenous variables. Equation 14.6.3 has two exclusion restrictions; neither X_3 nor X_4 appears in it. It also has two endogenous right-hand-side variables, and hence two parameters, α_1 and α_2, which need to be identified. One instrumental variable cannot simultaneously identify both of those parameters, as demonstrated graphically in Figure 14.7. In this three-dimensional graph, each equation is represented by one plane in the graph; the intersection of the three planes determines the equilibrium. Let the gray plane represent the first equation, the white plane represent the third equation, and the red and pink planes represent two different positions of the second equation. A change in X_4, which appears only in the second equation, would shift the second equation from the red plane to the pink plane. The equilibrium point would then move along the line (solid black in the figure) where the first and the third equations (the gray and white planes) intersect. This lets us identify the slope of that line, but not the slopes of either of the two planes. If we want to know the slope of one of the planes, we have to see a change in X_3, which produces a shift in the both the red and white planes (not shown in the figure). This shift will move along the slope of a second line that also lies inside the gray

FIGURE 14.7
A Three-
Variable Model

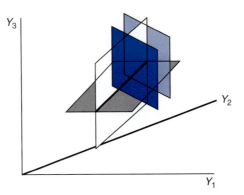

plane. From the slope of these two lines, we can infer α_1 and α_2, the slope of the plane that contains both of them.[8]

In general, to identify a linear equation, we need one instrumental variable for each endogenous right-hand-side variable. Equation 14.6.3 has two endogenous right-hand-side variables, Y_2 and Y_3, and two instrumental variables, X_3 and X_4, so it can be identified. Equation 14.6.4 cannot be identified; it has two endogenous variables and only one excluded exogenous variable (X_1). There are more than enough instrumental variables available to estimate Equation 14.6.5, which excludes X_1, X_2, and X_4, providing three instrumental variables for only two endogenous right-hand-side variables.

> **Definition 14.5** An equation is *overidentified* if it has more excluded exogenous variables to serve as instrumental variables than it has endogenous right-hand-side variables. An equation is *underidentified* if it has fewer instrumental variables than right-hand-side variables, and is *exactly identified* if it has exactly the required number of instrumental variables.

In the money market example, the money supply curve is overidentified (two instruments available where one is needed) and the money demand curve is underidentified (no instruments available where one is needed).

> **Theorem 14.4** If an equation is underidentified, then its parameters cannot be identified. An equation's parameters can be identified only if it is exactly identified or overidentified.[9]

[8] It is not necessary for one variable to shift only one equation. Equation 14.6.3 would still be identified if X_4 appeared in both Equations 14.6.4 and 14.6.5. What matters is that there be two different shifts in the other equations, shifting the equilibrium point along two distinct lines, which exactly determine the slopes of Equation 14.6.3.

[9] It is possible that the parameters of even an exactly identified or overidentified equation may be unidentified and not estimable. This happens when, although there are enough instrumental variables to identify the equation, their effects on the equilibrium of the system are linearly dependent, and thus do not uniquely determine the slopes of the equation that does not shift. In terms of Figure 14.6, this occurs if the two lines traced by the equilibrium in response to changes in X_3 and X_4 have the same slope, and thus do not determine α_1 and α_2 separately. A formal statement of the conditions under which this happens requires linear algebra and is beyond the scope of this book. Those conditions happen only extremely rarely. In practice, the parameters of exactly identified and overidentified equations are almost invariably identified, as long as the equations are linear. The identification of nonlinear equations is a considerably more difficult topic, which is also beyond the scope of this book.

Thus, in the money market demand, we can estimate the slope of the supply curve but not that of the demand curve. In the three-equation system above, the α and γ parameters are identified but the β parameters are not, because Equation 14.6.4 doesn't have enough exclusion restrictions (one rather than the needed two).

It might appear that, if an equation is underidentified and can't be estimated by two stage least squares, then perhaps we can estimate the reduced form and use the results to solve back for the original parameters. Unfortunately, this turns out to be impossible:

Theorem 14.5 The parameters of an equation of a structural model can be derived from the parameters of the reduced form of the model only if the equation is exactly identified or overidentified. If the equation is underidentified, there will be no solution for the structural parameters. If the equation is exactly identified, there will be a unique solution; if the equation is overidentified, there will be multiple solutions.

Thus solving the reduced form backward for the structural parameters works only in those cases where the two-stage least squares process also works.

If an equation is underidentified, there is nothing we can do to estimate its parameters. We can still estimate the reduced form of the model and understand how the exogenous variables shift the equilibrium of the model, but we cannot obtain estimated values for the parameters of the structural model itself. If we need to estimate those parameters, then we have to change the system of equations to make the given equation exactly identified or overidentified. We can do that in either of two ways. One is to drop a variable from the right-hand side of the model, thus reducing the number of instruments needed if we drop an endogenous variable or increasing the number of exclusion restrictions if we drop an exogenous one. This can be done only on the basis of an economic argument explaining why the dropped variable does not belong in the equation. But since we cannot estimate the system without dropping it, we cannot test whether or not it belongs in the equation. The other option is to add a variable to one of the other equations in the system, which then becomes an additional instrumental variable. However, if the system of equations was correctly specified to begin with, then no variables should need to be added.

Finally, it is worth noting that the standard deviations of parameter estimates are lower for overidentified equations than for exactly identified equations, and the more instruments we use in the estimation, the smaller the variances get (as long as the additional instruments are truly exogenous). This is true because each additional instrumental variable adds one more set of shifts to the system that can be used to infer the slopes of the structural equations; the more such shifts we observe, the more information we will have about the slope of the structural equations and the better our estimates of those slopes will be. For that reason, it is desirable to have as many exogenous variables in the system as possible, as long as they are statistically significant in at least one of the structural equations. If they are not statistically significant in any of the equations, however, then they do not cause the equilibrium of the model to shift and thus they are not useful as instruments. Furthermore, if an endogenous variable is mistakenly used as an instrument, then two-stage least squares becomes biased and inconsistent, just as OLS is. We must be careful not to use a variable as an instrument unless we are certain, through economic arguments, that it is exogenous to the economic model and hence to the econometric model as well.

14.7   THE EFFECTS OF ALCOHOL TAXES

We return to the problem with which we started the chapter: calculating the effects of an excise tax, which requires us to know the slopes of the supply and demand function. We use data on the price and consumption of alcoholic beverages in the United States to estimate the slopes and calculate the tax's effect. Let the supply curve be

$$\log Q = \gamma_0 + \gamma_1 \log P + \gamma_2 \log P_C + \gamma_3 \log W$$
$$+ \gamma_4 PR + \gamma_5 UR + \varepsilon_S \qquad \textbf{(14.7.1)}$$

and let the demand curve be

$$\log Q = \beta_0 + \beta_1 \log P + \beta_2 \log \text{Percapdisinc}$$
$$+ \beta_3 \log \text{Adpop} + \varepsilon_D \qquad \textbf{(14.7.2)}$$

where Q is the quantity of alcoholic beverages consumed in the United States, P is the price of alcoholic beverages, Percapdisinc is per capita disposable income, Adpop is the adult population, P_C is the price of cereal products, W is the wage rate of labor, Partrate is the labor force participation rate, and Unemprate is the unemployment rate. We use monthly data from April 1981 to December 1993, a total of 153 observations.

Price and quantity are of course endogenous, and all other variables are treated as exogenous. Income is expected to affect demand because a wealthier nation will consume more of all goods, including alcoholic beverages, and adult population is expected to affect it because a larger population will consume more, all else equal. We expect both β_2 and β_3 to be positive. Furthermore, we do not expect either of these variables to affect the supply curve. Therefore, they can be excluded from the supply curve and be used as instrumental variables to estimate γ_1. Most alcoholic beverages sold in the United States are made from cereal products, so we expect that higher prices for this input should reduce supply. The other three variables are all measures of the cost of labor. The wage rate reflects the direct cost of labor; the participation and unemployment rates measure the availability of labor.[10] We expect γ_2 and γ_3 to be negative, because higher prices increase costs and reduce supply. We expect γ_4 to be negative and γ_5 to be positive, because greater availability of employable workers reduces the costs of hiring labor. Furthermore, we do not expect any of these variables to affect the demand for alcoholic beverages, so they can be used as instruments to identify β_1. Last, we of course expect $\beta_1 < 0$ and $\gamma_1 > 0$, since supply should slope up and demand should slope down. We use the log-linear functional form for the regression so that we can interpret β_1 and γ_1 as elasticities of demand and supply, respectively. Both equations are overidentified, having one endogenous right-hand-side variable and at least two instrumental variables.

Because of the endogenous right-hand-side variables, we cannot estimate these equations by OLS. One option for dealing with the endogeneity is to solve the equations

---

[10] Previous research (Freeman, 2000) has shown that the labor force participation rate and the unemployment rate do significantly affect alcohol consumption. We might worry that these rates would affect demand for alcohol, rather than supply, but they are not statistically significant when included in the demand curve.

for their reduced form and then estimate the reduced-form equations by OLS. From Theorem 14.2, we know that the reduced-form equations will be:

$$\log Q = \alpha_0 + \alpha_1 \log \text{Percapdisinc} + \alpha_2 \log \text{Adpop}$$
$$+ \alpha_3 \log P_C + \alpha_4 \log W + \alpha_5 \text{Partrate} + \alpha_6 \text{Unemprate} + \varepsilon_Q \quad \textbf{(14.7.3)}$$

$$\log P = \delta_0 + \delta_1 \log \text{Percapdisinc} + \delta_2 \log \text{Adpop}$$
$$+ \delta_3 \log P_C + \delta_4 \log W + \delta_5 \text{Partrate} + \delta_6 \text{Unemprate} + \varepsilon_P \quad \textbf{(14.7.4)}$$

where the α and δ parameters will be complex combinations of the original β and γ parameters. The results of estimating the reduced-form equations are shown in Table 14.1. These equations give a useful description of what happens to the equilibrium price and quantity when one of the exogenous variables changes. For instance, a 10 percent increase in per capita income will increase quantity of alcohol consumption by 7.41 percent, and will increase its price by 2.92 percent. These results are consistent with the idea that an increase in income shifts the demand curve to the right, causing prices and quantities to rise as the equilibrium shifts along the supply curve. For a second example, the price equation results also imply that a 10 percent rise in grain prices should increase the price of alcohol by 4.54 percent. This makes economic sense; part of the rise in the input price is passed along to consumers, but part is absorbed by alcohol manufacturers. However, this shift in the supply curve should also result in a drop in quantity of alcoholic beverages consumed. The quantity equation results suggest that there is such a drop, but the estimated value is extremely small and is not statistically significantly different from 0.

More important, the reduced-form estimates do not tell us what we originally set out to know, which is the effect of an increase in the excise tax on alcohol consumption. To know

TABLE 14.1
Reduced-Form Equation Estimates for Alcoholic Beverages

Quantity Equation				
Variable	Parameter	Estimate	Standard Error	t Statistic for $\alpha = 0$
Intercept	α_0	−20.73	5.438	−3.81
Log per capita income	α_1	0.741	0.207	3.58
Log adult population	α_2	1.860	0.484	3.84
Log price cereal	α_2	−0.007	0.056	−0.12
Log wage rate	α_3	−0.874	0.294	−2.97
Participation rate	α_4	−0.011	0.008	−1.41
Unemployment rate	α_5	0.010	0.005	2.09

Price Equation				
Variable	Parameter	Estimate	Standard Error	t Statistic for $\delta = 0$
Intercept	δ_0	−21.37	4.223	−5.06
Log per capita income	δ_1	0.292	0.161	1.82
Log adult population	δ_2	1.831	0.376	4.87
Log price cereal	δ_2	0.454	0.043	10.50
Log wage rate	δ_3	−0.066	0.229	−0.29
Participation rate	δ_4	−0.015	0.006	−2.43
Unemployment rate	δ_5	0.018	0.004	4.82

TABLE 14.2
Estimated
Supply and
Demand
Curves for
Alcoholic
Beverages

Demand Curve				
Variable	Parameter	Estimate	Standard Error	t Statistic for $\beta = 0$
Intercept	β_0	−12.66	4.945	−2.56
Log price	β_1	−0.128	0.063	−2.03
Log per capita income	β_2	0.228	0.061	3.74
Log adult population	β_3	1.278	0.467	2.74

Supply Curve				
Variable	Parameter	Estimate	Standard Error	t Statistic for $\gamma = 0$
Intercept	γ_0	2.553	0.415	6.16
Log price	γ_1	1.124	0.333	3.37
Log price cereal	γ_2	−0.521	0.158	−3.31
Log wage rate	γ_3	−0.358	0.249	−1.43
Participation rate	γ_4	0.013	0.007	1.66
Unemployment rate	γ_5	−0.019	0.004	−4.34

that, we must know the elasticity of the supply and demand curves. To know those elasticities, we must estimate the structural equations of the model. Because of the endogenous right-hand-side variables in those equations, we must use two-stage least squares to estimate them.

Results of estimating these equations by two-stage least squares are found in Table 14.2, and generally conform to expectations. The price elasticity of demand is −0.128, which is statistically significantly different from 0. It indicates that demand for alcoholic beverages is inelastic, and the demand curve is quite steeply sloped. The income elasticity of demand is positive, as expected, though not very high; the estimated elasticity, 0.228, suggests that alcohol consumption rises only slightly as income rises. The estimated elasticity with respect to population is 1.278. We might expect that as the population grows, all else equal, alcohol consumption would rise proportionally. This implies that the true elasticity should be equal to 1. A t test of the hypothesis $\beta_3 = 1$ has the t statistic $(1.278 − 1)/0.467$, which is equal to 0.595. This is less than the critical value of 1.98 for 149 degrees of freedom; we do not reject the idea that an increase in adult population increases alcohol consumption proportionately.

In the supply equation, we find that the price elasticity of supply is 1.124, which is statistically significantly greater than 0. Higher cereal prices reduce supply, with an elasticity of −0.521, but the elasticity with respect to wages is not statistically significantly different from 0. The estimated coefficient of −0.358 is quite reasonable, but has a high standard error of 0.249. We cannot reject the null hypothesis that wages do not affect supply. The coefficient on unemployment is statistically significant at the 5 percent level; that on participation is significant only at the 10 percent level. Both take their expected signs.

From these results we can work out the effects of an excise tax on alcohol consumption. We need to rewrite Equation 14.1.2 slightly to allow for the fact that we have estimated elasticities of the supply and demand curves rather than their slopes. The equivalent equation is

$$\%\Delta Q = \%T(\beta_1 - \gamma_1) \qquad \textbf{(14.7.5)}$$

where $\%T$ is the tax rate stated as a percentage, and $\%\Delta Q$ is the resulting percentage change in the quantity of alcoholic beverages consumed. Plugging in $\beta_1 = -0.128$ and $\gamma_1 = 1.124$ gives

$$\%\Delta Q = \%T(-1.252) \qquad \textbf{(14.7.6)}$$

which suggests that a one percent increase in alcohol taxes should reduce consumption of alcohol by about 1.25 percent. A total tax of 20 percent would result in a decrease in consumption of about 25 percent. Or we can solve for the tax rate:

$$\%T = \%\Delta Q/(-1.253) \qquad \textbf{(14.7.7)}$$

which suggests that to reduce alcohol consumption by 10 percent, we would need a tax rate of about 8 percent. This information, which we can calculate once we can estimate the elasticities of the supply and demand curves, can be of great assistance to policymakers who are trying to set alcohol taxes in order to achieve desired social outcomes.

Chapter Review	

Chapter Review

- Many interesting economic models contain more than one *endogenous variable.* Any model that is solved by the intersection of two curves, for instance, will have two endogenous variables.

- If a variable is endogenous in an economic model, then its value will be correlated with the error terms of the structural equations of that model, and hence it will be econometrically endogenous as well.

- If an equation has an endogenous right-hand-side variable, then ordinary least squares is biased and inconsistent. It will not produce meaningful estimates of the parameters of those equations.

- We can solve the problem of endogenous right-hand-side variables by solving the model, eliminating the endogenous variables from the right-hand side, and estimating the result by least squares. This is known as estimating the *reduced form* of the model.

- Estimating the reduced form provides a good description of how changes in exogenous variables change the equilibrium of the model. But it does not produce estimates of the slopes of the structural equations themselves.

- We can also solve the problem of endogenous right-hand-side variables by observing the effects of *instrumental variables,* which shift one curve in the model but not another. The slope of the curve that does not move can be inferred by observing the shift of the curve that does move.

- Estimates produced by instrumental variables are consistent. They are biased, but as the sample grows larger the bias diminishes.

- We can estimate an equation with instrumental variables only if its parameters are identified, that is, only if there are enough instrumental variables to determine the values of the parameters of the endogenous variables mathematically.

- An equation can be *overidentified* if there are more instrumental variables than needed, just *identified* if there are exactly the number needed, and *underidentified* if there are not enough instrumental variables. It is possible for some equations of a model to be just identified or overidentified while others are underidentified, in which case the ones that are underidentified cannot be estimated, but the others still can be.

Computer Exercise

In this exercise we'll work with a two-equation model and show that least squares produces biased estimates of the results. The two equations will be

$$Y_1 = 20 - 2Y_2 + X_1 + \varepsilon_1$$

$$Y_1 = 5 + Y_2 + 3X_2 + \varepsilon_2$$

and the reduced forms of these equations are as follows (verify this for yourself by solving the two structural equations for Y_1 and Y_2):

$$Y_1 = 10 + \frac{1}{3}X_1 + 2X_2 + \frac{1}{3}(\varepsilon_1 + 2\varepsilon_2)$$

$$Y_2 = 5 + \frac{1}{3}X_1 - X_2 + \frac{1}{3}(\varepsilon_1 - \varepsilon_2)$$

1. Open Eviews and create a new workfile, undated, with 100 observations.
2. Type genr x1 = rnd(50)+10 and genr x2 = rnd(50)+20 to generate the exogenous variables of the model.
3. Type genr err1 = nrnd()*3 and genr err2 = nrnd()*4 to generate error terms.
4. Type genr y1 = 10 + x1/3 + x2*2 + (err1+2*err2)/3 and genr y2 = 5 + x1/3 − x2 + (err1-err2)/3 to generate the values of the endogenous variables.
5. Select a group containing Y_1 and Y_2 and graph their scatterplot. Is either of the two structural relationships between Y_1 and Y_2 visible in the graph?
6. Select a group containing Y_1, Y_2, Err_1, and Err_2, and verify that the correlations between each of the endogenous variables Y_1 and Y_2 and each of the errors Err_1 and Err_2 is not 0, even though Err_1 and Err_2 are uncorrelated.
7. Type ls y1 c y2 x1 to estimate the first structural equation. Is the estimated parameter for Y_2 significantly different from –2 or not? Is the estimated parameter for X_1 significantly different from 1 or not? Do these estimates seem to be close to the right value, or far from the right value?
8. Type ls y1 c y2 x2 to estimate the second structural equation. How close are the estimated parameters to the true ones? How close are they to the estimated parameters of the first equation?
9. Now we'll see if two stage least squares does a better job of estimating the structural parameters. Type tsls y1 c y2 x1 @ x1 x2 to estimate the first structural equation by two stage least squares, treating X_1 and X_2 as exogenous. Now are the estimated parameters significantly different from their true values?
10. Type tsls y1 c y2 x1 @ x1 x2 to estimate the first structural equation by two stage least squares. Are the estimated parameters of this equation significantly different from their true values?
11. Repeat steps 3–10 a few times and see how much the answers change from trial to trial.

Problems

1. In this problem we'll consider the relationship between crime rates and government spending to reduce crime. Load the data file crime, which contains data from the

50 U.S. states on the following variables: crimespendpc (spending on crime and corrections per capita in 1995); rate (crimes per 100,000 people in 1995); rate90 (crimes per 100,000 people in 1990); age1834 (percentage of population aged 18 to 34); over64 (percentage of population over age 64); under18 (percentage of population under age 18); democrat (fraction of votes for the Democratic candidate in the 1996 presidential election); expperstud (spending on education per student); fedfundspc (federal funds received by the state per capita); nonwhite (fraction of the state's population that is nonwhite); percapinc (per capita income); population (in thousands); poverty (percentage of households with incomes below the poverty line); staterevpc (state revenues per capita); and unemploy (unemployment rate). All financial variables are in dollars.

a. If government spending on crime and corrections encourages criminals to commit fewer crimes, would you expect Crimespendpc and Rate to have a positive correlation or a negative correlation?

b. Estimate the regression $\text{Rate}_i = \beta_0 + \beta_1 \text{Crimespendpc}_i + \beta_2 \text{Staterevpc}_i + \beta_3 \text{Expperstud}_i + \beta_4 \text{Percapinc}_i + \beta_5 \text{Nonwhite}_i + \beta_6 \text{Poverty}_i + \beta_7 \text{Under18}_i + \beta_8 \text{Age1834}_i + \beta_9 \text{Over64}_i + \beta_{10} \text{Democrat}_i + \varepsilon_i$. What sign do you get for β_1? Is it statistically significantly different from 0? If a state increases crime spending by $1, how much will the crime rate change? Is this what you expected based on your answer to part *a*, or not?

c. Perhaps this occurs due to a problem of endogeneity. Consider two states, identical except that one has a higher value of ε_i and thus a higher crime rate. Which state do you think would spend more on crime fighting, and why? Will crime spending and the error term have a positive correlation or negative correlation?

d. If the correlation from part c exists, will the estimate of β_1 be biased up or down? Does this help explain your finding in part *b*?

2. In this problem we'll use two-stage least squares to estimate the effects of crime spending on crime rates. Load the data file crime, which was described in problem 1.

To use two-stage least squares, we need a second equation that provides instrumental variables for the estimation of the other. The equation we're interested in determines the crime rate on the basis of things that determine the level of criminal behavior. We will specify the equation that determines the crime rate as

$$\text{Rate} = f(\text{Crimespendpc, Rate90, Staterevpc, Nonwhite, Democrat})$$

The second equation in our model determines the amount state spending on crime fighting on the basis of things that affect government finance. We will specify the equation that determines government spending as

$$\text{Crimespendpc} = g(\text{Rate, Over64, Staterevpc, Expperstud, Percapinc, Poverty})$$

a. Do you think it is reasonable to exclude Over64 from the crime rate equation? Why or why not? How do you think a high fraction of the population over age 64 would affect the ability of the government to spend money on fighting crime?

b. What variables are available as instruments to identify the parameter on the endogenous variable Crimespendpc in the first equation? Are the equations of this model underidentified, exactly identified, or overidentified?

c. Estimate the equation $\text{Rate}_i = \beta_0 + \beta_1 \text{Crimespendpc}_i + \beta_2 \text{Rate90}_i + \beta_3 \text{Staterevpc}_i + \beta_4 \text{Nonwhite}_i + \beta_5 \text{Democrat}_i + \varepsilon_i$, treating Crimespendpc_i as endogenous and the other right-hand-side variables as exogenous, and using the appropriate instrumental variables to identify β_1. Do you get a negative or positive estimate for β_1? Is it statistically significantly different from 0 or not?

d. Construct a 95 percent confidence interval for β_1. If the government spends $1 more per capita on crime fighting, how much will the crime rate (per 100,000 people) fall?

e. Suppose we failed to recognize the endogeneity of Crimespendpc. Estimate the same equation by least squares, treating Crimespendpc as exogenous. How different are the results?

3. We can also estimate the second equation in the two-equation system of problem 2.

a. What, in economic terms, are we assuming when we exclude Rate90 from the second equation in the system? Does this seem like a reasonable assumption?

b. Estimate the equation $\text{Crimespendpc}_i = \gamma_0 + \gamma_1 \text{Rate}_i + \gamma_2 \text{Over64}_i + \gamma_3 \text{Staterevpc}_i + \gamma_4 \text{Expperstud}_i + \gamma_5 \text{Percapinc}_i + \gamma_6 \text{Poverty}_i + \upsilon_i$, using Rate90_i, Nonwhite_i, and Democrat_i as instruments to identify γ_1. Is your estimate of γ_1 positive or negative? Is it statistically significantly different from 0, or not? When the crime rate rises by 100 crimes per 100,000 people, how much does government spending rise or fall?

c. Does an increase in the fraction of the population that is over 64 increase crime spending, decrease it, or have no significant effect? Does an increase in per capita income increase crime spending, decrease it, or have no significant effect? Do these answers seem reasonable?

d. Suppose we failed to recognize that crime rate was endogenous in this equation. Estimate this equation by least squares. How different are the results?

4. In this problem we'll use the results from problems 2 and 3 to graphically analyze the effects of a change in per capita income on both spending and the crime rate.

a. On a graph with crime spending on the horizontal axis and crime rate on the vertical axis, draw the first equation of the model. (Put the intercept in any convenient place, since its value depends on the values of the exogenous variables—but draw the slope accurately). What is its slope? Is it positive or negative?

b. Draw the second equation of the model. What is its slope, and is it positive or negative? Which curve represents the behavior of criminals, and which one represents the behavior of governments?

c. Now suppose there is an increase of $1,000 in per capita income in the state. Which curve shifts, the first or the second? Which way does it shift? Draw the shifted curve on your graph. At the new equilibrium, is the crime rate higher or lower than the old one? Is crime spending higher or lower than previously? Which variable has changed its value more, and why?

d. Explain how a change in per capita income affects crime rates, even though Percapinc doesn't appear in the equation with rate as the dependent variable.

5. We could alternatively have dealt with the problem of endogenous crime spending by estimating the reduced form of the model instead of the structural equations.

a. Estimate the equation $\text{Rate}_i = \beta_0 + \beta_1 \text{Rate90}_i + \beta_2 \text{Staterevpc}_i + \beta_3 \text{Nonwhite}_i + \beta_4 \text{Democrat}_i + \beta_5 \text{Over64}_i + \beta_6 \text{Staterevpc}_i + \beta_7 \text{Expperstud}_i + \beta_8 \text{Percapinc}_i +$

$\beta_9 \text{Poverty}_i + \varepsilon_i$. How many of the parameters are statistically significantly different from 0?

b. Estimate the equation $\text{Crimespendpc}_i = \gamma_0 + \gamma_1 \text{Rate90}_i + \gamma_2 \text{Staterevpc}_i + \gamma_3 \text{Nonwhite}_i + \gamma_4 \text{Democrat}_i + \gamma_5 \text{Over64}_i + \gamma_6 \text{Staterevpc}_i + \gamma_7 \text{Expperstud}_i + \gamma_8 \text{Percapinc}_i + \gamma_9 \text{Poverty}_i + \upsilon_i$. Does a state with higher crime five years ago spend more or less on crime fighting today? Why does a past level of crime affect spending today, in this model?

c. Does an increase in per capita income change crime spending per capita? Does it change crime rates? Are the changes significant?

6. Open the data file gasdemand, which contains monthly observations from January 1978 to August 2002 on the following variables: pricegas (cents per gallon); quantgas thousands of barrels per day); persincome (personal income, billions of dollars); and carsales (millions of cars per year). Consider the following supply and demand model for unleaded gasoline, where the first equation represents demand and the second represents supply:

$$\text{Pricegas} = \beta_0 + \beta_1 \text{Quantgas} + \beta_2 \text{Persincome} + \beta_3 \text{Carsales} + \varepsilon_D$$

$$\text{Pricegas} = \gamma_0 + \gamma_1 \text{Quantgas} + \varepsilon_S$$

a. What variables in this system are endogenous, and which are exogenous?

b. Is the demand equation overidentified, underidentified, or exactly identified? Is the supply equation overidentified, underidentified, or exactly identified?

c. Estimate the supply equation using two-stage least squares. What value do you get for $\hat{\gamma}_1$? Does it take the sign you expect and, if so, is it statistically significantly different from 0?

d. Can you estimate the demand curve by two-stage least squares? If not, what variables might you add to the supply curve, and exclude from the demand curve, in order to provide instruments to estimate the demand curve?

e. Estimate the demand curve by least squares. What is your estimated value for β_1? This estimate is biased—is it biased upward or downward? What can you conclude about the slope of the demand curve from this information?

7. Government efforts to reduce smoking in the United States have often been based on advertising; the government either restricts advertisements for cigarettes or runs advertisements encouraging people not to smoke. In this problem we'll measure the responsiveness of cigarette sales to cigarette advertising on cigarette sales, to assess whether these programs are likely to be effective or not. Load the data file cigads, which contains annual data from 1930 to 1978 on the following variables: logsales (log of sales per capita); logincome (log of real income per capita); logrealads (log of real advertising expenditures for cigarettes); lowtar (fraction of total sales that were low-tar cigarettes); filter (fraction of total sales that were filtered cigarettes); tobacpercig (tobacco per cigarette); d64 (a dummy that is 1 after 1964, the year the Surgeon General's warning against tobacco smoking was instituted); d71 (a dummy that is 1 after 1971, when cigarette advertising was banned on broadcast media); and fairdoc (amount of money spent on anti-smoking ads under the Fairness Doctrine program between 1967 and 1970).

a. Cigarette manufacturers have to pay money to run advertisements. Knowing this, would you expect advertising to increase sales, or decrease them?

b. Estimate the equation $\log \text{Sales} = \beta_0 + \beta_1 \log \text{Realads} + \beta_2 \log \text{Income} + \beta_3 \text{Tobacpercig} + \beta_4 \text{D64} + \beta_5 \text{Fairdoc} + \varepsilon_D$. Test the null hypothesis $\beta_1 = 0$. Do cigarette advertisements affect sales or not? If they do, do they increase sales or decrease sales? On the basis of this regression, would you conclude that regulating advertising is a good way to decrease cigarette consumption, or not?

c. Because this is time series data, perform the Durbin-Watson test on this regression. If you find first-order autocorrelation, add a correction for it and reestimate the equation. Now is β_1 significantly different from 0? If it is, does advertising increase sales or decrease sales? Does this match your economic intuition about what the effect of advertising should be, or not?

d. Suppose advertising were an endogenous variable. Could that explain your findings in part c? If so, briefly explain how. Would the correlation between advertising and the error in the sales equation have to be positive, or negative?

8. In this problem we'll consider a model where cigarette advertising is endogenous and estimate it using two-stage least squares. Load the data file cigads, which was described in problem 7.

a. Perhaps the amount of advertising a cigarette company chooses to do depends on its sales. We'll assume so, and we'll also assume it depends on things like the advertising brand, and the variety of products it has to offer. Let the second equation of the model be $\log \text{Realads} = \gamma_0 + \gamma_1 \log \text{Sales} + \gamma_2 \text{D71} + \gamma_3 \text{Fairdoc} + \gamma_4 \text{D64} + \gamma_5 \text{Lowtar} + \gamma_6 \text{Filter} + \varepsilon_A$. What variables from this regression can be used as instruments to estimate the demand equation given in problem 7, part b?

b. Estimate the equation $\log \text{Sales} = \beta_0 + \beta_1 \log \text{Realads} + \beta_2 \log \text{Income} + \beta_3 \text{Tobacpercig} + \beta_4 \text{D64} + \beta_5 \text{Fairdoc} + \varepsilon_D$ by two-stage least squares, using the instruments from part a and including a correction for first-order autocorrelation. Test the null hypothesis $\beta_1 = 0$. Do cigarette advertisements affect sales or not? If they do, do they increase sales or decrease sales? Does the instrumental variables technique seem to have improved the results? On the basis of this regression, would you conclude that regulating advertising could be a good way to decrease cigarette consumption, or not?

c. What is the elasticity of cigarette sales with respect to income? Test whether the elasticity is equal to 1. Are sales elastic, inelastic, or unit elastic with respect to income? Does this match your intuition or not? Why or why not?

d. Did the 1964 Surgeon General's warning have any effect on cigarette sales? How do you know? Did the 1971 ban on advertising have any effect on cigarette sales? How do you know?

Part **Six**

Advanced Topics

There is far more to econometric analysis than the core material presented in the first five parts of this book. In Part VI, we present a series of chapters dealing with advanced topics that are widely used in applied econometrics and within the grasp of undergraduate-level analysis. Each chapter deals with a specific issue beyond the basic least squares model—multiple equations, forecasting, time series analysis, models nonlinear in their parameters, and dependent variables that are discrete or have limited ranges—and shows how modern econometric methods handle those issues in analyzing economic problems.

Chapter **Fifteen**

Simultaneous Equations

Including the cost share equations in the estimation procedure has the effect of adding many additional degrees of freedom to the model without adding any unrestricted regression coefficients. This will result in more efficient parameter estimates than would be obtained by applying ordinary least squares to the cost function alone.

Laurits Christensen and William Greene (1976)

15.1 ESTIMATING MORE THAN ONE EQUATION AT A TIME

Most economic models involve more than one equation. Supply and demand models such as the one estimated in Chapter 14, most macroeconomic models, and any other model that involves two lines crossing on a graph include two (or more) equations. We know how to estimate each equation individually, but given the links between the equations, we might reasonably ask whether it is possible, or desirable, to estimate the equations jointly. Can we get more efficient estimates of the parameters of our model if we look at all of the equations in the model at once instead of looking at each one separately?

> **Definition 15.1** *Simultaneous estimation* is the process of estimating more than one equation at a time.

It turns out that it is possible to estimate equations jointly. Sometimes this improves the efficiency of the estimates, sometimes it has no effect on their efficiency, and sometimes it makes things worse than if we estimate the equations separately. In general, simultaneous estimation of two or more equations will not have any effect on the estimates unless there is some kind of relationship between the two equations. In that case we do better to choose estimated parameters for both equations at the same time, using our knowledge of their relationship, than if we estimate them separately and ignore that relationship.

There are two useful types of relationships between equations. First, there may be a relationship between the error terms of the two models. If so, then we should choose estimated values for the parameters of the model that reflect that relationship. Second, there may be relationships between the parameters of the model themselves, either because two parameters take the same value or because some more general mathematical relationship exists between two parameters. If so, then again we should choose estimates that obey the relationship that we think exists. If the relationship is true, then imposing it will increase the accuracy of the estimates. This chapter presents methods for simultaneous estimation of multiple equations and discusses conditions under which it is helpful and under which it is not.

15.2   SEEMINGLY UNRELATED REGRESSIONS

Consider a firm that is deciding how much labor to use to produce its output. The wage rate will certainly affect its decision; all else equal, a higher wage rate should encourage a firm to cut back on labor and use other inputs to make its output. For example, a firm might buy automated machinery in order to reduce the number of workers it requires. The prices of the other inputs matter also. A rise in those prices will encourage the firm to use less of those inputs, and more labor. Last, the amount of output the firm wishes to produce will affect its demand for labor. We can write the following labor demand function:

$$L = \beta_0 + \beta_1 P_L + \beta_2 P_K + \beta_3 P_O + \beta_4 Q + \varepsilon_L \qquad \textbf{(15.2.1)}$$

where L is labor demanded, P_L is the wage rate of labor, P_K is the price of capital, P_O is the price of other inputs the firm could shift to, and Q is the amount of output. We expect $\beta_1 < 0$, because as wages rise, firms should use less labor. We expect all other parameters except β_0 to be positive, because higher prices of all other inputs and higher output levels should cause the firm to use more labor.

At the same time that the firm is deciding how much labor to use, it must also decide how much capital to use; the decisions are linked because the firm must choose enough of both (and enough other inputs) to produce the required amount of output. The amount of capital the firm wants to use therefore depends on exactly the same variables as the amount of labor it wants: the prices of all inputs and the amount of output. The firm's capital demand function is therefore

$$K = \gamma_0 + \gamma_1 P_L + \gamma_2 P_K + \gamma_3 P_O + \gamma_4 Q + \varepsilon_K \qquad \textbf{(15.2.2)}$$

Furthermore, there should be a relationship between ε_L and ε_K; they should be negatively correlated. Holding the firm's output Q fixed, if a firm uses more labor than expected, it should use less capital than expected, and conversely.

We would like to use our belief that the errors are correlated to improve the quality of the estimation. To do that, we modify the least squares principle slightly. Suppose that we know the variances of the two errors, and also their covariance. When estimating two equations simultaneously, we will pick estimated values for the parameters not only to minimize the sum of squared residuals but also to make the covariance of the residuals of the two equations as close as possible to the desired covariance. If we know the covariance of the errors, then we know what the pattern of the residuals should be and we can choose the parameters to reproduce that pattern as closely as possible.

Mathematically, let σ_L^2 be the variance of ε_L, σ_K^2 be the variance of ε_K, and σ_{LK} be the covariance of ε_L and ε_K. Then we pick values for the β and γ parameters to minimize the function:

$$\frac{\sigma_K^2}{\Delta} \sum_{i=1}^{N} \hat{\varepsilon}_L^2 + \frac{\sigma_L^2}{\Delta} \sum_{i=1}^{N} \hat{\varepsilon}_K^2 - 2\frac{\sigma_{LK}}{\Delta} \sum_{i=1}^{N} \hat{\varepsilon}_L \hat{\varepsilon}_K \qquad \textbf{(15.2.3)}$$

where $\Delta = \sigma_L^2 \sigma_K^2 - (\sigma_{LK})^2$. The first term is proportional to the sum of squared residuals of the first equation, and the second term is proportional to the sum of squared residuals from the second equation—so we seek to make those as small as possible. However, we also try to minimize the value of the third term, $-2(\sigma_{LK}/\Delta) \sum_{i=1}^{N} \hat{\varepsilon}_L \hat{\varepsilon}_K$, which depends on the covariance of the two residuals. If σ_{LK} is positive, we will get a lower value for Equation 15.2.3 if we allow the covariance of the residuals, $\sum_{i=1}^{N} \hat{\varepsilon}_L \hat{\varepsilon}_K$, to be positive; and if σ_{LK} is negative, we get a lower value for the equation if we allow the covariance to be negative. Note also that the first term depends not only on the residuals from the first equation but also on σ_K^2, and the second term depends on the residuals from the second equation and on σ_L^2. These terms cause us to place relatively more weight on the equation with smaller error terms. This is conceptually similar to the weighted least squares technique we used to correct for heteroskedasticity in Chapter 13. As σ_L^2 rises, we will place a greater weight on the residuals from the capital equation and thus less weight on the residuals from the labor equation. Similarly, as σ_K^2 rises, we place more weight on the residuals from the labor equation and less on the (larger) residuals from the capital equation. And as σ_{LK} rises, we place greater weight on the covariance of the residuals.[1]

There is one problem: We generally do not know the variances and covariances of the two error terms. We solve this problem by first estimating the two equations separately by ordinary least squares (OLS). The standard errors of these regressions provide consistent estimates of the variances of their error terms, and using the residuals from this estimation, we can calculate a consistent estimate of the covariance of the two error terms. We then use those estimated values to perform the calculations above. Because there may not be any apparent link between the two equations being simultaneously estimated, this model is known as the *seemingly unrelated regressions (SUR) model*. It is also known as *multivariate least squares*. It produces estimates of multiple equations that are both consistent and efficient. The technique can be generalized in a straightforward way to the case of three or more equations.

Does it make a difference whether we estimate by SUR or by OLS? Under some conditions, the answer is no.

> **Theorem 15.1** If the error terms of the equations are uncorrelated, or if all equations in the simultaneous estimation have the same right-hand-side variables, then SUR and OLS will produce identical estimated values for the parameters of the equations. If one equation has more independent variables than the other, but all independent variables in the smaller equation are included in the larger, then SUR and OLS produce identical estimated values for the smaller equation (but not the larger one).

Under other conditions, SUR can be a better method.

> **Theorem 15.2** If the equations of the system have different right-hand-side variables and the error terms are correlated, then SUR and OLS will produce different

---

[1] If we assume $\sigma_{LK} = 0$, so that the third term cancels out of Equation 15.2.2, then we are simply minimizing the sum of squared errors of the residuals from both equations, weighted by the variance of the respective error terms. This is known as equation-weighted least squares. Its estimates are identical to those from ordinary least squares unless there are cross-equation restrictions on the parameters.

estimates of the β and γ parameters, as well as different estimated standard errors. If the Gauss-Markov assumptions are satisfied, then the SUR estimates will be consistent and more efficient (i.e., they will have lower standard errors) than the OLS estimates for sufficiently large samples.

Intuition tells us that this is true: If all of the equations have the same right-hand-side variables, then all of them have the same information available to predict the left-hand-side variable, and thus estimating simultaneously cannot help improve the fit. But if one equation contains a right-hand-side variable that does not appear in the other equation, then estimating jointly can be more efficient. Suppose X is an exogenous variable that appears on the right-hand side of the first equation. Clearly, it affects the value of $\hat{\varepsilon}_1$, the residual from the first equation. However, if the residuals are correlated, then it should also indirectly affect the value of $\hat{\varepsilon}_2$, the residual from the second equation. If we estimate equation by equation, we fail to use the information in the variable X to fit the residuals in the second equation. By taking advantage of that information, SUR is able to produce better estimates than single-equation OLS can produce.

We demonstrate these two theorems using data from urban bus companies collected by the Federal Transit Authority. We estimate Equations 15.2.1 and 15.2.2, using maintenance expenditure as the measure of capital expense and fuel as the other input. The variable F is the quantity of fuel used; P_F is its price. We also estimate an equation for fuel demand:

$$F = \delta_0 + \delta_1 P_L + \delta_2 P_K + \delta_3 P_F + \delta_4 Q + \varepsilon_F \qquad \textbf{(15.2.4)}$$

Labor is measured in number of full-time equivalent workers, fuel in thousands of gallons, and maintenance expenditure in thousands of dollars. Output is measured in vehicle-miles of bus service provided. The data are panel data on 238 firms from 1993 to 1995; there are 714 observations.

Because there are three equations in the system of Equations (15.2.1, 15.2.2, and 15.2.4), each observation provides us with the ability to calculate three residuals rather than just one. Accordingly, our estimates are more powerful than they would be if we were calculating only a single residual, based on a single economic relationship, between the variables we observe.

Definition 15.2 For a system of M equations with K total parameters and N observations, the degrees of freedom in the estimation are df $= (N \cdot M) - K$.

In this case, we have 714 observations, 3 equations, and 15 parameters, so the degrees of freedom of our estimation is equal to $(714 \cdot 3) - 15 = 2{,}127$.

We first estimate the equations individually by least squares. Results are shown in Table 15.1. The parameter estimates that are statistically significantly different from 0 are generally in accordance with expectations, but many of the parameter estimates are not statistically significant, because they have relatively high standard errors. All of the parameter estimates for output are positive and statistically significantly different from 0. Of the estimates of parameters on input prices, only three of the nine are significant, although all three of the significant ones take the expected sign. The results are not inconsistent with predictions of economic theory; but with so many insignificant results, it would be desirable to find a way to get more powerful estimates.

TABLE 15.1
Equation-by-Equation Least Squares Estimates

Labor Demand

Variable	Parameter	Estimate	Standard Error	t Statistic for $\beta = 0$
Intercept	β_0	155.8	47.87	3.25
P_L	β_1	−16.81	1.806	−9.31
P_K	β_2	−0.016	0.185	−0.09
P_F	β_3	52.36	58.05	0.90
Output	β_4	0.059	0.003	23.1

Maintenance Demand

Variable	Parameter	Estimate	Standard Error	t Statistic for $\gamma = 0$
Intercept	γ_0	−748.5	363.5	−2.05
P_L	γ_1	13.63	13.71	0.99
P_K	γ_2	1.894	1.411	1.34
P_F	γ_3	273.8	440.8	0.62
Output	γ_4	1.005	0.019	51.8

Fuel Demand

Variable	Parameter	Estimate	Standard Error	t Statistic for $\delta = 0$
Intercept	δ_0	140.9	40.60	3.47
P_L	δ_1	−0.562	1.532	−0.37
P_K	δ_2	0.642	0.157	4.07
P_F	δ_3	−247.6	49.23	−5.02
Output	δ_4	0.305	0.002	140.6

Table 15.2 shows the results of estimating the same three equations by SUR. As Theorem 15.1 suggests, the estimated coefficients are exactly the same, and the six parameters that were insignificant remain so. One option for increasing the precision of the estimates is to drop one or more insignificant variables from the equations. In the fuel equation, the only insignificant parameter is δ_1, so we drop the price of labor from that equation. In the labor equation, the t statistic for the hypothesis $\beta_2 = 0$ is −0.09, so we drop the price of maintenance. In the maintenance equation the t statistic for the hypothesis $\gamma_3 = 0$ is 0.62, so we drop the price of fuel.[2] This results in the following system of equations:

$$L = \beta_0 + \beta_1 P_L + \beta_3 P_F + \beta_4 Q + \varepsilon_L \qquad \textbf{(15.2.5)}$$

$$K = \gamma_0 + \gamma_1 P_L + \gamma_2 P_K + \gamma_4 Q + \varepsilon_K \qquad \textbf{(15.2.6)}$$

$$F = \delta_0 + \delta_2 P_K + \delta_3 P_F + \delta_4 Q + \varepsilon_F \qquad \textbf{(15.2.7)}$$

Now the right-hand-side variables of each equation are different, and in this case SUR and OLS should produce different parameter estimates, as well as different estimated standard

---

[2] You might ask whether, since we are dropping more than one variable, we ought to be doing an F test instead of t tests. In this case, t tests are acceptable, because the estimated parameters are identical to those produced by equation-by-equation OLS, and we are dropping only one variable from each equation. F test or Wald tests would give (approximately) the same answer, however.

TABLE 15.2
Seemingly
Unrelated
Equations
(SUR)
Estimates

Labor Demand

Variable	Parameter	Estimate	Standard Error	t Statistic for $\beta = 0$
Intercept	β_0	155.8	47.70	3.27
P_L	β_1	−16.81	1.800	−9.34
P_K	β_2	−0.016	0.185	−0.09
P_F	β_3	52.36	57.84	0.90
Output	β_4	0.059	0.003	23.2

Maintenance Demand

Variable	Parameter	Estimate	Standard Error	t Statistic for $\gamma = 0$
Intercept	γ_0	−748.5	362.2	−2.06
P_L	γ_1	13.63	13.67	1.00
P_K	γ_2	1.894	1.406	1.35
P_F	γ_3	273.8	439.2	0.62
Output	γ_4	1.005	0.019	52.0

Fuel Demand

Variable	Parameter	Estimate	Standard Error	t Statistic for $\delta = 0$
Intercept	δ_0	140.9	40.46	3.48
P_L	δ_1	−0.562	1.526	−0.37
P_K	δ_2	0.642	0.157	4.07
P_F	δ_3	−247.6	49.06	−5.05
Output	δ_4	0.305	0.002	141.1

errors. Table 15.3 shows the results of OLS estimation, and Table 15.4 shows the results of SUR estimation. This time, the parameter estimates for SUR are different and the SUR estimates are the more efficient of the two. However, the differences are quite small. The standard errors of the SUR estimates are, in general, lower, and in a few cases they are quite a bit lower. For example, the estimated standard error of δ_3, the effect of fuel prices on fuel demand, has an estimated standard error of 41.77 in the SUR results, as opposed to 49.13 in the OLS results. This is an exceptional case, however; in most cases the efficiency gains are smaller. Using SUR to jointly estimate the equations of the system, allowing for correlation between the errors of the equations, will improve the efficiency of estimation, but usually not much.

There is one potential problem with simultaneous estimation, which is that it requires the Gauss-Markov assumptions to be true for all equations. Suppose that the Gauss-Markov assumptions are true for one equation but not for another. For example, one equation might have an omitted right-hand-side variable or an endogenous one. Then estimating by SUR will generally no longer be unbiased or consistent for any of the equations. In such a case, OLS would remain unbiased and consistent for those equations for which the Gauss-Markov assumptions held. Estimating equation by equation has the advantage that, if there is a problem with one equation, the problem is limited to that equation and cannot spill over to the estimates of the parameters of the other equations.

TABLE 15.3

Equation-by-Equation Least Squares Estimates with Parameter Restrictions

Labor Demand

Variable	Parameter	Estimate	Standard Error	t Statistic for $\beta = 0$
Intercept	β_0	156.5	47.18	3.32
P_L	β_1	−16.83	1.798	−9.36
P_F	β_3	50.87	55.68	0.91
Output	β_4	0.059	0.003	23.3

Maintenance Demand

Variable	Parameter	Estimate	Standard Error	t Statistic for $\gamma = 0$
Intercept	γ_0	−546.1	161.1	−3.39
P_L	γ_1	13.17	13.69	0.96
P_K	γ_2	2.140	1.354	1.58
Output	γ_4	1.004	0.019	52.2

Fuel Demand

Variable	Parameter	Estimate	Standard Error	t Statistic for $\delta = 0$
Intercept	δ_0	134.7	36.84	3.66
P_K	δ_2	0.637	0.157	4.06
P_F	δ_3	−246.6	49.13	−5.01
Output	δ_4	0.305	0.002	144.1

TABLE 15.4

Seemingly Unrelated Equations (SUR) Estimates with Parameter Restrictions

Labor Demand

Variable	Parameter	Estimate	Standard Error	t Statistic for $\beta = 0$
Intercept	β_0	158.3	46.99	3.37
P_L	β_1	−16.85	1.792	−9.40
P_F	β_3	48.83	55.43	0.88
Output	β_4	0.059	0.003	23.4

Maintenance Demand

Variable	Parameter	Estimate	Standard Error	t Statistic for $\gamma = 0$
Intercept	γ_0	−573.3	144.5	−3.97
P_L	γ_1	15.91	11.63	1.37
P_K	γ_2	2.126	1.346	1.58
Output	γ_4	1.003	0.019	52.7

Fuel Demand

Variable	Parameter	Estimate	Standard Error	t Statistic for $\delta = 0$
Intercept	δ_0	146.4	31.75	4.61
P_K	δ_2	0.651	0.155	4.21
P_F	δ_3	−262.8	41.77	−6.29
Output	δ_4	0.305	0.002	144.9

15.3 RESTRICTIONS ON PARAMETERS IN DIFFERENT EQUATIONS

Up to now, we have not made use of the economic connection between the three equations in the system. We have allowed for the error terms to be correlated, and we have some economic ideas about why the errors would be correlated, but the errors might well be correlated by coincidence even if there was no economic link between the two equations at all. We may do better if we can use economic theory to suggest direct links between the parameters of the three equations of the system.

> **Definition 15.3** Restrictions on the values of parameters in two different equations are called *cross-equation restrictions*. For example, the restriction $\beta_2 = \gamma_1$ in Equations 15.2.1 and 15.2.2 is a cross-equation restriction.

Imposing cross-equation restrictions on the data will reduce the total number of parameters we have to estimate. More important, if a parameter occurs in two equations, then when we choose a value for it, we observe its effects on two sets of residuals, rather than just one. This not only gives us a greater ability to recognize a poor estimate of the value of the parameter but also allows us to be more confident in the correctness of the estimates we calculate, meaning they will have smaller standard errors. However, in order to do this, we have to use some explicit economic theory to demonstrate *why* there should be links between the parameters of the two equations.

In the case of the mass transit companies, we can rely on the following piece of economic theory. There is a relationship between the amount of labor, capital, and fuel a firm purchases and its total cost of doing business, which we represent by C:

$$C = P_L L + P_K K + P_F F \qquad \textbf{(15.3.1)}$$

We know that the amount of labor, capital, and fuel that a firm buys will depend on both the prices of labor, capital, and fuel and the amount of output the firm chooses to produce. We can therefore write a cost function for the firm:

$$C = f(P_L, \ P_K, \ P_F, \ Q) \qquad \textbf{(15.3.2)}$$

And it is possible to demonstrate the following:

> **Theorem 15.3** Shepard's lemma: The derivative of a firm's total cost with respect to the price of one of its inputs is equal to the total amount of that input the firm uses:[3]
>
> $$\frac{\partial C}{\partial P_X} = X \qquad \textbf{(15.3.3)}$$

where X is the amount of input used and P_X is its price.

---

[3] This may seem to follow obviously from Equation 15.3.1. However, remember that if, say, P_L changes, then the values of L, K, and F will all change also, because as the price of labor rises, the firm will use less labor and more capital and fuel. The proof of Shepard's lemma, which can be found in any graduate-level microeconomics textbook, is to demonstrate that the effects from changes in L, K, and F when P_L changes add up to exactly 0. When they cancel out, only the L term is left in the derivative.

Specifically, if we write the firm's cost function as a fully quadratic function of all of its right-hand-side variables:

$$C = \alpha_0 + \alpha_1 P_L + \alpha_2 P_K + \alpha_3 P_F + \alpha_4 Q + \alpha_{11} P_L^2$$
$$+ \alpha_{12} P_L P_K + \alpha_{13} P_L P_F + \alpha_{22} P_K^2 + \alpha_{23} P_K P_F + \alpha_{33} P_F^2$$
$$+ \alpha_{14} P_L Q + \alpha_{24} P_L Q + \alpha_{34} P_L Q + \alpha_{44} Q^2 \quad \text{(15.3.4)}$$

Then we can use Shepard's lemma to show that:

$$L = \frac{\partial C}{\partial P_L} = \alpha_1 + 2\alpha_{11} P_L + \alpha_{12} P_K + \alpha_{13} P_F + \alpha_{14} Q \quad \text{(15.3.5)}$$

and

$$F = \frac{\partial C}{\partial P_F} = \alpha_3 + \alpha_{13} P_L + \alpha_{23} P_K + 2\alpha_{33} P_F + \alpha_{34} Q \quad \text{(15.3.6)}$$

and we can see that Equations 15.3.5 and 15.3.6 are the same as Equations 15.2.1 and 15.2.4 with the parameters appropriately renamed, except that the parameters are now visibly related to the parameters of the cost equation. In particular, the parameter α_{13} appears in all three equations. Christensen and Greene (1976), in their study of costs in the electric power industry, pioneered the method of using Shepard's lemma to derive additional equations relating input demand and prices, and estimating those equations simultaneously with the cost function to improve the power of the estimates of the parameters.

To impose cross-equation restrictions, we must estimate the system of equations simultaneously; there is no way to require that the same estimated value be chosen for a parameter in two equations if they are estimated separately. To estimate a system of equations with cross-equation restrictions, we again choose the values of the parameters of the equations to minimize Equation 15.2.3. The primary difference is that, if a parameter such as α_{13} appears in more than one equation, then the choice of its estimated value affects the values of the residuals for all the equations it appears in, not just one. This makes only a small change in the estimation technique. We still choose the parameters to minimize the sum of the squared residuals from each equation and their covariances, appropriately weighted, using weights calculated from single-equation estimates of the residuals. The mathematics will be slightly more complicated because the parameter that appears in more than one equation will affect the residuals for more than one equation, so the derivative of the sum of squared residuals with respect to that parameter will be more complex.

Table 15.5 shows the results of estimating this system by seemingly unrelated regressions, imposing the cross-equation restrictions implied by Shepard's lemma. Because of the restrictions, some of the parameters appear in more than one equation; those parameters appear with an interaction term in the cost equation, Equation 15.3.4, and with a linear variable in one of the other two equations. The second column of Table 15.5 shows the relationships between the parameters of this table and those of the earlier tables.

Almost all of the standard errors for each parameter are lower in Table 15.5 than in any of the proceeding tables; all but two of the parameters are now statistically significantly different from 0. The standard error of α_2 (γ_0 in previous equations) has dropped from 144.5 in Table 15.4 to 9.172 in Table 15.5. The standard error of α_{33} (δ_3 in previous equations) has dropped from 41.77 in Table 15.4 to 22.46 in Table 15.5. The parameter α_{13} was

TABLE 15.5
SUR Estimates with Cross-Equation Restrictions

Parameter	Matches	Estimate	Standard Error	t Statistic for $\alpha = 0$
α_0	—	−2,235.1	401.4	−5.56
α_1	β_0	186.2	29.38	6.34
α_2	γ_0	25.78	9.172	2.81
α_3	δ_0	150.5	37.49	4.01
α_4	—	3.166	0.156	20.3
α_{11}	β_1	−8.695	1.196	−7.27
α_{12}	β_2 and γ_1	0.304	0.259	1.17
α_{13}	β_3 and δ_1	−1.441	1.428	−1.00
α_{14}	β_4	0.063	0.004	17.0
α_{22}	γ_2	−0.147	0.027	−5.30
α_{23}	γ_3 and δ_2	0.612	0.162	3.78
α_{24}	γ_4	0.008	0.002	3.53
α_{33}	δ_3	−123.3	22.46	−5.48
α_{34}	δ_4	0.304	0.002	136.2
α_{44}	—	2.1e-5	8.3e-6	2.50

FIGURE 15.1
Cost Curve with Variable Returns to Scale

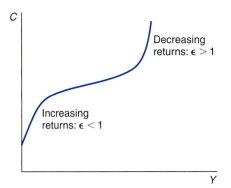

estimated twice in the earlier equations, once as β_3, the parameter on the price of fuel in the labor demand equation and once as δ_1, the parameter on the price of labor in the fuel demand equation. In Table 15.2, its standard error was 57.84 in the labor demand equation and 1.526 in the fuel demand equation. In Table 15.5 its standard error has dropped to 1.428. Not all the standard errors have dropped as far as these, and two have risen slightly, but on the whole the imposition of the cross-equation restrictions has substantially increased the precision of the parameter estimates. This occurs because we are using more information to estimate the values, and as long as our information is correct, using more of it will increase the precision of the estimates.

This is useful not only in terms of the parameters that appear in more than one equation; it also helps us estimate the parameters that appear in only one equation. In particular, this equation shows that α_{44}, the parameter on output squared in the cost function, is quite small but statistically significantly different from 0. This means that the elasticity of costs with respect to output increases as output rises, eventually reaching a point of decreasing returns to scale, as shown in Figure 15.1. This is an important finding for regulating the industry, as it implies that there is an efficient scale for firms in the industry, above which still larger firms are not more cost-effective than those at the efficient scale. This implies that it may become cost-effective to have more than one firm serving a market, and raises the possibility of allowing competition in the industry. In their study of the electric power industry, Christiansen and Greene found that electric power plants did indeed have a point of decreasing returns to scale and, furthermore, that electric power plants were, as of the time of their writing, beginning to reach that scale. Their findings were one of the initial discoveries that led to the restructuring of the electric power industry 15 to 20 years later.

15.4 MULTIPLE EQUATIONS WITH ENDOGENOUS RIGHT-HAND-SIDE VARIABLES

SUR is a useful technique for models that can be estimated by least squares. However, it cannot be used if the Gauss-Markov assumptions are not satisfied. In particular, if the equations contain endogenous right-hand-side variables, SUR will be biased and inconsistent. Anytime we have two equations solving for the values of two variables, such as the supply and demand model of Chapter 14, there will be endogenous right-hand-side variables and SUR will not be appropriate.

Fortunately, we can simultaneously estimate equations by two-stage least squares in exactly the same way that we simultaneously estimate them by ordinary least squares. Doing so requires a three-step process:

1. Regress each endogenous variable on all exogenous variables in the system of equations, and calculate predicted values for the endogenous variables.
2. Estimate the structural equations by least squares, replacing the endogenous right-hand-side variables with their predicted values from step 1.
3. Calculate the estimated variances and covariances of the residuals from step 2, and reestimate the structural equations using the SUR method.

This technique, known as *three-stage least squares,* is the instrumental variables equivalent to SUR. It has the same general relationship to two-stage least squares that SUR has to OLS. Its advantage is that it will be more efficient than two-stage least squares for large samples, as long as the right-hand-side variables of the equations are not the same in all equations. It is not unbiased—but two-stage least squares is not unbiased either, so that is not a disadvantage of three-stage least squares. Its main disadvantage is that, as with SUR, simultaneous estimation permits a violation of the Gauss-Markov assumptions in one of the equations to spread to the other equations.

Table 15.6 shows the results of estimating Equations 14.7.1 and 14.7.2, the supply and demand for alcoholic beverages, using three-stage least squares instead of equation-by-equation two-stage least squares. It is easy to see that the parameter estimates have changed very little and that the standard errors are generally 10 to 20 percent smaller for the three-stage least squares estimates. The estimated demand elasticity is only slightly different, -0.136 rather than -0.129, but the estimated supply elasticity has changed somewhat more substantially, falling to 0.712 from its previous value of 1.124. This changes the calculation of the effect of excise taxes as well. Plugging the three-stage least squares results

TABLE 15.6
Estimated
Supply and
Demand
Curves for
Alcoholic
Beverages

Demand Curve

Variable	Parameter	Estimate	Standard Error	t Statistic for $\beta = 0$
Intercept	β_0	−13.69	4.355	−3.14
Log price	β_1	−0.136	0.061	−2.24
Log per capita income	β_2	0.216	0.054	4.00
Log adult population	β_3	1.377	0.411	3.35

Supply Curve

Variable	Parameter	Estimate	Standard Error	t Statistic for $\gamma = 0$
Intercept	γ_0	2.402	0.313	7.69
Log price	γ_1	0.712	0.278	2.56
Log price cereal	γ_2	−0.374	0.137	−2.74
Log wage rate	γ_3	−0.031	0.201	−0.15
Participation rate	γ_4	0.011	0.006	1.93
Unemployment rate	γ_5	−0.015	0.004	−4.19

into Equation 14.7.5 suggests that a tax of about 11.8 percent is required to reduce alcohol consumption by 10 percent. The results are not mutually inconsistent. The 95 percent confidence interval for the supply elasticity from the two-stage least squares results is $1.123 \pm (1.96 \cdot 0.333) = (0.47, 1.77)$, and that interval contains the three-stage least squares estimated value of 0.711. Similarly, the 95 percent confidence interval from the three-stage least squares estimates is $0.711 \pm (1.96 \cdot 0.278) = (0.167, 1.255)$, and that interval contains (just barely) the estimated value of 1.123 from the two-stage least squares results. What the discrepancy really demonstrates is that the confidence intervals are, from a policymaking standpoint, quite wide, and can give a fairly broad range of figures for the size of the tax needed to reduce alcohol consumption by 10 percent. This suggests that we should be relatively cautious in making policy recommendations based on these results. It also suggests that we should use the most powerful techniques available to estimate the elasticities so that we can have as much confidence as possible in our findings. In this case, the three-stage least squares results have a lower standard error and therefore are the ones on which we should base our conclusions.

Chapter Review

- When there is more than one equation in an economic model, it is possible to estimate the equations simultaneously.
- To estimate two or more equations simultaneously, we choose parameters to minimize a weighted combination of the sum of squared residuals from each equation and their covariances. To do so, we first estimate the regressions individually and use the variances and covariances of the residuals from the individual regressions to estimate the necessary weights. This method is called *seemingly unrelated regressions (SUR)*.
- When two or more equations all have the same right-hand-side variables, then SUR and OLS provide exactly the same estimates.

- When the equations do not all have the same right-hand-side variables, then SUR is biased in small samples but is more efficient than OLS in large samples.
- When estimating equations simultaneously, we can impose *cross-equation restrictions* on the parameters of the model. Imposing cross-equation restrictions can substantially improve the precision of the parameter estimates.
- When we estimate equations simultaneously, specification errors in one equation or other violations of Gauss-Markov assumptions can bias the estimates of the parameters in all equations. If we estimate separately, this cannot happen.
- If the two equations involve endogenous right-hand-side variables, then we can perform simultaneous two-stage least squares by estimating the second stage of that method simultaneously. This method is called *three-stage least squares*. It is generally more efficient than two-stage least squares but is equivalent to two-stage least squares in certain cases.

Computer Exercise

In this exercise we'll estimate a system of equations by SUR and show that misspecification in one equation biases estimates of the parameters of both.

1. Open Eviews and create a new workfile, undated, with 250 observations.

2. Type genr x1 = rnd(50)+10, genr x2 = rnd(50)+20, and genr x3 = rnd(10)+x1*0.8+x2*0.8 to generate three exogenous variables for the model. Note that X_2 and X_3 will be strongly positively correlated.

3. Type genr err1 = nrnd() and genr err2 = nrnd()+err1 to generate error terms. The error terms will also be correlated.

4. Type genr y1 = 10 + x1 + err1 and genr y2 = 5 + 2*x2 + 4*x3 + err2 to generate the values of the endogenous variables.

5. Under the Objects menu, select New Object. In the resulting dialog box, select System for Type of Object, and give it any name you like.

6. In the open system object, type y1 = c(1)+c(2)*x1 and y2 = c(3)+c(4)*x2+c(5)*x3. This gives Eviews the equations you wish it to estimate.

7. In the system object, hit the Estimate button and select Ordinary Least Squares to estimate each equation separately. Because this is generated data, we know that the true value for $c(1)$ is 10, the true value of $c(2)$ is 1, the true value of $c(3)$ is 5, the true value of $c(4)$ is 2, and the true value of $c(5)$ is 4. How close are the OLS estimates to the true values? Are they within two standard errors?

8. Now hit the Estimate button again, and this time select SUR. Because the equations have different right-hand-side variables, the SUR estimates will be different. How different are they? Are they within two standard errors of the true values? Which estimates have smaller standard errors, SUR or OLS?

9. Hit the Spec button, and change the last line of the specification to y2 = c(3)+c(4)*x2. This will result in the second equation having omitted variable bias. Then hit the Estimate button again and select OLS. Are the estimated parameters for the first equation close to their true values? Are they within two standard deviations? Are they the same

as, or different from, the estimates from part 7? How are the estimates for the second equation? Which estimates appear to be biased?

10. Now hit the Estimate button one more time and select SUR. How close are the estimates of the first equation's parameters to their true values now?

Problems

1. In this problem we'll look at a multiple equation model of international trade flows, and show SUR provides more efficient estimates than least squares does. Open the data file intltrade, which contains monthly data from January 1990 to December 2000 on the following variables: tradedefcanada (U.S. trade deficit with Canada, millions of real U.S. dollars); tradedefjapan (U.S. trade deficit with Japan, millions of real U.S. dollars); exratecanada (Canadian dollars per U.S. dollar); exratejapan (yen per U.S. dollar); ratecanada (Canadian government bond interest rate); ratejapan (Japanese government bond interest rate); and rateus (U.S. Treasury bill interest rate).

   a. Estimate the regression $\log \text{Tradedefcanada}_t = \beta_0 + \beta_1 \text{Exratecanada}_t + \beta_2 \text{Ratecanada}_t + \beta_3 \text{Rateus}_t + \varepsilon_{Ct}$. Observe that we have chosen the semilogarithmic functional form. If the Canadian dollar depreciates from 1.1 per U.S. dollar to 1.2 per U.S. dollar, by what percentage does the U.S. trade deficit with Canada rise, fall, or not change? Does it move in the direction you would expect it to move?

   b. Estimate the regression $\log \text{Tradedefjapan}_t = \gamma_0 + \gamma_1 \text{Exratejapan}_t + \gamma_2 \text{Ratejapan}_t + \gamma_3 \text{Rateus}_t + \varepsilon_{Jt}$, also in the semilogarithmic functional form. Is it reasonable to exclude Exratecanada and Ratecanada from this equation? If Japanese interest rates rise from 3 to 4 percent, does the trade balance rise, fall, or not change? Is this the answer you expect?

   c. Would you expect ε_{Ct} and ε_{Jt} to be positively or negatively correlated? Why?

   d. Estimate both equations simultaneously using SUR. Have the parameter estimates changed a lot, or only slightly? Look at the standard errors of the parameter estimates. Are they larger or smaller than the standard errors of the single-equation estimates? Which technique is more efficient?

2. In this problem we'll see the effect of imposing a cross-equation restriction on the efficiency of SUR estimates. Open the data file intltrade, which was described in problem 1.

   a. Consider the equations $\log \text{Tradedefcanada}_t = \beta_0 + \beta_1 \text{Exratecanada}_t + \beta_2 \text{Ratecanada}_t + \beta_3 \text{Rateus}_t + \varepsilon_{Ct}$ and $\log \text{Tradedefjapan}_t = \gamma_0 + \gamma_1 \text{Exratejapan}_t + \gamma_2 \text{Ratejapan}_t + \gamma_3 \text{Rateus}_t + \varepsilon_{Jt}$. If a 1 percentage point increase in the interest rate of a foreign country has the same effect on trade for all countries, then what should be true about the model's parameters?

   b. Estimate each equation separately. What estimated values do you get for β_2 and γ_2? How far apart are the two values? What are their standard errors? Does it look plausible that they might have the same true value?

   c. Estimate the two equations by SUR, and test the null hypothesis $\beta_2 = \gamma_2$. Do you reject or fail to reject this hypothesis?

   d. Reestimate the system of equations, imposing the restriction $\beta_2 = \gamma_2$. What value do you get for their common value? If the interest rate of a foreign country rises by 1 percent, how much does the U.S. trade deficit with that country fall?

e. What is the standard error of the estimated value of β_2 and γ_2 when the restriction that they take the same value is imposed? What is its standard error in the previous regression without the restriction? Has the standard error gotten larger or smaller? How have the standard errors of the other parameters changed when this restriction was imposed?

3. In this problem we'll estimate a model of cigarette advertising using three-stage least squares. Open the data file cigads, which was described in problem 7 in Chapter 14, and consider the two-equation system, the first describing demand for cigarettes, the second describing the amount of advertising manufacturers choose to buy:

$$\log \text{Sales}_t = \beta_0 + \beta_1 \log \text{Realads}_t + \beta_2 \log \text{Income}_t$$
$$+ \beta_3 \text{Tobacpercig}_t + \beta_4 \text{D64}_t + \beta_5 \text{Fairdoc} + \varepsilon_D$$

$$\log \text{Realads}_t = \gamma_0 + \gamma_1 \log \text{Sales}_t + \gamma_2 \text{D71}_t + \gamma_3 \text{Fairdoc}_t$$
$$+ \gamma_4 \text{D64}_t + \gamma_5 \text{Lowtar}_t + \gamma_6 \text{Filter}_t + \varepsilon_A$$

a. Estimate the first equation by two-stage least squares, using D71, Lowtar, and Filter as instruments, and including a correction for first-order autocorrelation (this is time series data). How much does an increase of 0.1 in tobacco per cigarette increase sales? Is the effect statistically significant or not? Calculate a 95 percent confidence interval for the true value of β_3. Does 0 fall in the interval?

b. Estimate the second equation by two-stage least squares, using log Income and Tobacpercig as instruments. Does it seem reasonable to exclude these instruments from the second equation? If not, why not?

c. From the second equation, if sales increase by 10 percent, how much does advertising change? Is the effect statistically significant or not? Why do you think this might happen? Did the ban on broadcast advertising reduce the amount of cigarette advertising? How much? Is the effect significant or not?

d. Estimate the system by three-stage least squares. How have the parameter estimates changed? How have the standard errors changed? Which set of parameter estimates are preferable, and why?

e. Using the three-stage least squares results, calculate a 95 percent confidence interval for β_3. Is it wider or narrower than before? Which estimate is more precise? Test whether an increase in tobacco per cigarette increases sales. Is the answer different than your answer for the same test in part *a* with the two-stage least squares estimates? If so, why?

4. In this problem we'll omit a significant variable from the right-hand side of one equation, and show that under three-stage least squares this leads to omitted variable bias in both equations of the system, not just the one with the omitted variable. Load the data set cigads, which was described in problem 7 in Chapter 14.

a. Estimate the two-equation model given in problem 3 by three-stage least squares, treating log Sales and log Realads as endogenous, and including corrections for first-order autocorrelation in both equations. Test whether β_2 is statistically significantly different from 0. Does higher income increase cigarette demand, decrease it, or have no effect?

b. Now estimate the model

$$\log \text{Sales}_t = \beta_0 + \beta_1 \log \text{Realads}_t + \beta_3 \text{Tobacpercig}_t$$
$$+ \beta_4 \text{D64}_t + \beta_5 \text{Fairdoc} + \varepsilon_D$$

$$\log \text{Realads}_t = \gamma_0 + \gamma_1 \log \text{Sales}_t + \gamma_2 \text{D71}_t + \gamma_3 \text{Fairdoc}_t + \gamma_4 \text{D64}_t$$
$$+ \gamma_5 \text{Lowtar}_t + \gamma_6 \text{Filter}_t + \varepsilon_A$$

which (incorrectly!) omits log Income from the model. How much does the estimated value of β_1 change when log Income is omitted? Calculate a 95 percent confidence interval for the true value of β_1 using the first model's estimates. Does the estimated value from the second model fall inside this confidence interval or not? Has the omission of log Income from the model created bias in this equation's estimates, or not?

c. How much does the estimated value of γ_1 change when log Income is omitted? Calculate a 95 percent confidence interval for the true value of γ_1 using the first model's estimates. Does the estimated value from the second model fall inside this confidence interval or not? Has the omission of log Income from the first equation created bias in the second equation's estimates, or not?

d. Estimate the model by two-stage least squares, again incorrectly omitting log Income from the first equation. Which equations show omitted variable bias now, and which do not?

5. In this problem we'll show that the addition of irrelevant variables as instruments does not improve the estimates. Load the data file crime, which was described in problem 1 in Chapter 14. We described this data using a two-equation model, in which crime rates and crime spending by governments were the endogenous variables. The equations are:

$$\text{Rate}_i = \beta_0 + \beta_1 \text{Crimespendpc}_i + \beta_2 \text{Rate90}_i + \beta_3 \text{Staterevpc}_i$$
$$+ \beta_4 \text{Nonwhite}_i + \beta_5 \text{Democrat}_i + \varepsilon_i$$

and

$$\text{Crimespendpc}_i = \gamma_0 + \gamma_1 \text{Rate}_i + \gamma_2 \text{Over64}_i + \gamma_3 \text{Statercvpc}_i$$
$$+ \gamma_4 \text{Expperstud}_i + \gamma_5 \text{Percapinc}_i + \gamma_6 \text{Poverty}_i + \upsilon_i$$

a. Estimate the model by two-stage least squares, then by three-stage least squares. How have the parameter estimates changed? How have the standard errors changed? Which set of estimates is more precise?

b. Reestimate the system, this time adding two variables to both of the equations, Under18 and Unemploy. (Be sure to add them to the instruments list also.) Is either of them significant in either equation? Do they affect crime rates and crime spending, or not?

c. Estimate the model again, this time omitting Under18 and Unemploy from the equations, but including them on the instruments list. Are the standard errors from this estimation larger or smaller than the three-stage least squares estimates from part *a* of this problem? Did the addition of irrelevant instruments help the estimation, hurt it, or make little difference?

6. In this problem we'll demonstrate that using all relevant instrumental variables improves the estimation compared to the case when some relevant instruments are not used. Load the data file crime, which was described in problem 1 in Chapter 14.

   a. Estimate each equation of the system given in problem 5 by two-stage least squares, using all excluded exogenous variables as instruments in both cases. Then reestimate the first equation using only Over64 and Poverty as instruments (that is, not using Expperstud and Percapinc). How do the parameter values change? Does it appear that dropping two instruments has caused bias? How do the standard errors change? Does it appear that dropping two instruments has caused inefficiency?

   b. Reestimate the second equation using only Democrat as an instrument (omitting Rate90 and Nonwhite). Is the equation overidentified, or just identified? How do the parameter values change? How do the standard errors change? Does it appear that dropping two instruments has caused bias, inefficiency, or both?

Chapter **Sixteen**

Forecasting

California's economy grew by an incredible 32% in the past 5 years, fueling an increase of 24% in electricity consumption. In the 3 years following passage of the state's restructuring law, peak demand grew by a phenomenal 5,500 megawatts. To reliably supply such an increase in peak demand would require the maximum output of eleven 500 MW power plants. Yet, incredibly, there have been no major power plants built in California since the 1970s . . . Until California adds sufficient generating capacity to satisfy the state's demand for power, it will remain vulnerable to the market forces it uniquely created.

Douglas Biden, President, Electric Power Generation Association, March 2001

16.1 THE IMPORTANCE OF ECONOMIC FORECASTING

Many applications of economic analysis require anticipating events before they happen. The Federal Reserve Board can use monetary policy to stimulate the economy if it anticipates that the economy is starting to slow down. Governments need to know how much money they can expect to collect in taxes in the course of a year to know how much the government should plan on spending. Firm owners must know whether there will be sufficient demand for their products to justify building a new factory. Failure to correctly anticipate economic events can have serious consequences. The failure to build new power plants in the face of a steadily rising population was one factor (though far from the only one) that led to electricity shortages in California in the summer of 2001.

We would like to be able to use econometric analysis to be able to predict values of economic variables such as gross domestic product (GDP) growth, tax collections, and electricity demand. If the values we predict for those variables are available before the true values become known, and if the predicted values are close enough to the true values to be useful, then we can make better economic decisions by using the predicted values to help make decisions about monetary and fiscal policy and investment today.

> **Definition 16.1** *Forecasting* is the use of econometrics to calculate predicted values for future values of economic variables.

Econometrics is well suited to forecasting, for many reasons. Most important, econometrics takes advantage of economic relationships between variables to help forecast their future values. For example, we know that people with higher incomes demand more electricity than people with lower incomes; this suggests a relationship between electricity demand and income that is helpful in forecasting demand. If incomes are rising, we should expect demand to rise as well. Mathematically, regression analysis allows us to calculate a predicted value for a dependent variable on the basis of one or more independent variables and estimated parameter values. To create a forecast of a particular variable, we can estimate a regression with the variable on the left-hand side and variables we can observe on the right-hand side. We can then use the estimated parameters and the values of the observed variables to calculate a forecast for the left-hand-side variable that interests us. Furthermore, regression analysis lets us calculate not only predicted values but also standard errors of those predicted values. We can thus assess the reliability of our forecasts and determine not just a single forecast value but also a range in which the forecasted variable is likely to fall. This lets us plan optimistically or pessimistically if we wish to do so; it also allows us to determine whether or not the forecast value is sufficiently accurate to be useful. This chapter presents the methods used to calculate forecast values from econometric models and calculate their standard errors and then gives some simple examples of their use in electricity demand forecasting.

16.2   CALCULATING FORECASTS AND THEIR STANDARD ERRORS

On January 1, 1999, California's population was 33,140,000. Peak electricity demand that year came on July 12; it was 51,287 megawatts. On January 1, 2000, California's population had risen to 33,753,000. It would seem likely that California's peak electricity demand would be higher that year than in 1999, because of the higher population. How much higher would it be? Or, since that question cannot be answered with certainty, how much higher was it *likely* to be—in what range was the peak demand likely to fall? How much additional electricity would California's utilities have to purchase in order to be reasonably confident of being able to meet customer demand at its highest that year?

We can answer these questions if we know something about the relationship between electricity demand and population. It seems reasonable, at first approximation, to assume that the relationship between the two variables is linear; all else equal, twice as many people will use twice as much electricity. Thus, if we want to create an extremely simple forecast of electricity demand, we might write the equation

$$\text{Peakdem}_t = \beta_0 + \beta_1 \text{Pop}_t + \varepsilon_t \qquad \textbf{(16.2.1)}$$

where Peakdem_t is peak electricity demand for year t in megawatts; Pop_t is the state's population in year t in millions; and, assuming that the Gauss-Markov assumptions apply, ε_t is an error term with mean 0 and standard deviation σ. As Figure 16.1 shows, if we knew the values of β_0 and β_1, we could plug in a value of 33.753 for Pop and calculate a forecast of

FIGURE 16.1
Forecasting
When the True
Values of β Are
Known

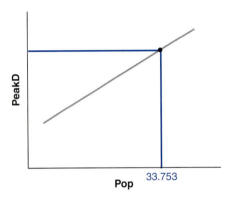

peak demand for a year with that population, using the equation

$$\text{Peakdemf}_{2000} = \beta_0 + \beta_1 33.753 \qquad \textbf{(16.2.2)}$$

where Peakdemf_{2000} is the forecasted value of Peakdem for the year 2000. However, the true peak demand will certainly be affected by things other than the state's population. These things are represented in Equation 16.2.1 by the error term, the factors that affect the real California economy but are not represented explicitly in the model. Those factors are not used in making the forecast, so the forecast will not be exactly equal to the right answer. We want to know how far off it is likely to be so that we can assess the reliability of the forecast.

Definition 16.2 The *forecast error* of a forecast is equal to the difference between the true value and the forecast value.

In this case, the true value of peak electricity demand in 2000 would be given by

$$\text{Peakdem}_{2000} = \beta_0 + \beta_1 33.753 + \varepsilon_{2000} \qquad \textbf{(16.2.3)}$$

which differs from Peakdemf_{2000} because it includes the error term. The forecast error would then be given by

$$\text{Peakdemerr}_{2000} = \text{Peakdem}_{2000} - \text{Peakdemf}_{2000} \qquad \textbf{(16.2.4)}$$

Substituting in Equations 16.2.2 and 16.2.3 produces

$$\text{Peakdemerr}_{2000} = \beta_0 + \beta_1 33.753 + \varepsilon_{2000} - (\beta_0 + \beta_1 33.753) \qquad \textbf{(16.2.5)}$$

which is just equal to ε_{2000}. That is, if we knew the true values of β_0 and β_1, the error of the forecast would just be equal to the error term of the equation for that particular observation. We could then conclude several things:

1. The forecast error would have an expected value of 0. The forecast would be an unbiased estimator of the true value.
2. The standard deviation of the forecast error would be the same as the standard deviation of the error term.

From the standard deviation, we could then work out confidence intervals in which the true value of peak electricity demand was likely to fall, assess the chance that the true value would be above or below any given value, and so forth.

FIGURE 16.2

**Forecasting
When the True
Values of β Are
Unknown**

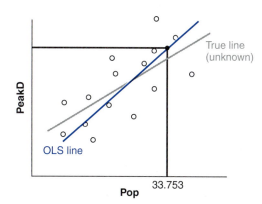

The problem, of course, is that we don't know the true values of β_0 and β_1. We have to estimate them, and to do that we need to have a sample. With that sample, we can calculate estimated values $\hat{\beta}_0$ and $\hat{\beta}_1$ and then work out the forecast using those values, as shown in Figure 16.2. Once we have those estimates, we can calculate the forecast value using the equation

$$\text{Peakdemf}_{2000} = \hat{\beta}_0 + \hat{\beta}_1 33.753 \qquad \textbf{(16.2.6)}$$

However, this changes the forecast error. It is now given by

$$\text{Peakdemerr}_{2000} = \beta_0 + \beta_1 33.753 + \varepsilon_{2000} - (\hat{\beta}_0 + \hat{\beta}_1 33.753) \qquad \textbf{(16.2.7)}$$

which can be rearranged to produce

$$\text{Peakdemerr}_{2000} = (\beta_0 - \hat{\beta}_0) + (\beta_1 - \hat{\beta}_1) 33.753 + \varepsilon_{2000} \qquad \textbf{(16.2.8)}$$

This equation shows that there are now three sources of possible error in the forecast. The forecast may still be wrong because of the error term ε_{2000}, which will cause the actual data point to lie above or below the line. But it may also be wrong because the value of $\hat{\beta}_0$ is not equal to the true value β_0, and because the value of $\hat{\beta}_1$ is not equal to the true value β_1. The estimated regression line is not the same as the true line that generated the data.

More generally, when we estimate a regression of the form $Y_i = \beta_0 + \beta_1 X_i + \varepsilon_i$ and we wish to forecast the value of Y^* that we predict when $X_i = X^*$, the forecast error will be given by

$$\varepsilon_{Fi} = (\beta_0 - \hat{\beta}_0) + (\beta_1 - \hat{\beta}_1) X^* + \varepsilon_i \qquad \textbf{(16.2.9)}$$

We can say the following things about ε_F:

Theorem 16.1 The expected value of the forecast error is equal to 0; even when the forecasting equation must be estimated by least squares, the forecast is an unbiased estimator of the true value of Y.

This is true because $\hat{\beta}_0$ is an unbiased estimator of β_0, and $\hat{\beta}_1$ is an unbiased estimator of β_1. Sometimes they will be overestimates, other times underestimates, but on average both $(\beta_0 - \hat{\beta}_0)$ and $(\beta_1 - \hat{\beta}_1)$ will be equal to 0. Since the expected value of ε_i is also 0, the expected value of ε_{Fi} is 0 as well.

Theorem 16.2 The standard deviation of the forecast error is equal to

$$\sigma_F = \sigma\sqrt{1 + \frac{1}{N} + \frac{(X^* - \bar{X})^2}{\sum(X_i - \bar{X})^2}} \qquad \textbf{(16.2.10)}$$

where N is the number of observations used to estimate the parameters and σ is the standard deviation of ε_t.

Unfortunately, we can't calculate this because we don't know the true value of σ. We can, however, replace it with its estimated value:

Theorem 16.3 The estimated standard deviation of the forecast error is equal to

$$\hat{\sigma}_F = \hat{\sigma}\sqrt{1 + \frac{1}{N} + \frac{(X^* - \bar{X})^2}{\sum(X_i - \bar{X})^2}} \qquad \textbf{(16.2.11)}$$

We can say quite a few things about this formula. The expression under the square root contains three terms, one for each of the three sources of error in the forecast.[1] The first term represents the variance due to the error term of the regression, the second represents the variance due to the estimation of $\hat{\beta}_0$, and the third represents the variance due to the estimation of $\hat{\beta}_1$. We can show the following:

> **Theorem 16.4** As X^* gets farther from $\bar{X}$, the forecast error gets larger. We can forecast better when the value of the independent variable is closer to the values we used to estimate the regression than we can when it is far from them.

This happens because the third term under the square root has $(X^* - \bar{X})^2$ in the numerator. The farther X^* gets from $\bar{X}$, the larger that term is and the greater the standard deviation of the forecast error becomes. We can also show the following:

> **Theorem 16.5** The forecast error is strictly greater than the standard deviation of the error term σ, but as the number of observations in the sample used to estimate the parameters rises, $\hat{\sigma}_F$ becomes approximately equal to σ.

We can see this mathematically from Equation 16.2.10. As the number of observations increases, the second term, $1/N$, will clearly go to 0. The third term will also go to 0; as we add more observations, there are more terms in the summation in its denominator, but the numerator does not change. Therefore, as N gets large, the expression under the square root will go to 1, and $\hat{\sigma}_F$ will go to $\hat{\sigma}$. Because $\hat{\sigma}$ is a consistent estimator of the true σ, both $\hat{\sigma}_F$ and $\hat{\sigma}$ will go to σ. However, since $1/N$ is greater than 0 for any finite number of observations, and so is

$$\frac{(X_i - \bar{X})^2}{\sum(X_i - \bar{X})^2}$$

(because all of its terms are squares), we know that $\sigma_F > \sigma$ for any real-world sample.

---

[1] Strictly speaking, there are actually four possible sources of variation in the forecast error; the variance of the regression error, the variance of $\hat{\beta}_0$ and $\hat{\beta}_1$, and the covariance between $\hat{\beta}_0$ and $\hat{\beta}_1$. The third term in the expression captures both the variance of $\hat{\beta}_1$ and its covariance with $\hat{\beta}_0$.

Economically, this means that as the sample gets larger, our forecasts will get more and more precise, but it will never get better than the limit imposed by the error term in the econometric model. This happens because $\hat{\beta}_0$ and $\hat{\beta}_1$ are consistent estimates of β_0 and β_1. As the sample gets larger, the estimated values become arbitrarily close to the true values and the forecast error becomes identical to the regression error. But the regression error represents economic factors that affect the real data generating process that are not included in the economic model we are using to forecast that data generating process. No forecast can ever hope to do better than the limits that the economic model imposes on it.

For an example of forecasting and forecast errors, we estimate Equation 16.2.1 using data from 1988 to 1997. Results are shown in Table 16.1. As expected, we find that β_1 is positive and significant; adding a million people to the state adds about 1,864 megawatts to peak demand. The parameter is statistically significantly different from 0 at the 5 percent level, with a t statistic of 4.27. However, the confidence interval for β_1 is quite wide, because its standard error of 436.8 is quite large in an economic sense. The figure of 1,864 megawatts is only an estimated value for the increase in peak demand from adding 1 million people; the true value may be higher or lower. The 95 percent confidence interval for that true value is equal to (857, 2,871), meaning that the actual increase in power demand when a million people arrive in California could be quite a bit higher than 1,864 megawatts. The state power authority may wish to plan conservatively and add rather more than 1,864 megawatts—the confidence interval, in this sense, may be a more useful piece of information than the forecasted value alone.

Also note that the intercept β_0 is negative; it is about $-12,900$. This suggests that the demand for electricity, if the population were 0, would be less than 0, which is clearly impossible. However, we need not be very disturbed, because the value is not statistically significantly different from 0; the standard error of β_0 is 13,356. We would not reject the null hypothesis that $\beta_0 = 0$. Furthermore, economically, $\beta_0 = 0$ is what we would expect; if there were no people in the state, electricity demand would be exactly 0. This suggests that our assumption that the relationship between population and peak demand is linear is probably a good one.[2]

TABLE 16.1
Results of Estimating Equation 16.2.1

Variable	Parameter	Estimate	Standard Error	t Statistic for $\beta = 0$
Intercept	β_0	−12,892.2	13,356.4	−0.97
Population	β_1	1,864.27	436.8	4.27
$N = 10$		$R^2 = 0.694$		SER = 1,811.3

[2] If β_0 had been negative and significant, that would be somewhat disturbing, because that would imply the true relationship between the two variables was not linear—it would have to bend upward as population fell, to avoid crossing the vertical axis. Even so, we might not worry too much, because 0 is a very unrealistic value for California's population, very far from the sample average population, and we would not expect to be able to estimate demand for a population value that far away away from the sample with any accuracy. As long as the forecasts for reasonable values of population were close to our economic expectations, that would suffice.

We can use these results and Equation 16.2.6 to work out a forecast value for peak demand in 2000. As stated earlier, California's population on January 1 of that year was 33,753,000. This implies a forecast peak demand of

$$\text{Peakdemf}_{2000} = \hat{\beta}_0 + \hat{\beta}_1 33.753 \qquad (16.2.12)$$

which equals 50,032 megawatts of electricity. We'd also like to know the standard deviation of the forecast error, since the true value won't be exactly equal to the forecast value. From Equation 16.2.11, we can estimate the forecast error; it works out to be 2,359.6 megawatts. This is a respectably small error; it is about 4.7 percent of the forecast value, and it is not a great deal higher than the standard error of the regression, which is 1,811 megawatts, the best we could hope to do. The 95 percent confidence interval works out to be 50,032 megawatts plus or minus 5,446 megawatts, which is (44,586, 55,478), a range of plus or minus 10.9 percent. California's maximum capacity on the day that peak demand occurred was 51,502. On the basis of this forecast, we would have been worried; it suggests a rather high chance that peak demand could have exceeded capacity.[3] Fortunately, actual maximum demand in 2000, which came on August 16, was only 49,097. With hindsight and Equation 16.2.4, we can say that the actual forecast error was $49,097 - 50,032 = -935$ megawatts; peak demand was in fact somewhat below the value predicted by the model.

16.3 CONDITIONAL FORECASTING

One drawback to the model presented in the preceding section is that it includes only one right-hand-side variable in the regression equation. In practice, demand for electricity depends on more than population. A somewhat more sophisticated model of peak electricity demand might be given by

$$\text{Peakdem}_t = \beta_0 + \beta_1 \text{Temp}_t + \beta_2 \text{Incpc}_t + \beta_3 \text{Pop}_t + \varepsilon_t \qquad (16.3.1)$$

where Incpc_t is income per capita of California citizens in year t, measured in thousands of dollars, and Temp_t is the statewide high temperature (calculated as the average temperature in six cities) on the day of maximum demand, in degrees Fahrenheit. People with higher incomes demand more of most goods, probably including electricity, so we would expect $\beta_2 > 0$. In the summer (when peak demand nearly always occurs) electricity demand is driven by air conditioners. The higher the temperature gets, the higher peak demand will likely be, and we would therefore expect $\beta_1 > 0$ also.

Results of estimating Equation 16.3.1 are shown in Table 16.2. Both temperature and per capita income take the expected positive sign. As is always the case when we add variables to a regression, the R^2 has risen. It is now a very respectable 0.956; this model fits the data well. For the same reason, the standard error of the regression has fallen quite a bit, down to 794 megawatts. Since that is the lower bound on our ability to forecast the data, we can hope that this model will forecast more accurately than the previous one. The intercept is still not statistically significantly different from 0, though its t statistic is getting larger. Oddly enough, however, β_3 is not statistically significant (the 5 percent critical value for the

---

[3] California regulators probably weren't quite so worried. They use a much more sophisticated forecasting model than the simple one used here, with a much smaller forecast error and hence a much narrower confidence interval for the true value of peak demand.

TABLE 16.2
Results of
Estimating
Equation
16.3.1

Variable	Parameter	Estimate	Standard Error	*t* Statistic for $\beta = 0$
Intercept	β_0	−30,818	18,681	−1.65
Temperature	β_1	709.6	136.7	5.19
Income per capita	β_2	1,351.6	620.0	2.18
Population	β_3	−797.8	915.4	−0.87
$N = 10$		$R^2 = 0.956$		SER = 794.6

t statistic is 2.447 for six degrees of freedom), and β_2 isn't either.[4] This occurs because population is highly multicollinear with income per capita (their correlation coefficient is 0.967) as both variables tend to rise over time. With only 10 observations we cannot effectively tell their effects apart.

This raises the question of whether we should drop one of the two variables from the model. On the one hand, doing so would give us more degrees of freedom and produce more accurate estimates of the other parameters. On the other hand, we are not interested in the parameter estimates themselves; we are interested in the forecast. Dropping a variable will reduce the fit of the model to the data. Furthermore, as economists we can be quite certain that both population and per capita income really do belong in the model; if we drop one, we raise the possibility of omitted variable bias. For the present, we will retain both of them; we will discuss the consequences of dropping one in Section 16.5.

When we turn to using the regression in Equation 16.3.1 to forecast peak demand, we quickly hit upon a problem. For the forecast to be useful, we need to calculate it before peak demand actually occurs; otherwise we could just use the true value instead, since we can observe it once it actually happens. Therefore, we need to be able to observe the values of the right-hand-side variables before the time of the forecast. For population and per capita income this presents no problem; we have been using their values as of January 1 in the regression, and those are available at the start of the year. But the temperature variable is not available in advance. We cannot know what the temperature will be on the day of peak demand until it actually happens; we cannot even know what day it will occur. Therefore, an attempt to calculate a forecast value for peak demand in 2000 using the equation

$$\text{Peakdemf}_{2000} = \hat{\beta}_0 + \hat{\beta}_1 \text{Temp}_{2000} + \hat{\beta}_2 \text{Incpc}_{2000} + \hat{\beta}_3 \text{Pop}_{2000} \qquad (16.3.2)$$

will fail; we do not have a value of Temp_{2000} to use.

The solution is simple: Use a weather forecast. We know the temperature on the day of peak demand for the years 1988 to 1997; we can take their average value as a reasonable guess for Temp_{2000} and use it in calculating Equation 16.3.2.

Definition 16.3 A *conditional forecast* is one that uses a predicted value for one or more of the right-hand-side variables to forecast the left-hand-side variable. An *unconditional forecast* is one that uses observed values for all right-hand-side variables.

In this case, we can produce a conditional forecast for peak demand based on some prediction about what the high temperature will be. The average value of Temp from 1988 to 1997

---

[4] In fact, β_3's estimated value is negative, but that is of no concern because of its being insignificant; it had at least a 5 percent chance to take either sign.

TABLE 16.3 Six Forecasts of Peak Demand for Electricity Conditional on Temperature

Temperature	Forecast Peak	Temperature	Forecast Peak
93	48,547	99	52,805
95	49,966	101	54,224
97	51,385	103	55,643

is 97.64 degrees, and the per capita income (real, not nominal, to avoid problems with inflation) of Californians on January 1, 2000, was $29,818. The forecast value is therefore

$$\text{Peakdemf} = -30,819 - (797.8 \cdot 33.753)$$
$$+ (1,351.6 \cdot 29.818) + (709.6 \cdot 97.64) \quad \textbf{(16.3.3)}$$

which works out to 51,840 megawatts.

This forecast is poorer than the previous forecast; the true value was 49,097, so its forecast error is $-2,743$ megawatts. Why does it do so badly? The reason is that it is based on a guess of 97.64 for the average high temperature, and in fact 2000 turned out to be a somewhat cool year; the actual value for the average high temperature that year was only 94.8. If, with hindsight, we used the correct value for temperature, instead of the sample average, the forecast value (calculated using Equation 16.3.3) would be 49,824 megawatts. This is much closer to the true value of 49,097; its forecast error is -727 megawatts. Unfortunately, there is no way we could do this in reality, since it relies on information about the actual temperature that we do not have in advance.

We could, however, calculate a range of forecasts based on a series of different assumptions about what the temperature might be. Table 16.3 shows the results of six forecasts based on temperatures between 93 and 103 (the actual sample range is 94 to 101). The advantage to doing this is that it shows us explicitly how our forecasts of peak demand are related to our temperature forecasts. It also allows us to calculate a range of forecasts based on optimistic and pessimistic assumptions about the weather, which may also be useful for planning purposes, because it is much worse to fall short of electricity than it is to have a surplus. Thus, both conditional and unconditional forecasts have their uses; the latter are better if we need a single forecast value, but the former let us understand how our forecast of the dependent variable is related to the value of the independent variable we can't observe in advance.

16.4 FORECASTING WITH AUTOCORRELATED ERRORS

All of the preceding discussion has been based on the Gauss-Markov assumptions; in particular, it has assumed that the error terms of the regression equation are not autocorrelated. If the error terms are instead autocorrelated, then we will have to make some adjustments to our forecasting methods. Suppose we are using time-series data to estimate a relationship of the form

$$Y_t = \beta_0 + \beta_1 X_t + \varepsilon_t \quad \textbf{(16.4.1)}$$

and the error terms of the econometric model follow a first-order autoregressive process:

$$\varepsilon_t = \rho \varepsilon_{t-1} + u_t \quad \textbf{(16.4.2)}$$

with $-1 < \rho < 1$ and u_t being uncorrelated over time. We would like to use a sample of T observations to predict the value of Y_{T+1}. Then we can use Equations 16.2.9 and 16.4.2 to write an expression for the forecast error when there is autocorrelation of the AR(1) form:

$$\varepsilon_{FT+1} = (\beta_0 - \hat{\beta}_0) + (\beta_1 - \hat{\beta}_1)X_{T+1} + \rho\varepsilon_T + u_{T+1} \quad \textbf{(16.4.3)}$$

In this case, we can say the following:

> **Theorem 16.6** If the error terms are autocorrelated, then the forecast error no longer has an expected value of 0 and the forecasts are no longer unbiased estimates. Instead, the forecast error has an expected value of $\rho\varepsilon_T$, that is, the error from the last period of the sample multiplied by the autocorrelation coefficient.

This result can be seen from Equation 16.4.3, all of whose terms have expected value equal to 0 except for $\rho\varepsilon_T$. This occurs because the error terms have patterns over time. If $\rho > 0$, then a positive error at time period T will tend to lead to another positive error at time $T + 1$, and a negative error will tend to lead to another negative error. The reverse is true if $\rho < 0$.

This bias is occurring because the forecasting method described above, which assumes that the error terms are uncorrelated, fails to recognize the pattern that the error terms are following. The solution is simply to take advantage of that pattern. We can use the residuals from estimating Equation 16.4.1 to form an estimate of ρ. Then we can use Equation 16.4.1 to calculate the forecast value of Y_{T+1}:

$$Y_{T+1} = \hat{\beta}_0 + \hat{\beta}_1 X_{T+1} + \hat{\rho}\hat{\varepsilon}_T \quad \textbf{(16.4.4)}$$

because the expected value of ε_{T+1} is $\rho\varepsilon_T$, and once we have estimated the regression, we can use $\hat{\rho}\hat{\varepsilon}_T$ as an estimate of ε_{T+1}.

We can easily adopt this approach to handle autocorrelation structures more complicated than AR(1). Suppose the error terms follow a general ARMA(P, Q), process of the type we studied in Section 6 of Chapter 12:

$$\varepsilon_t = \rho_1\varepsilon_{t-1} + \rho_2\varepsilon_{t-2} + \cdots + \rho_M\varepsilon_{t-M} + u_t$$
$$+ \lambda_1 u_{t-1} + \cdots + \lambda_Q u_{t-Q} \quad \textbf{(16.4.5)}$$

Then we can write the forecast as

$$Y_{T+1} = \hat{\beta}_0 + \hat{\beta}_1 X_{T+1} + \hat{\rho}_1\hat{\varepsilon}_T + \hat{\rho}_2\hat{\varepsilon}_{T-1} + \cdots + \hat{\rho}_P\hat{\varepsilon}_{T+1-P}$$
$$+ \hat{\lambda}_1\hat{u}_T + \hat{\lambda}_2\hat{u}_{T-1} + \cdots + \hat{\lambda}_Q\hat{u}_{T+1-Q} \quad \textbf{(16.4.6)}$$

Forecasting with autocorrelated errors is a somewhat strange exercise, however, because it involves using the estimated error terms from the sample. Doing so improves the forecast (eliminates their bias and reduces their variance), but it relies on information other than the exogenous variables in the model to create the forecast. There are times when relying on such information is not desirable, such as when we are interested in seeing how well our model can predict the data rather than using the regression residuals to get smaller forecast errors.

> **Definition 16.4** A *structural forecast* is one that ignores the autocorrelation of the error terms and calculates the forecasts by
>
> $$Y_{T+1} = \hat{\beta}_0 + \hat{\beta}_1 X_{T+1} \quad \textbf{(16.4.7)}$$

Structural forecasts are biased[5] and inefficient, but they do depend only on information in the economic model of the data generating process, rather than on the error terms. We can compare the structural forecasts given by Equation 16.4.7 to the standard forecasts given by Equation 16.4.6 to find out how much of our ability to forecast the data is due to our economic model and how much is just due to the tendency of the error terms to persist over time. If the structural forecasts are much worse than the standard ones, it is a sign that our economic model is a poor description of the data generating process and that we might wish to try to improve it.

16.5   THE PROBLEM OF A SHIFTING ECONOMIC MODEL

Economic forecasting is inherently based on the idea of looking at a sample of data that is observable in order to predict something that is not observable. In the case of predicting forward in time, it is thus based on using the past to predict the future. Like any other application of regression analysis, it depends critically on the idea that all of the observations, both those in the sample and those whose values are being predicted, are governed by the same data generating process.

That need not be true, and in many cases it isn't. The macroeconomy constantly evolves as new technologies are developed and new economic policies are applied. In forecasting with cross-section data, some units of the cross-section are observed and others are unobserved and hence need to be forecast. This implies that there must be some difference between the two groups that may affect the data generation process. For example, trying to predict trade flows with the transitional economies of Eastern Europe based on data on trade among the countries of the Organization for Economic Cooperation and Development (OECD) inherently relies on the assumption that the same trade equations, with the same parameter values, describes trade in both cases. This is a strong assumption; market institutions have only recently begun to develop in Eastern Europe since the fall of communism, whereas those of the OECD countries are mature. Therefore, it is unlikely that the same data generating process produces both.

When the data generation process is changing, forecasting inherently breaks down, because the relationship between the variables in the past doesn't hold for the future. This can lead to absurd forecasts, such as the following infamous example:

> In 1977, there were 37 Elvis impersonators in the world. In 1993, there were 48,000. At this rate, by the year 2010 one out of every three people in America will be an Elvis impersonator.

Mathematically, this is true enough, assuming constant exponential growth. The figures for 1977 and 1993 imply a growth rate of 56.5 percent per year, and extending that trend forward to 2010 produces a forecast of 97 million Elvis impersonators. The problem is that it

---

[5] Actually, in an *ex ante* sense structural forecasts remain unbiased. If we use only the estimated economic relationship and do not look at the values of the residuals, then the expected value of ε_T is 0, since even though the errors are correlated, they still are, overall, equally likely to be above or below the line. The forecast becomes biased only once we find out whether ε_T is positive or negative, and thus whether ε_{T+1} is likely to be positive or negative. If we do not look at the residuals, this information never comes up.

assumes that the growth rate of Elvis impersonation does not change over time. It ignores the fact that 1977 was the year of Elvis's death, and immediately afterward the growth rate of Elvis impersonators was very high. After a few years, it dropped off to almost 0, and it has almost certainly not risen much above 48,000 or may even have dropped as Elvis has become part of fewer and fewer living memories.

Economic examples rarely produce forecasts as obviously wrong as that one, but in some ways that makes the problem worse, not better. Consider the growth in the stock market that took place from 1995, when the Dow Jones index was around 4,000, to early 2000, when it peaked at nearly 12,000. During this period there was substantial debate over the reason for this increase. Some argued that it was due to a sharp increase in the growth rate that would eventually end in a crash. Others argued that it was due to a fundamental change in the American economy, caused by developments in high-technology industries, that would last far into the future (the so-called New Economy hypothesis). The drops of the following few years suggest that the New Economy idea was wrong, but the debate continues over whether at least some part of the increase in the trend is permanent. Despite this, many investors, including many pension funds, lost a great deal of money as the Dow receded from its peak value. Investors who assumed that the trend of 1995–2000 would continue into the new millennium were severely disappointed.

We would like to be able to assess whether our forecasts predict well or poorly for years not included in the sample used to estimate the regression. To do this, it is common practice to hold some of the available data out of the sample used to estimate the equation. This results in somewhat less precise estimates of the model's parameters than would be the case otherwise, but it means that there are several observations left over for which the true values of the dependent variable are known. We can then use the model to forecast values for those observations and see how well the model does.

We have already done this in the electricity example above; we estimated the regression using only data from 1988 to 1997, leaving the observations from 1998, 1999, and 2000 for forecast evaluation as described above. Table 16.4 shows forecast peak demand for all 13 years, as well as the forecast standard deviations, then true peak demand, and the actual forecast errors.

Definition 16.5 The *root mean squared error (RMSE)* of the forecast is equal to

$$\text{RMSE} = \sqrt{\frac{1}{T}\sum_{t=1}^{T}\varepsilon_{Ft}^2}$$

where T is the number of forecasts made. That is, we calculate the square of each forecast error, take the average squared error, then take the square root of the result.

The root mean squared error (RMSE) is a good measure of the accuracy of the forecast in hindsight. For this regression, the RMSE is 741.3, meaning that 741.3 megawatts is a reasonable expectation for the size of an average residual.[6]

---

[6] The purpose of the squaring is to avoid averaging positive and negative residuals. We can instead use the mean absolute value of the forecast errors, which will usually be a slightly smaller number; however, the RMSE is more widely used because it is immediately comparable to the standard error of the forecast and to the SER of the forecasting regression, which are also based on roots of squared errors.

TABLE 16.4
Actual and Forecast Peak Electricity Demand, 1988–2000

Year	Forecast	Standard Deviation	Actual Value	Actual Error
In Sample				
1988	40,514	978	40,091	−423
1989	39,715	936	39,948	+232
1990	44,199	931	44,421	+221
1991	41,420	979	41,501	+80
1992	44,658	895	45,941	+832
1993	43,669	886	42,396	−1,273
1994	45,119	925	45,058	−61
1995	44,812	892	44,855	+42
1996	46,408	900	47,331	+922
1997	50,066	1,061	49,493	−573
Out of Sample				
1998	51,540	1,248	50,049	−1,490
1999	52,062	1,739	51,287	−775
2000	49,824	2,359	49,097	−727

FIGURE 16.3
Actual and Forecast Values of Peak Demand, 1988 to 2000

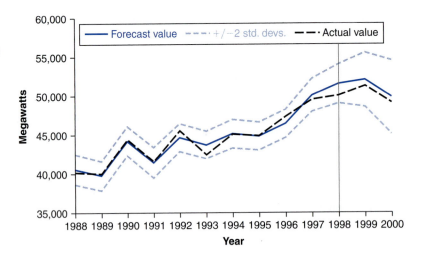

Figure 16.3 shows the results of the forecast graphically; the red line represents the forecast value and the dashed pink lines are two standard deviations on either side. Notice that the pink lines are substantially farther away from the red line for the years 1998 to 2000 (shaded in the graph) than for the others. This occurs because these observations have higher values of population and average income than the others. Those high values are farther away from the sample mean than the values from 1988 to 1997 (partly because the values from 1998 to 2000 were not included when the sample mean was calculated) and thus the forecast is inherently less reliable for them.

We can see that the forecast standard deviation does a reasonably good job predicting the true range of the forecast errors. We would expect that about two-thirds of the actual forecast errors would be within one standard deviation of the true values, and about

95 percent would be within two standard deviations.[7] In the real data, 10 of the 13, or 77 percent, are within one standard deviation of the true value, and all of them are within two. These results are, in fact, a bit better than we might have expected. Note, however, that not only do the forecast standard errors rise for the three out of sample observations, but the actual errors rise also. The three forecast errors for the years 1998 to 2000 are among the five largest in the entire 13-year sample. Furthermore, they are all negative. This suggests that the data generating process—that is, actual demand by California consumers for electricity—may have been changing as time passed. In particular, the popular press coverage of electricity shortages and the need to conserve electricity might have reduced demand below its level prior to restructuring in 1996. This would explain why all three errors are negative as well as why they are relatively large. More important, this suggests that the model may continue to perform poorly for 2001 and future years. It may be necessary to create a more powerful model that includes the effects of conservation efforts on demand in order to represent the data generation process accurately enough to produce useful forecasts.

On the other hand, there may be some things we can do to improve this model. In particular, remember that $\hat{\beta}_3$, the coefficient on population, was not statistically significantly different from 0 in the original model. We might try reestimating the model with population removed:

$$\text{Peakdem}_t = \beta_0 + \beta_1 \text{Temp}_t + \beta_2 \text{Incpc}_t + \varepsilon_t \qquad \textbf{(16.5.1)}$$

and see if we can forecast better with this model. Results of estimating Equation 16.5.1 are shown in Table 16.5, and forecasts and forecast errors are shown in Table 16.6. As expected, both $\hat{\beta}_1$ and $\hat{\beta}_2$ are positive and statistically significant; the R^2 of the regression has dropped, but only very slightly.

A comparison of the forecast values is, however, revealing. The first model, which included population, does better on the observations from the sample years 1988 to 1997. It has a smaller RMSE (615 versus 662) and a smaller average error (466 versus 510), and it produces a smaller error in 7 of the 10 years. But in the three years outside the sample, the model that excludes population is considerably better. Its errors are smaller in all three cases, and smaller on average. Furthermore, two of its errors are positive and one is negative; it describes the observations from outside the sample better than the model that includes population does.

Why does this happen? At heart, it is a consequence of the multicollinearity between population and per capita income. We do not have enough information to reliably

TABLE 16.5 **Results of** **Estimating** **Equation** **16.6.1**	Variable	Parameter	Estimate	Standard Error	*t* Statistic for $\beta = 0$
	Intercept	β_0	−43,522	11,480	−3.79
	Temperature	β_1	708.8	134.3	5.27
	Income per capita	β_2	828.9	154.8	5.35
	$N = 10$		$R^2 = 0.950$		SER $= 780.9$

[7] Actually slightly less than that; because we are using an estimated forecast error rather than the true forecast error, we should use the *t* distribution, and for only six degrees of freedom, the confidence intervals are rather wider than those for the normal distribution.

TABLE 16.6
Actual and Forecast Peak Electricity Demand Redux, 1988–2000

Year	Forecast	Standard Deviation	Actual Value	Actual Error
In Sample				
1988	40,383	950	40,091	−292
1989	39,584	908	39,948	+363
1990	44,141	912	44,421	+279
1991	41,246	941	41,501	+254
1992	44,883	842	45,941	+607
1993	43,884	836	42,396	−1,488
1994	45,451	828	45,058	−393
1995	45,033	840	44,855	−178
1996	46,283	873	47,331	+1,047
1997	49,692	954	49,493	−199
Out of Sample				
1998	50,926	1,012	50,049	−877
1999	50,936	1,143	51,287	+350
2000	48,386	1,655	49,097	+710

determine their effects separately. However, within the regression sample, we can *always* get a lower sum of squared residuals by using population than by excluding it. Even though the estimated value of $\hat{\beta}_3$ is negative, using that negative value improves the fit of the model to the data—within the sample. Outside the sample, however, it almost certainly won't. The negative value of $\hat{\beta}_3$, which is not statistically significantly different from 0, improves the fit within the sample only due to a coincidental match between the error terms and the two multicollinear variables. Outside the sample, that match is unlikely to repeat itself.[8] Economic intuition tells us that the true value of β_3, whatever it is, is certainly positive. Though we do not know its exact value, certainly 0 is a better estimate of it than −797.8 is. And indeed, the forecast works better—outside the sample—when we use a value of 0 by dropping the variable.

The moral of the story is simple: Regression analysis fits the model to the sample as well as possible, but when we are forecasting, we are trying to fit the model to data outside the sample. The model that fits the sample data best is not necessarily the best model to describe data outside the sample. This can come about either because of random patterns in the sample errors that won't exist outside the sample or because of fundamental changes in the data generating process. In either case, our knowledge of economics can tell us when our model is economically reasonable, in which case it will probably do well forecasting outside the sample, or when it is unreasonable, in which case it may do poorly outside the sample despite being the best possible (smallest sum of squared residuals) description of the sample. Calculation is not a replacement for thinking and economic judgment, and the better our theoretical understanding of an economic phenomenon is, the more likely we are to be able to produce an econometric model that produces useful forecasts of that phenomenon.

---

[8] If the multicollinearity between the variables does continue outside the sample used to estimate the regression, then it will not cause this problem.

Chapter Review

- If we have an economic relationship between two or more variables, and we can observe the values of the independent variables, we can estimate the relationship to *forecast* the value of the dependent variable.

- Under the Gauss-Markov assumptions, forecasts are unbiased estimates of the true values. The standard deviations of the forecasts are larger than the standard deviation of the regression's error term, but become equal as the sample grows.

- The standard deviation of the forecast becomes larger as the value of the independent variables gets farther from the sample average.

- If we do not observe the values of the independent variables, we can still make *conditional forecasts* based on predicted values for the independent variables.

- If the regression has autocorrelation, then the forecast error no longer has an expected value of 0 but instead depends on the value of the sample residuals. The sample residuals can be used to correct the resulting bias.

- Forecasting works only when the data generating process is the same in the regression sample and in the forecast sample. Economic knowledge can help us determine whether an econometric model is likely to describe data from outside the regression sample well or poorly.

Computer Exercise

In this exercise we'll create a data set of 100 observations, estimate a regression with 80 of the observations, and test the forecasts on the remaining 20 observations.

1. Open Eviews and create a new workfile, undated, with 100 observations.

2. Type genr x = rnd()*20 to generate a random independent variable, and genr regerr = nrnd()*5 to generate an error term for the regression. Then type genr y = 5 + 2*x + regerr to generate a dependent variable.

3. Last, type sort x to sort the data so the observations with the lowest values of X come first.

4. To limit the sample to the first 80 observations, type smpl 1 80. Then type ls y c x to estimate the regression equation. How far apart are the estimated parameters and the true parameters? What is the standard error of the regression?

5. Click the Forecast button to have Eviews forecast the data based on this regression. Set the forecast sample to 1 100; for the forecast name, enter YF; for the forecast error, enter Forese. What is the RMSE of this forecast? Is it larger or smaller than the standard error of the regression? How much?

6. Close the equation window, type smpl 1 100 to restore the full sample, then type genr forerr = y − yf to generate the actual errors of the forecasts. Display the histogram and statistics of the actual errors. What is the average error? Do they look approximately normally distributed or not?

7. Open a group containing the variables y, yf, foresee, forerr, and regerr. How many of the forecast errors are smaller than the forecast standard errors? (It should be about two-thirds.) How many are smaller than twice the forecast errors? (It should be about 95 percent.) How closely are the regression error terms and the forecast errors related?

8. How good are the forecasts for observations 81–100, that is, the ones that were not used in the regression? Do they look about as good as the forecasts for the observations that were used in the regression?

9. Now we'll examine the consequences of using a model that is not the correct model. Type genr y = 5 + 2*x + 0.1*x*x + regerr to generate a new dependent variable that depends on X^2 as well as on X. Repeat steps 4–8 with the new dependent variable, still using the regression ls y c x so that the regression model omits the X^2 term. Now how well does the model forecast for observations 81–100? How many of the forecast errors are positive in that group?

Problems

1. In this problem we'll consider forecasting interest rates. Interest rates are widely forecast, for several reasons. Because of their effect on savings and investment, they are closely related to macroeconomic performance; also, future interest rates are an important determinant of the relative value of short-term and long-term investments. Open the data file macro3, which contains annual observations from 1959 to 2001 on the following variables: primerate (the U.S. prime rate), nextrate (prime rate in the following year), inflation (inflation rate), gdpgrowth (annual growth rate of real GDP), debtgrowth (annual growth rate of federal debt), moneygrowth (annual growth rate of the real money supply), and nextmoney (money growth rate in the following year). All variables are measured in percentage points.

   a. Estimate the regression $\text{Nextrate}_t = \beta_0 + \beta_1 \text{Debtgrowth}_t + \beta_2 \text{Moneygrowth}_t + \beta_3 \text{GDPgrowth}_t + \beta_4 \text{Inflation}_t + \varepsilon_t$. How many of the parameters are statistically significantly different from 0? Reestimate the equation, dropping as many variables as you can.

   b. If inflation rises in the present year, do you predict a higher or lower interest rate for next year? If GDP grows at a faster rate in the present year, do you predict a higher or lower interest rate for next year? Do these results match your economic intuition or not?

   c. Use the resulting equation to calculate forecast values for Primerate, forecast errors, and standard errors for the forecasts. Graph the true and forecast values. The true value increases sharply around 1980 and then drops back toward its typical value. Does the forecast predict this increase well or not? How large is a typical forecast error?

   d. How large are the standard errors of the forecasts? Do these appear to be large errors or small errors? How many of the forecasts are within one standard error of the predicted value, and how many are not?

   e. In 2000, money growth was 2.63 percent, GDP growth was 3.75 percent, inflation was 3.36 percent, and debt growth was −2.63 percent. What value would you predict for the prime rate in 2001? What would the standard error of your forecast be? The true value was 6.92—how good was your forecast?

2. In this problem, we'll use the autocorrelation of the error term to improve the interest rate forecasts from problem 1. Open the data file macro3, which was described in problem 1.

   a. Estimate the equation $\text{Nextrate}_t = \beta_0 + \beta_1 \text{Debtgrowth}_t + \beta_2 \text{Inflation}_t + \varepsilon_t$, and perform the Durbin-Watson test for first-order serial correlation in the error term. Verify that there is autocorrelation, and reestimate the equation, correcting for it. What is the estimated value of ρ?

b. Calculate forecast values, forecast errors, and forecast standard errors based on the corrected regression. Graph the true and forecast values. Do the forecast values track the ups and downs of the cycle well, or not very well?

c. In 1996, inflation was 2.93 percent and debt growth was 2.02 percent. Calculate a structural forecast for the prime rate in 1997. Is your prediction above or below the true value of 8.44?

d. The value of the residual for the year 1995 was -0.84. Were interest rates below predicted values or above them in 1996? Would you expect residual for the year 1996 to be positive or negative? Use this value, and the estimated value of the autocorrelation coefficient, to predict the value of the prime rate for 1996. Is it closer to the true value than the structural forecast from part *c*? Why does this happen?

3. Changes in monetary policy may affect interest rates in the same period that the changes are made, since capital markets respond quickly to changes in money supply. But changes in monetary policy are not known in advance. In this problem we'll do conditional forecasting of interest rates based on predictions of changes in money supply. Open the data file macro3, which was described in problem 1.

a. Estimate the equation $\text{Nextrate}_t = \beta_0 + \beta_1 \text{Debtgrowth}_t + \beta_2 \text{Inflation}_t + \beta_3 \text{Nextmoney}_t + \varepsilon_t$. Does an increase in the money supply increase or decrease the interest rate in the same period? Does this match economic theory about the effect of money supply increases on interest rates?

b. Just to make sure that the effect of the money supply on interest rates happens within the same year, estimate the equation $\text{Nextrate}_t = \beta_0 + \beta_1 \text{Debtgrowth}_t + \beta_2 \text{Inflation}_t + \beta_3 \text{Nextmoney}_t + \beta_4 \text{Moneygrowth}_t + \varepsilon_t$. Test the null hypothesis that $\beta_4 = 0$. Do you reject, or fail to reject, this hypothesis? Does a change in money supply in one period affect the prime rate in the following period, or not?

c. In 2000, inflation was 3.36 percent and debt growth was -2.63 percent. Based on the regression from part *a*, what value would you conditionally forecast for the prime rate in 2001 if you assumed money supply growth in 2001 would be 1 percent? What value would you forecast if you assumed that money supply growth in 2001 would be 5 percent?

d. Find the level of money supply growth for 2001 that will produce a prime rate in 2001 of 6 percent.

e. Reestimate the equation from part *a* allowing for a first-order autocorrelation correction, and find answers to parts *c* and *d* based on the new regression results. How much do your answers change? If the goal of monetary policy is to target interest rates, does it matter whether interest rate forecasts include autocorrelation coefficients or not?

4. In this problem we'll do some forecasting out of sample, to see how our forecasts work when they are applied to years not used in the regression. Load the data file receipts, which was described in problem 6 in Chapter 10.

a. Using only the data from 1959 to 1996, estimate the regression $\text{Nextrevenues}_t = \beta_0 + \beta_1 \text{Currentrevenues}_t + \beta_2 \text{Persincome}_t + \beta_3 \text{Investment}_t + \beta_4 \text{Tbillrate}_t + \varepsilon_t$. Does higher investment increase next year's tax revenues? Is the effect statistically significant? Do all of the coefficients take the expected signs?

b. Calculate forecast values, forecast errors, and forecast standard errors for the period 1959–1996. How many of the forecast values are within one standard error of the actual value? How many are within two standard errors?

c. Now calculate forecast values, forecast errors, and forecast standard errors for the period 1997 to 2001, out of sample. Are the errors larger than previously? How many of the forecast values are within one or two standard errors of the true values now?

d. Actual tax revenues decreased fairly sharply in 2001 and 2002. Does the forecast revenues predict this decrease or not? What might have caused an unforecastable drop in tax revenues at this time? Is this a sign that the model is forecasting badly, or well?

5. In this problem we'll see what happens when we include irrelevant variables in our forecasts. Load the data file receipts, which was described in problem 6 in Chapter 10.

a. Using only the data from 1959 to 1996, estimate the regression $\text{Nextrevenues}_t = \beta_0 + \beta_1 \text{Currentrevenues}_t + \beta_2 \text{Persincome}_t + \beta_3 \text{Investment}_t + \beta_4 \text{Tbillrate}_t + \beta_5 \text{Unemployment}_t + \varepsilon_t$. Can you think of a theoretical reason why unemployment might help forecast next year's tax revenues? Is β_5 statistically significantly different from 0, or not?

b. Calculate forecast values, forecast errors, and forecast standard errors for the period 1959–1996. How many of the forecast values are within one standard error of the actual value? Are the standard errors larger or smaller than the errors from problem 4, which did not include unemployment in the regression? Are the forecast errors larger or smaller?

c. Now calculate forecast values, forecast errors, and forecast standard errors for the period 1997–2001. How many of the forecast values are within one standard error of the actual value? In the out of sample forecasts, are the forecast errors larger or smaller than the errors from problem 4, which did not include unemployment in the regression?

6. In the mid and late 1990s there was a sharp increase in American stock prices, followed by an even sharper drop, which some economists have labeled a bubble. In this problem we'll forecast the stock market value of American firms and see how the bubble affects our forecasting. Open the data set stockvalue, which contains quarterly observations from the first quarter of 1952 to the fourth quarter of 2002 on the following variables: realstockvalue (total value of American stocks), realgdp (real GDP), and bondaaayield (yield on corporate bonds rated AAA). Yield is measured in percentage points, other variables in billions of 2001 dollars.

a. The value of American firms should depend on the discounted future value of the profits they will earn. Estimate the equation $\text{Realstockvalue}_{t+1} = \beta_0 + \beta_1 \text{RealGDP}_t + \beta_2 \text{BondAAAyield}_t + \varepsilon_t$. Since this involves time-series data, perform the Durbin-Watson test for autocorrelation. What do you find?

b. To deal with the autocorrelation problem, let's estimate the equation in first differences. Estimate the equation $\text{Realstockvalue}_{t+1} - \text{Realstockvalue}_{t+1} = \beta_0 + \beta_1(\text{RealGDP}_t - \text{RealGDP}_{t-1}) + \beta_2(\text{BondAAAyield}_t - \text{BondAAAyield}_{t-1}) + \upsilon_t$. Do higher values of GDP today have a significant effect on future stock values? Is the effect positive or negative, and is this what you would expect? Do higher values of bond rates today have a significant effect on future stock values? Is the effect positive or negative, and is this what you would expect?

c. Calculate forecast values, forecast errors, and standard errors. How well does the model forecast the data prior to 1993? How well does it forecast the data after 1993? How large are the standard errors?

d. Perhaps the underlying regression equation changed at the start of 1993, due to the bubble. Do a Chow test for the stability of the regression equation, using the first quarter of 1993 as the breakpoint. Did the regression equation shift or not? If it did, did the parameter estimates change only slightly, or substantially?

e. Estimate the regression equation separately for the two periods, and calculate forecasts, forecast errors, and standard errors. Which model forecasts better from 1952 to 1992? Which one forecasts better from 1993 to 2002?

f. To forecast the value of the change in stock values for the coming quarter, would you use the regression from the entire data sample, the first period only, or the second period only? Explain your answer.

Chapter **Seventeen**

Economic Variables as Processes

> . . . some cast again,
> And by that destiny, to perform an act
> Whereof what's past is prologue, what to come
> In yours and my discharge.

William Shakespeare, The Tempest, *Act 2, scene 1*

17.1   A NEW WAY TO THINK ABOUT MACROECONOMIC MODELS

One point on which all macroeconomists agree is that, if left alone, economies will experience business cycles. The existence of business cycles suggests that the current state of the economy depends on where it has been recently. An economy that has started to slow down is likely to continue to slow down for one or two more years; but if it has been slow for longer than that, it is likely to begin a recovery in the near future. Conversely, an economy starting to boom is likely to do so for a few years, but eventually the recovery will end and the cycle will begin again. If we wish to model or predict the economy, we may do well to use models in which the present condition of the economy is a function of its recent past.

In Chapter 12 we suggested that econometric models of business cycles might have error terms that had serial correlation; their values depended on the values of error terms in previous periods. In this chapter, we will go one step further and consider the possibility that the variables themselves are serially correlated. That is, we will explicitly allow the variables to depend on their own past values. For example, we might model gross domestic product (GDP) growth with an equation such as

$$Y_t = \alpha + \rho Y_{t-1} + \varepsilon_t \qquad \textbf{(17.1.1)}$$

which suggests that GDP growth in year t is equal to some fraction of what it was in year $t - 1$, plus a random change for this year.

> **Definition 17.1** An *innovation* is a serially uncorrelated random shock that alters the current value of an economic variable.

In Equation 17.1.1, ε_t is an innovation affecting the value of GDP growth at time t. The innovation is essentially the same thing as an error term. We call it an innovation because

FIGURE 17.2
**Response of
Unemployment
Rate to an
Innovation over
Time**

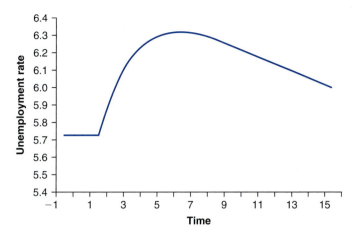

Definition 17.2 The *steady-state value* of a variable that follows an ARMA process is the value such that, if the variable takes that value in all time periods, then the equation describing the process holds in all time periods.

We solve for the steady-state value by setting $\text{Unemployment}_t = \text{Unemployment}_{t-1} = \text{Unemployment}_{t-2} = \bar{U}$, and solving for $\bar{U}$:

$$\bar{U} = 0.206 + (1.607 \cdot \bar{U}) - (0.643 \cdot \bar{U}) \qquad \textbf{(17.2.4)}$$

which can be solved to find $\bar{U} = 5.72\%$. We can also predict the consequences of an innovation to unemployment. Suppose unemployment was equal to the steady-state value in year 1, but in year 2, due to a bad economic shock, it rose to 6 percent. What would then happen? We can use the process in Equation 17.2.2 to predict unemployment in year 3:

$$\text{Unemployment}_3 = 0.206 + (1.607 \cdot 6) - (0.643 \cdot 5.72) \qquad \textbf{(17.2.5)}$$

which works out to 6.17 percent. By a similar process we can calculate predictions for all future values of unemployment. The results are shown in Figure 17.2. It suggests that the shock to unemployment will persist for a few quarters but will eventually peak and recede, with the economy returning to its steady-state value thereafter. We can view many macroeconomic variables as ARMA processes and use the processes to forecast the behavior of the variables. Much modern macroeconometric modeling is done in essentially this way.

17.3   THE PROBLEM OF UNIT ROOTS

The correlogram is very useful for revealing patterns that occur over time in economic variables. However, sometimes knowing those patterns creates more problems than it solves. Suppose that Y follows the process:

$$Y_t = \alpha + Y_{t-1} + \varepsilon_t \qquad \textbf{(17.3.1)}$$

which is an ARMA(1, 0) model with $\rho = 1$. We recognize this as the case of a unit root, which we initially discussed in Chapter 12, Section 12.5. We say that Y follows a random walk, and Y has the same problem that a regression error has in case of a unit root. An innovation in Y does not decay over time but instead persists undiminished through time; as the number of time periods, and hence the number of innovations, goes to infinity, so does the variance of Y. The same thing happens if $\rho > 1$ or if $\rho < -1$. In this case, not only do innovations not decay, but they grow increasingly larger over time, and again the variance of Y goes to infinity. The variance of Y can be finite only if $-1 < \rho < 1$ so that each innovation eventually disappears as time passes.

> **Definition 17.3** An AR(1) process with $-1 < \rho < 1$, for which the variance of Y is finite, is called *stationary*, because its values of Y have finite variance and tend to fall around the mean value. An AR(1) process with $\rho > 1$ or $\rho < -1$ is called *nonstationary*. Its variance is infinite, and its values do not tend to lie near its mean value.

There is, however, worse news yet.

> **Theorem 17.1** Suppose that we have a regression of the form
>
> $$Y_t = \beta_0 + \beta_1 X_t + \varepsilon_t \qquad \textbf{(17.3.2)}$$
>
> and Y is not stationary. Then OLS estimates of β_0 and β_1 are inconsistent and inefficient, and the estimated standard errors of the parameters are invalid.

We know intuitively that this happens because then mean value of Y is $\beta_0 + \beta_1 X_t$, and the residual is the distance between Y and its mean value. If Y is not stationary, then it has no tendency to be near the regression line and the residuals become arbitrarily large, making it impossible to infer the slope and the intercept of the regression line.[3]

Not only are the results of OLS invalid in this case, but they are invalid in a particularly misleading way. When two variables have unit roots and are regressed on one another, the variance of the parameter estimates is, not surprisingly, much higher than is the case if the variables are stationary. Suppose that the variables are, in fact, unrelated and therefore the true value of β_1 is 0. Then, because of its high variance, the estimated value of $\hat{\beta}_1$ is likely to fall quite far from 0. If, failing to realize that the variables have unit roots, we apply the critical values of the t distribution, we will tend to find that $\hat{\beta}_1$ is significantly different from 0, even though the hypothesis $\beta_1 = 0$ is true.

Because of this possibility that we will falsely reject $\beta_1 = 0$, any finding that two time-series variables are significantly related must be suspect unless we can be certain that the variables do not have unit roots. How can we tell whether or not they do? In principle, this should be easy: Estimate the equation

$$Y_t = \alpha + \rho Y_{t-1} + \varepsilon_t \qquad \textbf{(17.3.3)}$$

and test whether $\rho = 1$. However, this fails because of Theorem 17.1: OLS does not work appropriately on Equation 17.3.3 if the hypothesis $\rho = 1$ is true, because Y_t has a unit root in that case and is not stationary.

The solution is to estimate Equation 17.3.3 anyway but to realize that the estimate of ρ has a larger standard deviation than usual, and thus the t test we might normally perform

---

[3] It turns out that OLS is also inconsistent and inefficient if X is nonstationary, even if Y is stationary, but that conclusion is more difficult to prove and cannot be easily demonstrated intuitively.

is invalid. Dickey and Fuller (1979) calculated the true distribution of $\hat{\rho}$ when the hypothesis $\rho = 1$ is true, so we can calculate correct critical values for testing that hypothesis. To perform the test, we subtract Y_{t-1} from both sides of Equation 17.3.3:

$$\Delta Y_t = Y_t - Y_{t-1} = \alpha + \beta Y_{t-1} + \varepsilon_t \qquad \textbf{(17.3.4)}$$

where $\beta = \rho - 1$. The null hypothesis then becomes $\beta = 0$. It turns out that we can improve the power of test, when the null hypothesis is false, if we add lagged values of ΔY_t to the right-hand side of the equation:

$$\Delta Y_t = \alpha + \beta_1 Y_{t-1} + \beta_2 \Delta Y_{t-1} + \cdots + \beta_{M+1} \Delta Y_{t-M} + \varepsilon_t \qquad \textbf{(17.3.5)}$$

where the number of lags M is chosen to ensure that ε_t is not serially correlated. The test of $\beta_1 = 0$ from estimating Equation 17.3.5 is known as the augmented Dickey-Fuller (ADF) test, and is the most widely reported test for unit roots.

Table 17.2 shows the results of the ADF test for the null hypothesis that unemployment follows a unit root, using two lags of ΔUnemployment$_t$ on the right-hand side. The test statistic is exactly equal to the t statistic for the null hypothesis $\beta_1 = 0$, but the Dickey-Fuller critical value is larger than the critical values of the t distribution are; in this case, the 5 percent critical value is -2.880. The test is one-tailed, so we fail to reject the null hypothesis of a unit root for any test statistic greater than -2.880.[4] The test statistic is -2.461, so we cannot reject the null hypothesis that unemployment contains a unit root.

The results of the test suggest that we should not use Unemployment as a variable in an OLS regression, because the parameter estimates from such a regression will be inconsistent. Unfortunately, many macroeconomic variables appear to have unit roots on the basis of the Dickey-Fuller test. In part this occurs because the Dickey-Fuller test is not very powerful if the true value of ρ is only slightly below 1. If, for example, $\rho = 0.98$, then the Dickey-Fuller test is almost certain to fail to reject the presence of a root, even though the series is actually stationary. However, it is also quite plausible that many macroeconomic variables do in fact contain unit roots and that we need to develop

TABLE 17.2
Augmented Dickey-Fuller Test for Unit Root of Unemployment

Test statistic:	-2.461	10% critical value:	-2.576
		5% critical value:	-2.880
		1% critical value:	-3.473

Variable	Parameter	Estimate	Standard Error	t Statistic for $\beta = 0$
Intercept	α	0.192	0.083	2.313
Unemployment$_{t-1}$	β_1	-0.033	0.014	-2.461
ΔUnemployment$_{t-1}$	β_2	0.674	0.079	8.585
ΔUnemployment$_{t-2}$	β_3	-0.046	0.081	-0.566

[4] You might wonder why the critical value is a negative number. Because we are normally hoping to find a stationary series, we are looking for $\rho < 1$, and if that is true, $\beta_1 = \rho - 1$ will be negative. Most economic series do produce a negative estimate (though of course not always significantly different from 0) and thus we are usually concerned with the negative half of the distribution. Note that the critical value of -2.88 is larger (in absolute value) than the t distribution's critical value of 1.68. We would have rejected $\beta = 0$ if we had not realized that Unemployment follows a unit root when $\beta = 0$.

methods of estimating equations with nonstationary variables if we want to do econometric analysis with those variables.

17.4 ESTIMATING EQUATIONS WITH NONSTATIONARY VARIABLES

Suppose that we wish to estimate an equation of the form

$$Y_t = \beta_0 + \beta_1 X_t + \varepsilon_t \tag{17.4.1}$$

where either Y or X, or both, are nonstationary and thus least squares will not produce consistent estimates. There are two approaches to estimating such equations. The first is to do the same thing we did in Chapter 12, that is, take first differences on both sides of the equation. Equation 17.4.1 implies that

$$Y_{t-1} = \beta_0 + \beta_1 X_{t-1} + \varepsilon_{t-1} \tag{17.4.2}$$

and subtracting Equation 17.4.2 from Equation 17.4.1 produces

$$\Delta Y_t = \beta_1 \Delta X_t + \nu_t \tag{17.4.3}$$

where $\nu_t = \Delta \varepsilon_t$, the first difference of the error term. Under fairly general conditions, this equation can be estimated by least squares.

Definition 17.4 Suppose that Y_t is not stationary, but its first difference ΔY_t is stationary and follows an ARMA(P, Q) process:

$$\Delta Y_t = \alpha + \rho_1 \Delta Y_{t-1} + \rho_2 \Delta Y_{t-2} + \cdots + \rho_P \Delta Y_{t-P} + \nu_t$$
$$+ \lambda_1 \nu_{t-1} + \lambda_2 \nu_{t-2} + \cdots + \lambda_Q \nu_{t-Q} \tag{17.4.4}$$

Then we say that Y_t is *integrated of order 1*, and we say that Y_t follows an autoregressive integrated moving average, or ARIMA($P, 1, Q$), process. More generally, if Y_t must be differenced D times to produce a stationary series, then we say that Y_t is *integrated of order D*, and we say that Y_t follows an ARIMA(P, D, Q) process.

And we can say the following:

Theorem 17.2 Suppose we have a model of the form of Equation 17.4.1, and both X and Y follow ARIMA($P, 1, Q$) processes. Then least squares estimates of the first differenced Equation 17.4.3 produces a consistent estimate of β_1 that is the best linear unbiased estimator (BLUE).

This follows simply from observing that, under the stated conditions, ΔY_t and ΔX_t are stationary and that the Gauss-Markov theorem applies (assuming the rest of its assumptions are satisfied). Note, however, that Theorem 17.2 doesn't say anything about an estimate of β_0, the intercept of Equation 17.4.1. That is because β_0 cancels out in the subtraction that produces Equation 17.4.3, so estimating Equation 17.4.3 doesn't produce any estimate of β_0, consistent or otherwise.

This problem turns out to have economic implications that are rather severe. Estimating the regression in first differences tells us whether Y is going up or down but does not tell us what its level actually is, because we don't have information about its intercept β_0. The

FIGURE 17.3
Simulated X and Y Values from Equations 17.4.5 and 17.4.6

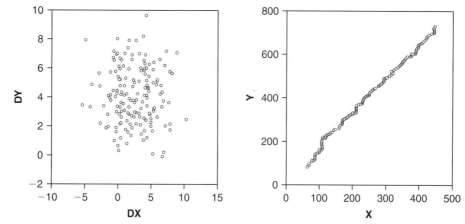

same is true of X. It can be the case that the levels of two variables are closely related, but their period-by-period changes are not. Suppose, for instance, that

$$\Delta Y_t = \alpha_1 + \varepsilon_{1t} \qquad \textbf{(17.4.5)}$$

$$\Delta X_t = \alpha_2 + \varepsilon_{2t} \qquad \textbf{(17.4.6)}$$

where ε_{1t} and ε_{2t} are independent of one another. Then ΔY_t and ΔX_t are also independent of one another, and $\beta_1 = 0$ in Equation 17.4.3. However, because of the α_1 and α_2 terms, both X and Y are growing over time (assuming α_1 and α_2 are positive), and this can cause the values of X and Y to be closely related even though their first differences are not related at all. Figure 17.3 shows the results of simulating Y and X from Equations 17.4.5 and 17.4.6. Observe that the graph of ΔY against ΔX shows no pattern at all, but that Y and X are very strongly related. Taking first differences to eliminate the unit roots from X and Y obliterates the relationship between them.

Similar problems occur in regressions with real economic data as well. For example, consider the regression

$$\log C_t = \beta_0 + \beta_1 \log Y_t + \varepsilon_t \qquad \textbf{(17.4.7)}$$

where $\log C$ is the log of real consumption in the U.S. economy, and $\log Y$ is the log of GDP. Before we estimate Equation 17.4.7 using OLS, we need to check whether or not $\log C$ and $\log Y$ have unit roots. It turns out that they both do; the Dickey-Fuller critical value is -2.92 and the test statistics are -1.22 for $\log C$ and -0.33 for $\log Y$.

There is a condition under which we can consistently estimate Equation 17.4.7 without taking first differences. Remember that the problem is that both variables follow random walks. They have no tendency to return toward their mean values if they are disturbed by an innovation. Thus, under general conditions ε_t will also follow a random walk, will not tend to be near 0, and will not average out to produce a consistent estimate of the parameters. Suppose, however, that the random walks of the two variables are linked in such a way that, though they do not return to their central values, they do stay near one another. That is, when there is an unexpected increase (or decrease) to income, there is an increase (or decrease) to consumption as well that is of approximately the same proportion. Then the ratio of C to Y will remain approximately constant and there will be a stable relationship between the two variables even though the variables themselves are not stationary. In that case, ε_t may be stationary even though $\log C$ and $\log Y$ are not. And if ε_t is stationary, then the residuals will average out and we can consistently estimate Equation 17.4.7 by least squares.

> **Definition 17.5** Two nonstationary variables X and Y are *cointegrated* if the innovation
>
> $$\varepsilon_t = Y_t - \beta_0 - \beta_1 X_t \qquad \textbf{(17.4.8)}$$
>
> is stationary for appropriate values of β_0 and β_1. Thus β_0 and β_1 are called the *cointegrating parameters* of the two variables.

If two variables are cointegrated, then we can estimate their relationship by least squares, because the error terms are stationary by definition and least squares provides unbiased and consistent estimates of the cointegrating parameters. In fact, not only does least squares produce consistent estimates of the relationship between them, but as the number of observations increases, the standard deviation of the estimator decreases faster than it does if X and Y are stationary. We say that the least squares estimator is *superconsistent* in this case.

We can also define cointegration for a set of three or more variables, by the natural extension of our definition for the two-variable case:

> **Definition 17.6** A set of M nonstationary variables X_1, X_2, ... X_M are cointegrated if the innovation
>
> $$\varepsilon_t = X_{Mt} - \beta_0 - \beta_1 X_{1t} - \beta_2 X_{2t} - \cdots - \beta_{M-1} X_{(M-1)t} \qquad \textbf{(17.4.9)}$$
>
> is stationary for appropriate values of the β parameters.

In this case there can be more than one cointegrating relationship between the variables, if they can be combined in more than one way to form a stationary error term. In general, a set of M variables can have any number of cointegrating relationships from 0 to $M - 1$, each with its own values for the cointegrating parameters. When a set of variables is cointegrated, equations containing all of them can be superconsistently estimated using least squares.[5]

To test whether two variables are cointegrated, we can simply estimate their relationship by least squares and test to see whether the residuals have a unit root, using the Dickey-Fuller test. Table 17.3 shows the results of estimating Equation 17.4.7 by least squares, using

TABLE 17.3 **Results of** **Estimating** **Equation** **17.4.7**	**Variable**	**Parameter**	**Estimate**	**Standard Error**	**t Statistic for $\beta = 0$**
	Intercept	β_0	-0.344	0.0630	-5.45
	$\log Y$	β_1	0.946	0.0076	124.9
	$N = 51$		$R^2 = 0.997$		$SER = 0.026$

[5] However, all of them must be included. It can be the case that X_1, X_2, X_3, and X_4 are cointegrated, but the subset X_1, X_2, and X_3 are not. If one wants to estimate an equation containing only X_1, X_2, and X_3, one must test whether or not that specific group of variables is cointegrated.

TABLE 17.4
Augmented Dickey-Fuller Test for Unit Root of Residuals from Equation 17.4.7

Test statistic:	−3.250	10% critical value:	−2.598
		5% critical value:	−2.921
		1% critical value:	−3.568

Variable	Parameter	Estimate	Standard Error	t Statistic for $\beta = 0$
Intercept	α	0.123	0.053	2.326
$\hat{\varepsilon}_{t-1}$	β_1	−0.953	0.293	−3.250
$\Delta\hat{\varepsilon}_{t-1}$	β_2	0.368	0.239	1.540
$\Delta\hat{\varepsilon}_{t-2}$	β_3	0.058	0.215	0.268

annual data from 1950 to 2000. Table 17.4 shows the results of the augmented Dickey-Fuller test for a unit root of the residuals. The test statistic of −3.250 is larger than the 5 percent critical value of −2.921. Thus we can claim that these residuals are stationary and that log C and log Y are cointegrated.[6] We can then treat the OLS results as consistent estimates of the true parameters.

Furthermore, because of the superconsistency of the estimators, we get very small standard errors for the parameter estimates. There is, however, one difficulty with OLS results, which is that the parameter estimates do not take normal or t distributions. Therefore, although we have a consistent estimate of the standard error of the parameter estimate, we cannot use the normal or t distribution critical values to calculate confidence intervals or perform hypothesis tests about its true value. Calculating correct intervals requires techniques more complicated than those presented here. But it remains true that the smaller standard errors do imply more precise estimates of the parameters.

17.5   MEASURING THE INFLUENCE OF ONE VARIABLE ON ANOTHER OVER TIME

Time-series models would not be very interesting if they contained only one variable that evolved over time. Macroeconomic models show relationships between a variety of variables—unemployment, inflation, money supply, national output—all of which can be expected to depend on their own past values. More important, some of these variables may depend on the past values of other variables as well. For instance, if we believe that increasing the money supply can stimulate the economy and increase employment, then we would expect changes in the unemployment rate at time t to depend on the history of the growth rate of the money supply as well as on its own past values. We then write the equation:

$$\Delta \text{Unemployment}_t = \beta_0 + \beta_1 \Delta \text{Unemployment}_{t-1} + \beta_2 \Delta \text{Unemployment}_{t-2}$$
$$+ \beta_3 \% \Delta M_{t-1} + \beta_4 \% \Delta M_{t-2} + \varepsilon_t \qquad \textbf{(17.5.1)}$$

A simple version of the monetarist theory of macroeconomics argues that changes in the money supply will affect only the price level, and will not affect any real variable such as the unemployment rate. This theory implies that $\beta_3 = 0$ and $\beta_4 = 0$ in Equation 17.5.1. By

[6] This is not the only way to test for cointegration. There are more powerful (but more complex) tests available which econometrics software may offer.

testing those hypotheses econometrically, we can also provide a simple test of the monetarist hypothesis.

> **Definition 17.7** A variable X is said to *Granger-cause* a variable Y if the present value of Y depends on past values of X as well as on its own past values. In the equation
>
> $$Y_t = \beta_0 + \beta_1 Y_{t-1} + \cdots + \beta_M Y_{t-M} + \gamma_1 X_{t-1} + \cdots + \gamma_M X_{t-M} + \varepsilon_t$$
>
> $$(17.5.2)$$
>
> if we reject the null hypothesis $\gamma_1 = 0$, $\gamma_2 = 0, \ldots, \gamma_M = 0$, then X Granger-causes Y. If we fail to reject that null hypothesis, then X does not Granger-cause Y.

To test for Granger causality, the variables X and Y must be stationary so that the equation can be correctly estimated. We determine the number of lags to use in Equation 17.5.2 in the same way we did when modeling variables as processes: Start with a large number of lags, and test to see how many are statistically significant.

Table 17.5 shows the results of estimating Equation 17.5.1 using quarterly data on unemployment and the money supply (measured by real M2) from the first quarter of 1962 to the fourth quarter of 2000. To test whether money supply growth Granger-causes changes in unemployment, we perform an F test of the null hypothesis $\beta_3 = 0$ and $\beta_4 = 0$. The test statistic is 8.75, and the critical value for 2 and 149 degrees of freedom is 3.06. We reject the null hypothesis that money supply growth does not affect changes in unemployment, and we conclude that money supply growth Granger-causes changes in unemployment.

What does this conclusion mean? In general, what does it mean to say that one variable Granger-causes another? Those questions have been the subject of intense debate among econometricians. The initial proposed answer was that if the money supply did not Granger-cause GDP, then it meant that changes in the money supply would not cause GDP to change, and if the money supply did Granger-cause GDP, then it meant that (contrary to the monetarist hypothesis) changes in the money supply would cause changes in GDP. This interpretation has generally been rejected, however, on the grounds that a regression equation cannot prove whether or not an independent variable causes changes in the dependent variable, as we discussed in Chapter 6. A conclusion about whether one variable causes a change in another depends on an economic model of how two variables are related, not just on showing that the slope of their relationship is statistically significantly different from 0. Since the test for Granger-casuality does not suggest any particular economic model, it does not, by itself, provide evidence for the claim that one variable causes another to change.

TABLE 17.5
Results of Estimating Equation 17.5.1

Variable	Parameter	Estimate	Standard Error	t Statistic for $\beta = 0$
Intercept	β_0	0.068	0.033	2.09
$\Delta \text{Unemployment}_{t-1}$	β_1	1.354	0.066	20.5
$\Delta \text{Unemployment}_{t-2}$	β_2	−0.554	0.063	−8.76
$\% \Delta M_{t-1}$	β_3	−0.079	0.043	−1.84
$\% \Delta M_{t-2}$	β_4	0.021	0.045	0.46
$N = 154$		$R^2 = 0.896$		$\text{SER} = 0.325$

Instead, we offer a somewhat more restricted interpretation of the meaning of Granger causality. What the test shows is that past values of one variable help us predict the value of the other. In this particular case, it shows that an increase in the growth rate of the money supply is associated with lower future values changes in unemployment, holding the present value of unemployment constant. Whether this implies that a change in money supply will cause changes in future unemployment depends on the choice of the economic model we use to interpret the regression. In many models that would be a reasonable implication to draw; in other models it might not be. The term Granger causality has come into use precisely to reflect that fact that Granger causality between a pair of variables suggests that the one causes the other to change but does not prove that it does so.

Having shown that money supply growth Granger-causes changes in unemployment, we might ask whether changing unemployment also Granger-causes money supply growth. To answer that question, we reverse the roles of M and Unemployment in the model, and estimate the equation

$$\%\Delta M_t = \beta_0 + \beta_1\%\Delta M_{t-1} + \beta_2\%\Delta M_{t-2} + \beta_3\Delta\text{Unemployment}_{t-1}$$
$$+ \beta_4\Delta\text{Unemployment}_{t-2} + \varepsilon_t \qquad \textbf{(17.5.3)}$$

The results of estimating this equation are found in Table 17.6. The test of Granger casuality is again whether $\beta_3 = 0$ and $\beta_4 = 0$; if so, then past changes in unemployment do not help predict today's value of M. The F statistic for this null hypothesis is 13.55, versus a critical value of 3.06. We conclude that changes in unemployment do Granger-cause the money supply.

It may seem odd that we have concluded both that the money supply Granger-causes unemployment and that unemployment Granger-causes the money supply. However, from a purely econometric standpoint it is perfectly plausible; it means that there is some dynamic relation between the two variables such that knowledge of each one's past values tells us something useful about each one's present values. It is also not difficult to provide consistent economic explanations of both findings. Money supply may Granger-cause (or even cause) changes in unemployment through effects on money markets that do not adjust instantaneously to changes in money supply. The negative coefficient for β_3 in Equation 17.5.1 suggests that, consistent with this explanation, unemployment falls following a positive shock to the money supply. The positive but smaller coefficient for β_4 suggests that this fall may subsequently be reversed in part as money markets continue to adjust to the change in monetary policy.

For the other finding, we can argue that changes in unemployment may Granger-cause (or even cause) money supply growth because if the economy rises very quickly, the Fed may

TABLE 17.6
Results of Estimating Equation 17.5.3

Variable	Parameter	Estimate	Standard Error	t Statistic for $\beta = 0$
Intercept	β_0	0.046	0.055	0.84
$\%\Delta M_{t-1}$	β_1	1.421	0.072	19.7
$\%\Delta M_{t-2}$	β_2	−0.455	0.075	−6.00
$\Delta\text{Unemployment}_{t-1}$	β_3	0.552	0.110	5.01
$\Delta\text{Unemployment}_{t-2}$	β_4	−0.378	0.106	−3.59
$N = 154$		$R^2 = 0.929$		SER $= 0.544$

respond by cutting the money supply to cool it down, or if the economy slows down the Fed may increase the money supply to stimulate it. This is consistent with the positive coefficient for β_3 in Equation 17.5.3. Of course, the two explanations describe two different relationships; the first describes the economic effects of a policy change, and the second describes the reactions of policymakers to economic events. But it is not difficult to explain how each of two variables could simultaneously Granger-cause each other. In general, two variables X and Y can both Granger-cause the other, or neither can Granger-cause the other, or one can cause the other but not vice versa. All statistical results are possible; it is up to the clever econometrician to explain the meaning of whatever result appears in the data.

17.6 TIME-SERIES MODELS OF SYSTEMS OF VARIABLES: VECTOR AUTOREGRESSION

Granger casuality describes relationships between a pair of variables evolving over time. More generally, we might want to think of a set of variables, all of which depend on the past values of every other variable in the set.

Definition 17.8 Given a set of stationary variables $Y_1, Y_2, \ldots Y_K$, a *vector autoregression (VAR)* is a set of equations of the form:

$$Y_{1t} = \beta_0 + \beta_{11} Y_{1(t-1)} + \cdots + \beta_{1M} Y_{1(t-M)} + \beta_{21} Y_{2(t-1)} + \cdots$$
$$+ \beta_{2M} Y_{2(t-M)} + \cdots + \beta_{K1} Y_{K(t-1)} + \beta_{KM} Y_{K(t-M)} + \varepsilon_t \quad \textbf{(17.6.1)}$$

that describe the evolution of a related set of variables over time.

We can write a VAR somewhat more compactly using summation notation:

$$Y_{it} = \sum_{k=1}^{K} \sum_{s=1}^{M} \beta_{iks} Y_{k(t-s)} + \varepsilon_{it} \quad \textbf{(17.6.2)}$$

where K is the number of variables in the set, M is the number of lags of each variable used in writing the equations, and there is one such equation for each of the K variables in the set. The number of lags is again determined by starting with a large number and dropping lags for which all parameters are statistically insignificant.

Note that Equations 17.5.1 and 17.5.3, considered together, are a VAR in which $K = 2$, the two variables being real GDP and money supply, and $M = 2$. Together, the two equations can be used to describe the future path that money supply and GDP will take as a function of their values at a given time and future innovations. VARs are widely used in macroeconomic forecasting and in other economic applications where the behavior of an economic model over time is of interest. Somewhat surprisingly, they often forecast macroeconomic performance much better than do complicated structural models of the type discussed in Chapter 15. They are easily estimated by least squares, as long as the variables in the VAR are all stationary. Consider, for example, a VAR containing three lags on each of four variables; the first differences of real GDP, the inflation rate, the federal budget surplus, and the money supply. It is necessary to use first differences to avoid problems with unit roots; in general, one should check for the presence of a unit root using a Dickey-Fuller test before using a variable in a VAR, taking first differences when necessary. The Dickey-Fuller test shows that all four of these first differences are stationary. The equations for this VAR are as follows:

$$\Delta G_t = \beta_{10} + \beta_{111}\Delta G_{t-1} + \beta_{112}\Delta G_{t-2} + \beta_{113}\Delta G_{t-3} + \beta_{121}\Delta \pi_{t-1}$$
$$+ \beta_{122}\Delta \pi_{t-2} + \beta_{123}\Delta \pi_{t-3} + \beta_{131}\Delta S_{t-1} + \beta_{132}\Delta S_{t-2} + \beta_{133}\Delta S_{t-3}$$
$$+ \beta_{141}\Delta M_{t-1} + \beta_{142}\Delta M_{t-2} + \beta_{143}\Delta M_{t-3} + \varepsilon_{1t} \tag{17.6.3}$$

$$\Delta \pi_t = \beta_{20} + \beta_{211}\Delta G_{t-1} + \beta_{212}\Delta G_{t-2} + \beta_{213}\Delta G_{t-3} + \beta_{221}\Delta \pi_{t-1}$$
$$+ \beta_{222}\Delta \pi_{t-2} + \beta_{223}\Delta \pi_{t-3} + \beta_{231}\Delta S_{t-1} + \beta_{232}\Delta S_{t-2} + \beta_{233}\Delta S_{t-3}$$
$$+ \beta_{241}\Delta M_{t-1} + \beta_{242}\Delta M_{t-2} + \beta_{243}\Delta M_{t-3} + \varepsilon_{2t} \tag{17.6.4}$$

$$\Delta S_t = \beta_{30} + \beta_{311}\Delta G_{t-1} + \beta_{312}\Delta G_{t-2} + \beta_{313}\Delta G_{t-3} + \beta_{321}\Delta \pi_{t-1}$$
$$+ \beta_{322}\Delta \pi_{t-2} + \beta_{323}\Delta \pi_{t-3} + \beta_{331}\Delta S_{t-1} + \beta_{332}\Delta S_{t-2} + \beta_{333}\Delta S_{t-3}$$
$$+ \beta_{341}\Delta M_{t-1} + \beta_{342}\Delta M_{t-2} + \beta_{343}\Delta M_{t-3} + \varepsilon_{3t} \tag{17.6.5}$$

$$\Delta M_t = \beta_{40} + \beta_{411}\Delta G_{t-1} + \beta_{412}\Delta G_{t-2} + \beta_{413}\Delta G_{t-3} + \beta_{421}\Delta \pi_{t-1}$$
$$+ \beta_{422}\Delta \pi_{t-2} + \beta_{423}\Delta \pi_{t-3} + \beta_{431}\Delta S_{t-1} + \beta_{432}\Delta S_{t-2} + \beta_{433}\Delta S_{t-3}$$
$$+ \beta_{441}\Delta M_{t-1} + \beta_{442}\Delta M_{t-2} + \beta_{443}\Delta M_{t-3} + \varepsilon_{4t} \tag{17.6.6}$$

where ΔG, $\Delta \pi$, ΔS, and ΔM are the first differences of real GDP, inflation, the surplus, and the money supply, respectively. Note the very large number of parameters in this model, a problem from which all VARs suffer. This VAR has a total of 52 parameters: three lags of each of four variables plus a constant in each of four equations. In general, a VAR with K variables and M lags will have $(K \cdot M) + 1$ parameters in each equation, and K equations, for a total of $(K^2 \cdot M) + K$ parameters. It is necessary to have enough observations to estimate the number of parameters required by the VAR structure.

Results of estimating Equations 17.6.3 through 17.6.6, using quarterly data from first quarter 1963 to third quarter 2000, are shown in Table 17.7.[7] If only because of the sheer number of parameters, an interpretation of these results is not straightforward. Each individual parameter is not too difficult to understand. For example, the result that $\beta_{10} = 18.64$ means that, if all the variables on the right-hand side of Equation 17.6.3 were equal to 0 (i.e., no change last quarter in GDP, money supply, inflation, or surplus) then real GDP would rise by $18.64 billion. The result that $\hat{\beta}_{142} = 0.065$ means that, all other variables held constant, a rise in money supply of $1 billion in year t would produce a rise of $65 million in real GDP in year $t + 2$.

Unfortunately, due to the structure of the model, other things are not held constant. Because the intercepts of three of the four equations are significantly different from 0, the variables tend to change value over time, so in general the right-hand-side variables will not be equal to 0. More important, a change in any one of the four variables at time t produces changes in all four of them at time $t + 1$ (though those changes are not necessarily statistically significantly different from 0). Then, the changes in each of those four variables at time $t + 1$ causes each of them to change again at time $t + 2$. And, because variables from

---

[7] Each equation is estimated separately. There is no need to estimate the equations jointly, as discussed in Chapter 15, because they all have exactly the same right-hand-side variables, so OLS and SUR give the same results.

TABLE 17.7
Results of
Estimating
Vector
Autoregression

GDP Equation			Inflation Equation		
Parameter	Estimate	Standard Error	Parameter	Estimate	Standard Error
β_{10}	18.64	6.224	β_{20}	−0.166	0.083
β_{111}	0.240	0.088	β_{211}	−1.29e5	0.001
β_{112}	0.136	0.091	β_{212}	0.001	0.001
β_{113}	0.065	0.090	β_{213}	0.0005	0.001
β_{121}	−8.760	7.274	β_{221}	0.483	0.096
β_{122}	−3.353	7.788	β_{222}	−0.195	0.103
β_{123}	5.892	6.837	β_{223}	0.433	0.090
β_{131}	0.091	0.192	β_{231}	0.005	0.003
β_{132}	0.388	0.199	β_{233}	0.001	0.003
β_{133}	−0.252	0.197	β_{233}	−0.0008	0.003
β_{141}	0.482	0.246	β_{241}	0.005	0.003
β_{142}	0.065	0.296	β_{242}	−0.009	0.004
β_{143}	0.062	0.243	β_{243}	0.013	0.003

Surplus Equation			Money Supply Equation		
Parameter	Estimate	Standard Error	Parameter	Estimate	Standard Error
β_{30}	−11.77	2.929	β_{40}	2.788	2.499
β_{311}	0.124	0.041	β_{411}	−0.032	0.035
β_{312}	0.065	0.042	β_{412}	−0.001	0.036
β_{313}	0.057	0.042	β_{413}	0.060	0.036
β_{321}	2.021	3.423	β_{421}	−5.561	2.920
β_{322}	−4.917	3.665	β_{422}	2.410	3.127
β_{323}	4.295	3.217	β_{423}	−5.235	2.745
β_{331}	−0.243	0.090	β_{431}	−0.191	0.077
β_{332}	0.091	0.094	β_{432}	0.007	0.080
β_{333}	−0.129	0.093	β_{433}	0.032	0.079
β_{341}	0.129	0.116	β_{441}	0.543	0.099
β_{342}	−0.040	0.139	β_{442}	−0.013	0.119
β_{343}	0.100	0.114	β_{443}	0.127	0.097

two time periods previously appear in Equations 17.6.3 to 17.6.6, the change at time t also causes each variable to change at time $t + 2$.

The full dynamics of the system are shown in Figure 17.4. Suppose, for the sake of example, that there is an innovation to money supply in period 1. In period 1, this innovation affects money supply, but no other variable, because only lagged values of ΔM appear on the right-hand side of the equations.[8] In period 2, the values of all four variables change

---

[8] This is true only if the innovations are uncorrelated, such that an innovation to money supply does not imply an innovation in any other variable. In reality, innovations usually are correlated. Then we must consider whether, when there is an innovation to one variable, we should also include the effects of innovations in the other variables due to correlation with the first innovation. The solution usually used is to order the equations in the VAR and to attribute all correlation between two innovations to the effects of the one listed first in the ordering. The consequence of this is that changing the order of the equations can significantly alter the response of the system to innovations. In principle, one should order the equations so that the one with the dependent variable that is likely to be determined first within a given time period is ordered first. In practice, the choice of ordering is usually not obvious from economic theory.

FIGURE 17.4

Effects of an Innovation at Time 1 on a Four-Equation Vector Autoregression (VAR)

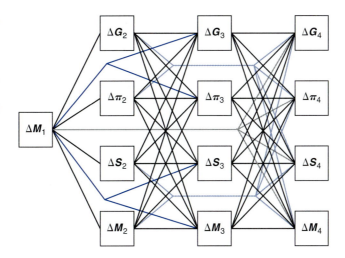

because ΔM_{t-1} appears in all four equations. This effect is represented by the first set of black lines on Figure 17.4. In period 3, there are two sets of effects. The first one is the direct effect of the change in ΔM_1 on ΔG_3, $\Delta \pi_3$, ΔS_3, and ΔM_3, caused by the ΔM_{t-2} terms in the four equations; these effects are represented by the red lines in the figure. The second set is the effects of changes in all four variables in period 2 on their values in period 3, shown by the second set of black lines in the figure. By period 4, there are three sets of effects; one for the $t - 1$ terms in the equation, one for the $t - 2$ terms, and one for the $t - 3$ terms. The effect of a change in ΔM_{t-3} on the four variables is shown by the gray lines on the figure; the effects of a change in the variables in period 2 on their values in period 4 is shown by the pink lines; and the effects of a change in the variables in period 3 on their values on period 3 is shown by the third set of black lines. To understand how a change in the money supply affects the macroeconomy for the following three periods (in this example, three quarters), it is necessary to calculate the values for all of these effects and sum them up to see what the total change in GDP will be.

The calculations are tedious but straightforward. If ΔM rises by 1 unit in period 1, then in period 2 ΔG will rise by β_{141}, $\Delta \pi$ will rise by β_{241}, ΔS will rise by β_{341}, and ΔM will rise by β_{441}. In period 3 things get more complicated. The total change in ΔG in period 3 will be equal to

$$\Delta G_3 = \beta_{111}\beta_{141} + \beta_{121}\beta_{241} + \beta_{131}\beta_{341} + \beta_{141}\beta_{441} + \beta_{142} \quad \textbf{(17.6.7)}$$

The first term is the effect on ΔG_3 of a change in ΔG_2 of size β_{141}; the effect is the parameter on ΔG_{t-1} in the ΔG_t equation (β_{111}) multiplied by the size of the change (β_{141}). The second, third, and fourth terms are the effect on ΔG_3 of the changes in $\Delta \pi_2$, ΔS_2, and ΔM_2, respectively, that were caused by the initial change to ΔM_1. The fifth and final term is the effect of ΔM_{t-2} in the ΔG_t equation. The changes in $\Delta \pi_3$, ΔS_3, and ΔM_3 can be worked out similarly. The calculations for the change in ΔG_4 are longer but conceptually identical.

Definition 17.9 In a VAR containing the variables $Y_1, Y_2 \ldots Y_K$, the *impulse response* of Y_i at time $t + s$ to a change in Y_j at time t is $dY_{i(t+s)}/dY_{jt}$, including the effects of changes in all variables between times $t + 1$ and $t + s$ on the value of

FIGURE 17.5 **Impulse Response of ΔG and $\Delta\pi$ to an Innovation in ΔM**

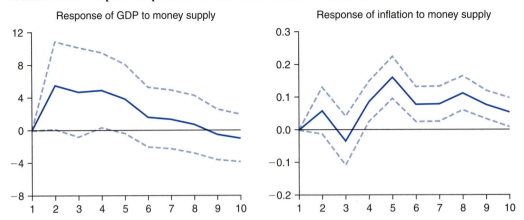

$dY_{i(t+s)}$. The *impulse response function* of Y_i to Y_j is a function showing the values of s and $dY_{i(t+s)}/dY_{jt}$ for a range of different s values.

It is also possible to calculate standard errors for the calculated values of $dY_{i(t+s)}/dY_{jt}$. Using those standard errors, we can test whether or not the response of one variable to another at any given time lag is statistically significantly different from 0.

Figure 17.5 shows the impulse responses of the first differences of real GDP and inflation to changes in the first difference of money supply, such as an unanticipated expansion of the money supply by the Fed. The graph is essentially a multiple-variable version of the graph shown in Figure 12.2 for a single variable. The horizontal axis shows the passage of time; in this case, 10 quarters are displayed. The vertical axis shows the value of ΔG and $\Delta\pi$ in each of the 10 quarters. The solid red line is the impulse response; the dashed pink lines plot a 95 percent confidence interval for the response, 2 standard deviations above and below the response itself. The left graph shows that in the short run, GDP responds positively to an innovation in the money supply and the effect is statistically significant in the first and third quarter following the innovation (and is significant at the 90 percent level in the second quarter following). After that, however, the response diminishes and is not statistically significantly different from 0 after the third quarter following the innovation. The graph on the right shows the reverse pattern. Inflation does not respond significantly to an innovation in the money supply for two quarters after the innovation; after that, there is a significant and positive response. The response begins to die off after the 9th quarter but remains significant as far as the 10th quarter, which is as far as the chart shows the response. (If we extend the chart, it becomes insignificant after the 12th period.)

These responses are consistent with standard macroeconomic models of monetary policy. In the short run (two or three quarters, in this data set) the aggregate supply curve is fairly flat and an increase in the money supply can cause GDP to grow faster than it otherwise would. After three quarters, however, the economy absorbs the effect of this shock and GDP growth returns to normal. Inflation does not initially respond to the monetary shock; but in the long run, when the aggregate supply curve is vertical, the effect of the money shock is (solely) to increase inflation.

The purpose of impulse response functions is to show precisely how the system evolves over time in response to a change in any one of its variables. For this reason, they, and VARs more generally, have become a standard tool for studying both the performance of the macroeconomy over time and other economic models in which a set of interrelated variables evolves dynamically.

Chapter Review	• Many economic models imply that one or more variables are functions of their recent past values. They can be modeled with equations of the form $Y_t = \alpha + \rho Y_{t-1} + \varepsilon_t$.

• Such variables can be modeled as ARMA processes, and the correlogram can be used to identify the AR and MA parameters of the model.

• The ARMA representation of the variable can then be used to forecast its future behavior.

• We may find that a variable follows a unit root process or some other nonstationary process. If so, then OLS regressions using that variable will be inconsistent and inefficient. They will tend to produce significant estimates of their parameters even when the two variables are in fact unrelated.

• The *augmented Dickey-Fuller test* can be used to determine whether or not a variable has a unit root. Unfortunately, the test has rather low power when the variable follows an AR(1) process with ρ close, but not equal, to 1.

• If one or more of the variables in a regression equation have unit roots, we can take first differences and estimate the resulting equation. But taking first differences can obscure important economic relationships.

• If the error term of a regression is stationary, even though the variables in the regression are not, then the variables are *cointegrated.* OLS is *superconsistent* in the case of cointegration, but the parameters are not normally distributed, so we cannot calculate confidence intervals or perform hypothesis tests in this case.

• Time-series variables may depend on the past values of other variables as well as their own. One variable *Granger-causes* a second variable if its past values are significant in a regression with the second variable on the left-hand side and past values of both on the right-hand side. It may be the case that one variable Granger-causes another, that both Granger-cause the other, or that neither does.

• The evolution of a set of related time-series variables can be described by a *vector autogression (VAR),* which can be estimated by least squares if the variables are stationary, or in their differences if not.

• VARs can be summarized by their *impulse response functions,* which show how the system of variables evolves over time in response to a change in one of its variables at a point in time.

Computer Exercise	In this exercise we'll generate some time-series variables, some stationary and some not, and examine the properties of regressions that use them.

1. Open Eviews, and create a new workfile: quarterly data, range 1976:1 to 2000:4 (100 observations total).

2. We'll start by setting some initial values. Type smpl 1976:1 1976:2 to set the sample to the first two quarters, then type genr y1=0 and genr y2=0 to create initial values.

3. Type smpl 1976:3 2000:4, then type genr e1=nrnd() and genr e2=nrnd() to create two sets of innovations, one for each variable.

4. Type genr y1 = 0.7*y1(–1) – 0.2*y1(–2) + e1 and genr y2 = 0.95*y2(–1) + e2 to create two variables which follow AR processes.

5. Double-click on y_1 to open it, and view its line graph. Does it look like a typical macro-economic variable? Then click the View button and select Correlogram. Look at the correlogram of the level with 12 lags. Which AR terms are significant? Do the same for y_2.

6. In the y_1 window, click the View button and select Unit Root test. Test the levels of y_1, with an intercept and 2 lagged values. Do you reject, or fail to reject, a unit root? Do the same for y_2. (The y_2 series is stationary, but not by much.)

7. Now we'll generate two series with unit roots. Type genr y1 = y1(–1) + e1 and genr y2 = y2(–1) + e2 to recreate the series, this time with unit roots.

8. Repeat steps 5 and 6 with the new variables. How do the correlograms look now? Do you reject or fail to reject unit roots in the data?

9. Type ls y2 c y1 to regress y_2 on y_1. We generated the two variables independently, so the true value of the slope parameter should be 0. Is its estimate significantly different from 0 or not? If you try it about 10 or 15 times, you should get mostly significant results.

Problems

1. In this problem we'll model U.S. interest rates as an ARMA process and see what we learn about their behavior over time. Load the data file rates, which contains annual observations from 1954 to 2002 on the variable fedfunds (the federal funds rate, in percentage points).

   a. Estimate the regression equation $\text{Fedfunds}_t = \beta_0 + \beta_1 \text{Fedfunds}_{t-1} + \varepsilon_t$. Does the federal funds rate appear to depend on its own past behavior, or not?

   b. Calculate the correlogram of Fedfunds. Does it depend on more than one year of its past behavior? Estimate the regression equation $\text{Fedfunds}_t = \beta_0 + \beta_1 \text{Fedfunds}_{t-1} + \beta_2 \text{Fedfunds}_{t-2} + \beta_3 \text{Fedfunds}_{t-3} + \beta_4 \text{Fedfunds}_{t-4} + \beta_5 \text{Fedfunds}_{t-5} + \varepsilon_t$. What is the longest lag that is statistically significant? Does this match the results from the correlogram? Test whether you can drop all longer lags and, if so, reestimate the equation. What type of process does the federal funds rate follow?

   c. Calculate the estimated innovations to the federal funds rate (they are just the residuals from your regression from part *b*). Is the estimated innovation for 2000 positive or negative? Calculate the correlogram of the estimated innovations. Do they appear to be serially correlated or not?

   d. Calculate the steady-state value of the federal funds rate. If the federal funds rate was at its steady-state value last year but had a positive 1 percent innovation this year, is it likely to be above or below its steady-state value next year? How much above or below? Is it likely to be above or below its steady-state value in two years? How much above or below? (Remember that it will not be at its steady-state value in one year.)

2. In this problem we'll look at the consumption function, and problems caused by units roots in the variables. Load the data file macro4, which contains quarterly data from 1948 to 2002 on the following variables: realconsumption (billions of 2001 dollars), realgdp, and fedfundsrate.

a. Estimate the equation $Realconsumption_t = \beta_0 + \beta_1 RealGDP_t + \beta_2 Fedfundsrate + \varepsilon_t$. What is the estimated value of the marginal propensity to consume (β_1)? What is its standard error? Do we have a relatively precise estimate of this parameter's value?

b. Test whether consumption, GDP, and the prime rate have unit roots, using the Dickey-Fuller test with two lags. Do you reject unit roots, or fail to reject them? What does this suggest about the regression results from part *a* of this problem?

c. Calculate new variables: deltac, deltagdp, and deltar, equal to the first differences of consumption, GDP, and the federal funds rate, respectively. Test the first differences for unit roots with the Dickey-Fuller test with two lags. Are the first differences stationary?

d. Estimate the equation $Deltac_t = \beta_0 + \beta_1 DeltaGDP_t + \beta_2 Deltar_t + \upsilon_t$. What value do you get for the marginal propensity to consume now? What is the standard error of the estimate? Is it larger or smaller than in part *a*?

3. One argument made in favor of tax cuts in the United States is that reducing revenue would force the federal government to reduce spending in the future. In this problem we'll look at federal expenditures and tax receipts and test whether these variables are in fact related over time. Load the data file receipts2, which contains annual observations from 1947 to 2002 on the following variables: govspend (federal expenditures), receipts (federal tax receipts), and cpi (the consumer price index).

a. First we'll test whether changes in taxes are followed by changes in expenditure. Estimate the equation $Govspend_t = \beta_0 + \beta_1 Govspend_{t-1} + \beta_2 Govspend_{t-2} + \beta_3 Receipts_{t-1} + \beta_4 Receipts_{t-2} + \varepsilon_t$. Perform the Granger causality test. Do changes in receipts influence future values of spending? Does this finding support the argument for cutting taxes, or refute it?

b. Test whether the error terms from the above regression are serially correlated. What do you find?

c. Next we'll test whether changes in expenditure are followed by changes in receipts. Estimate the equation $Receipts_t = \beta_0 + \beta_1 Govspend_{t-1} + \beta_2 Govspend_{t-2} + \beta_3 Receipts_{t-1} + \beta_4 Receipts_{t-2} + \varepsilon_t$, and perform the Granger causality test. What do we find now? Look at the estimated values of β_1 and β_2. Do increases in spending lead to increases or decreases in receipts? Is this what you would expect?

d. Perhaps the result is dependent on the length of the lags. Redo the tests using four lags of the variables rather than only two. Do the results change?

e. Perhaps the result would change if we used real values rather than nominal. Using the CPI variable, deflate both Govspend and Receipts, and repeat the tests (using two lags). Does this change the economic interpretation of the data and, if so, how?

4. In 1991, King, Plosser, Stock, and Watson, in an important test of real business cycle theory, proposed that the log of per capita consumption and the log of per capita GDP ought to be cointegrated, and that the log of per capita investment and the log of per capita GDP should be also. This occurs because the fraction of income that is consumed, and the fraction of income that is saved, should stay the same over time, even though productivity changes and hence total income rises. In this problem we'll test whether those cointegrating relationships exist. Load the data file cointegrate, which contains quarterly observations from the first quarter of 1949 to the last quarter of 2002 on the following variables: logrpccons (log of per capita consumption), logrpcinv (log of per capita investment), and logrpcgdp (log of per capita GDP).

a. First we should check and make sure the original data series have unit roots. Perform the Dickey-Fuller test for unit roots on the three variables, using four lags. Do the variables have unit roots?

b. Estimate the regression $\log \text{Rpccons}_t = \beta_0 + \beta_1 \log \text{RpcGDP}_t + \varepsilon_t$, and save the residuals. Test whether the residuals have a unit root, using the Dickey-Fuller test with four lags. Do these variables appear cointegrated, or not?

c. Now estimate the regression $\log \text{Rpcinv}_t = \beta_0 + \beta_1 \log \text{RpcGDP}_t + \varepsilon_t$, and save the residuals. Test whether the residuals have a unit root, using the Dickey-Fuller test with four lags. Do these variables appear cointegrated, or not?

d. We can also test whether all three variables together are cointegrated. Estimate the regression $\log \text{RpcGDP}_t = \beta_0 + \beta_1 \log \text{Rpccons}_t + \beta_2 \log \text{Rpcinv}_t + \varepsilon_t$. Save the residuals, and test whether they have a unit root. Do all three variables appear cointegrated? Is the theory that GDP, consumption, and investment all grow due to a common productivity shock supported by these results, or refuted?

5. During the 1990s, the American economy had one of the longest economic booms in its history and, simultaneously, a sharp rise in the value of the stock market. In this problem we'll explore whether the rising stock market might have boosted the performance of the economy (perhaps due to expectations of future wealth by investors) and, conversely, if the collapse of the market might have contributed to the recession. Load the data file stockvalue, which was described in problem 6 in Chapter 16.

a. If the variables have unit roots, we need to estimate the VAR in first differences. Test whether Realstockvalue and RealGDP are stationary, using the ADF test with four lags. If they are, test whether their first differences are stationary.

b. Calculate first differences of the two variables; call them dstockval and drealgdp. Estimate a VAR containing five lags of each of the first-differenced variable. Are any of the parameters on the fifth lags statistically significantly different from 0? If not, estimate the VAR with four lags, and test whether any of the fourth lags are significant. Keep dropping lags and testing until you find the last lag has at least one significant parameter.

c. Are any of the parameters on the lagged values of Dstockval significant in the DrealGDP equation? If so, are the values positive or negative? Does an increase in the total value of the stock market seem to raise GDP, decrease GDP, or have no effect?

d. Are any of the parameters on the lagged values of DrealGDP significant in the Dstockval equation? If so, are the values positive or negative? Does an increase in the GDP seem to raise the stock market, lower the stock market, or have no effect?

e. Calculate impulse response functions for the vector autoregression, using the ordering DrealGDP first, Dstockval second. Do changes in GDP respond to past changes in stock value or not? If they do, for how many quarters? Do changes in stock value respond to past changes in GDP? If they do, for how many quarters? Do the answers change if you use the ordering Dstockval, DrealGDP instead?

f. On the basis of these results, does it seem like the fall of the stock market could have contributed to the recession, or not? Does it seem like the recession could have contributed to the fall of the stock market, or not?

Chapter **Eighteen**

Nonlinear Models

The importance of changes in inventory investment in cyclical fluctuations has been widely documented. In eight postwar recessions, declines in inventory investment have on average accounted for more than 30% of the peak-to-trough declines (relative to trend) of real GNP, even though inventory investment itself represents a much smaller component of GNP.

James Kahn

18.1 AN ECONOMIC MODEL OF INVENTORY ADJUSTMENTS

Thus far, all of the models we have studied have been linear in their parameters. It is very convenient for least squares analysis for the model to be linear in the parameters, because then the derivatives of the sum of squared residuals with respect to the parameters are simple and the formula for $\hat{\beta}$ is not difficult to derive. For this reason, economists, especially in the era before computers, have long favored models that are linear in the parameters for econometric analysis.

There are many economic models that are not linear in their parameters and thus not suited for the least squares techniques we have studied so far. One such model is the stock adjustment model. Consider an industry in which buyers wish to choose a product from among an inventory that sellers must maintain. Automobiles, furniture, and musical instruments are three examples of industries with such a structure. We might think that the more sales the industry has, the larger an inventory it would like to maintain:

$$\text{Inv}_t^* = \beta_0 + \beta_1 \text{Sales}_t + \varepsilon_t \qquad \textbf{(18.1.1)}$$

where Inv_t^* is the desired inventory level and Sales is sales, both at time t. However, the firm cannot instantly adjust its inventory to the desired level. If there is an unusually large number of sales in a given period, the industry must produce more of the product, and it may take weeks or months before new products are available for sale. Conversely, if sales slow down, the industry may wish to reduce production, but the products already in production will be produced and inventories will build up for a while before the slowdown in production affects inventories. At any given time the industry probably does not have the exact amount of inventory it would like to hold, but is instead adjusting its inventory up or down. For a simple approximation of this, we might assume that the firm adjusts its inventory according to the following rule:

$$\text{Inv}_t = \text{Inv}_{t-1} + \lambda(\text{Inv}_t^* - \text{Inv}_{t-1}) \qquad \textbf{(18.1.2)}$$

That is, the firm's inventory level at time t is equal to the level from time $t - 1$, plus a fraction λ of $(\text{Inv}_t^* - \text{Inv}_{t-1})$, which is the difference between the amount the firm would like to have and what it actually does have. In this model, λ is a measure of how rapidly the firm can adjust its inventories to a change in sales, and we expect $0 < \lambda < 1$. If, at one extreme, $\lambda = 1$, then Equation 18.1.2 reduces to

$$\text{Inv}_t = \text{Inv}_t^* \qquad \textbf{(18.1.3)}$$

In this case, the firm can adjust its inventories to the optimal level instantly. If, at the other extreme, $\lambda = 0$, then Equation 18.1.2 reduces to

$$\text{Inv}_t = \text{Inv}_{t-1} \qquad \textbf{(18.1.4)}$$

In this case, the firm is unable to change its inventory at all. If $0 < \lambda < 1$, then the firm has some ability to change its inventory, but not as much as it would like. If we can estimate a value for λ, then we can measure how rapidly the industry is capable of adjusting inventories. Slow inventory response is one sort of economic "stickiness" that can help explain why there are business cycles, and thus measurements of the rapidity with which inventories actually adjust is of some theoretical interest.

The problem is that we cannot estimate Equation 18.1.2 to estimate a value for λ, because Inv_t^*, the level of inventory that the firm desires to hold, is unobservable. All we can observe is Inv_t, the level the firm actually does hold. If we could estimate the values of β_0 and β_1, we could calculate estimates of the values of Inv_t^*, but we cannot estimate that equation either; it also contains the unobservable variable Inv_t^*. The solution to the problem is to substitute Equation 18.1.1 into Equation 18.1.2 to eliminate Inv_t^*:

$$\text{Inv}_t = \text{Inv}_{t-1} + \lambda(\beta_0 + \beta_1 \text{Sales}_t + \varepsilon_t - \text{Inv}_{t-1}) \qquad \textbf{(18.1.5)}$$

which can be simplified to

$$\text{Inv}_t = \lambda\beta_0 + \lambda\beta_1 \text{Sales}_t + (1 - \lambda)\text{Inv}_{t-1} + \lambda\varepsilon_t \qquad \textbf{(18.1.6)}$$

which we can estimate, since it relates current actual inventory to current sales and last period's inventory. Unfortunately, this model is nonlinear in the parameters λ, β_0, and β_1, because of the terms $\lambda\beta_0$ and $\lambda\beta_1$. The techniques studied in this book so far apply only to models that are linear in their parameters. In this chapter we will extend the least squares principle to apply to nonlinear models as well. This will permit us to estimate the parameters of equations like Equation 18.1.6, calculate their standard errors, and test whether the estimated values are consistent with our economic ideas about the models.

18.2 APPLYING THE LEAST SQUARES PRINCIPLE TO NONLINEAR MODELS

To estimate linear models, we solved the equations for the error terms and wrote the sum of squared errors as a function of the parameters. For the linear model

$$Y_i = \beta_0 + \beta_1 X_i + \varepsilon_i \qquad \textbf{(18.2.1)}$$

solving for the error term produces

$$\varepsilon_i = Y_i - \beta_0 - \beta_1 X_i \qquad \textbf{(18.2.2)}$$

and we can then write the sum of squared errors as the familiar

$$\text{SSR} = \sum_{i=1}^{N}(Y_i - \hat{\beta}_0 - \hat{\beta}_1 X_i)^2 \qquad \textbf{(18.2.3)}$$

The linear least squares estimates $\hat{\beta}_0$ and $\hat{\beta}_1$ are the values that minimize Equation 18.2.3. This method generalizes very easily to the case of a nonlinear model. Suppose we have an econometric model that, solved for its error term, is of the form

$$\varepsilon_i = f(Y_i, X_1, \ldots, X_M, \beta_0, \beta_1, \ldots, \beta_K) \qquad \textbf{(18.2.4)}$$

where f is any function we can write down. All this requires is that the error term, in some way, be a function of a dependent variable Y, M independent variables $X_1, \ldots, X_M$, and $K + 1$ parameters $\beta_0, \beta_1, \ldots, \beta_K$. Note that the number of parameters and the number of variables need not be the same. Then we can write the sum of squared residuals for this model as

$$\text{SSR} = \sum_{i=1}^{N} f(Y_i, X_1, \ldots, X_M, \hat{\beta}_0, \hat{\beta}_1, \ldots, \hat{\beta}_K)^2 \qquad \textbf{(18.2.5)}$$

and again we can choose the values of $\beta_0, \beta_1, \ldots, \beta_K$ that minimize the sum of squared residuals as our estimates. The first-order conditions are

$$\sum_{i=1}^{N} \frac{\partial f}{\partial \beta_k}(Y_i, X_1, \ldots, X_M, \hat{\beta}_0, \hat{\beta}_1, \ldots, \hat{\beta}_K)^2 = 0 \qquad \textbf{(18.2.6)}$$

which give us a set of $K + 1$ equations in $K + 1$ unknowns. Unfortunately, we have no guarantee that this set of equations has a solution. Also, if it has a solution, it might have more than one solution. Suppose, for example, we have the following nonlinear regression model:

$$Y_i = \beta_0 + \beta_1 \beta_2 X_i + \varepsilon_i \qquad \textbf{(18.2.7)}$$

We solve this for the error term to get

$$\varepsilon_i = Y_i - \beta_0 - \beta_1 \beta_2 X_i \qquad \textbf{(18.2.8)}$$

and the sum of squared residuals is

$$\text{SSR} = \sum_{i=1}^{N}(Y_i - \hat{\beta}_0 - \hat{\beta}_1 \hat{\beta}_2 X_i)^2 \qquad \textbf{(18.2.9)}$$

We can see that there will be more than one solution for $\hat{\beta}_1$ and $\hat{\beta}_2$ if we minimize this sum of squared residuals, because different values of $\hat{\beta}_1$ and $\hat{\beta}_2$ will produce exactly the same residuals. Suppose we choose $\hat{\beta}_1 = 2$ and $\hat{\beta}_2 = 3$. Then the sum of squared residuals will be equal to

$$\text{SSR} = \sum_{i=1}^{N}(Y_i - \hat{\beta}_0 - 6X_i)^2 \qquad \textbf{(18.2.10)}$$

Suppose instead we choose $\hat{\beta}_1 = 3$ and $\hat{\beta}_2 = 2$. Then the sum or squared residuals will be exactly the same. In fact, we can choose $\hat{\beta}_1 = 1$ and $\hat{\beta}_2 = 6$, or $\hat{\beta}_1 = 12$ and $\hat{\beta}_2 = 0.5$, or any values for $\hat{\beta}_1$ and $\hat{\beta}_2$ that multiply to 6, and the sum of squared residuals will be the one given in Equation 18.2.10.

Definition 18.1 A model is *overparameterized* if multiple values of the parameters produce the same values for the residuals of the model. If a model is overparameterized, then at least some of its parameters cannot be estimated.

If a model is overparameterized, we can reparameterize it. For example, we can rewrite Equation 18.2.7 as

$$Y_i = \beta_0 + \gamma X_i + \varepsilon_i \qquad \text{(18.2.11)}$$

where $\gamma = \beta_1\beta_2$. That model is linear in the parameters and can be estimated by ordinary least squares (OLS). The resulting estimate for $\hat{\gamma}$ will also give us an estimate of the value of $\beta_1\beta_2$. But it will not give us individual values for $\hat{\beta}_1$ and $\hat{\beta}_2$. Depending on the economic problem we are trying to solve, it may be enough for us to have an estimate of $\beta_1\beta_2$, or we may need estimates of β_1 and β_2 separately. If the former, then estimating Equation 18.2.11 is fine. If the latter, then neither Equation 18.2.11 nor Equation 18.2.7 can tell us what we need to know. In that case, we need to use our economic model to derive another equation that we can estimate and that is not overparameterized.

18.3 THE PROPERTIES OF THE NONLINEAR LEAST SQUARES ESTIMATOR

Assuming that a unique solution to the first-order conditions given by Equation 18.2.6 does exist, then we can take the values of $\hat{\beta}_0, \hat{\beta}_1, \ldots, \hat{\beta}_K$ as the nonlinear least squares (NLLS) estimates of the parameters $\beta_0, \beta_1, \ldots, \beta_K$. These estimates have a number of properties—some useful, some not. One important one is that it may not be possible to explicitly solve the first-order conditions to derive formulas for $\hat{\beta}_0, \hat{\beta}_1, \ldots, \hat{\beta}_K$. For this reason, most computer software that provides NLLS estimation uses numerical methods to search for a solution to the first-order conditions instead of trying for a direct solution. NLLS estimators have two other important properties:

Theorem 18.1 Suppose that the nonlinear model we are estimating is correct; that is, the data generating process is given by $\varepsilon_i = f(Y_i, X_1, \ldots, X_M, \beta_0, \beta_1, \ldots, \beta_K)$. Suppose also that classical regression assumptions A2 through A5 hold. Then the NLLS estimates of the parameters $\beta_0, \beta_1, \ldots, \beta_K$ are consistent. If we add assumption A6, then as the sample size grows large, NLLS is efficient.

Note that, unlike the linear least squares estimator, the NLLS estimator is not unbiased, although because it is consistent, the bias goes to 0 as the sample gets large. Also, it is not necessarily efficient unless the error terms are normally distributed. Without the normality assumption, consistency is all we can get from the NLLS estimator, although that is enough to assure us that the estimator will be as good as we need it to be in the presence of enough data.

If we want to test hypotheses about the parameters, we also need to know their distribution function.

Theorem 18.2 Suppose that the nonlinear model we are estimating is correct, and suppose that classical regression assumptions A2 through A5 hold. Then the NLLS estimates of the parameters $\beta_0, \beta_1, \ldots, \beta_K$ are approximately normally distributed and the distribution becomes exactly normal as the sample size grows large.

This allows us to use the normal distribution table to calculate confidence intervals and hypothesis tests, as long as we remember that the intervals and tests are only approximately accurate. Like the parameters themselves, the standard deviations of the distribution of the parameters depend on the exact nonlinear function of the model. Econometric software will calculate estimated standard deviations of the parameters, using a variety of methods.[1]

For an example of NLLS, we estimate the stock adjustment model given in Equation 18.1.6, using data on inventories of U.S. domestic automobiles. Data are quarterly from the second quarter of 1967 to the fourth quarter of 2000; inventories and sales are measured in millions of cars per year. Results are shown in Table 18.1. Note that we give Z statistics rather than t statistics; this is because the parameters do not take the t distribution in small samples, and we must rely on the normal distribution for an approximate test of their significance. Because Equation 18.1.6 is nonlinear, the parameters do not have the usual interpretation of the result in a one-unit change in an independent variable. Instead, their meanings have to be derived from the structural equations of the model, Equations 18.1.1 and 18.1.2. From Equation 18.1.1, we interpret β_1 as the increase in inventory that auto dealers will choose if sales rise by 1 car per quarter. The value of 0.091 car more in inventory implies that it requires a $1/0.091 = 11$-car increase in sales to induce a dealer to hold 1 more car in inventory, a figure that matches economic intuition about dealer behavior.

The estimated value of the speed of adjustment parameter λ is 0.217, which falls within the expected range of (0, 1). The value is significantly different from both 0 (Z stat $= 4.28$) and 1 (Z stat $= (0.217 - 1)/0.051 = -15.4$); its 95 percent confidence interval is 0.217 plus or minus $1.96 \cdot 0.051 = (0.117, 0.317)$. This suggests that the speed of inventory adjustment in this industry is quite slow. In any given quarter, automobile dealers increase (or decrease) inventory by only 21.7 percent of the value they would like to change it on the basis of that quarter's sales. This may imply that sales are highly variable and thus dealers are unlikely to adjust much to what may be a transitory increase in sales. It could also mean that automobile factories are unable to quickly scale up production in response to an increase in demand.

TABLE 18.1 **Nonlinear Least Squares Estimates of Equation 18.1.6**

Parameter	Estimate	Standard Error	Z Statistic for $\beta = 0$
β_0	0.757	0.271	2.80
β_1	0.095	0.036	2.65
λ	0.217	0.051	4.28
$N = 135$	SER $= 94.4$	$R^2 = 0.704$	DW $= 1.975$

[1] There are, in fact, several different methods that can be used, and they can give substantially different answers. Different software packages, or the same package with different options set, can thus give rather different standard errors for the same regression.

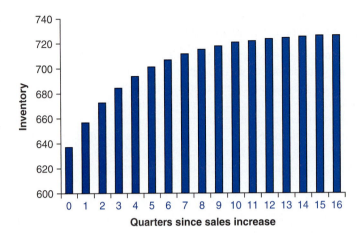

We can get a graphical interpretation of this parameter by calculating the response of inventory to a permanent increase in sales of 1 million cars. Equation 18.1.1 says that dealers would like to raise inventory by 91,000 cars as a result; but Equation 18.1.2 says that, in the first quarter, they can raise it by only 21.7 percent of that value, or 19,750 cars. In the next quarter, they are still 71,250 cars short of what they would like to have in inventory. As a result, they increase inventory by 21.7 percent of that value, or another 15,450 cars. As time passes, inventory levels rise toward the desired 91,000-car increase. Figure 18.1 shows the inventory of the industry as a function of time since the increase. After four quarters, only about two-thirds of the total adjustment has been made; it takes more than two years to get 90 percent of the way to the desired new inventory target. These calculations provide an economic interpretation to the estimate $\lambda = 0.217$ and support our conclusion that it represents a fairly slow response of inventories. NLLS permits us to estimate λ and see what the result implies for the original economic question about inventory adjustments.

For a second example, we consider the Cochrane-Orcutt transformation introduced in Chapter 12. The equation produced by that transformation is:

$$Y_t = (1 - \rho)\beta_0 + \rho Y_{t-1} + \beta_1 X_t - \rho\beta_1 X_{t-1} + u_t \qquad \textbf{(18.3.1)}$$

which is a nonlinear model in the parameters β_0, β_1, and ρ. In Chapter 12 we solved the problem of nonlinearity by reparameterizing the model as

$$Y_t = Y_t = \gamma_0 + \gamma_1 Y_{t-1} + \gamma_2 X_t + \gamma_3 X_{t-1} + u_t \qquad \textbf{(18.3.2)}$$

and estimating it with ordinary least squares. But, as we observed in Chapter 12, the model implies that $\gamma_3 = -\gamma_1\gamma_2$, and estimating by OLS will not necessary produce that result.

With nonlinear least squares, however, we can estimate Equation 18.3.1 directly, picking the values of β_0, β_1, and ρ that minimize the sum of squared residuals. Using the same data on savings rates and interest rates used in Chapter 12, we estimate the equation

$$\text{Savings}_t = (1 - \rho)\beta_0 + \rho\text{Savings}_{t-1} + \beta_1 \text{Interestrate}_t$$
$$- \rho\beta_1 \text{Interestrate}_{t-1} + u_t \qquad \textbf{(18.3.3)}$$

TABLE 18.2 **Results of Nonlinear Estimation of Equation 18.3.3**

Variable	Parameter	Estimate	Standard Error	t Statistic for $\beta = 0$
Intercept	β_0	5.971	0.382	15.6
Interestrate	β_1	0.083	0.049	1.71
Autocorrelation	ρ	0.735	0.064	11.5

Results are found in Table 18.2 and are essentially identical to those found in Chapter 12 with the autocorrelation correction. NLLS allows us to transform models in ways that make them nonlinear yet still estimate those models with the least squares principle.

18.4 TESTING NONLINEAR RESTRICTIONS ON THE PARAMETERS OF A MODEL

As noted in the preceding section, in a nonlinear model, the number of parameters and the number of variables need not be the same, which can result in the model being overparameterized. However, it can also produce a model in which the value for each parameter can be estimated in more than one way. For example, consider the following model:

$$Y_i = \beta_0 + \beta_1 X_{1i} + \beta_2 X_{2i} + \beta_1 \beta_2 X_{3i} + \varepsilon_i \qquad \textbf{(18.4.1)}$$

in which β_1 and β_2 both appear twice, once by themselves, once multiplied by the other. Clearly, we could get estimates of β_1 and β_2 from just the first two terms, without using the third term where they are multiplied together. To do that, we could reparameterize the model as follows:

$$Y_i = \beta_0 + \beta_1 X_{1i} + \beta_2 X_{2i} + \gamma_1 X_{3i} + \varepsilon_i \qquad \textbf{(18.4.2)}$$

where $\gamma_1 = \beta_1 \beta_2$. We could then estimate Equation 18.4.2 by OLS and have perfectly adequate estimates of β_1 and β_2.

If we did that, though, we would be failing to use the information that $\gamma_1 = \beta_1 \beta_2$, which the economic model gives us. We would do better to estimate Equation 18.4.1 by NLLS and force the estimation procedure to impose the restriction $\gamma_1 = \beta_1 \beta_2$ on the estimated parameters. Further, we can estimate Equation 18.4.2 and see whether the estimated value of γ_1 is close to the estimated value of $\beta_1 \beta_2$. If it is, that is a sign that the economic model that generated Equation 18.4.1 as a prediction about the data is a good one. If it is not, then the nonlinear restriction is probably false and the economic model may be flawed. We can construct a test of the nonlinear restriction and use it as a test of whether or not the economic theory behind the restriction is valid.

Many economic models involve nonlinear restrictions of this general form. In the rest of this section, we will consider a model of the effect of money supply on the unemployment rate.[2] In this model, we will assume that firms base their hiring decisions on the wages they

---

[2] This model is closely based on the model estimated by Robert Barro (1977), though he solves the model to a different estimating equation. This form is much closer to the one presented by Attfield, Demery, and Duck (1985) though it uses somewhat different variables.

expect to pay the workers in the future. If the money supply changes, it may affect the real value of the wages of the workers. Thus, a large increase in the money supply, which would lower real wages, might encourage a firm to hire more workers and thereby result in reduced unemployment. The problem is that the firm cannot know in advance what monetary policy will be. Firms must make a guess about the future value of money supply and hire on the basis of that guess. If it turns out that their guess is correct, they will not change their number of workers—and the unemployment rate will not change either. Only if their guess is wrong will they hire (or fire) workers, and only then will unemployment rise (or fall). This suggests that the unemployment rate is determined by

$$\text{Unemployment}_t = \beta_0 + \beta_1[\text{DM}_t - \text{E}(\text{DM}_t)] + \beta_2\text{Mil}_t + \varepsilon_t \quad \textbf{(18.4.3)}$$

where Unemployment_t is the unemployment rate in year t, Mil_t is the size of the active resident military population, DM_t is the growth rate of the money supply, and $\text{E}(\text{DM}_t)$ is the firm's expectation of what DM_t will be. This equation is constructed so that only the error in the firm's guess about the money supply, which is equal to $\text{DM}_t - \text{E}(\text{DM}_t)$, will affect the unemployment rate. Mil_t is in the equation because an increase in the military population will tend to reduce unemployment by taking young men and women out of the civilian labor force. Furthermore, suppose that the money growth rate is determined by the equation

$$\text{DM}_t = \alpha_0 + \alpha_1\text{DM}_{t-1} + \alpha_2\text{DM}_{t-2} + \alpha_3\text{DG}_{t-1} + \upsilon_t \quad \textbf{(18.4.4)}$$

where DG_{t-1} is the growth rate of government spending at time $t - 1$.

The only part of the model not yet specified is how firms form their expectations of DM_t. One possibility is that the firms form these expectations rationally. Observe that all the right-hand-side variables of Equation 18.4.4 are dated at time $t - 1$ or earlier, and thus are observable to the firm (except, of course, the error term). If the firm knew enough about the recent history of the economy, it could deduce the relationship described by Equation 18.4.4 and use it to form $\text{E}(\text{DM}_t)$ for use in hiring decisions. If the firm does that, then it would be the case that

$$\text{E}(\text{DM}_t) = \alpha_0 + \alpha_1\text{DM}_{t-1} + \alpha_2\text{DM}_{t-2} + \alpha_3\text{DG}_{t-1} \quad \textbf{(18.4.5)}$$

because $\text{E}(\upsilon_t) = 0$, as it is a regression error. We could then substitute Equation 18.4.5 into Equation 18.4.3 to produce

$$\text{Unemployment}_t = \beta_0 + \beta_1(\text{DM}_t - [\alpha_0 + \alpha_1\text{DM}_{t-1}$$

$$+ \alpha_2\text{DM}_{t-2} + \alpha_3\text{DG}_{t-1}]) + \beta_2\text{Mil}_t + \varepsilon_t \quad \textbf{(18.4.6)}$$

We estimate Equations 18.4.4 and 18.4.6 using seemingly unrelated regressions and impose the restrictions that the α parameters take the same values in both equations. The data are measured annually from 1962 to 1999. Results are shown in Table 18.3. The estimates of the α parameters suggest that money growth does depend on its past values, but not significantly on the past growth of government spending; $\hat{\alpha}_3$ is not statistically significantly different from 0. The estimates of the β parameters show that unemployment rises when there is an unexpectedly high increase in the money supply; this is what we expected, because the high money growth is inflationary and hence reduces real wages. A larger military significantly reduces civilian unemployment, also as expected.

TABLE 18.3
Nonlinear Least Squares Estimates of Equations 18.4.4 and 18.4.6

Parameter	Estimate	Standard Error	Z Statistic for $\beta = 0$
α_0	0.057	0.017	3.47
α_1	0.751	0.188	4.00
α_2	−0.493	0.181	−2.66
α_3	−0.230	0.152	−1.52
β_0	8.631	0.753	11.5
β_1	30.25	6.875	4.40
β_2	−339.4	88.90	−3.82

TABLE 18.4
Least Squares Estimates of Equations 18.4.4 and 18.4.7

Parameter	Estimate	Standard Error	Z Statistic for $\beta = 0$
α_0	0.008	0.010	0.80
α_1	0.959	0.147	6.53
α_2	−0.424	0.143	−2.97
α_3	−0.217	0.101	2.14
γ_0	6.749	0.817	8.26
γ_1	18.46	8.465	2.18
γ_2	−8.612	10.89	−0.79
γ_3	9.700	8.006	1.21
γ_4	16.20	5.726	2.83
γ_5	−396.4	99.96	−3.97

These results are all dependent on our assumption that firms have rational expectations; that is, that $E(DM_t)$ is indeed formed by Equation 18.4.5. That assumption might not be true, and it would be desirable to have a way to test that assumption. It turns out that we do have enough information in this model to conduct such a test. To do so, we reparameterize Equation 18.4.6, writing it as

$$\text{Unemployment}_t = \gamma_0 + \gamma_1 DM_t + \gamma_2 DM_{t-1} + \gamma_3 DM_{t-2} + \gamma_4 DG_{t-1} + \gamma_5 Mil_t + \varepsilon_t$$

(18.4.7)

where if expectations are rational, then $\gamma_0 = \beta_0 - \beta_1\alpha_0$, $\gamma_1 = \beta_1$, $\gamma_2 = -\beta_1\alpha_1$, $\gamma_3 = -\beta_1\alpha_2$, $\gamma_4 = -\beta_1\alpha_3$, and $\gamma_5 = \beta_2$. But if expectations are not rational, then the γ parameters would take different values.

We can estimate Equations 18.4.4 and 18.4.7 by OLS, since the nonlinear parameter restrictions are not imposed. From that, we can obtain estimates of the α parameters from Equation 18.4.4, and we can obtain an estimate of β_1 from the estimate of γ_1 in Equation 18.4.7. The rational expectations assumption implies that our estimate for γ_2 should be equal to our estimate for γ_1 (i.e., for β_1) multiplied by our estimate for α_1. We can test to see if that is true or not. If it is true, then it is empirical evidence in favor of the rational expectations hypothesis; if it is not true, then it is evidence against that hypothesis. Similarly, if expectations are rational, then $\hat{\gamma}_3$ should be equal to $\hat{\gamma}_1$ multiplied by $\hat{\alpha}_2$, and $\hat{\gamma}_4$ should be equal to $\hat{\gamma}_1$ multiplied by $\hat{\alpha}_3$.

We estimate Equations 18.4.4 and 18.4.7 using seemingly unrelated regressions, and annual data from 1962 to 1999. Results of the estimation are found in Table 18.4. Our estimate for $\hat{\gamma}_1$ is 18.46, and our estimate for $\hat{\alpha}_1$ is 0.959. These imply that, if expectations are rational, then $\hat{\gamma}_2$ should equal $-18.46 \cdot 0.959 = -17.70$. In fact, the value of $\hat{\gamma}_2$, -8.612, is rather far from -17.70, although because of its high standard error, we cannot reject the null hypothesis that it is equal to -17.70. For $\hat{\gamma}_3$ we expect $-18.46 \cdot -0.424 = 7.827$ and get an actual estimate of 9.700, and for $\hat{\gamma}_4$ we expect $-18.46 \cdot -0.217 = 4.006$ and get 16.20.

To formally test the null hypothesis $H_0 : \gamma_2 = -\gamma_1 \alpha_1$ and $\gamma_3 = -\gamma_1 \alpha_2$ and $\gamma_4 = -\gamma_1 \alpha_3$, we cannot use an F test, because we are estimating a multiple-equation model and so there is more than one sum of squared residuals to contend with. It is easier to test this hypothesis using a Wald test. The test statistic works out to 12.20, and has a chi-square distribution with three degrees of freedom (we are testing three joint restrictions on the parameters). The 5 percent critical value is 7.81, and the 1 percent critical value is 11.34. We can therefore reject the null hypothesis that $\gamma_2 = -\gamma_1 \alpha_1$, $\gamma_3 = -\gamma_1 \alpha_2$, and $\gamma_4 = -\gamma_1 \alpha_3$, and conclude that at least one of the equalities does not hold. This suggests that we can also reject the rational expectations hypothesis.

Alternate interpretations are possible, however, that could defend the rational expectations hypothesis. In particular, this test depends critically on the assumptions that DM_{t-1}, DM_{t-2}, and DG_{t-1} do not appear in Equation 18.4.3; they affect unemployment only insofar as they affect $E(DM_t)$. If that assumption is false, then the rational expectations hypothesis would not predict that $\gamma_2 = -\gamma_1 \alpha_1$, $\gamma_3 = -\gamma_1 \alpha_2$, and $\gamma_4 = -\gamma_1 \alpha_3$, and then the test would be invalid. This test rejects only the assumption of rational expectations in the model presented here. If some other assumption of the model is wrong, then it might be that assumption, and not the rational expectations hypothesis, that is causing H_0 to be rejected. We must be careful not to claim more than our econometrics results permit us to claim, and the more complicated the econometric model is, the more limits it places on our ability to draw strong conclusions from it.

Chapter Review

- Some economic models are inherently nonlinear in their parameters. If we wish to estimate the values of those parameters, we must extend the least squares principle to handle the case of nonlinear equations.

- Even when the model is nonlinear, we can still write the sum of squared residuals and choose as our estimates the values of the parameters that minimize it. These estimates are known as *nonlinear least squares (NLLS)* estimates.

- It may be the case that multiple values of the parameters give exactly the same formula for the residuals of the model. If so, the model is *overparameterized*. It cannot be estimated until it is reparameterized to eliminate the redundancy of the parameters.

- When a model is overparameterized, we can generally estimate some combinations of the parameters but not all of the parameters individually.

- If we have the correct nonlinear model, and the rest of the classical regression assumptions hold, then NLLS is consistent. However, it is not unbiased, and it may not be efficient unless the error terms have a normal distribution.

- NLLS estimates are approximately normally distributed, but for finite samples they do not have exactly the normal distribution, nor do they have exactly the t distribution. We conduct hypothesis tests using the normal distribution, and the tests are only approximately correct.

- If some of the parameters appear in more than one term of an equation, then it may be possible to estimate more than one value for them. If so, we can test whether the restrictions on the model's parameters implied by the multiple appearance of the same parameters are supported by the data, or rejected.

Computer Exercise

In this exercise we'll generate some data using a model that is not linear in the parameters, and test to see whether the bias is a problem in small samples or not.

1. Open Eviews, and create a new workfile, undated, with 15 observations. (The small sample will result in larger bias.)

2. We'll generate some data using the nonlinear relationship $Y_i = \beta_0 + \beta_1 X_{1i} - \beta_1^3 X_{2i}$. Type genr x1=rnd()*20 + 10 and x2=rnd()*20 + 10 to generate independent variables.

3. Type genr err = rnd()*20 − 10 to produce some (nonnormally distributed) error terms. Then type y = 500 + 3*x1 − 27*x2 to generate a dependent variable. The true value of β_0 is 500, and the true value of β_1 is 3.

4. Under the Quick menu, select Estimate Equation. In the resulting box, type y = c(1)+c(2)*x1−c(2)^3*x2 to enter the nonlinear equation we wish to estimate. Then hit the OK button to estimate. How close is the estimated β_0 to 500? How close is the estimated β_1 to 3? Are they significantly different from their true values, or not?

5. In an Excel spreadsheet or other analysis package, type the estimated values for β_0 and β_1 and their standard errors. Then repeat steps 3 and 4 twenty-four times, to produce a sample of 25 estimates of β_0 and β_1. How many times is the estimate of β_1 too low? How many times is it too high? Does it look normally distributed or not?

6. Calculate the average value of the estimated value of β_1 from your 25 samples. Is it close to 3? Is it too high or too low? Which way does it appear biased? Test whether the sample average of your 25 estimates of β_1 is significantly different from 3 or not. Is the bias significant or not?

Problems

1. In Chapter 6 we considered the problem of estimating the marginal propensity to consume (MPC) from the consumption function. In this problem we will use nonlinear least squares (NLLS) to estimate it from the reduced form of the macro model. Consider the two-equation model

$$Y = C + I + G + X$$
$$C = a + bY$$

where b is the marginal propensity to consume. Because Y is endogenous in this system, we need to solve for a reduced form. Eliminating C produces the equation

$$Y = \frac{a}{1-b} + \frac{1}{1-b}I + \frac{1}{1-b}G + \frac{1}{1-b}X$$

Load the data file multiplier, which contains annual data from 1949 to 2002 on GDP, investment, government expenditure, and net exports.

a. Estimate this model with NLLS. What value do you get for the MPC? What standard error do you get? Calculate a 95 percent confidence interval for the true value of the MPC.

b. To deal with the possibility of a unit root, take the first difference of this equation and estimate the resulting equation. Now what value do you get for the MPC? Calculate a 95 percent confidence interval for the true value of the MPC. How different is your answer?

2. NLLS can be used to fit curves to data that can't be described by linear models, such as the exponential decay model. Mansi and Phillips (2001) use this model to estimate the relationship between the interest rate on government bonds and the length of the bond. Load the data file yield2, which contains monthly data from January 1990 to December 2002, for government bonds of 1, 2, 3, 5, 7, and 10 years, on the following variables: term (length of bond in years), rate (interest rate), longrate (rate on the 10-year bond that month), and shortrate (length on the three-month bond that month).

a. Estimate the relationship $\text{Rate}_t = \beta_0 + \beta_1 \text{Shortrate}_t + \beta_2 \text{Term}_t + \varepsilon_t$. When the length of a bond rises by one year, how much does its interest rate rise? Is the effect statistically significant?

b. The linear functional form implies that each additional year adds the same amount to the interest rate, without an upper limit on the rate. This may be an unrealistic assumption. Instead, assume that there is a minimum rate r and a maximum rate R that the market will provide for any time period. Then the exponential decay model can be written as $\text{Rate} = R - (R - r)e^{-\beta_1 \text{Term}}$, where we expect $\beta_1 > 0$. As Term rises, what is the upper limit on rate? As Term goes to 0, what is the lower limit?

c. One problem with this model is that we cannot observe the maximum and minimum rates. Assume that the maximum is given by $\beta_2 \text{Longrate}$, where we expect $\beta_2 > 1$ so that the maximum is above the long rate, and the range of interest rates $R - r$ is equal to $\beta_3(\text{Longrate} - \text{Shortrate})$, where we expect $\beta_3 > 1$ also. Estimate the model $\text{Rate}_t = \beta_2 \text{Longrate} + \beta_3(\text{Longrate} - \text{Shortrate})e^{-\beta_1 \text{Term}} + \varepsilon_t$ using NLLS. Test the null hypotheses $\beta_2 = 1$ and $\beta_3 = 1$. Did you find what we expect?

d. What is your estimated value of β_1, the exponential decay rate? Using your estimated parameter values, plot the yield curve for terms between 0 and 30 years when the long rate is 6 percent and the short rate is 3 percent. What do you forecast for the rate on a 4-year bond? What do you forecast for a 20-year bond? What do you forecast as the upper limit as the term goes to infinity?

3. In this problem we'll look at inventory adjustments in the U.S. steel and iron industry and see how the adjustment rate in that industry compares to the adjustment rate in automobiles. Load the data file steel, which contains monthly data from January 1967 to December 2002 on inventories and shipments of steel and iron, both measured in millions of real 2002 dollars.

a. Using nonlinear least squares, estimate the equation $\text{Inventories}_t = \lambda \beta_0 + \lambda \beta_1 \text{Shipments}_t + (1 - \lambda)\text{Inventories}_{t-1} + \varepsilon_t$. What is your estimated value for λ? Calculate a 95 percent confidence interval for its true value.

b. Using ordinary least squares, estimate the equation $\text{Inventories}_t = \gamma_0 + \gamma_1 \text{Shipments}_t + \gamma_2 \text{Inventories}_{t-1} + \varepsilon_t$. How would you calculate values of λ, β_0, and β_1 from your estimates $\hat{\gamma}_0$, $\hat{\gamma}_1$, and $\hat{\gamma}_2$? Can you calculate a confidence interval for β_1 from these estimates or not? If you can, do so; if you cannot, explain why not.

c. Using the information in Table 18.1, calculate a 95 percent confidence interval for the speed of adjustment parameter for the automobile industry. Does it overlap the confidence interval you found in part *a*? If it does not, why do you think the speed of inventory adjustment might be different in the steel industry than in the automobile industry?

4. In this problem we'll consider an extension of the Cochrane-Orcutt transformation and estimate it with nonlinear least squares. Open the data file taxrcpt, which was described in problem 7 in Chapter 6.

   a. Estimate the equation $Receipts_t = \beta_0 + \beta_1 GDP_t + \varepsilon_t$, and test whether there is autocorrelation or not.

   b. The Cochrane-Orcutt transformation on the equation in part *a* produces the equation $Receipts_t = (1 - \rho)\beta_0 + \beta_1 GDP_t - \rho\beta_1 GDP_{t-1} + \rho Receipts_{t-1} + v_t$. Estimate this equation with nonlinear least squares. What is your estimated value for β_1? What is your estimated value for ρ? Is your estimate for ρ significantly different from 0? Does this match your finding in the Durbin-Watson test?

   c. Estimate the equation $Receipts_t = \gamma_0 + \gamma_1 GDP_t + \gamma_2 GDP_{t-1} + \gamma_3 Receipts_{t-1} + v_t$. The Cochrane-Orcutt equation suggests that γ_2 should equal $-\gamma_1\gamma_3$. Test this hypothesis. Do you reject it, or fail to reject it?

   d. The correlogram reveals that the autocorrelation structure in this equation actually is $\varepsilon_t = \rho_1\varepsilon_{t-1} + \rho_3\varepsilon_{t-3} + v_t$. Perform the appropriate transformation on the equation to correct this form of autocorrelation, and estimate the resulting equation. What is your estimated value of ρ_3, and is it statistically significantly different from 0, or not?

5. Consider an investor who wants to invest in U.S. Treasury bonds for six months. One possibility is to buy a six-month bond. Another possibility is to buy a three-month bond, let it mature, then use the proceeds to buy a second bond. If investors are risk neutral and have no liquidity preference, then we might believe the expected rate of return on those two investments should be the same. That is, we would believe $R6_t = 1/2R3_t + 1/2E(R3_{t+3})$, where $R6$ is the annual rate on the six-month bond, $R3$ is the annual rate on the three-month bond, and $E(R3_{t+3})$ is the present expected value of the three-month rate three months from now, when the investor plans to reinvest. To estimate this model, we need to write an equation for $E(R3_{t+3})$. A simple model is to let $E(R3_{t+3})$ depend on present and past values of the three-month interest rate. Load the data file yield, which contains monthly data from January 1983 to December 2002 on the following variables: rate3 (three-month bond rate), rate6 (six-month bond rate), and futurerate3 (three-month bond rate three months ahead).

   a. Using nonlinear SUR, estimate the system of equations

   $$Futurerate3 = \beta_0 + \beta_1 Rate3_t + \beta_2 Rate3_{t-1} + \varepsilon_t$$
   $$Rate6_t = \gamma_0 + \gamma_1 Rate3_t + \gamma_2(\beta_0 + \beta_1 Rate3_t + \beta_2 Rate3_{t-1}) + v_t$$

   where the first equation produces the expected value of future rates for the second equation. How many of the parameters are statistically significantly different from 0?

   b. Test the joint null hypothesis $\gamma_1 = 1/2$ and $\gamma_2 = 1/2$. Do you reject, or fail to reject, this null hypothesis? Is the theory described above supported or not?

c. Perhaps the six-month rate depends on the three-month rate and the future rate, but not in equal proportions. Test the null hypothesis $\gamma_1 + \gamma_2 = 1$. Do you reject, or fail to reject, this null hypothesis? What does this suggest about the market to you?

d. The theory described above also suggests $\gamma_0 = 0$. Test this null hypothesis. What do you find? Explain the result in terms of risk or liquidity preference.

e. We could multiply out the multiplication in the second equation to get

$$\text{Futurerate3} = \beta_0 + \beta_1 \text{Rate3}_t + \beta_2 \text{Rate3}_{t-1} + \varepsilon_t$$

$$\text{Rate6}_t = \alpha_0 + \alpha_1 \text{Rate3}_t + \alpha_2 \text{Rate3}_{t-1} + \upsilon_t$$

This model has the advantage of being linear. Can we test this problem's theory with the linear model? Briefly explain why or why not.

6. In this problem we'll deal with a model that produces a nonlinear equation similar to that of the stock adjustment model, but from rather different economic assumptions. Consider the effect of advertising on a firm's sales. Because advertisements build up a market presence for a firm, they can increase sales not only in the year they are run but in the future as well. Thus, present sales may depend on the history of advertisements run in the past:

$$\text{Sales}_t = \beta_0 + \beta_1 X_t + \beta_2 \text{Ad}_t + \beta_3 \text{Ad}_{t-1} + \beta_4 \text{Ad}_{t-2} + \beta_5 \text{Ad}_{t-3} + \cdots + \varepsilon_t$$

where X is any other variable affecting sales. This model contains an infinite number of parameters and cannot be estimated. To reduce the number of parameters, assume that the effect of advertising decays over time geometrically, so that $\beta_3 = \beta_2 \lambda$, $\beta_4 = \beta_2 \lambda^2$, $\beta_5 = \beta_2 \lambda^3$, and so forth. Then we can write the equation as:

$$\text{Sales}_t = \beta_0 + \beta_1 X_t + \beta_2 \text{Ad}_t + \beta_2 \lambda \text{Ad}_{t-1} + \beta_2 \lambda^2 \text{Ad}_{t-2} + \beta_2 \lambda^3 \text{Ad}_{t-3} + \cdots + \varepsilon_t$$

Adding this assumption produces a model known as the *Koyck model,* which is often used in situations where one variable has an effect on another over a long period. Lag this equation one period and multiply by λ to get

$$\lambda \text{Sales}_{t-1} = \lambda \beta_0 + \lambda \beta_1 X_{t-1} + \lambda \beta_2 \text{Ad}_{t-1} + \beta_2 \lambda^2 \text{Ad}_{t-2} + \beta_2 \lambda^3 \text{Ad}_{t-3} + \cdots + \lambda \varepsilon_{t-1}$$

Subtracting the last equation from the second-to-last cancels out all of the lagged advertising terms, leaving the equation

$$\text{Sales}_t = (1 - \lambda)\beta_0 + \lambda \text{Sales}_{t-1} + \beta_1 X_t - \lambda \beta_1 X_{t-1} + \beta_2 \text{Ad}_t + \varepsilon_t - \lambda \varepsilon_{t-1}$$

which contains a finite number of terms and can be estimated, although because Sales_{t-1} is correlated with ε_{t-1}, it must be estimated by two-stage least squares (see Chapter 14). Last year's advertising is a good instrument to use to identify the model. Load the data file salesads, which contains data for 52 different industries for the years 1998 to 2001 on the following variables: Sales, Advertising, Assets (book assets of industry firms), Lastsales (previous year's sales), Lastads, Lastassets, and dummy variables for each of the 52 industries in the data. All financial variables are measured in millions of dollars.

a. Using nonlinear two-stage least squares, estimate the equation $\text{Sales}_{it} = (1 - \lambda)\beta_0 + \lambda \text{Lastsales}_{it} + \beta_1 \text{Assets}_{it} - \lambda \beta_1 \text{Lastassets}_{it} + \beta_2 \text{Advertising}_{it} + \delta_i D_i + \varepsilon_t$, where D_i is a fixed effect dummy variable, using Lastads as an instrument to identify the model. Is β_1 statistically significantly different from 0? Does the amount of assets held by an industry affect its sales or not?

b. If you found that β_1 was not statistically different from 0, reestimate the model imposing the restriction $\beta_1 = 0$.

c. If a firm increases its advertising by $1 million, how much do its sales rise that year? Is the effect statistically significantly different from 0? It wouldn't make much sense for a firm to advertise if $\beta_1 < 1$, because the sales increase wouldn't cover the cost of the advertising. Test the null hypothesis $\beta_1 = 1$ against the alternative that $\beta_1 > 1$. What do you find?

d. Test whether $\lambda = 0$. If a firm increases its advertising by $1 million, how much do its sales increase the following year (holding its advertising the following year constant at the previous level)? How much does it rise two years in the future?

Chapter Nineteen

Dummy Dependent Variables

To all those who depend on welfare, we offer this simple compact: We will provide the support, the job training, the child care you need for up to two years. But after that, anyone who can work must work—in the private sector if possible, in community service if necessary. We will make welfare what it ought to be: A second chance, not a way of life.

President Bill Clinton, State of the Union address, 1994

19.1 WELFARE REFORM AND THE DECISION TO WORK

The Personal Responsibility and Work Opportunity Reconciliation Act of 1996 was promised to "end welfare as we know it." The centerpiece of this promise was to require welfare recipients to work, with the intention of getting them off welfare and back into the productive economy. To enforce this requirement, the act set a time limit on welfare payments; after their allotted time ended, recipients became ineligible for further welfare regardless of other qualifications for the program.[1] Critics of the act focused on the possibility that a recipient might be unable to find work on any terms, regardless of his or her incentive to do so. To deal with this criticism, the act contained provisions to assist recipients in finding work. Some of these provisions provided job training and other ways for recipients to acquire productive skills; others were intended to make working possible by providing transportation to job sites, child care, and so on.

The effect of those provisions depends on the extent to which welfare recipients respond to their incentives to join the labor force and obtain jobs. To assess the prospects for welfare reform—and the extent to which job training, child care, and similar programs can help move welfare recipients into the workforce—it is necessary to study the process by which people decide whether or not to work. Economic models of labor force participation are relatively straightforward. Potential workers weigh the benefits of work income against

---

[1] The limit was two years for any one period on welfare, with a five-year lifetime limit. However, states were allowed to make individual exceptions to the five-year limit, and the definition of *work* was left sufficiently vague that it was unclear how many recipients, if indeed any, would actually be removed from the welfare rolls when the five-year limit began to matter in 2002.

FIGURE 19.1
Data with a
Dummy
Dependent
Variable

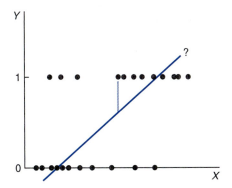

the benefits of other uses of their time, such as education and child rearing, and choose to work if the benefits of the former are greater than those of the latter.

Econometrically, however, these models differ from those studied earlier in this book, because the dependent variable—whether or not a person chooses to work—is a dummy variable that takes only two values. The least squares principle is fundamentally flawed for models in which the dependent variable is a dummy variable. Figure 19.1 shows a graph of an independent variable X, which is continuous and can take any value, and a dependent dummy variable Y. The data can lie only along two horizontal lines on the plot, one where $Y = 1$ and the other where $Y = 0$. However, the best-fitting line will invariably cross between the two lines where the data are grouped. Mathematically, the least squares principle still works; the red line in Figure 19.1 is the best-fitting line, and the pink line is the residual for the data point at the upper end of that line. Economically, however, this line is very difficult to interpret sensibly. The line has an equation of the form

$$\hat{Y}_i = \hat{\beta}_0 + \hat{\beta}_1 X_i \tag{19.1.1}$$

and the value of $\hat{Y}$ is not limited to 1 or 0—it can, and does, take any value. For the observation whose residual is shown, $\hat{Y}$ is about 0.6. However, what interpretation do we give to $\hat{Y} = 0.6$ when $Y = 1$ means that a person is working, $Y = 0$ means that the person is not working, and any other value has no meaning at all?

One possibility is to give $\hat{Y}$ a probability interpretation. We can take $\hat{Y} = 0.6$ to mean that there is a 60 percent chance that $Y = 1$ (the person works) and a 40 percent chance that $Y = 0$ (the person does not work).

Definition 19.1 The *linear probability model* of a dummy dependent variable assumes that P_i, the chance that the dummy variable Y_i is equal to 1 for observation i, is given by

$$P_i = \beta_0 + \beta_1 X_i \tag{19.1.2}$$

And we can show that the linear probability model works in a purely statistical sense:

Theorem 19.1 Suppose the true data generating process is the linear probability model, and we estimate the equation

$$Y_i = \beta_0 + \beta_1 X_i + \varepsilon_i \tag{19.1.3}$$

by least squares. Then the resulting estimates of $\hat{\beta}_0$ and $\hat{\beta}_1$ are consistent estimators of the true values of β_0 and β_1.

However, the model is not very satisfying on other grounds. Suppose the true values of β_0 and β_1 are 0.5 and 0.1, respectively, and for one particular observation, $X_i = 3$. Then the ordinary least squares (OLS) equation implies that $Y_i = 0.5 + (0.1 \cdot 3) + \varepsilon_i = 0.8 + \varepsilon_i$. Because it is a dummy variable, Y_i can only take the values 0 or 1. This implies that ε_i can take only the values 0.2 (to make $Y_i = 1$) or -0.8 (to make $Y_i = 0$). This would be a strange distribution for the error term to take. Worse, for a different observation, ε_i would have to take different values. Suppose for another observation, $X_i = 2$; then for that observation, ε_i can take only the values 0.3 or -0.7. The values that ε_i can take would be different for each possible value of X_i. This would imply that ε_i would be both heteroskedastic and not independent of X_i. Under those conditions, OLS is not very efficient.

Furthermore, the original problem of interpretation has not been completely solved. Suppose that for a third observation $X_i = 7$. Then for that observation we get $\hat{Y}_i = 1.2$. We cannot interpret this as meaning that there is a 120 percent chance that a person would choose to work. As Figure 19.1 shows, any fitted regression line whose slope is not exactly 0 will eventually rise above $Y = 1$ on the graph and will also drop below $Y = 0$. This means that there will always be some values of X for which we predict more than a 100 percent chance that $Y = 1$ and others for which we predict less than a 0 percent chance. There is no way to use the linear probability model to avoid this problem. For this reason, the linear probability model is no longer used in econometric analysis, although since it does produce consistent estimates, it was commonly used before newer methods were developed.

Ultimately, the problem is that the concept of least squares itself does not make sense in the context of a dummy dependent variable. When the only values that Y_i can take are 0 and 1, it does not make economic sense to draw a line on a graph like Figure 19.1, or to talk about how "close" the line is to the data. That is, $\hat{Y}_i$ should be equal to either 1 or 0, nothing else. This implies that the least squares principle itself is not useful for estimating models with dummy dependent variables. There are many economic models with dummy dependent variables: choosing to be in the labor force or not to be, finding a job or not finding one, owning a house or renting an apartment, buying a car or not, retaining earnings within a corporation or paying a dividend, and more. To give such econometric models a sensible economic interpretation, we will need to find a new approach to estimating their parameters. In this chapter we present an alternative approach that is useful in the case of dummy dependent variables and then show how to estimate and interpret the parameters of that model to reach economically useful conclusions.

19.2 MAXIMUM LIKELIHOOD: A NEW ESTIMATING PRINCIPLE

A person who is deciding whether or not to work must calculate the benefits of working, calculate the benefits of alternative uses of his or her time, and decide which is greater. We can write the net benefits of work as

$$\text{Net benefits} = \text{Benefits of work} - \text{Benefits of alternatives} \qquad \textbf{(19.2.1)}$$

and assert that the person will work if the net benefits are positive, and will not work if the net benefits are negative. We could then assert that the net benefits from working depend on exogenous variables like age, educational level and number of children, and on unobserved factors not in our model that produce an error term. We write:

$$NB_i = \beta_0 + \beta_1 Educ_i + \beta_2 Age_i + \beta_3 Kids_i + \varepsilon_i \qquad \textbf{(19.2.2)}$$

where NB is the net benefit of person i, Educ is his or her educational level, Age is age, Kids is the number of children the person has, and ε_i is the error term representing all the things that influence the person's decision to work that we do not observe.

Unfortunately, we cannot estimate Equation 19.2.2, because we cannot observe the net benefits a given person gets from working. All we know is whether or not the person chooses to work.

Definition 19.2 A *latent variable* is one we cannot observe. We must make an inference about its value on the basis of a related variable that we can observe.

Even though we cannot observe the latent variable NB_i, the net benefits of work, we can learn something about it from observing the person's work decision. If we observe a person working, we can conclude that the net benefit from work is positive, and if we observe a person not working, we can conclude that the net benefit is negative. Mathematically, if we observe $Y_i = 1$, we can infer $NB_i > 0$, and if $Y_i = 0$, we can infer $NB_i < 0$.[2]

It turns out that this knowledge about NB_i is enough to let us estimate the parameters of Equation 19.2.2. Because of the error term, the net benefits any one person receives from working are random. We can say that Y_i will equal 1 if

$$NB_i = \beta_0 + \beta_1 Educ_i + \beta_2 Age_i + \beta_3 Kids_i + \varepsilon_i > 0 \qquad \textbf{(19.2.3)}$$

and we can rearrange that condition as

$$\varepsilon_i > -\beta_0 - \beta_1 Educ_i - \beta_2 Age_i - \beta_3 Kids_i \qquad \textbf{(19.2.4)}$$

To simplify the notation, we define

$$\overline{NB}_i = \beta_0 + \beta_1 Educ_i + \beta_2 Age_i + \beta_3 Kids_i \qquad \textbf{(19.2.5)}$$

and we can write Equation 19.2.3 as $\varepsilon_i > -\overline{NB}_i$.

This condition is shown graphically in Figure 19.2. Because of the error term, NB_i is a random variable with some distribution function. This distribution function will be

FIGURE 19.2

Distribution of Net Benefits

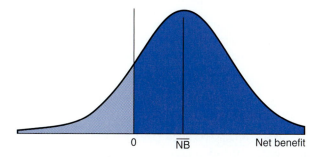

^{2} We do not worry about the case that $NB_i = 0$. Because NB_i contains the error term ε_i, it is random and can take any value. The odds that it will take *exactly* the value 0 are themselves 0 and can be ignored. If we prefer not to ignore it, we can assume that $D_i = 1$ if $NB_1 \geq 0$; the probability is exactly the same as the probability $NB_1 > 0$.

centered around $\overline{\text{NB}}_i$.[3] The chance that NB_i will be positive is equal to the red-shaded area in the figure; this is the chance that the person will choose to work. The chance that NB_i will be negative is equal to the pink-shaded area; this is the chance that the person will choose not to work. If $\overline{\text{NB}}_i > 0$, as drawn in the figure, there will be more than a 50 percent chance that the person will choose to work; if $\overline{\text{NB}}_i < 0$, then there will be more than a 50 percent chance that he or she will not work.

Whether $\text{NB}_i > 0$ depends on the error term ε_i as well as on $\overline{\text{NB}}_i$. If, as shown in Figure 19.2, $\overline{\text{NB}}_i$ is positive, then the person will choose to work if ε_i takes any positive value, or a negative value that is less (in absolute value) than $\overline{\text{NB}}_i$. The person will choose not to work only if the error term is negative, and larger (in absolute value) than the positive value of $\overline{\text{NB}}_i$, causing total net benefits from work to be negative and fall into the red region of Figure 19.2. If $\overline{\text{NB}}_i$ is negative, then the person will choose not to work for any negative value of the error term, or for any positive value of the error term smaller than the absolute value of $\overline{\text{NB}}_i$. Only if the error term is positive and larger than the absolute value of $\overline{\text{NB}}_i$ will the person choose to work.

We can write these results in terms of the distribution function of the error term. Let $F(\varepsilon_i)$ be the cumulative distribution function of ε_i. Then, whether $\overline{\text{NB}}_i$ is positive or negative, the pink area is the chance that $\varepsilon_i < -\overline{\text{NB}}_i$, which is $F(-\overline{\text{NB}}_i)$, and the red area is equal to $1 - F(-\overline{\text{NB}}_i)$, since the total area under the distribution function must be 1. We can then say that the probability that the person will choose to work is equal to $1 - F(-\overline{\text{NB}}_i)$, and the chance that he or she will choose not to work is equal to $F(-\overline{\text{NB}}_i)$.

With this, we can now draw a connection between the values of the $\hat{\beta}$ parameters and the chance that a given person will work or not. Replacing $\overline{\text{NB}}_i$ with its definition from Equation 19.2.5, we can say that the chance that a person works is equal to

$$\Pr(Y = 1) = 1 - F(-\beta_0 - \beta_1 \text{Educ}_i - \beta_2 \text{Age}_i - \beta_3 \text{Kids}_i) \qquad \textbf{(19.2.6)}$$

and the chance that the person does not work is equal to

$$\Pr(Y = 0) = F(-\beta_0 - \beta_1 \text{Educ}_i - \beta_2 \text{Age}_i - \beta_3 \text{Kids}_i) \qquad \textbf{(19.2.7)}$$

where Y is a dummy variable that is 1 if the person works and 0 if not.

> **Definition 19.3** The *likelihood* of the ith observation is the chance that Y takes the value we observe it to take. For a person who works, the likelihood is $\Pr(Y = 1)$; for a person who does not work, the likelihood is $\Pr(Y = 0)$.

The likelihood of each observation thus depends on the value of the β parameters and on whether or not the person chooses to work. We can also think about the likelihood of the entire sample, which is the chance that every person in the sample chooses to do what he or she is observed to do.

> **Definition 19.4** The *likelihood function* is the chance that Y_i takes the value we observe for every observation in the sample.

The chance that a group of observations takes the observed values for Y_i is equal to the product of the chances for each observation. We can therefore write the likelihood

---

[3] The figure is drawn with the assumption that ε_i is normally distributed, but that need not be the case; ε_i can take any distribution as long as the mean value is 0.

function as

$$L(\beta) = \prod_{Y=1} \Pr(Y_i = 1) \cdot \prod_{Y=0} \Pr(Y_i = 0) \qquad \textbf{(19.2.8)}$$

where the first term represents those observations where we observe $Y = 1$ and the second term represents the observations for which we observe $Y = 0$. Substituting Equations 19.2.6 and 19.2.7 into the likelihood function produces

$$L(\beta) = \prod_{Y=1} 1 - F(-\beta_0 - \beta_1 \text{Educ}_i - \beta_2 \text{Age}_i - \beta_3 \text{Kids}_i)$$

$$\cdot \prod_{Y=0} F(-\beta_0 - \beta_1 \text{Educ}_i - \beta_2 \text{Age}_i - \beta_3 \text{Kids}_i) \qquad \textbf{(19.2.9)}$$

We can see that the likelihood function depends explicitly on the β parameters of the model.

Definition 19.5 The *maximum likelihood principle* is to choose estimated values of the β parameters that maximize the likelihood function. The *maximum likelihood estimates* are the values for which the chance of observing the sample we actually observe is as large as possible.

The maximum likelihood estimates give us a way to calculate estimates of the parameters of the model without the use of residuals or other calculations that are not sensible in the case of dummy dependent variables.

The maximum likelihood principle is not limited to dummy dependent variables. It can be applied to any econometric model containing a random variable whose distribution function is known. For a simple case, consider the problem of estimating the probability that a coin will land heads when tossed. Let the chance of heads be μ and the chance of tails be $(1 - \mu)$, and suppose we observe that the coin produces 2 heads and 1 tails in three flips. The chance of getting 2 heads and 1 tails is equal to $3\mu^2(1 - \mu)^1$. The maximum likelihood estimate of μ is the value that makes that chance as high as possible, because 2 heads and 1 tails is what we actually observed. If we thought the coin was fair—that is, we took the estimated value to be $\hat{\mu} = 0.5$—then the chance of 2 heads and 1 tails would be $3 \cdot 0.25 \cdot 0.5 = 0.375$. But other values of $\hat{\mu}$ produce higher chances for observing 2 heads and 1 tails. If we instead assume $\hat{\mu} = 0.6$, then the chance is 0.432. We can find the value of $\hat{\mu}$ that maximizes the chance of getting 2 heads and 1 tails by taking the derivative of $3\hat{\mu}^2(1 - \hat{\mu})^1$ with respect to $\hat{\mu}$ and setting it equal to 0. The solution is $\hat{\mu} = \frac{2}{3}$. This value of $\hat{\mu}$ produces a chance of observing 2 heads and 1 tails equal to 0.444, which is higher than the chance produced by any other possible value of $\hat{\mu}$, and so $\frac{2}{3}$ is therefore the maximum likelihood estimate of μ from this sample.[4]

The maximum likelihood principle can also be applied to the classical regression model, as an alternative to the least squares principle for choosing estimated parameter values. If the Gauss-Markov assumptions are true, including assumption A6 (normal distribution of the

---

[4] In general it can be shown that the maximum likelihood estimator for the chance that the coin is heads will be equal to the fraction of tosses that are heads in the sample. If you set the derivative of $3\mu^2(1 - \mu)^1$ equal to 0 and solve the equation, you will find that it has two solutions, $\frac{2}{3}$ and 0. The second derivative test reveals that $\frac{2}{3}$ is a maximum value and 0 is a minimum value of the likelihood function.

error term), then maximum likelihood and least squares produce exactly the same formula for the estimated values of the parameters. However, the maximum likelihood method requires us to know the exact distribution of the error terms, whereas least squares remains unbiased and consistent without any such assumption. It is therefore generally better to use the least squares principle to calculate estimates where that is possible, turning to maximum likelihood in cases like the dummy dependent variable model, where least squares cannot be applied.

It turns out that calculating the values that maximize the likelihood function is a difficult task. It is easier to take the natural logarithm of both sides of Equation 19.2.9 to get

$$\log L(\beta) = \sum_{Y=1} \log[1 - F(-\beta_0 - \beta_1 \text{Educ}_i - \beta_2 \text{Age}_i - \beta_3 \text{Kids}_i)]$$

$$+ \sum_{Y=0} \log[F(-\beta_0 - \beta_1 \text{Educ}_i - \beta_2 \text{Age}_i - \beta_3 \text{Kids}_i)] \qquad \textbf{(19.2.10)}$$

which is called the *log likelihood function,* and which is easier to maximize in practical terms.

Theorem 19.2 The values of the β parameters that maximize the log likelihood function are the same as the values that maximize the likelihood function.

This is true because the log function is a strictly increasing function. For any two values of the β parameters, the one that gives a higher value of $L(\beta)$ also gives a higher value of $\log L(\beta)$. Therefore, the value of β that produces the highest possible value of $\log L(\beta)$ is the same value that produces the highest value of $L(\beta)$ and is thus the maximum likelihood estimate. The virtue of this theorem is that it assures us we can maximize either the likelihood function or the log likelihood function, whichever is more convenient, and get the same answer. In some cases, the equations found by setting the derivatives of the likelihood or log likelihood function equal to 0 can be solved to find values for the β parameters of the model. More frequently, they cannot be solved, in which case we use a computer to calculate the value of the function for different values of the β parameters, searching iteratively until we find the values that maximize the function.

How good are the estimates provided by maximum likelihood? In general, we can say the following:

Theorem 19.3 Under the assumption that the model is correctly specified, maximum likelihood estimates of the model's parameters are consistent and approximately normally distributed. As the sample size grows large, they are efficient.

Maximum likelihood estimates are not necessarily unbiased, but at least they tend toward the correct values as the sample grows larger, and for large enough samples they are better than any other consistent estimators available to us. We can also estimate their standard errors, and with their standard errors we can use the normal distribution table to calculate confidence intervals and test hypotheses about their values.

19.3   THE PROBIT MODEL OF A DUMMY DEPENDENT VARIABLE

Maximum likelihood gives us a method to estimate the parameters of a model with a dummy dependent variable, as long as we can write down a model of the data generating process like the one in the preceding section. To perform the maximization, however, we have to specify F, the cumulative distribution function of the error term.

Definition 19.6 The *probit model* assumes that the true likelihood function is given by

$$L(\beta) = \prod_{Y=1} \Pr(Y_i = 1) \cdot \prod_{Y=0} \Pr(Y_i = 0) \qquad \textbf{(19.3.1)}$$

where the error term that creates the probabilities is distributed normally with mean 0 and variance 1.

With this assumption, and with the knowledge of the normal cumulative distribution function, we can calculate the probability that each person in a sample of data will choose to work or not work, and pick the values of the β parameters that maximize the likelihood that we observe the decisions that the people in the sample actually made.

One difficulty with the probit model is that, as discussed in Chapter 3, we cannot write an equation for the normal cumulative distribution function. Instead, we define $\Phi(X)$ to be the standard normal distribution function, so that $\Phi(X)$ is the chance that a normally distributed random variable with mean 0 and variance 1 is less than X. For example, $\Phi(0.5) = 0.691$, as can be seen in Appendix A. When we estimate a probit model, we must use an approximation of $\Phi(X)$ to maximize the likelihood function.

To demonstrate the probit model, we consider a sample of the work decisions of 2,532 single women with children, taken from the Consumer Expenditure Survey published by the Bureau of Labor Statistics.[5] We refine Equation 19.2.2 in one way, which is to count separately the number of children ages 0–2, and the number ages 3–15. Younger children require more care, and there may be greater benefits to not working if a parent has younger rather than older children. The equation for the net benefits of work is thus

$$\text{NB}_i = \beta_0 + \beta_1 \text{Educ}_i + \beta_2 \text{Age}_i + \beta_3 \text{Kids02}_i + \beta_4 \text{Kids315}_i + \varepsilon_i \qquad \textbf{(19.3.2)}$$

and we expect that $\beta_3 < \beta_4 < 0$, because more children of any age should reduce the net benefit of work, but younger children should reduce it more.

The results of estimating Equation 19.3.2 by the probit model are shown in Table 19.1. The table reports Z statistics rather than t statistics because the parameters do not take the t distribution in small samples. Even the normal distribution is only approximate, as Theorem 19.3 says, so the Z statistics are themselves only approximately correct, but the

TABLE 19.1
Probit (Maximum Likelihood) Estimates of Equation 19.3.2

Variable	Parameter	Estimate	Standard Error	Z Statistic for $\beta = 0$
Intercept	β_0	−0.084	0.232	−0.36
Education	β_1	0.152	0.014	10.7
Age	β_2	−0.015	0.003	−5.06
Children ages 0–2	β_3	−0.794	0.101	−7.84
Children ages 3–15	β_4	−0.290	0.030	−9.53

$N = 2532$ ... $\log L = -930.1$

[5] We consider only single women to avoid dealing with the possibilities that a married woman's husband is also influenced by her decision to work and that his preferences may affect her decision as well as her own. This simplifies the economic model; if we included the husband's influence in the model, the econometric approach would be similar.

approximation gets better as the sample gets larger. The critical Z value for 5 percent significance is 1.96, and we can therefore conclude that all of the parameters (except the intercept) are statistically significantly different from 0. The maximized value of the log likelihood function is -930.1. (For the probit model, the value of the likelihood function is always negative, because the chance of each person working or not working is less than 1, so the log of each chance is always negative, and so is the sum of the logs of the chances.)

If we wish to know how well the model fits the data, we cannot use the R^2 measure that we use for least squares regression, because there is no sum of squared residuals (or total sum of squares) we can use to calculate it in the probit model. Instead, the probit model deals with the probability that the woman chooses to work or not work. We therefore look to see how well our model predicts the decisions of the women in the sample.

We can calculate estimated net benefits for every woman in the sample using the estimated parameters of the model:

$$\widehat{NB}_i = \hat{\beta}_0 + \hat{\beta}_1 Educ_i + \hat{\beta}_2 Age_i + \hat{\beta}_3 Kids02_i + \hat{\beta}_3 Kids315_i \quad \textbf{(19.3.3)}$$

where the difference between $\widehat{NB}_i$ and $\overline{NB}_i$ is that $\widehat{NB}_i$ uses the estimated $\hat{\beta}$ values whereas $\overline{NB}_i$ uses the true β values. We can then use $\widehat{NB}_i$ to forecast each woman's decision to work or not work. If $\widehat{NB}_i > 0$, then the chance that the woman will not work is less than 50 percent (because the chance that $\varepsilon_i < -\widehat{NB}_i$ is less than 50 percent) and so we predict that she will choose to work. If $\widehat{NB}_i < 0$, then the chance that the woman will not work is more than 50 percent, so we predict that she will choose to work.

> **Definition 19.7** The predicted value of Y_i from the probit model, $\hat{Y}_i$, is equal to 1 if $\widehat{NB}_i > 0$ and is equal to 0 if $\widehat{NB}_i < 0$.

We can then calculate the fraction of women in the sample for whom our prediction is correct (that is, $\hat{Y}_i = 1$ if $Y_i = 1$, and $\hat{Y}_i = 0$ if $Y_i = 0$) and use that as a measure of how well the model fits the data.

The parameter estimates in Table 19.1 correctly predict the work decision of 84.6 percent of the women in the sample. On the one hand, this seems like a very impressive fit. On the other hand, the fraction of women in the sample who work is 83.2 percent. Had we ignored our model, and simply predicted that all women work, we would have correctly predicted the work decision of 83.2 percent of the women in the sample. Our econometric model has not improved our ability to predict women's decisions very much, although it has improved it somewhat. This suggests that the model does not fit the data particularly well.

19.4 EFFECTS OF CHANGING INDEPENDENT VARIABLES IN THE PROBIT MODEL

The probit model tells us that the chance that a woman will choose to work is influenced by the dependent variables Age, Educ, Kids02, and Kids315. To use the results of estimating the model to analyze policies dealing with working women, we would like to know whether higher values of those variables increase or decrease the chance that a woman will work, and by how much it will change the chance. For a simple answer, we can use Equation 19.3.2 to interpret the signs of the $\hat{\beta}$ estimates. Because $\hat{\beta}_1$ is positive and significantly different from 0, an increase in a single woman's education increases her net benefits from working. Presumably, greater education makes it possible for her to earn a higher wage and hence a higher income if she chooses to work. The parameter $\hat{\beta}_2$ is negative, meaning that the older a woman is, the lower her net benefits of working; similarly, the parameters $\hat{\beta}_3$ and $\hat{\beta}_4$ are negative, meaning that the more children a woman has, the lower her net benefits of working (probably because the benefits of staying home are greater).

This, however, is not fully satisfying, because it describes only the effects of the independent variables on the latent variable, which we don't observe. We would prefer to know how a change in education or number of children affects the chance that a woman will choose to work or not work. Fortunately, the two are directly linked, because the chance that a woman works is equal to the chance that $NB_i > 0$. Therefore, anything that increases the expected net benefits of working increases the chance that the woman will choose to work, and anything that decreases the expected net benefits of working reduces that chance.

This point is demonstrated graphically in Figure 19.3. An increase in a woman's level of education increases $\widehat{NB}_i$, and hence shifts the distribution function of the random variable NB_i to the right. As the distribution shifts to the right, the chance that the woman will work rises, increasing by the red area in the figure. Conversely, an increase in the number of children she has decreases $\widehat{NB}_i$, and shifts the distribution function of NB_i to the left. This increases the chance that the woman will choose not to work.

More generally, suppose that the dummy variable Y_i is generated by the probit model, where $Y_i = 1$ if the latent variable $Y_i^* > 0$, and

$$Y_i^* = \beta_0 + \beta_1 X_{1i} + \beta_2 X_{2i} + \cdots + \beta_K X_{Ki} + \varepsilon_i \qquad \textbf{(19.4.1)}$$

Then we can say the following:

Theorem 19.4 If $\beta_k > 0$, an increase in X_{ki} increases the chance that $Y_i = 1$. If $\beta_k < 0$, an increase in X_{ki} decreases the chance that $Y_i = 1$. If $\beta_k = 0$, then an increase in X_{ki} has no effect on the chance that $Y_i = 1$.

We might, however, want to know more than this; we might want to know how much the chance that $Y_i = 1$ changes when one of the X variables changes. (Since it can be equal only to 1 or 0, it will change for some observations in the sample and not for others.) The size of the increase can be important. In the case of the decision to work, we might have one opinion about providing job training to welfare recipients if the training increases the chance that the trainee will work by 20 percent, and a very different one if the training increases that chance by only 0.1 percent.

FIGURE 19.3
Effect on an Increase in Education on Chance of Work

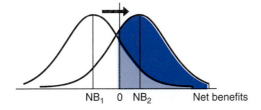

NB₁ 0 NB₂   Net benefits

Definition 19.8 The *probability derivatives* of the probit model are the change in the chance that $Y = 1$ that occurs when each of the independent variables X_k changes. That is, the probability derivative of Y with respect to X_k is equal to

$$\frac{\partial \Pr(Y_i = 1)}{\partial X_k} \qquad (19.4.2)$$

Unfortunately, calculating the probability derivatives turns out to be somewhat complex. The probability that an individual chooses to work is $1 - \Phi(-\text{NB}_i)$. Changing one of the X variables changes NB_i and therefore changes this probability. The derivative of NB_i with respect to one of the independent variables X_k is just β_k. Therefore, by the chain rule, the derivative of the probability of working with respect to X_k is equal to

$$\frac{\partial \Pr(D_i = 1)}{\partial X_k} = -\frac{d\Phi}{d\text{NB}_i} \cdot -\beta_k \qquad (19.4.3)$$

The derivative of Φ, the normal cumulative distribution function, is equal to the normal density function, as Figure 19.4 shows. $\Phi(X)$ is, by definition, the chance that a normally distributed random variable is less than X. If we raise X very slightly, the resulting increase in the area to the left of X under the curve is approximately equal to the height of the curve. The height of the curve is the normal density function, which we write as $\phi(X)$. Thus we have

$$\frac{d\Phi}{d\text{NB}_i} = \phi(\text{NB}_i) = \frac{1}{\sqrt{2\pi}} e^{-\frac{1}{2}\text{NB}_i^2} \qquad (19.4.4)$$

We can cancel the negative signs in Equation 19.4.3 and use Equation 19.4.4 to write

$$\frac{\partial \Pr(D_i = 1)}{\partial X_k} = \phi(\text{NB}_i)\beta_k \qquad (19.4.5)$$

That is, the probability derivative with respect to X_k is equal to its parameter β_k multiplied by $\phi(\text{NB}_i)$. Since we don't know the true values of either β_k or NB_i, we will replace them with their estimated values to calculate the probability derivatives in practice.

This formula for the probability derivatives has two features—one useful, one not. The useful one is that the probability derivative with respect to X_k is proportional to β_k. If β_1 is twice as large as β_2, then a one-unit change in X_1 has twice as much effect on the chance that the person will choose to work as a one-unit change in X_2 has. Thus the size of the β parameters is meaningfully related to the size of the effect of a one-unit change in the associated variable.[6] The feature that is not useful is that the value of $\phi(\text{NB}_i)$ depends on NB_i,

FIGURE 19.4
Effect of a
Small Change
in X on $\Phi(X)$

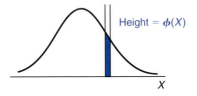

Height $= \phi(X)$

X

---

[6] Of course, if we change the units in which the X variables are measured, the estimates of the β parameters will change accordingly. As is the case with least squares, the effect of a one-unit change in X depends critically on what the units of X are. Two estimated parameters can be meaningfully compared only insofar as the units in which the variables are measured are comparable.

the net benefits of work for each person, and thus is different for each person in the sample. Therefore, we cannot talk about how much the chance of work changes when, for instance, education changes. The amount of change is different for each person in the sample.

In some ways this is not surprising. The results in Table 19.1 suggest that a young, highly educated, childless woman would be very likely to work. For a 30-year-old woman with a college degree and no children, we have

$$\widehat{NB}_i = \hat{\beta}_0 + \hat{\beta}_1 16 + \hat{\beta}_2 30 + \hat{\beta}_3 0 + \hat{\beta}_4 0 \qquad \textbf{(19.4.6)}$$

which, using the estimates in Table 19.1, works out to 1.892. This woman will choose to work as long as $\varepsilon_i > -1.892$. This is very likely; the chance that this woman will work is equal to $1 - \Phi(-1.892)$. Appendix A, the normal distribution table, shows that $\Phi(-1.892)$ is approximately equal to 2.9 percent. Therefore, the chance that this woman will work is about 97.1 percent. If this woman gains one additional year of education, then her net benefits are

$$\widehat{NB}_i = \hat{\beta}_0 + \hat{\beta}_1 17 + \hat{\beta}_2 30 + \hat{\beta}_3 0 + \hat{\beta}_4 0 \qquad \textbf{(19.4.7)}$$

which is equal to 2.044. The chance that she will then work is $1 - \Phi(2.044)$, which is 98.0 percent. The extra year of education increases the chance that she will work by only 0.9 percent. This happens because, when the chance of the woman working is 97 percent to begin with, an additional year of education can increase it by only a small amount.

Suppose we instead look at a woman with different values of the right-hand-side variables: a 35-year-old woman with a 10th-grade education and three children, all older than age 2. For this woman, the net benefits of working are

$$\widehat{NB}_i = \hat{\beta}_0 + \hat{\beta}_1 10 + \hat{\beta}_2 35 + \hat{\beta}_3 0 + \hat{\beta}_4 3 \qquad \textbf{(19.4.8)}$$

which works out to 0.033. This woman's predicted net benefits are very close to 0, suggesting that she is almost indifferent between working and not working. The chance that she will work is $1 - \Phi(0.033)$, which is 51.3 percent; the chance that she will not work is 48.7 percent. If she gains an extra year of education, then her net benefits rise to

$$\widehat{NB}_i = \hat{\beta}_0 + \hat{\beta}_1 11 + \hat{\beta}_2 35 + \hat{\beta}_3 0 + \hat{\beta}_4 3 \qquad \textbf{(19.4.9)}$$

which is 0.185. Now the chance that she will work is $1 - \Phi(0.185)$, which is 57.4 percent. For this woman, the additional year of education increases the chance of working by 6.1 percent. This occurs because her age, education, and number of children make working and not working nearly equally attractive. A change in her level of education makes a much larger difference in the chance that she will choose to work than it does for the college-educated 30-year-old. Figure 19.5 shows this graphically. The left side of the figure shows

FIGURE 19.5

Effect of a One-Year Increase in Education on Work Probability

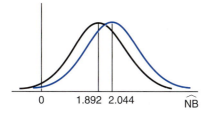
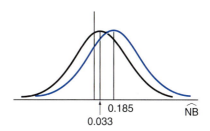

the case of the first woman. When $\widehat{NB}_i$ shifts from 1.892 to 2.044, the chance that the woman works changes little, because $\phi(NB_i)$, the height of the density curve, is very low at $\widehat{NB}_i = 0$, where the woman switches between working and not working. The area under the curve to the left of 0 changes very little when the curve shifts. The right-hand side of Figure 19.5 shows the case of the second woman. For her, the height of $\phi(NB_i)$ at $\widehat{NB}_i = 0$ is much larger, and the shift in the density function from the additional year of education has a much greater effect on the chance that she will choose to work.

Given that the probability derivatives are different for each individual in the sample, it is not clear how they should be reported for the sample as a whole. There are two common practices. The first is to calculate the average value of each right-hand-side variable in the regression and report the probability derivatives for an "average" person in the sample using those values. The second is to calculate the probability derivatives for every person in the sample and report the average value of the probability derivatives. Table 19.2 shows the probability derivatives for each of the right-hand-side variables in Equation 19.3.2, calculated both ways. The two methods produce nearly identical answers. They show that one additional year of education increases the chance that an average woman will work by 3.11 percent, and increases the average chance that a woman in this sample will work by 3.08 percent. The effects of having children are larger; one additional child between ages 3 and 15 reduces the chance (either of them) by about 6 percent, and an additional child between ages 0 and 2 reduces it by more than 16 percent. An increase in age has a very small effect on work chance, reducing it by about 0.3 percent, but this is because a 1-year increase in age is a very small effect. A 10-year change in age reduces the work probability by 3.1 percent, almost exactly the same amount as a 1-year increase in education increases the probability.

Using the probability derivatives, we can conduct economic analysis in the same way that we do with least squares models. The probability derivatives let us predict how much an increase in one of the independent variables will change the fraction of people who will choose to work. For example, our results suggest that if the government would spend more on education, allowing the average woman to have one more year of education than is currently the case, there would be about a 3 percent increase in the fraction of women who work in the United States. We must remember, however, that this statement applies to the average woman and thus might not apply in narrower populations. Increasing the amount of education available the average welfare recipient, for example, might have a larger or smaller effect on her chance of working than it does on the average woman in the entire population. If we wish to understand how education affects welfare recipients, we should use not the average probability derivative, but the probability derivative calculated with X values typical of welfare recipients. Or better, we should estimate the equation using a sample of only welfare recipients and use the average values from that sample. We must

TABLE 19.2

Probability Derivatives of Equation 19.3.2

Variable	Probability Derivative for Average Values of X Variables	Average of Probability Derivatives
Education	3.11%	3.08%
Age	−0.31	−0.31
Children ages 0–2	−16.25	−16.10
Children ages 3–15	−5.93	−5.88

remember that probability derivatives vary from individual to individual and account for that whenever we predict the consequences of a change in the independent variables of the model.

19.5 TESTING HYPOTHESES IN THE PROBIT MODEL

The probability derivatives in Table 19.2 suggest that having a child between the ages of 0 and 2 makes a woman less likely to work than having one between the ages of 3 and 15. However, we do not know whether or not the difference is statistically significant. To find out whether the difference between the two effects is real, or just a coincidence of the data, we need to be able to test hypotheses about the values of the parameters we get from the probit model. We can then use those tests to see whether or not the results of the model conform to our economic expectations about how women make work decisions.

If we want to do tests about the value of a single parameter, we can use the standard errors of the estimated values, using the fact that the estimates are (approximately) normally distributed.[7] We have already used this fact to test whether the estimated parameters are significantly different from each other, and we can use it to test any hypothesis we have that involves only one value of the parameters. However, if we wish to test a hypothesis involving two or more of the parameters, we cannot use the F test to do it. The F test involves the sum of squared residuals, and the probit model does not have a sum of squared residuals to use in the test.

We can, however, continue to use the idea of a restricted and unrestricted model. Suppose we wish to test the null hypothesis $\beta_3 = \beta_4$ against the alternative hypothesis that $\beta_3 \neq \beta_4$ (expecting that β_3 is larger in absolute value). For this null hypothesis, the restricted model is

$$\text{NB}_i = \beta_0 + \beta_1 \text{Educ}_i + \beta_2 \text{Age}_i + \beta_3(\text{Kids02}_i + \text{Kids315}_i) + \varepsilon_i \quad \textbf{(19.5.1)}$$

and the unrestricted model is Equation 19.3.2, which we have already estimated. We can estimate Equation 19.5.1 using the probit model also, as long as we generate the variable Kids, which is the sum of Kids02 and Kids315.

Results of estimating Equation 19.5.1 are shown in Table 19.3. The estimates for the parameters have not changed very much. The estimates for β_1 and β_2 are almost identical to

TABLE 19.3 Probit (Maximum Likelihood) Estimates of Equation 19.5.1

Variable	Parameter	Estimate	Standard Error	Z Statistic for $\beta=0$
Intercept	β_0	−0.214	0.230	−0.93
Education	β_1	0.157	0.014	11.0
Age	β_2	−0.013	0.003	−4.54
Children (all ages)	β_3	−0.334	0.029	−11.6

$N = 2,532$ $\log L = -941.5$

[7] It is not strictly correct to perform *t* tests, because the probit estimates do not take that distribution, even approximately. Because the *t* distribution and the normal distribution are so similar, especially for large number of degrees of freedom, a *t* test will usually give the same answer as a test using the normal distribution, but only the latter is statistically valid (and even then only as an approximation).

their earlier values. The estimate for β_0 has changed a bit more, but by less than one standard error. The estimated value for β_3 (and by the null hypothesis, for β_4 also), which is -0.334, is between the two separate estimates of -0.794 and -0.290 from the unrestricted model. The log likelihood is -941.5.

The question is, How much better is the fit of the unrestricted model to the data than the fit of the restricted model? For the F test, we looked to see how much lower the sum of squared residuals was in the unrestricted model, because least squares is based on making the sum of squared residuals (SSR) as low as possible. In the probit model, or any other maximum likelihood model, we are maximizing the likelihood function, and so the way to compare two regressions is to compare the value of the likelihood function. It must be larger for the unrestricted model than for the restricted model. If it is only slightly larger, then we can conclude that the restriction hurts the fit of the model only very slightly, and the restriction is acceptable. If the maximized value of the log likelihood is much larger for the unrestricted model than for the restricted model, then the restriction has hurt the fit and is therefore not acceptable.

> **Theorem 19.5** Let LL_{UR} and LL_R be the log likelihoods of the unrestricted and restricted models, respectively. Then, if the restrictions are true, the test statistic
>
> $$LR = 2(LL_{UR} - LL_R) \qquad\qquad \textbf{(19.5.2)}$$
>
> takes the chi-square distribution, with degrees of freedom equal to the number of restrictions imposed.

This test, known as the *likelihood ratio test,* is one of two ways to test multivariate hypothesis in the probit model, or other maximum likelihood models. It is also possible to test hypothesis by the Wald test in the maximum likelihood model, as it is in the least squares model.

To test the null hypothesis $\beta_3 = \beta_4$, that is, that the effect of children on the mother's chance of working is the same regardless of the child's age, we use Equation 19.5.2 to calculate the likelihood ratio test statistic, and compare it against the chi-square table in Appendix C at the end of the book. The test statistic is equal to $2[-930.1 - (-941.5)]$, which is equal to 22.8. The test statistic has one degree of freedom because we are imposing one restriction on the model. The 5 percent critical value for the chi-square distribution with one degree of freedom is 3.84. Since the test statistic is larger than this, we conclude that the difference in the likelihoods of the two models is large enough to be statistically significant. We therefore conclude that the restriction is not acceptable and the null hypothesis is false. Children under age 3 have a statistically significantly larger effect on the mother's decision to work than do children between the ages of 3 and 15.

We can test multiple restrictions with the likelihood ratio test as well. For instance, we can test the hypothesis that children, of any age, do not affect the mother's work decision. This economic hypothesis implies that $\beta_3 = \beta_4 = 0$. The restricted model derived from imposing this null hypothesis is

$$NB_i = \beta_0 + \beta_1 Educ_i + \beta_2 Age_i + \varepsilon_i \qquad\qquad \textbf{(19.5.3)}$$

Estimating this equation by the probit model produces a log likelihood of $-1,010.7$. The likelihood ratio test statistic for this null hypothesis is thus $2[-930.1 - (-1010.7)] = 161.2$. The 5 percent critical value for the chi-square distribution with two degrees of freedom is 5.99. Again, the test statistic is larger than the critical value; we conclude that the restriction is incorrect, and we reject the null hypothesis.

We can also use the likelihood ratio test to assess the validity of the model as a whole. To do this, we test the null hypothesis that all of the parameters of the model, except the intercept, are equal to 0. If we fail to reject this hypothesis, then we conclude that none of the right-hand-side variables affect the dummy dependent variable at all; if we reject it, then we conclude that at least one of them does. For Equation 19.3.2, the likelihood ratio test statistic for the hypothesis that β_1 through β_4 are all equal to 0 is 434.4. The 5 percent critical value for four degrees of freedom is 9.49. We conclude from this that the model does show a statistically significant relationship between a woman's decision to work and the right-hand-side variables.

19.6   AN ALTERNATIVE MODEL: THE LOGIT MODEL

The probit model assumes that the error term in the equation for the latent variable is normally distributed. That is not, however, the only possible assumption we could make. In fact, the normal distribution is difficult to work with, because of our inability to write an equation for $\Phi(X)$. With cheap and fast computing, it is feasible to estimate the probit model by using computer-calculated approximations of the $\Phi(X)$ function. However, another alternative, widely used when computer power was more expensive and still common today, is to specify a different distribution function for the error term, one that we can write down as an equation. In particular, we may assume that the error term takes the logistic distribution. The probability density function (PDF) of an error term with a logistic distribution is shown in Figure 19.6, along with the PDF for a standard normal random variable. Note that the two distributions are very similar in shape, except that the logistic PDF is wider and flatter than the normal PDF. In fact, this distribution is used precisely because it is very similar to the normal distribution but does not suffer from the normal distribution's drawback of not having an expression for its cumulative distribution function (CDF). Because the logistic PDF is wider, it has a higher standard deviation; its standard deviation is 1.81. The PDF for a logistically distributed random variable is given by the following equation:

$$L(X) = \frac{e^{-X}}{(1 + e^{-X})^2} \qquad \textbf{(19.6.1)}$$

FIGURE 19.6

The Logistic Random Variable

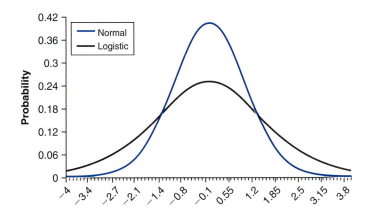

and the chance that a logistically distributed error term ε is less than X is given by

$$\Pr(\varepsilon < X) = \frac{1}{1 + e^{-X}} \tag{19.6.2}$$

Because we can write an equation for the chance that the logistically distributed error term is less than a given value, we can also write an exact equation for the likelihood function in Equation 19.2.10, rather than having to rely on approximations.

Definition 19.9 The *logit model* assumes that a dummy dependent variable Y is equal to 1 if a latent variable $Y^* > 0$, where

$$Y_i^* = \beta_0 + \beta_1 X_{1i} + \cdots + \beta_K X_{Ki} + \varepsilon_i \tag{19.6.3}$$

and ε_i takes the logistic distribution.

Using Equation 19.6.2, we can write the log likelihood function for the logit model as

$$\log L(\beta) = \sum_{Y=1} \log \left(1 - \frac{1}{1 + e^{-\beta_0 - \beta_1 X_{1i} - \cdots - \beta_K X_{Ki}}} \right)$$
$$\cdot \sum_{Y=0} \log \left(\frac{1}{1 + e^{-\beta_0 - \beta_1 X_{1i} - \cdots - \beta_K X_{Ki}}} \right) \tag{19.6.4}$$

and again we choose as estimates the values of the β parameters that maximize the log likelihood function.

We can estimate Equation 19.3.2 using the logit model instead of the probit model. Results of doing so are found in Table 19.4, and probability derivatives are found in Table 19.5. The parameters all take the same signs as they did when the equation was estimated using the probit model. Their values, however, are larger. The reason for this is that the

TABLE 19.4
Logit (Maximum Likelihood) Estimates of Equation 19.3.2

Variable	Parameter	Estimate	Standard Error	Z Statistic for $\beta=0$
Intercept	β_0	−0.455	0.434	−1.04
Education	β_1	0.285	0.027	10.5
Age	β_2	−0.026	0.006	−4.66
Children ages 0–2	β_3	−1.363	0.173	−7.90
Children ages 3–15	β_4	−0.499	0.053	−9.37
$N = 2{,}532$				$\log L = -931.4$

TABLE 19.5
Logit Model Probability Derivatives of Equation 19.3.2

Variable	Probability Derivative for Average Values of X Variables	Average of Probability Derivatives
Education	3.03%	3.21%
Age	−0.27	−0.29
Children ages 0–2	−14.50	−15.36
Children ages 3–15	−5.30	−5.62

FIGURE 19.7 **Shift in the Normal and Logistic Density Functions Required to Produce a Fixed Change in the Probability of $Y = 1$**

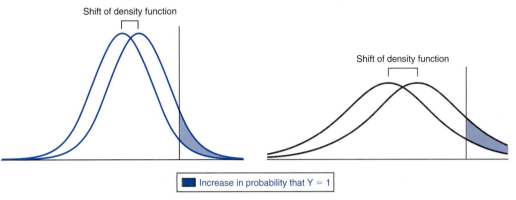

Shift of density function

Shift of density function

■ Increase in probability that Y = 1

standard deviation of the logistic distribution is higher. Figure 19.7 shows that the center of the logistic distribution must be shifted 1.81 times farther than that of the standard normal distribution to change the probability that $\varepsilon < X$ by a given amount. Because the logistic function is wider and less steeply sloped, a larger shift in the function is required to produce a change in probability equal to the pink area (which is the same in both graphs of Figure 19.7). Thus, the estimated parameters of the logit model are all roughly 1.81 times larger than the estimated parameters of the probit model. The standard errors are also roughly 1.81 times larger; the Z statistics are quite similar, though not identical. Table 19.5 shows that the probability derivatives for the two models are also quite similar, and the economic interpretation of the two models is thus very similar, although not quite identical. The logistic probability derivatives are in this case slightly smaller and, in particular, suggest slightly less importance of children in the work decision than the probit estimates do.

Which model should we prefer, the probit model or the logit model? That question has no easy answer. Theoretically, there may be some reason to prefer the probit model. If we believe that the error terms of our models are the result of many small, independent factors we cannot measure, summed up, then they should be approximately normally distributed (due to the central limit theorem). However, because the logit density is so close to the normal density, it may be just as good a model of an error distribution that is only approximately normal and not actually normal. The logit model was once widely used because it is easier to estimate numerically, but that is no longer an issue, because even a large probit model can be quickly estimated on even a small personal computer. At present, both are widely used. In practical terms, their results are usually so similar that the economic conclusions of the research are the same regardless of which is used.

Chapter Review

- Many economic decisions involve a question of whether to do something or not to do it, such as to work or not to work. Such decisions can be modeled with a dummy variable, where $Y = 1$ if the thing is done and $Y = 0$ if it is not.
- We can use the *linear probability model,* based on the least squares principle, to estimate models of such decisions, but the model is unsatisfactory because it is difficult to interpret economically in a sensible way.

- We can instead use the *maximum likelihood principle* to estimate models in which the probability that $Y = 1$ depends on a set of independent variables.

- To do so, we assume the existence of a *latent variable,* called Y^*, which is a linear function of the independent variables and an error term. We assume that $Y = 1$ if $Y^* > 0$ and that $Y = 0$ if $Y^* < 0$. We can then interpret Y^* as a measure of the net benefit of the decision in question.

- If we assume that the error term is normally distributed, the resulting model is known as the *probit model.*

- We can use the results of the probit model to calculate probability derivatives, which tell us how much the chance that $Y = 1$ increases when one of the independent variables changes.

- The *likelihood ratio test,* which is similar to the F test but is appropriate for maximum likelihood estimation, can be used to test hypotheses about the values of the parameters of the model.

- Alternately, we can assume the error term takes the logistic distribution, which is similar to the normal distribution but computationally easier to work with. The resulting model is known as the *logit model.*

- The logit and probit models can be given similar economic interpretations and usually provide very similar results. There is no strong reason to prefer one to the other in practice.

Computer Exercise

In this exercise we'll generate a latent variable and a dummy dependent variable based on it, and work through the details of the probit model.

1. Open Eviews, and create a new workfile, undated data, with 100 observations.

2. Type x1 = rnd()*2 and x2 = rnd()*3 to generate two independent variables.

3. Now, we'll create a latent variable based on these independent variables. Type yhat = 1 + 0.5*x1 – 0.7*x2 to generate this latent variable. (If we were working with actual data we could not observe this; but when generating our own data, we can.)

4. Next we'll add a normally distributed error term, so as to match the assumptions of the probit model. Type err = nrnd(), then type ystar = yhat + err. Open yhat and ystar as a group, and display their scatterplot. How closely are they related? Are there many cases where Yhat is positive and Ystar is negative, or vice versa? Or only a few?

5. Next we'll create a dependent dummy variable based on Ystar. Type y = (ystar>0). This will make $Y = 1$ if Ystar is greater than 0 and $Y = 0$ if Ystar is less than 0 (or equal to 0, but almost certainly ystar is not exactly equal to 0 for any of your observations, because of the random error term). Open Y and Ystar as a group, and verify that Y is 1 if Ystar is positive, and Y is 0 if Ystar is negative.

6. Type chance = @cnorm(-yhat). This will calculate the chance that $Y = 1$ for each observation in the sample. Open X_1 and chance as a group, and display their scatterplot. Does an increase in X_1 increase, or decrease, the chance that $Y = 1$? Do the same for X_2 and chance. How does X_2 affect the chance that $Y = 1$?

7. Type ls y c x1 x2 to estimate the linear probability model. How well does it work? Do you get estimates that are close to their true values?

8. Now type probit c x1 x2 to estimate the probit model. How good are the parameter estimates this time? Which model seems to be estimating the parameters more efficiently?

Problems

1. One important issue in developing countries is population growth. Reducing fertility allows women to work, and reduces the number of dependents in the economy. In this problem we'll look at the decisions of women in one developing country, Peru, to have children. Load the data file fertility, which contains observations from 1985 on 864 Peruvian women for the following variables: children (number of children the women has had); haschildren (a dummy equal to 1 if she has had children and 0 if not); age; married (a dummy variable equal to 1 if she is married and 0 if not); education (in years); fathereduc and mothereduc (education of the woman's father and mother); members (of the woman's household); adults (in the woman's household); householdexp (annual household expenditure); land (owned by the household, in hectares); rural (a dummy variable equal to 1 if she lives in a rural area and 0 if she lives in an urban area); and employee (a dummy variable equal to 1 if she works as an employee of a firm and 0 if she does not).

   a. Using the probit method, estimate a model in which the dependent variable is whether a woman has had children, and her latent net utility for having children is given by $Y_i^* = \beta_0 + \beta_1 \text{Age}_i + \beta_2 \text{Education}_i + \beta_3 \text{Married}_i + \beta_4 \text{Rural}_i + \beta_5 \text{Adults}_i + \beta_6 \text{Fathereduc}_i + \beta_7 \text{Mothereduc}_i + \beta_8 \text{Land}_i + \varepsilon_i$. How many of the parameters are significantly different from 0?

   b. Drop as many variables as you can, and perform a likelihood ratio test to verify that dropping those variables is statistically acceptable. How many variables are left? Do the parameters take the signs you would expect? Why or why not?

   c. If a woman is unmarried, how much does her utility for having children change, compared to being married? Does the chance of her having children rise or fall in this case? If a woman acquires an additional year of education, how much does her utility for having children change? Does the chance of her having children rise or fall in this case? Which has a larger effect, being married or having one more year of education?

   d. Based only on the results of this equation, what policies might you recommend to reduce fertility in developing countries?

2. In this problem we'll reestimate the model of problem 1 using the linear probability model. Load the data file fertility, which was described in problem 1.

   a. Using least squares, estimate the equation $\text{Haschildren}_i = \beta_0 + \beta_1 \text{Age}_i + \beta_2 \text{Education}_i + \beta_3 \text{Married}_i + \beta_4 \text{Rural}_i + \beta_5 \text{Adults}_i + \beta_6 \text{Fathereduc}_i + \beta_7 \text{Mothereduc}_i + \beta_8 \text{Land}_i + \varepsilon_i$. How many of the parameters are significantly different from 0?

   b. Estimate the model $\text{Haschildren}_i = \beta_0 + \beta_1 \text{Age}_i + \beta_2 \text{Education}_i + \beta_3 \text{Married}_i + \beta_5 \text{Adults}_i + \varepsilon_i$. Test whether this is an acceptable restriction on the regression in part *a*. Do the parameters take the same signs they did in problem 1? How are the estimated values different?

    c. According to this model, what is the probability that a married woman, 20 years old, with two adults in her household and eight years of education will have children? If she is single and has only one adult in her household, what is the probability that she will have children?

    d. Consider a married woman with two adults in her household and no education. How old would she have to be before the predicted probability that she has children will exceed 100 percent? Calculate the predicted probabilities of having children for all 864 women in the sample. How many are greater than 100 percent? How many are less than 0 percent?

3. In this problem we'll consider the chance that a Peruvian woman chooses to work. Open the data set fertility, which was described in problem 1.

    a. Estimate a probit model with the dependent variable Employee and a latent net utility for working given by $Y_i^* = \beta_0 + \beta_1 \text{Age}_i + \beta_2 \text{Education}_i + \beta_3 \text{Married}_i + \beta_4 \text{Rural}_i + \beta_5 \text{Haschildren}_i + \beta_6 \text{Land}_i + \varepsilon_i$. According to this equation, does having children make it more likely or less likely that a woman will choose to work? Does having an additional year of education make it more or less likely that a woman will choose to work?

    b. Estimate the restricted model $Y_i^* = \beta_0 + \beta_1 \text{Age}_i + \beta_2 \text{Education}_i + \beta_3 \text{Married}_i + \beta_4 \text{Rural}_i + \varepsilon_i$. Test, by likelihood ratio test, whether the restriction is acceptable. According to this equation, does having children make it more likely or less likely that a woman will choose to work?

    c. Find the average values in the sample of the variables Age, Education, Married, and Rural. Calculate the value of $\hat{Y}^*$ for the average woman in the sample. What is the chance that she chooses to work? Then calculate the probability derivatives for education and married at the mean values of the independent variables. If an average woman gets one more year of education, how much more likely is she to work as an employee? If she gets married, how much less likely is she to work as an employee? Are these relatively large effects or relatively small effects?

    d. Calculate the value of $\hat{Y}_i^*$ for all the women in the sample, and calculate the average value. What is the average chance that a woman in the sample chooses to work? How different is it from the chance that the average woman chooses to work that you calculated in part *c*? Calculate the probability derivatives based on the average values of $\hat{Y}_i^*$. How different are the results?

4. Another dummy variable of considerable interest to economists (and others) is whether people choose to buy houses, or live in a property owned by another person and pay rent. In this problem we'll examine the reasons why people do or do not choose to own a home. Load the data file homeown, which contains observations on 6,072 households on the following variables: owned (a dummy variable that is 1 if the household owns its own home and 0 if not); adults; kids; persons (number living in the household); income (of all people in the household, in thousands of dollars per year); cars (owned by all members of the household); age, education (of the head of household); haswealth (1 if the household has $25,000 in savings and 0 if not); married (1 if the head of the household is married, 0 if not); male (1 if the head of household is male, 0 if not); urban (1 if the household is in an urban area, 0 if not); metro (1 if the household is in a central city, 2 if it is in a suburb, and 3 if it is in a rural area); worked (1 if the head of household

worked in the last week, 0 if not); race (race of the head of household); aframer, asian, nativeam, hispanic, and minority (dummy variables that are 1 if the head of household is African American, Asian American, Native American, of Hispanic origin, and a member of any ethnic minority, respectively, and 0 if not). Data are from the U.S. Census Bureau's 2001 American Housing Survey.

a. Estimate a probit model with the dependent variable Owned, and latent net utility for ownership given by $Y_i^* = \beta_0 + \beta_1 Age_i + \beta_2 Adults_i + \beta_3 Cars_i + \beta_4 Education_i + \beta_5 Haswealth_i + \beta_6 Income_i + \beta_7 Kids_i + \beta_8 Married_i + \beta_9 Urban_i + \beta_{10} Worked_i + \beta_{11} Aframer_i + \beta_{12} Asian_i + \beta_{13} Nativeam_i + \beta_{14} Hispanic_i + \varepsilon_i$. How many of the parameters are significant? Which variable increases net utility for home ownership by the most when it increases by one unit? What variable decreases net utility the most when it increases by one unit? Does it make sense that these variables should affect a person's utility from owning his or her own home, or his or her utility from renting? Explain why.

b. Why does this model not include a dummy variable equal to 1 if the head of the household is Caucasian and 0 if not? What would have to be true about the parameters of this model if race did not affect one's chance of buying a home? Test this null hypothesis. What do you find? Does being a member of an ethnic minority increase the chance that a person will own their own home, decrease the chance, or have no effect on the chance?

c. We would expect that people with high income and wealth would be more likely to be able to afford their own homes. Do the variables indicating high income and wealth take the predicted signs, and are they statistically significant? Which has a greater effect on the chance of home ownership—having $25,000 in financial wealth, or an increase of $10,000 in annual income?

5. In this problem we'll do some forecasting with the probit model and see how accurate its predictions are. Load the data file homeown, which was described in problem 4.

a. Estimate a probit model with the dependent variable owned, and latent net utility for ownership given by $Y_i^* = \beta_0 + \beta_1 Age_i + \beta_2 Adults_i + \beta_3 Cars_i + \beta_4 Education_i + \beta_5 Haswealth_i + \beta_6 Income_i + \beta_7 Kids_i + \beta_8 Married_i + \beta_9 Urban_i + \beta_{10} Worked_i + \beta_{11} Aframer_i + \beta_{12} Asian_i + \beta_{13} Nativeam_i + \beta_{14} Hispanic_i + \varepsilon_i$. Calculate predicted net utilities for home ownership for each observation in the sample. What is the average net utility? What is the range between the maximum and the minimum net utility?

b. What is the probability that a household with the average net utility would live in a home it owns? Compare this to the fraction of households that actually do own the home they live in. How do they compare?

c. Calculate the predicted probability that each household in the sample will own its house. What is the average value of this variable? How does it compare to the fraction of households that actually do own the home they live in?

d. Using the predicted probabilities, predict whether each household in the sample owns its own home. How many observations are predicted to own their own home? How many of the predictions are correct? Without estimating a regression at all, we could have predicted that every household owns its own home and been correct 66.47 percent of the time. How much better are our predictions when we use the model?

6. In this problem we'll compare results of the probit model to those of the logit model. Load the data file homeown, which was described in problem 4.

   a. Estimate a logit model with the dependent variable owned, and latent net utility for ownership given by $Y_i^* = \beta_0 + \beta_1 Age_i + \beta_2 Adults_i + \beta_3 Cars_i + \beta_4 Education_i + \beta_5 Haswealth_i + \beta_6 Income_i + \beta_7 Kids_i + \beta_8 Married_i + \beta_9 Urban_i + \beta_{10} Worked_i + \beta_{11} Aframer_i + \beta_{12} Asian_i + \beta_{13} Nativeam_i + \beta_{14} Hispanic_i + \varepsilon_i$. Compare them to the parameter estimates obtained by estimating the same equation with a probit model. Which model's parameters have larger estimated values? Have they changed in exactly the same proportion? If not, have they changed in approximately the same proportion? Which have larger standard errors? Are any parameters significant in one model but not the other? If so, which ones?

   b. Calculated predicted probabilities of home ownership for each individual in the sample for both the probit and the logit models. Are they very different? Calculate the difference in predicted probabilities for the two models. What is the largest difference in predicted probabilities? For how many observations is one probability above 50 percent and the other below 50 percent?

   c. Calculate the probability derivative for an increase of one child in the household, using both the logit and probit models. (You can use either the derivative for the average household or the average derivative, whichever is easier with your econometric software.) How different are the derivatives?

   d. Does it make a difference whether we use the logit method or the probit method to estimate this model? Why or why not?

Chapter **Twenty**

Qualitative and Limited Dependent Variables

The marvelous richness of human experience would lose something of rewarding joy if there were not limitations to overcome.

Helen Keller

20.1 ECONOMIC AGENTS WITH RESTRICTED CHOICES

Anyone who has ever shopped for a new or used car has had the experience of driving from one dealership to another, looking for the perfect car—or at least the best car available whose price is within the budget. Each car has a different set of features, a different level of quality, and of course a different price. The buyer will purchase the car with the best combination of attributes. The buyer is not, however, the only agent interested in the process. To set prices at profit-maximizing levels, dealers need to understand how car buyers choose cars. Automobile manufacturers need to understand the value that buyers place on features and quality so that they can design the most economically attractive car possible.

To study consumer behavior in such situations, we need an econometric model that predicts which choice a consumer will make from a finite set of options. The probit and logit models of Chapter 19 do not quite fit the bill, though they come close. They can be used when there are only two options to choose from, such that the choice can be represented by a dummy variable; the consumer chooses either to buy the first choice or not (in which case the consumer must, by default, have selected the other). But in many situations, there are more than two choices: There are more than two brands of automobile available, there are more than two choices of Internet service provider for people who wish to use the Internet, students choosing majors have more than two to choose from, and graduates choosing industries and occupations have more than two to choose from. To study choices of this type, we need to be able to deal with a dependent variable that takes values other than 1 or 0; we need one that can represent a choice from among more than two alternatives.

> **Definition 20.1** An *index variable* is a variable that can take any value between 1 and M, depending on which of M discrete choices the economic agent has selected.

For example, we might let the variable Y be equal to 1 if a consumer purchases a Ford, 2 if she purchases a Toyota, 3 if she purchases a Chevrolet, 4 if she purchases a Volkswagen, and 5 if she purchases anything else. The numbers themselves have no meaning; they simply indicate which decision the consumer has made, and the order of the list is immaterial.

An index variable is a specific case of a more general category of variables:

Definition 20.2 A dependent variable is called a *qualitative response variable* if it takes only a finite number of values.

The probit and logit models are also examples of models whose dependent variables are qualitative response variables.

Because the values of qualitative response variables are not economically meaningful, least squares is not a fruitful approach for dealing with them as dependent variables. For such variables, the least squares concept of a residual is not economically sensible. If we define a residual as the distance between the observed value of the dependent variable and the predicted value from the model, then the residual will be able to take on only those values that produce the permitted values of the dependent variable. Furthermore, since the possible values of the residual will change as the predicted value changes, the distribution of the residual will be different for each observation. And even the concept of distance from the Y values may not make economic sense. If $Y = 1$ for a consumer who purchases a Ford, $Y = 2$ for a consumer who purchases a Toyota, and $Y = 3$ for a consumer who purchases a Chevrolet, what shall we do with a consumer whose predicted value of Y is 1.3? For all of these reasons, a model that relies on that concept will be difficult to interpret in economic terms.

There are also models in which the dependent variable is continuous but cannot take some values. For example, suppose we are interested in knowing the amount of money the consumer will spend on a car. In any given year, most consumers spend $0 on a car, because they do not buy one that year. However, some consumers will choose to buy one, and they could spend anywhere from less than $10,000 to more than $100,000. The data we observe are the results of two different decisions: first, whether or not to buy a car and, second, how much to spend if a car is bought. The people who chose not to buy a car, and hence spent $0, might have bought one had prices or features been different. Least squares will not describe this model well either, because a value of $0 does not necessarily imply that the consumer wants to spend $0; it just means that he or she did not buy any particular car at that particular time. The consumer's willingness to spend may be less than 0, or it may be more than 0 but not as high as the price of the cheapest available car.

Definition 20.3 A dependent variable is called a *limited dependent variable* if its value can fall only in particular ranges. We refer to an observation as *censored* if the observed value of the variable is at the limit of the permitted range.

In the car-buying example, spending must be greater than or equal to $0, so the variable is limited. If we observe a consumer whose spending is $0, that observation is censored; we don't know what that consumer would have spent, because he or she chose not to buy anything. Least squares will generally not work well on observations for which the data are censored by the observation process.

We will generally use maximum likelihood techniques to estimate both qualitative response models and limited dependent variable models. In the case of qualitative response variables, we write the chance of each of the possible outcomes as a function of independent variables and parameters, and choose parameter values that maximize the probability of observing the actual sample. In the case of limited dependent variable models, we consider the observed value of the variable if it is not censored, and we consider the probability of being censored if it is. In this chapter we will show how the maximum likelihood methods introduced in Chapter 19 can be extended to handle these somewhat more complex types of models.

20.2 INDEX VARIABLES AS DEPENDENT VARIABLES

Suppose we have a model in which the dependent variable is an index variable, representing the choice that a person or firm makes from among a finite set of options. Economically, such a model is quite similar to the probit and logit models from Chapter 19; we would expect people to make the choice that gives them the highest utility, or a firm to make the choice that gives it the highest profit, or in general the choice that provides the highest level of whatever the economic agent in question is maximizing. The only difference is that there are more than two choices. Suppose that there are J different possible choices, and we have a data set with N observations.

> **Definition 20.4** The *random utility model* of discrete choices assumes that the agent chooses the option with the highest utility and that the utility from choosing any one option is given by
>
> $$U_{ij} = \beta_{0j} + \beta_{1j}X_{1i} + \beta_{2j}X_{2i} + \cdots + \beta_{Kj}X_{Ki} + \varepsilon_{ij} \quad \textbf{(20.2.1)}$$
>
> where U_{ij} is the utility of choice j for person i, the variables $X_1, X_2, \ldots X_K$ are observable exogenous variables affecting the benefit of choice j, and ε_{ij} is an error term representing unobservable influences on the benefit of choice j.[1]

For example, we might estimate a model in which consumers choose among different Internet service providers (ISPs). Assume that each consumer has six choices of ISP: AOL, AT&T's Worldnet, BlueLight, Road Runner, @Home, or another.[2] Then any given consumer has six utility levels, one for each of the six options. If the benefit of choosing AOL (call this U_{iAOL}) is the highest of the six, that consumer will choose AOL. If the benefit of Road Runner (call this U_{iRR}) is the highest, the consumer will choose Road Runner, and so forth. Note that to the consumer, the utility is not random; the consumer observes the value of ε_{ij} for each choice and picks the one with the highest utility level, including the contribution of ε_{ij} to the utility. The utilities are random only to the

---

[1] This is a fairly general specification; we can impose restrictions on it if we wish. If we believe that some variables affect the benefit of one choice and not another, we can impose $\beta_{kj} = 0$ so that X_k does not affect the benefit of choice j. If we think that a variable has the same effect on two benefits, we can impose $\beta_{kj} = \beta_{kl}$ so that X_k has the same effect on choices j and l, or we can impose $\beta_{kj} = \beta_k$ for all choices if X_k has the same effect on every option. More complex restrictions can be imposed as well.

[2] *Another* means any ISP other than one of the listed five. In nearly all cases, the ISP selected in this case is a regional or local ISP offering a fairly basic dial-up service at a fairly common price. We are implicitly assuming that all observations in the sample will choose to have an ISP; we make this choice because the data we will use to estimate the model later in the sample contain only ISP customers. If we also had data on people who choose not to have Internet service at all, then we would need to include *none* as a seventh option.

econometrician. The error term represents those factors that affect the consumer's decision but cannot be measured with the available data and so cannot be predicted or included in the econometric model.

In order to estimate the model, we need to make one further assumption. We do not observe the actual level of utility of the option the consumer selects; we know only that it is higher than the levels of all other options. The same choices can result from different numbers for the utility of each choice. For example, the consumer will choose option 1 if the utilities for the six choices are 10, 4, 7, 3, 8, and 2, respectively. However, the consumer will also choose option 1 if the utilities are 20, 14, 17, 13, 18, and 12. To produce a unique set of utility numbers, we choose one option (any one will do) and set its utility level to 0. The utilities of the other choices are then interpreted as the relative utility of the given choice, compared to the choice whose utility has been set to 0. We impose this restriction by setting the values of the β parameters to 0 for the option whose utility level we wish to be equal to 0.

If there are only two choices, then the model is identical to the dummy variable model from Chapter 19. In that case, the consumer chooses choice 1 if

$$U_{i1} > U_{i2} \tag{20.2.2}$$

that is, if the benefit of option 1 is greater than the benefit of option 2. Subtracting U_{i2} from both sides gives

$$U_{i1} - U_{i2} > 0 \tag{20.2.3}$$

and, since $U_{i1} - U_{i2}$ is equal to the net utility of option 1, this is identical to the condition from Chapter 19 that the net utility be positive. The random utility model is thus a generalization of the dummy variable model to the case of more than two choices, in which the consumer chooses choice 1 if U_{i1} is greater than the benefit from all other choices.

As with the dummy dependent variable model, the model is not completely specified until we make some assumption about the distribution function of the error term.

> **Definition 20.5** The *multinomial logit* model assumes that the data are generated by the random utility model, and that the error terms are independent of one another and take the Weibull distribution function, whose CDF is given by:

$$\Pr(\varepsilon < K) = e^{-e^{-K}} \tag{20.2.4}$$

We specify the Weibull distribution for the error terms because it results in a particularly convenient expression for the probability that any given choice will be made.[3] Let Y be the dependent variable in the model, which takes an integer value between 1 and J. If the benefits of each option are as given in Equation 20.2.1, then it can be shown that the chance

---

[3] This assumption is made much more for mathematical convenience than because of the particular properties of the Weibull distribution itself. It is possible to estimate a random utility model in which the error terms take different distributions. We can, for instance, assume the error terms are normally distributed; the resulting model is called the *multinomial probit model*. However, the multinomial probit model is extremely difficult to estimate, because, as with all normally distributed random variables, the CDF cannot be written as a closed-form expression. For this reason the multinomial logit model is almost invariably used in economic analysis. It can be shown that if there are only two choices, the multinomial logit model is identical to the logit model from Chapter 19.

that a given option j will have the highest utility is given by

$$\Pr(Y_i = j) = \frac{e^{U_{ij}}}{\sum_{m=1}^{J} e^{U_{im}}} \qquad (20.2.5)$$

The likelihood function is then equal to the product of the likelihood that Y_i takes its observed value for all the observations:

$$L(\beta) = \prod_{i=1}^{N} \frac{e^{U_{iY_i}}}{\sum_{m=1}^{J} e^{U_{im}}} \qquad (20.2.6)$$

We estimate the parameters of the model by choosing the values that maximize the likelihood function. As in Chapter 19, for mathematical convenience, we actually maximize the log likelihood rather than the likelihood itself. We can also use the estimated parameters to calculate predicted net utility for each choice, predicted choices, and the percentage of correct predictions for the model, in the same way we did for the probit and logit models.

We can apply the multinomial logit model to the problem of consumer's choice of Internet service provider. Let the utility from choosing a particular provider be given by

$$U_{ij} = \beta_{1j} \text{Age}_i + \beta_{2j} \text{Exper}_i + \beta_{3j} \text{Emails}_i$$
$$+ \beta_4 \text{Price}_j + \beta_5 \text{Cable}_j + \varepsilon_{ij} \qquad (20.2.7)$$

where Age is the age of the consumer, Exper is the computer experience of the consumer in years, Emails is the number of e-mails sent by the user per month (a measure of the intensity of demand), Price is the cost per month of the service, and Cable is a dummy variable that is 1 if the service is provided by cable modem and 0 if it is provided by telephone dial-up. Note that some of the variables are different for each consumer but the same for each ISP (Age, Exper, and Emails) while others are the same for each user but differ between the ISPs (Price and Cable). We allow the value of the β parameters to be different for each of the ISPs when the variables differ by consumer, but require the values of the β parameters to be the same for each ISP when the data vary only by ISP. Therefore, Age is multiplied by the parameter β_{1j}, where the j subscript indicates different values for each of the six ISPs, but Price is multiplied by the parameter β_4, which takes the same value for all of the ISPs.

Results of estimating Equation 20.2.7 with the multinomial logit model and data on 126 ISP customers from December 2001 are found in Table 20.1. We set the utility of choosing another ISP (option 6) to 0, and we interpret all other parameters as increasing or decreasing the relative utility of a given ISP compared to that. Most of the statistically significant parameters are for Road Runner and @Home. The parameters for e-mail use, β_{34} and β_{35}, are significantly positive; users with high-intensity demand get a higher utility from these ISPs than from the others. This may be the case because of the greater bandwidth those ISPs offer. The parameters on age for those two ISPs, β_{14} and β_{15}, are negative; this means that older consumers get less utility from these ISPs, and are less likely to choose them. The other statistically significant result among the ISP-specific parameters is the negative estimate for experience for BlueLight, β_{23}, which implies that highly experienced users get a lower utility for this ISP. The lack of significant results for AOL and WorldNet suggests that the benefits those services offer to consumers may not differ much from those offered by the typical regional ISP that is represented by the choice of "another ISP."

TABLE 20.1
Multinomial
Logit
Estimates of
ISP Choice

		AOL		
Variable	Parameter	Estimate	Standard Error	Z Statistic for $\beta = 0$
Age	β_{11}	−0.192	0.212	−0.90
Experience	β_{21}	−0.079	0.128	−0.62
E-mails	β_{31}	0.001	0.007	0.13

		Worldnet		
Variable	Parameter	Estimate	Standard Error	Z Statistic for $\beta = 0$
Age	β_{12}	−0.561	0.973	−0.58
Experience	β_{22}	−0.241	0.654	−0.37
E-mails	β_{32}	−0.014	0.035	−0.41

		BlueLight		
Variable	Parameter	Estimate	Standard Error	Z Statistic for $\beta = 0$
Age	β_{13}	−1.325	0.893	−1.48
Experience	β_{23}	−1.235	0.509	−2.43
E-mails	β_{33}	−0.029	0.058	−0.50

		Road Runner		
Variable	Parameter	Estimate	Standard Error	Z Statistic for $\beta = 0$
Age	β_{14}	−1.518	0.521	−2.91
Experience	β_{24}	0.268	0.671	0.40
E-mails	β_{34}	0.027	0.011	2.33

		@Home:		
Variable	Parameter	Estimate	Standard Error	Z Statistic for $\beta = 0$
Age	β_{15}	−1.324	0.544	−2.43
Experience	β_{25}	0.137	0.687	0.20
E-mails	β_{35}	0.028	0.014	2.06

		Other Parameters		
Variable	Parameter	Estimate	Standard Error	Z Statistic for $\beta = 0$
Price	β_4	−0.210	0.108	−1.93
Cable	β_5	2.128	3.412	0.62

We can also provide economic interpretations of the parameters that do not vary from one ISP to another. The estimated parameter on the Price variable is negative, and statistically significant at the 10 percent level though not at the 5 percent level. The negative sign, if accepted as accurate, suggests that higher prices reduce the utility of service. The estimated parameter on the Cable dummy variable is not statistically significant different from 0, which is somewhat surprising; cable modems offer substantially higher bandwidth and faster access than dial-up service, which should increase the utility of these services.

The estimated value is indeed positive and is a relatively large number; it is not significant because of the large standard error. This may be the result of an omitted variable that is correlated with the Cable dummy. In particular, the cost of a cable modem and cable hookup may offset the gains in bandwidth from using cable technology, such that when these effects are included, cable modem service may not be particularly more attractive than dial-up service.[4]

If we wish to know how much these variables affect consumer choice, rather than just their signs, we can calculate probability derivatives, as we did in Chapter 19. We will normally want to do this in order to assess the economic importance of the variables in determining the consumer's choice. The chance that consumer i will choose ISP j is given by Equation 20.2.5. We can take the derivative of this probability with respect to any one of the variables, to calculate the effect of a one-unit change in the variable on the chance of that ISP being selected. Some calculus and algebra produces:

$$\frac{\partial \Pr(Y_i = j)}{\partial X_{ik}} = \frac{e^{U_{ij}}}{\sum_{m=1}^{J} e^{U_{im}}} \cdot \left(\beta_{jk} - \frac{\sum_{m=1}^{J} (e^{U_{im}} \beta_{mk})}{\sum_{m=1}^{J} e^{U_{im}}} \right) \qquad \textbf{(20.2.8)}$$

Because the terms in Equation 20.2.8 depend on i and j, the value of the probability derivative is different for each consumer in the sample, as they did in Chapter 19, and for each of the ISPs. We can either report the probability derivative for an average value of the X variables or calculate the derivative for each observation and report the average value.

Using the regression results from Table 20.1 and Equation 20.2.8, we can calculate the effect of a \$1 increase in an ISP's monthly payment on the chance that a consumer will choose that ISP. Because β_4, the coefficent on the payment variable, is negative (-0.209), and because an increase in AOL's monthly payment does not affect the utility of any other service, an increase in AOL's fee will decrease the chance that AOL will be selected. The average decrease for all the users in the data sample works out to -3.99 percent. The typical user has a 3.99 percent chance to switch ISPs if AOL raises its monthly price by \$1; put another way, AOL should expect such an increase to reduce its demand by 3.99 percent. The effect is smaller for Road Runner, for which the average change in the chance of selection is -1.66 percent. Intuitively, this occurs because Road Runner has a lower market share to begin with and thus is less likely to lose customers in response to a small change in price.

The multinomial logit model is a very useful tool for describing the chances that economic agents will make particular choices, and the way in which changes in exogenous variables alter those chances. However, it depends on a very specific assumption about the distribution of the error term, which is that the error terms take the Weibull distribution. This assumption turns out to have some important consequences. Suppose we eliminated one of the six alternative ISPs from the choice set. What would happen to the chance that the others would be selected? Clearly, the chance would rise, as the consumers who preferred the eliminated alternative switched to other ISPs. Mathematically, when there are six

---

[4] If we include the service's hookup fee in the regression, it is not significant, nor does the cable dummy become significant. This is the result of multicollinearity between the two variables; the hookup fees for cable service are much larger than those for dial-up.

choices of ISP, the chance that any one consumer will select AOL is equal to

$$\Pr(Y = \text{AOL}) = \frac{e^{U_{i\text{AOL}}}}{\sum_{m=1}^{6} e^{U_{im}}} \tag{20.2.9}$$

and when there are only five, the chance is

$$\Pr(Y = \text{AOL}) = \frac{e^{U_{i\text{AOL}}}}{\sum_{m=1}^{5} e^{U_{im}}} \tag{20.2.10}$$

The numerator of both chances is exactly the same, since the elimination of a competitor does not alter the utility a consumer derives from AOL. The denominator of Equation 20.2.10 must be smaller than the denominator of Equation 20.2.9, because it sums up five terms instead of only six.[5] Therefore, the chance of selecting AOL is higher when there are only five alternatives. How much the chance rises depends on how much the denominator falls when one fewer term is included.

Exactly the same argument is true for any other service. The chance that Road Runner will be selected when there are five options is

$$\Pr(Y = \text{Road Runner}) = \frac{e^{U_{i\text{RR}}}}{\sum_{m=1}^{5} e^{U_{im}}} \tag{20.2.11}$$

and the elimination of the @Home option from the denominator affects the chance of selecting Road Runner in exactly the same way it affects the chance of selecting AOL. That is, if we eliminate the possibility of choosing @Home, it will raise the chances of selecting AOL and Road Runner equally. Or, if we know that a consumer will not select @Home, then eliminating it from the choices does not change the chance that the consumer will choose either AOL or Road Runner.

Definition 20.6 The property of *independence of irrelevant alternatives (IIA)* implies that removing, or adding, an undesirable choice does not change the relative chance of selecting any other desirable choice.

The multinomial logit model has the IIA property. There can be cases where the IIA property is undesirable, because it does not match our economic intuition about how consumers make the choice we are studying. The original example used to introduce the IIA property is that of a commuter choosing whether to get to work on a car, a red bus, or a blue bus.[6] If we eliminate the choice of the blue bus, then the IIA property requires that both the chance that the commuter will choose the car and the chance that the commuter will choose the blue bus should rise proportionately. If 60 percent of the commuters choose car, 20 percent choose red bus, and 20 percent choose blue bus, then after the blue bus choice is eliminated, IIA requires that 75 percent will choose car and 25 percent will choose red bus (a one-fourth increase in the number of people choosing car and red bus). However, economic intuition tells us this is unlikely. People do not care what color the bus they ride is, so we would expect that if the blue bus option was taken away, most of the former blue bus commuters would switch to red bus, and few if any would switch to car. If

---

[5] All the terms must be positive, because *e* to any power is a positive number.
[6] This discussion is presented by McFadden (1981).

that is the case, then the decision rule used by commuters does not satisfy the IIA property and the multinomial logit model (which does) is probably a poor representation of the real decision rule.

The model of ISP choice may have the same problem. Road Runner and @Home are the only two cable modem providers among the five choices listed. It may be the case that consumers first choose whether they want cable or dial-up service, and only afterward choose which ISP they want. If so, then when @Home is eliminated from the list of choices, we would expect most consumers who had chosen @Home to switch to Road Runner. We would not expect a proportional increase among all of the ISPs, but the multinomial logit model would require one. If we think that that is a problem, then we might not want to use the multinomial logit model. We can still use the random utility model; we need only specify a different distribution for the error terms. We can either allow some correlation between the error terms so that a consumer with a high preference for one alternative will tend to have a high (or low) preference for another one as well. Or we can specify a different distribution for the error terms that does not imply the IIA property. In either case, however, we end up with a model that has a more complex equation for the chance of selecting any particular alternative, and the resulting model is more difficult to estimate computationally. It is therefore standard to use the multinomial logit model unless there is strong reason to believe that the IIA property will cause problems for the model.

20.3   CENSORED VARIABLES AS DEPENDENT VARIABLES

Suppose that, instead of being qualitative, the dependent variable is limited; it can fall only into a certain range of values. In this case, we have to explain two things about the data points we observe: whether or not they are censored, and what value they take if they are not censored. The most common model of limited dependent variables uses the idea of a latent variable, developed in Chapter 19, to handle both questions at the same time.

Definition 20.7 The *Tobit model*[7] assumes a latent variable Y^*, determined by

$$Y_i^* = \beta_0 + \beta_1 X_{1i} + \beta_2 X_{2i} + \cdots + \beta_K X_{Ki} + \varepsilon_i \qquad \textbf{(20.3.1)}$$

where X_1, X_2, ... X_K are observable independent variables, and ε is a normally distributed error term with mean 0 and variance σ^2. The observed variable Y is equal to Y^* if Y^* is greater than 0, and is equal to 0 if Y^* is less than 0.

The latent variable Y^* is then given an economic interpretation. In the case of a car purchase, we regard Y^* as the amount of money the consumer wishes to spend on a car. If that amount is positive, then the consumer buys the car, and we observe the amount he wanted to pay, which is equal to both Y and Y^* in that case. If the amount of money the consumer wishes to spend is negative, then the consumer chooses not to buy a car and we observe spending of 0.

---

[7] The Tobit model is named partly after its originator, James Tobin, and partly by analogy to the logit and probit models, which it resembles. The difference between the Tobit and the probit model is that in the probit model, $Y = 1$ if $Y^* > 0$, and in the Tobit model, $Y = Y^*$ in that case. They are otherwise identical.

FIGURE 20.1

Correlation of Dividend Income and Earned Income

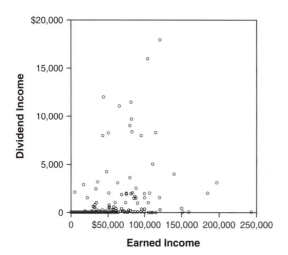

The Tobit model can be applied to any model where a variable is observed only if it is greater than 0.[8] We might, for example, use it to study forms of income that only part of the population earns. One such type of income is income from capital investments. Individuals can earn dividend income only if they have money invested in firms that pay dividends. Many people do not have enough income to have savings; many of those who do have savings have only a savings account or another form of savings that does not pay dividends out of firm profits. Figure 20.1 shows a scatterplot of dividend income against labor income for 10,000 households, using data from the U.S. Census Bureau's 1997 Survey of Program Dynamics. The figure shows a weak but generally positive relationship between labor income and dividend income for those households that have dividend income. However, most investments do not earn any dividend income; only 19.7 percent of households in the sample do. The other 82 percent of households do not have investments that pay dividends. For these households, $Y^* < 0$ and therefore we observe $Y = 0$ for them. For households that are wealthy enough to have such investments, $Y^* > 0$ and we observe $Y = Y^*$, whatever value it takes. The average household earns \$611 of dividends per year; however, this average is somewhat misleading, since it includes the households that earn no dividend income. Among those houses that earn dividend income, the average amount earned is \$3,103.

Economically, we wish to explain why some households have dividend income when others do not, and why, among those who do, some have more than others. We assume that households desire to have investments, if they can afford them; the amount of these investments will determine how much dividend income, if any, the household earns. We let the latent variable Y^* be equal to the amount of dividend income the household would receive from its desired level of investments. If the dividends paid by the family's desired level of investments is below 0, the reported value of dividend income will be 0. Many households will not have enough wealth to desire investments that pay dividends. The level of dividends a family desires will depend primarily on its income. It will also depend on the age of the household

---

[8] The model can be easily extended to allow a cutoff point different from 0, or an upper limit rather than a lower limit, or both. It can also handle the case where the sample only contains observations with $Y > 0$, and not ones with $Y = 0$. The model is known as the *truncated Tobit model* in that case.

members. Older households may be out of debt and be able to afford larger investments; they may also be closer to retirement and more conscious of retirement needs. Households with married couples have double the retirement needs of singles, so we include marital status as a dummy independent variable. On the one hand, households with more kids may have greater consumption requirements, leaving less money for investment; on the other hand, they may need additional investments to pay for college expenses. We therefore include the number of children in the household as an independent variable as well. The econometric model is thus

$$\text{Div}_i^* = \beta_0 + \beta_1 \text{Income}_i + \beta_2 \text{Age}_i + \beta_3 \text{Married}_i + \beta_4 \text{Kids}_i + \varepsilon_i \quad \textbf{(20.3.2)}$$

However, we cannot estimate Equation 20.3.2 directly, because the dependent variable Div^* is latent; it is not observable. When Div^* is positive, $\text{Div} = \text{Div}^*$ and we can observe Div, so in that case we know the value of Div^* also; but when Div^* is negative, all we observe is $\text{Div} = 0$. We do not know the value of Div^* in that case; it could be any negative number. One solution to this problem, not a good one, is to estimate

$$\text{Div}_i = \beta_0 + \beta_1 \text{Income}_i + \beta_2 \text{Age}_i + \beta_3 \text{Married}_i + \beta_4 \text{Kids}_i + \varepsilon_i \quad \textbf{(20.3.3)}$$

using the observable Div_i as the dependent variable and ignoring the problem that Div_i is not equal to Div_i^* when Div_i is 0.

Theorem 20.1 If the data generating process is correctly described by the Tobit model, but we estimate the regression equation by OLS using the observable variable in place of the latent variable, then the OLS estimates are biased and inconsistent.

Figure 20.2 demonstrates why OLS works badly when the true data generating process is the Tobit model. The gray line in the figure represents the true Tobit model. The gray and black data points are generated by this true model. The black data points are the ones for which $Y^* > 0$ and we observe $Y = Y^*$; these data points we can observe. The gray data points are the ones for which $Y^* < 0$ and we observe $Y = 0$. We do not observe the gray data points; instead, we observe the red data points along the X-axis, since $Y = 0$ for them. If we use OLS to estimate the model using the black and red data points, the estimated line (shown in red in the figure) will not lie near the true model, because it moves up the graph to go through the red data points, rather than the (unobserved) gray ones. This causes both the estimated slope and intercept to be biased. Because the red points must be above the gray ones, the intercept is biased upward (the estimated value is higher than the true value) and the slope is biased downward (the estimated line is flatter than the true model).

FIGURE 20.2
Bias of Least Squares in Data Generated by the Tobit Model

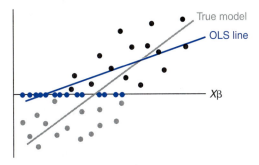

FIGURE 20.3

Bias of Least Squares in Data Generated by the Tobit Model in Limited Samples

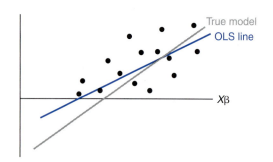

One possible solution to this problem is to ignore the red data points (that is, the ones for which $Y = 0$) and estimate the model using only the black data points. Those data points are not censored; for them, we know $Y = Y^*$ and the data points are in fact generated by the true model.

Theorem 20.2 If the data generating process is correctly described by the Tobit model, and we estimate the regression equation by OLS using only observations for which the observable variable is uncensored (greater than 0), the OLS estimates are still biased and inconsistent.

Because of Theorem 20.2 we cannot solve the problem of censored data by simply ignoring the censored observations. Figure 20.3 shows why the OLS line will still not be a good estimate of the true model in this case. Consider an observation for which the value of $X\beta$ is near the point where the true model (gray line) crosses the horizontal axis. This observation could have a positive error term, or it could have a negative error term. If it has a positive error term, it will lie above the horizontal axis, its value of Y^* will be greater than 0, and it will be observed. If it has a negative error term, it will lie below the horizontal axis, its value of Y^* will be less than 0, and it will not be observed; it will be censored and we will not use it in estimating the regression. Therefore, near the point where the true model crosses the horizontal axis, we will use the observations with positive errors, but not the observations with negative errors. This violates the OLS assumption that the expected value of the errors must be 0. Thus the Gauss-Markov theorem does not apply and OLS will be biased and inconsistent.

Therefore, instead of using least squares, we estimate the Tobit model by maximum likelihood. The expression for the likelihood of a single observation depends on whether or not the observation is censored. Suppose that, for the ith observation, we see that $Y_i = 0$; then all we know is that $Y_i^* < 0$. The probability that $Y_i^* < 0$ is given by the normal CDF:

$$\Pr(Y_i = 0) = \Pr(Y_i^* < 0) = \Pr(\varepsilon_i < -X\beta) = \Phi\left(\frac{-X\beta}{\sigma}\right) \quad \textbf{(20.3.4)}$$

where $X\beta = \beta_0 + \beta_1 X_{1i} + \beta_2 X_{2i} + \cdots + \beta_K X_{Ki}$, and the Φ function is the normal CDF. Suppose instead that we observe $Y_i > 0$. Then, because we know $Y_i = Y_i^*$ in that case, we know exactly what value the error term must take to produce that value of Y_i:

$$\varepsilon_i = Y_i - \beta_0 - \beta_1 X_{1i} - \beta_2 X_{2i} - \cdots - \beta_K X_{Ki} \quad \textbf{(20.3.5)}$$

and we know that the value of the normal PDF for that value of the error term is equal to $\phi[(Y - X\beta)/\sigma]$. The likelihood for the sample is, as always, the product of the likelihood for each of the observations, and we choose as estimates the values of the β parameters that maximize its value. Because the estimates are maximum likelihood estimates, they will be consistent and efficient as long as we have specified the model correctly.

Table 20.2 shows the results of estimating Equation 20.3.2 by maximum likelihood. They show that people with high incomes earn more dividend income; an extra dollar of earned income results in an extra 8.6 cents of dividend income. Older people earn more dividend income than younger ones; each additional year of age adds about $141 to predicted dividend income. This occurs because older people have had longer to save for investments and because their investments may have grown over time. Being married increases dividend income by about $1,450, and each additional child reduces it by $922. All estimated values are statistically significantly from 0 at the 5 percent (and 1 percent) level.

These results are quite different from those obtained by OLS regression, which are shown in Table 20.3, both for the full sample and for the uncensored sample. The differences occur because the Tobit estimates are consistent estimates of the true parameters, but the OLS

TABLE 20.2
Tobit (Maximum Likelihood) Estimates of Dividend Income

Variable	Parameter	Estimate	Standard Error	Z Statistic for $\beta = 0$
Intercept	β_0	−20,018	733.8	−27.3
Earned income	β_1	0.0862	0.0038	22.3
Age	β_2	141.77	14.57	9.73
Married	β_3	1,457.5	325.0	4.48
Number of children	β_4	−922.3	165.2	−5.58

Log likelihood = −23,231.3   Number of observations = 10,000

TABLE 20.3
Least Squares (Inconsistent) Estimates of Dividend Income

Full Sample				
Variable	Parameter	Estimate	Standard Error	Z Statistic for $\beta = 0$
Intercept	β_0	−1,210.4	158.4	−7.64
Earned income	β_1	0.0113	0.0011	10.0
Age	β_2	31.37	3.317	9.46
Married	β_3	166.5	84.28	1.98
Number of children	β_4	−134.8	33.80	−3.99

$R^2 = 0.026$ Number of observations = 10,000

Uncensored Sample				
Variable	Parameter	Estimate	Standard Error	Z Statistic for $\beta = 0$
Intercept	β_0	−3,607.9	891.0	−4.05
Earned income	β_1	0.0124	0.0047	2.62
Age	β_2	133.21	17.60	7.57
Married	β_3	422.15	428.9	0.98
Number of children	β_4	−504.6	190.3	−2.65

$R^2 = 0.046$ Number of observations = 1,969

estimates are not. In particular, the OLS estimates are all much smaller than the corresponding Tobit estimates. Because of this bias, the OLS estimates imply much smaller effects of the independent variables on dividend income than is really the case. For example, the OLS estimates show that an additional child reduces dividend income by only $504 (uncensored sample) or only $135 (full sample), rather than the $922 from the Tobit estimates. Economic interpretations of the data based on the OLS results would substantially underestimate the effects that income, age, and family structure have on the patterns of dividend income.

Chapter Review

- Least squares analysis assumes that the independent variable can take any value. There are many variables, in addition to dummy variables, of which this is not true.
- We can divide such variables into two broad categories; *qualitative response variables,* which take only a finite set of values, and *limited variables,* which can take any value within a prescribed range.
- Least squares works poorly on limited and qualitative response dependent variables. Instead, we use maximum likelihood to estimate the parameters of models with dependent variables of those types.
- The *random utility model* describes situations where an economic agent chooses one option from a finite list.
- The *multinomial logit model* is a random utility model where the error terms take the Weibull distribution, which is particularly easy to work with computationally.
- The multinomial logit model allows us to analyze reasons why agents make one choice rather than another.
- The multinomial logit model suffers from the property of *independence of irrelevant alternatives (IIA),* which may not be true of some real-world data generating processes. Alternative models which do not suffer from IIA are available but are more cumbersome to estimate.
- The *Tobit model* describes situations where the dependent variable is constrained to be greater than 0, and is censored if it is not.
- If the data are generated by a Tobit model, least squares estimates are biased and inconsistent, even when the censored observations are not used. Maximum likelihood of the true model provides consistent estimates of the parameters.

Computer Exercise

In this exercise, we'll generate a dependent variable that is censored. We'll estimate its data generating process with OLS and with the Tobit model, and show that the Tobit model provides better estimates of the true parameters, though not as good as OLS would provide if the latent variable could be observed.

1. Open Eviews, and create a new workfile, undated data, with 300 observations.
2. Type genr x1=rnd()*10 and genr x2=rnd()*10 to create two independent variables.
3. Type genr err=nrnd()*5 to create a random error term.
4. Type genr ystar = −5 + 2*x1 − x2 + err to generate an underlying dependent variable. Graph the histogram and descriptive statistics for Y^*. Does it have some positive and some negative values?

5. If Y^* is observable, we'd use least squares to estimate the model. Type ls ystar c x1 x2 to estimate the parameters. Do you get estimated values for β_0, β_1, and β_2 which are close to -5, 2, and -1, respectively?

6. The Tobit model applies to the case where Y^* cannot be observed. Type y = ystar* (ystar >0) to generate a variable Y that is equal to Y^* if Y^* is positive and equal to 0 if Y^* is negative. Open the variables Ystar and Y as a group, view them as a spreadsheet or as a scatterplot, and verify that they have this relationship.

7. For the rest of the exercise, we'll treat Y^* as unobservable and make all our inferences using the limited variable Y. Type ls y c x1 x2 to estimate the model by OLS. Are the resulting estimates close to the true values? Are they statistically significantly different from the true values? Do these estimates appear to be consistent or inconsistent?

8. In the regression output, press the Estimate button to reestimate the model. In the Sample box, type 1 300 if y >0, so that only uncensored observations will be used. Now how close are the estimates to the true values? Are they significantly different? How many observations were used. Do these estimates look better than those from step 6? Do they look consistent, or not?

9. Again, press the Estimate button. This time, go to the Method drop-down box and select the option for censored data models. Change the sample back to 1 300 to use the full sample, and hit OK. Make sure the maximum likelihood process converged. Look at the Tobit parameter estimates. Are they close to the true values? Are they statistically significantly different? Do these estimates look consistent or inconsistent? Are they as good as the OLS results from using Y^* as the dependent variable (compare the standard errors)?

10. Repeat steps 3–9 about five times to verify that the Tobit estimate consistently outperforms the OLS model on the censored dependent variable Y, but not on the latent variable Y^* if we use that (which in normal applications we can't, but in this computer exercise we can).

Problems

1. Multinomial logit models have often been used to explain, and forecast, decisions of workers regarding whether to use mass transit to get to work or to drive their own cars. Highway congestion can be reduced if people can be encouraged to use buses, rail systems, carpooling, or other alternatives to driving themselves to work. Load the data file worktrip, which contains observations on 3,782 workers who commute to a regular workplace on the following variables: age; distance (miles from home to work); education (years); male (dummy variable that is 1 for males, 0 for females); married (1 if the worker is married, 0 if not); salary (in thousands of dollars); time (minutes required to get to work); and transpmode (an index variable describing the mode of getting to work—1 = own vehicle, 2 = carpool, 3 = bus, 4 = rail system, 5 = walk or bicycle).

   a. To estimate a multinomial logit model, we need to specify the utility of each choice. Let the utility for choice j be equal to $U_{ij} = \beta_{0j} + \beta_{1j}\text{Age}_i + \beta_{2j}\text{Education}_i + \beta_{3j}\text{Salary}_i + \beta_{4j}\text{Distance}_i + \beta_{5j}\text{Male}_i + \beta_{6j}\text{Married}_i + \varepsilon_{ij}$.   In this model, the utility of each choice is affected by the same variables, and all the parameters differ between choices. Normalize the utility of driving one's own vehicle to 0. Then we interpret U_{ij} as the net utility for worker i for choice j, compared to driving one's own car. Estimate the model. Of its 28 parameters (7 for each of four choices other than the normalized one), how many are statistically significantly different from 0?

b. Look at the coefficients for distance (β_{41}, β_{42}, β_{43}, and β_{44}). Which choices become more attractive (higher net utility), relative to driving one's own car, as distance to work increases? Which choices become less attractive? How many of the effects are statistically significant? For which mode is the effect of distance smallest, and for which mode is it largest? Are these the results you would expect, or not?

c. Look at the coefficients for salary (β_{31}, β_{32}, β_{33}, and β_{34}). How many are statistically significant? Which options are more attractive to higher-paid workers, and which are more attractive to lower-paid workers? If two cities are identical except that one has higher salaries, which will have higher demand for its bus system?

d. Look at the coefficients for the male dummy variable (β_{41}, β_{42}, β_{43}, and β_{44}). Does gender appear to affect commute mode decisions? Test the null hypothesis $\beta_{41} = \beta_{42} = \beta_{43} = \beta_{44} = 0$. What do you find?

2. Another discrete choice people make is whether to live in a city, in a suburb, or in a rural area. Many of the problems of central cities are attributed to the departure of higher-income residents for the suburbs. In this problem we'll estimate a multinomial logit model of the location decision, and see to what extent it can be explained by income and by other factors. Open the data file homeown, which was described in problem 4 in Chapter 19.

a. The variable Metro is equal to 1 if a household lives in the central city of a metropolitan area, 2 if the household lives in a suburb (an urban area outside the central city), and 3 if the household lives in a rural area. Let the utility of living in the central city be 1, and let the utility of the other two choices be given by $U_{ij} = \beta_{0j} + \beta_{1j}\text{Age}_i + \beta_{2j}\text{Education}_i + \beta_{3j}\text{Income}_i + \beta_{4j}\text{Persons} + \beta_{5j}\text{Minority}_i + \beta_{6j}\text{Married}_i + \varepsilon_{ij}$. Estimate a multinomial logit model. How many of the 14 parameters are statistically significantly different from 0?

b. How does an increase in income affect the net utility of living in the suburbs? How does it affect the net utility of living in a rural area? Are these results consistent with the idea that people choose to leave central cities when their incomes rise?

c. Consider a household that has a utility of 0 for all three options. What are the probabilities of it making each of the three choices? Now suppose its value for the education variable rises by four years, the difference between high school and college education. What are its utilities for each of the three choices now? What are the probabilities that the household will choose each of the three options? How do rising education levels move population?

d. Consider a household that is not a member of an ethnic minority that has a utility of 0 for all three options. Now consider a household that is identical except that it is a member of an ethnic minority. What are its utilities for suburbs and rural living? What is the chance that this household will locate in a central city? What does this suggest about the ethnic distribution of households between cities and suburbs? What, if anything, does the model tell us about why this happens? What explanation might you suggest?

e. What does the assumption of independence of irrelevant alternatives imply for this data set? Does this implication seem a reasonable one to you? Why or why not?

3. The Tobit model is widely used to estimate spending patterns for goods which many households do not buy, particularly if households do not buy them because they cannot afford them, since in that case it makes sense to think of a demand for the good that is negative due to a low income. One good that is bought primarily by higher-income households, and whose demand is of economic interest, is air travel. In this problem we'll estimate a Tobit model of spending on air travel. Load the data file spending, which contains data from 1998 on 1302 households on the following variables: Income (of the household); members (people in the household); cars (number owned by the household); airtravel (spending on air travel); carloans (money owed on car loans); highered (spending on higher education); midwest; south; west; and urban (dummy variables equal to 1 if the household is located in the Midwest, South, West, or an urban area, respectively).

   a. What is the mean value of Airtravel? What is the median value? How many households spend money on air travel and how many do not?

   b. Using the Tobit model, estimate the equation $\text{Airtravel}_i^* = \beta_0 + \beta_1 \text{Income}_i + \beta_2 \text{Urban}_i + \beta_3 \text{Midwest}_i + \beta_4 \text{South}_i + \beta_5 \text{West}_i + \varepsilon_i$, where $\text{Airtravel}_i = 0$ if $\text{Airtravel}_i^* < 0$ and $\text{Airtravel}_i = \text{Airtravel}_i^*$ if $\text{Airtravel}_i^* > 0$. Test the null hypothesis $\beta_2 = 0$. What do you conclude about travel demand from the results? Test whether there are differences in demand among different regions of the country. What do you find?

   c. If income rises by \$1,000, how much more money does a household spend on air travel? Is the effect statistically significant? Find the amount of income at which an urban household in the Northeast has a 50 percent chance to buy airline tickets (i.e., the amount for which $\text{Airtravel}_i^* = 0$). Does it seem too high, too low, or about right?

4. In this problem we'll see what happens if we use the least squares model instead of the Tobit model. Load the data file spending, which was described in problem 3.

   a. Using the Tobit model, estimate the equation $\text{Airtravel}_i^* = \beta_0 + \beta_1 \text{Income}_i + \beta_2 \text{Urban}_i + \beta_3 \text{Midwest}_i + \beta_4 \text{South}_i + \beta_5 \text{West}_i + \varepsilon_i$, where $\text{Airtravel}_i = 0$ if $\text{Airtravel}_i^* < 0$ and $\text{Airtravel}_i = \text{Airtravel}_i^*$ if $\text{Airtravel}_i^* > 0$. Construct a 95 percent confidence interval for the true value of β_1. If income rises by \$1,000, in what interval should we expect the increase in spending on air travel to fall?

   b. Now use least squares to estimate the equation $\text{Airtravel}_i^* = \beta_0 + \beta_1 \text{Income}_i + \beta_2 \text{Urban}_i + \beta_3 \text{Midwest}_i + \beta_4 \text{South}_i + \beta_5 \text{West}_i + \varepsilon_i$, ignoring the problem of the many households that spend nothing on air travel. Construct a 95 percent confidence interval for the true value of β_1 from this regression. Does it overlap with the confidence interval from part *a*? If not, has using OLS biased the estimated value upward or downward? Are the results different from those for the equation in part *a* in any other way?

   c. Maybe we can solve the problem by using only the households that actually spend money on air travel. Reestimate the equation from part *b* using only the part of the sample for which $\text{Airtravel}_i > 0$. Calculate the 95 percent confidence interval for the true value of β_1 using these results. Does this confidence interval overlap with the one calculated in part *a*? Did using only the subsample of households that spend money on air travel solve the bias problem, or not? Graph a scatterplot with income on the horizontal axis and air travel spending on the vertical axis, and use it to explain why the bias has or has not been corrected.

5. The Tobit model can be used for other allocation decisions besides spending, as long as they can be represented by a model where the desired value of the variable can be positive or negative, and the observed value is 0 when the desired value is negative. In this problem we'll use the Tobit model to estimate the demand of households for debt, specifically for loans to buy automobiles. Load the data file spending, which was described in problem 3.

a. Let the household's desired amount of car loans be given by $Carloans_i^* = \beta_0 + \beta_1 Income_i + \beta_2 Income_i^2 + \beta_3 Urban_i + \beta_4 Highered_i + \beta_5 Members_i + \varepsilon_i$. If $Carloans_i^*$ is negative, then the household does not take out a car loan, and we observe $Carloans_i = 0$. If $Carloans_i^*$ is positive, then the household does take out a car loan, and we observe $Carloans_i = Carloans_i^*$. Estimate this model with the Tobit method. How many of the estimated parameters are statistically significantly different from 0?

b. Would you expect households with more members to have a higher desire for car loans, or lower? Test your answer. What do you find? Give one reason why households with higher college education bills might have a higher desire for car loans, and one reason why they might have a lower desire. Test whether there is a significant effect and, if so, what sign it takes. What do you find?

c. Calculate an expression for $\partial Carloans_i^* / \partial Income$. When income is low, does higher income increase or decrease the chance that the household will have a car loan? When income is high, does higher income increase or decrease the chance that the household will have a car loan? How do you explain this? (Hint: Under what conditions can you buy a car without taking out a car loan to do it?) Find the value of income that maximizes the household's desire to have a car loan.

6. Some variables are limited both in the sense of being censored and in the sense of being discrete. Consider, for example, the number of cars a household has. It must be positive or 0, and for some households it is exactly 0. It must also be an integer; a household can have 1 or 2 or 3 cars, but not 1.5 or 2.6 cars. Load the data file spending, which was described in problem 3.

a. We could use a Tobit model to describe the number of cars a household has, in which case there would be a desired number of cars and a household with a negative desired number would have 0. Or we could use a multinomial logit model in which households would have a net utility for having 0, 1, 2, 3, 4, 5, or 6 cars (6 is the highest value observed in the data) and would choose whatever number gave the highest net utility. What are the problems with each approach? (In considering about the multinomial logit model, think about IIA.)

b. Using the method you prefer, estimate a model for the number of cars a household owns, using Income, Members, Urban, Midwest, West, and South as explanatory variables. Test whether income increases the number of cars the household has, and if it does, how much. Also test whether there are differences in car desires between regions of the country and between rural and urban households.

c. Can you think of a better way to model the probability of the household buying any particular number of cars? If so, how?

Appendix A

Area in the Right Tail of Standard Normal Density Function

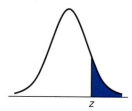

The number in the chart is the area to the right of Z under the standard normal density function, where Z is the sum of the row and column numbers. For Z below 0, look up $|Z|$ in the table and subtract from 1.

This table was generated using the Excel function NORMDIST.

Z	0.00	0.01	0.02	0.03	0.04	0.05	0.06	0.07	0.08	0.09
0.0	0.50000	0.49601	0.49202	0.48803	0.48405	0.48006	0.47608	0.47210	0.46812	0.46414
0.1	0.46017	0.45620	0.45224	0.44828	0.44433	0.44038	0.43644	0.43251	0.42858	0.42465
0.2	0.42074	0.41683	0.41294	0.40905	0.40517	0.40129	0.39743	0.39358	0.38974	0.38591
0.3	0.38209	0.37828	0.37448	0.37070	0.36693	0.36317	0.35942	0.35569	0.35197	0.34827
0.4	0.34458	0.34090	0.33724	0.33360	0.32997	0.32636	0.32276	0.31918	0.31561	0.31207
0.5	0.30854	0.30503	0.30153	0.29806	0.29460	0.29116	0.28774	0.28434	0.28096	0.27760
0.6	0.27425	0.27093	0.26763	0.26435	0.26109	0.25785	0.25463	0.25143	0.24825	0.24510
0.7	0.24196	0.23885	0.23576	0.23270	0.22965	0.22663	0.22363	0.22065	0.21770	0.21476
0.8	0.21186	0.20897	0.20611	0.20327	0.20045	0.19766	0.19489	0.19215	0.18943	0.18673
0.9	0.18406	0.18141	0.17879	0.17619	0.17361	0.17106	0.16853	0.16602	0.16354	0.16109
1.0	0.15866	0.15625	0.15386	0.15151	0.14917	0.14686	0.14457	0.14231	0.14007	0.13786
1.1	0.13567	0.13350	0.13136	0.12924	0.12714	0.12507	0.12302	0.12100	0.11900	0.11702
1.2	0.11507	0.11314	0.11123	0.10935	0.10749	0.10565	0.10383	0.10204	0.10027	0.09853
1.3	0.09680	0.09510	0.09342	0.09176	0.09012	0.08851	0.08692	0.08534	0.08379	0.08226
1.4	0.08076	0.07927	0.07780	0.07636	0.07493	0.07353	0.07215	0.07078	0.06944	0.06811
1.5	0.06681	0.06552	0.06426	0.06301	0.06178	0.06057	0.05938	0.05821	0.05705	0.05592
1.6	0.05480	0.05370	0.05262	0.05155	0.05050	0.04947	0.04846	0.04746	0.04648	0.04551
1.7	0.04457	0.04363	0.04272	0.04182	0.04093	0.04006	0.03920	0.03836	0.03754	0.03673
1.8	0.03593	0.03515	0.03438	0.03362	0.03288	0.03216	0.03144	0.03074	0.03005	0.02938
1.9	0.02872	0.02807	0.02743	0.02680	0.02619	0.02559	0.02500	0.02442	0.02385	0.02330
2.0	0.02275	0.02222	0.02169	0.02118	0.02068	0.02018	0.01970	0.01923	0.01876	0.01831
2.1	0.01786	0.01743	0.01700	0.01659	0.01618	0.01578	0.01539	0.01500	0.01463	0.01426
2.2	0.01390	0.01355	0.01321	0.01287	0.01255	0.01222	0.01191	0.01160	0.01130	0.01101
2.3	0.01072	0.01044	0.01017	0.00990	0.00964	0.00939	0.00914	0.00889	0.00866	0.00842
2.4	0.00820	0.00798	0.00776	0.00755	0.00734	0.00714	0.00695	0.00676	0.00657	0.00639
2.5	0.00621	0.00604	0.00587	0.00570	0.00554	0.00539	0.00523	0.00508	0.00494	0.00480
2.6	0.00466	0.00453	0.00440	0.00427	0.00415	0.00402	0.00391	0.00379	0.00368	0.00357
2.7	0.00347	0.00336	0.00326	0.00317	0.00307	0.00298	0.00289	0.00280	0.00272	0.00264
2.8	0.00256	0.00248	0.00240	0.00233	0.00226	0.00219	0.00212	0.00205	0.00199	0.00193
2.9	0.00187	0.00181	0.00175	0.00169	0.00164	0.00159	0.00154	0.00149	0.00144	0.00139
3.0	0.00135	0.00131	0.00126	0.00122	0.00118	0.00114	0.00111	0.00107	0.00104	0.00100

Appendix B

Critical Values of the T Distribution

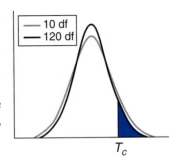

This chart shows the one-tailed critical T value for various percentage chances and numbers of degrees of freedom. For two-tailed critical values, divide the desired percentage by two and use the one-tailed value.

This chart was generated in Excel using the TINV formula.

df	Probability				
	0.1	0.05	0.025	0.01	0.005
1	3.07768	6.31375	12.70615	31.82096	63.65590
2	1.88562	2.91999	4.30266	6.96455	9.92499
3	1.63775	2.35336	3.18245	4.54071	5.84085
4	1.53321	2.13185	2.77645	3.74694	4.60408
5	1.47588	2.01505	2.57058	3.36493	4.03212
6	1.43976	1.94318	2.44691	3.14267	3.70743
7	1.41492	1.89458	2.36462	2.99795	3.49948
8	1.39682	1.85955	2.30601	2.89647	3.35538
9	1.38303	1.83311	2.26216	2.82143	3.24984
10	1.37218	1.81246	2.22814	2.76377	3.16926
11	1.36343	1.79588	2.20099	2.71808	3.10582
12	1.35622	1.78229	2.17881	2.68099	3.05454
13	1.35017	1.77093	2.16037	2.65030	3.01228
14	1.34503	1.76131	2.14479	2.62449	2.97685
15	1.34061	1.75305	2.13145	2.60248	2.94673
16	1.33676	1.74588	2.11990	2.58349	2.92079
17	1.33338	1.73961	2.10982	2.56694	2.89823
18	1.33039	1.73406	2.10092	2.55238	2.87844
19	1.32773	1.72913	2.09302	2.53948	2.86094
20	1.32534	1.72472	2.08596	2.52798	2.84534
21	1.32319	1.72074	2.07961	2.51765	2.83137
22	1.32124	1.71714	2.07388	2.50832	2.81876
23	1.31946	1.71387	2.06865	2.49987	2.80734
24	1.31784	1.71088	2.06390	2.49216	2.79695
25	1.31635	1.70814	2.05954	2.48510	2.78744
30	1.31042	1.69726	2.04227	2.45726	2.74998
35	1.30621	1.68957	2.03011	2.43772	2.72381
40	1.30308	1.68385	2.02107	2.42326	2.70446
45	1.30065	1.67943	2.01410	2.41212	2.68959
50	1.29871	1.67591	2.00856	2.40327	2.67779
55	1.29713	1.67303	2.00404	2.39608	2.66822
60	1.29582	1.67065	2.00030	2.39012	2.66027
80	1.29222	1.66413	1.99007	2.37387	2.63870
100	1.29008	1.66023	1.98397	2.36421	2.62589
120	1.28865	1.65765	1.97993	2.35783	2.61742
150	1.28722	1.65508	1.97590	2.35146	2.60901
200	1.28580	1.65251	1.97189	2.34513	2.60063
500	1.28325	1.64791	1.96472	2.33383	2.58569
∞	1.28156	1.64484	1.95996	2.32635	2.57583

Appendix C

Critical Values of the Chi-square Distribution

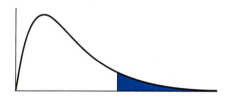

This chart shows the critical value for the chi-square distribution with various right-tail probabilities and degrees of freedom.
This table was generated using the Excel function CHIINV.

Degrees of Freedom	Right-Tail Probability				
	0.25	0.1	0.05	0.02	0.01
1	1.323304	2.705541	3.841455	5.411904	6.634891
2	2.77259	4.605176	5.991476	7.824071	9.210351
3	4.108342	6.251394	7.814725	9.837411	11.34488
4	5.385266	7.779434	9.487728	11.66784	13.2767
5	6.625678	9.236349	11.07048	13.38822	15.08632
6	7.840806	10.64464	12.59158	15.0332	16.81187
7	9.037146	12.01703	14.06713	16.62243	18.47532
8	10.21885	13.36156	15.50731	18.1682	20.09016
9	11.38875	14.68366	16.91896	19.67898	21.66605
10	12.54886	15.98717	18.30703	21.16075	23.20929
11	13.70069	17.27501	19.67515	22.6179	24.72502
12	14.8454	18.54934	21.02606	24.05393	26.21696
13	15.98391	19.81193	22.36203	25.47149	27.68818
14	17.11693	21.06414	23.68478	26.87273	29.14116
15	18.24508	22.30712	24.9958	28.25949	30.57795
16	19.36886	23.54182	26.29622	29.63316	31.99986
17	20.48868	24.76903	27.5871	30.99504	33.40872
18	21.60489	25.98942	28.86932	32.34617	34.80524
19	22.71781	27.20356	30.14351	33.68741	36.19077
20	23.82769	28.41197	31.41042	35.01962	37.56627
21	24.93478	29.61509	32.67056	36.34344	38.93223
22	26.03926	30.81329	33.92446	37.65948	40.28945
23	27.14133	32.00689	35.17246	38.96828	41.63833
24	28.24115	33.19624	36.41503	40.27033	42.97978
25	29.33885	34.38158	37.65249	41.56603	44.31401
30	34.79974	40.25602	43.77295	47.96179	50.89218
35	40.22279	46.05877	49.80183	54.24386	57.34199
40	45.61601	51.80504	55.75849	60.43607	63.69077
45	50.98494	57.50529	61.65622	66.55521	69.9569
50	56.33361	63.16711	67.50481	72.61322	76.1538
60	66.98147	74.397	79.08195	84.5799	88.37943
70	77.57665	85.52704	90.53126	96.3875	100.4251
80	88.13025	96.5782	101.8795	108.0693	112.3288
90	98.64992	107.565	113.1452	119.6484	124.1162
100	109.1412	118.498	124.3421	131.1417	135.8069

Appendix D

Critical Values of the F Distribution

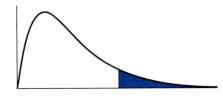

This chart shows the critical value for the F distribution with right-tail probabilities of 5 percent and 1 percent, and various degrees of freedom in the numerator and denominator.

This table was generated using the Excel function FINV.

Denominator Degrees of Freedom		Numerator Degrees of Freedom											
		1	2	3	4	5	6	7	8	9	10	11	12
1	5%	161.4	199.5	215.7	224.6	230.2	234.0	236.8	238.9	240.5	241.9	243.0	243.9
	1%	4052.2	4999.3	5403.5	5624.3	5764.0	5859.0	5928.3	5981.0	6022.4	6055.9	6083.4	6106.7
2	5%	18.51	19.00	19.16	19.25	19.30	19.33	19.35	19.37	19.38	19.40	19.40	19.41
	1%	98.50	99.00	99.16	99.25	99.30	99.33	99.36	99.38	99.39	99.40	99.41	99.42
3	5%	10.13	9.55	9.28	9.12	9.01	8.94	8.89	8.85	8.81	8.79	8.76	8.74
	1%	34.12	30.82	29.46	28.71	28.24	27.91	27.67	27.49	27.34	27.23	27.13	27.05
4	5%	7.71	6.94	6.59	6.39	6.26	6.16	6.09	6.04	6.00	5.96	5.94	5.91
	1%	21.20	18.00	16.69	15.98	15.52	15.21	14.98	14.80	14.66	14.55	14.45	14.37
5	5%	6.61	5.79	5.41	5.19	5.05	4.95	4.88	4.82	4.77	4.74	4.70	4.68
	1%	16.26	13.27	12.06	11.39	10.97	10.67	10.46	10.29	10.16	10.05	9.96	9.89
6	5%	5.99	5.14	4.76	4.53	4.39	4.28	4.21	4.15	4.10	4.06	4.03	4.00
	1%	13.75	10.92	9.78	9.15	8.75	8.47	8.26	8.10	7.98	7.87	7.79	7.72
7	5%	5.59	4.74	4.35	4.12	3.97	3.87	3.79	3.73	3.68	3.64	3.60	3.57
	1%	12.25	9.55	8.45	7.85	7.46	7.19	6.99	6.84	6.72	6.62	6.54	6.47
8	5%	5.32	4.46	4.07	3.84	3.69	3.58	3.50	3.44	3.39	3.35	3.31	3.28
	1%	11.26	8.65	7.59	7.01	6.63	6.37	6.18	6.03	5.91	5.81	5.73	5.67
9	5%	5.12	4.26	3.86	3.63	3.48	3.37	3.29	3.23	3.18	3.14	3.10	3.07
	1%	10.56	8.02	6.99	6.42	6.06	5.80	5.61	5.47	5.35	5.26	5.18	5.11
10	5%	4.96	4.10	3.71	3.48	3.33	3.22	3.14	3.07	3.02	2.98	2.94	2.91
	1%	10.04	7.56	6.55	5.99	5.64	5.39	5.20	5.06	4.94	4.85	4.77	4.71
11	5%	4.84	3.98	3.59	3.36	3.20	3.09	3.01	2.95	2.90	2.85	2.82	2.79
	1%	9.65	7.21	6.22	5.67	5.32	5.07	4.89	4.74	4.63	4.54	4.46	4.40

13	14	15	18	20	25	30	35	40	45	50	75	100	∞	
244.7	245.4	245.9	247.3	248.0	249.3	250.1	250.7	251.1	251.5	251.8	252.6	253.0	254.3	**1**
6125.8	6143.0	6157.0	6191.4	6208.7	6239.9	6260.4	6275.3	6286.4	6295.7	6302.3	6323.7	6333.9	6365.6	
19.42	19.42	19.43	19.44	19.45	19.46	19.46	19.47	19.47	19.47	19.48	19.48	19.49	19.50	**2**
99.42	99.43	99.43	99.44	99.45	99.46	99.47	99.47	99.48	99.48	99.48	99.48	99.49	99.50	
8.73	8.71	8.70	8.67	8.66	8.63	8.62	8.60	8.59	8.59	8.58	8.56	8.55	8.53	**3**
26.98	26.92	26.87	26.75	26.69	26.58	26.50	26.45	26.41	26.38	26.35	26.28	26.24	26.13	
5.89	5.87	5.86	5.82	5.80	5.77	5.75	5.73	5.72	5.71	5.70	5.68	5.66	5.63	**4**
14.31	14.25	14.20	14.08	14.02	13.91	13.84	13.79	13.75	13.71	13.69	13.61	13.58	13.46	
4.66	4.64	4.62	4.58	4.56	4.52	4.50	4.48	4.46	4.45	4.44	4.42	4.41	4.37	**5**
9.82	9.77	9.72	9.61	9.55	9.45	9.38	9.33	9.29	9.26	9.24	9.17	9.13	9.02	
3.98	3.96	3.94	3.90	3.87	3.83	3.81	3.79	3.77	3.76	3.75	3.73	3.71	3.67	**6**
7.66	7.60	7.56	7.45	7.40	7.30	7.23	7.18	7.14	7.11	7.09	7.02	6.99	6.88	
3.55	3.53	3.51	3.47	3.44	3.40	3.38	3.36	3.34	3.33	3.32	3.29	3.27	3.23	**7**
6.41	6.36	6.31	6.21	6.16	6.06	5.99	5.94	5.91	5.88	5.86	5.79	5.75	5.65	
3.26	3.24	3.22	3.17	3.15	3.11	3.08	3.06	3.04	3.03	3.02	2.99	2.97	2.93	**8**
5.61	5.56	5.52	5.41	5.36	5.26	5.20	5.15	5.12	5.09	5.07	5.00	4.96	4.86	
3.05	3.03	3.01	2.96	2.94	2.89	2.86	2.84	2.83	2.81	2.80	2.77	2.76	2.71	**9**
5.05	5.01	4.96	4.86	4.81	4.71	4.65	4.60	4.57	4.54	4.52	4.45	4.41	4.31	
2.89	2.86	2.85	2.80	2.77	2.73	2.70	2.68	2.66	2.65	2.64	2.60	2.59	2.54	**10**
4.65	4.60	4.56	4.46	4.41	4.31	4.25	4.20	4.17	4.14	4.12	4.05	4.01	3.91	
2.76	2.74	2.72	2.67	2.65	2.60	2.57	2.55	2.53	2.52	2.51	2.47	2.46	2.40	**11**
4.34	4.29	4.25	4.15	4.10	4.01	3.94	3.89	3.86	3.83	3.81	3.74	3.71	3.60	

Denominator Degrees of Freedom		Numerator Degrees of Freedom											
		1	2	3	4	5	6	7	8	9	10	11	12
12	5%	4.75	3.89	3.49	3.26	3.11	3.00	2.91	2.85	2.80	2.75	2.72	2.69
	1%	9.33	6.93	5.95	5.41	5.06	4.82	4.64	4.50	4.39	4.30	4.22	4.16
13	5%	4.67	3.81	3.41	3.18	3.03	2.92	2.83	2.77	2.71	2.67	2.63	2.60
	1%	9.07	6.70	5.74	5.21	4.86	4.62	4.44	4.30	4.19	4.10	4.02	3.96
14	5%	4.60	3.74	3.34	3.11	2.96	2.85	2.76	2.70	2.65	2.60	2.57	2.53
	1%	8.86	6.51	5.56	5.04	4.69	4.46	4.28	4.14	4.03	3.94	3.86	3.80
15	5%	4.54	3.68	3.29	3.06	2.90	2.79	2.71	2.64	2.59	2.54	2.51	2.48
	1%	8.68	6.36	5.42	4.89	4.56	4.32	4.14	4.00	3.89	3.80	3.73	3.67
16	5%	4.49	3.63	3.24	3.01	2.85	2.74	2.66	2.59	2.54	2.49	2.46	2.42
	1%	8.53	6.23	5.29	4.77	4.44	4.20	4.03	3.89	3.78	3.69	3.62	3.55
17	5%	4.45	3.59	3.20	2.96	2.81	2.70	2.61	2.55	2.49	2.45	2.41	2.38
	1%	8.40	6.11	5.19	4.67	4.34	4.10	3.93	3.79	3.68	3.59	3.52	3.46
18	5%	4.41	3.55	3.16	2.93	2.77	2.66	2.58	2.51	2.46	2.41	2.37	2.34
	1%	8.29	6.01	5.09	4.58	4.25	4.01	3.84	3.71	3.60	3.51	3.43	3.37
19	5%	4.38	3.52	3.13	2.90	2.74	2.63	2.54	2.48	2.42	2.38	2.34	2.31
	1%	8.18	5.93	5.01	4.50	4.17	3.94	3.77	3.63	3.52	3.43	3.36	3.30
20	5%	4.35	3.49	3.10	2.87	2.71	2.60	2.51	2.45	2.39	2.35	2.31	2.28
	1%	8.10	5.85	4.94	4.43	4.10	3.87	3.70	3.56	3.46	3.37	3.29	3.23
21	5%	4.32	3.47	3.07	2.84	2.68	2.57	2.49	2.42	2.37	2.32	2.28	2.25
	1%	8.02	5.78	4.87	4.37	4.04	3.81	3.64	3.51	3.40	3.31	3.24	3.17
22	5%	4.30	3.44	3.05	2.82	2.66	2.55	2.46	2.40	2.34	2.30	2.26	2.23
	1%	7.95	5.72	4.82	4.31	3.99	3.76	3.59	3.45	3.35	3.26	3.18	3.12
23	5%	4.28	3.42	3.03	2.80	2.64	2.53	2.44	2.37	2.32	2.27	2.24	2.20
	1%	7.88	5.66	4.76	4.26	3.94	3.71	3.54	3.41	3.30	3.21	3.14	3.07
24	5%	4.26	3.40	3.01	2.78	2.62	2.51	2.42	2.36	2.30	2.25	2.22	2.18
	1%	7.82	5.61	4.72	4.22	3.90	3.67	3.50	3.36	3.26	3.17	3.09	3.03
25	5%	4.24	3.39	2.99	2.76	2.60	2.49	2.40	2.34	2.28	2.24	2.20	2.16
	1%	7.77	5.57	4.68	4.18	3.85	3.63	3.46	3.32	3.22	3.13	3.06	2.99
30	5%	4.17	3.32	2.92	2.69	2.53	2.42	2.33	2.27	2.21	2.16	2.13	2.09
	1%	7.56	5.39	4.51	4.02	3.70	3.47	3.30	3.17	3.07	2.98	2.91	2.84
35	5%	4.12	3.27	2.87	2.64	2.49	2.37	2.29	2.22	2.16	2.11	2.07	2.04
	1%	7.42	5.27	4.40	3.91	3.59	3.37	3.20	3.07	2.96	2.88	2.80	2.74
40	5%	4.08	3.23	2.84	2.61	2.45	2.34	2.25	2.18	2.12	2.08	2.04	2.00
	1%	7.31	5.18	4.31	3.83	3.51	3.29	3.12	2.99	2.89	2.80	2.73	2.66
45	5%	4.06	3.20	2.81	2.58	2.42	2.31	2.22	2.15	2.10	2.05	2.01	1.97
	1%	7.23	5.11	4.25	3.77	3.45	3.23	3.07	2.94	2.83	2.74	2.67	2.61
50	5%	4.03	3.18	2.79	2.56	2.40	2.29	2.20	2.13	2.07	2.03	1.99	1.95
	1%	7.17	5.06	4.20	3.72	3.41	3.19	3.02	2.89	2.78	2.70	2.63	2.56
55	5%	4.02	3.16	2.77	2.54	2.38	2.27	2.18	2.11	2.06	2.01	1.97	1.93
	1%	7.12	5.01	4.16	3.68	3.37	3.15	2.98	2.85	2.75	2.66	2.59	2.53
60	5%	4.00	3.15	2.76	2.53	2.37	2.25	2.17	2.10	2.04	1.99	1.95	1.92
	1%	7.08	4.98	4.13	3.65	3.34	3.12	2.95	2.82	2.72	2.63	2.56	2.50

13	14	15	18	20	25	30	35	40	45	50	75	100	∞	
2.66	2.64	2.62	2.57	2.54	2.50	2.47	2.44	2.43	2.41	2.40	2.37	2.35	2.30	**12**
4.10	4.05	4.01	3.91	3.86	3.76	3.70	3.65	3.62	3.59	3.57	3.50	3.47	3.36	
2.58	2.55	2.53	2.48	2.46	2.41	2.38	2.36	2.34	2.33	2.31	2.28	2.26	2.21	**13**
3.91	3.86	3.82	3.72	3.66	3.57	3.51	3.46	3.43	3.40	3.38	3.31	3.27	3.17	
2.51	2.48	2.46	2.41	2.39	2.34	2.31	2.28	2.27	2.25	2.24	2.21	2.19	2.13	**14**
3.75	3.70	3.66	3.56	3.51	3.41	3.35	3.30	3.27	3.24	3.22	3.15	3.11	3.00	
2.45	2.42	2.40	2.35	2.33	2.28	2.25	2.22	2.20	2.19	2.18	2.14	2.12	2.07	**15**
3.61	3.56	3.52	3.42	3.37	3.28	3.21	3.17	3.13	3.10	3.08	3.01	2.98	2.87	
2.40	2.37	2.35	2.30	2.28	2.23	2.19	2.17	2.15	2.14	2.12	2.09	2.07	2.01	**16**
3.50	3.45	3.41	3.31	3.26	3.16	3.10	3.05	3.02	2.99	2.97	2.90	2.86	2.75	
2.35	2.33	2.31	2.26	2.23	2.18	2.15	2.12	2.10	2.09	2.08	2.04	2.02	1.96	**17**
3.40	3.35	3.31	3.21	3.16	3.07	3.00	2.96	2.92	2.89	2.87	2.80	2.76	2.65	
2.31	2.29	2.27	2.22	2.19	2.14	2.11	2.08	2.06	2.05	2.04	2.00	1.98	1.92	**18**
3.32	3.27	3.23	3.13	3.08	2.98	2.92	2.87	2.84	2.81	2.78	2.71	2.68	2.57	
2.28	2.26	2.23	2.18	2.16	2.11	2.07	2.05	2.03	2.01	2.00	1.96	1.94	1.88	**19**
3.24	3.19	3.15	3.05	3.00	2.91	2.84	2.80	2.76	2.73	2.71	2.64	2.60	2.49	
2.25	2.22	2.20	2.15	2.12	2.07	2.04	2.01	1.99	1.98	1.97	1.93	1.91	1.84	**20**
3.18	3.13	3.09	2.99	2.94	2.84	2.78	2.73	2.69	2.67	2.64	2.57	2.54	2.42	
2.22	2.20	2.18	2.12	2.10	2.05	2.01	1.98	1.96	1.95	1.94	1.90	1.88	1.81	**21**
3.12	3.07	3.03	2.93	2.88	2.79	2.72	2.67	2.64	2.61	2.58	2.51	2.48	2.36	
2.20	2.17	2.15	2.10	2.07	2.02	1.98	1.96	1.94	1.92	1.91	1.87	1.85	1.78	**22**
3.07	3.02	2.98	2.88	2.83	2.73	2.67	2.62	2.58	2.55	2.53	2.46	2.42	2.31	
2.18	2.15	2.13	2.08	2.05	2.00	1.96	1.93	1.91	1.90	1.88	1.84	1.82	1.76	**23**
3.02	2.97	2.93	2.83	2.78	2.69	2.62	2.57	2.54	2.51	2.48	2.41	2.37	2.26	
2.15	2.13	2.11	2.05	2.03	1.97	1.94	1.91	1.89	1.88	1.86	1.82	1.80	1.73	**24**
2.98	2.93	2.89	2.79	2.74	2.64	2.58	2.53	2.49	2.46	2.44	2.37	2.33	2.21	
2.14	2.11	2.09	2.04	2.01	1.96	1.92	1.89	1.87	1.84	1.80	1.78	1.78	1.71	**25**
2.94	2.89	2.85	2.75	2.70	2.60	2.54	2.49	2.45	2.40	2.33	2.29	2.29	2.17	
2.06	2.04	2.01	1.96	1.93	1.88	1.84	1.81	1.79	1.76	1.72	1.70	1.70	1.62	**30**
2.79	2.74	2.70	2.60	2.55	2.45	2.39	2.34	2.30	2.25	2.17	2.13	2.13	2.01	
2.01	1.99	1.96	1.91	1.88	1.82	1.79	1.76	1.74	1.70	1.66	1.63	1.63	1.56	**35**
2.69	2.64	2.60	2.50	2.44	2.35	2.28	2.23	2.19	2.14	2.06	2.02	2.02	1.89	
1.97	1.95	1.92	1.87	1.84	1.78	1.74	1.72	1.69	1.66	1.61	1.59	1.59	1.51	**40**
2.61	2.56	2.52	2.42	2.37	2.27	2.20	2.15	2.11	2.06	1.98	1.94	1.94	1.80	
1.94	1.92	1.89	1.84	1.81	1.75	1.71	1.68	1.66	1.63	1.58	1.55	1.55	1.47	**45**
2.55	2.51	2.46	2.36	2.31	2.21	2.14	2.09	2.05	2.00	1.92	1.88	1.88	1.74	
1.92	1.89	1.87	1.81	1.78	1.73	1.69	1.66	1.63	1.60	1.55	1.52	1.52	1.44	**50**
2.51	2.46	2.42	2.32	2.27	2.17	2.10	2.05	2.01	1.95	1.87	1.82	1.82	1.68	
1.90	1.88	1.85	1.79	1.76	1.71	1.67	1.64	1.61	1.58	1.53	1.50	1.50	1.41	**55**
2.47	2.42	2.38	2.28	2.23	2.13	2.06	2.01	1.97	1.91	1.83	1.78	1.78	1.64	
1.89	1.86	1.84	1.78	1.75	1.69	1.65	1.62	1.59	1.56	1.51	1.48	1.48	1.39	**60**
2.44	2.39	2.35	2.25	2.20	2.10	2.03	1.98	1.94	1.88	1.79	1.75	1.75	1.60	

Denominator Degrees of Freedom		Numerator Degrees of Freedom											
		1	2	3	4	5	6	7	8	9	10	11	12
65	5%	3.99	3.14	2.75	2.51	2.36	2.24	2.15	2.08	2.03	1.98	1.94	1.90
	1%	7.04	4.95	4.10	3.62	3.31	3.09	2.93	2.80	2.69	2.61	2.53	2.47
70	5%	3.98	3.13	2.74	2.50	2.35	2.23	2.14	2.07	2.02	1.97	1.93	1.89
	1%	7.01	4.92	4.07	3.60	3.29	3.07	2.91	2.78	2.67	2.59	2.51	2.45
75	5%	3.97	3.12	2.73	2.49	2.34	2.22	2.13	2.06	2.01	1.96	1.92	1.88
	1%	6.99	4.90	4.05	3.58	3.27	3.05	2.89	2.76	2.65	2.57	2.49	2.43
80	5%	3.96	3.11	2.72	2.49	2.33	2.21	2.13	2.06	2.00	1.95	1.91	1.88
	1%	6.96	4.88	4.04	3.56	3.26	3.04	2.87	2.74	2.64	2.55	2.48	2.42
85	5%	3.95	3.10	2.71	2.48	2.32	2.21	2.12	2.05	1.99	1.94	1.90	1.87
	1%	6.94	4.86	4.02	3.55	3.24	3.02	2.86	2.73	2.62	2.54	2.46	2.40
90	5%	3.95	3.10	2.71	2.47	2.32	2.20	2.11	2.04	1.99	1.94	1.90	1.86
	1%	6.93	4.85	4.01	3.53	3.23	3.01	2.84	2.72	2.61	2.52	2.45	2.39
95	5%	3.94	3.09	2.70	2.47	2.31	2.20	2.11	2.04	1.98	1.93	1.89	1.86
	1%	6.91	4.84	3.99	3.52	3.22	3.00	2.83	2.70	2.60	2.51	2.44	2.38
100	5%	3.94	3.09	2.70	2.46	2.31	2.19	2.10	2.03	1.97	1.93	1.89	1.85
	1%	6.90	4.82	3.98	3.51	3.21	2.99	2.82	2.69	2.59	2.50	2.43	2.37
120	5%	3.92	3.07	2.68	2.45	2.29	2.18	2.09	2.02	1.96	1.91	1.87	1.83
	1%	6.85	4.79	3.95	3.48	3.17	2.96	2.79	2.66	2.56	2.47	2.40	2.34
150	5%	3.90	3.06	2.66	2.43	2.27	2.16	2.07	2.00	1.94	1.89	1.85	1.82
	1%	6.81	4.75	3.91	3.45	3.14	2.92	2.76	2.63	2.53	2.44	2.37	2.31
200	5%	3.89	3.04	2.65	2.42	2.26	2.14	2.06	1.98	1.93	1.88	1.84	1.80
	1%	6.76	4.71	3.88	3.41	3.11	2.89	2.73	2.60	2.50	2.41	2.34	2.27
250	5%	3.88	3.03	2.64	2.41	2.25	2.13	2.05	1.98	1.92	1.87	1.83	1.79
	1%	6.74	4.69	3.86	3.40	3.09	2.87	2.71	2.58	2.48	2.39	2.32	2.26
300	5%	3.87	3.03	2.63	2.40	2.24	2.13	2.04	1.97	1.91	1.86	1.82	1.78
	1%	6.72	4.68	3.85	3.38	3.08	2.86	2.70	2.57	2.47	2.38	2.31	2.24
350	5%	3.87	3.02	2.63	2.40	2.24	2.12	2.04	1.96	1.91	1.86	1.82	1.78
	1%	6.71	4.67	3.84	3.37	3.07	2.85	2.69	2.56	2.46	2.37	2.30	2.24
400	5%	3.86	3.02	2.63	2.39	2.24	2.12	2.03	1.96	1.90	1.85	1.81	1.78
	1%	6.70	4.66	3.83	3.37	3.06	2.85	2.68	2.56	2.45	2.37	2.29	2.23
450	5%	3.86	3.02	2.62	2.39	2.23	2.12	2.03	1.96	1.90	1.85	1.81	1.77
	1%	6.69	4.65	3.83	3.36	3.06	2.84	2.68	2.55	2.45	2.36	2.29	2.22
500	5%	3.86	3.01	2.62	2.39	2.23	2.12	2.03	1.96	1.90	1.85	1.81	1.77
	1%	6.69	4.65	3.82	3.36	3.05	2.84	2.68	2.55	2.44	2.36	2.28	2.22
600	5%	3.86	3.01	2.62	2.39	2.23	2.11	2.02	1.95	1.90	1.85	1.80	1.77
	1%	6.68	4.64	3.81	3.35	3.05	2.83	2.67	2.54	2.44	2.35	2.28	2.21
800	5%	3.85	3.01	2.62	2.38	2.23	2.11	2.02	1.95	1.89	1.84	1.80	1.76
	1%	6.67	4.63	3.81	3.34	3.04	2.82	2.66	2.53	2.43	2.34	2.27	2.21
1,000	5%	3.85	3.00	2.61	2.38	2.22	2.11	2.02	1.95	1.89	1.84	1.80	1.76
	1%	6.66	4.63	3.80	3.34	3.04	2.82	2.66	2.53	2.43	2.34	2.27	2.20
∞	5%	3.84	3.00	2.60	2.37	2.21	2.10	2.01	1.94	1.88	1.83	1.79	1.75
	1%	6.63	4.61	3.78	3.32	3.02	2.80	2.64	2.51	2.41	2.32	2.25	2.18

13	14	15	18	20	25	30	35	40	45	50	75	100	∞	
1.87	1.85	1.82	1.76	1.73	1.68	1.63	1.60	1.58	1.54	1.49	1.46	1.46	1.37	**65**
2.42	2.37	2.33	2.23	2.17	2.07	2.00	1.95	1.91	1.85	1.77	1.72	1.72	1.57	
1.86	1.84	1.81	1.75	1.72	1.66	1.62	1.59	1.57	1.53	1.48	1.45	1.45	1.35	**70**
2.40	2.35	2.31	2.20	2.15	2.05	1.98	1.93	1.89	1.83	1.74	1.70	1.70	1.54	
1.85	1.83	1.80	1.74	1.71	1.65	1.61	1.58	1.55	1.52	1.47	1.44	1.44	1.34	**75**
2.38	2.33	2.29	2.18	2.13	2.03	1.96	1.91	1.87	1.81	1.72	1.67	1.67	1.52	
1.84	1.82	1.79	1.73	1.70	1.64	1.60	1.57	1.54	1.51	1.45	1.43	1.43	1.32	**80**
2.36	2.31	2.27	2.17	2.12	2.01	1.94	1.89	1.85	1.79	1.70	1.65	1.65	1.49	
1.84	1.81	1.79	1.73	1.70	1.64	1.59	1.56	1.54	1.50	1.45	1.42	1.42	1.31	**85**
2.35	2.30	2.26	2.15	2.10	2.00	1.93	1.88	1.83	1.77	1.69	1.64	1.64	1.48	
1.83	1.80	1.78	1.72	1.69	1.63	1.59	1.55	1.53	1.49	1.44	1.41	1.41	1.30	**90**
2.33	2.29	2.24	2.14	2.09	1.99	1.92	1.86	1.82	1.76	1.67	1.62	1.62	1.46	
1.82	1.80	1.77	1.71	1.68	1.62	1.58	1.55	1.52	1.48	1.43	1.40	1.40	1.29	**95**
2.32	2.28	2.23	2.13	2.08	1.98	1.90	1.85	1.81	1.75	1.66	1.61	1.61	1.44	
1.82	1.79	1.77	1.71	1.68	1.62	1.57	1.54	1.52	1.48	1.42	1.39	1.39	1.28	**100**
2.31	2.27	2.22	2.12	2.07	1.97	1.89	1.84	1.80	1.74	1.65	1.60	1.60	1.43	
1.80	1.78	1.75	1.69	1.66	1.60	1.55	1.52	1.50	1.46	1.40	1.37	1.37	1.25	**120**
2.28	2.23	2.19	2.09	2.03	1.93	1.86	1.81	1.76	1.70	1.61	1.56	1.56	1.38	
1.79	1.76	1.73	1.67	1.64	1.58	1.54	1.50	1.48	1.44	1.38	1.34	1.34	1.22	**150**
2.25	2.20	2.16	2.06	2.00	1.90	1.83	1.77	1.73	1.66	1.57	1.52	1.52	1.33	
1.77	1.74	1.72	1.66	1.62	1.56	1.52	1.48	1.46	1.41	1.35	1.32	1.32	1.19	**200**
2.22	2.17	2.13	2.03	1.97	1.87	1.79	1.74	1.69	1.63	1.53	1.48	1.48	1.28	
1.76	1.73	1.71	1.65	1.61	1.55	1.50	1.47	1.44	1.40	1.34	1.31	1.31	1.17	**250**
2.20	2.15	2.11	2.01	1.95	1.85	1.77	1.72	1.67	1.61	1.51	1.46	1.46	1.24	
1.75	1.72	1.70	1.64	1.61	1.54	1.50	1.46	1.43	1.39	1.33	1.30	1.30	1.15	**300**
2.19	2.14	2.10	1.99	1.94	1.84	1.76	1.70	1.66	1.59	1.50	1.44	1.44	1.22	
1.75	1.72	1.70	1.63	1.60	1.54	1.49	1.46	1.43	1.39	1.32	1.29	1.29	1.14	**350**
2.18	2.13	2.09	1.99	1.93	1.83	1.75	1.70	1.65	1.58	1.49	1.43	1.43	1.20	
1.74	1.72	1.69	1.63	1.60	1.53	1.49	1.45	1.42	1.38	1.32	1.28	1.28	1.13	**400**
2.17	2.13	2.08	1.98	1.92	1.82	1.75	1.69	1.64	1.58	1.48	1.42	1.42	1.19	
1.74	1.71	1.69	1.63	1.59	1.53	1.48	1.45	1.42	1.38	1.32	1.28	1.28	1.12	**450**
2.17	2.12	2.08	1.97	1.92	1.81	1.74	1.68	1.64	1.57	1.47	1.41	1.41	1.17	
1.74	1.71	1.69	1.62	1.59	1.53	1.48	1.45	1.42	1.38	1.31	1.28	1.28	1.11	**500**
2.17	2.12	2.07	1.97	1.92	1.81	1.74	1.68	1.63	1.57	1.47	1.41	1.41	1.16	
1.74	1.71	1.68	1.62	1.59	1.52	1.48	1.44	1.41	1.37	1.31	1.27	1.27	1.10	**600**
2.16	2.11	2.07	1.96	1.91	1.80	1.73	1.67	1.63	1.56	1.46	1.40	1.40	1.15	
1.73	1.70	1.68	1.62	1.58	1.52	1.47	1.44	1.41	1.37	1.30	1.26	1.26	1.09	**800**
2.15	2.10	2.06	1.96	1.90	1.80	1.72	1.66	1.62	1.55	1.45	1.39	1.39	1.13	
1.73	1.70	1.68	1.61	1.58	1.52	1.47	1.43	1.41	1.36	1.30	1.26	1.26	1.08	**1,000**
2.15	2.10	2.06	1.95	1.90	1.79	1.72	1.66	1.61	1.54	1.44	1.38	1.38	1.11	
1.72	1.69	1.67	1.60	1.57	1.51	1.46	1.42	1.39	1.35	1.28	1.24	1.24	1.01	**∞**
2.13	2.08	2.04	1.93	1.88	1.77	1.70	1.64	1.59	1.52	1.42	1.36	1.36	1.01	

Appendix **E**

5 Percent Critical Values of the Durbin-Watson Statistic

Autocorrelation is:

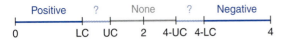

Number of Parameters Estimated (Including Intercept)											
Observations		**2**	**3**	**4**	**5**	**6**	**7**	**8**	**9**	**10**	**15**	**20**
10	LC	0.879	0.697	0.525	0.376	0.243	—	—	—	—	—	—
	UC	1.320	1.641	2.016	2.414	2.822						
15	LC	1.077	0.946	0.814	0.685	0.562	0.447	0.343	0.251	0.175	—	—
	UC	1.361	1.543	1.750	1.977	2.220	2.472	2.727	2.979	3.216		
20	LC	1.201	1.100	0.998	0.894	0.792	0.692	0.595	0.502	0.416	0.100	—
	UC	1.411	1.537	1.676	1.828	1.991	2.162	2.339	2.521	2.704	3.542	
25	LC	1.288	1.206	1.123	1.038	0.953	0.868	0.784	0.702	0.621	0.275	0.065
	UC	1.454	1.550	1.654	1.767	1.886	2.012	2.144	2.280	2.419	3.119	3.702
30	LC	1.352	1.284	1.214	1.143	1.071	0.998	0.926	0.854	0.782	0.451	0.195
	UC	1.489	1.567	1.650	1.739	1.833	1.931	2.034	2.141	2.251	2.823	3.368
35	LC	1.402	1.343	1.283	1.222	1.160	1.097	1.034	0.971	0.908	0.604	0.340
	UC	1.519	1.584	1.653	1.726	1.803	1.884	1.967	2.054	2.144	2.619	3.099
40	LC	1.442	1.391	1.338	1.285	1.230	1.175	1.120	1.064	1.008	0.731	0.477
	UC	1.544	1.600	1.659	1.721	1.786	1.854	1.924	1.997	2.072	2.473	2.892
45	LC	1.475	1.430	1.383	1.336	1.287	1.238	1.189	1.139	1.089	0.838	0.598
	UC	1.566	1.615	1.666	1.720	1.776	1.835	1.895	1.958	2.022	2.367	2.733
50	LC	1.503	1.462	1.421	1.378	1.335	1.291	1.246	1.201	1.156	0.927	0.703
	UC	1.585	1.628	1.674	1.721	1.771	1.822	1.875	1.930	1.986	2.287	2.610
60	LC	1.549	1.514	1.480	1.444	1.408	1.372	1.335	1.298	1.260	1.068	0.874
	UC	1.616	1.689	1.689	1.727	1.767	1.808	1.850	1.894	1.939	2.177	2.434
70	LC	1.583	1.554	1.525	1.494	1.464	1.433	1.401	1.369	1.337	1.172	1.005
	UC	1.641	1.672	1.703	1.735	1.768	1.802	1.837	1.873	1.910	2.106	2.318
80	LC	1.611	1.586	1.560	1.534	1.507	1.480	1.453	1.425	1.397	1.235	1.106
	UC	1.662	1.688	1.715	1.743	1.772	1.801	1.831	1.861	1.893	2.059	2.238
90	LC	1.635	1.612	1.589	1.566	1.542	1.518	1.494	1.469	1.445	1.318	1.187
	UC	1.679	1.703	1.726	1.751	1.776	1.801	1.827	1.854	1.881	2.025	2.179
100	LC	1.654	1.634	1.613	1.592	1.571	1.550	1.528	1.506	1.484	1.371	1.253
	UC	1.694	1.715	1.736	1.758	1.780	1.803	1.826	1.850	1.874	2.000	2.135
150	LC	1.720	1.706	1.693	1.679	1.665	1.651	1.637	1.622	1.608	1.535	1.458
	UC	1.746	1.760	1.774	1.788	1.802	1.817	1.832	1.847	1.862	1.940	2.023
200	LC	1.758	1.748	1.738	1.728	1.718	1.707	1.697	1.686	1.675	1.621	1.554
	UC	1.778	1.789	1.799	1.810	1.820	1.831	1.841	1.852	1.863	1.919	1.991

Source: Extracted from N. E. Savin and K. J. White, "The Durbin-Watson Test for Serial Correlation with Extreme Sample Sizes and Many Regressors," *Econometrica* 45, no. 8 (November 1977), pp. 1994–1995, and from J. Durbin and G. S. Watson, "Testing for Serial Correlation in Least Squares Regression, II," *Biometrika* 38 (1951), p. 173, with permission of the Econometric Society and Oxford University Press.

References

Adams, Walter, and James W. Brock. *The Structure of American Industry,* 9th ed. Englewood Cliffs, NJ: Prentice Hall, 1995, pp. 65–92.

Attfield, Clifford; David Demory; and Nigel Duck. *Rational Expectations in Macroeconomics.* Oxford: Basil Blackwell, 1985.

Barro, Robert. "Unanticipated Money Growth and Unemployment in the United States." *American Economic Review* 67, no. 2 (March 1977), pp. 101–15.

Christensen, Lauritis, and William H. Greene. "Economies of Scale in US Electric Power Generation." *Journal of Political Economy* 84, no. 4 (1976), pp. 655–76.

Cosamano, Michael A. *The Japanese Automobile Industry.* Cambridge MA: Harvard University Press, 1985.

Dickey, D., and W. Fuller. "Distribution of the Estimators for Autoregressive Time Series with a Unit Root." *Journal of the American Statistical Association* 74 (1979), pp. 427–31.

Durbin, James, and G. S. Watson. "Testing for Serial Correlation in Least Squares Regression, II." *Biometrika* 38 (1951), p. 173.

Freeman, Donald G. "Alternative Panel Estimates of Alcohol Demand, Taxation, and the Business Cycle." *Southern Economic Journal* 67, no. 2 (October 2000), pp. 325–44.

Hendry, David. "Econometrics—Alchemy or Science?" *Economica* 47 (November 1980), pp. 387–406.

Kahn, James. "Inventories and the Volatility of Production." *American Economic Review* 77, no. 4 (September 1987), pp. 667–79.

Keynes, John Maynard. *The General Theory of Employment, Interest, and Money* (1936). Vol. VII in *The Collected Writings of John Maynard Keynes.* London: MacMillan Press, 1973.

King, Robert; Charles Plosser; James Stock; and Mark Watson. "Stochastic Trends and Economic Fluctuations." *American Economic Review* 81, no. 4 (September 1991), pp. 819–40.

Lewis, Michael. *Liar's Poker.* New York: W. W. Norton, 1989.

Long, John, and Charles Plosser. "Real Business Cycles." *Journal of Political Economy* 91, no. 1 (February 1983), pp. 39–40.

Mansi, Sattar, and Jeffrey Phillips. "Modeling the Term Structure from the On-the-Run Treasury Yield Curve." *Journal of Financial Research* 24, no. 4 (Winter 2001), pp. 545–64.

Markowitz, Sara, and Michael Grossman. "Alcohol Regulation and Violence Towards Children." National Bureau of Economic Research Working Paper 7129.

McCloskey, D. N. "Economical Writing." *Economic Inquiry* 23, no. 2 (April 1985), pp. 187–222.

McFadden, Daniel. "Econometric Models of Probabilistic Choice." In *Structural Analysis of Discrete Data with Econometric Applications,* eds. Manski and McFadden. Cambridge, MA: MIT Press, 1981.

Murray, Michael. "Econometrics Lectures in a Computer Classroom." *Journal of Economic Education* 30, no. 3 (Summer 1999), pp. 308–21.

Nerlove, Marc. "Returns to Scale in Electricity Supply." In *Measurement in Economics: Studies in Mathematical Economics and Econometrics in Memory of Yehuda Grunfeld,* ed. Carl Christ. Stanford, CA: Stanford University Press, 1963.

Phillips, A. W. "The Relation between Unemployment and the Rate of Change of Money Wage Rates in the United Kingdom, 1861–1957." *Economica* 25, no. 100 (November 1958), pp. 283–99.

Samuelson, Paul. *Foundations of Economic Analysis.* Cambridge, MA: Harvard University Press, 1947.

Sargent, Thomas. *Macroeconomic Theory,* 2nd ed. San Diego, CA: Academic Press, 1987.

Savin, N. E., and K. J. White. "The Durbin-Watson Test for Serial Correlation with Extreme Sample Sizes and Many Regressors." *Econometrica* 45, no. 8 (November 1977), pp. 1994–95.

Sims, Christopher. "Macroeconomics and Reality." *Econometrica* 48, pp 1–47.

Index